UPON THIS ROCK

A New History of the Trenton Diocese

Edited by
Rev. Monsignor Joseph C. Shenrock

THE DIOCESE OF TRENTON

Trenton, New Jersey

Printed and bound in the United States of America

Cardinal Publishing Company
Pennington, New Jersey

Backes Graphic Productions
Princeton, New Jersey

Library of Congress Catalog Card Number 93-070520
ISBN: 0-9638128-0-7

Feast of St. Teresa of Avila
October 15, 1993

WITH GRATITUDE TO
MOST REVEREND JOHN C. REISS, D.D., J.C.D.
EIGHTH ORDINARY OF TRENTON
FOR HIS DEDICATED PASTORAL LEADERSHIP
ON THE OCCASION
OF HIS
TWENTY-FIFTH ANNIVERSARY
AS A BISHOP

CONTENTS

PART ONE
BEFORE THE
DIOCESE OF TRENTON

PART TWO
THE DIOCESE OF TRENTON, 1881–1993

Most Reverend John C. Reiss, D.D., J.C.D., Bishop of the Diocese of Trenton

FOREWORD

◆

WHEN WE ARE FACED WITH DIFFICULties and challenges, we are tempted to look back in time to the "good old days" for solace. In so doing, however, we may be shocked to find that the "good old days" do not exist. Such looking back is actually nothing other than coming into contact with our history.

History does not merely record facts and seek explanations for past events; it also teaches. In reviewing the history of a nation, of the Universal Church, or of our Diocese of Trenton, we will gain both knowledge and insight about the problems that beset our predecessors, how they solved them, what should be avoided, and what can help us now. We will be taught and, at the same time, encouraged to face our own challenges with trust and dependence on God.

Our diocese observed its 110th anniversary in 1991, and on that occasion, a strong determination was made to compile its history. The project has not been an easy one, not only because of the lengthy period of time to be covered but also because of the lack of necessary archival records and materials. The disastrous fire of March 24, 1956, destroyed the cathedral, the rectory, and the Chancery Office, which contained the older records. Thus, research was hampered, and extra time had to be spent to fill in gaps by using alternative sources.

In order to compile the history of the diocese, a person with special qualities was needed. We found this person in Monsignor Joseph C. Shenrock, pastor of Saint Elizabeth Ann Seton parish, Whiting, New Jersey, and vicar of social services. First of all, Monsignor has a love for history, and with that goes the dedication that is needed for searching out documents and source material. At the same time, he has the quality of leadership that is required to direct such a time-demanding project and to apply the spur to bring the work to completion.

I am most grateful to Monsignor for accepting the commission and for guiding the project. Despite the call for sacrifice in terms of his time and energy, I am sure that he has found the effort to be rewarding and interesting.

It is my hope that all who read *Upon This Rock* will also discover the same interest and be rewarded. I congratulate Monsignor Shenrock and his collaborators on producing this marvelous history of the Diocese of Trenton. It is my hope and prayer that the reading of *Upon This Rock* will raise our hearts in thanksgiving to God for what we have learned and will fill us with the same trust, hope, and courage as exhibited by our predecessors as we face current challenges.

May our future be one of Faith, Hope, and Charity.

John C. Reiss

John C. Reiss
Bishop of Trenton

PREFACE

◆

IN A CERTAIN SENSE, THIS NEW HISTORY of the Diocese of Trenton began thirty-five years ago, when I was stationed at St. Paul's Parish in Burlington, New Jersey. Burlington is one of the oldest cities in New Jersey, and it played an important role in the early history of the Catholic church in New Jersey. While in Burlington, I began to do research on the life of John Tatham, who came to Burlington in 1685 and in whose house Mass was celebrated at that time.

A new history of the Diocese of Trenton is long overdue. Rev. Walter T. Leahy wrote the first history of the diocese in 1906 on the occasion of the Silver Jubilee of the diocese. Since that time, pamphlets and newspaper articles on the diocese have appeared, but no one has undertaken to write a new history.

In the fall of 1990, Bishop John C. Reiss appointed me archivist of the diocese and entrusted to me the task of producing a new history of the diocese. With the help of other interested persons, we have finally produced this history. We hope that it will inspire others to further levels of research and interest in our 112-year experience.

We dedicate this new history to Bishop John C. Reiss, who this year celebrated twenty-five years as a bishop. Without his encouragement and support of the project, this new history would never have seen the light of day.

The local church of Trenton, built on the rock that is Peter, gives thanks to God for Bishop Reiss's twenty-five years as a bishop and for his unswerving interest in all aspects of this new history of the church of Trenton.

Joseph C. Shenrock
January 10, 1993

ACKNOWLEDGMENTS

I T WOULD TAKE ANOTHER BOOK TO AD-
equately thank all the people who have
assisted me in preparing and writing this
new history of the Diocese of Trenton. First
and foremost, I again thank Bishop John C.
Reiss for his encouragement in bringing the
project to completion and Bishop Edward
U. Kmiec, who supported me in this history
until the day he left our diocese for Nashville, Tennessee.

To the pastors of the diocese who answered my letters and phone calls; to the
chancery staff, who cooperated with me in
doing much of the research; and to Joseph
Donadieu, editor of *The Monitor*, and his
staff for allowing me to use the files and past
issues of that publication, I express my
thanks. To the contributors of the articles
on the history, whose names appear in the
opening pages of this book, I extend my
thanks for their loyal cooperation and interest in the project.

If it were not for James F. O'Neill Jr., a
student at Stevens Institute of Technology in
Hoboken, who gave long hours, night and
day, in working on the project, there would
never have been a new history of the diocese
at this time. To the staff of St. Elizabeth Ann
Seton parish, and especially Marian Pernetti,
I owe a debt of gratitude for putting up with
me and for their cooperation in the final
production of this new history.

The following people made special ef-
forts to offer me assistance and support in
this endeavor: Fr. Raymond J. Kupke, Dio-
cese of Paterson; Dr. Joseph J. Casino,
archivist of the Archdiocese of Philadelphia;
C. Adrienne Murphy, executive director of
Joseph Greaton Institute, Old St. Joseph's
Church, Philadelphia; Rebecca B. Colesar,
New Jersey State Library, Trenton; Rev.
Canon James Green, rector of St. Mary's
Episcopal Church, Burlington; Marilyn Se-
quin, secretary of St. Patrick's Parish,
Montreal, Quebec; Sr. Marguerite Smith,
archivist of the Archdiocese of New York;
Margaret Boese, Ocean County College,
Toms River; Sr. John Berchmans, St. Francis
Hospital, Trenton; Fr. Bruno Harel, P.S.S.,
Grand Séminaire de Montréal, Montreal
Quebec; Msgr. Francis R. Seymour, vice-
chancellor for archives of the Archdiocese of
Newark; Msgr. William N. Field, director of
special collections for Seton Hall University
and university archivist; Msgr. Charles S.
Giglio, vicar of communications of the Dio-
cese of Camden; Timothy D. Cary, archivist
of the Archdiocese of Milwaukee, Wiscon-
sin; Fr. Gerald P. Fogarty, S.J., University of
Virginia, Charlottesville, Virginia; Sr.
Aloysia, archivist of the Daughters of Charity, Emmitsburg, Maryland; Barbara Anne
Cusack, associate chancellor of the Archdiocese of Milwaukee, Wisconsin; Dr. Jef-
frey Burns, archivist of the Archdiocese of
San Francisco; Msgr. Theodore A. Opdenaker, priest of the Diocese of Trenton;
Fr. John Catoir, director of the Christophers

movement, New York; Msgr. Joseph Punderson, priest of the Diocese of Trenton; Brother Thomas W. Spalding, Spalding University, Louisville, Kentucky; Christine McCullough, assistant archivist, Archdiocese of Philadelphia; Fr. Robert F. Trisco, Catholic University of America, Washington, D.C.; Brother Philip Hurley, O.S.P., assistant archivist of St. Vincent Archabbey, Latrobe, Pennsylvania; Fr. John W. Bowen, S.S., archivist of the Sulpician Fathers, Baltimore; Dr. Joseph F. Mahoney, Seton Hall University, South Orange; Fr. Peter M. J. Stravinskas, editor of *The Catholic Answer* magazine; Fr. James Dubell, priest of the Diocese of Trenton; Very Rev. Thomas J. Ertle, O.P., provincial of the Dominicans in the New York Province; Fr. Augustine Curley, O.S.B., Newark Abbey, Newark; Fr. Paul K. Thomas, archivist of the Archdiocese of Baltimore; Vincent A. Weiss (deceased), founder and editor of *The Monitor*, diocesan newspaper of the Diocese of Trenton; Henry Murphy, Trenton; Mary Dalton, retired secretary to bishops of the Diocese of Trenton; Thomas Wade, controller of the Diocese of Trenton; Msgr. Edward F. O'Brien, rector of North American College, Rome, Italy; John J. Treanor, archivist of the Archdiocese of Chicago; Fr. Arthur F. Smith, O.S.M., archivist of the Augustinians, Villanova, Pennsylvania; Fr. James C. Sharpe (deceased), librarian at Seton Hall University, South Orange; Marie H. Coen, former teacher at Wayne Valley High School, Wayne, New Jersey; Fr. Joseph M. LaForge, priest of the Diocese of Trenton; Diane L. Backes and Karen L. Mamo, Backes Graphic Productions; and Claude Mastrosimone, Cardinal Publishing Company.

CONTRIBUTORS

Donald P. Delany, former editorial writer at the diocesan newspaper, *The Monitor*, and writer at the *Trenton Times*, Trenton, New Jersey, who lives in West Trenton, New Jersey.

Rev. Msgr. John K. Dermond, pastor of St. Francis Church, Trenton, and judicial vicar of the Diocese of Trenton.

Rev. Vincent E. Keane, director of Aquinas Institute, Princeton, New Jersey.

Regina Waldron Murray, free-lance writer, Princeton, New Jersey.

James F. O'Neill Jr., senior at Stevens Institute of Technology, Hoboken, New Jersey.

Rev. Eugene M. Rebeck, pastor of St. Catharine's Church, Holmdel, New Jersey.

Rev. G. Scott Shaffer, parochial vicar of St. Joseph's Church, Toms River, New Jersey.

Rev. Msgr. Joseph C. Shenrock, pastor of St. Elizabeth Ann Seton Church, Whiting, New Jersey; archivist of the Diocese of Trenton; and curial vicar of social services of the Diocese of Trenton.

Rev. Gregory D. Vaughan, pastor of St. Mary's Church, New Monmouth, New Jersey.

PART ONE

BEFORE THE DIOCESE OF TRENTON

CHAPTER ONE

COLONIAL DAYS
1665~1776

BY MONSIGNOR JOSEPH C. SHENROCK

 IN ORDER TO UNDER-stand the early history of the Roman Catholic Church in New Jersey, one should also have an understanding of English history during American Colonial days. The following is an excerpt from Rev. John T. Catoir's pamphlet *A Brief History of the Catholic Church in New Jersey.*[1]

The Origins of English Supremacy
In the year 1660, Charles II ascended the throne of England. He was ambitious for world supremacy and wanted to control all the colonies in the new world. English troops were already in Virginia, Maryland, Massachusetts, Connecticut, Rhode Island and northern New York. To realize his dream Charles needed the New York harbor and the territory to the west of the Hudson which is known today as New Jersey.

In 1665 New Jersey was governed in the north by the Dutch who had crossed over from their colony on Manhattan Island. Swedes were living southward in the area which is today called Gloucester and

Salem Counties. The British were ancient sea rivals of both the Dutch and the Swedes, and so their new world possessions were doubly tempting for the power seeking King of England.

England had begun a war with Holland over trade disagreements back in 1652, and in spite of superficial attempts at peace-making, the sea battles continued. Charles knew that the Dutch settlement of New Amsterdam, little old New York, was poorly defended. In 1664 he decided to seize it.

British war vessels sailed up the Hudson River on September 7, 1664, and caught the Dutch by surprise. Dutch resistance quickly dissolved at the sight of the overwhelming display of strength. Charles had captured his prize with a mere show of power.

He then deeded the new acquisition to his brother James, Duke of York. James in turn divided the territory west of the Hudson between two men, Sir George Carteret and John Lord Berkeley. Berkeley, Carteret and the Duke decided that the land would be called New Jersey in honor of Carteret's brilliant defense of the Island of Jersey during the Parliamentary Wars.

King Charles II had no legitimate sons. When he died in 1685 the Crown passed to his brother James who was a Catholic.

James II (1685–1688) inherited a difficult Parliament. Although loyal to the Crown, Parliament had a strong determination to preserve the Established Church of England. Laws had been passed which struck fiercely at the "dissenters," a name used to describe all Christians not in affiliation with the Church of England. The Corporate Act ordered that every office holder in an incorporated town would receive Communion in the Established Church. This aimed at eliminating dissenters from holding public office anywhere in the Empire.

Under the reign of Charles these harsh enactments were not allowed. Charles had favored more religious toleration for the dissenters, including Catholics. No doubt Charles' brother James had a strong influence on his attitude since James had become a Catholic in 1668. As a Catholic, King James faced an antagonistic Parliament when he ascended the throne. Parliament was disturbed because of two conflicting traditions, the one being loyalty to the Crown, and the other a rigid determination to block any competition with the Established Church of England. The reign of James, a Catholic King, in a Protestant land, was destined to be short and turbulent.

Period of Proprietary Rule

Although James' grant of New Jersey to Carteret and Berkeley did not transfer any autonomous right to govern, they did issue a document of rule entitled *Concessions and Agreements*. This document reflected the liberal religious attitudes of Charles and James, and therefore it displeased Parliament. The following is an excerpt from it:

> No person was to be disquieted in matters of religious concernment who does not actually disturb the peace of the said Province.

Memorial erected in 1927 to commemorate 1677 landing of first settlers in Burlington.

After the issue of *Concessions and Agreements*, colonists began pouring into New Jersey. Under this liberating legal protection, religious freedom seemed secure in the new territory. Congregationalists, Episcopalians and Presbyterians settled in northern New Jersey, while Baptists moved to the south. Members of the Dutch Reformed Church settled in Passaic, Hackensack, and Raritan. Catholics arrived in very small numbers during the 17th Century, and when they did come they settled in the larger cities of New York and Philadelphia.

The property then began changing hands. In 1674 Berkeley sold his property rights to Edward Byllings. Byllings later transferred a portion of his share to William Penn and two other Quakers. Carteret died in 1680 leaving West New Jersey to his widow. She in turn sold his share at public auction to twelve men, among whom were Penn and Byllings.

King James II was disgruntled by these developments in the new colony. He decided to regain control, and challenged the proprietors to show by what right they held title to their property. The pressure he brought to bear eventually forced the collapse of proprietary rule.

In his efforts to solve one problem, James managed to create three new problems. He was politically naive. He believed

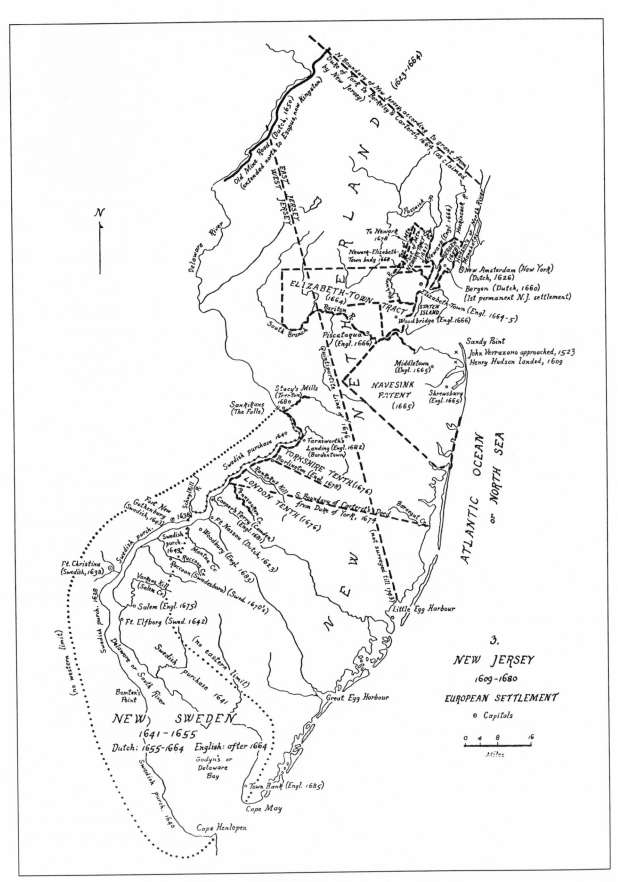

The European Settlement in New Jersey from 1609 to 1680.

that a decree from the King could correct years of blundering politics. With one simple, sweeping decision in 1687 he reunited all of New Jersey, New York, and New England. As though to insure a successful outcome of his rash plan, he appointed Sir Edmund Andros the governor of the whole territory.

From the summer of 1688 until the autumn of 1692 there was no governor actually residing in New Jersey. A government does not run well without a chief. The trouble came quickly. Factional disputes broke out among the landholders and a spirit of anarchy spread among the people. Parliament was highly dissatisfied with King James. When James' wife, Mary of Modena, gave birth to a son, the new prince was baptized a Catholic, and became the direct heir to the throne. Parliament could not bear the thought of continuing under another Catholic and it took action.

In 1688, the "Glorious Revolution" as it is called in history, removed James from the throne and drove him to France in exile. William of Orange had been enlisted to invade England for this purpose. When the overthrow was successfully accomplished, Parliament side-stepped the Catholic Prince and offered the Crown to another Mary and her husband, William III of Holland. This Mary was the Protestant daughter of James by his first wife. The royal couple accepted the honor and agreed to carry out the traditional policy which rejected "Papists."

William and Mary issued the famous Toleration Act in 1689. It was formally adopted in a New Jersey Assembly in 1698, and stated:

> No person or persons whatsoever are to be molested or deprived of any civil Right or Privilege, or rendered incapable of holding any office or employment in the Government because of their religious principles, the Province being planted by Protestant People of Divers Persuasions to whom that liberty was an original encouragement. . . . It shall not extend to any of the Romish Religion the right to extend their manner of worship contrary to the laws of the statutes of England.

Queen Mary died in 1694, and her husband ruled alone until his death in 1702. Mary's younger sister Anne, a less gifted woman, came to power and spent most of her reign unhappily involved in the struggle between Parliament's two political parties, the Whigs and the Tories. The Whigs fought bitterly to establish the supremacy of Parliament over the Crown; the Tories struggled to maintain the traditional power and prestige of royal authority.

Period of Royal Control
The legacy of disorder in New Jersey left by James II was not easily corrected. The absence of strong rule had developed into disunity. The economic effects of local disputes were disastrous, and Jerseyites were finally forced to turn to the Queen for help. As a price for her intervention Queen Anne (1702–1714) made the colonists sign over their respective charters and concede to her the right to govern. This virtual surrender took place on April 17, 1702.

The Queen appointed her cousin Lord Edward H. Cornbury the first governor. In her instruction to him she was very explicit in her thinking on the religious question. ". . . permit a liberty of conscience to all persons except Papists. . . ." She also required an Oath of Supremacy of the Assembly. It was anti-Roman in character, and anyone who refused to take it was to be

"...esteemed and adjudged a Popish Recusant Convict and as such to forfeit and be proceeded against."

In succeeding assemblies there were no new legislative enactments concerning religious freedom, but each succeeding governor did receive the same set of instructions. Some historians argue that Cornbury had actually established the Church of England in New Jersey, but this is unlikely. There is no specific act on record which explicitly established any official religion of the state. The fact that the assembly was predominantly Quaker would argue further against it. Whether any legal act declared it or not, the Crown often presumed the Church of England to be established by the mere presence of English rule. This presumption was of course taken less seriously in areas where there were few Anglicans living. At this time there were hardly any Anglicans living in New Jersey.

Though Catholics were not actually forbidden to exercise their religion, they were held down severely for many decades. For instance, in 1776 the First Constitution of New Jersey continued the long established custom of implicitly excluding Catholics from holding office:

> There shall be no establishment of any one religious sect in preference to another; and that no Protestant inhabitant of this Colony shall be denied the enjoyment of any civil right merely on account of his religious principles ... but that all persons professing a belief in the faith of any Protestant sect shall be capable of being elected into any office of Profit or trust, being a member of either branch of the legislature, and shall fully and freely enjoy every privilege and immunity.

The Revell House
The oldest house in Burlington built 1685.
Mr. Revell was clerk of the Courts of Burlington.

It is interesting to note that Catholics were prevented from holding office in New Jersey by Constitutional Law until 1844. In that year a new Constitution was framed and the religious test finally was eliminated.

JOHN TATHAM
1685~1700

Despite discriminatory laws and a general anti-Catholicism of the time period, Catholics did settle in New Jersey. One of these early settlers was John Tatham. According to most religious histories of the Colonial period, John Tatham was a prominent Catholic citizen in the city of Burlington during the years 1685 to 1700. He arrived in Philadelphia in 1685 and lived for a while in Bucks County, Pennsylvania, until he moved to Burlington and built a beautiful home known as the Stately Palace.[2]

In an interesting article in *The Pennsylvania Magazine*, Dr. Henry H. Bisbee gives us a key to understanding the life of this mysterious person:[3]

One major key lies in the name John Gray, which Tatham used for a time while living in Bucks County. It was by this name that William Penn first knew him, describing him in 1685 as a gentleman and a scholar. A year later, however, Penn had learned additional facts about Gray's career and sought to keep the information secret. In 1686, he wrote to Thomas Lloyd, "Gray is a Benedictine monck of St. James, left them and his vows, was married there, the congregation has spoak to the King about him, and to me. Keep this to thy selfe." Within the year, despite his intentions, Penn had apparently become irritated with Gray's land purchases and made his background more generally known. Thus, using the names Tatham and Gray and the clue of the Benedictines of St. James' Convent, John Tatham's English background can be pieced together.

John Tatham was born in Yorkshire, England, around 1642. In 1657 he was sent to Douai University in France to study for the priesthood and entered the Benedictine Order. He was professed at St. Gregory's, Douai, France, and remained there until about 1676 at which time he was acting as subprior. Shortly afterwards, Father Bede Tatham, the religious name he had chosen, was sent to the "Southern Province of the English missions!"

Tatham was in England scarcely more than a year before the Titus Oates plot put Catholics, in general, and then priests, in particular, in peril of their lives. It is reasonable to conjecture that Tatham left the priesthood and the Benedictine Order at this time and used the name of John Gray. Under this name he met William Penn; purchased a large plot of land in Bucks County, Pennsylvania, in June, 1684; and shortly after, sailed for America.

John Gray of London, friend of William Penn, would hardly as a monk have acquired the means to undertake this new venture in America. Some think that Gray absconded with a large amount of money and books from St. James Abbey in London and came to America. We know that, in 1685, a lawsuit was instituted against Tatham by the English congregation.

After coming to Burlington, Tatham became very active in the public life of that city and of West Jersey. Some think he was the first Catholic to perform the duties of governor of West Jersey in 1691.

He made his last will on July 15, 1700, and died shortly after, because the will was probated on July 26, 1700, leaving his wife, Elizabeth, his sole executor. From the inventory of his will we learn that he had many articles that were used in Catholic worship: relics, crucifixes, chalices, and several Catholic books, including one on the "Holy Mass." At the time of his death, he probably had one of the largest libraries in the state of New Jersey, about 500 volumes.[4]

An early missionary priest traveling from New York to Philadelphia stopped at Tatham's home to celebrate Mass. John McCormick states, "About 1691–92, a priest, traveling under the name of John Smith, left New York. He crossed New Jersey, arrived at Burlington and stopped at the home of John Tatham."[5]

*Collins House, 1808, Burlington,
Home of Isaac Collins, founder of State's
first newspaper. In his office, in Trenton,
Mass was celebrated.*

There are many unanswered questions about the life of John Tatham, but it seems safe to say he was one of the first Catholics in New Jersey. Considering the times, he practiced his faith to the best of his ability.

MISSIONARY
PERIOD
IN NEW JERSEY

Jesuits, Augustinians, and Sulpicians were among the early missionary priests who came to serve the Catholics of New Jersey. The earliest were four Jesuit priests who year after year traveled throughout the state on foot, on horseback, or by carriage. They tried to administer the Sacraments to the few, scattered Catholics who existed in those early years.

John Ury

To understand the hardships endured by the early missionaries, it might be well for us to look at the life of John Ury. His sufferings, and eventual martyrdom, serve as an example of the extreme anti-Catholicism of the time period. In 1739 John Ury taught school in Burlington, New Jersey, for a year.[6] He then went to New York City and was indicted as a Catholic priest and tried in 1741 in the case of the "Negro Plot." There was a rumor in New York City that the Negroes of the city were going to burn the city down and massacre the inhabitants. From the trial it is evident that the people's great fear of the Papacy had as much to do with the whole matter as their fear of the insurrection of the Negroes. On September 29, 1741, John Ury was hanged in New York City because he was a Catholic priest. However, Father Peter Gilmary Shea, a great Catholic scholar, doubts very much whether John Ury was a priest.[7] Most historians believe he was a defrocked Anglican clergyman. The story indicates the hatred that existed in Colonial days for Catholics and Catholic priests.

Father Theodore Schneider, S.J. 1743–64

According to Father Joseph Flynn's book, *The Catholic Church in New Jersey*, Father Theodore Schneider earned the title "first missionary in New Jersey."[8] Father Schneider was born in Geinsheim, Germany, on April 7, 1703, and entered the Jesuit Society on September 25, 1721. On September 19, 1740, he received his orders from his superiors to go to America and work in Pennsylvania. We know he arrived in New Jersey in

Father Farmer—circa 1759
Going on missions in New Jersey.
No picture of him is extant, but we are told
that he was "of slender form, having a
countenance mild, gentle, and bearing an
expression almost seraphic."

August 1743 and visited the home of Martin Lorentz, near Salem, New Jersey. We know that in 1744 he traveled to the northern part of New Jersey, stopping at Bound Brook.

It is safe to say that Father Schneider visited every village, out-of-the-way farm, and settlement within the territory of New Jersey in his quest for Catholics. He spent much time visiting Burlington and Trenton on his journeys.

Father Farmer, another Jesuit missionary who was to follow in the footsteps of Father Schneider, said that he often had no bed or food on his fatiguing journeys. At last, worn out in the service of the Lord, Father Schneider broke down suddenly in 1763, after more than twenty years of toil. His provincial superior contemplated recalling him to Philadelphia to recuperate, but, before this happened, he died on July 10, 1764, after an illness of four weeks. Father Farmer buried his colleague at the foot of the altar of the church Father Schneider had built at Goshenhoppen, Pennsylvania, and preached the sermon at his funeral Mass. Father Farmer was to look after Father Schneider's flock as best he could after his death.

Father Ferdinand Steinmeyer, S.J. "Father Farmer" 1752–86

Another Jesuit missionary was Father Ferdinand Steinmeyer, commonly known as "Father Farmer." He was born in Weisserstein, Germany, on October 13, 1720. His parents "lived in comfortable circumstances and his studious habits as a boy early marked him for one of the learned professions."[9] Father Farmer entered the Jesuit community on September 28, 1743, in Landsberg, Germany. He volunteered for the missions in China. His wishes were not granted, but he was for a time one of the noted professors at the University of Freiburg. He was sent after that to the

Old St. Joseph's Church in 1776—first Catholic church in Philadelphia.

missions in America and probably landed in Philadelphia in the company of Father Sillensbergh, S.J., on June 20, 1751. He was appointed to the mission of Lancaster, Pennsylvania, and after spending six years in Lancaster, he was transferred to Philadelphia in 1758 to assist Father Harding and Father Schneider in their missionary work. He was to spend almost thirty years as a missionary in New Jersey and New York.

Father Farmer must have had an unusual constitution because the registers of the Sacraments indicate that he covered considerable distances in one day, even though the laws of New Jersey and New York were anti-Catholic. His first pastoral function in New Jersey occurred on March 15, 1759, when he baptized in the home of Matthew Geiger in Salem County.

During his twenty-eight years in Philadelphia, he served as assistant to the pastor of Old St. Joseph's Church and once a year made his necessary journeys to New Jersey and New York. Father Farmer, happy to hear that Father John Carroll, S.J., had been appointed prefect apostolic of the church in America, wrote him a letter of congratulation. He also believed that the new church in America needed a bishop; in fact, he wrote to Father Carroll on January 19,

1785, stating, "I cannot conceive how we could be a body without a Bishop for a head!"[10]

During the year 1784 he still covered the length of the state of New Jersey; he undoubtedly visited Catholics in Burlington and the Trenton area. Even though he was sick, he made a trip into New Jersey just six weeks before he died, to witness a marriage on August 2, 1786. He died on August 17, 1786, at the age of 65, worn out after years of missionary work.

Father Carroll, bereaved over the loss of his best priest, wrote to Cardinal Leonardo Antonelli in Rome that "Father Farmer was a priest who had spent many years in Philadelphia in the practice of all kinds of virtues and labor for the salvation of souls, and concluded his life full of merits by which his may well be regarded as a most holy death."[11]

It was during Father Farmer's time in Philadelphia and as a missionary to New Jersey that Pope Clement XIV suppressed the Jesuit Society on August 16, 1773, by publishing a brief called "Dominus ac Redemptor Noster." The Society remained suppressed until July 31, 1814, when it was restored by Pope Leo XII.

Father Lawrence Graessl
November 1787–November 1793

Following the death of Father Farmer, the West Jersey Mission was attended to by Father Lawrence Graessl. Father Graessl was born August 18, 1753, at Rumansfield, Bavaria; entered the Jesuit novitiate in 1771; and was invited by Father Farmer to labor for the American mission. The absence of any baptismal records between 1787 and 1790 prevents us from following Father Graessl in his early missionary trips. Consequently, not till 1791 are his West Jersey labors known.

Father Graessl's constitution was not as robust as that of Father Farmer, and in the early part of 1793, he contracted a severe cold, which, aggravated by the hardships of missionary life, soon brought on consumption. So great was his zeal, however, that even when not on missionary duty in New Jersey or Delaware, he continued ministering to the Catholics of Philadelphia and vicinity, providing more evidence of a saintly life that was the wonder of priests and the laity alike.

Father Graessl always kept up a correspondence with his parents and friends in Germany both for their edification and for his own encouragement. The following extract from a letter to his parents, dated June 19, 1793, from Philadelphia, will speak for him:[12]

Dearest Friends,
I am sick and according to human understanding, my days are counted, probably before you read this, my body will rest in the grave, but let the splendid view of eternity be our consolation. My sickness I caught during my last mission through the extremely sandy roads of Nova Caesera [New Jersey] on a hot summer day. Pains in the chest, short breath, a dry cough, fever setting in every evening, nightly sweats, are the symptoms of the sickness whatever you may call it.

Old St. Joseph's Courtyard, 1733.

The election took place in the beginning of May, and dearest Parents, the choice fell on your poor Lawrence. Whilst my name, birthplace, etc., went to Rome to receive the approbation of the Pope, I shall leave this world to rest forever from the sufferings of my early pilgrimage.

Your affectionate, until death faithful,
Lawrence Graessl

As the good missionary had announced to his friends across the sea, he had been selected as coadjutor bishop to Bishop Carroll of Baltimore in May 1793, and the recommendation to the appointment had been forwarded to Rome for ratification. In January 1794, Rome confirmed the bishop's choice, and the bulls of his appointment were returned to America. By the time they finally arrived, however, Father Graessl had already passed on months before. Due to

the slow modes of travel, the letter had taken three or four months to reach Rome in the first place. Father Graessl's was the death of a saint, for when, in 1793–94, that dreadful plague of yellow fever ravaged Philadelphia, he contracted the disease on sick-call duty and died a martyr to charity in November 1793.[13] Father Graessl was the last of the early missionaries to do regular missionary work in New Jersey. However, the Jesuits remained in charge of these missions until 1797.[14]

Father Leonard Neale
1793–98

After Father Graessl's death, Father Leonard Neale, who had the shortest term of all the Jesuit missionaries, was placed in charge of the area during the years 1793 to 1798. Father Neale had come from Maryland to assist his brother priests in plague-stricken Philadelphia. In 1798 he was re-called from the New Jersey missions and named president of Georgetown College. Two years later, he was appointed coadjutor bishop of Baltimore and the first Catholic bishop consecrated in the United States. He succeeded Archbishop Carroll in that see in 1815. Father Neale was the last of the early Jesuits in charge of missionary work in West Jersey. When he left for Georgetown in 1798, there was not a single Catholic church structure anywhere in New Jersey.

The records and lives of the early Jesuit missionaries show that the two cities they visited most to celebrate the Sacraments and

Mass were Trenton and Burlington, within the present territory of the Diocese of Trenton.

Augustinian Missionaries

The next group of missionaries to visit New Jersey was the Augustinians, who arrived in Philadelphia in 1795. In 1801, Father Matthew Carr, O.S.A., built a large church at Fourth and Vine streets in Philadelphia and called it St. Augustine. It was from this church the early Augustinians continued their missionary work in New Jersey.

Father Flynn in his history *The Catholic Church in New Jersey* states, "After the death of Father Farmer, the Augustinians took up missionary work in New Jersey and the Catholics of this state must ever hold the members of this Order in grateful remembrance."[15]

Among the Augustinian priests who served in New Jersey was Father George Staunton, O.S.A. His missionary records indicate that he visited Burlington. He "baptized two children of John Gerard and his wife, Eleanor, born at Burlington, New Jersey. The names of the children are Caroline Eugenie, born June 20, 1797, and Henrietta May, born June 21, 1799, both at Burlington."[16]

Father Staunton did missionary work in Trenton and he baptized children there as the following indicates:

In 1804 there are five entries for Trenton, or "born near the town of Trenton," as follows: Peter Callan, born near Trenton, February 22, 1804, baptized November 1,

1804; Eleanor McDonough, born August 9, 1804, baptized November 1, 1804; Edward Sheridan, born June 1, 1804, baptized November 4, 1804; Peter Place, born October 17, 1802, and William Place, born November 3, 1804, at Trenton, baptized November 5, 1804. All these Trenton baptisms are entered under the name of Father Philip Stafford.

In 1805 the following baptisms are marked "at Trenton": Teresa Henrietta Sartori, baptized by Fr. Carr, April 23, 1805. On the same day Mary Magdalen Ellis, adult, was baptized. The following day, also at Trenton, Fr. Carr baptized John Baptist, Edward Duville and James Reily, the latter "born at Monmouth in the State of New Jersey." In August of this same year, 1805, there is a record of four baptisms by Fr. Carr at Trenton—"in civitate Trenton." Again, in 1806, April 7, the baptism of two children is recorded at Trenton, Bertrand and Margaret Léfèbvre. Bertrand was born October 5, 1800, Margaret April 6, 1803. In September of the same year, 1806, Fr. Carr records eight baptisms in New Jersey, Charles Sartori, "born at Lamberton, near Trenton," the others named Reily, Mullen, Sheridan, Hanlon, Hamilton, McCafarty, MacAllister, "born at Lamberton."

These facts from the Sacramental Registers seem to make it evident that Catholics living in what was then "West Jersey" were depending on the priests at Saint Augustine's for the Sacraments and ministrations of religion during the first ten years of the century.

An entry in Bishop Kenrick's Diary in 1830 will show that the Friars from St. Augustine's were still taking care of "West" or "South Jersey" at the beginning of the third decade of the century:[17]

August the fifteenth day [1830] I blessed the cemetery and church of St. Mary of the Assumption in a place commonly called PLEASANT MILLS, in Gloucester county in the State of New Jersey. About two hundred Catholics were present from various places, some distant six miles, some twelve or more miles from the church. The people are employed about the furnaces and works of this kind. The Rev. William O'Donnell, O.S.A., exercises the office of a pastor among them. He visits them from the city once in the space of two months.

There are said to be many other Catholics living scattered in the southern part of this state. I am told that in order to minister to their needs a church should be built in a place called MELVILLE [Millville]; and that, if a priest were stationed there with a love and zeal for souls, he could by visiting other parts bring back to the way of salvation, many whose parents had been Catholics.

At present there is no other church in that part of this state which belongs to this diocese, but one in the town of Trenton, which is also visited by the same priest [Father William O'Donnell] once every month.[18]

Sulpician Missionary

The last missionary that we shall mention is Father Pierre Babad, a Sulpician priest from Baltimore. His missionary work in Burlington is detailed in a book called *Mrs. Seton*, by Father Joseph I. Dirvin, C.M.

Father Dirvin mentions, in his scholarly work on the life of Elizabeth Ann Seton, that Father Babad, while doing missionary work in Burlington, was recalled by Archbishop Carroll to Emmitsburg to receive Harriet Seton, sister-in-law of Mother Seton, into the church. Father Babad arrived back in Emmitsburg to receive Harriet into the church in July 1809.

Father Babad was born at Fort-de-Veyle, in France, was ordained in France, and came to America, as did many Sulpicians during the French Revolution. After twenty years of work as a missionary and seminary professor, he returned to France and died on June 13, 1846.

REFERENCES

1. Permission was obtained from Rev. John T. Catoir, a priest in the Diocese of Paterson, to use an excerpt from his *Brief History of the Catholic Church in New Jersey*. Copyrighted and privately published in 1965, pp. 1–7.

2. Given, Lois V. "The Great and Stately Palace." *The Pennsylvania Magazine of History and Biography*. Philadelphia: The Historical Society of Pennsylvania, 1959, LXXXIII: 265. With permission.

3. Bisbee, Henry H. "John Tatham, Alias Gray." *The Pennsylvania Magazine of History and Biography*. Philadelphia: The Historical Society of Pennsylvania, 1959, LXXXIII: 261–263. With permission.

4. McCormick, John D. "John Tatham, New Jersey's First Catholic Governor." *The American Catholic Historical Researches*. Philadelphia: Martin I. J. Griffin, 1888, V: 89.

5. McCormick, John D. "Appendix II. John Tatham, New Jersey's Missing Governor." *The History of the Colony of Nova-Cæsaria, or New Jersey*, by Samuel Smith.

Spartanburg, South Carolina: The Reprint Company, Publishers, 1975, p. 575.

6. Flynn, Rev. Joseph M. *The Catholic Church in New Jersey*. New York: The Publishers' Printing Co., 1904, p. 21.

7. Shea, John Gilmary. *The Catholic Church in Colonial Days*. New York: Edward O. Jenkin's Sons, 1886, p. 399.

8. Flynn, p. 31.

9. Schrott, Rev. Lambert, and Rev. Theodore Roemer. *Pioneer German Catholics in the United States*. New York: The United States Catholic Historical Society, 1933, p. 57.

10. Schrott, p. 64.

11. Schrott, p. 66.

12. Leahy, Rev. Walter T. *The Catholic Church of the Diocese of Trenton, N.J.* Princeton: Princeton University Press, 1906, p. 18.

13. Leahy, p. 18.

14. Leahy, p. 18.

15. Flynn, p. 60.

16. Tourscher, Fr. Francis Edward, S.T.M. *Old Saint Augustine's in Philadelphia*. Philadelphia: The Peter Reilly Company, 1937, p. 32.

17. Tourscher, p. 33–34.

18. *Diary and Visitation Record of the Rt. Rev. Francis Patrick Kenrick*. Under the direction of the Most Rev. Edmond F. Prendergast, Archbishop of Philadelphia. Lancaster, Pennsylvania: Wickersham Printing Co., 1916, p. 30.

OTHER SOURCES

1. Ahlstrom, Sydney E. *A Religious History of the American People*. New Haven and London: Yale University Press, 1972, p. 341.

2. Bayley, J. R. *A Brief Sketch of the Early History of the Catholic Church on the Island of New York*. New York: United States Catholic Historical Society, 1973, reprinted from the 1870 edition, Monograph Series XXIX, pp. 42–47.

3. Daley, John M., S.J. *Ferdinand Farmer, S.J. Pioneer Missionary (1720–1786)*. September 1944. A thesis presented to the faculty of the Department of History, Georgetown University, in partial fulfillment of the requirements for the degree of Master of Arts.

4. Dirvin, Rev. Joseph I., C.M. *Mrs. Seton*. New York: Farrar, Straus and Giroux, 1962, 1975, p. 246.

5. Griffin, Martin I. J. "John Ury." *Records of the American Catholic Historical Society of Philadelphia*. Philadelphia: American Catholic Historical Society, September 1928, vol. XXXIX, no. 3, pp. 225–238.

6. Schrott, Rev. Lambert, and Rev. Theodore Roemer. *Pioneer German Catholics in the United States*. New York: The United States Catholic Historical Society, 1933, pp. 43–47.

7. "The Trial of John Ury." *American Catholic Historical Researches*. Philadelphia: Martin I. J. Griffin, January 1899, vol. XVI, no. 1, pp. 1–58.

CHAPTER TWO

DIOCESES OF BALTIMORE, PHILADELPHIA, AND NEW YORK, 1788~1853

BY MONSIGNOR JOSEPH C. SHENROCK

PRIOR TO 1784, THE Catholics of the United States were under the jurisdiction of the ordinary in London, England. In 1790, a bishop was consecrated for the United States with the see located at Baltimore, Maryland. His territory included the entire country, as it was then, until 1808, when four new dioceses were created. Until 1853, the Diocese of Philadelphia covered West Jersey; the Diocese of New York included the territory of East Jersey.

FIRST BISHOP OF BALTIMORE: JOHN CARROLL, 1790~1815

Father John Carroll was born in Upper Marlboro, Maryland, on June 8, 1735. He studied at St. Omer College in France, joined the Jesuits in France, and was ordained a priest in 1769. After the suppression of the Jesuit order on July 21, 1773, Father Carroll returned to his home and family in Maryland. He then played an important role in defending the Catholic faith in the thirteen colonies.

On June 9, 1784, Father Carroll was appointed prefect apostolic of the church in the United States and was then informed he would be appointed the first Catholic bishop in the United States as soon as the necessary information on the state of the church in the United States was received by authorities in Rome. On September 7, 1788, Pope Pius VI created the first diocese in the United States, namely, Baltimore. Father Carroll (as the first bishop) was ordained a bishop on August 15, 1790, by Bishop Charles Walmesley in Ludwirth Castle, Dorset, England. He returned to the United States

Bishop John Carroll

after his ordination to take up the new position in Baltimore.

Bishop Carroll knew of the missionary work of the early Jesuits in Pennsylvania and New Jersey and often referred to them in his writings. He referred to the German Jesuit missionaries in the highest terms as "men of much learning and unbounded zeal."[1] Bishop Carroll said expressly that Father Schneider, moreover, "was a person of great dexterity in business, consummate prudence and undaunted magnanimity."[2]

Rev. Charles H. Wharton

A cousin of John Carroll and an ex-Jesuit priest, Rev. Charles H. Wharton, was elected rector of St. Mary's Episcopal Church in Burlington on September 5, 1798. Charles Wharton was born in St. Mary County, Maryland, on May 25, 1748. In 1760, at the age of 12, he was sent to study at the Jesuit School at St. Omer, France. He was ordained a Jesuit priest in September 1772. On July 21, 1773, one year after his ordination to the priesthood, the Jesuits were suppressed. Rev. Charles Wharton had a great love for the Jesuits to his dying day, on July 23, 1833. He had been rector of St. Mary's Episcopal Church in Burlington for thirty-five years.

Wharton had several public disputes in writing on the subject of the Catholic faith with his cousin Archbishop John Carroll. He justified his proclaimed entry into the Protestant Episcopal Church by disagreeing with certain dogmas and practices of the Roman Catholic Church, which are found in his famous pamphlet "A Letter to the Roman Catholics of the City of Worcester."[3] His cousin responded to the letter in the 115-page "Address to the Roman Catholics of the United States of America."[4] These two letters appear in the second volume of *The Remains of the Rev. Charles Henry Wharton, D.D., with a Memoir of his Life.* Bishop George Washington Doane, bishop of the Episcopal Diocese of New Jersey, wrote the two-volume history of Rev. Charles H. Wharton in 1834.

It is said of Wharton that when a servant of his household was stricken with a mortal illness, and realizing the impossibility of getting a priest from Philadelphia for she was a Catholic, Wharton said to her, "Although I am a parson, I am also a Catholic priest and can give you absolution in *your* case." She made her confession to him and he absolved her, thus giving her that little comfort before she died. Wharton's nephew, a good Catholic and a judge in Washington D.C., is responsible for this story.[5]

Recently, interest about Charles H. Wharton has appeared in two articles, one by Brother Thomas Spalding, in the *Catholic Historical Review* of October 1985,[6] and an article in *Rome: Anglican and Episcopal History* of June 1987,[7] by Toby Terrar. Surely the ex-Jesuit priest was a concern to his cousin, John Carroll, and to the early Catholics in the Burlington area, later a part of the Diocese of Trenton.

Carroll's Visitation to Trenton

We know that there was trouble in the early church in Trenton according to a letter written by Archbishop Carroll to Mr. James Barry on September 8, 1803:[8]

Philada. Sep. 8—1803—

My dear & much respected Sir
Your joyful tidings of Anne's convalescence, & the probability of my having the happiness of your family's company to Boston were received, before I left Baltimore—; and pray, let my joy be compleat, let not a part only, but the whole of your family be of the party.

Next Monday, the 12th, I will leave this for the neighbourhood of N. York. The Devil is always busy to raise obstacles in my way; he, or his agent has made a disturbance at Trenton, where I did not expect any business, which will perhaps cause me some delay—; so that I do not expect to cross Hobuck ferry before Wednesday. Indeed I am much perplexed by the situation of N. York. Mr. Carr here says, that Mr. Morris's house is so much in or contiguous to the

suburbs of N. York, that I shall be subjected to quarantine, if I go thither. I write to day for an immediate answer, & whether a boat can be got, which without touching at the city, will conduct me to the Narrows. Excuse haste. Assure your dear & respectable family of the constant attachment of, Dr. Barry, Yrs J. B. of B.
ALS AAB

Creation of New Dioceses and Archdiocese

Bishop Carroll continued to lead the church in America. However, on April 8, 1808, four new dioceses were created by Pope Pius VII with sees at Philadelphia, New York, Boston, and Bardstown, Kentucky. Bishop Carroll was promoted to archbishop for the new Archdiocese of Baltimore. Official news of the new dioceses did not arrive in Baltimore until August 1810. A Dominican living in Rome, Father Richard L. Concanen, O.P., was appointed bishop of New York; Father Michael Egan was selected for Philadelphia. On November 1, 1810, Father John Cheverus was ordained in St. Peter's procathedral, Baltimore, as bishop for the new Diocese of Boston. Three days later, Father Benedict J. Flaget was consecrated bishop of Bardstown at St. Patrick's Church, Fells Point, Maryland (near Baltimore).

New Jersey had been divided into East and West Jersey in 1664 between Lord Berkeley and Sir George Carteret. "In 1664, about the colony of New Jersey, it had been granted to Lord Berkeley and Sir George Carteret by James, Duke of York, by his brother, Charles II of England,"[9] hence its partitions into West and East Jersey. The exact line of partition was a disputed issue for years.

Further confusion over the partitionings arose in 1808, with the establishment of the Dioceses of Philadelphia and New York. The official documents, known as bulls, which created New York and Philadelphia as Sees, gave no clear indication of where the division of the state of New Jersey would take place, since there were few Catholics in the central part of the state. The boundary remained uncertain until June 18, 1834, when Pope Gregory XVI described the boundaries of the new dioceses in the United States. The line separating New Jersey from Philadelphia given in this official document followed the old maps representing the East and West Jerseys.

The *Catholic Press*, on October 30, 1830, published a letter containing additional information. "When a Bishop was sent from the Holy See to New York, the Jerseys were divided according to the old division line (which runs from Easton, Pa., to Little Egg Harbor) between the dioceses of New York and Philadelphia."[10] Most of the territory of the future Diocese of Trenton was under the jurisdiction of the bishop of Philadelphia.

FOUNDER OF THE CHURCH IN TRENTON: JOHN BAPTIST SARTORI

In 1804, Catholic services were held in Trenton at the printing offices in the house

John Baptist Sartori

of Isaac Collins, which stood on the corner of Broad and State streets. We do not know whether Mr. Collins was a Catholic or not, but that he allowed Mass to be celebrated in his printing offices indicates he must have been a Catholic or had a great love for the Catholic faith.[11]

From 1811 to 1814, services were held in the home of John Baptist Sartori, who well could be called the father of the Diocese of Trenton. When early Catholics in the Trenton area decided they needed a church for Mass and the Sacraments, they approached Bishop Michael Egan of Philadelphia for advice and permission. In 1814, Sartori and Captain John Hargous purchased a lot on the corner of Lamberton and Market streets. A brick church was erected and called St. John's Chapel of West Jersey.

It was the first Catholic church in the state of New Jersey. The church and a cemetery were blessed by Bishop Egan on June 12, 1814. Rev. John P. Mackin built Trenton's second church, which opened for mass on Christmas 1847. He and most of the congregation moved to that church. Use of Trenton's first Catholic church ended because the remaining Germans were unable to support it. However, in 1851, Peter A. Hargous, son of Captain Hargous, purchased the building. As early as 1852, mass was offered for the Germans. This group would soon develop into St. Francis of Assisium Parish.

One of the original founders of Trenton's first Catholic church, John Baptist Sartori was born in Rome in 1765. He was the son of the pontifical jeweler; his father worked for several Popes. John Sartori emigrated to America in August 1793 and settled in Philadelphia.

Bishop Carroll of Baltimore knew John Sartori. In fact, he wrote a letter about him

On the Delaware River in Trenton, mansion of Mr. and Mrs. John Baptist Sartori.

to Cardinal Leonardo Antonelli, describing him as a good, practicing Catholic:[12]

> Baltimore September 23, 1793
> Most Eminent Cardinal,
> A month ago, an impressive and very refined young man, John Baptist Sartori, presented me with a letter of introduction from Your Eminence. What particularly pleased me about him was that he did not, as do so many who come to us from Europe, begin to be lax in his religious conduct. I thought I should mention this to Your Eminence so that you might know how deeply he took to heart that advice which in your wisdom and zeal you gave him at his departure from Rome.

Bishop Carroll reported in a later letter, of July 3, 1794, to Cardinal Antonelli that John Baptist Sartori married a woman by the name of Teresa Musgrove in Philadelphia on March 19, 1795:[13]

> A frank and open young man, John Baptist Sartori, about whom I wrote on September 23 last year, recently married a good girl, the daughter of very respectable parents. The girl had been brought up in the sect of Shakers, popularly called Quakers, and she was still unbaptized. But before the wedding she was instructed in our faith by the priests in Philadelphia, and she was admitted to baptism. She now professes the Catholic faith. John Baptist asked that I explain the facts to you, most eminent Prince of the Church, so that on the one hand you may know that he did nothing unworthy of a man whom you had recommended, and on the other that his parents might learn from you that everything was in accord with ecclesiastical law.

During the time that he was living in Philadelphia, Sartori had dinner with William Seton, husband of Elizabeth Ann Seton, later canonized as the first American saint. William Seton wrote to his wife from Philadelphia on July 26, 1794, to report this event:[14]

> I dined yesterday with my friend Sartori. His wife is a most agreeable little woman, and I was highly gratified at the many compliments passed on my *Cara Sposa*. Mrs. S[artori]. declares she must see you, and I have invited them to pass some days with us before they go to Italy, which will be in the month of September. I am sure you will be most pleased with her.

Sartori was appointed U.S. consul to the papal states by President John Adams on June 26, 1797. After his time in Philadelphia, John Baptist Sartori returned to Rome with his wife.

No record remains of the death of Mr. Sartori's first wife, but from existing records it is evident that he returned to the United States in April 1800 and settled in Trenton, New Jersey, as the Pope's consul general in New York City.

Four years later, John Baptist Sartori married Henriette de Woofooin, age 17. Together they built a beautiful home on the Delaware River. To this marriage, fourteen children were born, eleven growing to maturity. Henriette Sartori died in 1828 at this home following the birth of twins.

On March 16, 1815, Bishop Carroll wrote as follows to John Grassi:[15]

> Allow me the liberty of introducing to you Mr. Sartori, your respectable countryman, of whom you must have heared: he has resided more than twenty years in this country, for his first wife an American, whom he carried to Rome, & who was very particularly noticed by Pius 6th; the Father of Mr. Sartori having been in a distinguished employment under his Holiness. The bearer of this has the singular merit of having preserved in this country of infidelity the integrity of his faith, and attachment to the practices of our Holy religion. He has children growing up, and amongst them a Son almost ripe for a College; on which account, as well as to afford him the pleasure of seeing you, I shall place the letter in his hands. . . .

From a letter written by Bishop Henry Conwell of Philadelphia to Archbishop

Henriette Sartori

Ambrose Marechal of Baltimore on April 8, 1821, we learn that John Sartori was in Philadelphia on that date visiting the bishop, requesting a dispensation for his wife's niece:[16]

> . . . Signore Sartori from Trenton was here today requiring a dispensation for a German Baron to be married to his former wife's niece. . . . I could not gratify him. But I promised to write to you for it, hoping that if you had the faculty for any case or number of cases of that degree you would extend it to him but I found you had not. The Baron anxiously expects your answer.

Bishop Kenrick, in his diary on March 4, 1832, speaks of John Sartori: "The church property is held in the name of John Baptist Sartori, who, however, is now preparing to convey the same to me, to be held by me, in trust, for the congregation."[17]

As a result of his work for the early church in Trenton, Sartori received a letter from Peter Francis Cardinal Galletti dated December 16, 1828:[18]

> Being charged with providing in foreign ports persons designated to look after the interests and to the protection of commerce and of the pontifical subjects; and being persuaded of the ability and honesty which characterizes you, as the representative of His Holiness Leo XII, and by the authority of our office of Camerlengo, we have decided to nominate you, Giovanni Battista Sartori, Consul General of the ports of the United States of America, residing in Trenton, with ordinary faculties to exercise con-

sular jurisdiction and to enjoy all the honors and privileges and emoluments which are joined to this charge, similar in all things to those practised by the representatives of other nations. . . . We further give you the faculty to select and designate, subject to our approval, according to the needs or advantages of commerce and pontifical navigation, vice consuls and consular agents, according to the greater or less importance of the port in the places subject to your consular jurisdiction.

> We beg all authorities whom this may concern to recognize and treat with Sig. Giovanni Battista Sartori in his capacity as Consul General. . . .

After the death of his wife, Henriette, in 1828, Sartori began to lose interest in his work as consul. After many years in the United States he returned to Leghorn, Italy, and died in 1853 at the age of 88.

All these early records indicate that John Baptist Sartori was an outstanding Catholic in the early days of New Jersey and rightly won for himself the right to be called founding father of the church of Trenton.

EARLY BISHOPS OF PHILADELPHIA

Most of the present Diocese of Trenton was under the jurisdiction of the bishop of Philadelphia until 1853, at which time all of New Jersey was under the bishop of Newark.

On October 28, 1810, at St. Peter's procathedral, Baltimore, Father Michael Egan was consecrated the first bishop of

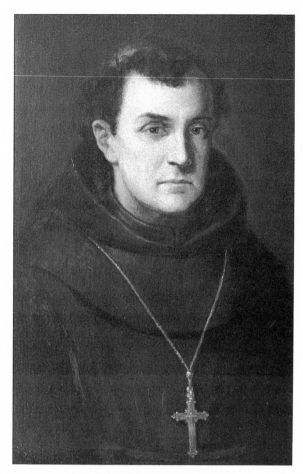

Bishop Michael Egan, O.S.F.
1810–1814
First bishop of Philadelphia

Philadelphia. As we have already mentioned, Bishop Michael Egan came to Trenton on June 12, 1814, to bless the first Catholic church in New Jersey, known as St. John the Baptist Church.

As far as records show, the second bishop of Philadelphia, Bishop Henry Conwell, never set foot in New Jersey but knew of the Catholics in the Trenton area from John Sartori, who paid him a visit on April 8, 1821.

The third bishop of Philadelphia was Bishop Francis Patrick Kenrick. Entries in his diary detail visits to the Trenton area on many occasions. Some of the places he

Bishop Henry Conwell
1820–1842
Second bishop of Philadelphia

First St. John's Church, Trenton,
dedicated June 12, 1814,
by Bishop Michael Egan of Philadelphia.

visited are the subjects of the following excerpts:[19]

August the fifteenth day [1830] I blessed the cemetery and church of St. Mary of the Assumption in a place commonly called PLEASANT MILLS, in Gloucester county in the state of New Jersey. About two hundred Catholics were present from various places, some distant six miles, some twelve or more miles from the church. The people generally are employed about the furnaces and works of this kind. The Rev. William O'Donnell, O.S.A., exercises the offices of a pastor among them. He visits them from the city once in the space of two months.

Bishop Francis Patrick Kenrick
1842–1851
Third bishop of Philadelphia

There are said to be many other Catholics living scattered in the southern section of this state. I am told that in order to minister to their needs a church should be built at a place called MELVILLE; and that, if a priest were stationed there with a love and zeal for souls, he could, by visiting other parts, bring back many to the way of salvation, whose parents had been Catholics.

At present there is no other church in that part of this state which belongs to this diocese, but one in the town of Trenton, which is also visited by the same priest [Father O'Donnell] once every month. . . .

March the fourth day [1832]. I visited the congregation of St. John the Baptist, in the town of Trenton in the state of New Jersey. I confirmed forty-nine persons; and seventy-five received Holy Communion. Religion is strong here under the prudent care of the Rev. Thomas Gegan. The number of Catholics resident in this town and vicinity is not large. But just at present there are a great number of Irish Catholics, who are employed on public works. The church property is held in the name of John Baptist Sartori, who, however, is now preparing to convey the same to me, to be held by me, in trust, for the congregation. The church is still burdened with debt, which the pastor, however, hoped to pay off, depending mainly on the generous contributions of the working men.

My companion on this journey [to Trenton] was the Rev. William Whelan, who came here on the second day of March from the diocese of Bardstown. . . .

November the nineteenth day [1837]. I visited the town of Trenton [New Jersey], and I blessed the cemetery near the church of St. John the Baptist in the town of Bloomsbury. I confirmed more than thirty persons. The Rev. Mr. Barron preached. . . .

November the fifteenth day [1840]. I confirmed thirty-seven in the church of St. John the Baptist in the town of Bloomsbury near Trenton. My brother preached. The Rev. Mr. John Gilligan celebrated the Mass. . . .

October the twenty-sixth day [1845]. I confirmed thirty in the church of St. John the Baptist, Trenton, New Jersey. . . .

June the twenty-seventh day [1847]. I laid the corner-stone of a new church in the town of Trenton [St. John the Baptist]. . . .

October the twenty-second day [1848]. I confirmed forty-three in the church of St. John the Baptist, in the town of Trenton. . . .

August the twenty-sixth day [1849]. I confirmed twenty in the church of St. Paul, Burlington [New Jersey]. . . .

After twenty-one years of service in the Diocese of Philadelphia, Francis P. Kenrick became archbishop of Baltimore. That circumstance played a major part in the appointment of his successor, for in Baltimore, Kenrick walked to St. Alphonsus Church every week to seek confession with Father John N. Neumann, C.Ss.R.

Bishop Neumann came to New Jersey in 1853 to the town of Progress, now known as Riverside. The saintly bishop visited the town of Progress to receive from Mrs. Bechtold a plot of ground for a church. He also had dealings with St. Francis Church, Trenton, and St. Paul's Church, Burlington. It was during Bishop Neumann's time, on July 29, 1853, that Pope Pius IX created the Diocese of Newark, which was to include the whole state of New Jersey.

Bishop John Neumann, later St. John Neumann
1852–1860
Fourth bishop of Philadelphia

OUTSTANDING EARLY PASTOR: FATHER JOHN P. MACKIN

One of the first priests whom Bishop Kenrick ordained was Rev. John P. Mackin, who was to play an important role in the early history of the Catholic church in the Trenton area.

Father Mackin was born in County Armagh, Ireland, in 1819. At an early age, he showed an inclination for the priesthood, and with the consent of his parents and spiritual advisers, he began his studies for the priesthood at the Theological College, connected with the Archdiocese of Armagh. At the conclusion of his studies, he emigrated to the United States in 1839, entering St. Charles Borromeo Seminary in Philadelphia.[20]

He was ordained to the priesthood in St. John's, Philadelphia, by Bishop Kenrick on December 24, 1843. Father Mackin's first assignment was in St. Peter's Church, Lancaster, Pennsylvania. In June 1844, he was transferred to St. John the Baptist Church in Trenton. At that time there were but few Catholics in New Jersey. Father Mackin's mission extended over a wide and scattered territory. He was obliged to attend the missions at Bordentown, Mount Holly, Lambertville, and Burlington, New Jersey, as well as at Bristol, Pennsylvania.

In 1844, he purchased a plot of land on Broad Street in Trenton, and, on this, he erected the second Catholic church in Trenton. On August 27, 1848, the church was dedicated by Rev. Francis Gartland, who was vicar-general of Philadelphia and pastor of St. John's Church in Philadelphia.[21]

Father Mackin was granted a leave of absence and an extended vacation by Bishop James R. Bayley of Newark in 1855. During this time, he visited England and Ireland. He wrote a letter to Bishop Bayley in 1855, thanking the bishop for his letter of introduction, which gave him access to many of the outstanding Catholic leaders in England and Ireland, among them Dr. John Henry Newman. Speaking of Dr. Newman, he said:[22]

[Your letter] secured for me the kindest attentions. I had the honour of spending a pleasant hour with many of the high dignitaries of the Church, all of whom made many enquiries regarding his Lordship of Newark, and I was certainly pleased to have the occasion of saying what I thought of the excellence of my own Bishop.

With Dr. Newman I had a delightful interview at the University; he is one of the most charming clergymen I have ever met. You see that he is the great and good man, but it is in his efforts to conceal his greatness that it most shows itself. He has about him the simplicity of manner almost of a child and this seems only to manifest his greatness of soul.

Father Mackin died on March 27, 1873, in his rectory in Trenton. Bishop Corrigan had not yet been ordained bishop but celebrated the Mass for Father Mackin's funeral. In his diary, Bishop Corrigan speaks about the funeral of Father Mackin:[23]

March 27th. The Rev. John P. Mackin, senior Priest of this Diocese died suddenly today. He had been infirm for many weeks, however, and had already received the last Sacraments some time since. Father Mackin was a scholarly man, with many good qualities. He studied in the Seminary of Philadelphia [St. Charles Borromeo] before the formation of this diocese, and being on the mission in that part of Philadelphia Diocese which was ceded to Newark, became thus one of our Priests. He built St. John's Church, Trenton, and freed it from debt. Afterwards, losing his health, he went abroad, and finally returned in 1870, and on the removal of F. Smith to the New Church (St. Mary's), Trenton, went back to his old charge. F. Mackin was particularly kind to me, though so much younger and unfit to rule. At my suggestion, he founded a Burse for Ecclesiastical Seminary, besides leaving $5,000 for a protectory, etc.

Monday 31st. Funeral of Father Mackin at Trenton. A large concourse of Priests and people. Just before the Mass, a panic occurred in the church, in consequence of the breaking of a bench in the gallery, and dreadful confusion ensued, during which several persons—all Protestants, as it happened, but one—were injured very severely by being trampled on by the frantic crowd.

Father Leahy, in his history of the Diocese of Trenton, comments on the life of Father Mackin with these words:[24]

Age and hardship had shattered his once powerful constitution, and he lingered on, a relic of his former self, till 1873, when he died among the people he loved so much and who loved him unto the end. The crowds that thronged old St. John's on the day of his funeral testified better than any monument to his worth. He was buried near the entrance of the church, where his remains rested till they were transferred to the cemetery of the Sacred Heart.

EARLY BISHOPS OF NEW YORK

The northern part of the current territory of the Diocese of Trenton was under the jurisdiction of the bishop of New York. According to the division of 1808, East Jersey fell under the jurisdiction of New York. Thus, parts of Monmouth, Mercer, and Ocean counties were taken care of by priests and bishops of New York. One thought to remember is that in the early days, there were very few Catholics in this area.

On April 8, 1808, New York was declared a diocese with Rev. Richard L. Concanen, O.P., appointed as the first bishop of New York. Father Concanen was ordained bishop on April 24, 1808, in the Dominican Church of St. Catherine in Rome. At the request of Bishop Concanen, Archbishop John Carroll appointed a vicar-general—Rev. Anthony Kohlmann, S.J.—for the New York diocese in 1808. Unfortunately, Bishop Concanen died suddenly on June 19, 1810, in Naples, Italy, before he ever sailed for New York. Father Kohlmann led the diocese until the second bishop of New York arrived in 1815.

On October 4, 1814, Father John Connolly, O.P., another Dominican in Rome, was appointed by Pope Pius VII as the second bishop of New York. He was ordained bishop on November 6, 1814. At the age of 68, he arrived in New York City on November 25, 1815, after a sixty-seven-day voyage from Dublin, Ireland.

The great American church historian Monsignor Peter Guilday said of Bishop Connolly: "It may well be doubted if, in the entire history of the Catholic Church in the United States, any other bishop began his episcopal life under such disheartening conditions."[25] With the many difficult problems facing the Catholics in New York City, the new bishop had little or no time to turn to the missions in New Jersey. Bishop John Connolly died on February 6, 1825, in his residence at 512 Broadway, New York City.

The third bishop of New York was Father John Dubois. Father Dubois was a professor and superior at Mount Saint Mary's College in Emmitsburg, Maryland. He attended Mother Elizabeth Ann Seton on her deathbed in January 1821. She was destined to become the first American to be canonized saint on September 14, 1975.

Father Dubois was appointed bishop of New York on May 23, 1826. He was consecrated a bishop on October 29, 1826, in Baltimore by Archbishop Marechal and installed in New York on November 4, 1826. At the time of his installation as bishop of New York, Bishop Dubois thought there were about 20,000 Catholics in East Jersey.

An interesting aspect of Bishop Dubois's life is that in New York on June 25, 1836, he ordained to the priesthood John N. Neumann, who was destined to become the fourth bishop of Philadelphia and canonized a saint on June 19, 1977.

One of the great problems facing the Catholic church in those early days was trusteeism. Great fights took place in the parishes between the bishop and the people over finances and appointments of pastors. Also, facing the Catholics of those days were organized anti-Catholic movements.

Father John Hughes was appointed coadjutor bishop to Bishop Dubois on August 8, 1837, and was consecrated on June 7, 1838, at St. Patrick's Cathedral, New York City. In August 1838, due to the failing health of Bishop Dubois, the Holy Father appointed Bishop Hughes administrator of the diocese. Upon the death of Bishop Dubois on December 20, 1842, Bishop Hughes became the fourth bishop of New York.

Bishop Hughes sent Father John Scollard to Princeton as pastor and missionary and he began his labors in Princeton without a church but with a band of sterling Catholics. He founded the future St. Paul's Parish in Princeton.[26] Historical records indicate that Bishop Hughes spent the summer of 1848 in a seaside resort in Long Branch, New Jersey, and said Mass in the old Cooper house in Long Branch.[27]

It was on July 29, 1853, that Pope Pius IX established the Diocese of Newark, with the entire state of New Jersey as its territory. He appointed Father James Roosevelt Bayley as the first bishop of New Jersey.

REFERENCES

1. Schrott, Rev. Lambert, and Rev. Theodore Roemer. *Pioneer German Catholics in the United States.* New York: The United States Catholic Historical Society, 1933, p. 47.
2. Schrott, p. 47.
3. Doane, George Washington, D.D. *The Remains of the Rev. Charles Henry Wharton, D.D., with a Memoir of his Life.* Philadelphia: William Stavely, 1834, vol. 2, p. 3.
4. Doane, p. 39.

5. Flynn, Rev. Joseph M. *The Catholic Church in New Jersey*. New York: The Publishers' Printing Co., 1904, p. 59.

6. Spalding, Thomas W. "John Carroll: Corrigenda and Addenda," *Catholic Historical Review*, LXXI, October 1985, pp. 505–518, esp. 513–514.

7. Terrar, Toby. "Episcopal–Roman Catholic Ecumenism and Church Democracy During North America's Revolutionary Era: The Life and Times of Liberation Theologian Charles H. Wharton," *Anglican and Episcopal History*, LVI, June 1987, pp. 163–196.

8. Hanley, Thomas O'Brien, S.J., ed. *The John Carroll Papers*. Notre Dame, Indiana: University of Notre Dame Press, 1976, vol. 2, pp. 424–425.

9. *American Catholic Historical Society*, vol. VI, 1895.

10. Flynn, p. 38.

11. Leahy, Rev. Walter T. *The Catholic Church of the Diocese of Trenton, N.J.* Princeton: Princeton University Press, 1906, p. 22.

12. Hanley, vol. 2, p. 104.

13. Hanley, vol. 2, p. 116.

14. Rev. Paul K. Thomas, archivist for the Archdiocese of Baltimore, was very helpful in finding this reference to Sartori. The original letter was never found. However, Father Thomas sent a copy of the letter from *Historical Records and Studies*, "Giovanni Battista Sartori," by Thomas R. Meehan, 1936, vol. 26, p. 176. Meehan copied the letter from *Memoir, Letters and Journal of Elizabeth Seton* by her grandson, Archbishop Robert Seton, 1869, vol. I, p. 16.

15. Hanley, vol. 3, pp. 327–328.

16. Personal letter from Bishop Henry Conwell of Philadelphia to Archbishop Ambrose Marechal of Baltimore, dated April 8, 1821. Archives of the Archdiocese of Baltimore, #6 14V6.

17. *Diary and Visitation Record of the Rt. Rev. Francis Patrick Kenrick*. Under the direction of the Most. Rev. Edmond F. Prendergast, archbishop of Philadelphia. Lancaster, Pennsylvania: Wickersham Printing Co., 1916, p. 68.

18. Meehan, Thomas F., ed. *Historical Records & Studies*. New York: The United States Catholic Historical Society, 1932, vol. XXI, p. 245.

19. *Diary and Visitation Record of the Rt. Rev. Francis Patrick Kenrick*, pp. 30–31, 68–69, 154, 198, 237, 244, 251, 257.

20. Paraphrased from Father Mackin's death notice given in *The Catholic Standard* on April 5, 1873.

21. Leahy, p. 24.

22. Yeager, Sr. Mary Hildegarde, C.S.C. *The Life of James Roosevelt Bayley, 1814–1877*. Washington, D.C.: The Catholic University of America Press, 1947, p. 142.

23. Permission was received to use passages from *The Diocesan Journal of Michael Augustine Corrigan, Bishop of Newark, 1872–1880*, edited by Joseph F. Mahoney and Peter J. Wosh. Newark and South Orange: New Jersey Historical Society and the New Jersey Catholic Historical Records Commission, 1987, p. 7.

24. Leahy, p. 26.

25. Cohalan, Rev. Msgr. Florence D. *A Popular History of the Archdiocese of New York*. Yonkers, New York: United States Catholic Historical Society, 1983, p. 31.

26. Leahy, p. 45.

27. 100th Anniversary (1886–1986) booklet of St. Michael's Church, Long Branch, New Jersey.

OTHER SOURCES

1. Griffin, Martin I. J. "History of Rt. Rev. Michael Egan D.D., First Bishop of Philadelphia." *American Catholic Historical*

Researches. Philadelphia: Martin I. J. Griffin, vol. X, pp. 161–162.

2. Guilday, Peter. *The Life and Times of John Carroll.* Westminster, Maryland: The Newman Press, 1954.

3. Meehan, Thomas F., ed. *Historical Records & Studies.* New York: The United States Catholic Historical Society, 1931, vol. XX, pp. 8–11.

4. Meehan, 1936, vol. XXVI, pp. 170–176.

5. Meehan, Thomas F., Stephen Farrelly, and Rev. Joseph F. Delany, D.D., eds. *Historical Records and Studies.* New York: The United States Catholic Historical Society, 1919, vol. XIII, pp. 61–83.

6. Wynne, George. *Early Americans in Rome.* Rome, Italy: Daily American Printing Co., 1966, pp. 6–7.

CHAPTER THREE

NEW JERSEY, NEW DIOCESE, JULY 29, 1853

BY MONSIGNOR JOSEPH C. SHENROCK

ON JULY 29, 1853, Pope Pius IX designated the entire state of New Jersey as a diocese in the New York Province of dioceses. He appointed James Roosevelt Bayley as the first bishop of Newark. Before the establishment of the Diocese of Trenton in 1881, Bishop Bayley and Bishop Michael A. Corrigan served as bishops for New Jersey, including the present territory of the Trenton diocese.

FIRST BISHOP OF NEWARK: JAMES ROOSEVELT BAYLEY, 1853~1872

Bayley's background, conversion to Catholicism, ordination to the priesthood, and consecration as first bishop for the state of New Jersey have been excerpted, with per-

mission, from *The Bishops of Newark*, prepared under the direction of the New Jersey Catholic Historical Records Commission.[1]

Background of James Roosevelt Bayley
The background of the first Bishop of New Jersey was a lineage of three distinguished names: Bayley, Roosevelt, and Seton. Through the first name he was related to one of America's first and outstanding physicians; by the second he was to be related to American presidents; and in the third name he claims relationship to the founder of the Sisters of Charity and of parochial education in the United States.

The boyhood of James Roosevelt Bayley was spent in the comfortable and pleasant surroundings of Mamaroneck [New York]. The home life was religiously oriented, and his father, Dr. Bayley, served as a vestryman of the new Episcopal parish. After the death of his mother when James was 13, the family moved to New York City.

Bayley prepared for college at the Mount Pleasant Classical Institution in Amherst, Massachusetts. However, he changed objectives and decided on a naval career, obtained a midshipman's commission and earned the sobriquet "Commodore." Again he changed his mind, and in 1831, having decided on a college education, entered Amherst College. Although he remained there only two years, he was carried on the alumni list and returned for a reunion in 1871.

In 1833 he entered Washington (now Trinity) College in Hartford, Connecticut, graduating in August 1835 and determined, like his father and grandfather, to follow a career in medicine. (While at Washington College, he was active in the Literary Society, the Athenaeum, to which he contributed later when he was Bishop of Newark.) During post-graduate study at Trinity, the 22-year-old Bayley changed his mind again and decided to enter the Episcopal ministry instead of pursuing medical studies. For several years, he studied with Samuel Farmer Jarvis, a learned Episcopal clergyman, in Middletown, Connecticut, and his mentor's library of over 10,000 books—including the collected works of the Fathers of the Church—became his daily companion and a major influence.

His father had moved his family to Harlem and was a vestryman at St. Andrew's Episcopal Church. When the rector of the parish became ill, James Roosevelt Bayley substituted for him during the winter of 1839–1840. After the summer of 1840 at Zion Church at Avon, near Rochester, New York, he accepted a call to St. Andrew's. In October 1840 he was ordained to the Episcopal clergy by the Rt. Rev. Benjamin T. Onderdonk in Bayley's Harlem parish. But, by the fall of 1841, doubts about the validity of the Episcopal ordination led James to resign and pursue his inclination toward the Catholic Church.

Bayley's Catholic Life and Ordination

Two major influences are evident in the journey to Catholicism of James Roosevelt Bayley: his extensive readings in the Fathers and early Church history while with Dr. Jarvis, and his newly made friendships with Catholic priests. Of the former he would write that "... high churchmanship led me to Rome.... It was the respect for the Antiquity, and testimony of the Fathers, which I learned in the course of instruction recommended by him [Jarvis]."

Among his Catholic priest friends the most influential was Rev. John McCloskey, pastor of St. Joseph's and teacher at St. John's College, Fordham. McCloskey was to become president of St. John's in 1841, and 34 years later, Bayley, as Archbishop of Baltimore, was to bestow the red biretta on America's first cardinal.

Bayley's grandfather was particularly disturbed by his grandson's inclination and, in the hope that a visit to Rome would enlighten this young, determined clergyman about the true nature of the Catholic Church, he sent young Bayley off on his first visit to the City of Rome. The opposite result came with Bayley's general confession, conditional Baptism, Confirmation, and First Communion "from the hands of Cardinal Franzoni in the Chapel of St. Ignatius" on Thursday, April 28, 1842.

The 18 months following his entry into the Catholic Church were spent in Europe traveling through Holland, England, Scotland, and Ireland. He spent one year in the Seminary of St. Sulpice in Paris where he found the strict and thorough training to his liking, made friends with others destined for prominent roles in the Church such as Nicholas Wiseman (future Cardinal Archbishop of Westminster) and John Williams (future Archbishop of Boston). In

August of 1843 his own bishop, John Hughes of New York, visited him and advised him to complete his training in New York. Bayley had written a year previously to his cousin Catherine Seton:

> I, at first, had some strong inclinations to enter one of the Religious Orders, but now I believe that it is the will of God that I should go back to my own country, and employ such abilities as he may have given me, among his poor and neglected flock: I have written to the bishop since I came to Paris, telling him of my intentions and asking his advice and commands. I trust, however, that he will allow me to remain where I am at least a year.

James R. Bayley's ordination to the Catholic priesthood was less than five months away when he returned to a somewhat confused family and to his studies at St. John's College, Fordham, where the seminary was conducted by the Lazarists. In old St. Patrick's on Mott Street, the morning of March 2, 1844, he was among three candidates ordained by Bishop John Hughes.

There would be nine years for Bayley to use his talents in New York; this scion of family affluence and prestige proved to be a tireless worker. Bishop Hughes, beset by many problems of growth, bigotry, nativism, and immigration, eagerly employed the talents of the genial priest. . . .

Bayley Consecrated First Bishop of Newark

One of 41 theologians picked to assist at the First Plenary Council of the American hierarchy in Baltimore, May 1852, Father Bayley saw that council petition the Holy See. The petition brought quick action: in 1853, 10 new dioceses were created, among them,

Newark. On July 29, 1853, Pope Pius IX by the bull *Apostolici Ministerii* designated the entire State of New Jersey as a diocese in the New York province and appointed Bayley as its first bishop.

In old St. Patrick's on Mott Street, on October 30, 1853, nine years after his ordination to the priesthood, Father Bayley became Bishop—as did John Laughlin for Brooklyn and Louis DeGoesbriand for Burlington, Vermont. The busy Bishop Hughes, however, was not the consecrator. Archbishop Cajetan Bedini, Papal Nuncio to Brazil, visiting the United States in a time of violent anti-Catholicism, performed the ceremony and none of the incidents which later marred Bedini's visit took place at the Consecration.

The October boat ride across the Hudson had been a rough one, and the train from what is now called Jersey City to Newark was hardly more comfortable. At 10 o'clock in the morning, "thousands upon thousands" greeted him at the center depot in Newark, forming a procession over a mile in length. Three bands, Sunday School children, laity and clergy conducted him to his residence at St. Patrick's on Washington Street; and the new Bishop felt this was his missionary area given to his charge by God himself. He would never again be truly happy and content away from his state.

On November 1st, the faithful came in great numbers to the newly designated Cathedral Church. It was a beautiful Indian summer day and, according to the new rector of the Cathedral, Rev. Bernard J. McQuaid, there were three crowds in the church; one standing on the floor, one sitting, and one standing on the backs of pews. Father McQuaid had planned thoroughly and the installation Mass, offered by Dr. J. W. Cummings of St. Stephen's in

New York, and the banquet for the bishops and 50 priests that followed, were elaborate and dignified. It was only 25 years since a handful of Catholics had begun to worship in tiny St. John's Church. This growing, vigorous, working-class diocese would need the acumen, polish, and kindliness of its accomplished shepherd.

Bayley's Work Within Trenton Diocese's Present Boundaries

Bishop Bayley began work in his new Diocese of Newark with twelve resident priests, who attended many missions, and only four church buildings, some of which were only temporary makeshifts and none of which had a decent rectory. These early priests lived as best they could. Their only desire being to keep and encourage their people, some of them suffered much from privations and hardships, but they knew their good people were enduring similar trials.

During Bishop Bayley's nineteen years as bishop of Newark, he established many new parishes. On July 15, 1866, he laid the cornerstone of St. Mary's Church in Trenton. He returned five years later on New Year's Day 1871 to bless and dedicate this new church under the patronage of St. Mary of the Assumption; the church would be designated the cathedral for the Diocese of Trenton, created in 1881.

In 1863, George P. Fox offered land in New Monmouth to Bishop Bayley for a church, but the bishop turned the offer down because the United States was in the middle of the Civil War. In 1868, Bishop Bayley established the Manchester Mission, forerunner of St. John's in Lakehurst. In

Bishop James Roosevelt Bayley

1871, he transferred the Hornerstown mission parish to the Conventual Franciscan Fathers of Trenton. In 1873, Father Peter Jachetti, O.F.M. Conv., built a church for the mission, the first church in nearby New Egypt.

On January 9, 1871, Bishop Bayley appointed Father Frederick Kivelitz as first pastor of St. Rose of Lima Parish in Freehold. Father Kivelitz traveled by saddle horse to serve his parish and missions scattered over 125 square miles. He was the first hardworking missionary priest in that area.

On July 30, 1872, Bishop Bayley was transferred from Newark to the Archdiocese of Baltimore and promoted to archbishop. On December 23, 1873, from

Baltimore, Archbishop Bayley wrote to Father Michael A. Corrigan in Newark:[2]

> I have seen for some time that if I did not secure you that you would be put into the first vacancy in the Province of New York, and I had made up my mind to ask you for my Coad. [coadjutor bishop of Newark] when this unfortunate Baltimore business came to spoil my plans. I intended also to ask for the division of the Diocese, which in fact is absolutely necessary.

Bayley, thus, informed Corrigan that he would most likely be made bishop of Newark, and that division of the Diocese of Newark was needed. However, the division was not to take place until 1881, when the Diocese of Trenton was created.

An appraisal of Bishop Bayley's accomplishments in New Jersey is found in the New York *Tablet*:[3]

> Faithfully and well has he governed for years the diocese which he found a new one,— comprising the entire state of New Jersey,—and now when his piety and zeal have built institutions, provided a numerous and efficient clergy, and, in short, completed the superstructure of religion in that important diocese, it is sad for the people who so loved him, who so cheerfully seconded all his efforts for the advancement of religion to see him taken from their midst and given to another diocese, with all his noble qualities of head and heart, his genial, unaffected kindness of disposition, his zeal for religion, his exhaustless charity. None but those who know Bishop Bayley personally can form any correct idea of the atmosphere of love and kindness and winning gentleness that surrounds him in his daily life, or the strong hold he had on his clergy and his people.

SECOND BISHOP OF NEWARK: MICHAEL AUGUSTINE CORRIGAN, 1873~1880

On October 9, 1872, Bishop James R. Bayley left Newark by train to go to Baltimore.[4] Following the firm and energetic Bishop Bayley came the courteous and pious Rev. Dr. Michael A. Corrigan, who was called from the presidency of Seton Hall College to lead the growing Diocese of Newark. He had been elected as administrator of the diocese until a new bishop could be appointed. On February 11, 1873, Father Corrigan was appointed as the second bishop of Newark. The date of his episcopal consecration was May 4, 1873.

Father Corrigan's constant associations with Bishop Bayley in administrative work had fitted him well for his new position, so that, although only 34 years of age, he entered upon his duties as one well prepared. Some thought his youth and inexperience as a pastor made him unfit for this new position, but they were mistaken. His administration of seven years proved that he was not only scholarly and pious but also shrewd in the management of all details, for he put every department of the diocese in the best possible condition. Upon taking up office he found twenty-five parishes and twenty-six missions in South Jersey. By the time he left, the numbers had increased very considerably, and his energy and zeal seemed to have infused themselves among the priests and the people. The Diocese of Newark was the school in which he prepared himself for the greater task of leading the Archdiocese of New York. In his dealings with priests and people, he was gentle but firm, knowing that oftentimes broad-mindedness meant neglect of duty, that a good bishop always meets criticism when he attempts to regulate things that have gone wrong for years, and that no matter what he did, there would always be some who thought they could have done it better.

The Most Rev. Michael A. Corrigan, D.D., was born in Newark, New Jersey, on August 13, 1839. He attended old St. John's School, Mulberry Street, Newark, and in 1855 St. Mary's College, Wilmington, Delaware. While at St. Mary's College, the young Corrigan was confirmed in St. Peter's Church, Wilmington, by Bishop John N. Neumann, C.Ss.R., fourth bishop of Philadelphia and later canonized a saint. Michael Corrigan then went to Mount Saint Mary's in Emmitsburg, Maryland. From there he went to Rome, where he became one of the first students to enter the American College of that city. Ordained September 19, 1863, he returned to Newark and was made professor of dogma and sacred scriptures in the seminary at Seton Hall. From this position he moved to the charge of the seminary, then to the vice presidency of the college, later becoming president of that institution. On February 11, 1873, he was appointed second bishop of Newark, succeeding Bishop Bayley. The new bishop at once took up and carried out the plans formulated by his predecessor.

Bishop Corrigan was always most assiduous in visiting the parishes of his dio-

Bishop Michael Augustine Corrigan

cese. In fact, according to his journal entry for December 15, 1879, he claimed to have visited every single church in New Jersey since his return from Rome in 1877.[5] So scattered and poor were the Catholics of South Jersey that the appointment of a priest to this district was considered the equivalent of banishment to Siberia. For a long time it was called the Siberia of the Diocese.

Corrigan's Work with Trenton Diocese's Present Boundaries

To understand Bishop Corrigan's contribution to the Diocese of Trenton, we can look at his diary to learn how often and with what zeal he visited the churches that would compose the Diocese of Trenton in 1881.

Some of the language and abbreviations Corrigan used have been updated in this book for the reader. Full names have been included when appropriate. Comments are set off by brackets. For a more literal copy of Michael Augustine Corrigan's journal, readers can refer to Joseph F. Mahoney's and Peter J. Wosh's work.[6]

Eighteen Hundred Seventy-three
March 27th. The Rev. John P. Mackin, senior Priest of this Diocese [of Newark] died suddenly today. . . .

Monday [March] 31st. Funeral of Father Mackin at Trenton. . . .

Previous to, or about this time [July 7th], the following appointments were made: Rev. Patrick Byrne to St. John's Church, Trenton, Rev. Patrick A. Treacy to Oxford Furnace & Washington. . . .

Rev. Joseph Butler, O.F.M. Conv. [a Conventual Franciscan], of Trenton, having obtained his secularization papers from Rome, left the Diocese, October 8th, to go to Ogdensburgh [to serve as a diocesan or secular priest]. . . .

18th [October]. Feast of St. Luke the Evangelist. Admitted to the triennial Vows Sisters Agnes Baudermann and Clara Carnahan, Benedictines, the latter a cousin of Archbishop John J. Hughes. In the afternoon I went to Bordentown. Father Patrick Leonard had invited the people to receive Holy Communion from the new Bishop, so that it was almost like a Mission. Four of us were busy hearing Confessions until a late hour. At my Mass on Sunday a very large proportion of the Parish communicated. It was a beautiful day, and the people flocked in from the country for miles around. Confirmation was administered to about 300. Father Byrne of Trenton preached at the last Mass. The people stood on the seats of the pews to obtain a look at the new Prelate. In the evening, I lectured on the Catacombs. The Church was well filled, many Protestants attending. Some $400 realized for the schools.

Monday [October 20th]. Fathers Hugh J. McManus & Patrick Leonard assisted me in admitting Miss Mary Russell, in Religion Sister Mary Clare, to her profession as a Sister of Mercy. Mass was then said for the first time in the domestic Oratory, in the old Parochial House, and the blessed sacrament placed in the Tabernacle. The chalice used at mass was that presented to the Church at Bordentown, by Joachim Murat, the ex-King of Spain, 40 years ago. The Sisters of Mercy are already beginning to do good, and their influence felt in the schools and also in the good conduct of the children. . . .

Eighteen Hundred Seventy-four
February [1st]. Spent Sunday in Lambertville, with Rev. Patrick F. Connolly. In the evening I lectured for the benefit of the Church, to a very large audience, and next morning, after blessing the candles and saying the Parochial Mass (Father Connolly being unwell), proceeded to Burlington.

English military barracks purchased in 1845 by St. Paul's Parish for use as a church, in Burlington.

St. Francis Hospital, Trenton, as it appeared in 1890.

Examined Books, etc., visited Church and Schools, and proceeded to Mount Holly. Father Michael J. Kirwan kindly sent me over in his buggy. It was a terrible day, cold & stormy. Saw the beautiful new church [St. Mary's] at Mount Holly, dined with Father Thaddeus Hogan and returned with him and Mr. Thomas Foy, in the carriage of the latter to Burlington, thence by cars to Bordentown, Trenton, & Newark, returning to [Seton Hall] College in the evening. . . .

[around March 7th] Appointments . . . Rev. Thaddeus Hogan to East Newark; Rev. Samuel J. Walsh to Mount Holly and Moorestown . . .

[April 19th] Went to the Hospital in Trenton, a fine, spacious building, with 2½ acres land attached. Cost $36,000. Present debt $19,000. The Superioress gave a very modest account of the persecution raised against the Hospital by the Pastor of St. John's. I promised my protection. The people of St. John's have been forbidden to contribute to the Hospital, and even required to take back their free offerings, although the Institution had the sanction of the Bishop at the time, of the former Pastor of St. John's, and of all the Priests of Tren-

ton. A strange illustration of the bad effects of misguided zeal and honesty of purpose!

On Sunday, May 31st, I confirmed 72 boys & 91 girls at St. Mary's Church, Trenton, and afterwards 125 at the German Church, St. Francis. Father Bonaventure Frey, O.F.M. Cap., New York, Father Anthony Smith of St. Mary's, Father Theophilus J. Degen of Millville, and several Conventual Fathers present. In the afternoon grand processions of the various Catholic Societies to the Hospital. During the Ceremony of blessing this Institution, Father Bonaventure preached in German, in the open air, and the Bishop succeeded him in English. A vast assemblage from the three Parishes [St. John, St. Francis, and St. Mary], and outsiders. In the evening I lectured on the old subject, the Catacombs, in St. Mary's Church, and retired thoroughly fatigued.

Monday [June 1st] morning at 7 o'clock consecrated 5 Altar Stones for Father Smith, inserting relics of Saints Eusebius and Lucy. Father Patrick Delaney, O.F.M. Conv., Father Anthony Smith, and Father Peter Jachetti, O.F.M. Conv., assisted. Visited the Schools, after Mass, and took the 10:35 train home. On arriving found telegrams announcing the return of my brother Joe & his wife & George Corrigan from Europe. . . .

[around June 6th] Appointments . . . Rev. James J. Curran to St. John's Trenton.

[June 7th] Confirmed about 150 at Red Bank. The day was intensely hot. Mr & Mrs. Felix O'Rourke, Mr. Bryan Laurence, and Mrs. & Dr. Van Buren dined with Father John F. Salaun. In the evening, Father Frederick Kivilitz came over from Freehold and preached at Vespers.

Monday [June 8th] said Mass at 5:30, assisted at Father Walter M. Fleming's Mass,

& took the 7 o'clock boat to New York. Met Mr. & Mrs. Felix O'Rourke, Mr. Thomas B. Kinney, Judge Frederick Halsted Teese, etc.

August 17th. Spent a few days at Shrewsbury with Mr. Felix E. O'Rourke, thence went to Cape May, & confirmed 21 on the 21st, thence to Swedesboro, & confirmed 56, on Sunday, 23rd. Lectured in the evening.

Received into the Diocese Rev. Charles A. Vogl, from Auburn, New York. Appointed him to build a new church in Newark in honor of St. Augustine. Site selected on St. Augustine's Feast, August 28th. Item, gave faculties to Rev. Mr. Stanislaus Danielou, from Diocese of Burlington, an old friend of Father John F. Salaun. Came to the U.S. together 19 years ago. For the present, being in infirm health, Rev. Mr. Danielou will remain at Red Bank with Father Salaun. Appointed [Conventual] Franciscan Fathers to build a small church at Florence, Burlington County. . . .

On Saturday, the 19th [September], went to Riverside, to give Confirmation. On Sunday the 20th, confirmed 105 persons. The church here was built by the Redemptorists from Philadelphia but is now attended by the Franciscans from Trenton. The Franciscan Sisters have lately taken charge of the Schools, and things are in good condition. During the Low Mass, the Philadelphia Cathedral Orchestra played several pieces, also after High Mass, etc. It was intended to have a grand procession to Beverly, but the rain prevented. At Beverly, that afternoon I confirmed 34 persons, after Vespers. The Church at Beverly is an old Masonic Lodge, and is a poor affair, very small, and shaky.

At Riverside was entertained by Mr. Ellis J. Little, a good and intelligent Catholic, who has a very extensive Canning establishment. Number of cans filled this season, to date, 453,000. He gave very interesting account of progress of the art of canning fruit, the methods employed, etc.

Monday [September 21st], Father Antonius M. Grundner, O.S.M., Servite, came from Philadelphia, Father Joseph Thurnes from Camden, Fathers Anthony Smith, Patrick Delaney, Peter Jachetti, O.F.M. Conv., Dominic Marzetti, O.F.M. Conv., and Andrew Avellinus Szabo, O.F.M. Conv., from Trenton to dine with Mr. Henry Orsprong, a Hollander, long settled in Jersey.

Father Peter Jachetti, O.F.M. Conv., accompanied me to Manchester. We had to take the freight train, and to finish our journey on the locomotive, in order to save time, and arrive that night. At Manchester, slept at the house of Mr. William McLaughlin, in a "cranberry bog." An ex-Presbyterian minister (Mr. Torrey) sent his carriage for the Bishop next morning (Manchester not having any livery stables) and placed it at his disposal during the day. St. John's Church, Manchester, was built by Father John F. Salaun, who attended to this Mission, until the Franciscans took charge of it, a couple of years ago. The Church is small, but neat. The ground was donated by Mr. Torrey (or Terry), the ex-Clergyman. Father Salaun having asked for a donation was upbraided for his audacity in requesting what he himself would most assuredly not do for a Protestant Church. Father Salaun explained the difference between Catholic & Protestant principles, and received the following reply by note, "As I despair of bringing you (Catholics) to the true faith, and as any religion is better than none, I donate ground for church and Cemetery."

In this district, there are 34,000 acres belonging to a single firm in Wall Street (Brown Bros), intended for the culture of the cranberry. Father Patrick Delaney, O.F.M. Conv., has been attending this Mission, and is much beloved. After Mass, we blessed the grave-yard, and Father Delaney bade farewell to the congregation, Father Stanislaus Danielou coming in his place, from Red Bank.

Fathers Salaun and Danielou, and Mr. Harper, an Ex-Anglican Clergyman, brother to Father Harper, S.J., dined at Mr. William McLaughlin's.

In the afternoon we started for Freehold, visiting on the way the marl pits at Farmingdale, arriving at Freehold about 5 P.M. Here we found Father Albinus of the Incarnate Wisdom Magno, C.P., Passionist, and Father Henry T. Martens, of New Brunswick. The Pastor, Father Frederick Kivilitz, had gone on a sick call 14 miles distant. That evening the Forty Hours' Adoration closed with Benediction, and the Litanies. [The Litany of Saints, an invocation of all the blessed, regularly concluded the Forty Hours' Devotion.]

On Wednesday morning [September 23rd], I confirmed 139 persons and returned to Newark that evening.

Father Kivilitz almost lives on horseback, having a large circuit to attend to. He is thoroughly familiar with condition of his numerous Missions, and evidently is full of zeal. During his residence at Freehold he has enlarged the church—& purchased & paid for Pastoral House. . . .

[December 12th] Went to Burlington. On 13th, confirmed 51 persons. Blessed the New Bell (600 lbs), and lectured in the evening on the Testimony of the Catacombs. Monday morning, visited [Episcopalian] Bishop [George Washington] Doane's grave, then went to Philadelphia to see about Father Mackin's legacy. In the evening arrived at New Egypt, Ocean County. Weather intensely cold.

On Tuesday [December 15th], Octave of the Immaculate Conception, dedicated new church in honor of the Assumption of the Blessed Virgin Mary [New Egypt]. Nothing was ready in the church: windows not yet put in; "opus festinatum" [a hurried work]. The Presbyterian Minister sent his Organ for the occasion, and the Methodist Clergyman volunteered his choir. Singers came, however, with Father Patrick Leonard from St. Mary's, Bordentown. Church is a frame building 30 x 60, cost about $2,000. It replaces an old building formerly owned by the Mormons, and after their departure 15 years ago for Salt Lake [City, Utah] purchased by Father Mackin for $600, and moved from Hornerstown to a sand-bank about two miles distant, as a more central position for the scattered Catholics of the neighborhood. There is only one Catholic family in New Egypt, Mr. Thomas Finegan's, where Fathers Peter Jachetti, O.F.M. Conv., Patrick Delaney, O.F.M. Conv. (the Pastor), Leonard and myself were entertained most kindly. A great many Protestants were present at the ceremony in the Church. Some of them, especially a Mr. John L. Hulme, very kind.

Returned to Bordentown, by way of Allentown. Visited St. John's Church, purchased from the Episcopalians by Father Mackin for $2,000, and enlarged by Father Leonard. Saw all the Catholics of the place. Next morning, after Mass, took early train for Newark, and assisted at the Second Examination in Moral Theology. Two did quite poorly; the others, remarkably well . . .

Eighteen Hundred Seventy-five

On Sunday, April 25th, the Chapel of Our Lady of Lourdes, attached to the Franciscan

House of Studies at Chambersburg (Trenton), was blessed, as also the [Franciscan] College itself. The Franciscans have built this structure, which is 80 x 40 (about), large and commodious, amidst many difficulties. They have a fine site, a substantial building, and will have in time a large Congregation. The Provincial, Father Bonaventure Keller, sang the Mass. The Bishop preached on devotion to the Blessed Virgin, giving an account of the apparitions and wonders wrought at Lourdes. Father Antonius M. Grundner, O.S.M., of Philadelphia, Father Anthony Smith of Trenton, Father Peter Jachetti, O.F.M. Conv., Rector, and several other Franciscan Fathers present. Father Grundner preached in German at Vespers. . . .

[June 13th] Confirmed [158] at St. Paul's, Princeton. On Sunday night, the weather became suddenly cold, so that ice formed in New York state, and a heavy frost in various parts of this state, particularly Morris County, injuring the crops. Lectured on the Catacombs, Sunday night, unexpectedly, to please Father Thomas R. Moran, who has done a great deal for Princeton, reviving the frequentation of the Sacraments, and introducing habits of sobriety amongst a demoralized people. Everything very neat about the church and grounds. . . .

On July 7th, omitted above, the addition to St. James Church, Red Bank, was blessed. Afterwards I celebrated Pontifically. Spent a few days at Long Branch, preached on Sunday, exhorting the people to build a new and more suitable Church, and returned to Newark to take part in the Retreat, as mentioned above. . . .

[August 8th] Preached in the Church at Red Bank in order to put down malicious gossip. Spent a couple of days at Dr. Van Buren's, Shrewsbury, with Archbishop Bayley. Afterwards went to Madison to be present at the close of the Sisters' Retreat. Admitted fourteen Sisters to their vows. On the 14th, Saturday evening, returned to Long Branch, and on Sunday afternoon (Feast of the Assumption) laid the corner stone of the new church. Dimensions of the church to be 115 x 45. It will be church and House combined and will cost about $20,000. . . .

On Sunday, September 5th, I confirmed 450 persons at St. John's Church, Trenton, of whom 20 were converts, and on Monday I assisted at the inauguration of the splendid school-house erected by F. Byrne, at an expense of $50,000, with accommodations for 1200 children, and with residences at either end for Brothers and Sisters. [Seven Sisters of Charity and three Brothers of the Holy Cross conducted the school, which opened with 700 pupils.]

On Sunday, the 12th, I confirmed 44 children at Mount Holly, and in the afternoon 90 at Moorestown. As this was the first visit of a Bishop to Moorestown, they made a grand demonstration of welcome. The whole town was alive with excitement, and the Church packed to its utmost capacity. . . .

Eighteen Hundred Seventy-six
[March 25th] On the Feast of the Annunciation, at the 8 o'clock Mass, the following Orders were conferred: Tonsure & *Minor Orders* on Brother Angelus Goessman and Brother Hyacinth Fudzinski, Professed Clerks of the Order of Minors Conventuals of St. Francis; *Subdeaconship* on Brother Conrad Elison, of the same Order, of Trenton. *Deaconship* on Rev. George Sylvester Collins, O.P., of Newark.

[March 26th] On the day following, namely the 4th Sunday in Lent, the Rev. Conrad Elison was ordained Deacon, at the

Solemn Pontifical Mass, and the Rev. George Sylvester Collins, Priest. Fathers Patrick Byrne, Patrick V. Keogh, & Collins, all Dominicans assisted. . . .

On Sunday, April 30th, I confirmed 155 persons in St. Mary's church, Trenton, and preached in the evening. Visited the Franciscan College, the Hospital, the Parochial Schools, etc.

[June 7th] Went with Father Thomas M. Killeen to South Amboy. The whole town with bands of music, societies in regalia, etc., turned out in honor of the occasion. Afterwards we rode over to Keyport and confirmed 117, and spent the day pleasantly. . . .

July 1st. I have made the following appointments which take effect to-day:

Rev. Secundinus Pattle, appointed Pastor of Burlington.

Rev. John F. Salaun, Pastor of Long Branch.

Rev. Michael E. Kane, Pastor of Red Bank.

The usual difficulties follow the making of these appointments. Time will tell whether the objections made by certain disappointed parties are well grounded or not. It is impossible to please all, and to find candidates with all the qualities desirable in a good, active, pious Pastor. So one must do what he deems best in the sight of God, and leave the issue to Divine Providence.

On Sunday, July 9, I blessed the beautiful new Church of Our Lady, Star of the Sea, at Long Branch. It is a frame building, in the Gothic Style, 105 feet long, 55 wide, with a transept measuring 70 feet, with rooms in the rear for the accommodation of the Pastor. The building cost, including ground, $25,000. Father Hector Glackmeyer, S.J., preached a short sermon. Three

or four Priests were present, besides the Pastor Rev. John F. Salaun.

In the afternoon, I confirmed about 30 children, returning to Newark Monday. Was the guest of Mr. Louis S. Binsse, at Long Branch. . . .

On Sunday, October 15th, the Feast of the Maternity of the Blessed Virgin Mary and the fourth anniversary of the blessing of the new church, I confirmed 130 children and adults at the first Mass in St. Mary's, Bordentown. Having appointed the Pastor, the Rev. Patrick Leonard, to take charge of St. John's Parish, Newark, I found the people of Bordentown very much depressed at the anticipation of parting with their Pastor, who had done so much for them and whose administration had been more successful than that of any of his predecessors. In fact, Father Leonard found the Parish in a sorry condition, and leaves it well provided, with new church, and Pastor's Residence and flourishing Schools. I preached to the people at the High Mass, explaining the reasons for the promotion of Father Leonard, and paving the way for his successor, the Rev. Patrick F. Connolly, of Lambertville. The transfer takes place Sunday October 22nd.

In the afternoon, Reverend Misters Patrick Leonard and Hugh J. McManus accompanied me to Allentown, where I confirmed 95 persons, and lectured for an hour in the evening. On both occasions the little church was crowded with Protestants, it being the first time a Bishop officiated in Allentown. Governor William A. Newell, Mr. George Middleton, Member of Congress, & and many other Protestants present.

Monday [October 16th] met Father Joseph M. Flynn at Bordentown, and proceeded to Mr. Daniel Dougherty's, Philadelphia, where we were most hospitably entertained for the balance of the week, during our visit to the "Centennial."

On Sunday, October 29th, I confirmed 65 persons at New Egypt, after the last Mass. Preached on Charity. Amongst those Confirmed were seven children of one family (Spence) and three or four of several others, so that there was manifest need of this Sacrament. After Confirmation, the graveyard adjoining the Church was blessed. A great many Protestants attended, and were very respectful all through the services. The Cemetery is well laid out, with a large wooden Cross in the Centre according to the Ceremonial. After this, an old lady over 70 years of age was baptized. Mr. Thomas Finegan entertained us: Father Peter Jachetti, O.F.M. Conv., Father Patrick Delaney, O.F.M. Conv., Mr. Thomas Foy, Mr. James & Mrs. Joanna Hylan, Mrs. Eliza Woodward [wife of D^r. Charles Woodward], etc. For a long time, Mr. & Mrs. Finegan were the only Catholics in Egypt; during the past year another Catholic family, named Nash, has settled there. The other Parishioners are scattered through the country, on farms from three to eight miles distant. Mr. Foy drove me to Mount Holly, sixteen miles, where I lodged with Father Hugh J. McManus, and saw the new residence which he has just moved into the past week. The school is closed at Mt. Holly on account of the hard times. For the same reason, nothing of consequence has been done towards finishing the Church, plastering, etc., during the past year. Made the Visitation at Mount Holly Monday morning, thence returned home.

Rev. Michael J. Connolly has been appointed Pastor of the Church of St. John Evangelist, Lambertville, October 22, instead of Rev. Patrick F. Connolly, transferred to Bordentown, and Rev. Martin

Van den Boogaard to the new [St. Joseph's] Parish of Bound Brook & Millstone, separated from Raritan. . . .

Eighteen Hundred Seventy-seven
[July 8th] Preached at St. Mary's, Trenton, at the High Mass, and 3 P.M. went by special excursion train to Hopewell, 13 miles distant, to bless the corner stone of a church in honor of St. Alphonsus Liguori. The Church will be a frame building, 36 x 72, slated roof, with spire 103 feet high, to cost $3,500. There are two and a quarter acres of ground attached to the Church, purchased for $725. About 2,000 people attended the Ceremony; the very best of good feeling prevailed; many non-Catholics were present. . . .

[August 10th] Blessed Stations of the Cross in the Church of Our Lady, Star of the Sea, Long Branch. Father James A. Walsh is doing wonders here, and is very popular. As many as a hundred carriages crowd around the Church on Sundays. The Stations were a gift from Colonel Edward McK. Hudson, U.S.A., a recent Convert, whom I met at his brother-in-law's, Mr. Louis S. Binsse's, where I was staying. Father Walsh has erected a neat Pastoral Residence, but the walls are not yet sufficiently dry for habitation.

[August 11th] Went to Philadelphia to consult Archbishop James F. Wood about a proposed foundation of a Passionist Monastery near Philadelphia, but in this Diocese. His Grace was so much opposed to the foundation, on various grounds, that the idea was abandoned.

[August 12th] Blessed the church of St. Clare, Florence, built by the Franciscans of Trenton. The building is frame, 24 x 40, cost $3,000, and has a debt of $950. Preached at the High Mass, confirmed 30 children after Vespers, and preached at Burlington in the evening. Peace and harmony flourish in the latter place, much to the delight of the Parish. . . .

[October 11th] Visited St. Joseph's Church, Keyport, and confirmed 22 persons, picked up since recent Confirmation. The church is still very badly provided, its wardrobe of sacred linens, etc., consisting of two purificators, 2 corporals, 1 alb, one white and one black vestment; no cope; no Confessional; only 2 altar cloths; a miserable and patched Ciborium, no Vespers or benediction; a leaky roof. The Sacred Particles in all three of these Parish churches renewed only once in two weeks, contrary to Council of Baltimore. [The Second Plenary Council of Baltimore, echoing other instructions, required that the Sacred Host be renewed at least weekly.]

[October 12th] Visited Church of Our Lady, Star of the Sea, Long Branch. Father James A. Walsh has done wonders during the Summer, creating great enthusiasm amongst the people, and in proportion collecting resources to reduce the debt. He has built a fine Pastoral Residence near the Church. Everything in good order . . .

On Monday morning, October 15th, Father Henry T. Martens accompanied the Bishop to Freehold. After the High Mass, 215 were confirmed. In the afternoon, Father Frederick Kivilitz, the active and most zealous Pastor, drove me to Farmingdale, 9 miles distant, where the people assembled at the house of a good Catholic named John Neastor. I made an address to them, and inspected the Vestments. Father Kivilitz has purchased 16 new sets of the five different colors, for the out Missions, besides others already in use. During the winter, when the people are free from work, he visits one or two of his Missions daily, instructing the children, and preparing them for the Sacraments, etc.

[October 17th] Wednesday morning, we went to Perrineville, 9 miles. As the house where Mass is said is small, the project of a new church was broached. One of the men offered half an acre of ground, and $200 were subscribed on the spot. The site was visited and approved, and the Bishop promised to return in the Spring to bless the Corner Stone.

In the afternoon, we visited Colts Neck, six miles from Freehold, and addressed the people in Mrs. Catherine Guire's house, and afterwards Big Woods. The people were earnestly urged to build a small Church, which they promised to do, and a subscription list was opened on the spot. At present, weather permitting, Mass is said under the trees, for want of a room sufficiently large. That night, a Committee came to see about getting an Irish Priest, if possible. They were composed of drinking men and careless Catholics, members of the A.O.H.

On Thursday, the 18th, Father Frederick Kivilitz started with the Bishop for the Parish of St. James', Red Bank. It happened to be the day of the Firemen's Parade, and the town was all aglow with the excitement. About 20,000 had tumbled into it, from various parts of Monmouth County.

Confirmation was given to 206 persons. The night was spent at the house of Mr. Felix E. O'Rourke at the Highlands, where Father Michael E. Kane and the Bishop said Mass in the morning. The site of the proposed new church was seen and approved. It is the gift of Mr. O'Rourke, and if a church be built there, it will be the first object to greet the emigrant as he nears the New World. [A church spire rising from such elevation might then indeed have been the immigrant's first sight of the New World.]

Went to Manchester by the noon train, about 30 miles below Red Bank, and confirmed 20. This place has 32 Catholic families. The people are very poor, as is the Church. Some necessary improvements, since carried out, were suggested at the time of visitation. The Bishop preached in the evening, and gave the Papal Blessing, here, as in every church where the people had been prepared to receive it, after Mass next morning.

Tom's River, and Bricksburg [Lakewood], each having only 3 Catholic families are also attended by Father Stanislaus Danielou from Red Bank; as also Riceville, 2 families, New Monmouth, 50 families, Highlands 15 families, Morrisville and Sandy Hook.

From Manchester, I went to Shrewsbury to call on Dr. William H. Van Buren, who had attended Archbishop James Roosevelt Bayley in Europe, and who was positive that the illness of which the Archbishop died was Bright's disease of the kidneys. From Red Bank, I went to Elizabethport, and thence by the New Bound Brook and Philadelphia line to Trenton.

[October 21st] Gave Confirmation at the Church of St. Francis [Trenton] to 84. Visited the fine new Schools. All things in good order. In the afternoon, assisted at Vespers and administered Confirmation in the Chapel of Our Lady of Lourdes. There was an immense throng. Confirmed 33. Next morning, said Mass in St. Francis Hospital [Trenton], confirmed 5 invalids who could not be brought to the Church the day previous, and made the visitation of St. John's [Trenton] and St. Mary's [Trenton]. There had been a general cleaning up in the former, and the Sacred Vessels were in good condition. The vestments in the latter church are remarkably well kept, especially the precious ones. Visited the Schools and returned to Newark. . . .

Saturday. October 27th, visited the Church of the Assumption, New Egypt. The church has only 2 decent vestments. People dissatisfied with existing arrangements, & clamoring for a Priest who can properly instruct them, etc.

October 28, 1877. Said early Mass at Mount Holly, and made visitation. Preached at late Mass at Moorestown and confirmed [unknown number]. In the evening preached at Mount Holly.

[October 29th] Confirmed 52 at St. Paul's, Burlington.

Tuesday morning, went in the storm to Bordentown. On account of bad weather, visitation to Allentown postponed. Gave homily in the evening and Solemn Benediction.

Wednesday, 31st, gave Confirmation to 53 in Beverly. Poor and shabby vestments there. Ordered them to be repaired or renewed. Drove over to Riverside; met Trustees. Condemned white vestment, and ordered black to be mended. The Trustees desire the services of a settled Pastor, complaining that the present Superior of the Mission [Andrew Avellinus Szabo, O.F.M. Conv.] is too easy, and his subordinates devoid of authority . . .

[November 15th] Confirmed 45 persons in St. Paul's Church, Princeton. Everything in good shape, except gas jets around Ostensorium. [The ostensorium is a liturgical vessel for the public display of the Sacred Host. Although gas was acceptable for general illumination of the church, the Holy

See had forbidden its use both as a substitute for wax candles and in any location on the altar.]

[November 16th] Visited St. Mary's Church, Trenton, trying to avert impending lawsuit between Pastor [Anthony Smith] and Colonel Joseph Wagner; went with Rev. Maurice O'Connor and Rev. Michael J. Connolly, Pastor of Lambertville, to Flemington . . .

Eighteen Hundred Seventy-eight

[February 12th] On Tuesday night, on my return from Baltimore, 70 adults were confirmed in St. John's Church, Trenton, at the close of a successful Mission conducted by three Fathers of the Holy Cross. . . .

On Sunday, February 17, at the close of the Mission conducted by Fathers Albinus of the Incarnate Wisdom Magno, C.P., and Alexander of St. Paul Hughes, C.P., Passionists, 216 persons, many of them adults, were confirmed. On the next morning, Father Frederick Kivilitz brought me 14 miles to Clarksboro to confirm an old lady, Mrs. Bridget Hylan, who is paralyzed, and who has been living in the woods for nearly half a century. Tuesday went to Keyport to see and bless the new Parochial House built by Father Augustine G. Spierings. . . .

March. On Sunday, March 3, at end of Mission given by Fathers Peter J. Cooney, C.S.C.; John M. Toohey, C.S.C.; and William O'Mahoney, C.S.C., 78 persons were confirmed at Moorestown. The people still clamor for a Priest, although the present Pastor of Mount Holly [Hugh J. McManus] is very attentive to their spiritual progress.

56 persons were confirmed the next night at Mount Holly. . . .

[June 12th] On Wednesday morning confirmed 176 persons at St. Joseph's,

Keyport, many of them adults. This Confirmation is mainly the result of the Redemptorist Mission recently given, during which 1,200 Communions were received. Many were brought back to the practice of their Religion, such particularly as had become careless on account of the infrequency of Mass, etc., previously. The new Pastor, Father Augustine G. Spierings, has purchased a new organ, procured Statues, made Confessionals himself, and infused new life into the Parish. . . .

[June 15th] Clerical Changes . . . Rev. Joseph Borghese, Pastor St. John's, Allentown, . . .

Said Mass next morning, September 21, at Bordentown, and received profession of Sisters of Mercy. Miss Mary C. Burke, of Albany, and Miss Mary Ryan, of Portland, Maine, both novices, took the veil under the names of Sister Mary Xavier Joseph and Mary Vincent. Reverend Misters Patrick F. Connolly, Patrick J. Connolly, Secundinus Pattle, Joseph Borghese, and James J. Curran assisted. . . .

Sunday, September 29, confirmed 300 at the 8 o'clock Mass [Trenton St. John's]. Lectured in the evening . . .

[October 13th] Confirmed 57 at Riverside, NJ. Held visitation publicly. No Baptismal Font. No ambry. A shabby black vestment condemned. Exhorted the people to provide against next visitation all that is necessary for decency of divine worship.

Mr. Henry Orsprong drove Father Peter Jachetti, O.F.M. Conv.; Bonaventure Frey, O.F.M. Cap.; and myself to Beverly, where I confirmed 11 persons. No font, etc. Only two vestments, namely white & black. Returned home by way of Bristol [Pennsylvania], where I saw Father Patrick A. Lynch. . . .

On Sunday, the 20th [October], the neat Church of St. Alphonsus at Hopewell was blessed. It has been built chiefly by the efforts of Rev. Michael J. Holland, under the supervision of Father Anthony Smith, of St. Mary's, Trenton. It is furnished with a fine, dry basement, and is neatly frescoed. With Flemington, or some other place, it will make a Parish, next year.

In the afternoon confirmed 159 in St. Mary's, Trenton. The church was intensely crowded. . . .

[Around November 11th] Changes . . . During the past fortnight, the Rev. Patrick Byrne of St. John's Trenton has withdrawn from the Diocese, and been replaced by Father Thaddeus Hogan. . . .

Eighteen Hundred Seventy-nine

[January 1879] Clerical changes. Rev. James A. McFaul has been transferred to St. Mary's, Trenton, Rev. Michael J. Holland from St. Mary's, Trenton, to St. Joseph's, Newark, . . .

[January 29th] Feast of St. Francis de Sales. Blessed a bell weighing 1,600 lbs. and preached. The church [in Keyport] very crowded . . .

Wednesday, February 12. Conference held in basement of St. John's Church [Trenton]. Rev. Thaddeus Hogan, Rev. Anthony Smith and Rev. James A. McFaul elected Officers.

In the evening there were recitations and tableaux at St. John's School [Trenton]. The Brothers of the Holy Cross and the Sisters of Charity are succeeding admirably.

Visited the State Prison [Trenton], saw Gershom Mott, the Superintendent, and others. About 850 prisoners; one third of the men are Catholics, say 150 in all; only two or three women. The officers at present allow every facility for the performance of religious duties by the prisoners. Confessions heard regularly. The Moral Instructor is an Episcopalian Clergyman, salaried by the State. He preaches before the cells, the inmates being behind the bars. . . .

[April 29th] Arrived during the storm in Burlington. Addressed the people that night, and gave Benediction with the Blessed Sacrament. Made the visitation the following day. Condition, in general, very satisfactory. The school which is held in the basement of the Church ought to be replaced by another. The Rector [Secundinus Pattle] is raising funds for this purpose. A few days after my visit, he had a sort of apoplectic attack, in consequence of which he was advised to take rest and a long sea voyage. He sailed a few weeks later for Spain, hoping to return in the Autumn.

Made the Visitation of the Sisters' Chapel. Found the Cup of the Ciborium to be plated merely, instead of silver. In the afternoon the Pastor and I crossed the Delaware to pay a visit of charity to Rev. Patrick A. Lynch, who was reported to be extremely ill. We found him already dead. R.I.P.

Wednesday, April 30th. After Mass in Burlington rode with Father Peter Jachetti, O.F.M. Conv., to St. Clare's Church, Florence. There are thirty-five families in this Mission. They have Mass twice a month. Exhorted them to pay their debts, and to keep up the Temperance Society. Met the Provincial of the Franciscans, Father Joseph Lesen from Syracuse; dined with my old friend, Matthew Gaynor, President of the Temperance Society, to whose efforts the building of the Church is largely to be attributed.

[May 1st] Preached at Bordentown that evening on Visitation and devotion to the Blessed Virgin. Made the Visitation next morning, and exhorted the people to procure a Baptismal font, which is lacking. Made the visit also to the Cemetery here as at Burlington, and to the Sisters' Chapel. Found the cup of the Ciborium plated only, as in many other places for economy.

On Friday May 2nd, made the Visitation at St. John's Allentown. The Rector, Rev. Joseph Borghese, has accomplished much during the short period of his Pastorship, having bought a House and three acres of ground for new Church, School, etc., furnished House and Church, and paid off over a thousand dollars. He was very lonely, however, in the country, and did not well understand the character of his flock; so falling sick a little later of Malarial fever, he sought and obtained permission to return to his native Diocese in Sicily [Italy]. He sailed with Father Januarius de Concilio in the new Guion steamer *Arizona* on June 17, and crossed the ocean in seven days and 23 hours, the fastest trip on record thus far.

The whole Congregation turned out on this occasion, and more than filled the Church. We both heard many Confessions, for the Jubilee, the people having come miles from their homes in the country.

Saturday morning, May 3rd, visited the Church of Our Lady [of the Assumption], New Egypt, formerly attended from Allentown and to be reunited to it, in August. . . .

May 5th, 1879. Made the Visitation at Mount Holly. Everything satisfactory. The Rector [Hugh J. McManus] is finishing the new Church, which will be dedicated in October, and is holding service temporarily in the old Church, or School House.

Wednesday, May 6, visited Moorestown. As usual a great crowd came to see the Bishop. Visited the Cemetery also at Mount Holly, processionally, and recited the prayers prescribed in the Pontifical. . . .

[June 20th] Friday went to Trenton,

meeting General Hooper, of Sonoma, California, in the train. Confirmed 133 in St. John's Church. . . .

[June 27th] Blessed the Corner Stone of the new St. Joseph's Church, Keyport. It was intensely hot in the sun. Father Michael J. Brennan made a very good address after the Ceremony in the old church. Then Confirmation was administered to 50 candidates.

Made the prescribed Visitation. Tabernacle revolves. The interior lining is of *red* silk; cup of ciborium not of silver. No veil for Ciborium. No throne for Blessed Sacrament. Baptismal font at present is kept in the Sacristy. No ambry. Only two altar cloths. No antependium, except for Requiem Masses. No Sacrarium. No record of erection of Way of the Cross. No school as yet. When Father Augustine G. Spierings took charge of this Mission, there was only an alb, one purificator and one vestment. He has lately received an excellent and abundant supply from a pious Association in Belgium. Everything seems to be flourishing in this Parish, and to promise well for the future. Went to Dr. William H. Van Buren's, Shrewsbury, for the night.

[June 28th] Confirmed 59 in St. James', Red Bank. The Church is quite out of debt. The zealous Pastor, Father Michael E. Kane, is now erecting a large brick School House, from designs furnished by Mr. Keely, and has the greatest part of the necessary funds on hand to pay for it.

[June 29th] Said Mass in Mr. Charles F. Meert's House on Sunday morning, and drove to Long Branch. Confirmed 55 and preached on the Primacy. Met Bishop John J. Conroy and Mr. Simon J. Ahern. Visited the new Pier, for which the President sent me a Season ticket. In the afternoon, Mr. & Mrs. Felix E. O'Rourke came to take me for a little rest to their delightful home in the Highlands.

[July 1st] The Rev. Cornelius Cannon, for many years attached to this Diocese sailed today for his native Diocese, Derry, intending to spend the remainder of his days in Ireland.

[July 6th] The Church of the Sacred Heart, Riverton, was blessed today. It was built by Father Peter Jachetti, O.F.M. Conv., and is a frame building 22 x 42. Mr. D. Leeds Miller kindly entertained me in his house, and another Protestant gentleman insisted on us all. We called on Mr. David S. Davis, a Presbyterian, who gave the site for the new Church. Present debt about $900 . . .

[August 10th] The Corner Stone of the new St. Peter's Church, Riverside, was blessed by Rev. Anthony Smith, of Trenton.

[August 17th] The Corner Stones of St. Mary's Church, Colts Neck, and St. Joseph's, Perrineville, both in the Parish of Freehold, were laid by Msgr. Robert Seton, in the midst of a storm of rain. The Monsignor preached in the morning. . . .

On Sunday, October 19, the beautiful new Church of the Sacred Heart, Mount Holly, Rev. Hugh J. McManus, Rector, was blessed. Rev. William McNulty sang the Mass. Bishop preached. Father Thaddeus Hogan, Patrick Leonard, Bernard H. Ter Woert, Nazarenus Graziani, O.F.M. Conv., Peter Jachetti, O.F.M. Conv., and others attended. Description of Church in weekly Catholic papers. [See *Catholic Review*, October 25, 1879.] Father Patrick F. Connolly preached at Vespers. . . .

[November 23rd] St. Mary's Church (Immaculate Conception) at Colts Neck was blessed today. It is of brick, 30 x 55, from designs of Mr. Austin H. Paterson, of

Monmouth County: Gothic style, the monotony relieved by ornaments in *terra cotta*. After Mass and a homely lunch in the Sacristy, after all had departed, drinking our cold coffee from lager beer bottles, Father Frederick Kivilitz and I drove eight miles to the residence of Dr. William H. Van Buren in Shrewsbury, where I remained overnight. Said Mass next morning in Red Bank, returned to Newark and thence proceeded to the Conference in Jersey City. A number of Priests, amongst them the Vicar General, Father Hugh P. Fleming, of Orange; Father William H. Dornin, of Belleville; Father Pierce McCarthy of East Newark dined at the House-warming of the new Parochial Residence attached to St. Michael's, Newark. . . .

[November 26th] Conference in Trenton. Blessed Statue of the Sacred Heart in Sisters' House, attaching Indulgence of 40 days for 1 Pater and three Hail Marys. Went to Mr. Farren's in the evening. . . .

[December 14th] Blessed the new brick Church of St. Peter, Riverside, 45 x 70 (cost $8,000), at Riverside, and at the 8 o'clock Mass conferred Subdeaconship on Rev. Henry Kavanagh, S.J., of St. John's College, Fordham. Confirmed one person privately.

In the evening confirmed 26 at St. Paul's, Burlington, preached, and blessed Statue brought from Lourdes by the Rev. Rector [Secundinus Pattle], attaching Indulgence.

[December 15th] Made Visitation in St. Francis' Church, Trenton, thereby completing the round of *all* the Churches in the Diocese since my return from Rome, 1877.

Confirmed four persons privately in St. Francis' Hospital [Trenton], and blessed and enriched with Indulgence of 40 days, Statue of "La Pieta," of Our Lady of Sorrows, presented to the Sisters by Mr. & Mrs. Joseph Wagner, for the New chapel now in course of erection.

Missions have been going on, as usual, in many places. Amongst others, . . . Father Albinus of the Incarnate Wisdom Magno, C.P., gave two Missions, in Moorestown and Mount Holly.

Fathers Benedict of St. Francis Murnane, C.P., and Vincent Nagler, C.P., in Princeton. 975 Communions . . .

December 28th, 1879. St. Joseph's Church [Perrineville], 30 x 55, brick, with terra cotta trimmings costing about $2,500 was blessed today. The principal attraction is the Altar, which is 27 feet high. Father Sebastian G. Messmer and Mr. Henry M. Efferz, Seminarian from Overbrook, assisted. Father Frederick Kivilitz, the Pastor, sang the Mass. Everything required by the Rubrics was sung. Introit, Kyrie, Gradual, Gloria, Credo, Offertory, Sanctus, Communion. We dined with Judge William P. Forman, an ex-Member of the Legislature, Mr. George Ely, and others at Martin Nolan's. Vespers and short Sermon, and Benediction in Freehold . . .

Eighteen Hundred Eighty
[March 7th] Blessed the new Chapel of Our Lady of Sorrows, attached to St. Francis' Hospital, Trenton . . .

[March 15th] Divided the parish of Mount Holly and Moorestown, putting Rev. James McKernan in charge of the latter church. There is a debt of $5,500 on the Church, and he has begun by increasing it to $10,000 by the purchase of the adjoining residence, and two lots. But as he is a good manager, all ought to go on well. . . .

[March 28th, Easter Sunday, **Msgr. George H. Doane**] At the close of the Mass, the bishop spoke substantially as follows, "Before imparting the Papal blessing, my dear Brethren, I have an announcement to make to you which I am sure will fill your hearts with joy, and add a crowning glory to this beautiful feast of Easter. This morning a cable dispatch was received from Rome, announcing that the Holy Father had been pleased to number your beloved Pastor [Rev. George H. Doane] among the Prelates of his household, and to make him an officer of the Roman Court. The Papal Brief constituting him Domestic Prelate has already been expedited, and will no doubt be received in a very few days. I am sure you will all rejoice, with me, at this honor conferred on your Rt. Rev. Pastor who has been so faithfully in your midst for so many years. It is a special joy to me to be able to make this announcement on this day of days, and it is my privilege to impart the glad tidings. The abiding presence in your midst of a Dignitary of the Papal Household will form a new bond of union with the Holy Father himself, in whose name and as a pledge of whose love I will now impart the Apostolic Benediction."

This news spread like wildfire through the city, and by telegraph next day through the country, and created very general satisfaction.

The *Daily Advertiser* gives the following notice of the new Monsignor. Right Rev. Msgr. George H. Doane was born in Boston, September 5, 1830. His father was then Rector of Trinity Church, Boston, but in 1833, was elected second Protestant Bishop of New Jersey. George Hobart Doane studied medicine at Jefferson College, Philadelphia, was graduated in 1850, but never practiced. Soon after graduating, he began his Ecclesiastical studies, for the Episcopal Ministry, and was ordained Deacon by his father at St. Mary's, Burlington,

New Jersey, and sent to Grace Church, Newark, where he assisted Rev. Mr. William H. N. Stewart, for four months. In 1855, he was received into the Catholic Church by Bishop James R. Bayley, was sent to Paris (St. Sulpice) and to the Collegio Pio, Rome. He was ordained in the Cathedral, Newark, September 13, 1857, where he has since remained, as Secretary, Chancellor, and later Vicar General. . . .

[June 8th] Tuesday morning, the 8th, left Vineland for Trenton. On the way, met Rev. Hugh J. McManus of Mount Holly, who was en route for New York, to sail next day by the *Algeria* for Ireland. He died a few days after arriving (June 25th). Made Visitation in St. John's, Trenton; visited all the classes in the schools, etc., etc. Father Thaddeus Hogan is full of zeal, but too fond of making expensive improvements. He is now remodelling the old Orphan Asylum, unnecessarily, I think, as a Select School. . . .

September 1, 1880. The Rev. Robert E. Burke, of St. Mary's Church, Hoboken, has been promoted to the Rectorship of Mount Holly, vacant by death of Rev. Hugh J. McManus. . . .

[September 19th] On Saturday afternoon went to Mount Holly, and after Mass on Sunday morning (19th). Feast of that Apostle, 1879. Father Isaac P. Whelan sang the Mass. Mr. Thomas Foy drove us over & back. Lecture in Mount Holly in the evening . . .

[October 10th] Said Mass at Church of Our Lady of Lourdes, Chambersburg [Trenton], and gave Minor Orders to [unknown number of] Franciscan Students. Confirmation before the High Mass. In the afternoon, confirmed 65 at St. Francis' Church, Front Street [Trenton]; visited Sisters and Brothers, etc. . . .

Conclusion of Corrigan's Tenure as Bishop of Newark

Finally, after laboring throughout the state of New Jersey for more than seven years, Bishop Corrigan was promoted in October 1880 to coadjutor archbishop to His Eminence John Cardinal McCloskey, archbishop of New York. Bishop Corrigan departed from Newark on November 9, 1880.

It is interesting to note that in his annual report to Rome in 1876, Bishop Corrigan again requested that the Diocese of Newark be divided. He suggested the city of Trenton for the location of a new see.

REFERENCES

1. Permission was received to extract material from *The Bishops of Newark 1853–1978*, which was prepared under the direction of the New Jersey Catholic Historical Records Commission. Information about Bishop James R. Bayley was extracted from pages 6–13.

2. Yeager, Sr. Mary Hildegarde, C.S.C. *The Life of James Roosevelt Bayley, 1814–1877*. Washington, D.C.: The Catholic University of America Press, 1947, p. 354.

3. Yeager, p. 338.

4. The introductory section about Bishop Michael A. Corrigan was based on pages 122 and 123 in Rev. Walter T. Leahy's *The Catholic Church of the Diocese of Trenton*, published in 1906 and printed by the Princeton University Press in Princeton, New Jersey.

5. Permission was received to use passages from *The Diocesan Journal of Michael Augustine Corrigan, Bishop of Newark, 1872–*

1880, edited by Joseph F. Mahoney and Peter J. Wosh. Newark and South Orange: New Jersey Historical Society and the New Jersey Catholic Historical Records Commission, 1987, p. 212.

6. Passages from Bishop Corrigan's journal appear on pages 7, 14, 19, 20, 29–30, 33–34, 37–38, 43, 44, 47, 49–51, 59–60, 65–66, 72, 75, 76, 76–77, 90, 95, 100, 103–104, 109–110, 114–115, 125, 127–128, 134, 135, 136–137, 138, 140, 145, 145, 146, 161–162, 162, 169, 170, 170, 171, 175, 179, 179, 180–181, 186–187, 188, 198, 200–201, 203, 207, 210, 210, 212, 213, 216, 217, 218–219, 238–239, 245, 247, and 248.

PART TWO

THE DIOCESE OF TRENTON 1881–1993

CHAPTER FOUR

FIRST BISHOP: MICHAEL J. O'FARRELL 1881~1894

BY FATHER G. SCOTT SHAFFER

ONE OF THE MOST gorgeous ecclesiastical pageants ever seen in New York was that which occupied exactly four hours in the [Saint Patrick's] Cathedral on Tuesday, November 1st [1881]. The occasion was the consecration of Right Reverend Michael J. O'Farrell, D.D., formerly the pastor of St. Peter's Church. An enormous congregation filled the pews and the side aisles of the cathedral before 10 a.m. . . . No more beautiful or gorgeous service has been held in any New York church since Archbishop McCloskey was made a Cardinal. At 10 o'clock the procession of ecclesiastics paced slowly around from the vestry to the sanctuary. There were not less than two hundred persons in it from the Cardinal to the choirboys. . . . (*Catholic Standard*, 12 Nov. 1881)

Thus reads the account of the beginning of Reverend Michael J. O'Farrell's tenure as the first bishop of Trenton. This holy and learned man from Ireland brought with him to the episcopacy, however, a wealth of experience and dedication to the faith about which this writer would be remiss if it were not recounted herein. It is hoped that through the following pages, the reader will come to know Bishop O'Farrell as a kind and loving man who dedicated himself to his people and his Lord. He was tireless in promoting and defending the faith and education, working always to educate his people into a deep love of God and their holy Roman Catholic Church.

EARLY HISTORY

Michael Joseph O'Farrell was born in Limerick, Ireland, on December 2, 1832, and was baptized on the Feast of Saint Francis Xavier, apostle of the Indies. The loving environment within the O'Farrell family inspired several of its sons to the service of the altar. Young Michael entered the Missionary College of All Hallows in 1848, where he devoted three years of study to the classics, philosophy, and theology. In August 1851 he enrolled in the seminary at Issy, France, to study philosophy and, a few months later, the historic seminary of St. Sulpice in Paris, where he became professor of dogmatic theology. During the next three years, he received the four minor orders in the Church of Saint Sulpice.[1] He returned to Limerick and was ordained a priest on August 18, 1855.

The year 1854–55 found Father O'Farrell making the "Solitude in Issy," which was a special preparatory program for admission into the Society of Saint Sulpice. His superiors decided he should fill the chair of dogmatic theology in the seminary. This was quite an honor for such a young priest in an institution of such renown.[2] Father O'Farrell taught at Issy for one year, but his health was affected by excessive study. He was then sent to teach theology at the Grand Seminary in Montreal.[3]

MONTREAL

The young priest enjoyed teaching, yet a problem arose with some of his confreres. During his two years at the Grand Seminary, certain Sulpicians were favoring "Gallican" doctrines, the French clergy were breaking ties with Rome, and the liberties of the French church were being jealously insisted upon. The doctrine of papal infallibility was bitterly discussed in the intellectual circles of the church. This French nationalistic thinking disturbed Father O'Farrell, and he voiced his outrage at the faculty members' disloyalty. It is reported that, in 1855–56, Father O'Farrell's colleagues challenged his position in support of the church in Rome.[4] No longer was he such a welcomed addition.

With the intellectual and theological climate not being favorable to Father O'Farrell's health, he left the faculty of the Grand and sought mission work in the area of Saint Bridget's and Saint Patrick's Hospital. During this time the Irish Catholics of the East End of Montreal were eager to erect a church they could call their own. To this end, the industrious Fathers O'Farrell and O'Brien undertook to raise a collection among the Irish Catholics of the whole city. They had hoped that with their collection of 800 pounds Canadian, they would justify the sanction of the project and secure from the Diocese of Montreal's leader, Bishop Bourget, permission to build. During the next eight years, however, the project never received approbation, but O'Farrell was remembered fondly for his efforts.[5]

Not being able to stay away from education, Father O'Farrell accepted a position at the College of Montreal, where he taught philosophy from 1860 to 1863, and was then made pastor of St. Anne Church, where he served until 1869. During his time in Montreal, Father William Quinn of Saint Peter's Church in New York City persuaded Father O'Farrell that parish work was his true forte.

NEW YORK

In July 1869, Father O'Farrell left the Society of Saint Sulpice, was accepted as a priest of the New York Diocese, and began as Father Quinn's assistant at Saint Peter's Church on Barclay Street.[6] Father O'Farrell "remained there for three fruitful years evincing a zeal in his flock that won universal confidence."[7] He was then appointed pastor of Saint Mary's Parish in Kingston/Rondout, New York, in July 1872. Although he remained there less than a year, before being recalled to Saint Peter's as its pastor in May 1873, he was remembered at Saint Mary's as "a most distinguished scholar and with his aid and that of his extensive library, the great Dominican, Father Thomas Burke, here prepared many of his famous lectures and addresses."[8]

Father Burke had been requested to defend the honor of Ireland against the arguments of English historian James Anthony Froude, who had come to America to lecture with the goal of convincing Americans that England was justified in her oppression of Ireland. He became the "David" to Froude's "Goliath." Father Burke sought out Father O'Farrell's scholarship and vast stories of Irish wisdom, for he knew his homeland's history as well as he knew his own prayers. Father O'Farrell, the quiet, unassuming parish priest of Rondout, "furnished the stones and fitted them in the sling that laid the giant low and put an end to his lecture course."[9] The result of the confrontations with Froude was clearly stated by William Cullen Bryant: "Mr. Froude, you left England with a reputation, and you are going home without one."[10]

Father O'Farrell succeeded Father Quinn at Saint Peter's. The office of parish priest in a large, busy city parish is no easy position, if its duties are conscientiously performed.

> There is one way, of shutting one's self in a pleasant library amid the companionship of books, enjoying all the emoluments of the office, and relegating to assistants all its duties. There is another way, of being a real father to the poor, a spiritual physician to the tempted, an instructor of the ignorant, a consoler of the afflicted. To be a real pastor of the flock, one must be in touch with the people; must have a kind, sympathizing heart, which will draw the poor and the afflicted to him; must be willing to spend and be spent in the service of the Lord.
>
> That Father O'Farrell was all this, the Catholic people of New York City and Montreal will gladly testify.[11]

Knowing the parish well, from his earlier assignment, Father O'Farrell immediately assumed the helm of pastoral responsibility and pursued a plan for the erection of a school, which had long been in the dreams of the people who realized the need for Catholic education. Much of Father O'Farrell's life would be dedicated to the promotion and defense of Catholic education. On June 11, 1874, he purchased an old factory and in just four months made the necessary alterations to provide space for classrooms. On the eighth of September the school opened its doors to educate young Catholic children of New York. Father

O'Farrell visited the school often and exhibited great fondness for the children, becoming their beloved father.

Because running a school created a great expense for the parish, Father O'Farrell "organized the whole parish into units and a ten cent collection per family was taken up weekly for this need."[12] Working together in this way, the parish grew and prospered. Saint Peter's School was regarded as a fine school, and it became the model for others throughout the Northeast.

During this time, Father O'Farrell was in great demand as homilist for many church functions in the metropolitan area. A couple of his sermon topics were "The action of the Church in relation to civilization" and "I believe in the Holy, Catholic Church." Referring to the former address, given at Saint John's, Archbishop Michael Corrigan of Newark noted fondly in his journal that Father O'Farrell's talk was "very good."[13] While he was still laboring for the welfare of his people and the intellectual and moral education of their children in Saint Peter's, word was sent July 17, 1881, that the Diocese of Newark, comprising the entire state of New Jersey, had been divided into two dioceses by Pope Leo XIII.

Selection of the Bishop

In New Jersey and New York it was generally known or rumored that division was imminent, and speculation was rife regarding the successor of Archbishop Corrigan in Newark and the new bishop of Trenton. In accordance with the procedure in effect at that time, Cardinal John McCloskey, archbishop of New York, called together the bishops of the ecclesiastical Province of New York on November 17, 1880, to discuss the selection of a new bishop for the vacant See of Newark as well as the possible division of the diocese. Present at the meeting at the cardinal's residence were the cardinal and his coadjutor, and the bishops of Buffalo, Rochester, Albany, Brooklyn, and Ogdensburg.[14] On his way from Rochester, Bishop Bernard J. McQuaid stopped in Paterson to see Father McNulty. Many years had elapsed since the bishop had left Newark for Rochester, and he was wholly a stranger to the priests of New Jersey. He inquired of Father McNulty who was the fittest man in the diocese to succeed Archbishop Corrigan. After some thought, McNulty replied that the only man worthy to be chosen would be Father Winand Wigger of Madison, New Jersey.[15]

At the November gathering, it was agreed that a scholarly man should be appointed to Newark to consult the best interests of the diocesan college. At that time, the bishops drew up two lists of candidates: one list for Newark, one for the proposed See of Trenton. Father Michael J. O'Farrell was placed at the head of the list for Newark, followed by Father Wigger, with Father Patrick Smyth as the third. The bishops considered Father O'Farrell to be "in robust health, frugal and well versed in the administration of temporal goods."[16]

Father Winand Wigger was then the first candidate to be proposed for Trenton. He was 39 years old, was born in New York, and had completed his theological studies at the seminary of Brignole-Sale in Genoa. He had obtained a doctorate in Rome and was ordained in 1865. He was fluent in French, German, and Italian and had held numerous diocesan positions. The bishops considered him to be "in good health, though not robust," and well versed in the administration of temporalities. They regarded him as "prudent and meticulous with a delicate conscience."[17] Monsignor George Hobart Doane, a convert from the Episcopal church, was placed second on the list. Although he had been honored as a monsignor, the bishops regretfully noted that Msgr. Doane had rather "worldly habits," which they attributed to his Protestant background. The third man on the list for Trenton was Father Patrick MacSweeney, 45, who was born in Ireland and educated in Rome. He was a good administrator who had served both in the City of New York and in other outlying areas of the archdiocese.[18]

Appearances are sometimes deceiving. Two lists were sent to Rome, one for each diocese, recommending three men on each list. However, the first man on the Newark list became bishop of Trenton, and the first man on the Trenton list became bishop of Newark. What happened?

In a meeting of July 7, 1881, the consultors of the Propaganda were asked to offer their opinion on several matters:

— The proposed division of the Diocese of Newark and the erection of the new Diocese of Trenton (question one) and

— The naming of "the respective bishops" (questions two and three).

From the way the questions were proposed, one would expect that, once they had approved the division of the Diocese of Newark, the consultors would then have voted on the next bishop of Newark and finally on the first bishop of Trenton. The minutes of the meeting, however, report the decisions in the following manner:

— To the first question, all the consultors were in favor of an affirmative response.

— To the second question, eight voted to recommend that His Holiness name Wigger, two voted for MacSweeney, and five voted for Doane (the Trenton list).

— To the third question, nine voted to recommend O'Farrell, five voted for Wigger, and one voted for Smyth (the Newark list).

The matter was then discussed in the General Congregation of the Propaganda on July 11, and the recommendations of the Propaganda were presented to Pope Leo XIII by Cardinal Franzelin on July 17, 1881, in what appears to be a more logical order, but still not indicating the diocese for which each candidate was being recommended:

— To the first question, affirmative.

— To the second question, the Rev. Michael O'Farrell is recommended to His Holiness.

— To the third question, the Rev. Winand M. Wigger is recommended to His Holiness.

When the papal briefs were issued, however, O'Farrell was named to Trenton and Wigger to Newark. The result was that the new bishop of Newark had been the provincial bishops' first choice for Trenton and only their second choice for Newark, and the first bishop of Trenton had been their first choice for Newark and not even on their list for Trenton![19] The contraposition of the names became widely known, causing "considerable discussion, and various groundless causes were alleged therefor."[20] One opinion was that the German Cardinal Franzelin had used his influence to give the larger and more important See of Newark to another German, leaving the smaller new See of Trenton to the Irish O'Farrell. As the Irish author Flynn expressed it:

> With that racial loyalty which is characteristic of the German family his eminence, [Card. Franzelin,] perceiving that Doctor Wigger was first on one list and second on another, contended, and successfully, that the more important diocese should be assigned to him.[21]

Robert Wister, in examining the Propaganda archives, found no reason for the apparent switch but did find letters written in support of Wigger by two priests of Newark, Gennaro de Concilio and Sebastian Smith (a German whose name was originally Schmidt).

So it happened that Doctor Wigger was called to become bishop of Newark and Father Michael J. O'Farrell was elected to the newly erected See of Trenton on August 11, 1881.

The Consecration

On the Feast of All Saints Day 1881, with a special dispensation from the Holy See, the consecration of Rev. Michael J. O'Farrell to the episcopacy was celebrated at Saint Patrick's Cathedral in New York City. As the *Catholic Standard* reported, the four-hour ceremony was quite impressive. His Eminence Cardinal McCloskey, metropolitan of the Province of New York, was the ordaining prelate, assisted by Archbishop Corrigan, who was coadjutor of the cardinal. Also in attendance were Archbishop Lynch of Toronto and Bishops Loughlin of Brooklyn, Lynch of Charleston, McNierny of Albany, Fabre of Montreal, McQuaid of Rochester, Grondell of Vancouver Island, Crinnon of Hamilton, Wigger of Newark, Conroy of Albany, Ryan of Buffalo (who was the homilist[22]), Wadhams of Ogdensburg, and Shanahan of Harrisburg. In addition to the ecclesiastics, F. B. McNamee, president of Saint Patrick's Society of Montreal, was present, in full dress, replete with heavy gold collar and medal. That evening, Mr. McNamee presented a purse of $2000 to Bishop O'Farrell from the inhabitants of that Canadian city where Bishop O'Farrell had long ministered.[23]

THE NEW BISHOP AND HIS NEW DIOCESE

The fourteen counties of Middlesex, Monmouth, Somerset, Warren, Hunterdon,

Bishop O'Farrell's coat-of-arms.
"Suffer the little ones to come unto me."

were considered to be faithful people, with the majority of them reported as making their Easter duty, but there were some pastoral problems. The major danger to the faith was judged to be indifference, and there seemed to be widespread alcoholism among the population. Another very real pastoral problem facing the new bishop was the diffusion of the Catholic population. The Catholics were not located in population centers, as their counterparts were in North Jersey and New York. Rather they were spread throughout the area and mixed among the non-Catholic population.[25]

Just eight days after his consecration, Bishop Michael O'Farrell arrived in Trenton and quickly set about the difficult task of organizing his new diocese, which, at that time, consisted of just 51 priests, 69 churches, 23 parochial schools, and 40,000 Catholic souls.[26] Of the 51 priests, only 10 were natives of the new diocese. The remainder were from Germany, Ireland, Holland, and elsewhere in the United States.[27] Choosing Saint Mary's Church as his cathedral, Bishop O'Farrell was installed with impressive ceremonies. He rented a house on West State Street and resided there until 1883, when the episcopal residence was erected on North Warren Street under the supervision of the Very Reverend Anthony Smith, pastor of Saint Mary's and the first vicar-general of the new diocese.

Upon his arrival, the bishop had found that women religious were a rarity, groups serving in only 14 of the missions. He discovered that he had inherited two foundations of the Sisters of Mercy from the parent community of Manchester. He

Mercer, Burlington, Ocean, Camden, Gloucester, Cumberland, Cape May, Salem, and Atlantic in the southern two thirds of the state now constituted the new Diocese of Trenton. In 1880, this area boasted a modest population of 413,693, of which approximately 10 percent were Catholic. It was noted at the time of the creation of the diocese that it

> . . . will not be rich but will find itself in better condition than many other dioceses at their foundation. Moreover, with the establishment of a new diocese, Catholicism will become a more powerful force not only for the new immigrants but for the conversion of the inhabitants.[24]

Most of the growing Catholic population had emigrated from Ireland. The people,

wanted religious teachers for the extensive parochial school system he planned to develop. On December 12, 1881, about six weeks after Bishop O'Farrell's consecration, he attended the Congregation of Mercy's Golden Anniversary of its founding. The local jubilee was held in Saint Mary's Church in Bordentown, New Jersey.[28] The bishop spoke to the congregation on the necessity of Catholic education and the promotion of it as his chief concern. During this visit, he proposed to the two communities of Mercy Sisters in Bordentown and Princeton that they form a union, suggesting Bordentown as their official center. The amalgamation was accomplished by spring of 1882, with the bishop favoring the sisters with a special solicitude for the remainder of his life.[29]

On December 18, 1881, the first ordination in the new diocese was celebrated. Bishop O'Farrell ordained an enthusiastic young graduate of St. Charles in Catonsville, Maryland, and of the Seminary of the Immaculate Conception in South Orange, New Jersey. The new priest, Rev. John T. Dwyer, was a native of Trenton. Not only was Father Dwyer's ordination the first in the diocese, but he was also the first Trentonian to be elevated to the dignity of the priesthood.[30]

Bishop O'Farrell immediately became popular with his priests and people. The clergy he found in Trenton were willing and zealous. They welcomed him with open arms. He knew how to elicit from them "not the unwilling, superficial work of place-hunters and time-servers, but the spontaneous homage of generous soldiers who had sacrificed much for God's holy name."[31]

He was known to be a man of influence, education, and gentle manner. The Catholic press received the new bishop with great excitement and anticipation: "The fervor with which Bishop O'Farrell has entered the duties of his new See . . . justifies the joy with which the priests of his new Diocese have hailed him. We are to look for telling results of his zealous management."[32] John Talbot Smith described Father O'Farrell as a man who

enjoyed a reputation for wit and bibliomania, for oratorical and social charm . . . he became the preacher and orator for notable occasions, stored up a magnificent library, and helped to bring about that smoothness of clerical social life which was later to become the normal condition. His oratory was marked by elegance of diction, deep sentiment and fine arrangement, rather than by force, and his writings had the same character, being very rich in allusion and quotation, as became a great reader of books.[33]

Another account describes O'Farrell as "an eloquent speaker in the pulpit and on the lyceum platform . . . constantly in demand."[34] Yet another reporter describes the bishop's homely nature as he visited Sacred Heart College in Vineland, where, because of time limitations, no formal program was offered and "perhaps for this very reason the exercises were more gratifying to the distinguished prelate, whose modesty is

Bishop Michael J. O'Farrell

account of Bishop O'Farrell's life. The proceeds from the *Saint Mary's Messenger* funded Saint Mary's Union, which was organized to enable the diocese "to provide the necessary means for the protection, education and moral improvement of homeless children."[36] These funds supported Saint Mary's Orphanage in New Brunswick and, later, Saint Michael's Orphan Asylum and Industrial School in Hopewell, which was one of Bishop O'Farrell's dreams. The Sisters of St. Francis from Glen Riddle, Pennsylvania, had established the orphanage in New Brunswick, but after six years it had become overcrowded. The bishop then set about launching plans for the building of what would eventually become known as St. Michael's Children's Home.[37]

so well known, than if elaborate presentations had been made for his reception."[35]

With the support of his priests, O'Farrell sought to imbue his people with pride in a strong Catholic identity. One of the bishop's first projects was the establishment of Saint Mary's Union, a forerunner of Catholic Charities, which constituted a response to the abuses that Bishop O'Farrell observed in the state of New Jersey's expenditure of public funds for proselytizing in state institutions for adults and children. Membership dues in the union were twenty-five cents a month, for which one received the publication called *Saint Mary's Messenger*. The first issue of the *Messenger* contained an

CATHOLIC EDUCATION

The Diocese of Trenton, under Bishop O'Farrell's leadership, was poised for growth. We know that by 1883 a clerical fund had been established by the new bishop for the education of seminarians.[38] Because of the bishop's tremendous interest in education, a great campaign of parochial school building was begun. O'Farrell believed strongly in the merits of Catholic education and was quite outspoken on the topic. In fact, late in his episcopate, great excitement was caused among the clergy and laity throughout the Diocese of Trenton and the country by the announcement in the public press that Bishop O'Farrell had accepted the invitation of a Dr. Brann to take the place of the papal nuncio, Archbishop Satolli, first apostolic delegate to the United States, in a New York debate on public education.

Archbishop Corrigan of New York and Bishop McQuaid of Rochester were openly hostile to the public schools of the United States. O'Farrell was poised to take his stand as one of the leading spirits against the public schools of America, a stand that was not necessarily in line with the Holy Father and his delegate, Archbishop Satolli. In Bishop O'Farrell's 1883 Pastoral Letter on Christian Education[39] were these words, ordered to be read by all the priests of the diocese every year:

> We are obliged in conscience to condemn the present godless, anti-Christian, anti-parental system of public schools [in the United States].

Compare this language with the much gentler and more politically correct, yet suppressed, propositions of Satolli:

> No. 2—When there is no Catholic school at all, or when the one that is available is little fitted for giving the children an education in keeping with their condition, then the public schools may be attended with a safe conscience.

> No. 5—We strictly forbid anyone, whether Bishop or priest, ... through the Sacred Congregation, either by act or threat, to exclude from the sacraments as unworthy, parents who choose to send their children to the public schools. As to the children themselves, this enactment applies with still greater force.[40]

Not only were new schools being built under O'Farrell's aegis, but new churches were built and dedicated as well. By the end of Bishop O'Farrell's first five years, the diocesan complement of parish churches had been augmented by 14.[41] Bishop O'Farrell was concerned about the coastal areas of the diocese as well. As early as 1883, in a letter to Bishop Wigger of Newark, he writes,

> I am about to leave from this place [Long Branch] for Cape May, where I lecture next Sunday evening. I am trying to provide for the wants of the coast, where so many summer residents are. I hope that I may have next year a home down here where you might come for a time to recruit your strength and health.[42]

Bishop O'Farrell became a community leader and involved himself in the affairs and issues that affected him and his people in Trenton. He was known to possess an exceptional Catholic library, "an immense and varied collection of books, constituting possibly the finest private library of its kind in the city."[43] In New York City, the keepers of the old bookstalls knew him well, and the Catholic University of America, in Washington, was grateful to him for the large addition he made to its library.[44] He was also a prime mover for the monument in Trenton at the top of Warren Street. Shortly after his arrival in Trenton and upon the recommendations of the Rev. Dr. John Hall, D.D., a renowned historian of the Presbyterian church, Bishop O'Farrell was elected to one of the most respectable bodies of the state, the New Jersey Historical Society.[45]

ON TEMPERANCE

O'Farrell was greatly concerned with family life. His first pastoral letter, given at Trenton on Good Friday of 1882, was a beautiful treatment on Christian marriage.[46] One of the major threats to the quality of family life to which Bishop O'Farrell gave much attention was that of intemperance. He saw that many of his people were struggling to make ends meet by working long, hard hours in the many factories of the Trenton area. Local taverns and saloons, however, never seemed to be lacking for customers, and many of their patrons were Catholic husbands and fathers. In addressing this issue, an order was sent forth from the decrees of the First Diocesan Synod in Trenton that saloons should be closed on Sundays. It was also stated that those engaged in liquor traffic on Sundays could not approach the sacraments unless they abandoned the practice.[47]

In early March of 1887, the Citizens League of Trenton held a meeting at the Taylor Opera House seeking to enforce strict observance of the law regulating the sale of intoxicants. Bishop O'Farrell presided and gave the opening address. He rarely spoke on public platforms except for sacred or charitable causes. He said that he could advocate temperance with all his heart, and he spoke to the assembly not as he would from the Catholic pulpit. He appealed to dealers not to break state laws.

Selling liquor on Sundays was "one of the worst violations of the law."[48]

In support of the sanctity of the sabbath, O'Farrell said that it was in the best interest of both the workingman and the saloon keeper to observe the Sunday law. "If I were addressing a Catholic audience tonight, I would require much more than I here require."[49] He had already given orders to his Catholics to sell no liquor to minors and requested that no one go to saloons after 11 p.m. on Saturday nights. The end of the meeting was met with a standing ovation in response to a resolution to endorse the work of the Citizens League.

In November 1884, the Third Plenary Council of Baltimore was convened, and Bishop O'Farrell was invited to be an active member of the council as well as to deliver an address. The bishop had also already attended the Provincial Council of New York in the previous year. In Baltimore, Bishop O'Farrell gave an outstanding homily on the Christian family. Many of the issues he touched upon are relevant even to this day as he decried the horrors of child abuse and broken homes.[50] Bishop O'Farrell was "considered to be one of the most eloquent and gifted speakers"[51] of the council.

FIRST DIOCESAN SYNOD

Upon the bishop's return to Trenton, plans were laid to call the First Diocesan Synod. However, on December 4, 1886, ten days before the opening of the synod, Bishop O'Farrell celebrated a Solemn Pontifical Mass of Requiem for the repose of the soul of John O'Farrell, his father. After living for over 80 years in the humble town of Limerick, Mr. O'Farrell passed into new life on November 30, 1886. Many of the clergy and vast numbers of the faithful were present for the somber ceremony, which was described as "a most imposing service, with the altars all draped in purple."[52]

The aim of the synod was to ratify the decrees of both the Third Plenary Council of Baltimore and the Provincial Council of New York and to formulate rules in accordance therewith for the future government of the diocese. Its deliberations resulted in the full acceptance of the Decrees of the Third Plenary Council and the appointment of new diocesan officials.

Every priest of the diocese was present in cassock and surplice as the synod opened with a procession, low Mass, chants, a talk of purpose, a solemn profession of faith, and a customary oath of allegiance. The decrees of the Baltimore Council were read, commented on by the bishop, and then accepted by the synod. The bishop addressed them again, led Solemn Benediction, and adjourned for dinner at 2 p.m.

The appointment of diocesan officials was announced the next day. An interesting feature of the synod was that four permanent pastorates were named: one tenth of all diocesan pastors could be made irremovable. They were Father Thaddeus Hogan at Sacred Heart in Trenton, Father John O'Grady at Saint Peter's in New Brunswick, Father Peter Fitzsimmons at Immaculate Conception in Camden, and Father John Kelly at Saint Mary's in South Amboy. The latter two were appointed as deans and Father Hogan as defender of the sacrament of matrimony. Father Anthony Smith was named vicar-general.[53] In addition to these, there were appointed the chancellor, secretary and council, synodal examiners, promotor fiscalis, and examiners of schools.[54]

This Synod of Trenton was the first occasion on which the entire clergy "gathered and shows that our priesthood is of the progressive kind".[55] Two other decrees were issued from the synod, which closed saloons on Sundays and showed disfavor of picnics, fairs, and balls as church fund-raisers. Any fund-raisers of this type would first require the permission of the bishop. The statistics of the diocese indicated much growth, boasting 14 counties, 84 churches, 75 priests, 26 parochial schools, 8 academies, 1 hospital, 1 orphan asylum, 12 convents, and 50,000 Catholics.[56]

Five years later, Bishop O'Farrell celebrated the tenth anniversary of his consecration with a Pontifical Mass in St. Mary's Cathedral. Serving with the bishop were Arch-Priest, Rev. James A. McFaul; Deacon, Rev. William O'Farrell (bishop's brother); Sub Deacon, Rev. John Gummel; Master of Ceremonies, Rev. Cornelius F. Phelan; two Franciscan fathers serving as Deacons of Honor; and Rev. P. F. Connelly of Bordentown as homilist.[57] There was an afternoon parade of children's societies from the parish, with blessings of their banners by the bishop. After Solemn Vespers, a reception was held in the rooms of the New Jersey Catholic Union. Once again the diocese had grown. Now, in 1891, there were 88 priests, 87 churches, and 60,000 Catholics in the diocese.[58]

Two months later, the bishop addressed the first annual convention of the Trenton Diocesan Union, made up of Catholic Young Men's Associations. Bishop O'Farrell addressed them and their spiritual adviser, Rev. James McFaul, for the excellent diocesan union they had formed. He favored the idea of these diocesan unions' growing into a national union so that the Catholic young men of the country "could leave their impress on national affairs."[59]

When the bishop was not engaged in defending Catholic education, visiting his priests, parishes, and schools, or decrying the social ills of his day, he was often involved in another of his passions, that is, speaking and teaching about his beloved homeland. Orally he would paint pictures of the early surroundings that had given him "such a deep and lasting love for the land of his birth; the beauty of river and dell, the greenness of the verdure, the sweet song and poetic legend, the famous old historic towers and the trailing vines, and the sweet innocent home-life of the peasantry."[60] His memories were not all pleasant, though. He knew scenes of desolation as well: the roofless cathedrals, the ruined abbeys, and the desolated homes that showed that Ireland had been a nation that knew great sorrow.

In Trenton and New York, many lectures were offered by the bishop on topics such as "A Visit to Ireland's Shrines and Sanctuaries" and "Ireland's Aspirations." The former address delighted over 700 people on the evening of St. Patrick's Day 1887 in the Trenton Cathedral. In his "eloquent" talk ("one of the best ever by O'Farrell in Trenton"), the bishop:

> in an interesting way, led the hearers up and down the Green Isle and along every coast, pointing out everywhere the ruins of famous shrines of piety and learning, and all showed plainly the ancient civilization of Catholic Ireland.[61]

It was said of the bishop that his heart was in what he said, and his love for Ireland was so deep that "his heart would fill to overflowing and abundant tears would flow from his eyes."[62] His love for Ireland evidenced itself especially in the publication of his book, *The Life of Saint Patrick*. It was a popular life of the saint and was intended principally for the younger generation of Irish Catholics. The bishop stated that his chief desire in writing the book was to instruct the young and that:

> I shall consider myself fully rewarded if the memory and the feast of our national saint receive thereby any increase of veneration and of respect, or if it serve to console, to encourage, or to enlighten even one of his children.[63]

THE TREACY AFFAIR

It was a case of "disordered intellect" that made the front pages of the *New York Times* for seven months in 1893. It is ironic that the bishop, who had such a great love for his homeland, had to suffer so much anguish at the hands of two of his fellow Irishmen. In a correspondence to Bishop Wigger of Newark, Bishop O'Farrell wrote, "I thank you for your kind words of sympathy in regard to W. Treacy's affair. The man is really insane, and his statements as to the way I have treated him entirely false."[64]

In early January 1893, Bishop O'Farrell had ordered Father P. A. Treacy of Burlington to be removed from his pastorate and placed in Trenton Psychiatric Hospital because of his violent temper and the disturbance he was causing in the parish. Treacy was subsequently released on a promise to travel in Europe, but all he did was go to Rome and make charges against Bishop O'Farrell. Immediately, his brother, the Reverend William P. Treacy of Swedesboro, came to his brother's defense and encouraged him in all his strange actions. This case was given to the papal delegate, Msgr. Satolli, who recommended that both priests be relieved of their duties.

Father P. A. Treacy responded publicly by claiming that Msgr. Satolli had given him a written agreement promising him a parish within two months. He was then upset that the "Papal Delegate has violated his repeated and written promise, and has indorsed the Bishop's arbitrary measures."[65] The Treacy brothers refused to acknowledge the authority of either Bishop O'Farrell or Satolli.

The Swedesboro Treacy then released this letter of defiance:

I beg to say that Bishop O'Farrell of Trenton, who acted so cruelly and tyrannically last Summer in kidnapping the Rev. P. A. Treacy and imprisoning him against the laws of God and man, and depriving him of his parish, is the same Bishop O'Farrell who now attacks the Rev. William P. Treacy of Swedesborough, who so gallantly defended his brother against the tyranny of Bishop O'Farrell, and wants to deprive him of his parish. But the pastor of Swedesborough will not tamely submit to be dragged from his home by Bishop O'Farrell. He has made his appeal to Rome, and he and his congregation will employ every lawful means in resistance to Bishop O'Farrell's arbitrary measures.[66]

In their boldness, they dared the bishop to violate their appeal to Rome.[67] Things went steadily downhill from this point on. Bishop O'Farrell sent Father Walter Leahy[68] down to Swedesboro to take control of the parish, but the Treacy brothers refused to let him take possession of the church and parish. Both sides retained counsel and "dug in" for the fight.

On March 7, 1893, Vicar-General McFaul issued a proclamation excommunicating the brothers Treacy. This action was taken at the request of the bishop because of the brothers' continued disobedience to Msgr. Satolli.[69] Soon, civil authorities were called in to determine whether or not Fr. Treacy would have to leave the rectory, which he had not yet given up.

While Father Leahy was offering Mass in the church, Father Treacy and a few of his loyal followers would celebrate Mass in the rectory. Those who attended the Masses of the outlaw priest were similarly excommunicated.[70] Bickerings and legal manipulations continued throughout the months of March and April, with Father William Treacy always ready to court the press. When it was announced by Father Leahy that Bishop O'Farrell was to visit Swedesboro on the Sunday following Saint Patrick's Day, Treacy commented sarcastically "that it would be a good thing, for it would be his first visit to the parish in seven years, and he would have an opportunity of learning for himself how things stood."[71]

After much litigation, the courts of Trenton decided that Msgr. Satolli's power in this case was supreme and that no appeal from his decisions would be entertained by the Pope. Soon after this, on Tuesday, April 25, 1893, Father Treacy called on Msgr. Satolli and prayed to be relieved of his sentence of excommunication. Satolli offered to grant his request provided Treacy would apologize to the bishop for his offenses. In turn, Treacy agreed to this provided his parish at Swedesboro be restored to him. When told that the matter of restoration would rely solely on the discretion of Bishop O'Farrell, Treacy refused to apologize and left.[72] Finally, on August 11, 1893, the Treacy brothers were restored to full communion with the church.[73] It is uncertain what the circumstances were surrounding their reinstatement; however, one can infer that an apology was eventually offered by the brothers and accepted by the benevolent bishop.

> Neither of them ever regained the confidence of priests or people. But it seems that in the life of every Bishop there must be some martyr ready to give up his place of

Bishop Michael J. O'Farrell

peace of mind for the principles he himself never attempted to put in practice. . . .

> To be constantly harassed by difficulties, to meet ingratitude where we expect kindness, affects even the calmest and most pious people.[74]

THE BISHOP'S DEATH

In the following spring of 1894, although the troubles with the Treacys had ceased, the good bishop, affected and troubled deeply by the scandal, died on April 2, with his naturally kind heart chilled and embittered. Together with the bishop in his residence at the time of his death were his closest friend, Vicar-General James McFaul, and Fathers Phelan and Kenny of St. Mary's Cathedral. At 5:30 in the morning, the bishop died peacefully of kidney trouble, which had been ailing him for approximately six weeks. He was 62 years old.[75]

Funeral services for the first bishop of Trenton were celebrated in St. Mary's Cathedral on Thursday, April 5, 1894, by Archbishop Michael Augustine Corrigan of New York. In attendance were over two hundred priests and dignitaries of the church. The Jesuit Father Thomas Campbell, president of St. Francis Xavier College of New York, in his homily gave a touching tribute to the lamented bishop:

> The presence of so many high ecclesiastics, the great number of priests, and the large gathering of people showed the esteem in which the dead prelate was held, and the sad countenances of all told better than the dark drapery of the church the grief occasioned by his death.[76]

A somber procession was preceded by the hearse drawn by four black horses and surrounded by the Guard of Honor chosen by the rectors of the parishes in Trenton City. Following the hearse rode the bishop's brother, Rev. William O'Farrell, and his sister-in-law of Brooklyn, widow of another of the bishop's brothers. All the Catholic societies of the city were in line following with no mounted men, in respect for the deceased prelate. The streets along the route of the procession were filled with people longing to bid farewell to this beloved man of the church, whom they had come to know, love, and respect as their father in faith.[77]

The funeral cortege terminated its route at St. Mary's Cemetery, where the bishop's remains were then buried. They were later disinterred and reburied, on June 26, 1905, in a crypt at St. Michael's Home Chapel in Hopewell, by order of his friend and successor, Bishop James A. McFaul. His remains were located "in a building which he had seen only in his mind's dreams, near an altar he had never known, giving him a resting place among the orphans he loved in life."[78] In 1973, Bishop George W. Ahr requested the first bishop's remains to be moved once again because of the closing and subsequent razing of St. Michael's Home. They were removed from the crypt at St. Michael's on June 7 and reburied in St. Mary's Cemetery, in the circle, next to the other bishops of the Diocese of Trenton on October 19, 1973.[79]

CONCLUSION

Bishop Michael J. O'Farrell was considered to be kind and paternal to those under him, yet, as noted above, when the principles of truth and justice were being undermined, he could be stern and uncompromising. He was a man of great humility and compassion, always seeking to build up, rather than to tear down. His love of education inspired and encouraged him in the rearing of intelligent, conscientious, and patriotic citizens. The promotion of strong Christian families, ties of affection and brotherhood, and deep faith rooted in action were the hallmarks of his episcopacy and his legacy to the great Diocese of Trenton. We owe much to this man of the church, who guided and shepherded us to the future, firmly rooted in the truths and traditions of the past.

REFERENCES

1. Walter T. Leahy, *The Catholic Church of the Diocese of Trenton* (Princeton: University Press, 1906), 145.
2. Theodore A. Opdenaker, Ph.D., D.Min., *Most Rev. Michael Joseph O'Farrell, D.D., Builder of Christian Families and a Great Diocese*, chap. in *People of Faith—Profiles of Early Catholics and their Effect on the Diocese of Trenton* (New Jersey: Privately printed for the Diocese of Trenton Centennial Celebration, 1981), 7.
3. Leo Raymond Ryan, A.B., M.S., *Old St. Peter's: The Mother Church of Catholic New York (1785–1935)*, in *United States Catholic Historical Society Monograph Series XV* (New York: United States Catholic Historical Society, 1936), 35.
4. Rolland Litalien, ed., *Le Grande Séminaire de Montréal 1840–1990* (Ville d'Anjou, Quebec: Metropole Litho Inc., 1990), 100.
5. J. J. Curran, J.S.C., *Golden Jubilee of Saint Patrick's Orphan Asylum—The Work of Fathers Dowd, O'Brien and Quinlivan* (Montreal: Catholic Institution for Deaf Mutes, 1902), 25.
6. *The Catholic Standard*, 12 November 1881.
7. Opdenaker, 7.
8. *Centenary, St. Mary's Parish, Kingston, New York 1842–1942* (New York: Privately Printed, 1942), 11.
9. Alexander P. Doyle, C.S.P., Sermon on the Month's Mind of Requiem for Rt. Rev. Michael J. O'Farrell, Archives of Saint Patrick's Parish, Montreal, 6.
10. Opdenaker, 8.
11. Doyle, 7.
12. Ibid.
13. Joseph F. Mahoney and Peter J. Wosh, eds., *The Diocesan Journal of Michael Augustine Corrigan, Bishop of Newark, 1872–1880* (Newark and South Orange: New Jersey Historical Society and the New Jersey Catholic Historical Records Commission 1987), 53.
14. Robert J. Wister, "Diocese of Trenton Founded in 1881," *The Monitor* (Trenton), 6 August 1981.
15. Joseph M. Flynn, *The Catholic Church in New Jersey* (New York: The Publishers' Printing Co., 1904), 478.
16. Wister, 5.
17. Ibid. Here Fr. Wister quotes from the original letters of recommendation from the bishops of New York to the Sacred Congregation for the Propagation of the Faith.
18. Ibid, 7.
19. Robert J. Wister, "The Establishment of the Apostolic Delegation in the United States of America: The Satolli Mission, 1892–1896 (H.E.D. dissertation, Pontifical Gregorian University, Rome, 1981), 229–231.
20. Flynn, 478.
21. Ibid.
22. For excerpts of Bishop Ryan's sermon, see Appendix 4.
23. *The American*, 3 November 1881.
24. Wister, quotation of Cardinal Pier Francesco Meglia at the May 1881 General Meeting of the Congregation for the Propagation of the Faith, 3.
25. Ibid., 5.

26. *New York Times*, 2 November 1891, 6.2.

27. Wister, 3.

28. *The Freeman's Journal and Catholic Register* (New York), 24 December 1881.

29. Marie La Salle O'Hara, R.S.M., *The First Fifty Years* (Plainfield, New Jersey: The Hibbert Printing Company of New Jersey, 1981), 22.

30. *The American*, 23 December 1881.

31. Doyle, 8.

32. *Freeman and Catholic Register*, 24 December 1881.

33. John Talbot Smith, *History of the Catholic Church in New York*, vol. 2 (New York: Hall and Locke, 1905), quoted in Ryan, *Old St. Peter's*, 219.

34. Trenton Historical Society, *A History of Trenton 1679–1929*, vol. 1 (Princeton: Princeton University Press, 1929), 180.

35. *New Jersey Catholic Journal*, 29 January 1887.

36. Opdenaker, 8.

37. *The Monitor*, 18 May 1973. Bishop O'Farrell purchased the 464-acre Van Dyk farm in Hopewell for the site but died before construction even began. The five-story, 450-child-capacity home of red brick was built in 1895–96. Bishop O'Farrell had endowed the project with $25,000 from his estate. Colonel Daniel Morris of Atlantic City also contributed to the fund with a $50,000 gift.

38. Michael J. O'Farrell, Long Branch, NJ, to Winand Wigger, Newark, 3 July 1883. Archbishops and Bishops Correspondence, Archives of Archdiocese of Newark, Seton Hall University, South Orange, NJ. O'Farrell states, "I have received your note enclosing the check for $2405.00 for the clerical fund. I am sincerely grateful to you for your kindness. I also thank you for writing to Genoa, about the free places for my students."

39. See Appendix 3.

40. *New York Times*, 23 January 1893, 10.

41. See Appendix 1.

42. O'Farrell, Long Branch, to Wigger, Newark, 3 July 1883.

43. Trenton Historical Society, 181.

44. Doyle, 7.

45. Opdenaker, 8.

46. For the Pastoral Letter on Christian Marriage, see Appendix 2.

47. *New Jersey Catholic Journal*, 1 January 1887.

48. *New Jersey Catholic Journal*, 5 March 1887.

49. Ibid.

50. Opdenaker, 9.

51. Leahy, p. 145.

52. *New Jersey Catholic Journal*, 4 December 1886.

53. *New Jersey Catholic Journal*, 18 December 1886.

54. Richard H. Clarke, LL.D., ed., *Illustrated History of the Catholic Church in the United States* (Philadelphia: Gibbie and Company, 1891), 69.

55. *New Jersey Catholic Journal*, 4 December 1886.

56. At the close of the Fourth Synod of the Diocese of Trenton on December 8, 1991, the diocese consisted of 4 counties (Mercer, Monmouth, Burlington, and Ocean) with 124 parishes, 67 parochial schools, 5 private academies, 2 hospitals, and 1 nursing home and residence. There were 261 priests combined with 54 religious orders in serving the Catholic population of 659,994.

57. On November 1, 1892, Father McFaul was appointed vicar-general of the diocese. He was made administrator of the diocese on the occasion of the bishop's death, April 2, 1894. On July 20, 1894, McFaul succeeded his friend as the second bishop of Trenton.

58. *New York Times*, 2 November 1891, 6.2.
59. Ibid., 11 January 1892, 5.3.
60. Doyle, 6.
61. *New Jersey Catholic Journal*, 19, 20 March 1887.
62. Doyle, 6.
63. Michael J. O'Farrell, *The Life of Saint Patrick* (New York: P. J. Kenedy & Sons, no date given), Preface.
64. O'Farrell, Long Branch, to Wigger, Newark, 30 November 1892.
65. *New York Times*, 21 February 1893, 4.5.
66. Ibid., 6 March 1893.
67. Ibid., 25 February 1893. These are the grounds assigned by the priests for their actions: (1) Because Msgr. Satolli has forfeited his right of deciding without appeal by having subdelegated his authority in the case to Bishop O'Farrell. (2) Because the Rev. P. A. Treacy had already placed the case before the Pope and the cardinals personally before Msgr. Satolli's arrival in America. (3) Because Msgr. Satolli, in his letter to the Poles, laid down principles that utterly disqualify him from acting as an impartial judge. (4) Because Msgr. Satolli has violated his repeated and written promises to both the Rev. William P. Treacy and the Rev. P. A. Treacy.
68. This is the same Walter Leahy who, in 1906, wrote *The Catholic Church of the Diocese of Trenton*, which was the first and only history of this diocese published to this date.
69. Ibid., 8 March 1893.
70. *Trenton Times*, 13 March 1893, 1, 8. In a meeting held in the Swedesboro Parish, Father Leahy stated, "Those who attended mass conducted by Mr. Treacy—notice I say Mr. Treacy—for now and here, . . . I do promulgate the excommunication of William P. Treacy and all those who may now be attending a service of the Church of Rome being conducted by him. None of them is a Catholic and not one can receive absolution except by individual decree from Msgr. Satolli. They will be denied Christian burial and all rights and comforts of the Catholic Church. They are out from among us."
71. *New York Times*, 20 March 1893, 4.7.
72. Ibid., 28 April 1893, 1.4.
73. Ibid., 21 August 1893, 1.4.
74. Leahy, 146.
75. *Trenton Times*, 2 April 1894.
76. Flynn, 388.
77. *Trenton Times*, 5 April 1894.
78. Leahy, 146.
79. *Burial records: Ledger No. 13145A*, Murphy Funeral Home, Trenton, New Jersey.

BIBLIOGRAPHY

American, 3 November, 23 December 1881.

Archdiocese of Newark. Collection of papers of Winand Wigger in Archbishops' and Bishops' Correspondence, Seton Hall University, South Orange.

Archdiocese of Philadelphia Archives and Historical Collection. Archbishops' Correspondence, St. Charles Seminary, Philadelphia.

Archival Collection of Archdiocese of New York. Archbishops' Correspondence, St. Joseph Seminary, Dunwoody.

Archives, Company of Saint Sulpice, Paris.

Centenary, St. Mary's Parish: Kingston, New York 1842–1892. New York, 1942.

Clarke, Richard H., LL.D., editor. *Illustrated History of the Catholic Church in the United States Vol. I.* Gibbie and Company: Philadelphia, 1891.

Code, Joseph Bernard. *Dictionary of the American Hierarchy (1789–1964)*. New York: Joseph F. Wagner, Inc., 1964.

Curran, Hon. J. J., J.S.C. *Golden Jubilee of St. Patrick's Orphan Asylum. The Work of Fa-*

thers Dowd, O'Brien and Quinlivan. Montreal: Catholic Institution for Deaf Mutes, 1902.

Doyle, Alexander P., C.S.P. Sermon on the Month's Mind of the Rt. Rev. Michael J. O'Farrell, given at St. Mary's Cathedral, Trenton, New Jersey, May 4, 1894. Archives of Saint Patrick's Parish, Montreal.

Flynn, Joseph M. *The Catholic Church in New Jersey.* New York: Publishers' Printing Co., 1904.

Freeman's Journal and Catholic Register, 24 December 1881.

Leahy, Walter T. *The Catholic Church of the Diocese of Trenton.* Princeton: Princeton University Press, 1906.

Litalien, Rolland. *Le Grande Séminaire de Montréal 1840–1990.* Ville d'Anjou, Quebec: Metropole Litho Inc., 1990.

Lonsway, Jesse W. *The Episcopal Lineage of the Catholic Hierarchy in the United States 1790–1963.* Cincinnati: Charger Press, 1965.

Mahoney, Joseph F., and Peter J. Wosh, eds. *The Diocesan Journal of Michael Augustine Corrigan, Bishop of Newark, 1872–1880.* Newark: New Jersey Historical Society, 1987.

New Jersey Catholic Journal, 4, 18 December 1886; 1, 29 January 1887; 5, 19, 20 March.

New York Times, 2 November 1891; 11 January 1892; 23 January 1893; 21, 25 February; 6, 8, 20 March; 28 April; 21 August.

O'Farrell, Michael J. *The Life of Saint Patrick.* New York: P. J. Kenedy and Sons, no year given.

O'Hara, Sister Marie La Salle, R.S.M. *The First Fifty Years.* Plainfield, New Jersey: Hibbert Printing Company of New Jersey, 1981.

Opdenaker, Theodore A., Ph.D., D.Min. *People of Faith: Profiles of Early Catholics and Their Effect on the Diocese of Trenton.* Trenton: Privately published, 1981.

Ryan, Leo Raymond, A.B., M.S. *The Mother Church of Catholic New York 1785–1935: Old St. Peter's, New York.* United States Catholic Historical Society, Monograph Series XV. New York: United States Catholic Historical Society, 1935.

Sulpician Archives Baltimore, SAB-RG 38—Box 1.

Trenton Historical Society, *A History of Trenton 1679–1929*, Vol. 1. Princeton: Princeton University Press, 1929.

Trenton Times, 13 March 1893; 2, 5 April 1894.

Wister, Robert J. "Diocese of Trenton Founded in 1881," *The* (Trenton) *Monitor*, 6 August 1981.

Wister, Robert J. "The Establishment of the Apostolic Delegation in the United States of America: The Satolli Mission, 1892–1896." H.E.D. dissertation, Pontifical Gregorian University, Rome, 1981.

APPENDIX 1

Churches Established During Bishop O'Farrell's Tenure

1882	Immaculate Conception	Somerville
	Saint Joseph	North Plainfield
1883	Saint Joseph	Beverly
	Our Lady of Perpetual Help	Highlands
	Saint Joseph	Toms River
1884	Saint Joseph	Sea Isle City
	Our Lady Star of the Sea	Atlantic City
	Holy Cross	Rumson
1885	Saint Gabriel	Marlboro
	Saint Michael	Long Branch
	Saint Anthony of Padua	Hightstown
	Our Lady of Victories	Sayreville
	Sacred Heart	Camden
1886	Saint Joseph	Hammonton
1887	Saint Mary	Colts Neck
	Saint Mary	East Vineland
	Saint Bridget	Glassboro
1889	Saint Joseph	East Millstone
1890	Saint Stanislaus	Trenton
	Saint Agnes	Atlantic Highlands
	Saint Mary of the Lake	Lakewood
1891	Holy Cross	Trenton
	Saint Joseph	Trenton
1892	Saint Joseph	South Camden
	Saint Patrick	Belvidere
	Saint Stephen	Perth Amboy
1893	Saint Joseph	Carteret
	Saint James	Woodbridge
	Saint Joseph Pro-Cathedral	Camden
1894	Saint Augustine	Ocean City

APPENDIX 2

Pastoral Letter on Christian Marriage

Michael Joseph, by the grace of God and the favor of the Apostolic See, Bishop of Trenton, to the Clergy and faithful of his Diocese, health and benediction.

BELOVED BRETHREN OF THE CLERGY, AND DEAR CHILDREN OF THE LAITY:

On this solemn day, when the Catholic Church commemorates, with such touching and mournful ceremonies, the passion and death of Our Blessed Saviour, we wish to address you on some practical truths which we believe to be of the greatest importance for the welfare of your souls. Having completed the penitential exercises prescribed for the due observance of Lent, and having been frequently instructed by your pastors, during this holy season, on your chief duties as Catholics, we feel convinced that you will be more than ever disposed to listen to the voice of your bishop who speaks to you to-day, in God's name, with all the affection and earnestness of one who knows that he is obliged to watch over you, as "having to give an account of your souls" to the Good Shepherd and Chief Pastor of all. What we say to you, dear brethren, will not be regarded by you in the light of human opinions ever variable and inconstant, but as the expression of the teachings of our Holy Church, "the pillar and the ground of truth."

In this our first pastoral letter to you, we had intended to explain the importance and necessity of Catholic education for your children. That subject has been always most dear to us, not only from our desire to carry out in all things the doctrines and teachings of the Holy See, so clear and explicit on the necessity of Catholic schools, but also from a long and close study of the many evils resulting to faith and morals from the mixed or godless system of education. But on reflecting that Catholic schools and Catholic education cannot produce by themselves all the true fruits of religion; that they require to have as a foundation, upon which they can firmly stand, the home education of the family; and that, without this basis of parental direction, the fruits of the labors of Christian teachers will be very much diminished, if not completely neutralized, we felt that before examining the question of education in schools, it would be necessary to enter into the family circle and consider the sacred duties of parents towards their children in the training of their hearts and minds, that they may be fitted to become good and useful citizens, and noble, zealous Christians.

But here, again, we find another problem underlying this one. How can fathers and mothers realize the importance and the sacredness of their obligations towards their offspring, unless they understand the true nature of Christian marriage, and the duties which that holy state necessarily imposes on them? If marriage be simply a civil union or contract, if it can be made and unmade, either at the pleasure of the parties themselves, and by mutual agreement as in other contracts, or by the power of the state allowing divorce for various causes, then we can well understand how the Christian ideas of duty and obligation to the children would become clouded and gradually disappear. It is easy to see that only a Christian marriage—Christian in its true sense—can produce true Christian ideas as to the training of children. Hence, behind the question of education, rises up the question of the nature of Christian marriage, and to realize the importance of the former, it will be necessary to find out what constitutes the latter. Therefore, dear brethren, instead of addressing you at once on the subject of Catholic education, we deem it essential to begin by the study of Catholic or Christian marriage, reserving that of Catholic education for a future occasion, being well convinced that if this question be properly understood, it will be very easy to explain the other truths that are so intimately connected with it.

The greatness and the importance of this question of Christian marriage will appear evident to you from the fact that all society rests upon the family, that the family is the unit from which the aggregate of human society is constituted, and that if the family ties be loosely joined or easily broken, society would lose its consistency and cohesive power, and soon relapse into barbarism and anarchy. But it is in its Catholic meaning that we wish you, dear brethren, specially to consider it. The Church teaches us that our Blessed Redeemer raised the natural contract of marriage to the dignity of one of the Sacraments of the New Law, that He made it a sacred and indissoluble union between husband and wife, that He constituted it the great and mysterious symbol of His own perpetual union with His Church, and that He expressly declared the law that "what God hath joined together, let no man put asunder."[1]

Hence, the Catholic Church has always proclaimed to the world that the sacrament of marriage is <u>one</u> and cannot be dissolved, that the union must be of one man with one woman, that this union must last for life, and that death alone can break it. It was by insisting on these principles that the Church civilized the barbarous nations of Europe and built up Christendom and Christian civilization. It was by refusing to even powerful monarchs the right to trample upon the marriage ties, as their lusts and unbridled passions often prompted them, that the Christian family was saved, the dignity of woman was exalted, and the character of wife and mother made so holy in true men's eyes. Rather than allow the violation of this sacrament, the Church, to her great sorrow, saw the English nation dragged from the unity of Christian faith by the ungovernable passions of Henry VIII. It was upon broken marriage ties and broken religious vows that the reformation of the 16th century was built.

By the teaching of the Catholic Church, the evil system of polygamy, the curse of pagan and idolatrous nations, was made hateful to the Christian world, and if so great an abhorrence of Mormonism is truly felt by so large a proportion of the American people, it is due to the fact that the Catholic Church is so deeply impressed with the truth of the singleness of marriage upon the consciences of Christian peoples, that even three centuries of erroneous teachings have not been able to entirely eradicate it.

Catholics, therefore, should hold most firmly those doctrines which have constituted in the past the most solid basis of the prosperity of nations. Let it, then, be clearly understood by all that the bond of Christian marriage is so firm that no earthly power can sever it and that no laws made by earthly legislators can justify in conscience absolute divorce between persons lawfully married. As the Apostle of the Gentiles declared, "A woman is bound by the law so long as her husband liveth,"[2] and by parity of reasoning, that the man is equally bound as long as his wife is living, so no state, no nation, no legislation can dissolve the marriage tie, for "What God has joined together let no man put asunder."[3]

But this perpetuity and indissolubility of marriage will often be considered a great hardship, and so it must prove where God's law is not observed. Men's passions will long for a change, and human frailty and fickleness revolt against a constant yoke.

The Catholic Church alone possesses the remedy and the antidote. She teaches that marriage, being a Sacrament, possesses within itself, and bestows on those who worthily receive it, all the graces and helps necessary to support and strengthen them amidst the crosses and cares and sorrows that

---

[1]Matthew, 19:6.
[2]1 Corinthians, 7:5,59.
[3]Matthew, 19:6.

so often accompany it. She teaches that God grants through this Sacrament all the blessings that will enable a husband and wife to live happy together and to bring up their children in the fear and love of God and that by those graces the inconstant human heart can be kept faithful and true to its early love. If Her counsels and commands were well observed, so many unhappy marriages would not exist, so many homes would not be made wretched, so many scenes of hatred and violence and so many scandalous lawsuits would not be known.

We desire, then, to call your attention to some of the rules and regulations which the Catholic Church has wisely prescribed, as we are all well assured that their strict observance will bring upon you and your children many blessings in this life and eternal happiness in the next.

1. The Banns Of Marriage—The Church, acting on the principle that marriage is honorable in all, has prescribed that the banns of marriage should be published previous to the celebration in the parish church. She does so, not only that whatever obstacle or impediment to the due solemnization of the sacrament should exist may be made known and thus removed while there is still time, but also to interest in the happiness of the young couple the faithful amongst whom they live. She does so especially for the sake of the future wife, to protect her from deception, as far as possible, and to shield her from any slur that might be thrown upon her good name in after years, if her marriage were clandestine or secret. No true Catholic woman, then, should ever consent to be married, unless in very rare cases, without the publication of the banns, in order to show that she is not ashamed of her marriage. We desire the pastors and rectors of the different churches to explain these and other reasons for the law of banns, and to apply for no dispensation from them, except in rare and exceptional cases.

2. The Celebration of the Marriage—Since marriage is a sacrament of the living, it must be received in the state of grace. It is therefore always desirable that it should be preceded by a good Confession and Communion. But if the conscience were burthened (sic) by sin, then the Confession would become necessary; otherwise the reception will be a sacrilege, and the graces destined by God to strengthen and comfort the married couple will not be given. Hence so many wretched marriages. How can such marriages be blessed by God? At the wedding of Cana, in Galilee, our divine Master and His Holy Mother assisted and sanctified the marriage by their presence, and even the miracle was wrought by the Son of God, as if to show all how He will bless those to whose marriage He is lovingly invited. But alas! How many marry without a thought of their Saviour? How many enter into that sacred union without any knowledge of its importance, of its nature, and of its true end and with low, earthly motives, or the mere promptings of passion and sinful desire? Hence we may well imagine that, instead of being blessed by the presence of the Son of God and His pure, virgin Mother, such nuptials have as a guest only the archenemy of all to bring malediction upon them. To guard against such evil marriages, entered into with so much haste and so little deliberation, with so little respect for their sanctity that confession is omitted, even when the conscience is burthened with crime and the union is thus contracted in sin, we recommend earnestly our people to dispose themselves by prayer and the sacraments for the worthy reception of marriage, and to implore the divine assistance with all their heart. The Catholic Church also desires most earnestly that all should be married in the morning and with a special nuptial Mass, and so great is her maternal anxiety to procure every blessing for the young couple, but especially on the young wife, that she obliges her ministers to interrupt the adorable sacrifice in order to pronounce the most solemn and touching blessings upon her. The Priest prays that all the gifts bestowed by the Most High upon the noble and saintly women of the old law may descend upon her; that her name, like that of Sarah, Rebecca, Rachel, and Esther, may be in benediction forever; and that she may live to see her children and children's children to the third and fourth generation. Now the Church allows no such interruption in any other Mass, except in the blessing of the holy Oils, for the administration of the sacraments, and in the Mass for the ordination of her own ministers and priests.

We command, therefore, that, after the reading of this pastoral, no marriages shall be celebrated in this diocese, either during the afternoon or at night, and that all shall be celebrated in the morning and with a nuptial Mass. We are certain that our people will reap abundant graces and blessings from following this holy law. Already this is the custom in many parishes of the diocese, to the great edification of the community, and we see no reason why the other parishes should not do the same. We prescribe, then, that marriages shall henceforth be celebrated always in the morning and with a nuptial Mass wherever it is possible.

Having thus seen the mind of the Church with regard to the manner in which Catholics should prepare themselves for the due reception of the sacrament of marriage, and her anxiety lest they should be deprived of any of its blessings, we will more easily understand the indignation and sorrow and horror with which she regards the conduct of those unfaithful children, who, instead of profiting by the advantages she offers them, turn their backs upon her and seek to be united in marriage outside of her pale and by others than her priests. Truly their conduct must be considered as sacrilegious, as manifesting a contempt for their Church, and as a complete disregard of her sacrament. What excuse can be offered for such a crime? What motive can justify them, particularly when in this country marriage before the priest is invested with all legal effects? Hence the severest punishments have been threatened by the Church against such offenders. Sentence of excommunication has been pronounced against them, and priests are not allowed to absolve them without special permission from the bishop. But, as in despite of past warnings and menaces, there are still to be found some Catholics, either so ignorant as not to know them or so reckless as to disregard them, we, knowing well from experience, that those who thus marry outside of their Church care very little about their own souls or about the religious training of their children, who are almost invariably brought up in ignorance, if not in contempt of their faith, moved by the earnest desire of our hearts to save them and others from such evils, in the name of God and by the power invested in us, now solemnly command the pastors to announce to their people, that, in future, after this letter has been clearly explained, with our reasons and motives developed before the congregations, all Catholics belonging to this diocese, who shall marry before anyone not a Catholic priest, shall not and cannot be absolved by any priest of this diocese, until they shall have done penance publicly in the church and either by themselves or by the priest speaking publicly at the Mass for them, shall ask pardon of the congregation for the scandal and bad example which they have given, and only upon the accomplishment of this penance shall we authorize the pastors to grant absolution. We also command and enjoin most strictly upon the pastors not to admit to be churched, after childbirth, any woman who shall be married in this way, after the publication of this letter, until she first perform public penance for it, in the manner just described.

3. Mixed Marriages—Another great evil, which the Church very much deplores, arises from mixed marriages, which are, unfortunately, but too common in some sections of the country. Whatever reasons may have existed in the past, from necessity or other powerful motive, to justify them or at least render them less dangerous, it is seldom that, in present circumstances, and with the increasing number of Catholics, any solid motives can be found to justify them. They are in themselves most dangerous to the faith of the Catholic party; they are opposed to the mutual confidence and complete union of heart and soul which should ever subsist between husband and wife and without which marriage loses one of its chief blessings; they are most hurtful to the religious training of the children, who will naturally feel less the importance of doctrines about which they not only see their parents divided but, perhaps, have to listen to bickerings and quarrels concerning them, so that even if all the promises, which must be made by the non-Catholic party before the marriage can be celebrated at all, should be faithfully and honorably kept, many dangers will still exist.

But that you may most fully appreciate the gravity of this evil, we will quote for you the testimonies and solemn declaration of the highest authorities in the Church. We begin with the supreme authority of the Holy See. In an instruction addressed in the year 1858 to all the archbishops and bishops of the Church, it is explicitly declared that "the Church has always reprobated these marriages, and has held them to be unlawful and pernicious; as well because of the disgraceful communion in divine things, as because of the peril of perversion that hangs over the Catholic party to the marriage, and because of the disastrous influences affecting the education of the children." And then the Holy See reminds us "that if the more recent constitutions of the Sovereign Pontiffs relax the severity of the canons in some degree, so that mixed marriages may occasionally be allowed, this is only done for the gravest reasons and very reluctantly, and without the express condition of requiring beforehand those proper and indispensable pledges which have their foundation in the natural and divine law."

Still later, in the year 1868, the Sacred Congregation of the Propaganda issued a new and even stronger instruction. It enjoins upon the bishops that "lest perchance from misunderstanding, the people confided to you should suffer any harm, you are earnestly exhorted to take proper occasions studiously to teach and inculcate both on the clergy and the laity committed to your care, what is the true doctrine and practice of the Church respecting these mixed marriages." The instruction concludes with these solemn words: "Wherefore we earnestly request of your charity, that you strive and put forth your efforts, as far as in the Lord you can, to keep the faithful confided to you from these mixed marriages, so that they may cautiously avoid the perils which are found in them. But you will gain this object the more easily if you have care that the faithful be instructed on the special obligation that binds them to hear the voice of the Church on the subject and to obey their bishops, who will have to give a more strict account to the Eternal Prince of Pastors, not only for sometimes allowing these mixed marriages, for most grave reasons, but for too easily tolerating the contracting of marriages between the faithful and non-Catholics, at the will of those who ask it." Can anything be added to these very earnest words? Nothing except by showing that the bishops throughout the Catholic world have everywhere sought to put them in practice. In our own country, all the bishops assembled in the council of Baltimore, and since then in various provincial councils, have all deplored the evils of mixed marriages and have repeatedly, in their pastoral letters, most earnestly urged upon their people to avoid them. And at the other extremity of the globe, the voice of the Australian bishops is found to be in unison with that of the head of the Church, and in a late synod they proclaimed, with no uncertain or ambiguous sound, this very important doctrine. We give for your instruction, dear brethren, this admirable passage from their synodal address: "The frequency of mixed marriages," say the Right Rev. Prelates, "is a terrible blot upon the character of our Catholic community. It is sad to think with what facility Catholic parents consent to such irreligious connections, and with how little caution they expose their young people to social intercourse, where passionate fancy and the thoughtlessness of youth are certain to entail the danger of mischievous alliances. It is in the main the fault of the parents more than of the children, who hear so little warning against mixed marriages—so the denunciation and deprecation of their dangers and miseries. If young people did hear from the clergy and from parents as often and as explicitly as they ought about the sense and doctrine of the Church concerning such marriages, they would be a far rarer calamity than they are. The generosity of the young would revolt from such unions if they saw them in their true light, as a danger and a disgrace. Yes, a disgrace, not, perhaps, always in the eye of the world, but always in the eye of the Church. How are they to be interpreted? On one side there is the Church teaching that matrimony is a sacrament; that married life has its own great duties, its own difficulties, for which special graces of God are necessary, and which are provided by Him; that the state is to be entered upon thoughtfully and solemnly, with careful preparation of mind and heart; that spouses are to be of mutual help and encouragement in the grand end of all human life, the life for God and the next world. This is on one side, and on the other, what is there? A mere fanciful or passionate attachment, with little enough of worth about it, even when pure with the utmost natural purity it can have—a mere passionate attachment, overlooking, or at least most certainly undervaluing, the great considerations we have just stated. Is not this a disgrace? Or if the motive to mixed marriage be an advantageous alliance in respect of money prospects, is it not even more disgraceful to soil a sacred thing with the sordid calculations of a commercial bargain? Or, if the mixed marriage be coveted because one of the parties possesses some little higher worldly standing of fashion, or connection, or style, why, is not the thing still more contemptibly disgraceful, at least for the Catholic, with his or her belief about the one Church, the holiness of sacraments, the preciousness of God's grace, and the true end of life?

From these testimonies it must appear evident that mixed marriages, no matter what precautions may be taken, are always more or less dangerous. Of course, there are exceptions. There are cases where such marriages have had happy results. But they are rare, they are exceptional, and we have no right to expect from God any special favors, when we act directly against the well-known wishes and even laws of His Church. There must be grave reasons and "even grave difficulties impending over the faithful, that cannot otherwise be removed, before they can be allowed to expose their faith and morals to grave risks." Such are the terms of the Sacred Congregation of the Propaganda, in the Pope's name, in 1868. Hence our people will see that the bishop should not grant a dispensation for such marriages except in cases where grave difficulties and serious risks might otherwise be feared. It would, therefore, be a great fraud for a Catholic to engage himself or herself to marry one who is not a Catholic and then plead the engagement as a ground for dispensation. It would be a fraud to settle everything for such marriage and then give as a reason for requiring dispensation that everything is ready and that they cannot draw back. No Catholic is justified in contracting such an engagement until a dispensation has been previously obtained.

We so earnestly desire no such marriage should take place at all that we request the pastors not to apply for dispensations for mixed marriages, unless they find the reasons very great and convincing.

This, we trust, dear brethren, will prove sufficient to convince you of the evils of mixed marriages and that we shall not have the grief of seeing any of them in future in our young diocese.

For a more complete development of the entire subject of marriage from a Christian point of view and of mixed marriages in particular, we strongly recommend for your perusal and serious consideration two little works lately published by Benziger Brothers: one is entitled "A Sure Way to a Happy Marriage," and the other is "An Instruction on Mixed Marriages," by the Right Rev. Dr. Ullathorne.

4. Other Rules For the Married—We would also most earnestly urge upon Catholic women to strive by all means to make religion known and loved in their households; to impress upon the children, from their tenderest years, the importance of prayer; and as they grow up to imbue their young minds with love of the Sacraments. Mothers will be well rewarded for all this care, when they witness the unfolding of their children's minds and their growth in the true wisdom and loveliness of virtue. We would also suggest that Catholic women, when they find the time of maternity approaching, should know where to find a conscientious physician or faithful and skillful woman to take care of them and should be determined, in case of danger, to refuse to allow those horrible devices by which the child's life is often ruthlessly sacrificed. A Catholic mother must know how to die rather than permit what is truly a great crime.

Such are some of the rules and regulations which we deem important to send to you for the beginning of the Easter time. We hope and confidently trust, through the mercies of the risen Saviour, that they will contribute much to your spiritual advancement and to the growth of the Catholic faith throughout our diocese. The more faithfully we practice the doctrines of our glorious Church, the more will her beauty and majesty shine out in the eyes of all. She is so beautiful and strong in spite of her nineteen centuries of labors, of conflicts, and of victories that even our shortcomings and failings cannot conceal her loveliness. But how much more radiant will she appear, if we, her children, seek to reflect her beauty in the holiness of our lives.

We write these words on Good Friday, with the shadows of the Passion around us, but with the merciful cry of the dying Saviour ringing in our ears: "Father, forgive them, for they know not what they do!" and, therefore, we cannot forget to turn towards those children of the Church who have almost forgotten their Holy Mother, who have been so long estranged from her practices, and who have violated her laws. To them we address our most earnest prayer to return to God and to their Church. We conjure them, by the blood of the Saviour, by the scourging and crowning with thorns and nailing to the cross, by the ardent cry of Jesus, "I thirst," to cast themselves at the feet of their merciful Lord and seek His pardon. The very rocks were split by His death; let not our hearts prove harder. We say to all that, whatever violations of ecclesiastical law may have taken place in the past, whether through ignorance, more or less culpable, or even through malice, now sincerely repented of, we shall most willingly authorize the pastors to grant any indulgence that lies in our power, and if application should be necessary to ourselves, we promise any concession that the repose of troubled consciences may require. May we not trust, then, dear brethren, that the feast of Easter will bring joy to you all and that the peace of the Lord Jesus—that peace which He won by His victory over death and hell, that peace "which surpasseth all understanding"—will descend upon you and your families and remain with you forever.

This letter shall be read at all the Masses in the churches where there are resident priests, on the Sunday immediately after its reception, and in the mission churches, at the earliest opportunity.

Given at Trenton, this 7th day of April (Good Friday), 1882

MICHAEL JOSEPH,
Bishop of Trenton

The Rev. Clergy are requested to add henceforth to the prayers at Mass the "Oratio pro Papa," until further notification.

APPENDIX 3

Pastoral Letter on Christian Education

Michael Joseph, by the grace of God and the favor of the Apostolic See, Bishop of Trenton, to the Clergy and Faithful of his Diocese, health and benediction.

Dearly Beloved Brethren: In addressing you during this holy season of Lent last year, we stated that it would have been our wish to treat, in our first pastoral letter, of Christian education, as the subject most dear to our heart and most important to your souls. But, as we felt that Christian education supposes naturally a Christian home and that such a home cannot exist without Christian marriage, we decided to begin our public instructions to you upon that fundamental doctrine. We pointed out to you the true teaching of the church with regard to the <u>unity</u>, the <u>perpetuity</u>, and the <u>indissolubility</u> of the marriage bond; how all the modern notions of divorce are contrary to the teachings of the Gospels, as well as injurious to the best interests of the family and the state—teaching founded on the sentence pronounced by our Divine Lord Himself, that "what God has joined, let no man put asunder."[1] The Catholic Church, with the wisdom given to her by her Founder, and from the ever-flowing fount of His graces, has provided a constant supply of blessings for those who enter into the holy state of matrimony, to strengthen them against the natural fickleness of the human heart. Finally, we insisted upon the due observance of the practical rules laid down for us by the Church in order to secure these blessings. And now, dearly beloved, we have reason to thank God and to congratulate you for the good success that has attended our exhortations. From every parish we have received most consoling accounts of the docility and obedience of our faithful people. Marriage is felt to be an honorable and holy institution and is treated as such. Our young people have come to ask the Church to bestow her most solemn blessings on their union, and the adorable sacrifice of the Mass is offered up, in most cases, for the spiritual and temporal welfare of the married couple. Clandestine, disgraceful, uncatholic unions have entirely disappeared; evening marriages are now unheard of; and the pastors rejoice over the improvement of their flocks. Even when one or two exceptions occurred in opposition to this Christian spirit, the sorrow and the public apology of the repentant sinners soon consoled us for the violation of the law.

Such, then, dearly beloved brethren, is your spirit with regard to Christian marriage. You believe it to be a Divine Sacrament instituted by Christ to give every grace to the husband and wife to live happy together and to bring up their children in the fear and love of God. As the primary object of the institution of marriage was to perpetuate the human race, so the chief end of Christian marriage is to beget children for God, to bring up a godly race of Christian men and women, and to add new living members to the body of Christ, until the number of the elect is completed. Hence it is evident that a Christian education should follow a Christian marriage and that Christian parents are necessarily bound to bring up their children in a Christian way. It is upon this most important truth that we wish to address you; and we pray you with all the earnestness and affection of your heart to give the deepest attention to our words and to show the same docility to our teachings as you have hitherto done. We know of no subject more important to you and to your children in all its bearings or more far-reaching in its consequences. May the Author of Light, He "Who enlighteneth every man that

---

[1]Matthew 19:6.

cometh into this world"[2] guide and direct and enlighten us in the elucidation and in the practice of this grand principle!

That every parent, still more every Christian parent, should provide for the wants, both temporal and spiritual, of his or her child seems almost a self-evident truth. The child is entrusted, in a most helpless condition, to the care of its parents. It can do nothing for itself; it has not even the instinct of animals to protect itself. To the love of its parents it must be indebted for everything. The parents must assist it in its growth and development. Now, as the child is a complex being, consisting of a body and soul, its growth must be in this twofold capacity. It must grow physically in its body to become a man and capable of a man's duties. But it must also grow in its mind and its intellect, otherwise, it would not become a reasonable, intelligent being. It must also grow in its moral nature, otherwise it would not become a Christian.

Now, nature itself secures the growth of the body; the very fact of living brings physical development; and the common instincts of humanity induce parents to provide for the physical wants of their children. Even the most unprincipled seldom fail in this duty. There are of course exceptions to the rule. There are parents who, to gratify their own vile passions, especially when debased by the foul habit of intemperance, seem to lose their natural feelings and abandon their children to poverty and degradation. But these are exceptions; they are like monsters and are held everywhere in just execration. The brand of shame and dishonor is stamped upon them. Even the most wretched parents will try to find food and clothing for their little ones, and nature itself supplies what may be deficient. For do we not often see how strong and vigorous is the physical growth of the children of the poor, although oftentimes wanting what to many would appear the very base necessaries of life? We may trust the human heart, even when debased, unless in very rare exceptions, to provide for the material and physical wants of the young. No need, then, to insist upon this truth. But the chief growth—the most important development of the child—is in its intellect, in its spiritual nature. Man is distinguished from other animals by his soul and his intelligence. It is by the growth of his spiritual faculties that he becomes more and more a man. Now this growth will not come spontaneously from nature. It must be brought about and be carried on principally by outside influences. The truths which will develop (sic) the intellect must come from without. They will not grow in the minds themselves. They must be sown there by a friendly hand, as the good grain will not spring forth from the soil, no matter how fertile, unless the farmer has previously deposited it there. The education of the mind and soul of children must then come from external sources, from those who surround them and are interested in their welfare. And a <u>Christian education</u> must come from sources blessed and protected and directed by the Christian faith. Now the first and most natural source of growth must be the home—by the domestic hearth and fireside, by the side of the father and the mother. This <u>home teaching</u> for the children must be supplemented by the <u>Christian Church</u> and still further developed by the <u>Christian school</u>. Hence we have three distinct, yet thoroughly connected, sources of Christian education—the Christian <u>home</u>, the Christian <u>Church</u>, the Christian <u>school</u>. These three are essential for the full Christian growth of the child and should not, if possible, be separated. But the foundation is in the home. The most important is the home training, which may supply in a certain measure the absence of the other two but can scarcely be replaced itself. These are the points to which we intend to call your attention—the three centres for the Christian education of your children, and we earnestly hope and pray that you may be enabled to give them the inestimable benefits of the three—the Christian home, the Christian Church, and the Christian school.

---

[2]John 1:9.

I. Education In The Christian Home

Home! What precious memories this name invokes! What pure and holy joys, what noble thoughts, what sublime deeds have sprung from the Christian home! There did our intellect first receive the earliest rays of divine truth; there did our heart expand under the pure sunlight of a loving mother's smile; there did our soul grow strong under the mighty influence of a good father. Home is the first, the chief, the best centre for the education of the child. To the mother belongs the first part in this great work. For the earliest years her loving hand and her gentle touch are needed to direct the growth of the tender plant confided to her. What a wonderful privilege, what a glorious mission for her! The Almighty has entrusted chiefly to her, in those first years, the welfare on earth and the happiness in heaven, of her child. As she is the first to feed and nourish her infant, so she also is the first who can reach to the depths where its soul lies hidden; she can bring it forth by her loving call from its recesses and stamp her own image upon it. She can, as it were, touch this soul with her hand and fashion it as she pleases. Through her, the rays of truth and knowledge begin to beam upon the child's mind; through her, the mysteries of this life and of the life to come are gradually unfolded. From her loving heart and by her gentle words, her kindly tones, and her tender glances, the child is made to grow in the virtues of faith and hope and heavenly charity. By her side the child kneels in reverential posture, and an infant tongue lisps the sacred names of God and Jesus. How deeply the child drinks in the pious words which fall from the mother's lips! How the God to whom she looks up, the great Being of whom she speaks so reverently and so lovingly, becomes for the child wonderful in all His attributes, and most deserving of love, because of the example of the mother's love!

Prayer becomes sweet to the child; attendance at divine worship, a source of delight; religion, a consolation and a comfort. The intellect is awakened; the heart is lovingly drawn towards the beauties of faith. Childish joys are thus sanctified by and connected with the practice of religious duties. Ah! who can tell in adequate terms the wonderful influence of the Christian mother?

The pages of history attest that nearly all the great men, men distinguished above their fellows by extraordinary deeds—great saints or great sinners—men who strove best to benefit their race and country or who by their crimes inflicted most injury upon both, have nearly all been such as their mothers trained them. The mother makes the man. Without speaking now of the great men of the world, the great scholars, the conquerors of nations, of whom this observation has frequently been made by their biographers or historians, let us simply look to the lives of our great saints. It would be impossible here to enumerate the noble women who, from their own generous and devoted hearts, enkindle the fire of religious heroism in the souls of their children. Not to mention in the old law the mother of the Maccabees pointing out to her sons the noble pathway to heaven through most frightful sufferings, nor the mothers of the martyrs in the new, let us simply recall some of the mothers of the great saints and doctors of the church. St. Paul reminds his disciple Timothy of what he owed to "the faith unfeigned"[3] of his grandmother Lois and his mother, Eunice. St. Basil and his brother, St. Gregory of Nyssa, gloried in preserving the faith in which they had been trained by their grandmother St. Macrina. St. Gregory describes most minutely the manner in which his mother instructed his sister. St. Fulgentius owed his education, not merely in sacred science but also in polite literature, to the care of his mother, Mariana, "the religious mother," as she is called in his _Life_. The early education, both liberal and religious, of St. John Chrysostom was in like manner directed by his admirable mother,

---

[3] 2 Timothy 1:5.

Anthusa, whose conduct in this particular drew from the pagan sophist Libanius the exclamation "Ye gods of Greece, how wonderful are the women of the Christians!"

Who has not read or heard of the touching story of St. Monica guiding the early steps of St. Augustine, and when the violence of his passions led her son astray from truth and virtue, she followed him through all his wanderings with her advice, her prayers, and her tears, until at length she was consoled by his return to God, and the words of St. Ambrose were verified, "that the child of such tears could not perish." How well St. Augustine himself understood how much he was indebted to his mother for his conversion, and his happiness may be seen from the touching words of his *Confessions*.

And again, many of you may have listened to the story of Queen Blanche of Castile, mother of Louis IX, king of France, whom in his childhood, when seated on her knee, she thus addressed: "My Louis, I love you above everything in this world, but I would rather see you fall dead at my feet than know you committed a single mortal sin." How well that boy remembered those lessons of his mother can be seen in his afterlife, so manly, so heroic, and so holy that he has merited the honor of being proclaimed by the Church of God, and proposed to the veneration of the people, as the model of Christian kings and the type of the Christian gentleman.

The father, too, has his recognized place, as the head of the Christian family in the great work of home education. Without his example to fortify, his authority to confirm and support her, the teachings of the mother would very often lose their efficacy. The boy, who in his earliest years can be directed safely by the mother, needs, as he grows older, the sterner hand and the strong will of the father to restrain him. In vain will the mother point out to the wayward child the beauty of virtue if his father does not convince him of its manliness also. But when both parents work harmoniously and lovingly, when their authority is combined for the one great purpose, when father and mother place their chief care in the religious development of their child, then God's blessing seldom fails to descend upon them.

It will thus be seen that the first, the best, the most solid foundations of a Christian education are laid in the Christian home, where the gentleness and love of the mother, encouraged, sustained, and developed by the manliness, honesty, integrity, purity, and high-mindedness of the Christian father, gradually form the character, bring forth all the good instincts of the soul, strengthen and guide the efforts of the intellect, repress and diminish the evil inclinations of the heart, so that when their child is exposed to the dangers of the world, he is equipped and prepared to take his part in the battle of life and almost certain to gain the victory. Happy is the man who can look back to the holy memories of such a home. He may, no doubt, have forgotten for a time those precious lessons; his passions, like an impetuous torrent, may have swept him from the path of honor and virtue; yet, sooner or later, amidst all his temptations, the image of his Christian mother will rise up before him and like a guardian angel draw him back even from the very edge of the abyss. It was the memories of his home that touched the poor prodigal son of the Gospel in the midst of the husks of swine and brought him back, sorrowful and repentant, to the feet of his generous father.

But, on the other hand, how miserable, how pitiable the lot of the child who never had a Christian home! For him no holy lessons remembered; no prayers said at his mother's knee; no wise counsel from his father's lips. He was neglected and abandoned to himself. Like a young plant which no skillful hand has cultivated, he has grown up in all the wild exuberance of his passions. He learned not of the goodness of God, nor of His greatness; neither the glories of heaven nor the horrors of hell. Perhaps he heard God's name pronounced only when it fell from the lips of a blaspheming father. What virtues could he acquire? Could he learn <u>industry</u> from an idle or dissolute father, <u>sobriety</u> from a drunken one, <u>probity</u> from a dishonest one, <u>self-respect</u> from a mean and worthless one? How could he acquire strength of soul against temptation, steadfastness of purpose in the pursuit of truth, integrity and uprightness of heart when all the lessons of his home, all his surroundings, and all the examples of his parents teach him the very contrary? What charms can have virtue for him? No wonder that the enemy of souls finds him an easy prey and an apt pupil for every lesson in vice and that the street becomes his school, in which he learns with marvelous facility the various phases of crime. From the unchristian, bad home to the streets is an easy step for both boy and girl, and from the streets to dens of infamy and to the prisons is a still easier one. And though the boy and the girl should stop short of that infamous goal, what a wreck they become for the Church and for God! The young man grows up without religion; he does not comprehend her beauty; he learns to despise her commands. This world becomes everything to him, and to succeed in it his sole ambition. His passions are his law and his pleasures his chief motives of action. Worldly prudence may restrain him where excess might bring danger, but he will not love virtue for itself, nor will he seek truth for its own sake. Religious dogmas are cast aside as too great a restriction upon his mind. Religious duties are discarded as too great a burthen (sic) for his heart. He has no religious principles to support him, no religious truths to enlighten him, no religious consolations to cheer him. This world is everything to him; beyond the grave all is dark and gloomy, and he does not wish to look into it. Is it not from an unchristian home, or from unchristian teachings and examples in the home, that so many men have derived their contempt of religion, their scorn of its teachings, their mockery of its votaries? Is it not thus that religious indifference begins, to be turned oftentimes to religious hatred? How many an infidel can trace back his loss of faith to the want of religious teaching in his home or, what is even worse, to the false, distorted, harsh, truly unchristian views of God and His dealings with His creatures! Alas! How many of our own children, in years past, have been perverted from the faith of their fathers and drawn into the proselytizers' nets to become the worst enemies of that religion which was stolen from them! How many, in the large cities and throughout the country, have been kidnapped, their names changed, and their religion destroyed! How many thousands, nay, we might say millions, have been thus stolen from the ranks of the Church to become her most bitter foes! And this principally because they had bad homes and wretched, unnatural parents who would have sold them body and soul for the gratification of their own vile passions.

How unhappy, then, is the man or woman who has no tender memories of home, no recollections of childhood! When he thinks of the mother who neglected him, of the father who misdirected him, who abandoned him without care or love, he must feel tempted to curse those who so foully betrayed their most sacred duties and allowed or even forced him, by their vices, to grow up without religion, without honor or true Christian manhood. His blood will surely cry to heaven for vengeance against those guilty parents.

But you, dearly beloved brethren, are already, we trust, convinced of these important and terrible truths. You know the maxim of Holy Writ, "Train up a child in the way he should you, and when he is old, he shall not depart from it."[4] You have understood that your children are a sacred treasure confided to you by heaven and that you have no more important duty than to train them for heaven. You provide for the wants of their body: you feed and you clothe them. This is right and proper. Hence you justly consider that the father who neglects his work, indulges in vice, squanders his earnings in debauchery and intemperance, and thus renders himself incapable of supporting, feeding, and clothing his children is a monster who deserves the execration and loathing of all honest men. But the feeding and caring for the body are not all. The caring for the immortal soul and the feeding of

---

[4]Proverbs 22:6.

the imperishable mind are of far more importance, and as far exceeds the former as the immortal spirit is superior to the body which it inhabits. Hence you, we hope, are convinced, dear brethren, that the parent, whether father or mother, who neglects this duty, who allows the mind of his child to grow up in ignorance and like a fair field, when uncared for, to become filled with thorns, thistles, and noxious or poisonous weeds, is guilty of a greater crime than if he had brought his child to the grave by deliberate starvation or cold-blooded murder. Listen to the terrible words of St. Paul, which should strike fear into the heart of every Christian parent: "If any man have not care of his own, and especially of those of his house, he hath denied the faith and is worse an infidel".[5] Are there any amongst you to whom these words can be applied? We trust not, dear brethren; we earnestly pray that there may be none. But we ask you to open your hearts and your minds more fully to the divine truths which we proclaim to you and to become more firmly convinced that there is no more important duty, none that will bring truer consolation in this life and more solid hopes for happiness in heaven, than to give to your children that blessed home training which will make the yoke of the Lord sweet to them from their youth and prepare them for a Christian manhood. Thus you will secure to them what we have called the first, the best, and the most lasting foundation of a truly Christian education—the education of a Christian home.

II. Christian Education By The Church

The education begun at home must be continued by the Church. The teachings of the father and mother must be supplemented, developed, and strengthened by the instructions of the ministers of religion, who are divinely appointed by Christ to teach the nations and to instruct them unto justice. It is a remarkable fact, and worthy of being mentioned, that in the early ages of the Church, no special provision seems to have been made for the instruction of the children of the faithful. For the catechumens, adults, and converts from paganism, a long course of sermons, homilies, and catechetical discourses was fixed by the discipline of the Church, but for the children of Christians, the little ones of the faith, there is no mention of any instruction. It would seem as if it were universally felt that instruction in the Christian home was quite sufficient, and no fears were entertained that Christian parents would ever neglect so important and sacred a duty as the teaching of Christian doctrine to their children. But as time elapsed and faith grew somewhat cold, many parents became indifferent and careless. Then the Church made it a special obligation for her priests and sacred ministers to look after the little ones, the young lambs of the flock. In our days especially, when parents for the most part are engaged in the arduous labors of modern industry and when, because of the difficulties and trials of their own childhood, many of these parents have not been able to acquire such a knowledge of their religion as to be able to impart it in an interesting way to their children, it becomes absolutely necessary to come to their aid and to supply, by instruction in the Church, what they themselves either have not the time or have not sufficient knowledge to communicate or, still worse, have not sufficient love for the faith to make them feel it a joy and a privilege. Therefore, catechism classes, or, as they are nowadays styled by the very pretentious and deceiving title of "Sunday schools," have been established in all churches wherever the priest of God has found it possible. Here the young mind is brought directly under the teaching power of the Church. Here the priest, taking the parents' place, but acting as the representative of our Lord Jesus Christ, unfolds the wonderful story of God's

---

[5] 1 Timothy 5:8.

dealings with men. Here the most sublime truths are adapted to the weak minds of the children and are accepted by them almost as self-evident. Truths and mysteries such as the greatest of the pagan philosophers could never conceive, or at the best could only guess at in a doubtful groping way, are presented as the most elementary principles by men consecrated for that purpose by God's providence, specially commissioned by His Church, and who speak without hesitation, with positive certainty, as men having authority to speak, and not as the scribes and Pharisees and all false teachers.

What a glorious mission is this of the priest, to be brought so closely to young hearts yet untainted by the world, and to have the charge of unfolding them, expanding them, under the influence of divine grace! Next to the mission and dignity of the mother comes this privilege of the Christian priest. How consoling, how refreshing to the soul of the true priest is this companionship with childhood! Like his Divine Master, he desires to have the young near him, and he cries out, "Suffer the little children to come to me." When these children come from Christian homes, where the foundations of piety and knowledge were deeply laid, this work becomes a labor of love. When he speaks of God and His infinite love for souls, when he unfolds the wonderful life of the Redeemer, His boundless tenderness to the poor and the suffering, and then leads them through the awful scenes of His passion and death, the priest does not speak to those children in an unknown tongue, nor of wonders which they never heard of before. A loving mother has already given them the outlines of this grandest story that human ears have ever listened to, and they can follow, with beating hearts and eager minds, the beautiful details which the priest's greater knowledge enables him to supply. How glorious, too, becomes the history of the rise and establishment of the Church of Christ; of her early suffering under the persecutions of the Roman emperors; of the heroic constancy of her martyrs; of the myriads of Christians of both sexes, the strong and the feeble, the learned and the ignorant, joyfully pouring out their blood for the faith of Christ! Then the immortal life of that Church through all ages down to us, in spite of every storm and tempest that the malice of men or the rage of demons could incite against her. What a noble work for the priest to develop the germs of virtue, to show the loveliness of holiness, to pluck up the seeds of vice which contact with the world or evil example may have sown in these young hearts, as the gardener carefully roots up the weeds that would soon choke his fairest flowers! To love their God and their neighbor, to cherish truth and to hate falsehood, to work for all that is good and noble, and to seek the crown of immortal bliss—this is what the priest can teach them. What merely human teacher can have such a mission, and what human knowledge can equal it in grandeur? We say it, and we say it most sincerely, that for the true priest of God's Church there is no more glorious work, no sweeter employment, no better recompense than this religious instruction of the little ones. When discouraged by the dreary scenes of vice and crime that meet his gaze so often during the labors of his ministry, it is a consolation to turn to the pure hearts and guileless souls of children. It is like coming to a green and fertile oasis in the desert, where the traveller, weary with his march through arid and desolate plains, can sit down to rest and gather fresh strength for his onward journey.

Yet, this consolation comes only to the priest when he has to deal with children who have a Christian home and are under the direction of Christian parents, for then their hearts are gentle and easily guided to what is good, and their intellects awakened to the beauties of truth. But when they have no Christian home nor Christian parents, then there is labor and toil for the priest, and little consolation. These hearts, that, if taken in time, would have been like soft wax to receive and retain the holiest impression, have now through neglect, through want of instruction, through evil example become hard and unyielding almost as flint. How will the priest speak of the love of God to children who never learned it in their homes? how inculcate the necessity of prayer, when perhaps they never saw their parents on their knees? how make them feel the shocking sin of blasphemy or of irreverence to God's name, when they seldom heard that name except when it fell in curses from their father's lips? how teach them to value purity, honesty, truth, and all the other virtues, when they perhaps were familiar at home with only the contrary vices? Every priest who has worked in the large missions of towns and cities can testify to the exceeding great difficulty he experiences in preparing such children for the reception of the Sacraments. Yes, this is the labor, the cross, the deep sorrow of the priest. He feels that he is building without a foundation and that his work will not be durable. Give him the work of Christian parents to build upon, and see what a glorious structure he will erect. But to expect that he will accomplish the mighty work of training these children to grow up to be noble men and women, in a half hour or so, once a week, on Sunday; that he will impress the most sublime truths upon their minds perhaps entirely unprepared or even indisposed to receive them; and that he will do this, when already so busy with his Sunday duties—this is to expect an impossibility. Yet, this is what many parents count upon. This is what many Catholics imagine to be quite sufficient for their children. They neglect these children at home, they leave them without religious instruction for the entire week, and then they expect that a tired and exhausted priest will be able, in a half hour on Sunday, to give to careless, undisciplined children a sufficient dose of religion which will last for the coming week. What folly! But this grand name of Sunday <u>school</u> satisfies their sleeping consciences. A half hour or an hour on Sunday; a few lessons recited, in a careless manner, by giddy, thoughtless children longing for play and having little relish for the dry pages of the Catechism and no comprehension of the divine truths underlying them—this is enough, according to such Catholics, for these children; this will make them good and noble men and women, will make them love the cross of their Savior and bear opprobrium and insult for His sake; this will make them strong against the religious indifference or the hatred of religion so common around them; this will make them prefer the poverty and lowly condition of their Church to the honors and riches which they might often obtain by forsaking her. The Sunday school is to accomplish all this! No thinking, serious Catholic could imagine it; and those who speak most of the Sunday school and its advantages are often the same who most neglected the home education.

III. Christian Schools

But will home teaching, even when united to the teaching in the Church, be sufficient to form a thorough Christian education? This is a question that needs the deepest consideration by all who are anxious for the Christian training and development of the rising generation. To answer it properly we must lay down some preliminary truths. In the first place, we must bear in mind that the vast majority of parents, and certainly of Catholic parents, belong to the working and industrial classes and that it is difficult, not to say almost impossible, after the severe and exhausting labors of the day, that they can find time or strength, even if they always had the requisite knowledge, to develop the Christian growth of their children. Then again how many poor people, though full of faith and anxious for their children's welfare, are not well qualified to instruct the bright little ones who fill their home! On the other hand, the work of the priest is very limited; the time that he can spare very short. He can see these children only on Sunday, as a general rule, and then he has many other duties to fulfill, and we have seen how little can be effected in the short time at his disposal. But during the week, during all the time when the children are neither at home nor in church, during those hours of mental activity in their school studies, what will enable them to grow in their faith and in the knowledge of their religion if they have no assistance and no teaching? Here, then, appears the necessity of Christian schools, to continue the work of Christian parents, to help in the work of Christian ministers, and to complete the work of Christian education. What the parents began in their homes, what the priest continues in the church, the school must develop and fortify. This is what it behooves you to consider. This is a subject far more important than many Catholics imagine. The enemies of the Church instinctively realize it. From the conduct of those who make war upon religion and who with wonderful unanimity select as their favorite and most powerful weapon godless schools and mere secular teaching, sensible Catholics, even if they had no other motive to determine them, no authority to guide them, should learn what to think of such schools and such teaching. It is right to learn even from an enemy; and precisely, because the foes of Christianity attach such importance to the banishment of the religious element from schools, so should all sincere Christians unite most earnestly in preserving and guarding for the schools of their children the sacred influence of religion. But for you, my brethren, as we shall show you hereafter, there is higher ground than this to stand upon. There is the unanimous teaching of the Catholic hierarchy throughout the world; the voice of the Bishops of America as spoken in various Councils; the voice of the Bishops of Ireland, Germany, France, and England; the voice of the Bishops of the Old World and the New; and clear above them all, directing and guiding all, the voice of the chief Pastor of the flock, the voice of Christ's vicar, the voice of the successor of St. Peter who was charged with feeding both the lambs and the sheep of Christ. Never, except upon positive articles of faith, has there been such unanimity in the teachings of the chief pastors of the Church as with regard to the evils of godless schools. For you, dear brethren, this authority ought to be, and is, we trust, sufficient to determine your assent. But we desire to go more fully into the matter and to state some of the reasons which should make you, as Catholics, and which will also, we hope, soon induce every Christian man, every one who believes in Christ and who desires to save his soul, to feel, as certain and not to be doubted, that Christian schools are needed if we wish to train up the future generations as Christian, and that godless schools will not only destroy supernatural faith and all belief in revelation but will sap parental authority, undermine the family, and diminish the social and civic virtues.

In the first place, we need scarcely remind you that the Catholic Church has ever been the friend and protectress of all true knowledge. Her whole history proves how carefully she cultivated and fostered it in all ages. She established schools and universities in the darkest epochs; she made her monasteries storehouses of learning, where all the remains of Grecian and Roman literature that had escaped the invasions of the barbarians were carefully treasured up and lovingly transmitted down to our times by the indefatigable labors of her monks. The wonderful services which she rendered to human knowledge are now generally conceded even by those who do not submit to her teaching. The Church that founded all the great universities of the Old World; that established the first public schools for the children of the poor; that fostered all the fine arts; that invented Gothic architecture and reared those mighty temples which are even yet unapproachable in their majesty and sublimity; that gave a soul to painting and to music; that inspired Fra Angelico, Raphael, and Michelangelo; Palestrina, Mozart, and Haydan; that encouraged every invention, the art of printing, the mariner's compass, the discoveries of astronomy, the reformation of the calendar: the Church that fostered these and hundreds of other inventions of the human mind cannot be set down as opposed to knowledge and to science.

This is our first proposition, that the Catholic Church loves and protects knowledge within its natural limits; and this proposition will be easily admitted even by those outside of her, in proportion to the extent of their studies and researches in the domain of history and will be contested only by those shallow socialists who have picked up a little on its surface, without ever sounding its depths or by designing men who, wishing to undermine all religion, find it convenient to calumniate the Church, the true bulwark of Christianity, and therefore try to persuade thoughtless dupes that the Catholic Church is opposed to all knowledge. This is simply false, as it equally is that we are opposed to public schools in their true and full meaning.

The next point to which it may be well to call your attention is the common idea that the state has the right to teach. This is not a Christian idea; it is a pagan one. It was natural for the pagans who deified the state, and worshiped it as a divinity, to believe that the state could enter into the human conscience and take possession of the human soul. But Christianity, in casting down the old idols, raised up man from his degradation and made his conscience and his soul a temple into which no state, no earthly power, can enter. When the Lord laid down the law, "Render unto Caesar the things that are Caesar's and to God the things that are God's," He established the principle of God's sovereignty over the human soul. When the Apostles proclaimed that "it is better to obey God rather than men," they struck the keynote of true liberty, "that freedom wherewith has Christ made us free."[6] The state is not appointed to teach; the Church alone has that mission. The state cannot deprive a parent of the right to bring up his children in his own way, as long as he does not inflict an injury on the state. The father has a divine right and a divine obligation to educate his child, and it would be tyranny to deprive him of it, unless for a notorious abuse or violation of this right. The state may, and ought in certain cases, assist the parents; it may insist that the children shall be brought up as good citizens. But the state ought not and cannot dictate the entire scheme of education or take it out of the hands of the parents. This is a principle which needs to be well remembered, since the tendency of all modern governments and states is to encroach upon the domain of conscience and to usurp the rights of parents by withdrawing children from their authority in the arrangement of systems of education. But though we protest, as Christians, against this anti-Christian principle, we will not now combat it. We pass it by and proceed to the next point for your consideration, and that is, the true nature of education itself.

Education, in the full force of the term, and according to its derivation from the Latin words e and ducere, is the bringing up or a bringing forth of all the faculties of the child—the development of its entire nature. To develop one of the faculties at the expense of the others, or to the neglect of the others, is not education. To cram the child's memory without strengthening the judgment, for instance, is surely not education; to develop the understanding, without improving the heart, is likewise no education. Man is an intelligent being, but he is likewise a moral being, bound by certain laws and responsible for their violation. To give all attention to the intelligence and little or none to the moral side of our nature is not, then, true education. True education takes the whole child together, intellect and heart, all the longings of the mind and all the cravings of the heart, and gradually lifts him up, advances him all together. We charge the present public school system, as its first defect, that it does not educate, it only instructs; and we also charge that it does not even instruct well. It only instructs—it claims no more; it simply intends to supply to the memory and to the intelligence a certain number of facts and dates which have little or no influence upon the moral nature of the child. Granting for the moment that the instruction, as far as it goes, is true and correct, and that the intelligence of the child is not perverted by false knowledge, how will that

---

[6] 1 Galatians 4:31.

knowledge fit him for his duties in life to God and to his country? He has learned, we suppose, all the ordinary branches taught. He can read and write and cipher; he has learned a little of the sciences and as many other things of the kind as he is able to acquire. What then? Is his heart any way changed? Are his passions thereby conquered? Are the evil instincts of his soul thereby vanquished? He grows up a smart, intelligent boy, keen and bright-witted, able to hold his own against others. But what principle has he to guide him, what law to direct him, what motives to restrain him? His learning, separated from all religion, or only veneered by a weak coating of the vaguest morality, can serve only to make him more dangerous than even the ignorant man. The better armed he is by his knowledge, the more powerful he becomes for evil, unless religious principles restrain him. But those religious principles his education will not give him. It is not necessary, dear brethren, to point out to you in detail the evils arising from this godless education. You well know that the great crimes committed against society are not committed by illiterate men. Isolated cases of violence, robbery, and other sins are often perpetrated by the ignorant and the uneducated. But the crimes that go to the very heart of society and shake it to its foundations—the frauds on public funds, the robbery of savings banks and insurance offices, by which countless numbers are made to mourn; the public gambling in stocks; the unsettling of public credit; the squandering and the pilfering of the treasures of the state; the creation of those huge monopolies that threaten to destroy the very liberties of a nation; the unlimited power of corporations and industrial companies, by which the artisan and the laborer may be despoiled of the fruits of their honest toil—these, and many more such evils, are not the work of ignorant, illiterate, and uneducated individuals. When we see rich men growing richer and poor men growing poorer, when discontent is increasing and socialistic principles are spreading, when public honesty and public morality are at such a low ebb, it is time to feel that the public schools, under their present form, have not benefitted the country. We will not dwell on the moral corruption of those schools. We leave that painful subject to be treated by other pens. But we point out to you the loss of religious convictions, the growth of religious indifference, and the spread of infidelity as the necessary consequences of the absence of all religious teaching. The teachers, for instance, in the immense majority of schools, belong to different forms of religion. Now, without even supposing that these teachers go out of their way to attack our faith, if they have any settled convictions themselves—and what teacher worthy of the name is without such convictions?—will they not necessarily influence and warp the children's minds? Is any parent mad enough to believe that the teacher with decided religious convictions—not to speak of decided religious antipathies—can for six hours each day hold the closest relations with the child without, unconsciously if you will, influencing the doctrinal conviction of those with whom he is so associated, whose full and free confidence he has secured, of whose moral being he has made himself master? And when the child contrasts his gentlemanly teacher, who perhaps has no religion, with a poor, uneducated parent who teaches him badly his own faith, is it not very likely that he will lose all respect for religion and either despise or abandon it?

Then, again, from the companions of school hours, often well cared for in their homes, who have learned to sneer at Catholic doctrines and to speak with contempt of Catholic worship, another danger arises for Catholic boys. Who does not know how much a schoolboy dreads ridicule? And when he hears his Church assailed by vile calumnies which he does not know enough to refute, and by the jeers of his schoolmates, how often will he blush for his religion and be ashamed to belong to it? And if it should happen, as it only too often does happen, that at home he has an ignorant, brutal, intemperate father for whom he can have no respect, what will keep him true to his Church? Just as he learns from his comrades to ridicule the language or the country of his parents, he will quickly learn to despise their faith. Children, in school, influence each other more than many imagine, and an unfashionable religion finds no mercy from them.

But danger also comes to your children from the books used in these godless schools. Of course a great show of impartiality is made by eliminating what might be too offensive to Catholics; yet we know that many textbooks used in those schools contain vile calumnies against the Catholic Church, misrepresentations of her doctrines, and sneers at the nations who profess them. How many false statements in the textbooks of history! and how much suppression of the truth wherever Catholics are concerned! Who would know, for instance, if we read only the histories of America commonly used, that Catholics had any share in the early building up of this country or took any part in securing its freedom? Then, what real knowledge of history, geography, and several other branches of science can any one learn from those colorless, even if not falsified, accounts, where religion must be ignored and its influence on the destinies of the world entirely concealed? Hence we charge that these schools do not instruct well; for they do not and cannot find the truth upon many branches that have to be learned, and leave a greater chaos and confusion in the mind than if nothing at all had been taught upon those matters. We have not space in this letter to develop this idea at greater length, but we hope you yourselves will meditate upon it and see how important it is. Enough to say at present that religion has had too great a share in the molding of society and directing the destinies of nations to be completely ignored without giving a false coloring to all the history of the past.

Finally, the system is unjust, because of the taxation imposed upon those who do not believe in it and who cannot adopt it. It would be almost as fair to establish a system of religion to which all should come, and build temples of worship for which we should all pay. We, who believe that religion is the best part of education, and that the school should be like the porch part of education, and that the school should be like the porch through which the young are brought into the Church, feel it unjust to tax us for what our consciences will not allow us to use, unless in cases of extreme necessity, when we cannot go elsewhere.

Here, then, dear brethren, you see that these public schools, so much vaunted, (1) do not educate, for they do not improve the heart, but at the most instruct only the intellect; (2) they do not even instruct well, since many branches of learning can be studied only in connection with religion; (3) they are not truly American, since they abridge unnecessarily the rights of citizens and sap the foundations of authority by encroaching on the rights and authority of parents; (4) they are unchristian and are calculated to destroy Christian principles in the rising generations; (5) they tend to loosen moral laws and do away with all restraint upon the passions; (6) they impose an enormous tax, every year growing greater, upon the entire community, and a very unjust and unnecessary tax upon a large section of that community.

To you, dear brethren, and we think to all fair-minded persons who have any love for the Christian faith and who desire to see, for the honor of their country, a godly race of men and women growing up in the future, we think that the foregoing consideration will be amply sufficient to determine you against the present godless system of public instruction. But as, unfortunately, there are still some Catholics who, either because they have been brought up under the dark shadow of these schools, or because their personal interests are superior to their religious feeling, or because they are deeply influenced by public opinion, cannot be brought to see the evils inherent in the system, we deem it right to add to our own decision some of the judgments pronounced in the most solemn manner by those whose position in the Church entitles them to obedience on the part of all Catholics, and whose personal virtues, great talents, and deep love of truth and justice would even excite the admiration of those who are outside the Church. We shall give only a few of these decisions, as the limits of our Pastoral letter forbid any more.

The Holy Father, Pius IX, in the Syllabus of Errors he publicly condemns, marks the following proposition, as one which no Catholic can hold: "Catholics can approve of a system of educating youth which is unconnected with the Catholic faith and the power of the Church, and which regards the knowledge of merely natural things, and only, or at least primarily, the ends of social life." The whole Catholic world has accepted the condemnation of this proposition.

Again, in 1875, the sacred Congregation de Propaganda Fide sent a letter to all the bishops of the United States, giving them directions and instructions on this subject of the public schools. We quote from it the following passage: "This system the sacred congregation considers by its nature to be fraught with danger and very hostile to Catholicity. For, since the system of such like schools excludes all teaching of religion, the pupils neither learn in them the rudiments of faith, nor are instructed in the precepts of the Church: hence they will be deprived of the knowledge most necessary to man, without which a Christian life is impossible. Now, in this kind of school youths are instructed from their childhood, not to say from very infancy, at which age, as is evident, the seeds of virtue and vice take most tenacious root. And, certainly, it is an immense evil that such tender children should grow up without religion.

"Again, in the aforesaid schools, as they are divorced from the authority of the Church, teachers indiscriminately of every sect are employed; and as no law prohibits them from doing harm to youth, they are left free to sow errors and the seeds of vices in tender minds.

"Certain corruption likewise ensues from the fact that in these same schools or in many of them, youths of both sexes are congregated in the same room for the recitation of lessons, and males and females are ordered to sit on the same bench (in eodem scamno): all of which have the effect of lamentably exposing the young to loss in faith and endangering of morals.

"Now, if this proximate danger of perversion be not made remote, such schools cannot be frequented with a safe conscience."

To these declarations, so grave and so binding on all Catholics, we will add only the public decision of the Plenary Council of Baltimore, held in 1866, at which forty-four Bishops and two representatives of Bishops were present.

"The experience of every day shows more and more plainly what serious evils and great dangers are entailed upon Catholic youth by their frequentation of public schools in this country. Such is the nature of the system of teaching therein employed, that it is not possible to prevent young Catholics from incurring through its influence danger to their faith and morals; nor can we ascribe to any other cause that destructive spirit of indifferentism which has made and is now making such rapid strides in this country, and that corruption of morals which we have to deplore in those of tender years. Familiar intercourse with those of false religions, or of no religion; the daily use of authors who assail with calumny and sarcasm our holy religion, its practices, and even its saints—these gradually impair in the minds of Catholic children the vigor and influence of the true religion. Besides, the morals and examples of their fellow scholars are generally so corrupt, and so great their license in word and deed, that through continual contact with them, the modesty and piety of our children, even of those who have been best trained at home, disappear like wax before the fire."

We also refer you to a little work entitled "The Judges of Faith and the Godless Schools," for a fuller development of this side of the question.

No Catholic can refuse to listen and to obey such positive instructions from the supreme Head of the Church and Her Divinely appointed pastors.

Hence we are obliged in conscience to condemn the present godless, anti-Christian, anti-parental system of public schools. But we are not obliged to condemn, and we do not condemn, public schools in themselves. We desire most heartily that there should be public schools for the education of all the children of the land; we wish to see ignorance banished and true knowledge exalted and honored. But these schools should combine secular and religious training. And let it not be said that such a system is impossible. It is not so. It has been established elsewhere and found to work well. It succeeded in France, until infidels resolved to make war upon religion; it succeeded in Germany, until a despotic minister, through selfish ambition, partly destroyed its good effects; and finally, passing over other countries, it has succeeded in Canada, our next neighbor. There the Catholic Bishops and priests are satisfied with the system which the Protestant majority of Upper Canada, or Ontario, has established. Cannot we, in this great republic, receive at least as much consideration as Catholics living under the British crown? and cannot our statesmen as easily devise a method satisfactory to all as Canadian politicians? We hope so; we believe so. We trust that the era of conciliation and good feeling is approaching, that our just claims will be considered favorably, and that all Christian men will combine to make our schools truly Christian, in order that our children may be prepared for the great struggle against infidelity and atheism which is rapidly coming upon us. We appeal to American fair play and to American honor, and we are not doubtful of our claims being heard.

But, in the meantime, we must support our own schools, at whatever sacrifice they may impose. Our children's souls must be saved and their faith preserved, and we are certain that those who so generously have built our churches and raised up so many glorious temples to the majesty of the Catholic faith will not hesitate to make equal sacrifices for the erection and maintenance of our religious schools, without which our children will be exposed to the greatest dangers for their faith. And we firmly believe that there will be too many churches, too many empty ones, in the future, if the children of the faith should be now neglected. We hope that our wealthy Catholics will come to our help and, by aiding us to build new schools and to endow the old ones, acquire for themselves true glory on earth and a generous reward in heaven.

IV. Good Reading

But education is not confined to the school. It is always going on, improving or retrograding, but never standing still. The mind is constantly receiving new kinds of food upon which it may grow strong or by which it may be seriously injured. This food is supplied principally by reading, and just as the reading is, so the mind will gain or lose. In this country, reading is universal, we might say; our children have a great thirst for it. There is little need to stimulate it, but it has to be wisely directed. Reading gives the turn to the minds of children; hence Christian education will gain or lose its effect, according to the reading of the child.

Here, dear brethren, we would have many things to say to parents upon the necessity of watching over carefully, and directing prudently, the tastes of their children in the selection of their reading books. How many parents never take the trouble to see what their children are reading, never advise them, never sympathize with them, never try to gain their confidence, so that the children might be inclined to consult them and rely upon them! The vilest trash, the most obscene stories, the most irreligious tracts may fall into the hands of these young people, who become interested, excited, and inflamed with what they read. Their minds become unbalanced, their intellects darkened, their hearts corrupted, their morals depraved, and the father calmly goes on his way and never pays attention. His child is devouring poison; he never minds. We see every day the evil effects of such reading, crimes most serious and most vile committed under its influence, children abandoning their homes for wild adventures, boys learning dishonesty, girls losing their purity. This evil is spreading to an enormous extent and is all the more dangerous because it does not always work openly. The evil of intemperance is very great, no doubt, and temperance societies do well to wage war upon it. But the effects of drunkenness are apparent; all can see the ruin and the desolation it causes. Not so with bad reading. It works stealthily upon the mind; it poisons slowly all the faculties; it dries up the generous impulses of the heart; it inflames all the corrupt passions of our nature; it enkindles a fire which consumes and withers up all God's graces. Oh, would that our temperance societies and our other beneficial societies would unite in a crusade against bad reading! It is from it that evils worse even than drunkenness flow. Irreligion, impiety, infidelity are some of its fruits. Yet how many fathers care nothing, do nothing to save their children! How few, even Catholic parents, supply good books, good newspapers, interesting histories for them! The daily papers, with all their shocking narratives of vice and crime, with their bigoted attacks upon the Church and their distorted reports of Catholic affairs, are eagerly read, while perhaps not one Catholic paper ever enters the house. The child reads slanders about his Church; he never reads the answer. The poison is swallowed and no antidote is at hand. We earnestly recommend you, then, dear brethren, to provide according to your means for the wholesome reading of your children. Few families but could afford to subscribe to one or two Catholic papers. We have now several good ones, well written, full of interesting matter, and able to furnish useful and varied information. Then we have the <u>Catholic World</u> and the <u>Catholic Quarterly</u>, which treat of the most interesting questions of the day. For the parents themselves we recommend two little books lately published, called the <u>Christian Father</u> and the <u>Christian Mother</u>, in which they will fully learn all their duties to their children. Last, we earnestly urge upon the parents to make religion pleasant, to make the home lovable, to win the confidence of their children, and then, by the help of the Sacraments and by prayer, they will lead them on gently, yet firmly, in the pathways of virtue and honor.

Such, dearly beloved, are the reflections and considerations which we have felt it our duty to lay before you on this most important subject of Christian education. In this holy season of Lent, you will have more leisure to meditate upon them. We are obliged by our charge to preach the Word to you in season and out of season. The Bishop, like the prophet of old, has to be on the watch to announce the danger and to summon to the battle for right and truth. To him is addressed the demand of the Lord, "Watchman, what of the night? Watchman, what of the night?"[7] Soldier of the Lord, what dost thou see amidst the shadows of the night, threatening the peace and the happiness of my people? Look carefully; strain thy sight; turn thy ear to catch every sound. There may be danger in the darkness; the enemy with silent footfall may be approaching, and thy people are calmly slumbering, relying on thy vigilance. "Watchman, what of the night?" And shall we be able to reply in the words of the same prophet, "The watchman said, `The morning cometh, also the night: if you seek, seek; return, come'"?[8]

Yes, we hope, the morning with its beauty and its light is coming to us all. Seek for help, O dearly beloved brethren! Return to God with your whole hearts. The light of divine faith, the morning of religious truth, will beam upon us, but this will come only through a Christian education, and this education, we repeat in closing, must consist of the education of the

_____
[7]Isaiah 21:11.
[8]Isaiah 21:12.

Christian home, the education of the Christian Church, and the education of the Christian schools. Give this education to your children and they will rise up around you "and call you blessed."[9]

This letter shall be read, either altogether or in part, at all the Masses in the churches where there are resident priests, on the first Sunday after its reception. Or the clergy can divide it into parts and explain them each Sunday, until the whole is read. In the mission churches, the pastors will read it at the earliest opportunity.

Given at Trenton, this 7th day of March, the Feast of St. Thomas of Aquin, Doctor of the Church, in the year of our Lord 1883.

MICHAEL JOSEPH O'FARRELL
Bishop of Trenton

JAMES A. McFAUL, Secretary

---

[9]Proverbs 31:28.

APPENDIX 4

Excerpt of Bishop Ryan's Sermon as Recorded in the *Catholic Standard*, 12 November 1881

We celebrate today . . . a glorious and joyous festival—the day of all saints. We have left for a time this earth and have been gathered into the heavenly Jerusalem. Commingling there with the myriads of white-robed saints we have joined in their everlasting hallelujahs. We seem to catch the songs of the angels here in this crowd of surpliced Levites, white-robed priests and purpled prelates around the Cardinal. It seems to preclude any other subject, and yet the solemn consecration of a Bishop, the ceremony you have witnessed, opens another subject. What is the New Jerusalem, but the Church of God on earth, the true spouse of Christ, the fruitful mother of saints? She points today to the conscious souls reigning about God in heaven, whom she has begotten to Christ and nurtured, and whose triumph she has crowned with complete beatitude.

It cannot be necessary in talking to Christians to say that Christ established a church on earth with power to perpetuate its corporate existence. All Christians believe that God became incarnate and that Jesus Christ, the God-Man, died on the cross of Calvary. Has He, then, left His work unfinished? What means did He adopt to perpetuate His Church? He was not always to remain on earth. He gathered around Him twelve disciples, whom He sent abroad to preach the Gospel. He said to them that whatsoever they should bind on earth should be bound in heaven, and whatsoever they loosed on earth should be loosed in heaven, that promising them the grant of the ample powers which after His resurrection He really gave them. One He singled out from the rest. Simon He called Peter, and He gave him the keys of the heaven. At the Last Supper, when He instituted the adorable sacrament of the altar, He made them His priests that they might consecrate the elements. He promised to send the Holy Ghost, the spirit of truth. After He had sealed His own divinity by His death and resurrection, His first care in His risen life was to reassure His disciples, and this He does by crowning His former work and affirming the seal of divinity to their commissions. He confirms Peter's power and by almost the last act of His glorified presence on earth makes him the supreme pastor.

Here, we are the Church of God fully organized. The apostles are now ready to start out on this mission, but they are bidden to tarry in Jerusalem. One promise is yet unfinished. They tarry ten days and then comes the Pentecost. As the Church was organized by Jesus, so must she be today, and such we affirm is the Holy Catholic Church. Who can fail to recognize that she is the Church as it came from the hands of Jesus? Peter lives today in the glorious Pontiff reigning in Peter's chair, tracing his lineage in unbroken succession. Leo XIII today exercises the powers of Peter, and today the Bishops succeed to the apostles, as Leo succeeds to the powers and office of supreme pastor. I could not stop now to demonstrate that the Bishops are in the succession, but Augustine and Cyprian, and Cyril, in fact, all the Fathers have said it. Could anyone, then, ask for a greater proof that our Church is identical with the Church of the apostles than this ceremony we have seen today? The Church has raised a new See. It has consecrated a priest of your own city to be its Bishop. He has new spiritual power. He has jurisdiction of the newly created See of Trenton. His authority is of Divine origin but comes from God through the Supreme Pontiff. This consecration today corresponds to the consecration of the apostles at Pentecost. It raises him to the rank of the apostles. He is the equal of all, even of the Supreme Pontiff. Others are his superiors in jurisdiction, but none are superior to him in order.

APPENDIX 5

Will of Bishop O'Farrell

In the name of the most Holy Trinity, I, Michael Joseph O'Farrell Bishop of Trenton in the State of New Jersey, being of sound disposing mind and memory, and desirous of arranging my worldly affairs, do hereby make, publish and declare this my last will and testament in the words, figures and manner following to wit;

First. I direct that all my just debts and the expenses of my funeral be paid by my executors hereinafter named as soon after my decease as may be convenient and practicable; and it is my will that my funeral be conducted with full ecclesiastical ceremonies suitable to and becoming a bishop, but at the same time without extravagance or worldly pomp. It is also my will and I do hereby direct that a suitable monument be erected over my remains and to be surmounted with a Celtic cross, and that the expense thereof be borne by my estate and by my executors.

Second. I give and bequeath my books and library and everything contained therewith to my executors in trust to transfer the same to my successor, when lawfully appointed, for his use as such bishop, and it is my will that the same be transferred for the like use to his successor.

Third. I give and bequeath to my beloved parents all the personal property owned by me individually and not belonging to the Church at the time of my decease; and in case both of my beloved parents should die before me, I give and bequeath the same to my brothers and sisters as follows; viz. one half thereof to my brother James, but in the event of his death before me I give the same to his children in equal portions share and share alike; the other half thereof I give and bequeath to my brother John and my sister Mrs. Mary Rowe in equal portions share and share alike; and it is my will that in case my brother John and my sister Mary Rowe should die before me, the portions hereby given to them respectively shall not lapse but go to their respective children, the children of each taking the share the parent would be entitled to under this my will, if living at the time of my decease.

Fourth. I give, devise and bequeath all the property and estate remaining to me, whether real or personal or mixed held by me as bishop of Trenton and belonging to the diocese thereof and devoted to ecclesiastical uses wherever the same may be situated, to the Most Rev. Michael Corrigan, coadjutor Archbishop of New York, and the Right Rev. Stephen M. Ryan, Bishop of Buffalo, as joint tenants in trust to transfer the same to my successor when lawfully appointed.

Fifth. I hereby nominate, constitute and appoint the most Rev. Michael Corrigan, coadjutor Archbishop of New York, and the Right Rev. Stephen M. Ryan, Bishop of Buffalo, executors and trustees of this my last will and Testament and do not require that they or either of them shall give any security in order to qualify as such executors and trustees.

Sixth. I hereby revoke and annul all other or former wills by me made and declare this to be my last will and Testament.

In witness whereof I have herewith subscribed my name and affixed my seal this   day of September A.D. One thousand eight hundred and eighty three.

APPENDIX 6

Inventory—Estate of Bishop O'Farrell

Policy # 360,674 New York Life Insurance Company	$25,000.00
Policy # 382,522 New York Life Insurance Company	10,000.00
Policy # 473,020 Mutual Life Insurance Co. of N.Y.	10,000.00
Cash Deposit, Trenton Banking Company	92,309.00
Due bill Rev. Wm. J. Fitzgerald for insurance value of policy transferred Jan. 8/94	1,050.00
Note Sacred Heart Church, Riverton	1,000.00
Interest thereon from July 2, 1893, 5% 76.35	1,076.35
Note St. Mary Star of the Lake, Lakewood	200.00
Note P.J. Petrie St. Monica's Church, Atlantic City	200.00
15 shares Capital stock, Ontario Bank, Canada	1,400.00
2 Dividend drafts, Ontario Bank	105.00
Library and works of art, estimate	3,000.00
Cathedrolium collected in cash	2,832.33
Total appraisement	55,786.77

CHAPTER FIVE

SECOND BISHOP: JAMES A. McFAUL 1894~1917

BY MONSIGNOR JOHN K. DERMOND

ON THE DAY FOLLOWING his consecration as second bishop of Trenton, on Thursday, October 18, 1894, James Augustine McFaul shared the pages of the *Daily State Gazette* with reports of the 72nd annual meeting of the Presbyterian Synod, the Mercer County Republican Convention, and the apprehension of suspected train robbers in Quantico, Virginia.[1] Coincidental in their juxtaposition, these other events in retrospect signaled the advent of a bishop whose service to the church would reach beyond the boundaries of the Diocese of Trenton, embrace more than the Catholic faithful entrusted to his care, and influence the political, economic, educational, and social life of his time. Father Walter Leahy, writing twelve years later, said:

There are few men who . . . can stand the constant strain of American public life, and always appear at their best. Especially is this the case with an American Bishop, for he has a varied part to play. Not only must he be a pious, painstaking priest, but he must be a good financier, . . . able to rule men who enjoy the possession of personal liberty in a country where that liberty often degenerates into license. Then, in his capacity of citizen, he must be able to meet his fellow citizens in press or on platform, and to defend his faith against all who attack it.

To occupy such a position creditably is no easy task, but to hold it honorably . . . means the possession of good judgment as well as excellent ability. Such a Bishop is the Rt. Rev. James A. McFaul, D.D., LL.D, Second Bishop of Trenton. From his first induction into office he has been constantly before the American public in press and pulpit, in the legislative halls and on the lecture platform, exhorting, refuting, pleading and reproving, battling for right and justice for Catholics. . . .[2]

James Augustine McFaul was born in Rory's Glen at Kilwaughter,[3] near the village of Larne, County Antrim, Ireland, on

June 6, 1850.[4] The son of James and Mary Heffernan McFaul,[5] the infant James emigrated to the United States with his parents when he was less than a year old.

James and Mary McFaul had owned and farmed land in Rory's Glen, but in 1850 there was widespread famine as well as hope of a far better life in America. The McFauls resolved to take the next ship bound for New York City, like so many of their countrymen. Among the traditions passed on to family members was the story "that on the way to Ballymena on the morning they left Rory's Glen, James asked to halt the cart at Shane's Hill, he lifted his son high above his head, looked back at Larne and said, 'Farewell, but I shed no tears for I have known little but poverty and hardship, but we will go forward now with faith and trust in God.'"[6]

The McFaul family remained in New York City for four or five years, where two more children were born.[7] They moved then to Bound Brook, New Jersey. Young James McFaul attended the public schools in the hamlets of Weston and Millstone and earned a reputation as a good student. Fathers Connell and Leahy relate that there were few Catholics in the Bound Brook area and no Catholic church. The McFaul family, like other faithful Catholics, had to travel to New Brunswick or Raritan for the Mass. When prevented from doing so by weather or illness, they prayed the rosary together at home at the time for Mass. Their example of fidelity in the midst of adversity was not lost on young James McFaul. He remained close to the church, receiving his first Communion and Confirmation at about nine years of age from then Bishop Bayley, in Saint Peter's Church in New Brunswick. He was influenced by the example and dedication of Father Rogers—a secular priest—and two Benedictines—Father William Walter and Father (later Bishop) Rupert Seidenbusch. During James's youth, the Benedictines had begun to gather the Catholics in Bound Brook for Mass, which young James McFaul would sometimes serve. Father Walter thought enough of the youth's talents to suggest he study for the priesthood, and James McFaul assented.

Acting on his advice, the young man entered Saint Vincent's College at Beatty, Westmoreland County, Pennsylvania, where he remained four years. He then entered Saint Francis Xavier's College, New York City, where he completed his classical course and fitted himself for the Seminary. His theological studies were made at Seton Hall College, South Orange, New Jersey, where he was ordained to the holy priesthood on May 26, 1877.[8]

Newly ordained, Father McFaul was first stationed in churches in Paterson and Orange, substituting for priests who were ill. Then Bishop Michael Augustine Corrigan, second bishop of Newark, who had ordained him, assigned Father McFaul to Saint Patrick's Church in Jersey City. From there he was transferred to Saint Patrick's Cathedral in Newark and then served, in turn, at Saint Peter's Church in New Brunswick and Saint Mary's Cathedral in Trenton. With the establishment of the

Bishop James A. McFaul

Diocese of Trenton, Father McFaul was sent to Saint Mary, Star of the Sea Church, in Long Branch. After seven years at that parish, during which he built the Church of Saint Michael at Elberon, Father McFaul was recalled to the cathedral in Trenton and appointed chancellor of the diocese.[9] On November 1, 1892, after completing a new Saint Joseph's School in East Trenton, Bishop Michael O'Farrell appointed Father McFaul vicar-general. In 1894, with the death of Bishop O'Farrell, Father McFaul was chosen administrator of the diocese; on July 20, 1894, he was appointed its second bishop.[10]

During the week preceding Father McFaul's consecration, the *New Jersey State Gazette* reported an outbreak of cholera in China, attacks by Pottawatomie Indians in Kansas, the train robbery in Quantico, Virginia, the meetings of the Presbyterian Synod, several local accidents, and stories of fraud, murder, beatings, and burglary. To the editorial writers of the paper it seemed neither a particularly peaceful nor auspicious time for celebration, as there was so much to lament about the deterioration of society.[11] Yet the celebration for the new Bishop James Augustine McFaul was in no way muted. Now archbishop of New York, the Right Reverend Michael Augustine Corrigan, the same prelate who ordained James Augustine McFaul as priest, on October 18, 1884, consecrated him bishop. Bishops Bernard J. McQuaid of Rochester and Charles E. McDonnell of Brooklyn served as co-consecrators. Bishops and clergy of "half the States in the Union," local and state government officials and dignitaries, and "well-known Protestants and clergymen of all denominations were guests and were given seats in the main body of the church."[12] Outside the cathedral stood more people than were seated inside. Flowers and flags, candles and colors of all sorts festooned the church and the surrounding streets. The press accounts were extensive in the *Gazette* and the *Daily True American*, the two papers published at that time in Trenton.

The new bishop was well-known, beloved, and jubilantly welcomed as the second bishop of Trenton. His coat of arms depicted the Virgin Mary with child, a lion on guard, and an eagle. The lion, it was said, represented Pope Leo XIII, who had established the Diocese of Trenton and appointed Bishop McFaul its shepherd. Bishop McFaul took as his motto *Gratia Dei, sum id quod sum* (By the grace of God, I am what I am) (1 Cor. 15:10). His crozier was a gift of friends and former parishioners of Star of the Sea Church, Long Branch, fabricated by the Gorham Company. A lamb in the center of the crook is surrounded by figures of Jesus, Mary, and the four Evangelists.[13]

Bishop McFaul's episcopacy saw a rapid expansion of the church in what was then the Diocese of Trenton. From the time of his appointment in 1894 to the time of his death in 1917, 65 parishes were established in the 14 counties that composed the diocese:[14]

Bishop McFaul's coat-of-arms.
"By the grace of God, I am what I am."

Sacred Heart	
South Amboy	1895
St. Ann	
Wildwood	1895
St. Joseph	
Woodstown	1895
St. Rose of Lima	
Haddon Heights	1896
St. Lawrence	
Lindenwold	1896
St. Peter	
Pleasantville	1896
St. James	
Pennington	1897
Our Lady of Perpetual Help	
Bernardsville	1898
Holy Trinity	
Perth Amboy	1899
Ss. Peter and Paul	
Trenton	1899
St. Mary	
Deal	1901
St. James	
Penns Grove	1901
St. Catharine	
Spring Lake	1901
St. Joachim	
Trenton	1901
St. Mary	
Alpha	1902
Our Lady of Victories	
Landisville	1902
St. Michael	
Minotola	1902
Our Lady of Hungary	
Perth Amboy	1902
St. Mary of Ostrabrama	
South River	1902
Our Lady of Mount Carmel	
Berlin	1903
St. John	
Collingswood	1903

St. Peter	
Merchantville	1903
St. Ann	
Raritan	1903
St. Stephen the King	
Trenton	1903
St. Michael	
Atlantic City	1904
St. Cecilia (mission)	
Monmouth Junction	1904
St. Ladislaus	
New Brunswick	1904
Most Holy Rosary	
Perth Amboy	1904
St. Hedwig	
Trenton	1904
Our Lady of Mount Carmel	
Asbury Park	1905
St. Dorothea	
Eatontown	1905
St. Mary of Mount Virgin	
New Brunswick	1905
St. Ann	
Browns Mills	1906
Holy Family	
Carteret	1906
St. Elizabeth	
Far Hills	1906
Holy Trinity	
Long Branch	1906
St. Vincent de Paul	
Mays Landing	1906
St. Anthony of Padua	
Port Reading	1906
St. Catharine	
Seaside Park	1906
Sacred Heart	
South Plainfield	1906
St. Mary	
Williamstown	1906
St. Elizabeth	
Avon	1907
Ascension	
Bradley Beach	1907

St. Stephen Protomartyr	
South River	1907
Holy Spirit	
Atlantic City	1908
Our Lady of Pompeii	
East Vineland	1908
St. James (mission)	
Rocky Hill	1908
St. Denis	
Manasquan	1909
All Saints	
Burlington	1910
Sacred Heart	
Carteret	1910
Holy Trinity	
Helmetta	1911
St. Paul	
Stone Harbor	1911
Our Lady of the Mount	
Warren	1911
St. Catherine	
Farmingdale	1912
St. Paul the Apostle	
Highland Park	1912
St. Joseph	
Raritan	1912
Blessed Sacrament	
Trenton	1912
Holy Name	
Camden	1913
St. Casimir	
Riverside	1913
Sacred Heart	
Bay Head	1914
St. Mary	
Bound Brook	1914
St. Elizabeth of Hungary	
Carteret	1914
Holy Assumption	
Roebling	1914
St. Stanislaus Kostka	
Sayreville	1914
St. Matthew	
National Park	1915

In an address delivered in the Taylor Opera House in Trenton on November 27, 1906, the celebration of the Silver Jubilee of the diocese, Bishop McFaul expressed what moved him to establish more than 30 churches in the first 12 years of his episcopacy.[15] Among his reasons were the sheer size of the territory; the rapid increase in Catholic population, more than doubling, from 40,000 in 1881 to 99,000 in 1906;[16] the lapse of Catholic people from the church for want of priests and churches; and immigration "reaching into the millions, old and young, most of whom have come to this country in the last fifteen or twenty years."[17]

Among Bishop McFaul's pastoral concerns were the care of those in special need, in particular, orphans and the indigent elderly. Bishop O'Farrell had laid plans for the establishment of Saint Michael's Orphan Asylum and Industrial School and had left a sum of $60,000 toward its construction. It fell to Bishop McFaul, however, to secure additional funding and land and to construct and staff the institution. He obtained an additional gift of $50,000 from Colonel Daniel Morris and from other "offerings made through St. Michael's Union, a society organized under the auspices of the Bishop."[18] To enable the home to be self-supporting, Bishop McFaul purchased 150 acres of the adjoining Drake farm. Construction of Saint Michael's home began on October 18, 1896, and was completed with the blessing of the building on May 30, 1898. The Sisters of Saint Francis were missioned for the care of "about two hundred boys and girls, giving them not only a

Bishop James A. McFaul

safe and comfortable home but also a good Catholic training, away from the vices of large cities."[19] To care for the aging, Bishop McFaul received a legacy of $50,000 from Colonel Morris and expended in excess of $100,000, "only a small part of which he has succeeded in collecting," to erect Morris Hall. "This home for the aged poor . . . [is] situated in the midst of a fertile farm, conveniently located near the beautiful village of Lawrenceville, and is about five miles from Trenton."[20] In addition, Bishop McFaul supported Saint Joseph's Home for the Indigent Poor in Beverly, which was also staffed by the Franciscan Sisters.[21] In 1891, he wrote to Father John Sheppard, vicar-general of Newark, about his concern for the pastoral care of Catholics in the "Trenton Asylum." Although attended from the cathedral, priests were granted access to

The Diocese of Trenton, 1881–1993

patients, called "inmates," only at the request of their families. Alluding to similar problems, "the case in Jamesburg, in the State Prison, in the Alms House, in other public institutions," he spoke of the need for greater cooperation between himself and the bishop of Newark in order to obtain concessions from the state to allow clergy free access to Catholic residents of these institutions, not only for sacramental ministration but also for Catholic education.[22] On August 3, 1891, he wrote expressing his pleasure that the bishops were able to secure "Mr. Earley as a candidate for steward of the Asylum. . . . Having a Catholic appointed to some prominent position in the Asylum" would, he hoped, facilitate the pastoral care of Catholic residents there.[23]

Two consistently pressing concerns throughout his episcopacy were Catholic education and family life. Six of Bishop McFaul's 32 published addresses dealt directly with these concerns, and others contained mention of them.[24] He was convinced that religious schools were necessary for the education of youth. He distinguished between instruction, meaning the imparting of information, and education, meaning the formation of persons. The free public schools of the United States could accomplish the former, but not the latter, because they could not impart the religious and moral training so necessary to the formation of the whole person.[25] Bishop McFaul insisted that the manner of funding schools was inherently unjust, because the "equal benefit" clause of the existing state law to fund its schools could not be fulfilled without also funding the religious schools, and the existing public schools could not accommodate the students then enrolled in religious schools. He proposed a historic compromise:

> 1. Let our schools remain as they are. 2. Let no compensation be made for religious instructions. We do not desire it. . . . Our principle is, "let the pastor take care of his flock and live by the flock." 3. Let our children be examined by a State or Municipal Board, and, if our schools furnish the secular education required, then let the State pay for it.[26]

Bishop McFaul supported the establishment of Mount Saint Mary College in North Plainfield in 1908 and its reconstruction after a fire in 1911.[27] During his tenure as bishop, 38 Catholic elementary schools were established in the parishes, which he erected in the 14 counties of the diocese.[28] He invited and welcomed religious communities to the diocese to teach—in particular, the Sisters of Mercy, the Franciscans, and the Sisters of Charity.[29]

In "The Christian Home," Bishop McFaul set out a charter for stable Christian family life, against the tenor of the times. He urged the scriptural pattern for home life, discussing the roles of husband, wife, and children, as well as the need to avoid what he called the "enemies of the home": unbelief, divorce, socialism, the tenement, intemperance, and ignorance of household duties. He taught good order, praying together, religious instruction at home, and fair, just, and gentle treatment of domestic help.[30] In

1899, he obtained the services of three Mission Helpers from Baltimore to establish a day nursery for the children of working mothers.[31]

Early in his episcopacy, Bishop McFaul anticipated the need for organization and cooperation among the many societies that Catholics were then establishing within and outside their parishes. His experience as arbitrator of a dispute between Irish societies in 1897[32] and his concern for the protection of the rights of Catholics in the pluralistic society of the United States led him to undertake the formation of the American Federation of Catholic Societies. In an address to the Federation on August 9, 1908, in Boston,[33] Bishop McFaul acknowledged that the idea for the federation originated with the Knights of Saint John. After consultation with several other ecclesiastics, Bishop McFaul reported, "the organization was established at Long Branch and Cincinnati, whence it spread to other cities."[34] He explained the various purposes of the Federation throughout his address: "to convince Catholics of the necessity of using the press for the dissemination of the truth,"[35] to unify the various ethnic groups ("nationalities"), to "banish divorce and Socialism," to create a "Catholic public opinion on the problems of the day and the dissemination of their solution," and to provide "agitation on the public school question."[36] In sum,

> The American Federation of Catholic Societies is an organization formed of subordinate societies for the advancement of the civil, religious and social interests of

Catholics. It will not interfere with the aims, objects or autonomy of existent organizations.[37]

Apparently there had been difficulty on several fronts in securing the establishment of the federation. Certainly its nature and purpose were misunderstood. One may infer from the words of Bishop McFaul that some thought the federation a grievance committee, others an effort to organize a Catholic political party. His response suggests he was thinking more along the lines of influencing the existing parties and processes:

> There was a tax bill introduced into the [New Jersey] legislature the phraseology of which was ambiguous and was liable to be interpreted as directing the taxation of parish schools. I had some influential Catholics wait upon the introducer of the bill, but he replied that it would have to stand. Then I directed a committee from the New Jersey Federation of Catholic Societies to wait upon the legislator. When he discovered who these men were and what they represented, he answered: "Gentlemen, don't raise a hornet's nest because of this bill; just sit down and write out what changes you want in the wording of it and they will be made. There is no desire to tax the parish schools." That is the kind of politics there is in the federation. If the politicians know that you have a strong, substantial body of people behind your claims, they will cheerfully grant them. It is certainly time we began to know how to employ the prerogatives of American citizenship.[38]

There was also difficulty in securing the cooperation of the various societies and ethnic groups. In a letter to Vicar-General Sheppard of Newark, Bishop McFaul suggested that "both bishops write a circular letter to all the Pastors asking each to appoint one delegate to represent each parish. . . . Let us at the same time issue a call for a State Convention of these delegates in Trenton, to put the machinery in motion."[39] As late as 1909, he had decided "to establish the Holy Name in every parish and unite all societies by means of the Holy Name societies."[40] Later that same year he commented:

> I have found that, while we have Federation in this City and Atlantic City, it will be impossible to cement all the societies together without some stable basis such as the Holy Name Society. Hence I have appointed an energetic young priest to organize the Holy Name Society in every parish of the Diocese. While his work is under way, I shall have him take up the Federation work also. The growth here is slow, too slow to suit me, but I'll succeed.[41]

No doubt he did, for at his death, the *Daily State Gazette* reported that the "Federation of Catholic Societies now has a membership of more than two million."[42] There was a notice in the *State Gazette* from the Mercer County chapter, scheduling a special meeting to "prepare for the annual convention of the Diocesan Federation of Catholic Societies, which is scheduled to be held in this city."[43]

In his efforts to secure civil legislation beneficial to the family, Bishop James Augustine McFaul was influential in organizing a group of religious leaders of various denominations in its pursuit. On January 30, 1906, the *Daily State Gazette* reported a conference of "prominent clergymen and citizens," among whom were listed Bayard Stockton, Charles B. Case, and Peter Backes—citizens—and, among the clergy, Bishop McFaul, Bishop Lines of the Episcopal Diocese of Newark, and the Reverends Henry Collin Minton, Hugh B. MacCauley, G. B. Wright, Rev. Mr. Nash, and others.[44] The conference sought to propose legislation to restrict the licensing and sale of liquor and to regulate the location and hours of tavern operation. A regulation already in place was not sufficiently effective to prevent public drunkenness, the sale of liquor to minors, the location of taverns near or next to churches, and the opening of taverns by unlicensed, or improperly licensed, proprietors.[45]

By February 15, 1906, opposition to the work of this conference had materialized, and the *Gazette* reported statements by the clergy to clarify their position.[46] The broad base of support for their effort was next reported in the *Gazette* on February 24. Two bills, numbered 136 and 137, had been introduced in the state senate, and the conference favoring them had grown to "about 200 delegates representing Catholics, Episcopalians, Presbyterians, Methodists, Baptists and Congregationalists."[47] Then in March, the Episcopal Bishops Scarborough and Lines and the Catholic Bishops McFaul and John Joseph O'Connor of Newark took strong public stands in favor of the legislation, and the *Gazette* began calling these the "Bishops' Bills."[48] In correspondence with Vicar-General Sheppard,

Bishop McFaul had written: "It would be too bad that any blunder should retard our progress or prevent unity of action with the different denominations, as the bill can be passed only by the combined strength of all."[49] On February 12, he noted: "This is the first time we have joined with the sects, so we must win."[50]

In sermons reported in the press, Bishop McFaul stressed the need for this legislation to protect the family by securing safety in their neighborhoods, preventing consumption of liquor by minors, enforcing the ban on Sunday sale of liquor, and preventing the location of taverns near churches and schools, where public safety would be endangered by intoxicated persons.[51] Debate in the legislature packed both houses in March; the *Gazette* heralded: "Great Day for Bishop Bills."[52] Opposition led to amendments, but on April 6, 1906, the bills passed the senate, and on April 12, the house.[53] On April 13, favorable editorial comment noted that the bills had passed in amended form, that there was broad public support for them, and that an equitable compromise had been achieved.[54] Yet on November 30, 1907, Bishop McFaul had reason to write to Vicar-General Sheppard of Newark, requesting statistics on the nonobservance of the new legislation so that he might approach the incoming governor about enforcement.[55]

Bishop McFaul had other occasions to be involved in public life. He wrote and spoke against "lynchings," which meant death by hanging imposed by an angry mob, and received public commendation for his stand from the local chapter of the Afro-American Council.[56] In 1914, he wrote a brochure on tuberculosis, for distribution among the faithful,[57] and a pastoral letter on the subject, which was read in all the churches of the diocese. He served actively as a member of the United States Catholic Historical Society, the Irish American Historical Society, the New Jersey State Tuberculosis Association, and the Trenton Chamber of Commerce.[58]

In his private life, he was also a man of great compassion. The story was recounted at the time of his death that in 1915 he had received a bequest of $11,000. Not long after that, he discovered that the donor's sons and daughter were in want, and so he returned the money to them.[59]

Bishop McFaul became ill about a year before his death, but he remained active until the early part of June 1917.[60] He had already designated that he should be buried at Morris Hall, in Lawrenceville. The place had been marked with a granite shaft on which his coat of arms and motto were to be carved.[61] By the time of his passing, on Saturday, June 16, 1917, World War I had broken out. Each day the press carried stories of ships being sunk by submarines, the sale of liberty bonds, and mobilization for war.

Bishop McFaul had already had something to say about war. On May 29, 1892, he had addressed members of the Grand Army of the Republic in St. Mary's Cathedral. He recalled the battle for the republic on Trenton's soil, as well as the more recent fight to preserve the Union. He expressed hope that the pursuit of virtue and *education* would lead to a temperate and just people in the United States and safeguard liberty without war.[62] Yet on July 24, 1898, he was called upon to address soldiers about to depart for another war. Bishop McFaul recalled the words of the First Letter to the Corinthians, Chapter 9, verse 25: The athlete "refraineth himself from all things: and they indeed that they may receive a corruptible crown; but we an incorruptible one"; and he exhorted these young men to guard their faith, to remember the favors of Providence with which America has been blessed, to acknowledge the spiritual destiny for which all are created, and to be pure and brave in battle.[63]

On the day of Bishop McFaul's funeral, Bishop O'Connor of Newark officiated, and—as at the bishop's consecration—hundreds of clergy and laity were present. Monsignor John H. Fox had been appointed administrator, and the Diocese of Trenton awaited its next bishop.[64]

REFERENCES

1. *Daily State Gazette*, 19 October 1894, 4.
2. Rev. Walter T. Leahy, *The Catholic Church of the Diocese of Trenton, N.J.* (Princeton, N.J.: 1906), 173.
3. Mrs. Margaret McIlgorm, Larne, County Antrim, Ireland, to Rev. Msgr. Joseph C. Shenrock, Whiting, New Jersey, 27 April 1992, 1 and 3. Mrs. McIlgorm identifies herself as grand-niece of Bishop McFaul by marriage to his grand-nephew, Edward McIlgorm.
4. Rev. Bernard T. Connell, "Sketch of Bishop McFaul," *Daily True American*, 19 October 1894, 6. This text, attributed to Father Connell in the *Daily True American*, was printed as background to the report of Bishop McFaul's episcopal consecration. It appears to be the source for all subsequent biographical data about Bishop McFaul. Almost in its entirety it appears in the Leahy work cited in note 2, on pages 173 and 174, and it is repeated in part in newspaper articles at the time of Bishop McFaul's death. It even seems to be known to Mrs. Margaret McIlgorm's sources. Because Father Connell's "Sketch" underlies nearly all the available sources concerning this period of Bishop McFaul's life, it will be closely followed and cited often.
5. McIlgorm, 1.
6. Ibid., 4. "The family had a smallhold in Rory's Glen, Kilwaughter, and the father, James McFaul, his wife and young son, born in June, 1850, were to take the emigrant ship for America and New York. Times were very bad in Ireland after the famine years, there was widespread emigration, and Larne was no exception. The story was always told by the family that on the way to Ballymena on the morning they left Rory's Glen, James asked to halt the cart at Shane's Hill, he lifted his son high above his head, looked back at Larne and said, 'Farewell, but I shed no tears for I have known little but poverty and hardship, but we will go forward now with faith and trust in God.'"
7. Ibid.
8. Connell, 6. "Catholics were few in that part of the State. There was no church in Bound Brook, and so to hear holy mass the journey to New Brunswick or Raritan had to be made. How faithful the old people

were in performing this holy duty is a tradition throughout the whole neighborhood. Never, when circumstances did not render it impossible, were they absent from the holy sacrifice. On stormy days the mother and father would gather the children around them, and as they could not reach the distant churches they would kneel (at least during the time of the mass), and devoutly recite the beads and present themselves in spirit at the divine mysteries. Under such training it was impossible but that the future Bishop should acquire deeply the spirit of strong enduring faith which is characteristic of him. At the early age of nine years he was prepared by good old Father Rogers for his first Holy Communion and Confirmation, which he received at the hands of lamented Archbishop Bayley. The Benedictines began to establish a mission at Bound Brook about this time and gradually gathered a number of Catholics of the neighborhood together. The house is still standing where the first mass was said, and which was used for a church for many years. Here the subject of our sketch served Mass and was so prudent and docile in his bearing as to attract the attention of the good priest who advised him to devote the talents God had given him to the service of the Church." Leahy, 174, identifies the priest who encouraged James McFaul to consider serving the church as Father William Walter, O.S.B., and the priest who prepared him for Communion and Confirmation as Father Seidenbusch, a Benedictine.

9. Leahy, 174.
10. Ibid., 175.
11. *New Jersey State Gazette*, 43 (15–17 October 1894), especially pages 1–5 of each issue.
12. Ibid., 19 October 1894, 4.
13. "The Consecration of Rt. Rev. Jas. A. McFaul, D.D., Bishop of Trenton," *Good Tidings*, November 1984, 6.
14. Compiled from *The Official Catholic Directory* (New Providence, N.J.: P. J. Kenedy and Sons, 1992), 161–163, 564–566, 1036–1038; and compared with the *1991 Catholic Telephone Guide*, (New Rochelle, N.Y.: The Catholic News Publishing Company, 1991), 209–212, 218–221, 240–243.
15. James A. McFaul, D.D., LL.D., "The Diocese of Trenton," in *The Pastoral Letters, Addresses and Other Writings of the Rt. Rev. James A. McFaul, D.D., LL.D., Bishop of Trenton*, ed. Rev. James J. Powers (Trenton, N.J.: State Gazette Publishing Company, 1915), 199–206.
16. Ibid., 203.
17. Ibid., 205.
18. Leahy, 214.
19. Ibid.
20. Ibid., 216.
21. Ibid.
22. Bishop James A. McFaul to Vicar-General John Sheppard, 22 July, 1891. In # 436, *Vicar General John Sheppard Papers*, Record Group 4 of the *John J. O'Connor Papers*, Archives of the New Jersey Catholic Historical Society, Seton Hall University, South Orange, New Jersey.
23. Ibid., 3 August 1891.
24. *The Pastoral Letters*. Bishop McFaul's "Address to the Graduates at Seton Hall," "Catholics and American Citizenship," "The Christian Home," "The Christian School," "Some Modern Problems," and "Infidelity in our Universities" directly treat education and family life.
25. James A. McFaul, D.D., LL.D., "The Christian School," in *The Pastoral Letters*, 207–236.

26. Ibid., 233–234.

27. "College of Mount Saint Mary," in *The Monitor*, 21 December 1912, 49.

28. Compiled from *The Official Catholic Directory* (New Providence, N.J.: P. J. Kenedy and Sons, 1992), 161–163, 564–566, 1036–1038.

29. Leahy, 219–224.

30. James A. McFaul, D.D., LL.D., "The Christian Home," in *The Pastoral Letters*, 167–195.

31. Leahy, 224–225.

32. "Decision of the Rt. Rev. James A. McFaul, Arbitrator, Between the A.O.H. of America, and the A.O.H. of the U.S.A. in Affiliation with the B. of E.," in *The Pastoral Letters*, 99–103.

33. James A. McFaul, D.D., LL.D., "The American Federation of Catholic Societies," in *The Pastoral Letters*, 269–280.

34. Ibid., 271.

35. Ibid., 272.

36. Ibid., 276.

37. Ibid., 275.

38. Ibid.

39. Bishop James A. McFaul to Vicar-General John Sheppard, 22 January 1906, in # 436, *Vicar General John Sheppard Papers*, Record Group 4 of the *John J. O'Connor Papers*.

40. Ibid., 16 March 1909.

41. Ibid., 8 May 1909.

42. *Daily State Gazette*, 18 June 1917, 3.

43. Ibid.

44. *Daily State Gazette*, 30 January 1906, 1.

45. Ibid.

46. *Daily State Gazette*, 15 February 1906, 1.

47. *Daily State Gazette*, 24 February 1906, 1.

48. *Daily State Gazette*, 3 March 1906, 1, and 5 March 1906, 1. "Bishop Bills" appears first on 7 March 1906, 1.

49. Bishop James A. McFaul to Vicar-General John Sheppard, 8 February 1906, in # 436, *Vicar General John Sheppard Papers*, Record Group 4 of the *John J. O'Connor Papers*.

50. Bishop James A. McFaul to Vicar-General John Sheppard, 12 February 1906.

51. *Daily State Gazette*, 5 March 1906, 1.

52. *Daily State Gazette*, 7 March 1906, 1.

53. *Daily State Gazette*, 12 April 1906, 1.

54. "The Bishops' Bill," *Daily State Gazette*, 13 April 1906, 4.

55. Bishop James A. McFaul to Vicar-General John Sheppard, 30 November 1907, in # 436, *Vicar General John Sheppard Papers*, Record Group 4 of the *John J. O'Connor Papers*.

56. *Daily State Gazette*, 13 February 1906, 6.

57. James A. McFaul, D.D., LL.D., "Tuberculosis, Its Prevention and Relief," 1914, in *The Pastoral Letters*, 367–379.

58. *Daily State Gazette*, 18 June 1917, 3.

59. Ibid.

60. Ibid.

61. Ibid.

62. James A. McFaul, D.D., LL.D., "Our Country's Defenders," in *The Pastoral Letters*, 57–64.

63. James A. McFaul, D.D., LL.D., "The Athlete of Christ," in *The Pastoral Letters*, 125–130.

64. *Daily State Gazette*, 18 June 1917, 3.

APPENDIX

Extracts from Bishop McFaul's Pastoral Letter on Education

THE CHRISTIAN SCHOOL

James Augustine, by the grace of God and the favor of the Apostolic See, Bishop of Trenton, to the Clergy and Faithful of his Diocese, health and benediction.

Venerable Brethren of the Clergy, and Beloved Children in Christ Jesus:

In our Pastoral Letter on "The Christian Home," we described the nature of the home, the relations of husband and wife, of father and mother; enumerated their rights and duties, and portrayed the happiness which always dwells within the true home. Then we mentioned the dangers to the home and the blessings it confers upon the individual and society. We maintained that there are three great educators: *The Christian Home, the Christian School* and *the Christian Church.* Having considered already the first of these institutions, we shall devote this letter to the Christian School.

HISTORY OF EDUCATION.

Before treating of the nature and end of education, it is advisable to relate briefly its history and progress. The heathen mind was materialistic. Whatever education the pagan obtained was mainly directed towards his material welfare....

JEWISH.

Turning to the Jewish people, we naturally expect to find their education molded likewise after their religion. Let us here lay stress again on the fact that a nation's civilization, its education, its whole character are fashioned after its religion....

CHRISTIAN SCHOOLS.

Upon the establishment of Christianity, a new order of things commenced. The good of the individual became paramount; the bond and the free are equal before God. All have the same eternal destiny; all the same means to obtain it; all are redeemed by the same Savior; all are His brethren. The Church in fulfilling her divine mission of teaching the gospel, of planting a new civilization was necessarily brought into conflict with Roman and Grecian culture. Her children retained what was good and true in that civilization, and elevated and ennobled it by making it conform to the spirit of Christ— that spirit which is as broad as humanity, which reaches to Heaven and embraces all men in the bond of divine charity. Hence, we see the Church not only preaching, but also teaching. Thus grew up the catechumenal schools for the instruction of the children of believers, and of converts coming from the Jews and pagans.

CATECHUMENAL AND CATHEDRAL.

Frequently during the week the Catechumens met in the porch of the church or in some other place to receive instruction in Christian doctrine. Through these schools, supplemented by home training, the children were educated. The catechumenal were also called catechetical schools, although this name gradually came to designate the great schools, such as those presided over by the renowned Origen at Alexandria and Caesarea. Out of the catechumenal schools there arose the cathedral schools, which, along with the monastic, made up the educational system of the Middle Ages....

CHANTRY, GUILD, MONASTIC, ETC.

In the course of time there grew up many private schools, especially in Italy. The Chantry schools were very numerous. These were so-called

in Italy. The Chantry schools were very numerous. These were so-called because they were presided over by priests who received support from pious foundations of Masses. The part of the church, where these were sung, was called the Chantry, and the name came to be applied to the endowment itself. These might be called the parish schools of the Middle Ages. They were of all grades, and in some the tuition was free.

The Guild schools were occasionally taught by clergymen; later on burgh schools arose. The secular authorities had more or less control over these schools and gave them support. Lay teachers taught in them as well as clerics....

FREE PUBLIC SCHOOLS IN THE UNITED STATES.

From the beginning of the Colonies, Americans have been profoundly interested in education. The Colonial grammar school was an offshoot of the English public schools. It differed from them only in receiving support from the colonies and town governments and being under their control.

To the Congregationalists of New England, however, our present system of public schools may be attributed. It had its origin in Massachusetts, and, strange to say, had many of the features of our parish school. The money required for support was either raised by taxation of the property in the district, or by a per capita tax on the scholars who attended the school....

PARISH SCHOOLS.

The Catholic parish schools in the United States had their origin in the European Catholic schools. It was natural enough that the founders of schools in this country should copy after those with which they were familiar at home.

The parish school has kept pace with the growth of the Church. After the church was built for divine worship, priest and people immediately recognized the necessity of the school, where the children would be trained in knowledge and virtue, if religion and morality were to increase, and the sacred edifice continue to be frequented. We find the parish school in connection with the church, in the days before the Revolution. It dates as far back as the foundation of the colony of Catholics in Maryland.

Passing by the different systems of education which have been introduced by the Jesuits, the Christian Brothers, Pestalozzi, Herbert and others, we shall now inquire what is true education.

MEANING OF EDUCATION.

The word "educate" is derived from a Latin word which means to lead out, to develop. This development should extend to our whole being. It must, therefore, be physical, mental, moral and religious. Education, by taking hold of all our faculties, should bring them into harmonious relation with themselves and the external world. It begins with the child and ends really only with death. Our theme, though in some respects viewing education in its universal sense, is restricted to that period when education is the work of the teacher in the school, and lasts during certain hours of the day when the teacher assumes the place of the parent.

There is a vast difference between mere instruction and education. Education includes instruction, but instruction never attains to the dignity of education. Instruction is a mere furnishing, a storing of the mind with knowledge. It neither develops nor gives productive power; it is unable to place us in complete agreement with our environment. Education is a development of all the faculties of the soul toward the perfection of which they are capable and supposes the simultaneous acquisition of knowledge. True education is, therefore, round and symmetrical. To train the reason and neglect the will is not education.

The Catholic must have a higher aim than the formation of merely intellectual culture. His view of education must be based upon man's nature and destiny. He must never forget that man is created to God's image and likeness; that this life is a stepping stone to the next. He must be qualified to live in accordance with the will of the Creator, who has prescribed all the relations and all the duties of life. His conception of education must not be confined to man's mere physical, ethical and intellectual development; it should be broader, higher, nobler, an education which fits for eternity as well as for time.

That education, whose value ends with the few fleeting years of this earthly life, is of comparatively little importance, seeing that our future weal or woe depends upon the life we have led in this world. Thomas a'Kempis asks: "What doth it avail thee to discourse profoundly on the Trinity, if thou be void of humility, and consequently displeasing to the Trinity? In truth, sublime words make not a man holy and just; but a virtuous life maketh him dear to God. I had rather feel compunction than know its definition. If thou didst know the whole Bible by heart, and the sayings of all the Philosophers, what would it all profit thee without the love of God and His grace?" The same thing our blessed Lord said long before: "What doth it profit a man to gain the whole world and suffer the loss of his own soul." [Matt XVI., 26] Man is therefore infinitely more important than science. Science is the servant; he is the master. Science should assist him in the attainment of his destiny.

Man was made the lord of creation. For him the seasons annually return, the earth is covered with verdure and filled with innumerable forms of life; for him are mountain and plain, river and ocean, the storm and the calm, the sunshine and the rain; for him the universe itself was framed. For him, too, the complete machinery of human life has been established, the family, society and government. All our institutions, civil and religious, are but means enabling him to reach his end. The Savior teaches this truth in the Gospel when He says: "Be not solicitous, therefore, saying, what shall we eat, or what shall we drink, or wherewith shall we be clothed? For after all these things do the heathens seek. For your Father knoweth that you have need of all these things. Seek ye, therefore, first the kingdom of God and His justice, and all these things shall be added unto you." [Matt. VI., 31.]

THE END OF EDUCATION.

Here is the object to be unceasingly kept in view: "The kingdom of God and His justice." That man may possess these, everything else is provided. If then we would have a true idea of education, of the Christian school and of the benefits it imparts, we must judge them by this standard. It applies equally well to the primary school, the college and the great university, for they are all only means to an end. These questions are, therefore, paramount: Does our education bring us nearer to God; do the buildings, the teachers, the equipment, the studies, the discipline, all minister to the entire well-being of the scholar? In a word, does the educational training received make us physically, mentally, morally and religiously healthier and stronger? If it does not, it is a failure; nay more, it may be a danger, a hindrance, an obstacle to our present and future welfare and happiness....

EDUCATION NOT A PANACEA.

Too much must not be expected of secular and religious education even when combined; for the teacher's work is not always fruitful. Much assuredly depends upon the person with whom he deals. Where there is very little to develop; where the disposition is degraded and vitiated; where the home environment is pernicious, it is difficult, if not impossible, for good results to follow. The school, then, must not always be blamed if the pupil gives little or no evidence of its beneficial results on his character and the tenor of his life. Children are not mere passive instruments in the hands of the teacher; they have their own inclination and their own individuality. How frequently we find children, surrounded by the most adverse influences,

by pious parents, rushing into danger, yielding to the first impulse of temptation and living the lives of reprobates thereafter. Nevertheless, it still remains true that education is the ordinary means of building up character, even if in some instances it fails, not because of anything lacking in itself, or in those who impart it....

THE RIGHT TO EDUCATE.

Having stated what education truly means, an important question suggests itself. Who has the right to educate?...

What is the province of the Church as regards education? Inasmuch as she is the divinely constituted interpreter of God's laws, all Catholics are obliged to educate and rear their children in harmony with her doctrines and practices.

But has the State any right to educate? Not in the strict sense. It can take the place of the parents only with their consent. It cannot lawfully interfere with the education of the child, unless the parents neglect their duty and the child is in danger of becoming a harmful member of society, for it is certain that the State can legitimately use all means requisite for its own protection....

INJUSTICE OF THE PUBLIC SCHOOL SYSTEM.

The State then may furnish education, provided that in so doing it does not infringe upon the rights of the parents. It may not, however, lawfully select a system of public education which many of its subjects are unable to conscientiously patronize. The rule of the majority may be just as tyrannical and unjust as that of the greatest despot. A minority, even as a minority, has inalienable rights, although their exercise is prevented by the power of the majority.

"Vox populi vox Dei." "The voice of the people is the voice of God," is not universally true. When the State establishes a system of public education, it must adopt one which is acceptable to the minority as well as to the majority. If it chooses a system which the minority cannot use without a violation of conscience, then it has committed an injustice....

THE CATHOLIC POSITION.

At all events, we are unable to recede from our position. We must have religion taught in our schools. The atmosphere of the school during the entire day must be religious, must tend to the development of Christian character and Christian life. No other system can satisfy the conscience of Catholics.

We cannot allow any man, or body of men, any system of education, to undermine the faith of our children, any more than we can grant the power of any man to tell us what we shall believe or not believe. Considering our Church the only Church of Christ to which all who are called to salvation must conform, we can tolerate no minimizing of doctrine, and must have all Christianity. No human authority shall interfere with our religion. God alone is our teacher through His divinely commissioned representatives.

CATHOLICS NOT ALONE IN THIS VIEW.

Many non-Catholic citizens see danger in the present public school system. They perceive clearly that, if the head alone is educated and the heart left fallow, injury is done both to the individual and society....

President Roosevelt voices the sentiments of Catholics in his address before the Long Island Bible Society, thus: "There is no word in the English language more abused than that of education. The popular opinion is that the educated man is the one who has mastered the learning of the schools and the colleges. * * * It is a fine thing to be clever, to be able and smart. But it is a better thing to have the qualities that find their expression in the Decalogue and the Golden Rule."...

RELIGIOUS DENOMINATIONS AND THE PUBLIC SCHOOLS.

Religion and morality cannot be taught by the different denominations in the schools under our present system; for all our citizens, irrespective of creed, have the same rights under the laws of the State and nation. Religious convictions, therefore, cannot be interfered with. The Catholic cannot introduce his religion into the public schools, and the same is equally true of the Protestant....

The problem then has been reduced to this: We are agreed that religious is more important than secular education for the stability, purity and perfection of human institutions,...

To secure this we build our parish schools and support them. In them we teach religion and morality, while we at the same time, give as good and often better secular education than the State requires.

PROPOSED SOLUTION.

At this stage it may be asked, what is the solution of the educational difficulty which has been proposed? In reply we quote from an address which we delivered in Cincinnati:...

"What is the compromise we propose? 1. Let our schools remain as they are. 2. Let no compensation be made for religious instruction. We do not desire it. We have seen what has happened in countries where the clergy are the hirelings of the State. Our principle is, 'let the pastor take care of the flock, and live by the flock.' 3. Let our children be examined by a State or Municipal Board, and, if our schools furnish the secular education required, then let the State pay for it."...

ERECTION OF PARISH SCHOOLS.

As the State is not inclined as yet to make any concession in favor of our parish schools, we must continue to bear the double burden of supporting both public and parish schools. We are strongly convinced that the parish school is absolutely necessary for the maintenance of the faith and the practices of religion in the rising generation. Wherefore, we earnestly exhort all Rectors to make provision for parish schools where none now exist, and to do everything in their power to extend the usefulness of those already erected.

These are the thoughts, Dearly Beloved, which we have deemed proper to bring to your attention during the holy season of Lent. And now, let us conclude with the words of the Prince of the Apostles: "You, therefore, brethren, knowing these things before, take heed, lest being led aside by the error of the unwise, you fall from your own steadfastness. But grow in grace, and in the knowledge of our Lord and Savior Jesus Christ. To Him be glory both now and unto the day of eternity. Amen." [II. Pet. III., 17, 18.]

Given at Trenton, this second day of February, the Feast of the Purification of the B. V. M., in the year of our Lord, 1907.

The Pastoral Letters, Addresses and Other Writing of the Rt. Rev. James A. McFaul, D.D., LL.D., Bishop of Trenton. Ed. Rev. James J. Powers. Trenton, New Jersey: State Gazette Publishing Company, 1915. pp. 207–236.

CHAPTER SIX

THIRD BISHOP: THOMAS J. WALSH 1918~1928

BY REGINA WALDRON MURRAY

AT THE DAWN OF THE twentieth century, waves of European immigrants, bright with promise, flooded the shores of America. But hundreds of the newcomers, unable to adapt to the language and customs of this country, could not find jobs and suffered severe hardships. In despair, scores of them, including many Catholics, lost both their hope and their faith.

Early in the new century, the Rev. Thomas J. Walsh was ordained to the priesthood for the Buffalo diocese. After becoming aware of the immigrants' problems, he quickly assumed the role of their advocate. Later, while serving successively as the third bishop of the Diocese of Trenton, the fifth bishop of the Diocese of Newark, and the first archbishop of the Archdiocese of Newark, he continued his work on their behalf. His efforts resulted in unprecedented educational expansion and innovative social work programs.

Bishop Walsh was a man for all missions. Charged with energy, he was both an astute businessman and a persuasive salesman for the church. Fluent in four languages, he was equally at ease with unschooled immigrants, members of the church hierarchy, and the prominent donors he solicited for his projects.

During his years in New Jersey, Bishop Walsh, who was often called the "apostle of education and charity," dramatically changed the scholastic landscape of the entire state.

Thomas Joseph Walsh, eldest of the four sons of Thomas and Helen Curtin Walsh, was born on December 6, 1873, in Parkers Landing, Pennsylvania. While attending the public and parochial schools of Pikesville and Wellsville, New York, he maintained a high scholastic record while remaining active in sports and music.

Following his decision to become a priest, young Walsh was educated at the College and Seminary of St. Bonaventure, in Allegany, New York. On January 27, 1900, he was ordained in the Chapel of the Blessed Sacrament in Buffalo, site of the future St. Joseph's Cathedral. The Most Rev. Bishop James E. Quigley, bishop of Buffalo (later archbishop of Chicago), presided.

With both an astute mind and great spirituality, Father Walsh moved quickly up the ecclesiastical ladder. Six months after his ordination, he was appointed to the dual office of secretary to the bishop and chancellor under Bishop Quigley. (He later served in the same capacity under Bishops Charles H. Colton, D.D., and Dennis J. Dougherty, D.D., who was later appointed cardinal archbishop of Philadelphia.) Together with an accountant, Father Walsh organized and systematized the finances of the Buffalo diocese.

In 1907, Father Walsh was sent to study at the University of St. Appolinaris, in Rome, Italy, where within one year he received a doctorate in sacred theology and a doctorate in canon law.

After his return to Buffalo, Father Walsh resumed his duties as chancellor and was also the master of ceremonies at many ecclesiastical functions. During these years, he experienced deep empathy with the struggling Catholic immigrants of the diocese. At the time, there were about 125,000 immigrants, mainly Italians and Poles, in the Diocese of Buffalo alone.

In 1911, in an attempt to help the immigrants and to assist in other charitable activities, Father Walsh organized the Mount Carmel Guild. The guild, which was a forerunner of Catholic Action groups, was an association of Catholic women who volunteered their services to charitable causes.

The guild was an instant success. Buffalo's civic leaders publicly acknowledged its importance. The *Buffalo Express* wrote that the guild was "an important factor in local charitable and educational work." Branches mushroomed in other industrial cities.

Because of his keen interest in public affairs, Father Walsh joined the Buffalo Chamber of Commerce. During World War I, the young priest, who was intensely patriotic, served as a member of the executive committee of the Red Cross and was active in the sale of war bonds. In December 1917, he conducted the first public novena in the United States for the success of its armed forces.

Throughout his life and especially during national crises, he encouraged priests to become chaplains. Father Walsh often referred to himself as being in the service of "God and Country."

On May 10, 1918, when His Holiness, Pope Benedict XV, selected Father Walsh to become the third bishop of Trenton, New Jersey, there were both pride and a sense of loss among the residents of Buffalo. An article in the *Buffalo Courier* referred to Bishop-Elect Walsh as "one of the best known and beloved priests of this city."

In an editorial on May 11, the *Buffalo Evening Times* said:

The designation of Chancellor Thomas J. Walsh as Bishop of Trenton, New Jersey, places at the head of that important diocese a distinguished Buffalo ecclesiastic, and is a deserved promotion of a great theologian. The Bishop-Designate of Trenton is one of the most scholarly men in the country and his eloquence and executive ability are equal to his scholarship. The Catholics of Buffalo and the community at large will feel deeply the loss of Chancellor Walsh, but they take pride in the appointment of this eminent cleric and citizen to a post of such exalted responsibility and honor as that which he will have in Trenton.

On July 25, 1918, in St. Joseph's Cathedral, Buffalo, Thomas Joseph Walsh was consecrated bishop of Trenton by His Eminence, John Cardinal Bonzano, the apostolic delegate to the United States. Only eighteen years had elapsed since Bishop Walsh's ordination to the priesthood.

Bishop Walsh's coat-of-arms.
"Pour forth your grace unto us."

Before leaving Buffalo, the new bishop attended a series of farewell dinners given by both religious and civic groups. In one farewell speech, Bishop Walsh, alluding to the world war being fought on the battlefields of Europe, spoke about patriotism:

> . . . I believe that every man here is one hundred percent American, just as I am. Service in the time of war means sacrifice. Every man today is under obligation to sacrifice according to his means and position. I have tried quietly and simply to do my duty as I saw it. . . . I take advantage of this time to urge all to redouble their sacrifice. . . . I am happy if the city realizes that I have done my duty as an American citizen. Good-bye and God bless you!

On July 30, 1918, the new bishop arrived in Trenton by train. Despite a heavy rainstorm, he was warmly greeted at the Trenton railroad station by 2,000 people, including Trenton's Mayor Frederick W. Donnelly. Catholics, as well as the general public, were anxious and curious about the successor of Bishop James A. McFaul.

Following the death of Bishop McFaul, Trenton had been without a bishop for a year. During the interim, the affairs of the diocese were administered by the Right Reverend John H. Fox (upon whom the title of protonotary apostolic was later conferred).

On July 31, 1918, Bishop Walsh was installed as the bishop of Trenton in St. Mary's Cathedral by His Eminence, John Cardinal Farley, archbishop of New York.

At that time, the Diocese of Trenton was composed of the fourteen central and southern counties of New Jersey, an area of

Bishop Thomas J. Walsh

5,756 square miles. The Diocese of Newark embraced the seven northern counties, an area of 1,699 square miles. There were 186,000 Catholics in addition to 191 secular and 35 religious priests in the Trenton diocese. There were 133 parishes, 55 mission chapels, 49 grammar schools (with about 16,000 pupils), and 5 parochial high schools (with 548 students).

The new bishop faced a monumental task. Soon after his installation, Bishop Walsh visited all the corners of the diocese. In the ensuing years, his pace never slackened.

During his ten years in Trenton, Bishop Walsh established 21 new parishes as follows: Holy Family (later called St. James), Holy Angels, St. Anthony, and St. Michael,

Trenton; Sts. Peter and Paul, Great Meadows; Our Lady of Lourdes, Milltown; Our Lady of Mt. Carmel, Woodbridge; St. Ann, Westville; Our Lady of Peace, Fords; Sacred Heart, Manville; St. Paul, Highland Park; St. Andrew, Avenel; Our Lady of Perpetual Help, Maple Shade; St. Anthony, Red Bank; St. James, Ventnor; St. Cecilia, Iselin; Our Lady of Lourdes, Whitehouse Station; St. Ann, Keansburg; St. Joseph, New Brunswick; Christ the King, Haddonfield; and St. Aloysius, Oaklyn.

Through a program of annual parish taxation, a fund was established to build and support churches and chapels in the poorer sections of the diocese. Under this plan, ten additional mission chapels were built.

Bishop Walsh's goal was to make high-quality Catholic education available throughout the diocese. "A schoolroom for every child," was his motto. After establishing more parishes, Bishop Walsh built additional schools. Within ten years, he increased the number of parochial elementary schools in the Diocese of Trenton from 49 to 89. In 1927 alone, Bishop Walsh established eight new schools. While he was bishop of Trenton, grammar school enrollment increased by over 100 percent. After setting up stricter standards of study for Confirmation, he gave the children verbal examinations before confirming them.

Bishop Walsh also increased the number of parochial high schools from 5 to 20. In addition to establishing the new high schools, he improved the quality of existing ones by adding new classrooms, science laboratories, cafeterias, libraries, and gymnasiums.

Shortly after his arrival in Trenton, Bishop Walsh saw the need for organizing the Mount Carmel Guild in the diocese. On January 6, 1920, the guild was formally inaugurated, and within three months it had 600 members. Through the guild's Americanization Department, prominent Catholic citizens were enlisted to give a lecture series. Visits to homes and prisons were made through the Adult Reform Department. Sunday schools were run by the Catechetical Department. Members of the Physical Relief Department visited and gave relief to families in need. In addition, appropriate cases were handled by the guild's Probation Department and the Juvenile Reform Department.

Under the auspices of the Mount Carmel Guild, the first Parent-Teacher Association was formed in Trenton. Five years later, in response to the growing number of PTAs in other communities, Bishop Walsh established the Diocesan Council of Parent-Teacher Associations.[1,2,5]

Higher education was not neglected in the bishop's long-range plans. The motherhouse of the Sisters of Mercy of North Plainfield housed a novitiate, an academy, and the College of Mount St. Mary's. Because of overcrowding at the North Plainfield site, the bishop and the sisters agreed that the college needed a separate location.

When Georgian Court, the beautiful 200-acre Lakewood estate of George Jay Gould, son and heir of railway magnate Jay Gould, went on the market, the sisters and Bishop Walsh became interested. Lakewood, a small town nestled in the pines of south-central New Jersey, had once been a winter resort for many wealthy and famous people.

With a college in mind, Bishop Walsh visited the estate. He toured the Gould Mansion, where he admired the huge frieze of the Canterbury Pilgrims, the carved and gilded furniture, and imported marble. He walked through the formal gardens, marveled at the white marble fountains, and inspected the tennis courts and golf course.

Then the bishop visited the Casino, a huge recreational complex, which provided Gould and his sports-minded friends a place to exercise in inclement weather. Bishop Walsh recognized that the enormous tan-bark ring, which Gould had used as an exercise run for polo ponies, could easily be adapted for both indoor collegiate sports and concerts. The Casino included a swimming pool and numerous rooms that could be used as dormitories.

The bishop and the sisters agreed that the Gould estate could successfully be adapted to a women's college. Under the bishop's guidance, the Sisters of Mercy purchased the estate with funds raised through a diocesan campaign.

In 1924, the College of Mount Saint Mary's was officially moved to Lakewood. Although the sisters initially proposed to rename the college St. Thomas in honor of the bishop's patron saint, Bishop Walsh declined. Acquiescing instead to a request from the Gould family, the sisters agreed to retain the original name of the estate. Georgian Court is now on the National Register of Historic Places.[3,12] (In 1992, Sr. Barbara Williams, R.S.M., president of Georgian

Court College, said that "throughout the years the sisters completed payment on the mortgage and then repaid the loan they received from the diocese."[10])

The problems of many immigrants living in Trenton were similar to those in Buffalo and other industrial cities. Detached from society by language, hundreds of immigrants, especially Italians, were unable to get jobs.

In an earlier effort to resolve the problem in his own parish, Monsignor Aloysius Pozzi, founding pastor of St. Joachim Church, in Trenton, went to Italy in 1910 seeking nuns to staff his new parish school. He was especially interested in the Religious Teachers Filippini (Maestre Pie Filippini).

The Pontifical Institute of the Religious Teachers Filippini was founded in 1692, when (Saint) Lucy Filippini of Corneto, Tarquinia, and Cardinal Mark Anthony Barbarigo opened schools in Montefiascone, Italy, for "the Christian education of young ladies." Although the dynamic Lucy was only 20 years old, the cardinal appointed her the mother superior. As the reputation of the schools spread, more were opened, and at the time of Lucy Filippini's death in 1732, 52 schools had been established.

When Monsignor Pozzi first approached Mother Rosa Leoni, superior general of the Religious Teachers Filippini, regarding his plan, she responded that it was impossible to spare any sisters for a mission to the United States.

Undaunted, the monsignor took his case directly to Pope Pius X. The Pope subsequently issued orders to the mother general to send five sisters of the Religious Teachers Filippini to Trenton. (A large picture of Pius X, which hangs in the present motherhouse in Morristown, bears an inscription and his blessing on the pioneer sisters who came to America.)

After a two-week transatlantic crossing, the first group of Italian nuns arrived in Trenton on August 17, 1910, and were greeted by a marching band accompanied by over 1,000 parishioners. On September 3, the sisters, who didn't speak any English, opened the school doors to 133 children in kindergarten and first grade.

When the sisters first saw their makeshift convent, they were appalled. There was scarcely any furniture, and the straw mattresses on the rusty beds were alive with insects. The building had no heat, and during cold weather, the sisters had to break through the ice of the holy water font in order to bless themselves. To earn enough money for food, they were forced to supplement their meager pittances by sewing and embroidering after school hours.

In the midst of continuing hardships and confusion, the discouraged sisters asked permission to return to Italy. But the pastor, by appealing directly to Rome, gained time. The sisters stayed, albeit reluctantly.

Three days after Bishop Walsh's installation as bishop of Trenton, Sr. Ninetta Ionata, M.P.F., the nuns' young superior in America, met with him. When the new bishop conversed with her in fluent Italian, she immediately felt at ease but told him that the mother general had already given the sisters permission to return to Italy. As she explained the problems the sisters had encountered since coming to Trenton, she showed him a copy of the community's constitution. After a study of the documents, the bishop made an official visit to the Trenton convent.

While acknowledging the validity of their complaints, Bishop Walsh recognized the sisters' enormous potential to help the diocese's immigrant Italians. In order to counter their imminent recall to Rome, the bishop sent a cable to the superior general of the Religious Teachers Filippini in Rome: THE GOVERNMENT FORBIDS DEPARTURE. The superior general was uncertain whether the "government" was civil or ecclesiastical. The bishop did not volunteer an explanation, and the sisters remained in the United States.

In order to Americanize and enlarge the American community of the Religious Teachers Filippini, the bishop needed a suitable site for an American motherhouse. The twenty-acre Fisk estate, which overlooked the Delaware River and was located near Trenton, became available. Although the property was ideal, the bishop lacked the funds to acquire it.

Through Monsignor Fox, an appointment was made for Bishop Walsh to meet James Cox Brady, a wealthy New York financier who was not then a Catholic but was eventually received into the church. When he walked into Brady's office, Bishop Walsh announced candidly that he was there to ask for money. If the financier had time to hear his story, Bishop Walsh would tell it; if not, the bishop would not waste the businessman's time. Brady told him to sit down. In his forthright manner, the bishop outlined why the estate was needed for the sisters. The financier, impressed with Bishop Walsh's candor and business acumen, donated $50,000 for the purchase of the Fisk property.

Later, Brady donated $1000 a month for five years to be used for the upkeep of the motherhouse. In his will, he left the same amount, in perpetuity, to the community.

In addition to preservation of the magnificent paneling, chandeliers, and other exquisite furnishings, the mansion was remodeled for use as a motherhouse. After an additional purchase of thirty-five adjoining acres, the river frontage eventually extended 2,500 feet.

In memory of the benefactor's wife, Victoria Mary Perry Brady, the motherhouse was called "Villa Victoria." By papal decree, Villa Victoria was declared the first motherhouse of the Religious Teachers Filippini in America. Among the 15,000 people present at the May 22, 1921, dedication ceremony were Mother Rosa Leoni and twenty young sisters who arrived from Rome to join the original American group.

Pope Benedict XV granted Bishop Walsh the jurisdiction to direct and govern the Religious Teachers Filippini in this country. Under the bishop's supervision, balanced meals and proper medical care were provided to maintain their health. To encourage regular exercise, the athletic bishop personally taught many groups of religious life aspirants how to play baseball.[4]

In order to prepare the sisters as teachers, Bishop Walsh devised a comprehensive program of academic studies, including an intensive course in English. The Sisters of Mercy, other religious, and members of Trenton's Catholic laity assisted in the ambitious program. To gain teaching accreditation for their high school and normal school, the sisters were sent to Georgian Court College, as well as other colleges, to pursue undergraduate degrees.

A high school and a normal school were established at Villa Victoria along with a novitiate, a postulancy, and a juniorate. (The juniorate provided, without charge, academic and religious training for girls of high school age who felt that they had a vocation. After graduation, they were under no obligation to enter the convent.)

The high school was initially staffed by the Sisters of St. Francis of Glen Riddle, Pennsylvania, who were affiliated with Immaculate Conception High School in Trenton. By 1928, when the state board of education granted a separate charter to Villa Victoria High School, there were enough college graduates from the Religious Teachers Filippini to staff the school themselves.[3,6]

Music continued to be important in the bishop's life. A frequent attendee at the opera and symphony, he made certain that music was also an integral part of the Villa's curriculum. Sister Mary Beatrice, a member of the Order of the Sisters of Mercy of North Plainfield, joined the team of Professor and Mrs. Nicola A. Montani of Philadelphia to head the music department. Under their experienced guidance, many of the young sisters developed into excellent music teachers. Eventually, Villa Victoria's musical programs brought considerable prestige to the school. In addition, Sister Beatrice established an outstanding music department at Georgian Court College, where the annual concerts gained national acclaim.

Between 1922 and 1928, four additional schools staffed by the Religious Teachers Filippini in America were inaugurated in the Diocese of Trenton: St. Joseph's, Hammontown; St. Mary's of Mt. Virgin, New Brunswick; St. James, Trenton; and Most Holy Rosary, Perth Amboy. There was also one each in New York and Baltimore.

Bishop Walsh's long-range plan was to fully Americanize the Religious Teachers Filippini. In 1922, at the bishop's urging, thirty-four Italian-born members of the order became American citizens. Bishop Walsh also encouraged vocations among young Italian-American women. Occasionally, he personally recruited them.

One sister who entered the juniorate at Villa Victoria and remained to become a religious recalled an occasion when Bishop Walsh visited her family in Trenton. Although she was then only 8 years old, the bishop asked her if she would like to become a sister. She later acknowledged that the seed for her spiritual vocation was planted at that time.[4]

Bishop Walsh's mission to help Italian immigrants and bring high-quality education to their children resulted, in many instances, in the revival of their faith.

In 1925, the San Alfonso Retreat House at West End was opened. A few years earlier, the Redemptorist Fathers had purchased the former summer home of Nicholas Brady as a summer and rest home for the community. With Bishop Walsh's support, its use was expanded to offer retreats for laymen during the summer months.

On March 2, 1928, Pope Pius XI selected Bishop Walsh to succeed the Most Rev. John J. O'Connor as bishop of Newark. Reaction to the news of his transfer was similar to that in Buffalo when he was named bishop of Trenton.

An editorial in the *Trenton State Gazette* of March 8, 1928, read:

> It is not easy for Trenton to rejoice over the great honor that has come to Right Reverend Thomas J. Walsh who has been Bishop of the Catholic Diocese of Trenton for ten years . . . When Bishop Walsh goes to his new and larger field of labor, Trenton will lose a valuable citizen and his Church an inspiring and deeply spiritual leader . . . The record of accomplishment established by Bishop Walsh during the ten years of his service . . . is one which would have done credit to a lifetime.

The *Trenton Evening Times* editorial of March 8, read:

> From the civic as well as the religious point of view, Trenton will suffer a great loss in the removal of the Right Reverend Thomas J. Walsh to the Bishopric of Newark. For the past decade, he has exerted a vital

influence upon the life of this community. It is inevitable, therefore, that the joy of his many friends over his advancement to a larger field of endeavor should be tempered by a deep and sincere regret that the well earned complement to the Bishop's spiritual leadership and executive capacity involves the termination of his Trenton career . . . Newark is to be congratulated upon securing the services of this eminent leader.

Although honored by his appointment to the See of Newark, on March 10 Bishop Walsh expressed his appreciation of the cooperation he had experienced in Trenton:

> I am pleased, honored, and gratified in my promotion to the great city of Newark as an expression of approval of my administration of the important Diocese of Trenton. All my official accomplishments in Trenton were the achievements of this holy, capable, loyal, responsive, kind and united priesthood, sisterhood, brotherhood and people. I know I am fortified and consoled in the knowledge that I will find in Newark the same qualifications, dispositions, sentiments, and perfect relationship which graced and gladdened my episcopal life in Trenton.

A series of farewell luncheons, receptions, and dinners were held before his departure to Newark. Speakers at the Community Testimonial Dinner, which was sponsored by the Chamber of Commerce, included former Governors Edward C. Stokes and Harry Moore. Governor Moore said that Bishop Walsh would always be remembered in Trenton "because he lived here and labored here and left an impression on the hearts and lives of its people, the fine influence of which will long endure."

On April 26, 1928, Bishop Walsh returned briefly to St. Joseph's Cathedral in Buffalo to assist at the episcopal consecration of his successor in Trenton, the Most Rev. John J. McMahon. On May 19, 1928, when Bishop McMahon was installed in St. Mary's Cathedral, Trenton, Bishop Walsh delivered the sermon. He said:

> The Diocese of Trenton is prosperous spiritually and financially. The Diocese of Trenton is rich in institutions; in a clergy, regular and secular, unsurpassed for obedience to authority, zeal for souls, and sacred scholarship; in hundreds of holy, capable, and loyal religious brothers and sisters teaching and serving in its schools and institutions; in a faithful, docile, and generous Catholic laity; and in a fair-minded, good-willed, and sympathetic non-Catholic people.

(Rt. Rev. Monsignor Maurice R. Spillane, LL.D., who had been Bishop McFaul's secretary, served as chancellor of the diocese and secretary to the bishop under Bishop Walsh. He was also rector of the Church of St. Mary of the Lake, Lakewood, until Bishop Walsh's successor, Bishop McMahon, appointed him vicar-general of the Diocese of Trenton and the fourth rector of St. Mary's Cathedral, Trenton. Upon the death of Bishop McMahon in 1932, Monsignor Spillane served as administrator of the diocese until the installation of Bishop Moses E. Kiley, D.D., in 1934.)

The news of Bishop Walsh's transfer to Newark caused some anxiety among the Religious Teachers Filippini in Trenton,

and Bishop Walsh, after deciding to transfer the motherhouse to the Newark diocese, purchased Tower Hill, a beautiful estate on the outskirts of Morristown. The new motherhouse was originally called "Villa Lucia," in honor of Lucy Filippini, the order's foundress, for whose beatification and eventual sainthood Bishop Walsh worked tirelessly.

The record of Bishop Walsh's accomplishments in the Trenton diocese preceded him to his new post. He was without peer as a diocesan administrator. His efforts in directing the parochial school system and in social work in the Trenton diocese were known throughout the country. During his decade in Trenton, Bishop Walsh, builder and innovator, was also the shepherd whose flock dramatically increased.

On May 1, 1928, Bishop Walsh was installed as the fifth bishop of Newark. His Eminence, Patrick Cardinal Hayes, archbishop of New York, presided at the ceremony in the unfinished Cathedral of the Sacred Heart, Newark. There were about 4,000 in attendance, including 15 bishops, many monsignori, and 1,000 priests.

Bishop Walsh quickly established in Newark many of the same programs that he organized in the Diocese of Trenton. The Conservation of the Faith was modeled on the program he began in Trenton. Twenty-eight Mount Carmel Guild Centers, which ministered to the poor, were started. He also supervised educational and recreational improvements at Seton Hall College and founded the Diocesan Institute of Sacred Music under the direction of Professor

Montani. The Catholic Youth Organization was sponsored in every parish of the diocese. Bishop Walsh conducted a broad building program, which included schools, churches, convents, rectories, mother-houses, colleges, and hospitals.

Within a few weeks of his installation as the bishop of Newark, Bishop Walsh visited Immaculate Conception Seminary in Darlington. The seminary, which was founded by Bishop James R. Bayley, has had several homes. In 1854, Bishop Bayley purchased a farm in Madison, where he hoped "to open a college in which the young men of the diocese who give signs of a vocation to the priesthood will be trained."

Four years later, Bishop Bayley decided to transfer Seton Hall College closer to Newark and "to unite to it a theological school . . ." A property in South Orange, consisting of 66 acres, was purchased. In 1862, the bishop sent his first diocesan report to the Holy See and referred to the seminary as being in its second year. (Seton Hall was named for Bishop Bayley's aunt, St. Elizabeth Ann Bayley Seton.)

By 1926, as both the college and the seminary grew, a Darlington estate of 1,100 acres was purchased for a separate, expanded seminary. The following year, the seminary at South Orange was closed, and the seminarians were sent to Darlington.

In 1928, following his first pontifical visit to Darlington, Bishop Walsh approved a budget for current repairs and expenses. Because the estate's manor house did not have adequate living quarters for the growing number of seminarians, Bishop Walsh engaged an architect to draw plans for a new seminarians' residence. However, before the end of 1929, the Seminary Fund was exhausted and a building campaign fell far short of the estimated operating expenses. During the Great Depression, when the nation's economy collapsed, plans for the seminary were scrapped.

By 1935, after the economy improved, Bishop Walsh announced that fresh plans were being drawn for the seminary. A building campaign to cover the architects' estimate of costs realized $1,679,348. On September 26, 1937, Bishop Walsh laid the cornerstones for the Seminary Church of Christ the King and the seminarians' residence (later known as Walsh Hall). By the beginning of the next academic year, both buildings were completed. Later, after becoming archbishop of Newark, he continued to oversee the scholastic reorganization of the seminary's curriculum.[7,8,9]

(In 1984, the seminary returned to the campus of Seton Hall University in South Orange. Archbishop Peter L. Gerety authorized the sale of the Darlington property and the seminary's move back to the urban campus. It was his conviction that "seminarians should not be isolated from the real world but should have direct contact with the intellectual and social community of the university.")[11]

On April 30, 1928, the day before his installation as bishop of Newark, Bishop Walsh arrived at his residence on the campus of Seton Hall College. He told students that it was his intention to give a great deal of attention to Seton Hall. In fact, he became

Seton Hall's greatest booster, overseeing both its physical development and its scholastic rise. He was a vigorous rooter at sports events and, with no apologies, he often urged students at other colleges to transfer to Seton Hall.

Although Seton Hall was indeed special to the bishop, he was also a faithful overseer of the religious communities of sisters in the Newark diocese. During a visit to St. Elizabeth's Convent, College and Academy in Convent Station, he saw that larger quarters were needed to accommodate the aged and infirm Sisters of Charity. Within three years, St. Anne's Villa was dedicated. To encourage vocations, a juniorate was established at Convent Station.

Juniorates were also established in the motherhouse of the Benedictine Sisters in Elizabeth and of the Sisters of St. Dominic in Caldwell. In 1933, the juniorate that was started for the Religious Teachers Filippini at Villa Victoria was moved to the new motherhouse in Morristown. As their founder in the United States, Bishop Walsh continued to maintain close ties with the teaching order.

Among the numerous new buildings erected under his direction were a new chancery office in Newark, a motherhouse

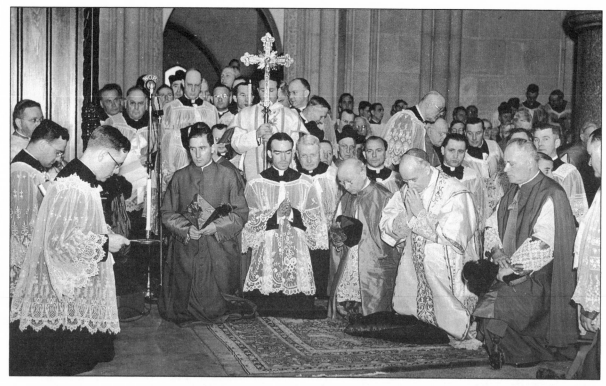

The Most Reverend Thomas Joseph Walsh, wearing skullcap, kneels in prayer during the impressive and solemn ceremonies in the new Cathedral of the Sacred Heart, Newark, April 27, 1938, at which he was elevated to archbishop of the newly created See of Newark. Thousands witnessed his installation, among them scores of high dignitaries of the Roman Catholic Church.

of the Sisters of Christian Charity in Mendham, and many churches. But new schools were again at the forefront of Bishop Walsh's long-range program. In 1931, at the dedication of St. Andrew's School, Westwood, he said, "I'd rather lay the cornerstone of one Catholic school than lay the cornerstone of ten Catholic churches."

In 1928, Bishop Walsh dedicated a remodeled Newark church for the benefit of Spanish-speaking and Portuguese-speaking Catholics. In 1930, he established two parishes for members of the black communities in the diocese. They were the Queen of Angels Church in Newark and the Church of Christ the King in Jersey City. In 1935, he personally baptized the 1,000th convert from the Queen of Angels Church.

In 1930, Bishop Walsh promoted the reopening of St. Peter's College, Jersey City. The Jesuit-administered college had remained closed since 1918, after World War I.

Because of New Jersey's increasing Catholic population, Newark was raised to the status of archdiocese. On December 10, 1937, Bishop Walsh was appointed its first archbishop. The installation ceremony was held on April 27, 1938, in the still unfinished Sacred Heart Cathedral of Newark. His Eminence, Patrick Cardinal Hayes, archbishop of New York (of which the Province of Newark had been a part), performed the installation ceremony. More than 6,000 people crowded into the cathedral, in which pews had not yet been installed, to witness the service.[12]

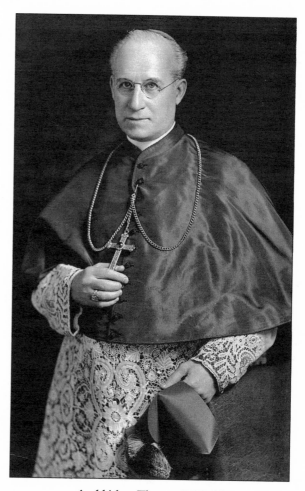

Archbishop Thomas J. Walsh

In his new role, Archbishop Walsh continued to expand the parochial school system and to build more parishes.

On January 27, 1940, the 40th anniversary of the archbishop's ordination to the priesthood, Sister Ninetta announced that Villa Lucia would be known in the future as "Villa Walsh." It was the highest honor that the Religious Teachers Filippini could give to their American founder who had helped so many Italian Americans.

Shortly before the Japanese attack on Pearl Harbor on December 7, 1941, the archbishop wrote to all the priests of the archdiocese, inviting them to contribute to the spiritual welfare of the armed forces by volunteering for service as chaplains. Archbishop Walsh led special prayer services for peace and participated in numerous campaigns for the support of war victims.

During his lifetime, Archbishop Walsh received numerous religious and civil honors. In 1913, he was awarded an honorary Doctor of Laws degree by St. Bonaventure's College. In 1922, he was made assistant at the pontifical throne by His Holiness, Pope Pius XI. In 1921, he was given the title of commandership of the Order of the Crown of Italy and in 1926, the honorary commandership of the Order of Sts. Maurice and Lazarus was bestowed on him by the Royal Italian government. In 1929, in recognition of his work for Newark's Spanish/Portuguese colony, King Alfonso XIII of Spain made him a knight commander of the Royal Order of Isabelle the Catholic.

On June 6, 1952, two years after the celebration of his golden sacerdotal jubilee, Archbishop Walsh died at the age of 78. Two days after his passing and five days before the Solemn Requiem Mass and burial,

November 1946, Villa Victoria Academy, Trenton. From left to right: Sr. Katherine Jonata; Sr. Assunta Crocenzi, treasurer of the Religious Teachers Filippini; Mother Teresa Saccucci, mother provincial; Archbishop Thomas J. Walsh; Mother Ninetta Jonata, superior of the community in the United States, who became mother general of the worldwide order; Sr. Carolina Jonata, music director at Villa Victoria; and Sr. Carmelina Mugnano, principal of Villa Victoria Academy. Srs. Katherine and Carolina Jonata, who were sisters, were also Mother Ninetta Jonata's cousins.

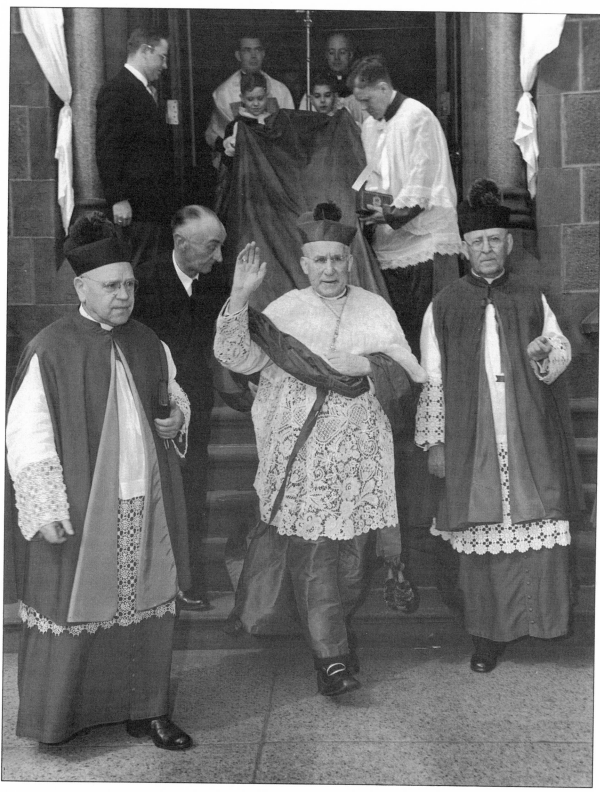

Archbiship Thomas Walsh leaving old St. Mary's Cathedral.
At his right is Rev. Msgr. Maximilian F. Wujek. At his left is Rev. Msgr. Linus A. Schwarze.

THIRD BISHOP: THOMAS J. WALSH

Seton Hall commencement exercises were held. The entire academic procession of administrators, faculty, graduates, and numerous visitors filed through his official residence to pay their last respects to their friend, Archbishop Thomas Joseph Walsh.

An earlier editorial tribute (*Trenton Sunday Times-Advertiser,* March 11, 1928), which had marked Bishop Walsh's departure from Trenton, was especially applicable at his death: "One may well recall at this parting hour what was said of Sir Christopher Wren, architect of the famous St. Paul's: 'If you seek his monument, you have but to look around.' "

REFERENCES

1. *The Most Reverend Thomas Joseph Walsh, S.T.D., J.C.D.,* by Reverend Joseph H. Brady, S.T.D., Ph.D., Seton Hall College (published in 1950).

2. Catholic Historical Records, Seton Hall College.

3. History of the Religious Teachers Filippini, Province of Saint Lucy, Villa Walsh, Morristown, New Jersey (from *A Pictorial History of the Saint Lucy Filippini Chapel,* by Margherita Marchione, M.P.F.).

4. Interview at Villa Victoria, Trenton, with Sr. Victoria Dal Corso (April 1, 1991).

5. *Trenton Sunday Times-Advertiser* (October 27, 1929, Part 5).

6. Filmstrip, "Robe of Glory," on the occasion of the 50th Sacerdotal Anniversary of Archbishop Thomas J. Walsh. Religious Teachers Filippini, Villa Walsh, Morristown, New Jersey.

7. Telephone conversation with Monsignor John F. O'Brien, S.T.L., retired vice rector and former member of the faculty, Immaculate Conception Seminary (September 16, 1991).

8. *The Centennial History of the Immaculate Conception Seminary, Darlington, New Jersey,* by Henry G. J. Beck (published in 1962).

9. *The Bishops of Newark, 1853–1978* (prepared under the direction of the New Jersey Catholic Historical Records Commission).

10. Sr. Barbara Williams, president, Georgian Court College (letter of March 2, 1992).

11. Conversation with Archbishop Peter L. Gerety (September 24, 1992, Princeton, New Jersey).

12. Personal recollections of the author. Bishop Walsh, whose official residence was nearby, was a frequent visitor to her family's home in Trenton, New Jersey. Her father, Thomas F. Waldron, a newspaper editor and publisher, accompanied the bishop when he toured the Gould estate in Lakewood, New Jersey, prior to its acquisition as a women's college.

The author was present at Sacred Heart Cathedral, Newark, New Jersey, when Bishop Walsh was installed as the first archbishop of the Newark archdiocese.

When the author's class graduated from Georgian Court College, Archbishop Walsh returned to confer the diplomas.

CHAPTER SEVEN

FOURTH BISHOP: JOHN J. McMAHON 1928~1932

BY FATHER EUGENE M. REBECK

WHEN THE MOST REV. John J. McMahon took his first vacation after coming to the Diocese of Trenton in August of 1928, it was to Rome. He said the vacation was made possible by the excellent condition in which his predecessor, the Most Rev. Thomas J. Walsh, had left diocesan affairs.[1] Though Bishops Walsh and McMahon were close friends, each had a different charisma that they brought to the Diocese of Trenton, and each one left the diocese richer for his presence and ministry. Perhaps the editorial of the *Trenton Evening Times* marking the passing away of Bishop John J. McMahon best sums up the personality of the fourth bishop of Trenton. It states that he was a man of "spiritual devotion, greatness of soul, and gentleness of manner and tireless, self sacrificing labor under great physical difficulties for the temporal and eternal welfare of those who came under his charge."[2]

The way that many people today wonder what impact the legacy of Pope John XXIII or Pope John Paul I would have had on the church had they had longer pontificates, we also wonder what impact a longer episcopacy of Bishop John J. McMahon would have had on the church of the Diocese of Trenton, had he lived longer.

"Bishop McMahon's spiritual leadership was augmented by his abilities as an organizer and administrator, and his broad vision, exemplified in his modern ministry to youth, the high value which he placed on well-supervised activities for youth, and the competency he had in directing diocesan affairs despite economic hardships of those years. Throughout his episcopacy, the qualities that work for religious advancement were always evident."[3]

John J. McMahon was born September 27, 1875, in Hinsdale, New York, the third of nine children born to Martin and Margaret McMahon. His higher education began in 1893, when he entered St. Bonaventure College at Allegany, New York, where he completed a four-year college program in three years and received his bachelor's degree summa cum laude.

After spending a year studying theology at St. Bonaventure Seminary, he was chosen to complete his studies at the Urban College of the Propaganda. On May 29, 1900, he was ordained in St. Peter's Basilica, in Rome, Italy.

When he returned to Buffalo, he served in various parishes, in addition to serving as superintendent of Catholic Schools of the Diocese of Buffalo. In 1906, he was named pastor of Our Lady of Mount Carmel Church on Buffalo's waterfront, becoming the first American-born priest to be chosen as pastor of an Italian parish in the diocese. This role of "parish priest" was the part of ministry that Bishop McMahon cherished most.

When he was assigned, in 1908, to establish the new St. Mark's Parish in North Buffalo, there were only thirty-two Catholic families in the area. In 1928, when he left for Trenton, the parish was a thriving community with a new church, school, and rectory. It was also distinguished by a stone tower, built in 1926 as the first memorial in the United States to the promulgation by the Holy Father of the universal Feast of Christ the King.

John J. McMahon was not only a competent administrator and good shepherd. He was also a person of tremendous education who possessed many natural gifts and

Bishop John J. McMahon

talents as well. He enjoyed particular facility with languages, becoming fluent in Latin, Greek, Hebrew, Spanish, French, and German. He delivered sermons in twenty different Italian dialects during his career. His hobbies included the study of archaeology, which took him to the grave of Tutankhamen, in the Valley of Kings near Thebes, as a member of the first party to visit the tomb with the consent of the British government. In addition to his more serious hobbies, his avid love of sports in all forms would eventually benefit the youth of the diocese where he would become bishop.

This gifted priest of the Buffalo diocese was to become a gift to the Diocese of Trenton. When Bishop Thomas J. Walsh was appointed bishop of Newark in the

Bishop McMahon's coat-of-arms.
"We are renewed by grace."

spring of 1928, His Holiness, Pope Pius XI, appointed as his successor Rev. John J. McMahon, pastor of St. Mark's, Buffalo. It should be noted that Bishops Walsh and McMahon experienced a close friendship that began in their seminary days. Both were sports enthusiasts and rival handball players while they attended St. Bonaventure College. The journey of their lives seemed to place them in similar situations throughout their church ministry. From their common schooling, they advanced to positions as officials in the Diocese of Buffalo. When Bishop Walsh was qualifying for his doctorate in sacred theology in Rome, Bishop McMahon took on Bishop Walsh's responsibilities as chancellor, in addition to maintaining his own roles as superintendent and

pastor. It is also interesting that both felt special concern for the wave of immigrants coming to the United States and were especially devoted to work among the Italian immigrants. The ultimate similarity is, of course, Bishop McMahon's succession of Bishop Walsh as bishop of Trenton.

On April 26, 1928, Bishop McMahon was consecrated at St. Joseph's Cathedral in Buffalo, New York. The Most Rev. William Turner of Buffalo was consecrator, with the Most Rev. Thomas J. Walsh of Newark and the Most Rev. Edmund F. Gibbons of Albany as co-consecrators. On May 10, 1928, Bishop McMahon was installed as the fourth bishop of the Diocese of Trenton in St. Mary's Cathedral by His Eminence Patrick Cardinal Hayes, archbishop of New York. The three-hour service was witnessed by the prelate's 78-year-old mother, Margaret McMahon.

As Bishop McMahon took on the duties of the diocese, he reappointed the Right Reverend Monsignor John H. Fox as vicar-general as well as rector of the cathedral. The Right Reverend Monsignor Maurice Spillane was reappointed as chancellor, and Reverend Thomas U. Reilly was reappointed as secretary. All three had served, in their respective capacities, under Bishop Walsh.

In the short period of less than four years that he was ordinary of the Trenton See, Bishop McMahon was successful in directing the construction of new buildings for Morris Hall Home for the Aged at Lawrenceville and of an annex at St. Michael's Children's Home in Hopewell. Those years were not times of prosperity, because the nation was in the grip of the Great Depression. However, diminished funds do not diminish needs, and in 1931, Bishop McMahon undertook the project of bettering these two important institutions of the diocese. At that time, there were 432 children at St. Michael's Orphanage, and 127 aged residents at Morris Hall.

As Bishop McMahon stated in his letter to the priests and people of the diocese, "Many more are knocking at their doors and crying for shelter and for food, but 'there is no room for them in the inn.' These helpless souls are crying to us for assistance, and we cannot turn a deaf ear to their prayers."[4]

And so, due to overcrowded conditions and needed improvements at both facilities, Bishop McMahon began a campaign to raise money for the addition of a separate unit at St. Michael's Orphanage, which would cost $175,000, and for similar improvements and additions at Morris Hall, which would cost $137,000. Both institutions served a tremendous need within the diocese, and the bishop and his predecessor regarded improvement of these facilities as answering the call of the Gospel "to care for the least of His brethren."

Bishop McMahon's untiring interest in the youth of the diocese and in their direct religious supervision caused him to conceive of and construct Camp McMahon, a diocesan camp for boys, during the years 1929 and 1930. The camp, with 135 acres of field and woodland and a 10-acre lake, was on a beautiful site in the sloping and picturesque hills of Hunterdon County, 5

miles from Clinton, New Jersey. The camp opened in 1930, and its first season promised a good future. It provided an all-encompassing program, consisting of spiritual exercises (including daily Mass), athletic activities, and educational opportunities. The project was "wrapped in the warmth of the happy hearts of those who have trodden the pathways of the Camp in its first and successful season of 1930."[5] The camp was a great haven for young boys, especially during the particularly harsh years of the Depression.

Many pictures of the camp show a tremendous number of boy campers who came from families of means in addition to those who came from poor families. Some parents were able to pay; others who could not received an award from their parish.

The camp and its quarry-stone cottages on the lake must have been a welcome relief for the boys, who for a few short weeks were able to leave the reality of the Depression behind. It was here that they could enjoy the benefits of the outdoors, summer sports, good food prepared by chefs from the preparatory school in Lawrenceville, and nourishing produce—the fresh vegetables and fruit from local farmers. The camp offered a truly rich, sorely needed, and most enjoyable experience for boys from the urban areas of the Trenton diocese. Though the camp functioned for only a few seasons, it constitutes the basis of good memories and stories that many campers still relive and tell to this day.

One of those campers was Jim Pippitt, who recalls the sacrifice his parents made in

Outside the dining hall

Boxing ring at the camp

Lake at Camp McMahon

Bishop McMahon at Camp McMahon

order to scrape up twenty-five dollars for his two weeks at the camp. He also remembers Bishop McMahon's great interest in the camp, which was evidenced by the bishop's many visits. Mr. Pippitt fondly reminisces about the many friends he had at the camp among his elementary school peers, and especially among the counselors, some of whom were high school students and some, seminarians preparing for priesthood. He recalls seeing the seminarians in a rowboat in the middle of the lake, praying the Divine Office.[6]

The same interest and concern for youth, which had led to the conception and construction of Camp McMahon, prompted Bishop McMahon to form the Diocesan

Basketball Leagues and establish the annual track meets in Trenton. These programs had a long, successful history in the Diocese of Trenton.

The gentle shepherd of Trenton took on the administration of the diocese with great care and concern for his flock, with visits to the many parishes in his diocese. He particularly enjoyed visits to parishes for Confirmation celebrations and for the blessing and dedication of parish buildings whose construction had begun under the guidance of his predecessor, Bishop Walsh, that were completed during his own term. Due to the Depression, as well as his short term as bishop, not many new parishes were started. However, records indicate that Bishop McMahon established Holy Savior Parish in Westmont in December 1928, officiated at the laying of the cornerstone of the four classrooms and new addition of the Church of Our Lady of Perpetual Help in Maple Shade in 1929, and established the parish of St. Theresa of the Infant Jesus in Runnemede as an independent parish on June 22, 1929. It had formerly been a mission of St. Rose of Lima in Haddon Heights. He also incorporated St. Thomas More Church in Old Bridge on November 21, 1932.

Though he was innovative and forward thinking in his episcopal ministry, he still reflected the caution of most Catholic clergy when it came to ecumenical matters. When he was asked to give his endorsement to the project of erecting a memorial chapel to be called the Cathedral of the Air, at Lakehurst, New Jersey, he sought out the advice and counsel of Cardinal Patrick Hayes, archbishop of New York. This chapel was to be nonsectarian and used by various religious groups, including Catholics, for weekly Divine Worship. The cardinal replied, "If specific provision is made for Catholic service, that is, if a Catholic altar is separated and reserved from possible use by another religious body, it might justify your giving approval and support. Otherwise, I do not see how you, the Bishop, could *publicly* endorse the project."[7] However, the cardinal went on to suggest that the local pastor or chaplain be given permission to show some interest.

Seeing the need for clearer diocesan guidelines and directives, Bishop McMahon, with the vote of his consultors, promulgated a decree on November 25, 1930, that there was to be a diocesan synod and that preparation for it would begin immediately.

The special preparatory commissions that were set up by the bishop worked diligently on all that was assigned to them, and they made their opinions known in writing to the general commission, which consisted of the diocesan consultors and other persons selected from the secular and religious clergy. The general commission, after further deliberation, drew up the materials in the form of statutes.

Bishop McMahon announced that the Third Synod was to be held on June 9, 1931, the 50th anniversary of the formation of the Diocese of Trenton.

A few days before the synod, all the priests, both secular and religious, of the entire diocese gathered together to express their opinions, to suggest, and to make corrections, additions, and withdrawals to the proposed statutes. This meeting was presided over by the Right Reverend Monsignor Maurice R. Spillane, vicar-general.

The day of the synod began with the celebration of a Solemn Pontifical Mass in honor of the Holy Spirit. Once the decree concerning the synod had been read, the names of synod officials were promulgated and the Profession of Faith was said. Finally, after various approvals and necessary dialogue, the statutes of the synod were read and approved by the bishop. Along with the published statutes of the Third Diocesan Synod were appendixes, which dealt with various aspects of diocesan policy. Issues addressed included the Diocesan Clerical Fund for the support of priests actively involved in the diocese and chancery regulations reminding priests that all business with the chancery must be transacted by mail because "The telegraph or telephone should not be used except in unforeseen and urgent cases." Dispensation procedures and special permissions were also covered. There were instructions on civil marriage regulations and church music guidelines (reminding priests of the "White List" of music approved by the church), as well as regulations of canonical visitation and legal directions for church corporations in the state of New Jersey. The approval and the bishop's benediction concluded the Third Synod of the Diocese of Trenton.[8] It would be some sixty years before another synod would be

called for the Diocese of Trenton, under the guidance and direction of the Most Rev. John C. Reiss.

Bishop McMahon suffered from poor health, which forced him to reduce his episcopal duties for the three years prior to his death, approximately three quarters of his brief episcopate. The illness prevented him from being as active in church and civic affairs as he would have liked to be. As a *Trenton Times* editorial stated at the time of his death:

> It cannot be truthfully said that Bishop McMahon was well known to the people of the City of Trenton. Since coming to Trenton he has made few public appearances aside from those connected with the performance of his religious duties and those arising from his deep interest in recreative activities for children. It is not to be assumed that he was aloof or indifferent to community affairs. In fact, Bishop McMahon was a friendly, cordial man with a community interest that was naturally active and intense. The almost constant impaired condition of his health made it necessary that he restrain his desire for participation in civic affairs.[9]

Shortly before Thanksgiving of 1932, after having had two serious operations at St. Francis Hospital in Trenton, Bishop McMahon decided, while visiting in Buffalo, to have his brother, a physician, examine him. Following a brief return to his duties in Trenton, Bishop McMahon entered Mercy Hospital in Buffalo shortly before Christmas. On December 31, 1932, Bishop McMahon died in the hospital at the age of 57, as he was preparing to celebrate Mass.

The funeral was held Tuesday, January 3, 1933, in St. Mark's Church in Buffalo, his former pastorate. That night his remains were taken to Trenton, where he lay in state at the cathedral. On Wednesday, a special Mass was celebrated with thousands of schoolchildren attending. On Thursday morning at 10:30, the Most Rev. Thomas J. Walsh, bishop of Newark, celebrated the solemn Pontifical Requiem Mass. Burial was in St. Mary's Cemetery in Trenton.

To those who remember him, Bishop McMahon was a man of compassion, love, and tenderness—a truly gentle man. In his sermon at the funeral Mass, Bishop Gibbons of Albany described him as "always a profoundly spiritual man, extremely conscientious in the performance of his priestly duties, a model to his fellow priests and a source of deep edification to this faithful people. . . . He was as humble and docile as a child . . . but showed force and character when entrusted with responsibility."[10]

The Church Universal was touched deeply by the short reigns of Pope John XXIII and Pope John Paul I, and the church of Trenton was deeply touched by the all too short reign of a gentle shepherd, Bishop John J. McMahon.

REFERENCES

1. *Trenton Evening Times*, Thursday, January 5, 1933.
2. *Trenton Evening Times*, Saturday, December 31, 1932.
3. *Trenton Evening Times*, Tuesday, January 3, 1933.
4. Letter of the Most Reverend John J. McMahon, Bishop of Trenton, to Priests and Laity Concerning the Building Campaign for Morris Hall and St. Michael's Orphanage, Archives of Our Lady of Angels Convent, Ashton, Pennsylvania 19014.
5. *Camp McMahon, the Ideal Camp for Catholic Boys.*
6. Personal reflections of Mr. James Pippitt.
7. Letter of the Most Reverend John J. McMahon, Bishop of Trenton, to His Eminence, Cardinal Patrick Hayes, and Cardinal Hayes's response. Archives of the Archdiocese of New York, Saint Joseph's Seminary, Dunwoodie, Yonkers, New York 10704.
8. *Synodus Diocesana Trentonensis Tertia Acta Synodi.*
9. *Trenton Evening Times*, Tuesday, January 3, 1933.
10. The Most Reverend Edmund F. Gibbons, D.D., Bishop of Albany, *Burden of the Episcopate*, eulogy offered at the Funeral Mass of the Most Reverend John J. McMahon, Bishop of Trenton.

CHAPTER EIGHT

FIFTH BISHOP: MOSES E. KILEY 1934~1940

BY FATHER VINCENT E. KEANE

ONE OF THE DISTIN-guishing and distinctive characteristics of the Most Reverend Moses Elias Kiley was that he was very tall, approximately 6'6". One of his first requests after becoming bishop of Trenton and looking over the episcopal residence at 901 West State Street was for a longer bed. When he came back to Trenton as archbishop of Milwaukee for Bishop Griffin's Funeral Mass in 1950, his miter fell off on his way out as he passed under the main door of St. Mary's Cathedral. Bishop Kiley was not only tall but also an imposing and patriarchal (even in name) figure who spoke with a powerful and low-pitched voice. In spite of his noble appearance, however, he was a humble man with no frills.[1]

Bishop Kiley served as the bishop of Trenton for only six years before being elevated to the metropolitan Province of Milwaukee as archbishop on January 1,

1940, succeeding Archbishop Samuel Stritch, who had been transferred to Chicago. Bishop Kiley's tenure in Trenton was not an easy one, however, especially as far as finances were concerned. The country was in a severe economic depression, and Bishop Kiley had to keep a watchful eye on the finances of the diocese, which at that time was under the complete jurisdiction of the bishop.[2] Bishop Kiley himself took no salary because of the critical financial situation in the diocese. During his earlier years in Trenton, some seminarians had had to be turned away because the diocese was not able to finance their seminary education. There was much cost cutting across the board.

Another special challenge that faced the bishop occurred when the Diocese of Camden was carved out of the Diocese of Trenton on December 10, 1937. Newark was also made an archdiocese, and the Diocese of Paterson was established. This was a significant event, an immediate result of this diocesan split being an acute shortage of

Procession of Funeral Mass for Bishop Wm. Griffin, January 5, 1950. From left to right: Most Rev. Moses E. Kiley, archbishop of Milwaukee; Most Rev. Francis P. Keough, archibishop of Baltimore; Rev. Joseph W. McLaughlin, crossbearer; Rev. Msgr. Thomas U. Reilly, vicar-general. Left of Archbishop Walsh, Rev. Lawrence Horvath. Behind Archbishop Walsh, altar boy Edward U. Kmiec, future bishop.

priests, which Bishop Kiley addressed by recruiting additional priests from certain other dioceses that had an oversupply of clergy.

YOUTH

Moses Elias Kiley was born on November 13, 1876, in Margaree, Cape Breton, in Nova Scotia, the son of John and Margaret McGarry Kiley, both of whom were natives of Ireland. Moses was one of seven children. His uncle, Mrs. Kiley's brother, Moses McGarry, was a Holy Cross priest. His brother Myles was later ordained in 1900 as a priest in the Archdiocese of Boston. Moses Kiley received his early education in the public schools of Baddeck, Nova Scotia.

John Kiley, Moses' father, was a farmer, and the family was serious, hardworking, and sober minded.

When Moses was 18, his family moved to Somerville, Massachusetts, where, to earn money to further his education, he worked as an errand boy, as a department store floorwalker, and in a carriage factory founded by his brothers.

SEMINARY

Exactly when Moses Kiley first began to think about becoming a priest is a matter of speculation. Undoubtedly, his uncle who was a priest and his brother who was ordained a priest when Moses was 24 had some influence on his decision. At any rate, in 1903, at 27, Moses Kiley began his studies for the priesthood at St. Laurent College in Montreal, where his uncle, Reverend Moses McGarry, C.S.C., was president of the college. Here he first met the saintly Brother Andre, C.S.C., founder of St. Joseph's Oratory on Mt. Royal in Montreal, who was beatified in 1982. During summer vacations, Moses was a trolley car motorman in Boston.

In 1906, Kiley entered St. Mary's Seminary in Baltimore, where, a year later, he received a B.A. degree magna cum laude. He was then sent to complete his studies for the priesthood at North American College in Rome. He earned a Ph.D. degree in 1909 from the Dominican-operated St. Thomas University, and two years later, the degree of Doctor of Sacred Theology (S.T.D.) from the Propaganda University in Rome.

Apparently, while he was still in Baltimore, Kiley came into contact with Archbishop James E. Quigley of Chicago, who invited him to study for the Archdiocese of Chicago. He realized that if he applied for incardination into his home archdiocese in Boston, he would have to serve as a curate for a long time before being named pastor in that priest-rich archdiocese. So he decided to accept Archbishop Quigley's offer and move west. The years that he spent in Rome had imbued in Kiley a deep-seated conservatism and loyalty to Rome that manifested itself in many ways, especially when he became bishop of Trenton and then archbishop of Milwaukee. For his part, he always cherished a special devotion to Pope St. Pius X, who was pope when he studied in Rome. Kiley considered himself to be thoroughly Roman in thought and outlook, and he took pride in his Roman education.[3]

PRIESTHOOD

Moses E. Kiley was ordained a priest at the age of 34, on June 10, 1911, for the Archdiocese of Chicago, in the Basilica of St. John Lateran in Rome by Patriarch Giuseppe Cezpetelli. After his ordination, he was assigned to Chicago's South Side, where he served as an assistant at St. Agnes Church from 1911 through 1916.

In 1916, Father Kiley began his work with the homeless men in Mission of the Holy Cross (still in existence and now also called Cooke's Manor), which he established in an old warehouse adjacent to the Des Plaines Street Police Station, located within St. Patrick's parish in Chicago. At times, the mission slept and fed more than 250 men. Father Kiley was known as "the janitor" of the Archdiocese because he wasn't afraid to work in overalls. Two years later, he was named by Archbishop Mundelein as the first director of Associated Catholic Charities for the Archdiocese of Chicago. In 1921, he helped to found Misericordia Maternity Hospital in Chicago. In the spring of 1924, Father Kiley was named a papal chamberlain by Pope Pius XI, with the title of very reverend monsignor in recognition of his singular accomplishments.

SPIRITUAL DIRECTOR AT NORTH AMERICAN COLLEGE

The year 1926 proved significant for Monsignor Kiley. Monsignor Edward Mooney, who was later to become cardinal archbishop of Detroit and who had been spiritual director of North American College in Rome, was appointed apostolic delegate to India, creating a vacancy at North American. Monsignor Eugene S. Burke of the Archdiocese of Newark (then rector of North American College) nominated Monsignor Kiley, his former classmate, to succeed Archbishop Mooney as spiritual director, undoubtedly with the permission of Archbishop Mundelein. The trustees of the college soon gave their approval to Monsignor Kiley, who was well-known as director of Catholic Charities in the Archdiocese of Chicago. Monsignor Kiley took up his new position

as spiritual director on March 26 of that year.

During the summer of 1926, Monsignor Kiley returned to Chicago as private secretary to John Cardinal Bonzano, who was papal legate to the International Eucharistic Congress held at that time. Upon his return to Rome, he was named a domestic prelate, with the title of right reverend monsignor, conferred by Pope Pius XI.

In addition to his duties as spiritual director, Monsignor Kiley was also appointed American member of the Supreme General Council of the Society for the Propagation of the Faith when Pius XI reorganized that confraternity in 1926. He was also made a consultor of the Sacred Congregation of the Oriental Church in 1929, and in 1930, consultor of the Pontifical Committee of Russia. However, his chief curial job was at the Supreme General Council, a position that in the Vatican at that time made him privy to much that was going on in the Catholic missionary world. He was later to recall, "It was a listening post for the financial problems of dioceses throughout the world, and of course we got the worst problems."[4] North American College was then in the process of acquiring property on the Janiculum Hill in Rome (not far from the Vatican) to build on its new site.

BISHOP OF TRENTON

On February 12, 1934, Gaetano Cardinal Bisletti made a special visit to North American College in order to announce to the gathered seminarians that their spiritual director, Monsignor Kiley, had been appointed bishop of Trenton. Pope Pius XI had personally called Monsignor Kiley to the Vatican two days previously to inform him of the appointment.[5] Monsignor Kiley was consecrated as a bishop in Rome on March 17, 1934, by Raphael Carlo Cardinal Rossi, O.C.D., secretary of the Sacred Consistorial Congregation, with Bishop Walsh, the third bishop of Trenton and then bishop of Newark, and Archbishop Carlo Salotti of Rome as co-consecrators in the American Church of Santa Susanna. Many seminarians from North American College attended and participated in the ceremony. In attendance as well were Monsignor Kiley's brother, Reverend Myles D. Kiley of St. Ann's Church in Gloucester, Massachusetts; Governor A. Harry Moore of New Jersey; Mayor George B. LaBarre of Trenton; and many other relatives and friends. On May 8, 1934, the new Bishop Kiley was installed as the fifth bishop of Trenton by Patrick Cardinal Hayes, archbishop of New York, at St. Mary's Cathedral in Trenton.

Bishop John McMahon, the fourth bishop of Trenton, died on December 31, 1932, so the diocese had been without a bishop for about a year and a half. At that time, the diocese as well as the rest of the country was in the midst of a severe economic depression, and it was known that the diocese had financial problems. Therefore, Bishop Kiley had his work cut out for him when he came to Trenton.

He first addressed the financial problems of the various parishes in the diocese and made certain recommendations to the pastors. The diocese had embarked on a massive building campaign under Bishop Thomas J. Walsh (1918–28) and was experiencing problems paying off those debts and bank loans, which amounted to approximately $10 million. Bishop Kiley helped to renegotiate some of the loans made to the parishes from a high rate of 6 percent interest to a manageable 3 percent with the help of both the Reconstruction Finance Corporation (a government agency) and Father Richard T. Crean, who was the vice-chancellor at that time.

Bishop Kiley separated Trenton Cathedral High School into a boys' division (later called Trenton Catholic High School) and a girls' division (later called Cathedral High

Bishop Moses E. Kiley

School), much to the dismay of some people. He requested that all the pastors inaugurate Confraternity of Christian Doctrine programs within their individual parishes.

A special 25th Anniversary Mass celebrating Bishop Kiley's ordination to the priesthood took place at St. Mary's Cathedral in Trenton on June 10, 1936, followed by a Silver Jubilee Luncheon at the Stacy-Trent Hotel. One of the masters of ceremonies at that Jubilee Mass was Father John Joseph Carberry, then a priest on loan to Trenton from the Diocese of Brooklyn. Bishop Kiley knew Father Carberry while he was a student at North American College and when he did graduate work in Rome. When Bishop Kiley came to Trenton, he needed a priest with a doctorate in canon law in the Chancery Office and secured the permission of Bishop Molloy of Brooklyn (Father Carberry's home diocese) for him to come to Trenton for a period of five years. Father Carberry, who later became archbishop of St. Louis and a cardinal in 1969, served as secretary to Bishop Kiley at that time.

In December of 1937, the six southernmost counties of the diocese were split off from Trenton to become the newly established Diocese of Camden. This reorganization was, generally speaking, unanticipated and a surprise to many. The Diocese of Trenton was left with 8 counties and 212 diocesan priests, 62 religious order priests, 121 parishes, 70 parishes with parochial schools, and a Catholic population of 210,114.[6] The Trenton diocese lost 75 diocesan priests, 49 parishes, 30 parochial schools, and a Catholic population of 105,246 to the new Camden diocese. Trenton also was deprived of its vicar-general, Monsignor Maurice R. Spillane, who was a pastor in Atlantic City, now part of the new diocese. Bishop Kiley had to recruit new priests for the diocese due to the split. He accomplished this by recruiting priests from New England dioceses and at least 50 new seminarians. Bishop Kiley kept a relatively low profile while bishop of Trenton, allowing Archbishop Walsh of Newark to take the lead in reordering the dioceses in New Jersey.

Only two parishes were established during Bishop Kiley's tenure in Trenton: St. Anne's in Lawrenceville (1937) and Our Lady of Sorrows in Mercerville (1939), which had been a mission of St. Anthony's, Trenton.

Unfortunately, many of the papers from Bishop Kiley's tenure in Trenton were destroyed during the Chancery Office and cathedral fire in March 1956. However, it was apparent that Bishop Kiley had proved himself to be an "exceptional administrator" of the Diocese of Trenton.[7]

ARCHBISHOP OF MILWAUKEE

Bishop Kiley was appointed archbishop of Milwaukee on New Year's Day of 1940. A farewell dinner with more than 200 clergy in attendance was held for him at the Stacy-Trent Hotel, Trenton, on March 24, 1940. During the event, Archbishop-Elect Kiley was referred to as "a charming companion, an inspiring example and an incomparable bishop" by priests of the Trenton diocese. Monsignor Thomas U. Reilly, the vicar-general, presented the bishop with a golden vessel of chrism to be used in the administration of the sacrament of Confirmation and which was inscribed with the words "To Archbishop Kiley, from the priests of Trenton, 1940." At the event, Bishop Kiley told the Trenton priests, "This parting comes just at the time when we are getting things at that satisfactory stage we all desire. For whatever has been accomplished here . . . after God's help . . . the major portion of the credit is yours, not mine." When Bishop Kiley left Trenton for Milwaukee, an edito-

rial in the *Trenton State Gazette*, dated March 26, 1940, stated:

> By reason of a retiring disposition and an intense preoccupation with the spiritual and temporal responsibilities of his office, Bishop Kiley had not become well-known to the people of Trenton during his six years of labor here. To a greater degree than any of his predecessors, some of whom have taken an active part in civic affairs, he has remained aloof from public life, devoting himself exclusively to his exacting duties as a spiritual leader. Necessarily, Trenton loses by the departure of Bishop Kiley from this city today. Without ostentation, but with zeal and devotion, wisdom and centering energy he has labored in behalf of a better community and has accomplished great good.[8]

Most Rev. Moses Elias Kiley, archbishop of Milwaukee, in front of St. Mary's old cathedral with Msgr. James E. Harding to his left and Fr. Lawrence Horvath to his right.

A special ten-car train that included 1,000 honorary escorts, comprising priests from Trenton as well as Milwaukee and religious and laypersons carried Archbishop-Elect Kiley to Milwaukee. The train stopped briefly at Chicago so that the archbishop-elect could say Mass at the Holy Cross Mission that he had founded 24 years previously for homeless men. Archbishop Kiley was installed as archbishop of Milwaukee by the Most Rev. Amleto Giovanni Cicognani, apostolic delegate to the United States, on March 28, 1940, in the Gesu Church because the Cathedral of St. John was being reconstructed due to a fire in 1935.

Among his many accomplishments while serving 13 years as archbishop of Milwaukee were the remodeling of St. Francis Seminary and the remodeling of Pio Nono High School into St. Francis Minor Seminary. He

Bishop Kiley's coat-of-arms.
"That I may be faithful."

Second Vatican Council (1961–65). Archbishop Kiley had been in poor health with heart problems for some time. His Pontifical Requiem Mass was said on April 21 by the Most Rev. Roman R. Athielski, auxiliary bishop of Milwaukee; the eulogy was preached by Samuel Cardinal Stritch, archbishop of Chicago and predecessor of Archbishop Kiley in Milwaukee. The casket was then taken down to the bishops' crypt beneath the baptistery, where Archbishop Moses E. Kiley was laid to rest in the cathedral he loved so dearly.

The motto found in the Archbishop's coat-of-arms reads, "That I may be faithful." Archbishop Kiley embodied that motto, for he was most faithful to his people whether in Trenton or in Milwaukee. He remained faithful to his church and his God to the end.

REFERENCES

1. Phone interview on October 26, 1992, with Bishop James J. Hogan, retired bishop of Altoona-Johnstown.
2. The New Code of Canon Law (1983) requires a diocesan finance council and a finance officer (see Canons 492–494).
3. Interview with John Cardinal Carberry, archbishop emeritus of St. Louis, on August 6, 1991.
4. "At 72, the Archbishop Is Working Hard," *Milwaukee Journal*, November 14, 1948.
5. *Catholic Herald Citizen* (Milwaukee), March 30, 1940.
6. *The Official Catholic Directory*, P. J. Kenedy & Sons, 1938.
7. *Brooklyn Tablet*, April 18, 1953.
8. *Trenton State Gazette*, March 26, 1940.
9. "The World of Moses E. Kiley," *Salesianum*, Fall/Winter 1985.

also completed rebuilding St. John's Cathedral. According to one of his biographers, Fr. Steven M. Avella, "By all accounts, Moses E. Kiley was the 'Rock': tough, hard, impenetrable, a man often more feared than loved by priests and laity alike. Simply put: Kiley was, in many respects, the product of his environment."[9]

Archbishop Moses E. Kiley died on April 15, 1953, at the age of 76, in St. Mary's Hospital, Milwaukee, after a long illness. He actually died in the arms of Bishop Albert Meyer of Superior, Wisconsin, while Meyer was reciting the prayers for the dying. Bishop Meyer was subsequently named to succeed Archbishop Kiley as archbishop of Milwaukee. Later he became the cardinal archbishop of Chicago and one of the American hierarchy's leading spokesmen at the

SIXTH BISHOP: WILLIAM A. GRIFFIN 1940~1950

BY FATHER GREGORY D. VAUGHAN

O N MAY 18, 1940, THE Most Rev. William Aloysius Griffin was appointed to the Trenton See by His Holiness, Pope Pius XII. On July 23 of that year, he was installed as the sixth bishop of Trenton in Saint Mary's Cathedral, Trenton, by His Excellency, the Most Rev. Thomas J. Walsh, archbishop of Newark and metropolitan of the Province of New Jersey. The first native of New Jersey to become bishop of Trenton, Bishop Griffin was born in Elizabeth on November 20, 1885, the son of John and Catherine Lyons Griffin.

Graduating from Saint Patrick's High School, Elizabeth, in 1903, he entered Seton Hall College, South Orange, where he was president of the class of 1907. He studied for the priesthood at Immaculate Conception Seminary, which was then in South Orange, and was ordained by the Most Rev.

John J. O'Connor, fourth ordinary of Newark, on August 15, 1910. After his ordination, Father Griffin was made a member of the faculty of Seton Hall, serving as headmaster at Bayley Hall. Later, he was assigned to the faculty of Seton Hall High School, and subsequently he was appointed professor of Latin and philosophy at the college.

On December 23, 1924, Bishop O'Connor appointed Father Griffin as the first director of the Society for the Propagation of the Faith in the Diocese of Newark, an office he retained for over fourteen years. For a time, he served as administrator of Saint John's Church, Newark, and later as administrator of Saint Augustine's Church, Newark. In January of 1929, the then Bishop Walsh appointed Father Griffin to the pastorate of Saint Michael's Church, Jersey City. On August 10 of the same year, His Holiness, Pope Pius XI, raised the energetic young priest to the rank of papal chamberlain with the title of very reverend monsi-

Bishop Griffin's coat-of-arms.
"Show yourself to be a mother."

gnor. He remained in charge of Saint Michael's Church until his consecration as auxiliary bishop of Newark in Sacred Heart Cathedral, Newark, on May 1, 1938. At this time, Bishop Griffin was also named rector of Immaculate Conception Seminary in Darlington.

Upon Bishop Moses E. Kiley's promotion to the Archdiocese of Milwaukee, the Diocese of Trenton became vacant, and it was to this see that Bishop Griffin was called in the spring of 1940. At his installation in July, the closing paragraphs of his address outlined the Roman Catholic Church's remedies for the evils in the world.

We shall have no other remedy to offer but the remedy of personal moral integrity . . . of the sanctification of wholesome family life and all social relations, of the Christian education of youth, of the dignity of honest labor, of genuine patriotism . . . of concord and "peace with justice" among nations.

What few people in the cathedral realized that day was that during the next decade, Bishop Griffin would work tirelessly to apply these same remedies to the needs he found within the Diocese of Trenton.

A significant influence in the thinking of Bishop Griffin was the philosophy held by the National Catholic Rural Life Conference, of which he was a member, as well as its national president in 1946. The purpose of the Rural Life Bureau was to call the attention of both urban and rural people to the truth that the well-being of the nation rested, to a large measure, on a healthy agrarianism. The bureau regarded the betterment of rural conditions as the starting point in the regeneration of society. It declared that for the full development of the human personality and the greater good of the family, rural living, with its wholesomeness, integrity, and responsibility, was the most desirable mode of life. It also stated that the welfare of the church and the safeguarding of democracy depended on a balance between people in cities and people on the land, giving a 50-50 ratio, rather than the 20-80 ratio of the day.

Bishop Griffin took hold of the reigns in Trenton, and after noting that only Mercer and Middlesex counties could be considered urban in the eight-county diocese, he declared, "We must take Christ to the Catholic people in the rural areas." To this end he expended an abundance of energy, establishing thirty-five parishes within the diocese, a number of them in the agrarian sections of central New Jersey. New parishes were formed in such areas as Baptistown, Basking Ridge, Blairstown, Bradley Gardens, Breton Woods, Bricktown, East Keansburg, Englishtown, Flagtown, Hainesport, Medford, Monmouth Beach, New Market, Seaside Heights, South Bound Brook, South Plainfield, Spotswood, Tuckerton, and Union Beach.

Certain that Catholic rural living was the direction in which he should be leading his people, Bishop Griffin appointed Rev. James S. Foley as director of Catholic Rural Life, so that he might assist him in this major endeavor. The more deeply the two delved into the issues surrounding rural life, the more they were convinced that, for too long, the church in America had been preoccupied with the masses in industrial urban centers, showing little or no concern for the spiritual, economic, and social needs of agrarian centers.

Several priests of the diocese did not share the bishop's view on this matter, questioning the wisdom of establishing so many rural parishes. Undaunted, Griffin remained steadfast in his effort to reach out to the agrarian areas of the diocese. He also realized, however, that extending understanding and sympathy toward a rural apostolate would take time, as the majority of priests, sisters, and brothers ministering in the diocese were urban born and trained. To help alter this situation, Bishop Griffin was influential in conducting training programs at the Rural Life Conventions and school programs during the summer months.

Stemming from his involvement with the Rural Life Bureau, Bishop Griffin came to understand that the life span for the average city parish, from its founding to well beyond its ascendency, was hardly fifty years, and the elements of evident decline usually set in long before the half-century mark. On the other hand, he saw the rural parish that is short-lived as the rare exception.

> Rural parishes may have a greater need for financial assistance in the beginning, but the investment is small and the material needs so few that money is not only not wasted but actually pays rich spiritual dividends in a more healthy, more vigorous and more enduring Catholic life.

The exalted aim and the well-conceived plan of the National Catholic Rural Life Conference was to get more Catholic people to settle on the land or at least to have one foot in the city and the other in the country. Throughout his term as chief shepherd of the Trenton diocese, Bishop Griffin demonstrated by word and action his commitment to the same aim and plan.

In his establishment of parishes, Bishop Griffin was not so blinded by his concern for the Catholics in agrarian centers of the diocese that he failed to see the needs of minorities living in the urban centers of central New Jersey. Always willing to reach out to those who were calling him, he responded to the blacks, Hispanics, and Portuguese of his flock and established parishes for them in Trenton, Asbury Park, New Brunswick, and Perth Amboy. The religious staffs were often interracial, because Griffin did not want to create the idea that he was an advocate of segregated parishes. His desire was to form interracial parishes, capable of responding to the specific needs of particular minority groups.

A global event that tremendously affected the episcopacy of Bishop Griffin, and the direction his leadership would take in guiding the people of Trenton, was U.S. entry into World War II. Within months of the attack on Pearl Harbor, he set up USO-NCCS clubs (United Service Organizations–National Catholic Community Service) in three cities of the diocese, all of which were adjacent to military reservations. During the five-year period (1942–47) that the Trenton, Long Branch, and New Brunswick clubs were supervised by local parishes, through their parent-teacher associations, well over 2.5 million servicemen took advantage of the hospitality offered by these "homes away from home." In fact, the clubs were so successful that Bishop Griffin was asked by the National Catholic Community Service to reopen the Trenton club in 1948 for the 18,000 soldiers stationed at Fort Dix during the postwar period.

Bishop Griffin also wanted the children of the diocese to be involved in the war effort. He accomplished this by having the Catholic elementary and high schools do their part through the war bond and stamp drive, which had been organized on the state level. This effort enabled the children to raise money for the purchase of jeeps for

Bishop William A. Griffin

the armed forces and, at the same time, to feel they were doing something constructive to help those fighting in the war.

As a result of Griffin's passionate pleas for involvement in the war effort, several priests of the diocese expressed a desire to serve as chaplains overseas. Bishop Griffin was very generous with his priestly resources, permitting many of his most talented priests to enter military service. He believed that service to God and country were intertwined, and what better way for this message to be expressed than by the example of service chaplains. Even when the war ended, he allowed his priests to remain in the

Reserves, so they could continue to minister to the needs of citizen-soldiers.

As the war was drawing to a close, Bishop Griffin became concerned with the peacetime welfare of service people upon their return home. He stressed the necessity for those on the home front to plan for the arrival of their soldiers, especially in terms of the soldiers' job placement and their reestablishment in civilian life. He felt strongly that to ignore such matters was to fail in the role all played in the war effort and to act contrary to the American ideals of wisdom, liberty, and peace.

After the war, Griffin oversaw the settlement of European Displaced Persons and the placement of European orphans within the diocese. In cooperation with an appeal from the National Catholic Rural Life Conference, he was able to encourage New Jersey farmers to offer employment to many displaced persons and to open their homes to the orphans. Never limiting himself to the boundaries that marked the Trenton diocese, Bishop Griffin was also influential in his personal appeals for the Bishops' Fund for Victims of War in Europe and the Orient. This fund assisted the millions of refugees and expellees starving in such countries as Germany and Japan. Because of the keen interest Griffin demonstrated in this matter, the Diocese of Trenton always exceeded its set goal throughout the postwar years.

A deep, personal commitment that Bishop Griffin brought with him, from his years in the Archdiocese of Newark, centered on the apostolic work of the Society for the Propagation of the Faith. He was not only the first director of the society while in Newark but also its national treasurer for a time, as well as a member of the society's national board of directors. With this as a background, it was only natural that during his episcopacy in Trenton, Bishop Griffin never missed an opportunity to stress to his priests, religious, and laity that there were over one billion people living in the world who had not heard the name of Jesus Christ. He urged them to accept their Christian responsibility to the missions by supporting those who had dedicated their lives to bringing the message of salvation to the pagan nations of the world.

Creating a sense of mission-mindedness within the diocese became a major goal for Griffin, and to help him in this project he appointed Rev. Emmett A. Monahan as director of the society for the diocese. They thought the best way they could build up the society was by following two specific guidelines established earlier by Pope Pius XI. One involved the organization of a diocesan-wide membership campaign for the Society for the Propagation of the Faith. In October 1940, Bishop Griffin mandated that parochial units be formed in every parish, so the Trenton branch of the society would be completely organized on a parochial membership basis by Mission Sunday of the following year.

In conjunction with the parochial units, a program to build up the interest of the children in Catholic schools was also planned by the bishop. The program eventually took the form of an annual Catholic Students' Mission Crusade Rally, which within a few short years became extremely popular. By the mid-1940s, the crusade was drawing thousands of young delegates not only from Catholic schools but also from a large number of parish confraternity programs.

The other guideline Bishop Griffin adopted fostered mission aid by encouraging dioceses throughout the country to offer missionary institutes and agencies the opportunity to make parish appeals for the alleviation of their respective mission needs. In turn, Griffin implemented a program called the Missionary Plan of Cooperation, whereby missionary congregations were allowed to appeal in a particular parish on an assigned Sunday during the year. The program was very successful, assisting more than thirty different mission institutes and allowing them a spiritual and material boom they had not experienced in several years.

Much of the success enjoyed by the mission programs of Bishop Griffin had to do with the limited number of appeals he was requesting. Both priests and laity were quite pleased that the number of collections for the missions was no more than two for the entire year. The Propagation of the Faith collection on Mission Sunday and the Missionary Plan of Cooperation appeal on a parish-appointed Sunday were just enough for the laity to appreciate that they were making a positive contribution to the missions but not being overly burdened with a financial responsibility they could not handle.

Pleased with the apostolic response that had taken place in both the parishes and the schools, Bishop Griffin viewed the diocese with satisfaction and pride. He never took even a moment's credit for the increased sense of mission the priests, religious, and laity now possessed but rather always praised his flock for their outpouring of love and generosity.

> We can look with a sense of real satisfaction on the apostolic accomplishments of the past few years and look forward with the genuine confidence that we have laid well the foundation of mission-mindedness, as well as of mission-aid in the diocese. This is true not only in the parishes, but even more especially in the schools. With congratulations and deep gratitude for your generosity, I encourage you to an even greater outpouring of love, if possible, in the years to come.

As a result of Griffin's forwarding of the mission cause during his episcopate, the Diocese of Trenton soon became one of the strongest benefactors of mission work on the East Coast.

Although Bishop Griffin devoted much time and energy to the development of new parishes, the rural life movement, the war and postwar efforts, and the Propagation of the Faith, he also took a deep interest in all parish societies. He organized the Saint Vincent de Paul Society on a diocesan level, as well as the Blessed Virgin Mary Sodality. The Mount Carmel Guild received a great deal of his personal attention, because its desire to foster a spirit of charity through humanitarian and religious care of the needy was a primary concern of the bishop. And the parish units of the parent-teacher association, who had helped him so ably in running the USO-NCCS clubs, were encouraged to continue with the valuable assistance they gave to the education of the young people attending Catholic schools in the diocese.

However, the parish organization that Bishop Griffin was particularly drawn to was the Holy Name Society. Early in his administration, the bishop had organized a campaign to rejuvenate the society within each parochial unit. His goal was to have every Catholic man of the diocese enrolled in the Holy Name. As a member, each man would have as his main priority the formation of a strong prayer life and frequent reception of the sacraments. Bishop Griffin felt that for a man to realize his spiritual potential, he needed the support and encouragement of men who shared similar values. In a word, the bishop believed that, inspired by their membership in a society dedicated to the noblest Christian ideals, good Catholic men could enrich their lives, their families, their communities, and their country.

Knowing that a well-organized Holy Name Society was capable of such inspiration, Griffin labored to carefully build up an organization of "personal interest, long-range planning, democratic discussion, intelligent direction, and specific activities that would not fail to elicit the interest of membership." To properly monitor the development of the units on the parish level, Bishop Griffin established a Holy Name Union, naming Rev. James P. O'Sullivan as spiritual director. The union basically func-

tioned on the diocesan level, bringing all the parochial units together in the spring at a convention in Trenton, and on the county level, calling the parochial units to gather in the fall at a rally in one of four district locations. By augmenting the Holy Name Society on these three levels, the bishop was sure the members would be in a good position to examine themselves in terms of spiritual growth, community service, and social development.

During the mid-1940s, a major social issue in which Bishop Griffin involved the Holy Name Union was that of labor-management relations. He declared that until labor unions were willing to extend their objectives beyond the consideration of wages, hours, and the ironing-out of grievances, it was useless to expect any real and permanent peace in the economic life of America.

> To achieve peace and the industrial progress we all hope for in the near future, labor must have a voice in the management of industry. Labor must form a partnership with management which will guarantee, as a practically working principle, a voice in the management and a reasonable share in the ownership and profits of the business.

Bishop Griffin continually reiterated to the Holy Name Union that union-management cooperation was the crying need of the hour. The need for job protection and a proper living wage as well as the need of the individual worker for self-expression and freedom at work were the economic principles being ignored, and, as a result, the economy of the country was being weakened.

A direct outgrowth of this concern was the Holy Name Labor School, which opened in January 1946 at Sacred Heart School in New Brunswick. Directed by Bishop Griffin and sponsored by the Diocesan Union of the Holy Name, the school was organized to further the cause of good unionism and to promote social justice through education. The program placed emphasis on the dignity of human labor and the rights and duties of labor, management, and government. The school taught both the employer and the employee along Catholic social lines, encouraging the men to recognize that only through labor-management cooperation and copartnership could they achieve reconstruction and lasting prosperity.

Although education in labor-management issues was a valuable contribution to many Catholics living in the Diocese of Trenton, the area of education where Griffin was most influential and forthright centered on the religious education of his flock. His ever-resounding plea to his priests, "*Euntes, ergo, docete, omnes gentes,*" carried with it his heartfelt message that "knowledge of faith meant more than merely believing."

Too often even so-called well-instructed Catholics are content with believing the truths of their holy religion without knowing them. As a consequence, they are not able to give a reason for the faith that is in them. Knowing implies something more personal and practical, more intimate and confidential than believing requires.

With this as his philosophy, Bishop Griffin asserted that it was impossible for one to defend a faith unless one first studied those truths in oneself and in one's relations to others.

Bishop Griffin wanted all his priests, sisters, brothers, and seminarians to "teach" the truths of the Catholic faith to the children and the adults alike in every corner of the diocese. Whether they were living in the city or the country, whether they numbered 500 or 5, it did not matter. The bishop wanted someone to go out to them, so they might be instructed. Particularly worried that families in several rural sections of central New Jersey were not being offered the opportunity to learn about their faith, religious of sixteen different orders were brought into the diocese to assist in this apostolate. Throughout his episcopate, Griffin remained steadfast in this mission, serving as the driving force that propelled the priests and sisters to maximize their skills as teachers.

Naturally, the primary source of religious education was found within the Catholic schools of the diocese, and over ninety parochial institutions of learning existed on the elementary, secondary, and college levels during the 1940s. In promoting Catholic education, Bishop Griffin, along with Rev. John J. Endebrock, secretary of education, encouraged parents to see the schools as extensions of themselves, where the religious training of their children would be further enhanced. Parochial school attendance increased dramatically during Bishop Griffin's time, growing from 22,543 boys and girls in 1940 to 31,541 in 1949. This increase of 40 percent along with a booming birth rate during the postwar years was enough for Griffin to realize the necessity of developing a plan for expansion in the very near future.

A source of religious education that Bishop Griffin believed equally important but also extremely wanting was the Confraternity of Christian Doctrine (CCD) program for Catholic children attending public schools. He found that in the diocese there were quite a few parishes with rather weak catechetical programs and numerous parishes with no catechetical program whatso-

Ordination, March 17, 1945, in St. Mary's Old Cathedral. Left to right: front row: the Revs. Albert Bielen of St. Stephen's Parish, Perth Amboy, NJ; Henry Joseph Burke of St. James' Parish, Red Bank, NJ; John Joseph Churak of Holy Trinity Parish, Perth Amboy, NJ; Francis Xavier Degnan of Our Lady of Mercy Parish, Forest Hills, NY; Thomas Campbell Jones of St. Vincent de Paul Parish, Albany, NY; James Augustus Reilly of Holy Cross Parish, Holyoke, MA; James Morgan Kelly of St. Peter's Parish, New Brunswick, NJ. Second row: the Revs. Frederick James Clancy of St. Rose of Lima Parish, Freehold, NJ; John Alexander Ozorowski of St. Hedwig's Parish, Trenton, NJ; Amadeo Louis Morello of St. Joachim's Parish, Trenton, NJ; Francis Vincent McCusker of St. Francis de Sales Parish, Revere, MA; Earl Anthony Gannon of St. John the Evangelist Parish, Syracuse, NY; Edward William Hughes of St. Joseph's Parish, Belmont, MA. Third row: the Revs. Vincent Arthur Lloyd of St. Ann's Parish, Keansburg, NJ; John Patrick Byrnes of Gate of Heaven Parish, South Boston, MA; John Charles Petri of Sacred Heart Parish, New Brunswick, NJ; Charles Joseph Platt of St. Thomas Aquinas Parish, Brooklyn, NY; His Excellency, the Most Rev. William A. Griffin, D.D.; Edward Joseph O'Connell of Our Lady of Refuge Parish, Bronx, NY; Nicholas Charles Murphy of St. Anthony's Parish, Trenton, NJ.

ever. To counteract this most serious injustice, the bishop appointed Rev. John E. Kelly as director of the Confraternity, and the two of them became devoted to organizing a CCD program that would enlighten by teaching the truths of the Catholic faith and would be expansive by reaching out to all areas of the diocese.

To help accomplish this goal, Bishop Griffin set up fourteen new parochial catechetical centers and developed eight regional catechetical centers. Several centers were established in the agrarian sections of the Trenton See, where there were the fewest religious education programs. As already stated, he brought in sixteen different orders of religious nuns to assist in the staffing of these centers. Many of the sisters traveled to the catechetical centers from the schools in which they taught; others, stationed in regional convents, moved from center to center. Bishop Griffin was also most persuasive in encouraging the laity to become catechists, as their help became necessary once there were more than 18,000 children seeking religious education in the late 1940s.

To supplement the work of the CCD in the diocese, Bishop Griffin established Religious Vacation Schools. Fearing that the weekly hour during the winter months was not a sufficient amount of time in which to instruct the children, the bishop hoped the more concentrated effort offered by the vacation schools would give children a better chance to learn about the truths and values they needed to lead a good Catholic life. The program, which was mandated in every parish and conducted by the priests, sisters, and seminarians, was extremely well received. By 1947, there were over 10,000 CCD children in the diocese attending the summer program.

Always wishing to improve on already existing programs, Bishop Griffin created two satellite projects to further the religious training of the children both in Catholic schools and in CCD classes. The first project involved two radio programs entitled "Catechism Comes to Life." One program was broadcast every Sunday morning from Trenton, and the other was on Sunday evening from New Brunswick. During each, there was a quiz in which children, chosen to represent their school or confraternity, were questioned on religious topics. The student who correctly answered the most questions was the winner, and he or she could return for the next broadcast. The format also included a brief talk by the priest-moderator, as well as music from local schools to open and close the half-hour program.

The second project consisted of two diocesan-wide religion contests held each year in the spring. Student representatives from all the Catholic schools, both secondary and elementary, competed in one contest, and elementary-school-age students from the numerous confraternities competed in the other. Winners were determined and announced in both contests, and they usually received an award from the bishop at a presentation ceremony in Trenton. The pupose of these satellite projects had been to motivate the boys and girls to study their faith, and the ensuing popularity of the broadcasts and the success of the contests indicated to everyone involved that both projects were most definitely fulfilling that purpose.

Bishop Griffin was also interested in the spiritual well-being of young men and women who had advanced to the college level of their education. He established a Newman Club in three secular colleges in the Trenton area, namely, Rider College, Trenton State College, and Trenton Junior College. The main thrust of these clubs was to gather the Catholic students enrolled in the college so they might share in some religious instruction, direction, and activity. Other major endeavors Griffin worked very hard to bring about were the establishment of Maryknoll Junior College in Lakewood and Saint Joseph's Mission House in Bordentown.

As to the religious education of adults, the bishop believed that Catholic men and women should indulge themselves in sound Catholic literature. He was a staunch advocate of the Catholic Press, and he felt that a Catholic weekly paper in every home was the best means for adults to stay well informed on theological issues and safely guided in moral values. Bishop Griffin stressed that whereas the Sunday sermon, the catechetical instruction, and the parish society meeting might supply the assistance one needed to approach many of life's problems, only regular reading of Catholic literature would propel that same one to lead a

more intelligent and more aggressive Catholic life.

Although the religious education of his flock was a priority throughout his episcopacy in Trenton, Bishop Griffin was a wonderful humanitarian as well as spiritual leader and teacher. His love of children was evident in his promotion of youth activities, particularly in the formation of Boy Scout and Girl Scout troops, in all the parishes of the diocese. And he always had a special affinity for children who had been orphaned or neglected, working with untiring zeal to make Saint Michael's Orphanage in Hopewell a home where each boy and girl would receive all the love to which he or she was entitled.

His works of mercy were also well-known in Trenton, as he spearheaded hundreds of campaigns and all types of programs to benefit the handicapped, the sick, the poor, and the aged. The bishop especially wanted to build up, and make more affordable, the institutions and hospitals associated with the diocese, so that people living on low incomes would be better able to receive the proper care they had a right to as God's children. And whenever Bishop Griffin was able to find a little time for himself, if he was not spending it with the children at Saint Michael's, he usually could be found visiting the aged and the infirm at Morris Hall in Lawrenceville or at Saint Joseph's Home in Beverly.

A final labor of love to which Griffin gave his enthusiasm and energy was the Apostolate of Vocations. This project, established in February 1941 and placed under the direction of Rev. Michael P. McCorristin, had for its purpose the fostering of vocations to the priesthood and religious life through prayer. To promote this apostolate, the bishop ordered a laminated plaque, with a prayer for vocations displayed on it, to be distributed to every church in the diocese. He told his priests they should encourage their parishioners to recite the prayer and should personally approach any young aspirants they might recognize in the parish. As a result of these prayers and the influential work of both priests and religious during Bishop Griffin's episcopate, there were over 100 men ordained to the diocesan priesthood and many others to the priesthood in various religious orders. In addition, 1,100 women were consecrated to God in religion.

With all his activity and involvement in the diocese, few people knew that for over two years Bishop Griffin had been ill and under a doctor's care. Then, on December 26, 1949, Griffin suffered a severe cerebral hemorrhage while visiting his sister, Mrs. Frank J. Curral, in Elizabeth. As the Holy Year 1950 was being ushered in, Rev. Alfred J. G. Curral, a nephew, administered the Sacrament of Extreme Unction to his uncle, and, shortly after, the bishop moved on to his heavenly reward at 2:36 a.m. At the time of his death, the bishop of the Trenton diocese was 64 years old.

The life of the Most Rev. William Aloysius Griffin was rich in the fruits of deep religious devotion and of ceaseless energy in the promotion of the spiritual welfare of his people. His work came to a sudden end, unfortunately, while the distinguished bishop was still at the height of his service to the over 300,000 Catholics who looked to him for guidance in matters that pertained not only to their faith but also to their daily life. Bishop Griffin added great luster to the roster of illustrious ordinaries of the Diocese of Trenton who had gone before him. He was a most gifted scholar and an able administrator, but he was above all a zealous, apostolic pastor, the kindly father of his flock, a truly priestly priest.

On speaking about Griffin and his dedication to the Diocese of Trenton, the Most Rev. Bartholomew Eustace, bishop of Camden, perhaps expressed it best when he spoke at the Solemn Pontifical Mass of Requiem.

Being by nature a kindly man, he found the sterner tasks more difficult. He was very just, moreover, and the ways of justice are rarely easy ways. But Bishop Griffin did not shrink from the difficult. He was neither deterred by fears, nor moved by flatteries. Above all else, he was zealous. It was his very zeal that hastened his demise. His thoughts were always on his diocese, his action always directed to the furtherance of its interests. For his diocese, he was completely ambitious. For himself, he was completely unambitious. . . . I can most truthfully say that I have never known, in my now lengthening experience, a more faithful bishop.

SOURCES

Catholic News (New Jersey Section)
Inquirer
Trenton Evening Times
Trentonian
Written Reflections of:
    Most Rev. John C. Reiss
    Rev. Msgr. Henry S. Bogdan
    Rev. Anthony L. Capitani
    Rev. Msgr. Bernard C. DeCoste
    Rev. Msgr. John J. Endebrock
    Rev. Msgr. James S. Foley
    Rev. Msgr. Joseph A. O'Connor
    Rev. Gerard S. Sloyan
    Rev. Msgr. Leonard R. Toomey
    Rev. Msgr. Thaddeus Wojciehowski

APPENDIX

Letters of Bishop William A. Griffin

BISHOP'S HOUSE
901 WEST STATE STREET
TRENTON 8, NEW JERSEY

Feast of the Holy Name of Jesus,
1948.

Dearly Beloved of the Clergy and the Religious:

Under separate cover I am sending you in the same mail with this letter the program of our "CRUSADE OF PRAYER" to be followed during the entire year of 1948, and afterwards if necessary, in conformity with our Christmas message to the people of the Diocese seconding the wishes of Our Holy Father expressed in his Encyclical, "Optatissima Pax," dated December 18, 1947.

You will note that, except for minor changes, there is nothing in the program which has not been given to our people during the past several years as an incentive to their devotion in various circumstances. Now, however, because of the critical year that lies ahead and especially because of urgent pleas of the Vicar of Christ, these separate devotions are assembled in the one program for the "CRUSADE OF PRAYER" which, if conscientiously carried out in practice, will make our people more deeply conscious of the critical situation we are facing in this year of decision. Thus more and more of them will listen to the promptings of the Holy Spirit and the "CRUSADE OF PRAYER" will gather momentum with each succeeding day. With a view to the active and sustained participation of the children in the "CRUSADE OF PRAYER" in accordance with the deliberately expressed wish of the Holy Father, copies of the program are being forwarded to the Superiors and Principals of the schools and catechetical centers.

The program is printed on stiff cardboard, to be hung in both sacristy and community room for reference as needed from time to time. Our sermons for the Forty Hours' Devotion, for the Holy Hour on the First Friday, and for the Lenten course could very appropriately derive their inspiration from the program for the "CRUSADE OF PRAYER," with emphasis on frequent and daily Communion, the nine First Fridays, the five First Saturdays, the Family Rosary, etc., etc.

Our own fervent prayer and personal zeal will prove to be the real measure of genuine success this time next year in the Diocese-wide "CRUSADE OF PRAYER" urged upon all, and particularly upon children by the Sovereign Pontiff for this critical, unpredictable year of 1948.

Begging of all our priests and religious this prayerful, zealous co-operation as an earnest of divine blessings upon them and their charges during the coming year, I remain,

With sentiments of deep gratitude,

Sincerely yours in Christ,

✠ WILLIAM A. GRIFFIN,
Bishop of Trenton.

FEAST OF ST. PETER'S CHAIR,
January 18, 1948.

THE CATHOLIC PRESS

Dearly Beloved of the Clergy, the Religious and the Laity:

February is CATHOLIC PRESS MONTH. Its observance affords the opportunity of taking stock every year of the amount of correct information and of sound knowledge we have acquired through the safe and secure medium of the Catholic Press.

No longer is it a matter of what Catholics CAN DO for the Catholic Press, but what the Catholic Press IS DOING for the Catholic cause and for every other worthy cause, not specifically Catholic, but contributing to the betterment of mankind.

In these trying days of social, political and religious conflict, Catholics can ill-afford to be ignorant and indifferent in regard to questions, policies and movements that vitally affect their welfare whether for good or for evil. They cannot sit idly by while the enemies of religion are endeavoring to drive a wedge between them and their divinely appointed leaders; while secularism, which is another name for Godlessness, stalks the land in the attractive and plausible guise of progressive knowledge and of civil and religious liberty; while the demon of lust continues to laugh to scorn virginal and conjugal chastity and to condone, sometimes even to extol, in press, motion-picture and radio the exploits of the gangster and the infidelities of people joined in wedlock. It would seem that Satan and the powers of darkness are having a holiday on earth in this post-war era. A sorry picture indeed; the more so when one stops to think that in 1947 there were at least 4,000,000 Catholic families that did not buy a single Catholic book. This one fact alone should make us Catholics hang our heads in shame; for the book we do not read, however good it may be, can do us no good. And the same is true of the paper.

We plead with our people, therefore, to keep themselves well-informed on problems and movements that reach down into their personal everyday life; that enter into the sacred precincts of the home; that change the whole course of education and of the religious training of youth; that enter with sinister purpose into the domain of industrial, political and social relations; that aim deliberately at destroying the very foundation of civil and religious liberty by attacking the Christian way of life in a free America. False prophets still go about the land in sheep's clothing, while inwardly they are ravening wolves feeding upon the fears, the confusion, the panic, and even the despair of well-intentioned souls whom they are leading with some degree of success to temporal and eternal ruin.

In this sad situation the serious obligation rests upon all our Catholic people to keep themselves well-informed on these present-day antisocial problems and movements, so as to meet them intelligently and courageously both for their own welfare and for the welfare of the nation and the world. For this exalted purpose the Sunday sermon and the occasional lecture are certainly not enough. Catholics must read consistently and habitually the kind of literature that will keep them on the alert in guarding the precious heritage of the Faith and the priceless treasure of God-given religious liberty. That is why we have been urging for years: "A CATHOLIC PAPER IN EVERY CATHOLIC HOME" as the minimum requirement for intelligent and articulate Catholicity among those who really appreciate the blessings of their Holy Religion.

In accordance with the custom of years, therefore, CATHOLIC PRESS EXHIBITS will be set up for one week during February at centers convenient for the majority of our people. This year the exhibits, showing the wide variety and extent of Catholic papers, books and magazines, will be held during the week of February 15th to 22nd in twelve regional school centers of the Diocese. These centers are as follows: Trenton, Cathedral Girls High School; Belmar, St. Rose's High School; New Brunswick, St. Peter's High School; Perth Amboy, St. Mary's High School; Phillipsburg, St. Philip and St. James High School; Red Bank, Red Bank Catholic High School; South Amboy, St. Mary's High School; Keyport, St. Joseph's Grammar School; Lambertville, St. John's Grammar School; Mount Holly, Mount Holly Regional Catholic School; Riverside, St. Peter's Grammar School; Lakewood, Georgian Court College.

The Reverend Pastors, the Principals, and the teaching staffs of these school centers spare no pains to make the Catholic Press Exhibits comprehensive and attractive for both adults and children. The Press Exhibits are for all the parishes in their respective regions. I beg all our people, especially the fathers and mothers and the young men and young women in our Catholic families, to heed the request of their Pastors to visit the exhibits and see at a glance the wide variety of Catholic papers, books and periodicals that are available for interested readers; and all Catholics worthy of the name should be interested. Admission is free and nothing is sold at the exhibits. May we hear that the exhibits during Catholic Press Week were well attended, and that all our Pastors and school faculties were gratified at the increased interest in the Catholic Press. Incidentally, here is but one more avenue for the exercise of practical zeal on the part of our Sodalities, Holy Name Societies and other parish organizations dedicated to the advancement of Christian principles and the progress of genuine virtue.

Trusting that serious thought will be given to this message, one of the most important of the year, to the great moral, spiritual and social benefit of our own Catholic people and of those not of our faith, and blessing all who further the Apostolate of the Catholic Press, I remain,

Sincerely yours in Christ,

✝ William A. Griffin,

Bishop of Trenton.

P.S. 1—Reverend dear Father:

On Sunday, February 15th, a Catholic weekly paper—one to each family—is to be given FREE after each Mass, the cost to be taken from the Church treasury. Kindly give sufficient advance notice to the publishers so that the required number of copies will be on hand for distribution.

Note that there are Twelve Press Exhibit Centers. Kindly urge your people and their children to attend the Catholic Press Exhibit in the school center nearest their Parish Church, announcing the convenient hours, afternoon and evening, when the Exhibits will be open. This information can be secured from the Pastor or Principal of the school center. Co-operation among all our Priests and Sisters during Catholic Press Month, and especially during the week of February 15th, will greatly enhance the cause of Catholic reading among our people.

The reading of this Pastoral is to take the place of the regular sermon next Sunday, January 25th, at all the Masses. Thank you.

P.S. 2—Septuagesima Sunday, January 25th, is "Biblical Sunday." Kindly bring the Bible, and especially the New Testament, to the attention of your people. Monsignor Stedman's "My Daily Reading from the Four Gospels" is worth recommending.

W. A. G.

Feast of the Conversion of St. Paul,
January 25, 1949.

Dearly Beloved of the Clergy, the Religious and the Laity:

By time-honored observance FEBRUARY IS CATHOLIC PRESS MONTH. As followers of Christ, we might well ask ourselves to what extent we have in the past taken advantage of this ready-at-hand means of learning to think with Christ and to spread His truth among others; for ourselves and for others we need the Catholic Press in its various forms; we need the Catholic weekly and monthly and pamphlet to keep ourselves well-informed on the momentous events sweeping down on an already distressed world like an avalanche; we need Catholic literature to help us to lead a more intelligent and a more aggressive Catholic life; and we need the Catholic Press to stem the tide of un-Christian and immoral filth in print that steadily flows into too many American homes; in a word, we need the Catholic Press to keep our minds attuned to the mind of Christ. There are worse evils than wars.

At no time more than the present has the obligation weighed so heavily upon Catholics of keeping themselves informed on events seriously affecting their faith, their moral life and their eternal salvation. Logically St. Paul makes clear for us as well as for the Corinthians of his own day that what is now happening to the courageous Cardinal Mindszenty in the Hungary of the twentieth century is a matter of deep concern to everyone professing the Christian faith, whether in Hungary or America or any other part of the world. Certainly by this time well-informed Catholics know that Doctor Michelfelder, an official of the Lutheran World Federation, has denounced the arrest of the Cardinal as "a travesty of justice" and the arrest of the gallant Lutheran Bishop Ordass, who refuses to resign, "as quite the same in all details as the policy" of the Nazi Regime; that the Anglican Archbishop Fisher of Canterbury this week denounced the imprisonment of the Hungarian Churchmen and expressed the sympathy of the Church of England in the "deadly struggle" and "grave assault" which has appeared in Hungary; that finally, this week also the exiled Unitarian Bishop of Hungary denounced the Communist Government of his country and spoke of the Cardinal as "the soul of integrity and honesty, respected by Catholics and Protestants alike, who know that he is innocent."

These facts and many like them Catholics who read their Catholic papers know and discuss intelligently. Catholics who do not read from the proper sources so as to keep themselves abreast of the times not only wallow in the mire of ignorance and indifferentism but do grave spiritual injury to themselves and their fellow-men and become serious obstacles to the progress of Christian civilization. The current situation in Hungary is only one example of apathy among too many Catholics; the imprisonment of Archbishop Stepinac of Yugoslavia three years ago is another. Anti-Christ is abroad in the world taking stronghold after stronghold, while Christians continue to adore the false gods of self-sufficiency and political expediency and social preferment. This is no cry of panic; but in God's Name I beg them to wake up and rout the wolf of apostasy at their very door with a courageous "Begone! Satan." Tomorrow may be too late.

Because we prayerfully desire soon to realize our ambition of "A CATHOLIC PAPER IN EVERY CATHOLIC HOME"—the minimum requirement for informed Catholic opinion on curren events, we respectfully ask our people to attend the Regional Catholic Press Exhibits to be set up during February at convenient centers. This year the Exhibits will be held during the week of February 13th to 20th in twelve regional school centers of the Diocese. These centers, in accordance with custom, have been designated as follows: Trenton, Cathedral Girls High School; Belmar, St. Rose's High School; New Brunswick, St. Peter's High School; Perth Amboy, St. Mary's High School; Phillipsburg, St. Philip and St. James High School; Red Bank, Red Bank Catholic High School; South Amboy, St. Mary's High School; Keyport, St. Joseph's Grammar School; Lambertville, St. John's Grammar School; Mount Holly, Mount Holly Regional Catholic School; Riverside, St. Peter's Grammar School; Lakewood, Georgian Court College.

The Reverend Pastors, the Principals and the teaching staffs of these school centers spare no pains to make the Catholic Press Exhibts comprehensive and attractive for both adults and children. The Press Exhibits are for all the parishes in their respective regions. I beg all our people, especially the Fathers and Mothers and the young men and young women in our Catholic families, to heed the request of their Pastors to visit the exhibits and see at a glance the wide variety of Catholic papers, books and periodicals that are available for interested readers; and all Catholics worthy of the name should be interested. Admission is free and nothing is sold at the exhibits. May we hear that the exhibits during Catholic Press Week were well attended, and that all our Pastors and school faculties were gratified at the increased interest in the Catholic Press. Incidentally, here is but one more avenue for the exercise of practical zeal on the part of our Sodalities, Holy Name Societies and other parish organizations dedicated to the advancement of Christian principles and the progress of genuine virtue.

Trusting that serious thought will be given to this message, one of the most important of the year, to the great moral, spiritual and social benefit of our own Catholic people and of those not of our faith, and blessing all who further the Apostolate of the Catholic Press, I remain,

Sincerely yours in Christ,

✠ William A. Griffin,
Bishop of Trenton.

P.S. 1. Reverend dear Father:

On Sunday, February 13th, a Catholic weekly paper—one to each family—is to be given Free after each Mass, the cost to be taken from the Church treasury. Kindly give sufficient advance notice to the publishers so that the required number of copies will be on hand for distribution.

Note that there are Twelve Press Exhibit Centers. Kindly urge your people and their children to attend the Catholic Press Exhibit in the school center nearest their Parish Church, announcing the convenient hours, afternoon and evening, when the Exhibits will be open. This information can be secured from the Pastor or Principal of the school center. Co-operation among all our Priests and Sisters during Catholic Press Month, and especially during the week of February 13th, will greatly enhance the cause of Catholic reading among our people.

The reading of this Pastoral is to take the place of the regular sermon next Sunday, January 30th, at all the Masses. Thank you.

P.S. 2.

Septuagesima Sunday—"Biblical Sunday" is on February 13th. Kindly bring the Bible, and especially the New Testament, to the attention of your people. Monsignor Stedman's "My Daily Reading from the Four Gospels" is worth recommending.

W.A.G.

Feast of Our Lady of Lourdes,
February 11, 1949.

Dearly Beloved of the Clergy, the Religious and the Laity:

Our Diocesan APOSTOLATE FOR VOCATIONS begins its 9th year today; and on it I beg you all—priests, religious and faithful—to join me in praying God's blessings for another year. During the last three or four years I have addressed my message on this always urgent subject only to the priests and religious of the Diocese because its contents mainly concerned them and their approach to the divine task of fostering vocations among the faithful; so that even now and in the immediate future Holy Mother Church may more easily fulfill her divinely appointed mission of teaching, sanctifying and saving the souls of men.

In addition to the revered clergy and religious this vocation appeal of 1949 goes out to you, the beloved laity of the Diocese. To increase the ranks of the Church Militant I bespeak your thoughtful and purposeful consideration, your willing and prayerful assistance. Trenton is a diocese with an admitted Catholic population of nearly two hundred and seventy-five thousand (275,000) souls. Its Catholic School population is approximately thirty thousand (30,000), with an equal number in the public schools mainly because of distance. During the past nine years one hundred young men were ordained to the diocesan priesthood and in addition many others to the priesthood in religious orders. Eleven hundred noble-souled women, consecrated to God in religion, are leading the young to the blessed feet of Christ or filling the needs of the aged and the orphan, the handicapped and the infirm. And this the Saviour Himself called "religion pure and undefiled before God and the Father." This is indeed a brilliant page of Catholic history and its brilliance must not be permitted to grow dim. Our present anxiety is that its brilliance may soon grow dim unless the ranks of both the clergy and the religious are notably increased. For never in this diocese or in the world at large have the fields been more "white for the harvest" and the need of laborers greater.

Now, dearly beloved, this is the end and aim, "the be-all and the end-all" of our Diocesan APOSTOLATE FOR VOCATIONS. What Catholic worthy of the name does not earnestly desire it to be a most fruitful apostolate. But to be fruitful, *abundantly* fruitful, the seed of vocations must be sown in the rich and fertile soil of prayer and labor and sacrifice.

We are well aware that it is God who gives the call to the priesthood and to the religious life, that "the Spirit breathes where He will," that the Saviour during His public life on earth personally called His apostles and that He enjoined upon all of us to "pray the Lord of the harvest that He send laborers into His harvest." We know too that when by a miracle He changed the persecutor Saul into the Apostle Paul and sent him to Ananias for spiritual guidance, He said: "I will show him what great things he must suffer for My Name's sake." Down through the centuries of Christianity the story of a vocation has always been the same. Miracles like that in St. Paul's conversion and vocation are exceptional. Yet the Lord finds His way into a generous heart and speaks to it in the atmosphere of a good family, in prayer, in the rearing of the children according to lofty Catholic ideals, in the genuine willingness to make sacrifices and in the spiritual guidance of a priest, particularly in the confessional.

Certainly all can say a prayer for vocations daily or at least frequently. Even a "Hail Mary" offered for such a noble and urgent purpose God will surely hear.

In the wisdom of God's designs vocations ordinarily come from the Tabernacle. Therefore let the Eucharistic life become more fervent and intense in all our Catholic families. Let frequent and even daily Holy Mass and Communion among children and grownups in our parishes become a more general practice as it was thirty and forty years ago in the days of Pius X, the Pope of the Eucharist, and for a long time after his death. Let parents set their children the example of frequent and daily Communion. Let our priests encourage this beautiful practice both in and out of the confessional. Let children, even the youngest, grow in the atmosphere of prayer in the family. Let them see their father and mother on their knees at least in the evening, even if it is to say together only one decade of the Rosary. Let the home be in child's mind the first religious house, the first seminary, the first monastery, the first convent, the father and mother the first superiors. Enthrone the Sacred Heart of Jesus in your home with the priest officiating. Let Christ be the Master of the house and Mary its Queen and be assured there Jesus and Mary will never usurp the authority of the parents. Your own diocese needs more vocations; America needs more vocations; distressed Europe needs more vocations; the Home and Foreign Missions need thousands more vocations; and in conformity with Our Divine Lord's own earnest wish and command, may I repeat that vocations innumerable will come only from God and only as the fruit of prayer, labor and sacrifice.

This grave responsibility, dearly beloved, "the Lord of the Harvest" imposes upon all of us in this our own generation. And may generations yet unborn bless us as we bless those of the past, particularly the generation spiritually begotten by the saintly Pius X, the Pope of frequent Communion.

May Christ the great High Priest reign over our hearts and our homes; may we be worthy of the breath of the Holy Spirit; and may Mary show herself our mother and protector and guide to the sanctuary and the cloister for our youth as each one of them hears the Divine call: "Come follow Me."

With a very grateful blessing upon all who by prayer, labor and sacrifice earnestly foster vocations among the young, I remain,

Sincerely yours in Christ,

✠ WILLIAM A. GRIFFIN,
Bishop of Trenton.

P. S.   REVEREND DEAR FATHER:

Please read at all the Masses on Sunday, February 20th.   May I also remind you of the annual Mass ex caritate for vocations?   (Postcard enclosed.)

P. S. 2.

May I ask all our priests and religious to intensify their efforts in prayer and apostolic work for the Apostolate for Vocations?   Many thanks.

W. A. G.

Feast of St. Joseph,
March 19, 1949.

Dearly Beloved of the Clergy, the Religious and the Laity:

The 1949 appeal for "THE BISHOPS' FUND FOR VICTIMS OF WAR" in Europe and the Orient will be made through the medium of a campaign opening on Sunday, March 20th and closing on Lætare Sunday, March 27th.

The goal of this appeal in the Diocese of Trenton is $75,000. This goal will not seem so great when it is remembered that two years ago the same campaign "for victims of war" reached $70,000. And the "BISHOPS' FUND FOR VICTIMS OF WAR" must pass the $5,000,000 mark throughout the country if the American Bishops are to continue the manifold relief services to which they committed themselves, their priests and their people at the end of the war.

The specific nature of "THE BISHOPS' FUND" appeal should make us Catholics in America do some very serious thinking, especially when we contrast conditions in Europe and the Orient with our own blessed situation at home. Official releases of "THE BISHOPS' FUND" appeal state explicitly with truth and authority that:

1. People are starving; multitudes are almost naked; many are sick unto death.
2. To feed the starving, to clothe the naked and to nurse the sick are fundamental works of mercy.
3. His Holiness, Pope Pius XII, the Vicar of Christ on earth, continues to plead for renewed efforts to relieve suffering overseas.
4. The charitable agencies of the Church abroad are striving to continue their great works of mercy, but their stocks are being depleted rapidly AND REPLENISHMENT OF THEM DEPENDS ON THE SUCCESS OF THIS APPEAL.
5. These charitable agencies are virtually the front lines of the titanic struggle now being waged between the forces of Christianity and of Communism.
6. We can fail neither them nor the people they serve.

The Bishops ask: "What will you give to help your neighbor overseas? The cost of a carton of cigarettes, of tickets to a good movie, of a trip to the beauty parlor, of a box of cigars? Compare how much you would spend in a year on luxuries such as those listed above. Then decide how much you will give to sustain life and to relieve suffering overseas. Let your love for Christ and His children be the measure of your generosity.''

In making this comparison and in reaching such a practical conclusion, let the words of Christ's Vicar be heard. Made aware of the forthcoming appeal for ''THE BISHOPS' FUND,'' His Holiness forwarded a grateful exhortation to the Catholics of the United States. ''In this hour of sorrow,'' said the Holy Father, ''we look more than ever to your great country for continued consolation and support. We feel confident that Our beloved sons and daughters in the United States will not fail to respond generously to the appeal which you will make to them in Our name and that they will enable Us to carry on and extend those works of charity by which We endeavor to alleviate the distress of Our suffering children. From Our heart We beseech Almighty God to reserve a bounteous share of recompensing grace for all those who have contributed or who will contribute towards Our crusade of mercy.''

The Campaign has been well organized by our zealous pastors and priests under the efficient supervision of Father Barron, the Diocesan Director of ''THE BISHOPS' FUND FOR VICTIMS OF WAR'' and eight County Priest-Directors.

With our beloved laity, pastors and priests generously co-operating in their respective parishes in this endeavor to attain the parish quota set and agreed upon, there is no reason why the Diocese of Trenton, through the whole-hearted combined effort of all its parishes, cannot reach the desired goal of $75,000.

Make Lætare Sunday, 1949, a day worthy to be remembered in ALMSGIVING in this Diocese and let our works of mercy for all races and creeds tell the current romantic story of genuine Catholicity in America.

With a grateful blessing upon all who co-operate with Christ and His Vicar in relieving the sufferings of the victims of war, I remain,

Sincerely yours in Christ,

✠ WILLIAM A. GRIFFIN,
Bishop of Trenton.

P.S. REVEREND DEAR FATHER:

The children of the Trenton Diocese are to be excused entirely from making any offering to the 1949 BISHOPS' FUND FOR VICTIMS OF WAR in view of their already generous contribution last September to the Holy Father for starving children abroad, as explained in my letter of August 22, 1948.

Kindly arrange to have this letter read at all the Masses on Sunday, March 20th. Thank you.

W. A. G.

May 6, 1949

WORLD SODALITY DAY PASTORAL

Dearly Beloved of the Clergy, the Religious and the Laity,

At the beginning of Lent your zealous priests made an urgent appeal to you, asking a more fervent, a more constant and a more deep-seated prayer-life and Eucharistic life in the Diocese in both adults and children. I heartily compliment both shepherds and sheep on the magnificent fruits of that appeal. The reports at the end of Lent showed clearly that you had entered into that self-sanctifying apostolate with an enthusiasm and a zeal worthy of the early Christians. Never have there been so many Holy Communions or so many people at daily Mass as during the past Lent. All will be pleased and edified to know this fact, and none more than those who assisted at the Holy Sacrifice and received Holy Communion every day during the Lenten season. I am sure their hearts were filled with a real, spiritual joy on the Feast of Christ's glorious Resurrection.

What I would like to impress upon all participating today in these annual Sodality Day rallies and paying child-like homage to God's own Mother and ours, is that our prayer-life and our Eucharistic life must not be a matter of a few weeks during Lent, but must be lived all the year through, not merely for one's own spiritual growth but for the betterment of the world as well. For the sinful and sorrow-stricken world needs you very much.

We are caught up in admiration at the many appearances of our Blessed Lady in various places during the past few decades, the Mother of God warning us that we had better pray more and do penance for our own sins and the sins of others; lest, perhaps, the wrath of God fall upon us; lest, perhaps, it be said also of us in this modern age that Her Divine Son "came unto His own and His own received Him not." (John 1, 11.) This was the Apostle John's lament only a few years after the death and Resurrection of the Saviour of mankind. Shall we deserve the rebuke uttered against those among whom during His sojourn on earth Jesus Christ lived, with whom He frequently conversed, whom He exhorted so strongly to a change to a better and a more spiritual life? Our Lady's message at Fatima is only the echo in our time of the repeated and insistent injunction of John the Baptist: "Repent, for the Kingdom of Heaven is at hand." (Mat. 3-2) Indeed Christ's whole Gospel is a gospel of penance.

Now in our own age who is so childish as to think that Our Lady's admonitions were addressed only to the three innocent children to whom She appeared at Fatima during the six months from May to October, 1917? Is Fatima to be merely a place in Portugal for us to read about, to discuss, then to forget? Is there to be no serious thinking, no meditation on the unusual supernatural events that took place at Fatima thirty years ago? In our Lord's own time people talked about His miracles; but unfortunately too many of them wondered and discussed the wonders and then promptly returned to the sinfulness and the sordidness of their old way of living. They gave no serious thought to the works and the words and the warnings of their Saviour appearing in the flesh and urging on His fellow-men a life of prayer and penance.

Yes, dearly beloved, Fatima is Christ's warning message spoken through Mary in her apparitions to our own generation. Fatima is all very personal, — personal to Jesus and Mary who so much desire our salvation, — personal to you and to me who are called upon to do penance and to pray, especially to pray the rosary daily, if we would first ensure our own salvation and then really help to save the world.

Surely the growth of our prayer-life and of our Eucharistic life will not remain a mere happy memory of the past Lent, but will become habitual and persevering, as taking our daily food and assimilating it into our very blood and bone and sinew.

Give the soul its food — prayer and the Eucharist. Let its food be taken daily, — especially the daily rosary and daily Mass and Holy Communion. And may Jesus through Mary nurture your prayer-life and your Eucharistic life. May they hear your humble prayers for a more peaceful world; and for each and all of us a happy eternity.

Blessing all in Jesus through Mary, I remain,

Sincerely yours in Christ,

✠ William A. Griffin,

Bishop of Trenton.

P.S. To be read at all the Masses on Sunday, May 8th, and at all the Sodality Day rallies. Thank you.
      W.G.

October 10, 1949.

Dearly Beloved of the Clergy, the Religious and the Laity:

Sunday, October 23rd, will be MISSION SUNDAY all over the world. By its religious observance we are brought closer to the spiritual needs of the pagan in foreign lands, who as yet has not begun to enjoy the saving fruits of Redemption, and of numerous non-Catholics in our own land, particularly in the South and the Southwest, who would gladly accept the true Faith and joyfully receive the ministrations of the Catholic missionaries, if he only had the material means to go to them.

It would indeed be unfortunate to let the world-wide appeal of MISSION SUNDAY go by unheeded—unfortunate for ourselves as well as for those helpless souls in whose behalf the appeal is made. On the other hand, it is a most blessed task providentially afforded us to be among those who directly or indirectly are privileged to bring the light of the Gospel and the means of grace and of salvation to these benighted peoples. The direct approach is made by the missionary; the indirect is made by mission-minded Catholics who by their alms and their prayers send him to the mission field and support him in his labors for souls.

This is why there is a MISSION SUNDAY. This is why there is the world-wide Pontifical Society for the Propagation of the Faith. It is not so much an occasion for a collection for the Missions as another golden opportunity for self-dedication to the Missions,— a day for the enrollment of oneself personally in the Mission apostolate—the universal Society for the Propagation of the Faith, which is the Pope's own instrument of Mission-aid.

Hearken, therefore, dearly beloved, to the call of Christ's Vicar pleading for your self-dedication to the mission cause of Holy Mother Church. Identify yourself personally with the Holy Father's own Mission-aid apostolate—the Society for the Propagation of the Faith. Let your daily prayer for the missions bring God's blessings upon you, the Mission-aid member, as upon the benighted souls to whom you make it possible for the missionaries to go and to bring them the saving fruits of Christ's Redemption. For this is what is meant by MEMBERSHIP in the Society for the Propagation of the Faith.

The Diocesan Director's report for last year shows the generous earnestness of your self-dedication to the mission cause; and I am confident the story of your self-dedication for the coming year will be even more inspiring and illuminating. As a means towards this happy result the Director will furnish all helpful information and guidance.

In solemn observance of MISSION SUNDAY it is my pleasure to invite all—Priests, Religious and laity to join me at the Cathedral on MISSION SUNDAY afternoon at 3:30 o'clock for the chanting of Pontifical Vespers to invoke God's blessing upon our Mission-aid efforts for the coming year. On that happy occasion the sermon will be preached by the Rev. Edward C. Kramer, D.D., Secretary-General of the Colored Mission Board and Promoter of the Society for Sisters' Sponsors among the colored people.

After MISSION SUNDAY we shall watch with real interest and with genuine pleasure the growth of the mission spirit and of the Mission-aid apostolate in this Diocese.

With a grateful blessing upon all who help in their own way, however humble, to promote the MISSION CAUSE, I remain,

Sincerely yours in Christ,

✠ WILLIAM A. GRIFFIN,
Bishop of Trenton.

P.S. REVEREND DEAR FATHER:

Kindly read this letter at all the Masses next Sunday, October 16th. In accordance with the suggestions of Monsignor Monahan, kindly enroll your people on MISSION SUNDAY, October 23rd, as members of the Society for the Propagation of the Faith.

October 24, 1949.

To the Beloved of the Clergy, the Religious and the Laity:

Since its institution and in accordance with traditional solemnity the Feast of Christ the King is observed throughout the Catholic World on the last Sunday of October. For a decade in this Diocese, Priests, Religious and people have never failed to exalt our Lord and King upon His Altar Throne, and as His loyal followers to offer Him their gifts of homage and thanksgiving. It will please our Eucharistic King very much if this year on His Great Feast we make no exception to our customary manner of observance but will intensify our devotion and to our profound homage and thanksgiving will add reparation.

It is not merely from motives of praise and thanksgiving but from motives of atonement and reparation that we keep the Feast of Christ the King as a FAMILY COMMUNION DAY, that we have Exposition of the Blessed Sacrament all day, that we multiply our visits during the afternoon and evening, that we increase our prayers and revitalize their fervor. That the need for reparation exists is more evident in this, our day, as we view the repudiation of Christ and His teachings and mark the indifference that attends the cause of Religion by millions throughout the world. The reasons that prompted the saintly Pontiff, Pius XI, to create the Feast of Christ the King still prevail, and greater reasons exist for a more faithful observance of the Feast.

Let us be mindful of the solemn observation of the saintly Pontiff when he said: "We grieve over the seeds of discord apparently sown everywhere, the rekindling of hatreds and rivalries between peoples which prevent the re-establishment of peace; we grieve over the unrestrained passions, so often hidden under the mask of the public good and love of country; . . . (we grieve) over domestic peace grievously disturbed because of the forgetfulness and the wilful disregard of family duties; (we grieve) over the natural unity and stability of the family broken, and last of all, over society itself shaken to its foundations and plunging headlong to ruin."

These words of the late beloved Pontiff remain a challenge to our efforts in behalf of the Kingship of Christ, and should persuade and encourage us to accept the task of atonement and reparation.

Praying that this message, occasioned by the annual recurrence of the Feast of Christ the King, will find a sympathetic and fruitful response in the hearts of Priests, Religious and people and bring greater glory and a richer harvest of souls to both the militant and the triumphant Kingdom of Christ, I remain,

With a blessing upon all,

Sincerely yours in Christ,

✠ WILLIAM A. GRIFFIN,

Bishop of Trenton.

P. S. May I ask that this letter be read in its full text at the Masses on the Feast of Christ the King.

W. A. G.

December 29, 1949.

REVEREND DEAR FATHER:

Permit me to confirm the telephone communication which you received on December 24th relative to the permission for Midnight Mass on New Year's Eve.

On the occasion of the solemn opening of the Holy Year of Jubilee, His Holiness, Pope Pius XII, has graciously deigned to permit the celebration of ONE Holy Mass, private or solemn, in all Churches and Oratories serving the faithful, at midnight between December 31, 1949, and January 1, 1950. At this Mass, or immediately thereafter, the faithful properly disposed may receive Holy Communion, observing the usual Eucharistic fast from midnight. Needless to mention, Pastors availing themselves of this faculty must exercise great caution in eliminating any danger of irreverence or of possible profanation.

The above-mentioned permission of His Holiness, transmitted through the Sacred Congregation of the Sacraments, further stipulates that a service of *two hours* duration must be organized for the occasion. Apart, therefore, from the Holy Sacrifice of the Mass, and possibly a sermon, at midnight, additional prayers, perhaps in the form of a Holy Hour beginning at 11 P. M. must be offered to Almighty God and to the Blessed Virgin Mary for the Holy Year intentions of the Sovereign Pontiff. The Holy Father's intentions may be summarized as follows: The sanctification of souls through prayer and penance, and unshaken fidelity to Christ and to His Church; the defense of the rights of the Church against her enemies and the conversion of those outside the fold; the establishment of peace among all nations and especially in the Holy Land; the welfare of all who toil and the increase of charitable work in behalf of the needy.

With renewed prayerful best wishes for a happy, blessed New Year, I remain,

Sincerely yours in Christ,

✠ WILLIAM A. GRIFFIN,
Bishop of Trenton.

P. S.—The program to be observed in this Diocese for the Holy Year will be mailed shortly.

W. A. G.

CHAPTER TEN

SEVENTH BISHOP: GEORGE W. AHR 1950~1979

BY DONALD P. DELANY

GEORGE W. AHR SERVED as bishop of Trenton for a longer period than any of his predecessors—29 years. And that period, from 1950 through 1979, was an exciting as well as a difficult one for the faithful of the diocese and for their chief shepherd. It was a time of enormous growth and dramatic change within the diocese. The Catholic population of the eight central New Jersey counties that then constituted the Diocese of Trenton tripled during Bishop Ahr's episcopate, eventually resulting in the division of the diocese and the creation of the new Diocese of Metuchen.

Bishop Ahr oversaw the establishment of more than 50 new parishes, together with the construction of scores of schools, parish centers, rectories, health care institutions, and other new buildings. The ethnic and racial makeup of the diocese changed significantly over the years with the influx of large numbers of Hispanic and black Catholics.

It was an era of social and moral upheaval in the secular world, which inevitably had a profound impact on the church. Traditional standards of morality came increasingly under attack in the 1960s and 1970s, and, within the church, some people openly questioned basic doctrines. The 1973 decision by the U.S. Supreme Court legalizing abortion split the country into those who upheld the right of the unborn to life and those who supported what was called women's "right to choose." The numbers of priests and religious in the country and the diocese declined alarmingly.

During this period, the historic Second Vatican Council took place. All of its sessions were attended by Bishop Ahr, who enthusiastically welcomed the liturgical and other changes that came from the council.

Bishop Ahr's service years were marked by stark tragedy and deep personal sorrow.

On March 14, 1956, the diocese's mother church, St. Mary's Cathedral in Trenton, and its adjoining chancery and rectory were destroyed by fire, which took the lives of the rector—Msgr. Richard T. Crean, who was chancellor and vicar-general of the diocese and a close friend of Bishop Ahr—and two housekeepers in the rectory—Miss Mary Brennan and Miss Mary Donnellan. Bishop Ahr then supervised the construction of a magnificent new cathedral, which he consecrated on March 14, 1959.

Bishop Ahr, then, had to deal with issues, problems, and changes largely unknown to those who had preceded him. And due in great measure to his strong personality and firm guiding hand, the diocese met the formidable challenges of the mid-twentieth century and remained at the close of his tenure a vibrant bastion of faith.

Bishop Ahr was a man ideally equipped to lead the diocese during those troublesome times. Prior to his selection by Pope Pius XII to succeed Bishop William A. Griffin, his priestly career had been devoted principally both to teaching in and directing a seminary and to preparing young men for the priesthood. His seminary experience and his solid grounding in the dogmas of the church gave him an image of strength and authority, which served him well as bishop. As a theologian, he was esteemed throughout the country and his opinions were sought by his colleagues at bishops' conferences.

George William Ahr was born in Newark on June 23, 1904, the oldest of three children of George and Mary Mueller Ahr.

The family subsequently moved to Irvington. Young George graduated from St. Ann's School in Newark and attended St. Benedict's Preparatory School, also in Newark, for a year. He completed his high school education, then three years of college at St. Vincent's College in Latrobe, Pennsylvania. In 1925, he graduated from Seton Hall College in South Orange, New Jersey.

Although Bishop Ahr later commented that he could not remember when or under what circumstances he received the call to the priesthood, he said it probably was during his high school days. As a boy he occasionally dreamed of becoming a fireman. But while playing in the schoolyard one day with a few friends, he made a remark that would prove to be prophetic. One of the parish priests standing nearby playfully asked, "Any of you boys going to become priests someday?" Young George replied, "Nah, I'm going to be a bishop!"

When he made his decision to enter the priesthood, Newark diocesan authorities recognized his potential and sent him to Rome to complete his studies. In October 1925 he arrived at the North American College in the Eternal City, studying there for four years.

They were four crowded years. The young student came under the tutelage of gifted professors, including Ernesto Cardinal Ruffini, who taught him sacred Scripture; Gregory Cardinal Agagianian, rector of the Armenian College, sacramental theology; Msgr. Antonio Baranzini, rector of Lombard College and later archbishop of Syracuse, dogmatic theology; Redemptorist

Fr. Cornelius Damen, a famous Dutch theologian, moral theology; and Franciscan Fr. D'Ambrosio, procurator general of the Conventual Franciscans, canon law.

University officials had a routine designed to familiarize the students with Roman and church history and to maintain their good health. Each afternoon at 4 o'clock, classes would halt, and the students, in groups of ten with two escorts, would take an hour's walk, visiting historic sights. On their return, they were refreshed in mind and their education enhanced. Young Mr. Ahr served as prefect for a year, in charge of the student group he accompanied.

He was ordained July 28, 1928, by Bishop Alfonso M. DeSanctis of Segni, in the chapel of the Leonine College, the Vincentian seminary in Rome. He was the first candidate for the priesthood to be ordained by Bishop DeSanctis since DeSanctis's consecration as bishop.

Present in the crowded chapel were the new priest's parents, who had made the trip from Irvington. That afternoon, young Fr. Ahr took his parents to Castelgandolfo outside Rome, where, at Santa Catarina Villa, he celebrated Benediction for the children there. The next day, Mr. and Mrs. Ahr attended their son's first Solemn Mass, celebrated in a school chapel in Rome dedicated to St. George, Fr. Ahr's patron saint, and the English martyrs.

After receiving his Doctor in Sacred Theology degree from the Propaganda University in July 1929, Fr. Ahr returned to the United States and appropriately celebrated his first Solemn Mass at home in St. Ann's Church in Newark, where just a few years earlier he had served Mass as an altar boy. Again his parents were present, as were his sister and brother, Eleanor and Wilbur Ahr. Assisting at the Mass were Fr. Michael Mechler, pastor of St. Ann's; Fr. Louis Remmele, assistant pastor; and Fr. Justin J. McCarthy, who in later years became bishop of Camden.

Fr. Ahr then began a short period of parish work. His first assignment was as assistant at St. Mary's Church, Jersey City, where he served for two and a half months while another priest was hospitalized. Then he was assigned to St. Venantius Church in Orange, remaining there also only a few months before being assigned to teach at Seton Hall Preparatory School. Three years later, in June 1933, he joined the faculty of Immaculate Conception Seminary in Darlington, New Jersey, in the Archdiocese of Newark.

During the next 17 years, Fr. Ahr served at the seminary as professor of dogmatic theology and metaphysics and then as professor of pastoral theology. In September 1947, he was appointed rector of the seminary to succeed Bishop Thomas A. Boland, who had been named the first bishop of Paterson and who later became archbishop of Newark. On December 24, 1947, Pope Pius XII named Fr. Ahr a domestic prelate with the title of right reverend monsignor.

Many priests of the Trenton diocese, as well as hundreds of others from other dioceses in and near New Jersey, came under the influence of Fr. Ahr during his years at

Darlington. His students also included five who later became bishops, including his auxiliary and successor, John C. Reiss.

His students remembered him as a tough but fair taskmaster who was determined that they would learn the lessons that he himself had learned so well. Bishop Reiss recalled that, as a teacher, Bishop Ahr stayed very close to the textbook. "He made sure that the important things were highlighted for us," he said. "He would give necessary explanations so that we would understand all the nuances of a doctrine. He made sure that we were always in accord with what the church was teaching. He inspired us to do that."

Bishop Reiss agreed that Bishop Ahr was a stern instructor but also a caring one. "If you had a problem and approached him and explained what was bothering you, he would do anything he could to help you. If a student had trouble with his studies, he would help him along, tell him where to find the material that would solve his problem."

Bishop Ahr was an authority in his field, his successor said. "Although his doctorate was in moral theology, he taught dogmatic theology for almost 16 years, and he was brilliant in that. During the Second Vatican Council, some of the other bishops looked to him as an authority in moral theology."

On another occasion, Bishop Reiss characterized Bishop Ahr as a "man of one book," a teacher who used a single textbook on theology. "Rather than bring in all kinds of authors and comparing and selecting, he stuck to the book, so that his students

Bishop Ahr and Bishop Hodges outside St. Peter's Basilica in Rome after a session of the Second Vatican Council.

would have a solid foundation in theology. Later on, the student could branch out.

"Thus, knowing that 'one book,' in its entirety, was the task we students had before us. We had to study each dogmatic thesis and learn its theological content; the official pronouncements of the church in ecumenical or lesser councils; the appropriate texts from sacred Scripture; the pertinent writings of the fathers of the church; and, finally, the proper theological reasoning. If the student acquired this array of knowledge, the professor would naturally feel that he had accomplished his goal."

Bishop Walter W. Curtis of Bridgeport, Conneticut, who also studied under Msgr. Ahr, said, "He was feared. Unfortunately

Second Vatican Council at St. Peter's in session—Bishop George W. Ahr is in second seat of third row. Second Vatican Council opened October 11, 1962, and closed December 9, 1965.

for us students, he expected performance and hard work. An easy way to be feared by your students!"

But five years later, Bishop Curtis said, as a fellow member of the seminary faculty with Msgr. Ahr, "His deep and wide qualities as a person became evident to me." A pillar of strength on the faculty, Msgr. Ahr as rector gained the affection of all, he said. "Historians of Darlington Seminary from 1934 to 1950 will need to include a large chapter with the initials G.W.A. If, in the beginning, he was feared for sternness and magisterial demands, he became loved for

the obvious fairness and justice that marked his life and his dealings with students. He hewed to the path of truth and justice and became revered accordingly."

Another of his students, in a humorous tribute to Bishop Ahr in later years, recalled that early in his teaching career, Bishop Ahr received the nickname "the Baron." That was because "like the barons of literature he was the complete autocrat in the classroom, both while lecturing and especially while conducting a test.

"No one dared to joke or make wisecracks, because to quote the renowned comedian of that time, 'Here only the Baron makes the jokes,'" he said. On occasion, he added, when he was in an especially demanding mood, Bishop Ahr would shorten the normally allotted time for a test from two hours to one.

But later, he said, Bishop Ahr's classroom demeanor underwent a noticeable metamorphosis. He became more affable, a smile or two was noted, and "concern for the seminarians began to blossom." As a result, a new nickname was coined—"Papa." Bishop Ahr earned the sobriquet because of "his paternal interest in those under his care. Like a father he could still correct when necessary and apply the rod, figuratively speaking. Like a father he was deeply committed to seeing that the men be properly trained as future priests. The interest was not just for their academic and technical training, but also for their development as individuals and as persons."

On New Year's Day 1950, Bishop William A. Griffin passed away. Four weeks later, on January 28, 1950, Pope Pius XII announced the appointment of Msgr. Ahr as the seventh bishop of the Diocese of Trenton.

As soon as the appointment was made public, Msgr. Thomas U. Reilly, vicar-general of the diocese and administrator since Bishop Griffin's death, wired the bishop-elect: "May you as our Chief Shepherd direct and guide us for many fruitful years."

For the diocese's 300,000 Catholics, the natural question was, "Who is Msgr. Ahr?" He was known, of course, to diocesan officials and to the many young men who had studied for the priesthood under his guidance at the seminary. But to the average family in the diocese, he was a stranger except through the photographs that appeared in newspapers at the time of his appointment.

To learn more about this obviously gifted and highly thought-of teacher, the *Trenton Times* sent a reporter and photographer to interview Msgr. Ahr. Vincent A. Weiss, who three years later was to become founding editor of *The Monitor*, the diocesan newspaper established by Bishop Ahr, met with the 45-year-old bishop-elect, together with photographer Martin D'Arcy, at St. Michael's Convent in Englewood Cliffs, where Msgr. Ahr was to attend a luncheon with some 40 priests.

Following a discussion that lasted more than an hour and a half, Weiss reported the next day that he had found Msgr. Ahr to be a man "possessed of a pleasing personality," extremely modest, with an engaging smile. When asked if he had a message for the people of the diocese, Msgr. Ahr responded with good humor, "I am not accustomed to issuing statements." Then he added, "Let me have your pencil and paper." He proceeded to write his message.

"I have been profoundly moved by and am deeply grateful for the many expressions of loyalty and goodwill that have come from Monsignor Reilly, the priests and people of Trenton," he wrote. "I know how fortunate I am to have been sent to a field so well prepared by the zealous and untiring efforts of my illustrious predecessor, Bishop

Griffin, whose priests are known for their zeal and whose people are renowned for their loyal, vigorous Catholicity.

"While I beg the continued prayers of all for abundant graces from on high, I pledge my complete dedication to the welfare of their souls."

Then, as Weiss read over the message, Msgr. Ahr asked with a laugh, "What's the rate, 20 cents a line?" When Weiss asked where he learned this advertising terminology, the bishop-elect replied that as a boy he had delivered advertising notices to newspaper offices for his father, who was a funeral director.

Msgr. Ahr told Weiss that members of his family were as much surprised as he was by the announcement of his elevation. The news sparked a brief family reunion in Irvington on the afternoon of the announcement, after which Msgr. Ahr motored to Englewood Cliffs for a ceremony at St. Michael's Convent, motherhouse of the Sisters of St. Joseph of Newark.

Msgr. Ahr said with regret that his many years of teaching had prevented him from being associated with parish organizations, that he was happy to learn of thriving groups in the Trenton diocese such as the Holy Name Society, the St. Vincent dePaul Society, and the Young Ladies' Sodality, and that he was looking forward to working with them.

When Msgr. Ahr joined the priests for luncheon, Weiss reported, he was greeted by a "terrific" round of applause. Fr. James Healy, chaplain of the convent,

commented that "the people of Trenton are getting a wonderful person in Bishop Ahr."

Meanwhile, plans were going forward for Msgr. Ahr's consecration and installation as bishop. Those solemn events took place on March 20, 1950. Diocesan and city officials left no stone unturned to make the diocese's new shepherd welcome.

On the day before, Sunday, March 19, 1950, Msgr. Ahr left the Immaculate Conception Seminary, receiving a warm farewell from his successor as rector, Msgr. Thomas Powers. He arrived at the episcopal residence at 901 West State Street in Trenton in mid-afternoon. The house was draped outside with the papal colors, gold and white. There he met with the Diocesan Board of Consultors, and it was at this session that he actually became Bishop Ahr. He presented the papal bull from Pope Pius XII commissioning him bishop of Trenton. It was thereupon examined and accepted by the consultors.

After the meeting, Bishop Ahr issued a statement noting he was keenly aware of the responsibilities facing him. "I appreciate the singular importance of this city, the capital of New Jersey and the seat of the state government. Good government, which seeks the welfare of all the citizens, is obviously a matter of concern to every one of us, interested as we are in the progress of our state.

"I know I speak for all of the Catholics of this diocese when I promise wholehearted support and cooperation in every genuine endeavor to promote the common good. And I shall frequently beseech our Blessed Lord

Bishop George W. Ahr on the day of his consecration as a bishop in old St. Mary's Cathedral. On his left is Msgr. Emmett A. Monahan.

The Diocese of Trenton, 1881–1993

to guide and strengthen our governor and the representatives of our people in their determination to fulfill their duties with a spirit of justice and charity toward all."

The consecration and installation rites the following day, March 20, 1950, in St. Mary's Cathedral were marked by the traditional, centuries-old splendor and solemnity of the church. Fourteen bishops, four abbots, more than 40 monsignori, upwards of 600 priests, more than a hundred nuns, and a hundred laypersons witnessed the three-hour ceremonies.

Shortly before 9:30 a.m., Bishop Ahr was escorted from the episcopal residence to the chancery office, then adjoining the cathedral on North Warren Street, by Trenton Police Chief William Dooling, Captain John Ryan, and a squad of motorcycle officers. More than a thousand persons, unable to gain admittance to the cathedral, stood in a roped-off area and cheered as Bishop Ahr alighted from his automobile.

Just before 10 a.m., the priests and religious brothers marched in procession from the cathedral auditorium on Bank Street; then the monsignori, robed in purple, from Cathedral High School; and the bishops and abbots from the chancery office. Finally came Bishop Ahr, with Archbishop Moses E. Kiley of Milwaukee, who had been bishop of Trenton from 1934 to 1940; Archbishop Francis P. Keough of Baltimore; Archbishop Thomas J. Walsh of Newark, the third bishop of Trenton, who was the consecrator; and Bishops Bartholomew J. Eustace of Camden and Thomas A. Boland of Paterson, the co-consecrators, all with their attendants.

His Holiness, Pope Pius XII, at the Vatican with Msgr. Richard T. Crean at his left and at Monsignor Crean's left, Msgr. John E. Grimes.

Fourth Degree Knights of Columbus of Bishop Griffin General Assembly, in full regalia, stood at the cathedral entrance as an honor guard. Congressman Charles Howell, Trenton Mayor Dönal Connolly, and members of the City Commission were among the lay dignitaries present. Music was rendered by the Schola Cantorum of the Immaculate Conception Seminary at Darlington, composed of seminarians.

Like the episcopal residence, the exterior of the cathedral was draped in the papal colors of gold and white, which also were much in evidence inside, draped from column to column. American and papal flags were suspended from every pillar. And the main altar, at which the consecration and installation ceremonies took place during a Solemn Pontifical Mass, was bedecked with hundreds of Easter lilies in gold vases.

Bishop Ahr's parents occupied a front pew. With them were their daughter, Eleanor Ahr, and their other son, Wilbur, his wife, and their three children, Peter, 9; David, 7; and Paul, 5. Directly behind the family was Marchesina Elena Rossignani Pacelli, niece of Pope Pius XII. She was visiting the United States and was a guest at Villa Walsh, motherhouse of the Religious Teachers Filippini in Morristown.

Msgr. Richard T. Crean, chancellor of the diocese and rector of the cathedral, read the apostolic mandate from Pope Pius XII. Msgr. Reilly served as assistant priest at the Mass, and Msgr. James J. Hogan, vice-chancellor of the diocese, was assistant master of ceremonies for the consecration-installation ceremonies.

Deacons of honor were Msgr. Linus A. Schwarze, pastor of St. Anthony's Church, and Msgr. Maximilian Wujek, pastor of St. Mary's, South Amboy. Master of ceremonies to Bishop Ahr was Msgr. Emmett A. Monahan, who had been secretary to Bishop Griffin and later pastor of St. Mark's Church, Sea Girt. Assisting was Fr. Joseph A. O'Connor, assistant at the cathedral.

Twelve priests of the diocese served as minor ministers at the Mass. They were Fr. Francis J. Russo, assistant at St. Anthony's, Trenton, book bearer; Fr. Thomas J. Frain, assistant at Holy Angels, Trenton, later diocesan superintendent of schools,

bugia bearer; Fr. Joseph A. Bischoff, assistant at Sacred Heart, Trenton, crosier bearer; Fr. William H. McKenna, assistant at Our Lady of Good Counsel, Moorestown, miter bearer; Fr. Francis E. Grabowski, assistant at Holy Cross, Trenton, gremiale bearer; Fr. John B. Cook, assistant at Incarnation, Trenton, cross bearer; Fr. Dominic A. Turtora, assistant at St. Joachim's, Trenton, and Fr. John J. Churak, assistant at Ss. Peter and Paul's, Trenton; Fr. Morgan J. Kelly, chaplain at St. Michael's Children's Home, Hopewell, and Fr. John E. Sullivan, assistant at Our Lady of Victories, Sayreville, acolytes; Fr. Robert P. Murray, Princeton, thurifer; Fr. Thaddeus J. Wojciehowski, assistant at St. Hedwig's, Trenton, processional cross bearer.

The sermon was preached by Auxiliary Bishop James A. McNulty of Newark. He was followed by Archbishop Walsh, who paid eloquent tribute to the new prelate, and by Msgr. Reilly, who welcomed Bishop Ahr to Trenton.

One of the most solemn moments of the ceremonies occurred when, with the entire congregation kneeling, the bishop-elect prostrated himself at the steps of the altar. For the next 15 minutes, the Schola Cantorum sang the Litany of the Saints. Near the end of the litany, Archbishop Walsh, taking his crosier in his left hand, asked God to bless Bishop Ahr. He then made the sign of the cross three times over the prostrate prelate. As the last phrase of the litany died away, Bishop Ahr rose to a kneeling position, and Archbishop Walsh placed the book of Gospels on his neck and shoulders so that the printed page touched his neck. With that, the consecrator and co-consecrators touched the head of Bishop Ahr, saying "Receive the Holy Ghost."

Bishop Ahr, in his remarks, declared: "To teach, to rule, to sanctify—this is the obligation of every bishop primarily concerned with the salvation and perfection of the souls entrusted to his care. This, I know, has been the ideal of all my predecessors, and it will be mine."

He warned of the evils of communism. "These indeed are difficult times for the church of Christ," he said. "The spread of communism—fanatically bent on promoting atheism, destroying all religion, and making every man a slave of a small group which seizes control of the state—makes us realize the need of diligent and persistent efforts to protect our church and safeguard the liberties we enjoy in our great country."

The new bishop also cited the "baneful influence of the secularist attitude" as a source of serious harm to the individual, the family, and the state. That attitude, he said, inclined many people to be careless and indifferent toward religious truth and moral principles.

"But the church of Jesus Christ is accustomed to face dangers and crimes of every kind," he continued. "She will endure to the end of time, for the gates of hell shall not prevail against her. The Son of God cannot be conquered."

Bishop Eustace escorted Bishop Ahr through the aisles of the cathedral as the new bishop imparted his blessing to the people. Returning to the sanctuary, Bishop Ahr gave the final blessing of the Mass.

That evening, Bishop Ahr was guest of honor at a dinner attended by the other bishops, priests, and religious at the Stacy-Trent Hotel in Trenton.

One of the new bishop's first acts was to choose a coat-of-arms, in conformity with centuries-old ecclesiastical tradition. Bishop Ahr selected a heraldic device bearing the words "Maria, Spes Mea" ("Mary, My

Dinner and reception following consecration of Bishop George W. Ahr. From left to right: Right Rev. Msgr. Thomas U. Reilly, V.G.; Most Rev. Thomas Walsh, archbishop of Newark; Most Rev. George W. Ahr; Most Rev. Moses Elias Kiley, archbishop of Milwaukee.

Bishop Ahr's coat-of-arms.
"Mary, My Hope."

Hope"), Bishop Ahr's lifelong motto. His coat-of-arms bore the insignia of the Diocese of Trenton—a golden moline cross signifying the mill that Trenton founder Mahlon Stacy built on the Delaware River. Red stag's antlers on a silver field signify the Ahr family's arms. A crescent is superimposed over the moline cross—this symbolizes the Blessed Virgin Mary, patroness of the Diocese of Trenton.

Bishop Ahr settled smoothly into the responsibilities and routine of his office. Less than two months after his installation, on June 3, 1950, he ordained his first class of priests in the cathedral. They were Fr. James Q. Bittner, Fr. Gerald J. Callahan, Fr. Francis X. Donovan, Fr. John A. Dzema, Fr. Raymond H. Griffin, Fr. Anthony M. Kramarz, Fr. Joseph M. Krysztofik, Fr. William J. Maguire, Fr. William H. Murray, Fr. Thomas C. Ryan, and Fr. Frederick A. Valentino.

On June 28, 1950, he ordained Fr. William F. Fitzgerald, who one day would become chancellor of the diocese.

On June 25, 1950, he blessed the new Christ the King Church in Manville, the first of some 250 blessings of parish structures at which he was to officiate during his episcopate.

The decade of the 1950s was marked by innovation, disaster, controversy, and personal sorrow for the new prelate. In early 1954, Bishop Ahr launched a weekly diocesan newspaper, *The Monitor,* in response to what he saw as "a clearly established and urgent need" to advance more effectively the cause of religion generally and the particular interests of the church's many institutions.

Noting that plans for such a publication had been conceived by Bishop Kiley and studied and developed under Bishop Griffin, Bishop Ahr said that *The Monitor* was primarily a medium through which the people of the diocese might gain a greater knowledge of all that concerned their faith.

"It is a means of education, an inspiration to greater zeal and devotion, an incentive to Catholic action in all that the term implies in the way of practical exemplification of Christian doctrine," he wrote in the paper's first edition, published February 5, 1954.

He said that *The Monitor* would present comprehensive coverage of news developments affecting the church, in world and national affairs, with particular emphasis on what was happening in the diocese and its churches, schools, and organizations, and what was happening among the men and women who labored in many ways for the faith and its advancement. The paper, he declared, would serve to bring the people of the widely scattered parishes together in a closer bond of friendship and unity, so that common causes might be advanced more effectively.

His goal, he made clear, was to see *The Monitor* in every home in the diocese and read by every family.

Bishop Ahr's devotion to *The Monitor* and his belief in its value never waned. At virtually every Confirmation ceremony through the years, he posed this question: "What is the 11th Commandment?" The boys and girls naturally were stumped, and he would answer his own question: "Read *The Monitor*!"

Vincent A. Weiss, an active Catholic layman and *Trenton Times* reporter who had interviewed Bishop Ahr following his appointment, was the bishop's choice to be *The Monitor's* editor. Weiss was a veteran newsman whose background made him ideal for the post. He had been associated with the *Trenton Times* for almost 25 years. As a reporter, he covered Trenton city hall with distinction for many years, later served as assistant city editor, and was widely respected for his journalistic skills. Through his membership and involvement in numerous Catholic organizations and causes within the diocese, he was well acquainted

with many pastors and lay diocesan leaders. Weiss served until his retirement a quarter century later. He continued to contribute to *The Monitor* until his death under the present editor, Joseph M. Donadieu.

Disaster struck on March 14, 1956, when a raging conflagration leveled St. Mary's Cathedral and the adjoining chancery/rectory, taking the lives of the rector, Msgr. Richard T. Crean, and two housekeepers, Miss Mary Donnellan and Miss Mary Brennan. Four priests staying at the rectory—Frs. Francis M. McGuinness, Peter J. Mooney, and Joseph O'Connor, assistants at the cathedral, and Fr. William F. Fitzgerald, at that time an assistant chancellor of the diocese—were saved, three of them with injuries, as was a cook at the rectory, Mrs. Vera Dzienis.

It was at 4:30 a.m. on that rainy morning when a man called a Bell Telephone operator from a coin box across from the cathedral and shouted that flames were pouring from the rectory windows. The operator sounded an alarm, and four more alarms were given within the next few minutes. When fire fighters arrived, they found the blaze had spread quickly to the cathedral. Soon flames were reaching 100 feet into the still-dark, early morning sky. Fire apparatus poured torrents of water on the blaze, with little effect.

Msgr. Crean, it was soon learned, gave his life trying to save the lives of the others. Fr. McGuinness, after being rescued, hysterically told the fire fighters that the rector was still in the building. Msgr. Crean had gone upstairs from his second-floor bedroom to the third floor to warn the others to get out as quickly as possible. Msgr. Crean apparently was making his way up the stairway when he was overcome by smoke. It was not until the fire subsided that fire fighters were able to remove the monsignor's body and those of the two housekeepers.

Fr. McGuinness was taken from the cross on the cathedral roof, on which he was hanging, by a fireman who went to his rescue on an aerial ladder, and only after the fireman got to him was he able to coax him down.

Fr. Mooney was rescued by fire fighters as he clung to a radio antenna outside his room. Fr. O'Connor was awakened by Msgr. Crean, who was calling the priests to alert them of the raging fire. He tried to contact Msgr. Crean but was unable to do so due to the dense smoke in the stairway. Msgr. Crean was on the stairs, almost to the third floor, and Fr. O'Connor could hear him calling out, but then there was silence. Fr. O'Connor tried to get through the door that led to the chancery offices, but smoke and flames made it impossible; he then went to the window and was able to open it enough to crawl out onto the window ledge and hang on until the rescuers arrived with a net and called to him to jump to safety.

Mrs. Vera Dzienis was rescued by a fireman who used an aerial ladder to the fourth-floor windows. She was on an air-conditioner unit and was assisted by the fireman down the ladder. She suffered some burns.

The police rushed to the episcopal residence, 901 West State Street, to inform Bishop Ahr of the fire. However, Bishop Ahr was staying overnight at St. Francis Hospital in Trenton for his annual physical checkup. Fr. John Reiss, who was then secretary to Bishop Ahr and lived in the episcopal residence with the bishop, answered the door and at once called St. Francis Hospital to inform the bishop of the fire. He came at once to the scene of the cathedral fire.

Fr. Reiss, on arriving at the fire scene, joined W. Traynor Staub, a maintenance employee at the cathedral, in racing into the burning edifice to the tabernacle, which Staub pried open with a crowbar so Fr. Reiss could save the Sacred Hosts. Staub had entered the cathedral earlier through a rear door and had run through the building to open the front doors to admit the firemen.

Fr. O'Connor was the most seriously injured of the four priests, suffering three broken vertebrae. Fr. Mooney suffered severe burns, and Fr. McGuinness was in shock. Fr. Fitzgerald escaped unharmed but spent a day resting in the hospital. The others were also hospitalized for a short time, as was Mrs. Dzienis, who was treated for shock and burns.

Fr. Fitzgerald reported that he had been awakened at about 4:30 a.m. by the sound of crackling and popping and that his room was bathed in an orange light. When he opened his door a few inches, flames shot into his face. He slammed the door shut, picked up a telephone to dial the operator, and got no answer. He unsuccessfully dialed the intercom numbers of the other rooms in the rectory, then decided to try to reach Msgr. Crean's room, but by this time the

Old St. Mary's Cathedral, Trenton, New Jersey.

Fire that destroyed St. Mary's Cathedral, Trenton, New Jersey.

door to his room was afire and his exit was blocked. Grabbing an armful of clothing, he went down the narrow stairs at the back of his room—the only such stairs in any room in the rectory. The stairs led to the kitchen, and he left the building by the kitchen door, stepping out barefooted into a narrow courtyard behind the rectory.

As he left, he saw raging flames extending out at least 10 feet from the second floor of the chancery. He heard the deep voice of a man crying "Help me! Help me! For God's sake, help me!" He believed it

to be the voice of Msgr. Crean. Standing in the bitterly cold rain, he raised his hand and gave final absolution to those trapped in the building, who obviously were beyond help.

As daylight came and as the blaze was finally brought under control, only smoldering walls remained of the 85-year-old cathedral and the adjoining buildings.

Because of the rapidity with which the flames had spread through the rectory, chancery, and the cathedral, the Trenton fire and police departments suspected from the be-

Msgr. Richard T. Crean
Died March 14, 1956

Celebrating Mass in St. Mary's Cathedral
Auditorium after the destruction of the
old cathedral in 1956. Parishioners of
the cathedral attended Mass in the
auditorium until a new cathedral was built.

ginning that it was a case of arson. Nine months later, in December 1956, a 41-year-old handyman from Florence, New Jersey, Elber Cooper Lucas, was arrested and charged with setting the fire. Lucas, according to the authorities, signed a confession admitting that he broke into the rectory on that early morning, tore up telephone books, and after pouring a flammable liquid on them, set them afire.

Lucas, who allegedly had set four other church fires later that year, was charged with murder in connection with the cathedral holocaust, was tried and found guilty by a jury on May 23, 1958, and was sentenced to life in prison. He was paroled in October 1976 and died three years later.

On the Monday following the conflagration, March 19, 1956, despite the worst blizzard in Trenton in more than 40 years, thousands of men, women, and children made their way to St. Anthony's Church in Trenton to pay their last respects to Msgr. Crean at his funeral. Because of the crowds, two Masses were celebrated: the first, a Solemn High Mass to which the cathedral parishioners and representatives of organizations with which Msgr. Crean was closely associated were invited, and the second, a Pontifical Requiem Mass celebrated by Bishop Ahr.

The sermons were preached by two of Msgr. Crean's close friends, Msgr. Joseph M. McIntyre, pastor of Christ the King Church, Haddonfield, and Msgr. Michael McCorristin, pastor of St. Anthony's. Both paid tribute to Msgr. Crean's sanctity, his zeal, his eloquence, and his tremendous accomplishments.

Bishop Ahr, after pronouncing absolution, led in the recitation of the first of nine public Rosaries, recited hourly until midnight.

Msgr. Crean was buried the next day in Calvary Cemetery, in Camden, his native city, following the celebration of a Mass in St. Anthony's Church by Bishop Ahr. The trip to Camden had to be postponed a day because of a snowstorm.

Bishop Ahr presided at a Solemn Requiem Mass for Miss Brennan three days after her death in the fire, in St. Anthony's Church. Miss Donnellan was buried in Valhalla, New York, following a Solemn Requiem Mass celebrated in St. John the Evangelist Church, White Plains, by her cousin, Msgr. Thomas A. Donnellan, an assistant chancellor of the Archdiocese of New York, later archbishop of Atlanta.

The grieving Bishop Ahr turned his attention to the task of dealing with the devastation caused by the fire. In *The Monitor* on March 23, 1956, he stated that it was impossible as yet to formulate definite plans to replace the cathedral but added, "Of this we may be sure: in God's good time, and we hope soon, the diocese again will have a cathedral, and Our Lady her church."

His prediction came true in a remarkably short time. Three years to the day following the fire, on March 14, 1959, a splendid new cathedral was blessed by Bishop Ahr on the site of the destroyed one. Archbishop Thomas A. Boland of Newark celebrated a Solemn Pontifical Mass of Thanksgiving, attended by many other members of the hierarchy and various civic dignitaries in the packed structure.

Designed by Ricker and Axt of West New York, New Jersey, architects, in modified Romanesque style, the new cathedral featured a 98-foot-high tower housing the original carillon and clockworks removed from the old cathedral, and the original bronze doors were reset in the main entrance to the tower and side transepts.

Highlighting the front facade was a large rose window with a Celtic cross sculptured in liturgical symbols. The front facade also contained statues of the Twelve Apostles and at the peak of the gable above the rose window, a life-size statue of Our Lady, patroness of the diocese.

The exterior walls of the fireproof structure were faced with Mt. Airy granite and limestone trim. The interior of the vestibule and baptistry were lined with imported marble. The nave and sanctuary interiors were lined from floor to ceiling with Briar Hill buff-colored sandstone. The floor of the sanctuary was of Roman Travertine marble with Virginia Greenstone borders. The new cathedral could seat 1,000 persons. The fireproof edifice was 216 feet long and 78 feet wide through the transepts. The sanctuary floor was more than 55 feet wide.

Woodwork throughout the cathedral, including the pews, confessionals, doors, trimming, wardrobes, and vesting cases, was of African mahogany.

Bishop Ahr began his sermon by recalling the pain and sorrow of that March 14, 1956, three years earlier, and of the days that followed. He paid tribute to Msgr. Crean, whose "heroic and sacrificial death," he said, "was but the culmination of a life of heroic sacrifice, and for me this new cathedral will be also a memorial of this noble soul, devoted friend, and exemplary pastor of souls."

He expressed gratitude to Msgr. McCorristin for his hospitality in permitting the use of St. Anthony's Church for so many ceremonies and functions following the cathedral's destruction, to Fr. Fitzgerald for assuming the responsibilities of providing for the spiritual needs of the bereft parish, and to Fr. John E. Grimes, rector of the new cathedral, for his work in connection with its construction.

After quoting the psalmist, in Psalms 35:18 "I will give thanks to Thee in a great church; I will praise Thee in a strong people," he dedicated the cathedral "to God under the title of Mary, our heavenly Queen, our Mother, and our Hope, confident that as we fly to her with filial love, with a mother's love she will shelter us under her protecting mantle and interpose her powerful intercession on our behalf with her Divine Son."

Following is the full text of Bishop Ahr's sermon:

"I will give thanks to Thee in a great church; I will praise Thee in a strong people." (Psalms 35:18)

Your Excellency, Most Reverend Archbishop; Your Excellencies, Most Reverend Bishops; Right Reverend and Very Reverend Monsignors, Very Reverend and Reverend Fathers; Reverend Sisters, distinguished guests and friends:

In the universal calendar of the Church the 14th day of March has no special significance. No mystery is celebrated; no saint is commemorated. But for us in the Diocese of Trenton it is a day which three years ago this very morning was painfully and indelibly imprinted upon our memories. For when that day dawned and the Angelus bell had sounded mournfully but defiantly for the last time from the blazing tower of the old cathedral, we recognized that a loving Providence had laid upon us a cross of sorrow in the destruction of our cathedral and chancery, and in the loss of three noble and devoted souls.

And so for us, forever more, the 14th of March will be a day of deep significance. For us there will always be a mystery to be celebrated on that day—the mystery of the loving Providence of God. For us there will ever be a commemoration of the holy souls who on that day God called into the joy of his presence.

Again, it is the 14th of March. Again, the Angelus bell has sounded but now triumphantly, for again the diocese has a cathedral and Our Lady her church. And now as each year we celebrate the mystery of Divine Providence we shall celebrate too the mystery of Divine Goodness, and our hearts will be filled with gratitude as we say as we do now: "I will give thanks to Thee in a great church; I will praise Thee in a strong people."

The days that immediately succeeded the fire were difficult ones indeed. You will pardon me, I hope, if, in the midst of what is essentially a joyous occasion, I revert for a brief moment to the sorrow of those days as we laid to rest the victims of the tragedy. They were my friends. Their loss was a personal and irreparable one. To their bereaved relatives I offer again sincere sympathy and the assurance of continued prayerful remembrance. It is but natural, I think, that the memory of Msgr. Crean, the beloved pastor of St. Mary's and vicar general of this diocese, should be recalled this morning. His heroic and sacrificial death was but the culmination of a life of heroic sacrifice, and for me this new cathedral will be also a memorial of this noble soul, devoted friend and exemplary pastor of souls.

It is a theological axiom that God exercises His care of us and extends His goodness to us for the most part through our fellow creatures. Never was this more forcibly demonstrated to me than in the months and years that have intervened since the fire. From far and near came expressions of sympathy and encouragement, offers of assistance and assurances of prayers. The priests, religious, and faithful of the diocese were magnificent in their faith and loyalty and generosity. And encouraged by their devotion and strengthened by their assistance, we set our hand to restoring the material losses we had sustained. And if today we are able to offer to Almighty God this magnificent temple, it is a tribute largely to them.

That is why it is most appropriate that every parish and community in the diocese participate in these ceremonies in the persons of the priests, religious and lay representatives here present, so that together we may share in the joy of our accomplishment, and together offer our thanksgiving to God for His goodness to us. And that is why as we say "I will give thanks to Thee in a great church" we add immediately "I will praise Thee in a strong people."

While I am deeply grateful to all who by their prayers and material generosity assisted us in our time of trial, I have particular debts of gratitude which cannot be passed over in silence.

Permit me then, in the first place, thus to acknowledge publicly my debt of gratitude and my deep appreciation to the members of the chancery staff, priests and laity alike. Their loyalty and devotion will always remain a bright page in the history of those dark days.

I am deeply grateful to Msgr. Michael McCorristin, our vicar general, for his gracious hospitality in permitting us to use St. Anthony's Church for so many ceremonies and functions since the destruction of our cathedral.

Fr. William Fitzgerald will always have my deep admiration and gratitude. In spite of his own harrowing experiences in the fire, he assumed and carried out with distinction the responsibility of providing for the immediate spiritual needs of a parish bereft at one stroke of its temple and its pastor.

Upon Fr. John Grimes, the present rector, fell the onerous task of rebuilding the cathedral. How well he has succeeded you are all witnesses today. But I would like to assure him now that I am deeply grateful to him for his capable administration, his unfailing cheerfulness and his indefatigable zeal.

The cathedral itself is eloquent testimony to the genius and competence of the architects, to the ability and fidelity of the contractors and workmen, and to the inspiration and artistry of the decorators. They have given us a substantial and beautiful House of God. And although we were told as early as last November that we could plan these ceremonies for today, I am conscious that it was only by the generous cooperation of all that our plans were realized. To all of them I am deeply grateful.

I am aware of the honor that has been conferred on us by the presence here today of Their Excellencies, the Most Reverend Bishops. In a particular way I wish to express my gratitude to His Excellency, our Most Reverend Archbishop, for his gracious presence and for having consented to offer this Mass of Thanksgiving.

And thus on this 14th day of March, with hearts filled with gratitude, we offer to Almighty God the new St. Mary's Cathedral.

Here we shall offer to Him our supreme act of worship in the daily renewal of the Sacrifice of Calvary, in adoration, thanksgiving, reparation and supplication.

Here under the sacramental veil His Incarnate Son, Body and Blood, Soul and Divinity, will dwell in our midst.

Here the parishioners of St. Mary's, the people of this city and its visitors will find an inexhaustible well-spring of divine grace and a fruitful source of spiritual blessing, strength and consolation.

In very truth it will be a House of God and a Gate to Heaven!

We dedicate this temple to God under the title of Mary, our heavenly Queen, our Mother and our Hope, confident that, as we fly to her with filial love, with a mother's love she will shelter us under her protecting mantle and interpose her powerful intercession on our behalf with her Divine Son.

But a cathedral is something more than a parish church. It is a symbol and an assurance of apostolic authority and the source of spiritual life for the entire diocese. The throne which graces the sanctuary of the cathedral is a constant reminder that the glorious heritage of truth and grace entrusted by Christ to His Apostles is still a living reality in this portion of His vineyard in the person of the one, however unworthy, appointed by the Successor of Peter to be numbered among the successors of the Apostles, and to inherit their pastoral power to teach, to rule and to sanctify.

In this sanctuary there will be consecrated the holy oils that will be mingled with the baptismal waters in every baptismal font in the diocese, and flow upon the head of every soul reborn in Christ; the sacred chrism that will sign with the sign of spiritual victory the foreheads of all those who are to be made perfect Christians and soldiers of Jesus Christ; the oil of the sick that will anoint the senses of the sick and dying of the diocese, to cleanse from their souls the remains of sin, to strengthen them in their agony and to prepare them to appear before their Judge.

Before this altar bishops will lay their hands on the heads of devout and eager young men; from the fullness of the priesthood pour into their souls a share of the Priesthood of Christ, and send them forth to preach the Gospel of Christ and dispense His mysteries in every portion of the diocese.

In very truth the cathedral is the Mother Church of the diocese, and the source of spiritual life to all the faithful.

From the flames and ashes of the old cathedral there has risen up the new. And in this resurrection we can find, I believe, a reminder of the indefectibility of the Church of Christ.

Though it may appear for a time that the forces of evil are in the ascendency, the spirit of Christ hovers ever over His Church in

New St. Mary's Cathedral, Trenton, New Jersey

fulfillment of His promises: "the gates of Hell shall not prevail" for "behold I am with you all days even to the consummation of the world." And so our new cathedral becomes for each of us a challenge that we walk worthy of the promises of Christ.

And thus to the glory of God, to the honor of His Immaculate Mother, for the salvation of souls and the edification of the Body of Christ which, in His Church, we dedicate this new St. Mary's Cathedral as with hearts filled with gratitude we say again: "I will give thanks to Thee in a great church; I will praise Thee in a strong people."

Present at the Mass of Thanksgiving were Bishop Martin W. Stanton, pastor of St. Aedan's Church, Jersey City, and Bishop Walter W. Curtis, pastor of Sacred Heart Church, Bloomfield, auxiliaries to the archbishop of Newark; Bishop Justin J. McCarthy of Camden; Bishop James A. McNulty of Paterson, Bishop John J. Carberry of Lafayette, Indiana; and Bishop Nicholas T. Elko of the Pittsburgh Byzantine Rite Diocese.

On Sunday, March 15, 1959, Bishop Ahr celebrated another Pontifical Mass in the new cathedral, and Bishop John J. Carberry preached at this Mass. Bishop Carberry had worked in the Diocese of Trenton under Bishop Kiley and eventually became cardinal archbishop of St. Louis, Missouri.

Following is the text of the sermon delivered by Bishop Carberry at the Mass:

"Peter addressed Jesus saying, 'Lord, it is good for us to be here.'" (Matt. XVII:4)

Your Excellency, Most Reverend Bishop Ahr, Right Reverend and Very Reverend Monsignors, Very Reverend and Reverend Fathers, esteemed religious brothers and sisters, and beloved members of St. Mary's Cathedral Parish.

The moving and touching words of St. Peter, "Lord, it is good for us to be here," seem to express perfectly the sentiments of all of us on this memorable occasion when we have gathered together in the newly restored St. Mary's Cathedral to assist at the Solemn Pontifical Mass offered by the beloved shepherd of the diocese, His Excellency, Bishop Ahr.

Yes, dear Lord, it is good for us, the members of St. Mary's Cathedral Parish, to be gathered around the altar of sacrifice as members of a loving family and to rejoice and thank Almighty God for His wondrous gift to us.

Yesterday, in the presence of the Most Reverend Archbishop of the Province of Newark and amidst all the beauty of the liturgy, St. Mary's Cathedral was rededicated by His Excellency, Bishop Ahr, and offered to Almighty God as His place of worship.

Today, however, in the warm simplicity of a parish gathering we have come together

The solemn blessing of the new St. Mary's Cathedral, by Bishop George W. Ahr. Left to right: Bishop Martin W. Stanton, auxiliary to the archbishop of Newark; Bishop Justin J. McCarthy of Camden; Archbishop Thomas A. Boland of Newark; Bishop George W. Ahr; Bishop James A. McNulty of Paterson; and Bishop Walter W. Curtis, auxiliary to the archbishop of Newark.

that we may relive the scenes of the past and pour forth sentiments of joy and gratitude to God for the gift of a new home for his beloved, revered, esteemed and treasured parish wherein the faithful of today and tomorrow will gather for prayer and sacrifice.

Truly, "it is good for us to be here." To be here to pray, and to rejoice and to assist at the Holy Sacrifice of the Mass, and to hear the Word of God and to reflect upon the true and real meaning of life, and to prepare ourselves in time for eternity.

Most humbly and prayerfully I say to Our Blessed Lord that I personally rejoice to be here on this historic occasion. The years from 1935 to 1940 which, in the Providence of God were permitted me to serve at St. Mary's Cathedral, are years never to be forgotten, precious years of grace, and years blessed with spiritual friend-

ships which have been a comfort, a consolation, a joy and an inspiration to me ever since. I express to His Excellency, Bishop Ahr, my gratitude for his thoughtfulness in permitting me to share in the happiness of St. Mary's Cathedral Parish today and of expressing on behalf of you, beloved parishioners, the joy which we know is in your hearts.

"God's ways are not men's ways, and God's thoughts are not men's thoughts," said the Prophet Isaiah centuries ago. God alone it is who can draw good from great sorrow and through suffering bring forth noble virtue and reveal sterling qualities of mind and heart.

Most of us present will never forget the heartsick and the grief-torn parishioners of St. Mary's Cathedral on the morning of March 14th, 1956, three short years ago. To behold the pride of the churches of the City of Trenton, to stand before the inspiring Gothic structure of one's beloved cathedral, and to see a work of generations of labor, suffering and love reduced to burning embers, a cluster of stones, is a memory that it seemed time could never erase. Helplessly, but without the loss of hope however, priests, religious, laity, and citizens of all faiths stood by and watched in profoundest sorrow and grief.

Yet, there was a deeper tragedy, the call to God of a beloved friend, trusted adviser to our Bishop, faithful and vigilant shepherd of his flock, Msgr. Richard T. Crean, a victim of the flames, together with the two faithful Marys whose lives were claimed in the holocaust of that hour. Mourning, dark and heavy grief weighed down the spirits of even the strongest. Some way or other it was hoped that the day would come when the walls of the cathedral would slowly rise again, when the chant of song and the sound of music would fill its spacious interior, when the sacrifice of the Holy Mass would be offered again for the living and the dead as before. Yes, all of this was hoped for, but everyone knew that Monsignor and the faithful women of the rectory service had solved the mystery of life never, never to return.

Of them we think and pray today, and they, on their part, are sharing with us in the place which God has rewarded them in the happiness of the Blessed.

The memory of our beloved Msgr. Crean is as fresh and vivid today as it was on the days before the tragedy. Please God he shall ever walk through the aisles of St. Mary's Cathedral, his kind smile, his total dedication to the service of God, his keen sense of judgment, his prudent and wise counsel, his love of God and his devotion to Our Lady can never be forgotten. These and other qualities are ever before our mind. Personally he daily shares in my prayers and Holy Mass, and in my own life and new responsibilities I ever ask Almighty God for the virtues which we so much admired and treasured in him. In moments of decision, in the face of difficulties, his manner of action comes to my mind and invariably I experience his helpful assistance which is so often sorely needed.

From the Solemn Blessing and opening of St. Mary Cathedral on January 1st in the year of 1871 down through the years the names of noble pastors have been written into the history of this parish. Fr. Anthony Smith, its first pastor; the Reverend James A. McFaul; and in our own times, the beloved Msgr. John H. Fox and Msgr. Maurice Spillane. These indeed were men of God, true shepherds of their flock, who left their impression upon the parish which they served so well. What a marvelous company of predecessors Msgr. Crean joined and how well he carried on the

traditions of a truly distinguished and blessed parish.

As one thinks of the great tragedy which befell the Diocese of Trenton in 1956 there comes to mind the history of a similar incident which affected the Universal Church in the destruction by fire of the well-known Basilica of St. Paul Outside the Walls of Rome in the year 1823. This great church had stood as a monument of antiquity from the sixth century. However, while repairing the roof one of the workmen in anger threw a pan of blazing charcoal at a fellow worker. One of the cinders unnoticed lodged in the roof and smoldered away. At 2 o'clock on the following morning great sheets of flame were seen from the nearby Benedictine monastery to ascend into the sky and in a short time the roof collapsed and all was destroyed but a portion of a wall, a few columns and the arch of the nave. Rome was stunned by the tragedy as Pope Pius VII lay dying. Word was kept from him of the disaster but before he died on that day he seemed to be possessed of a strange premonition of an impending disaster. The entire world, Catholic and non-Catholic as well as pagan, contributed to the rebuilding of a great monument of Faith. In 1854 on December 10th, some 31 years later, a new and more beautiful St. Paul's Basilica was rededicated by Pope Pius IX in the presence of prelates from all over the world.

There seems to be a striking parallel between the destruction of St. Paul's and its rebirth and our beloved St. Mary's Cathedral which has come back to life once more. Trenton and the whole country was stunned by the blow of its loss but now all rejoice in its reconstruction. Who could have ever predicted on that dark, rainy morning of March 14th, 1956, that within three years the Cathedral of St. Mary's would be alive once more, more beautiful, more spacious, more wonderful than ever before?

The rebuilding and rededication of St. Mary's Parish makes us conscious of the perpetual character of the Church of Christ. Tragedies occur and tragedies with God's grace pass into the realm of history. Men may come and men may go but the Word of God goes on forever. The loss of a great cathedral never interferes with the eternal mission of God's Church. "Behold I am with you all days, even to the consummation of the world." (Matt. 28:20). The love and service and dedication to Christ is the same whether it be offered to him in the humblest church located in the vastness of the forest or in the proudest cathedral in the center of a metropolitan city. The rebuilding and rededication of our cathedral make us realize, however, the strong, vital spirit of Catholicism which exists in the Diocese of Trenton.

His Excellency, our Most Reverend Bishop Ahr, asks for no praise, yet all who know and understand and see, realize that it was under his leadership and through the inspiration of his zeal for the House of God that plans were at once considered and carried out so that soon the foundations were being relaid and the actual walls of St. Mary's began to grow. We who know Bishop Ahr realize that he looks upon himself merely as the instrument in the hands of God, through whom the Cathedral of St. Mary's was given back to the Diocese of Trenton. Without a doubt all of us are convinced that the prayers of Msgr. Crean have overcome the innumerable obstacles which surely blocked the path of the reconstruction.

Today is a blessed day as Bishop Ahr, in humble gratitude, offers the Holy Sacrifice of the Mass in all the dignity of the Pontifical rite in his own church. His sentiments of appreciation and gratitude as expressed in the ceremony of yesterday go out to the wonderful, loyal, devoted priests, religious and faithful of the Diocese of Trenton through whose prayer, sacrifices and generosity the funds were supplied, without which the ruins of St. Mary's would never have been transformed into the inspiring edifice of today.

With the death of Msgr. Crean a great void had to be filled in the selection of a successor. Bishop Ahr realized where he could look for that successor in the present pastor of St. Mary's Cathedral, Fr. Grimes. He knew that Fr. Grimes was an assistant to Msgr. Crean and a devoted friend; he knew of the warm place which Fr. Grimes had in the hearts of the faithful of St. Mary's Parish; and he knew of his administrative abilities and accomplishments in his work as pastor of the church in Fords. He also was aware that his judgment in the selection of Fr. Grimes again was the work of prayers. The warmth of our joy today expresses itself in gratitude to Fr. Grimes for the masterly manner in which he has continued the traditions of St. Mary's Cathedral Parish.

In succeeding years undoubtedly the Parish of St. Mary's, like the great Basilica of St. Paul at Rome, will note with joy the anniversary of the rebirth of the cathedral and its rededication to the service of God. Parishioners of those days who look back prayerfully speak of the Faith and the courage and the love of the Bishop, his priests, his religious and his laity who indeed burned with zeal for the glory of the House of God.

May Our Lady, to whom the cathedral is dedicated under the title of her glorious Assumption, take unto herself once more this precious offering of the Diocese of Trenton in the form of a new home for her Divine Son. Most acceptable, indeed, will be this gift to her in which her children, like herself, may magnify the Lord and their spirit may rejoice in God their Savior.

Like the bewildered St. Peter of old as he gazed upon the brightness of Christ transformed before him on Mount Tabor so too we, overjoyed with happiness and gratitude, looking upon the new home of Our Dear Lord in this fair city, in the newly restored and beautiful Cathedral of Our Lady, can prayerfully and thankfully and lovingly say, "It is good for us to be here, O Lord." May God be thanked and praised forever and ever.

Accompanying the completion of the cathedral was the construction of a new chancery office on Lawrenceville Road, Lawrence Township, on the site of Notre Dame High School. Designed by Trenton architects William W. Slack & Son, the buff brick structure contained extensive office space, a boardroom, a courtroom, an assembly room, dining areas and a kitchen, a storage room, and lavatories.

On March 14, 1964, Bishop Ahr blessed a bronze plaque in the new cathedral in memory of Msgr. Crean, Miss Brennan, and Miss Donnellan, who died in the fire that had destroyed the old edifice.

Controversy made an appearance early in Bishop Ahr's reign, sparked by a young priest, the Catholic chaplain at Princeton University, who in the mid-50s sharply criticized certain university professors for what he charged was the atheistic and anti-Catholic nature of their teachings.

The university reacted with outrage, accused the priest, Fr. Hugh Halton, of personal and unsubstantiated assaults against esteemed educators, and demanded his removal. Eventually the university withdrew all campus privileges from Fr. Halton.

Bishop Ahr rejected the calls for Fr. Halton's replacement, staunchly defending him and his right to speak out to protect the faith of Catholic students at Princeton.

Fr. Halton, a Dominican priest then in his forties, was assigned to Princeton as Catholic chaplain in 1952 with Bishop Ahr's approval. His credentials for the position were impressive. He held Bachelor of Science, Master of Arts, Master of Literature, and Doctor of Philosophy degrees from Providence College and Harvard University. Six years after his ordination, he became the first American priest to receive a Doctor of Laws degree from England's Oxford University.

Even as a student, he served notice that he would not casually accept antireligious teaching. While at Harvard, he dared to question statements by the great Oliver Wendell Holmes Jr., then an associate justice of the U.S. Supreme Court, who in a lecture made demeaning references to the nature of humanity, declaring that "man is a cosmic ganglion not essentially distinct from a baboon or a grain of sand."

At Princeton, where he founded and directed the Aquinas Institute, a spiritual center for Catholic students, Fr. Halton came across some startling statistics. In compiling the names of Catholic graduates of Princeton, he found that 57 percent of them had fallen away from and died outside the church. He concluded that there was a connection between that figure and the university's curriculum, which, he had learned from students, was hostile to Catholicism.

In 1953, he publicly criticized a book, *Morals and Medicine*, by Dr. Joseph Fletcher, which had been selected as a textbook by the university. He charged that the book misrepresented Catholic teaching on such matters as euthanasia and abortion, pointing out 100 academic errors in the volume. Princeton was shocked that a chaplain would challenge an endorsed textbook. Willard Thorpe, professor of literary criticism, issued a statement: "Fr. Halton lacks decorum in daring to criticize any member of this faculty."

But the storm of controversy really broke on April 17, 1955, when Fr. Halton, speaking in the chapel of the Aquinas Institute, attacked the writings of Walter T. Stace, Stuart Professor of Metaphysics in the university's Department of Philosophy. In a textbook written by Stace, *Religion and the Modern Mind*, which was required reading at Princeton, the professor labeled all religious creeds as "myths," and faith itself "mere pig-headedness." He dismissed as an "opiate" the concept of a God who created the world and declared that since the world was ruled by blind forces, not a spiritual being, "there cannot be any ideals, moral or otherwise, in the universe outside us."

"Our ideals . . . must proceed only from our own mind," he wrote. "They are our own inventions. Thus the world which surrounds us is nothing but an immense spiritual emptiness. It is a dead universe."

Stace also declared, "The world . . . is purposeless, senseless, meaningless. Nature is nothing but matter in motion. The motions of matter are governed, not by any purpose, but by blind forces and laws. . . . Religion can get on with any sort of astronomy, geology, biology, physics. But it cannot get on with a purposeless and meaningless universe. If the scheme of things is purposeless and meaningless, then the life of man is purposeless and meaningless too. Everything is futile; all effort is in the end worthless."

Fr. Halton cited Professor Stace's statements as evidence of incompetence to teach religion in a university and said they posed a threat to the spiritual and moral life of Catholic students as yet ill equipped to judge them critically.

"My first concern is for the spiritual welfare of the boys whom I serve as chaplain," he wrote shortly afterward in *The Monitor*. "During their university years I want them not merely to keep the faith, but to grow in it and to deepen their understanding of classical Christian tradition.

"When they recite the Apostles Creed, I want them to know what they are saying. When they read in the Declaration of Independence that their Creator endowed them with certain inalienable rights, I want them to acknowledge their obligation to know, love and serve their Creator in such a way that gives rights their meaning. But what chance have they when Professor Stace (and I must insist he is not alone at Princeton) refers to their beliefs as 'opiates' and God as an 'illusion.' He violates the deepest convictions of their faith and reason, their very being.

"If Walter Stace is right, I'm wrong and so is the whole Christian cultural and spiritual tradition of the West. Are Christians and Jews adoring a myth? If Stace is right, we must get rid of the Creed and burn the Declaration of Independence."

The university community responded with indignation and anger. One of the most outspoken of the protesters was a Catholic member of the faculty, Hugh Scott Taylor, dean of the Graduate School. Taylor demanded that Fr. Halton desist, asserting that neither he nor the university would tolerate criticism of any teaching whatever by a priest.

In subsequent statements, Fr. Halton attacked all of the Catholic faculty members, as well as his predecessor as chaplain, Fr. Q. P. Beckley, for failing to speak out against the atheistic and anti-Catholic nature of much of the curricular material. Another book that earned an assault from the chaplain, one that was recommended to Princeton students, was *The Roman Catholic Controversy*, by George W. Elderkin, who had retired from the university in 1948 after 38 years in the Department of Art and Archaeology. In the book, Elderkin labeled the Vatican as the principal threat to democracy, traditionally hostile to popular rule, freedom of thought, and belief, and he accused the Papacy of collaborating with Hitler and other dictators.

Dean Taylor was particularly incensed by what he perceived as personal and vituperative attacks upon him by Fr. Halton.

The chaplain had referred disparagingly to Taylor's British citizenship after more than 20 years' residence in the United States, and he criticized the dean, who at the time was vice president of Princeton University Press, for acquiescing in the publication of books contrary to Catholic faith and morals.

Taylor began a long period of correspondence with Dominican and other church leaders, seeking redress for the "calumnies" against him. Ten Catholic faculty members complained in a letter to the provincial of the Dominican order in New York about Fr. Halton's attacks on Taylor, citing the dean's "selfless service in the cause of the Church." Provincial T. S. McDermott replied to one professor that "priests have their sphere of activity and cannot tolerate any interference with their sacerdotal duties on the part of any lay person." While Fr. Halton's Dominican superiors indicated they were uncomfortable with the tone of his attacks on the university figures, they made it clear that they would not act to replace him.

Taylor received considerable backing in the academic world, including expressions of support from a number of Catholic universities. In Princeton, substantial numbers of people agreed with Fr. Halton.

Bishop Ahr, meanwhile, was solidly in the chaplain's corner. When word reached him that Dean Taylor was contemplating carrying his case to the Vatican, the bishop let it be known that if that happened, he would go to Rome with Fr. Halton to present the chaplain's side.

In 1956, faculty resentment of Fr. Halton intensified. When the university invited convicted perjurer Alger Hiss to speak on campus on "The Meaning of Geneva," Fr. Halton declared that "spiritual, moral, and political subversion in our universities is a central threat to the Christian and American tradition." He arranged for Willard Edwards, who had covered the entire Hiss hearings before the U.S. Senate, to speak at Princeton the night before Hiss's appearance. A total of 578 persons jammed the hall to hear Edwards; Hiss drew 275. The press made much of the incident, to the university's chagrin.

Matters came to a head in June 1957, when the university board of trustees voted to withdraw from Fr. Halton all privileges at the university. The trustees then left it to Robert F. Goheen, the newly named president of Princeton University, to announce the action the following September.

The privileges rescinded from Fr. Halton included permission to march in academic processions, use of the university bulletin to publish schedules of Masses and other services at the Aquinas Institute, use of university rooms for lectures and guest speakers, and the listing of the Institute and himself in the university catalog.

Princeton maintained its action was not directed at the Catholic church. When another, more acceptable chaplain was appointed, the university said, all privileges would be restored. Speculation at the time was that because the suspension was announced by President Goheen, who was married to a Catholic and had five Catholic children, it was felt the university would be spared charges of religious bigotry.

Bishop Ahr refused to replace Fr. Halton. In a strongly worded statement, he supported Fr. Halton, declaring that "the basic issue is the right of a priest charged with the spiritual care of Catholic students in a secular university to speak out in defense of the faith and morals of those committed to his care."

He said the Aquinas Institute had been established and its director appointed under the authority of the bishop of Trenton, in order to care for the spiritual needs of Catholic students who attend Princeton University. "The first representations made to the bishop of Trenton in this matter by anyone of official standing at the university came in August when I was informed of the decision which the board of trustees had made in June. In my opinion, it was, in effect, an ultimatum from the board of trustees to remove Fr. Halton as director of the Aquinas Institute or have his recognition and privileges withdrawn by the university."

The bishop declared that to have removed Fr. Halton under those circumstances would have been "tantamount to placing the responsibility for the existing situation upon him. This I was unwilling to do.

"The published reports do not adequately present either the background of the situation or the basic issue involved," he continued. "The basic issue is the right of a priest charged with the spiritual care of Catholic students in a secular university to speak out in defense of the faith and morals of those committed to his care. The published reports do not recount the personal vilification that has been visited upon Fr. Halton in the Princeton community since first he undertook to speak."

Shortly afterward, on another occasion when Fr. Halton was present, Bishop Ahr referred to "the propaganda of silence" to which people were being subjected. He said, "We are being told that we should not speak about certain things lest we offend someone. An invitation was issued to us recently to inaugurate a kind of permanent 'be kind to atheists week.' . . . Is it unkind to point out that this gentleman (the atheist professor) is destroying the foundation of all religion and government?

"It is a strange anomaly that if you dare to present the truth you run the danger of being charged with anti-intellectualism. To be an intellectual you must not be intellectually committed to anything. As an intellectual you may have an opinion. But you must not say that you are right. And above all you may not say that anyone is wrong. This kind of intellectualism is the equivalent of universal skepticism."

A little less than a year after President Goheen's announcement, in August 1958, Fr. Halton was transferred from Princeton. Bishop Ahr announced that he had been notified by the provincial of the Dominican Fathers in New York, Fr. William D. Marrin, that the chaplain had been assigned to pursue advanced study and research at the University of Oxford.

Bishop Ahr commented, "I shall be sorry indeed to lose the services of this brilliant and dedicated priest. His sole purpose has been to safeguard in difficult circumstances the faith and morals of the students committed to his care, and he has carried out his responsibilities with extraordinary competence and great courage. My prayerful good wishes and gratitude go with him as he embarks upon his new duties."

Bishop Ahr experienced more personal sorrow during those early years of his episcopacy. On April 9, 1959, his father, George, died and on November 17, 1961, his mother, Mary, passed away.

But there were joyous occasions as well. In 1954, the bishop led Marian Year pilgrimages to churches dedicated to the Blessed Virgin Mary, patroness of the diocese, and there were two diocesan pilgrimages, which he headed, to the National Shrine of the Immaculate Conception in Washington, D.C.

On December 2, 1959, as the responsibilities of shepherding the rapidly growing diocese grew ever greater, Pope John XXIII named Msgr. James J. Hogan as the first auxiliary bishop of the Diocese of Trenton in its 79-year history.

Msgr. Hogan at the time was chancellor of the diocese and pastor of St. Catharine's Church, Spring Lake. His consecration took place on February 25, 1960, in St. Mary's Cathedral, with more than 1,200 members of the clergy, religious, and laity attending the traditional ceremony.

Bishop Ahr was the consecrator. Twenty-eight members of the hierarchy attended the colorful ceremony, and honored guests included Bishop Hogan's parents, Mr. and

Mrs. James F. Hogan of Camden, and his brothers and sisters and their families. Archbishop Thomas A. Boland of Newark, metropolitan of the Province of Newark, which embraces the entire state of New Jersey, preached the sermon. "Today, Bishop Hogan becomes another stone in the structure which is built on the Rock," he said. "Today he takes his place as one of the great Apostolic succession, which transmits from the first century to the 20th, and which will transmit from the 20th until the end of time the divine current of sacramental grace and revealed truth."

Bishop Hogan was born in Philadelphia October 17, 1911, the oldest of eight children. The family moved to National Park, and because there were no Catholic schools in that community, the Hogan children traveled each day to Camden to attend school. Bishop Hogan graduated from Camden Catholic High School and began his studies for the priesthood at St. Charles College in Catonsville, Maryland. In 1934, he was chosen by Bishop Moses E. Kiley of Trenton to complete his priestly studies in Rome. After completing studies at the North American College, he was ordained on December 8, 1937, in the college chapel, by Bishop Ralph L. Hayes, then rector of the college and later bishop of Davenport, Iowa.

He received his licentiate in sacred theology from the Jesuit Gregorian University in Rome in 1938, returning in that year to the United States. In 1941, he received the degree of Doctor of Canon Law from Catholic University of America. Bishop Griffin then assigned him as assistant chancellor of the diocese and parish assistant at St. Mary's Cathedral. Upon the death of Msgr. Reilly in 1953, Bishop Hogan succeeded him as pastor of St. Catharine's in Spring Lake, and he subsequently became chancellor of the diocese when Msgr. Crean was named vicar-general.

The following is Archbishop Boland's sermon.

"Behold I am with you all days even unto the consummation of the world." (Matt. 28:20)

Every consecration of a bishop witnesses another link in the chain of Apostolic office and tradition. It confronts the world across 19 centuries with those fishermen of Galilee whom Our Lord sent forth, clothed with His power and charged with the continuance of His work. Our Savior knew well that ages must roll by before this structure He planned could rise in its full glory; that the promise made to Peter, "upon this rock I will build my Church," implied a task of tremendous magnitude, of untold effort and struggle; that it would encompass and outreach the confines and the history of the world in which we live until at last God's children would attain "to the unity of Faith and of the knowledge of the Son of God." And because He knew the answer to the Psalmist's question, "Why have the gentiles raged and the people devised vain things?" He chose for His foundation a Rock so strong, unshakable and enduring that the very "gates of Hell" could not prevail against it.

Unity is the essential divine attribute and, consequently, the foremost test of all the works of God on earth. Unity is the prime requisite for order, peace and happiness among men, and, for that very reason, the first bulwark to suffer the vicious attacks of the "powers of darkness."

Hence it was that the divine Architect chose unity as the dominant note in His blueprint for the Church which was to perpetuate "grace and truth" among His followers until the end of time, and that He singled out Peter and through him his successors in the Papacy as the symbol and the guarantee of the unity of His Church.

And Peter understood that the supernatural strength that sank into his soul at that moment was not due to the ardent faith and unswerving loyalty that filled his breast, but as Our Lord had said to "His Father in Heaven."

Since the day on which this identity of teaching was made secure by Our Blessed Savior in the conferring of His authority on St. Peter, we have witnessed a unique phenomenon in history, the handing down, after the same manner, of an identical authority for nearly 2,000 years. Government, language, manners, the oldest viewpoints of life and society, social and economic conditions have changed and are changing, but the Catholic Church remains unchanged in her integral constitution, her teaching, her essential sacrificial worship and supernatural life.

Her episcopate yet stands for the Apostolic college that can never be said to die while the Apostles live in their successors. Her actual bishops are the last links in the unbroken chain of succession that goes back to Our Lord Himself, the first "Bishop and Pastor of our souls."

The Papacy today is a standing miracle, for only the "mighty wind" of Pentecost, the power of the Holy Ghost, could have carried through the centuries, from the Mediterranean basin to the farthest limits of the earth, the divine promise made at Caesarea Philippi, "Thou art Peter and upon this rock I will build my Church."

Today, Bishop Hogan becomes another stone in the structure which is built on that Rock. Today he takes his place as one of that great Apostolic succession which transmits from the first century to the 20th, and which will transmit from the 20th until the end of time, the divine current of sacramental grace and revealed truth.

What then does it mean to be a bishop? It means the possession of the fullness of the priesthood and a participation in the powers and privileges of the Apostles. It means to enter a new and special relationship with the Vicar of Christ, the Sovereign Pontiff of Christendom. For all bishops exercise their office of orders and of jurisdiction under the direction and authority of the Holy Father and in due submission to his primacy. It means the exercise of new and wonderful powers in the Mystical Body of Christ which is His Church. By the divine power of his orders he brings God's grace to man, and by the divine power of his jurisdiction he guides man unto God.

The power of orders needs little explanation. It works through the Sacraments of which the bishop is, by divine right, the dispenser and guardian. By virtue of the fullness of the priesthood which is in him, the bishop not only breaks the Bread of Life to his little ones and washes the prodigal soul in the Blood of the Savior, but he, because of spiritual generation, can perpetuate the life of the Church and transmit the power which Christ gave to His Apostles at the Last Supper when He said, "Do this in commemoration of Me." He alone can hallow men's hearts with that power of redeeming love, that power which Christ gave, when, breathing upon His Apostles, He said, "Receive ye the Holy Ghost, whose sins ye shall forgive they are forgiven." Thus, his power of orders means the efficacy which can create within men's souls the fullness of the gift and the fullness of the giving of the Grace of God.

The power of jurisdiction means the guidance of the Shepherd. Now the flock of Christ is led to God by the supernatural truth that enlightens the mind and the supernatural good that elevates the will. Therefore, the power of pastoral jurisdiction includes divine authority to teach and divine authority to command.

In simple, direct language fraught with meaning, the consecrating prelate declares these episcopal powers and duties to the bishop-elect after his mind and heart have been explored by the interrogations in the preamble to the ceremony—"It behooveth a bishop to judge, interpret, consecrate, ordain, offer sacrifice, baptize and confirm." Each of these acts pertains to a function vital in sustaining the unity, life and increase of the Mystical Body, and it is precisely through the exercise of these offices that the salvation of mankind is achieved.

In the acceptance of this divine institution we find the reason for the dignity conferred upon the bishop and the honor paid him by devout, loyal clergy and laity. Here may be found the reason why those outside the Church, even though they do not grasp the complete spiritual and sacred significance of the Catholic Episcopate, acknowledge the bishop as the leader of the Catholic flock, and give respect to his office and to his person.

Here, too, lies the reason for the fact that in time of persecution and assault upon the Church and Her rights, the enemies of religion have sought to silence the voice of the bishop, to restrict the liberty due him even as a citizen, and have not hesitated at imprisonment and death in an endeavor to stifle his power and influence. Just as in no century has the Church been devoid of a duly consecrated Episcopate carrying on the Apostolic succession and ministry, so there has been no century in which heroic bishops have not stood forth as witnesses unto Christ, even to the shedding of blood.

Ours is a day, too, when bishops in many parts of the world are languishing in prison for Christ, or driven into exile for Christ, or made to suffer tortures and humiliations for Christ. The disciple is not greater than his Master. It was no accident that the members of the Apostolic College made the Cross and the Sacred Passion of Our Savior the keynote in their lives, their teachings and their writing. The Savior's Death tuned the "glad tidings" of the Gospel to a mellow minor key, to the sound of which each one journeyed toward the martyr's crown.

The ceremonies of consecration are themselves the noblest proof of the esteem in which the Church holds the office. The Litany of the Saints fittingly introduces the central and essential act of consecration. Today the ancient prayer strikes us with rare solemnity. In majestic procession it takes us through the length and breadth of the Kingdom of God. From the all-holy throne of the Blessed Trinity it reverently winds its way through the realms of the angelic spirits and briefly halts at the "many mansions" in our Father's house which the Savior has lovingly prepared for His Apostles and Martyrs, Confessors and Virgins, and shortly we hear the inspiring prayer "that You may deign to bless, and sanctify and consecrate this bishop-elect." The solemn moment which is to witness the actual conferring of episcopal power has arrived.

Imposing their hands upon him, the three successors of the Apostles speak the exact words of Our Lord addressed to His Apostles, "Receive the Holy Spirit." Here and now with the recitation of the form there is fulfilled His divine promise: for the Holy Spirit, "Whom I will send you from the Father, the Spirit of Truth, Who proceedeth from the Father," descends into the soul of the new bishop and constitutes him, under the seal of the Blessed Trinity, a member of the ecclesiastical hierarchy in the long line of Apostolic succession.

It is significant that on other occasions when the Holy Spirit is given to men, such as Confirmation or the ordination of deacons and priests, the prayer always qualifies a specific power or function. We find no such qualification here; the Spirit descends in "His plenitude" even as He imparts "the plenitude of the priesthood." For here the Holy Spirit descends upon the Church, not alone as a Consoler and Guide, but as her Administrator and Head, as Provider for her life and great organic functions. He comes not principally for the personal benefit of the recipient of this exalted office, but for the common welfare of the faithful.

As in the beginning, so now in the constitution of bishops, we must acknowledge the influence of divine intervention in the selection and preparation of those who are to be bishops, i.e., witnesses unto Christ and his Church. No man assumes this burden to himself, and even when called, with fear and awe he approaches the altar of God to receive from the hands of the Consecrating Prelate the sublime and tremendous powers of the order.

For the 22 years of Bishop Hogan's priestly work in the Diocese of Trenton, God, in His inscrutable wisdom, was fashioning the soul and mind and heart of Bishop Hogan for the heavier and more responsible duties of the Episcopate. Whether as curate in St. Mary's or pastor in St. Catharine's, whether as Chancellor or Officialis, Delegate for Religious or Diocesan Consultor, Bishop Hogan brought to the work of his ministry an enthusiasm that never flagged, an exactness that never irritated, a courage that was never disheartened and a graciousness that was never affected.

These natural qualities of his character, made radiant and brilliant by grace, blended so easily with the supernatural powers of the priesthood as to form through the years the man, the priest and the leader admirably fitted for the Episcopate.

This day bespeaks two acts of high approval: one on the part of the Holy See, whose brief of appointment was read this morning, the other on the part of his beloved superior, Bishop Ahr. The fact that Bishop Hogan is to be associated with him as an Auxiliary of this great See of Trenton is a token of confidence of which he may be justly proud.

After Bishop Hogan's consecration, he gave the following talk at the dinner.

Your Most Reverend Excellencies, Archbishop Boland, Bishop Ahr and my brother Bishops; Monsignor Harding; Right Reverend and Very Reverend Monsignori; Very Reverend and Reverend Fathers:

You will all agree that on occasion old truths and old texts assume deeper significance than they ever had before. During the past few weeks, I have found so much more meaning and mystery in the divine reminder: "My ways are not your ways," as well as in the exclamation of the inscrutable designs of God.

My brother priests will know from confessional experience what a humiliating thing it so often is to leave the tribunal ashamed—shamed in the consciousness of eminent sanctity beyond the screen as compared to one's own. It is something of this humiliation I feel, despite all the generous sentiments so thoughtfully expressed, a confusion springing from consciousness of shortcoming, natural and supernatural, in relation to the exalted office which God has mysteriously deigned to bestow.

And yet it is a profound consolation to know from theology and from all Christian history that God, precisely to manifest His love, His power, His wisdom, can and frequently does employ the most unlikely of human instruments. Encouraging, too, is the conviction that what the liturgy has just now termed an "Onus" is really a sharing of Christ's burden, a "yoke which is sweet and a burden which is light." My concern, furthermore, is tempered by the multitude of reassuring messages speaking of Masses and prayers—especially from my brother priests.

To speak of my fellow priests is to be reminded, as I am, that the Holy Father through me has really honored them; that the Holy See has paid gracious tribute to our Most Reverend Bishop, to our priests, sisters and laity, for a work well done and for the mountainous task yet to be done. In this work of Holy Mother Church we are, all of us, His Excellency's auxiliaries. Insofar as the diocese has been honored in and through me, I am happy. But I am enormously proud, too, that God has numbered me among the dedicated, loyal clergy of Trenton—the finest priestly circle I know.

Just an hour ago, you joined in a litany for me. May I now recite one of my own—a litany of thanksgiving. If it be true, as

Ambrose puts it, "A man's greatest debt is the debt of gratitude," then indeed is my debt this day fathomless! I must thank God, however imperfectly, for this sacramental outpouring of His Holy Spirit, for this bestowal of spiritual dynamism which is the fullness of Christ's Priesthood; the Holy Father, Pope John XXIII, for his benevolence toward me and for his paternal solicitude toward the Church of Trenton; and His Excellency, Bishop Ahr, for the ineffable gift of episcopal consecration received by his imposition of hands, as well as for the confidence reposed in me and which, I beg God, will not have been misplaced. An expression of my deep appreciation is extended to Their Excellencies, Bishop McNulty and Bishop Griffiths, for the honor they have done me in the role of Co-consecrators. And what words could sufficiently thank His Excellency, Archbishop Boland, our Metropolitan, for the honor he has done all of us in making the day so much more significant by his beautiful sermon.

My gratitude goes out to Their Excellencies, my brother Bishops, and to my fellow priests, who by their sacrifice of time and effort saw fit to honor me and the diocese with their presence. In particular, it has been such a joy to meet again so many American college friends—some coming from a great distance.

To the priests and sisters who assisted with arrangements, with the ceremony and with the choir, I am deeply indebted—particularly to Frs. Grimes, Wagner, Reiss and Fitzgerald. Nor could I possibly fail to assure the Cathedral Choir, under the able direction of Mr. Godfrey Schroth Jr., of my grateful appreciation of its inspiring renditions.

If I may be permitted to extend the litany just a little, I should very much like to tell others of my gratitude today: My good parents, spared by God to see this occasion, my family, and all those priests and sisters and friends who have done so much by their inspiration, encouragement and help to nurture and to realize my vocation. My brother priests and the sisters who over the years have been so sympathetic and cooperative in my performance of official tasks. And members of the Trenton chancery staff, clerical and lay, who have always assisted me with uncommon patience, kindness, understanding and generosity.

And here, if I may, I would publicly say a word of heartfelt, grateful tribute to the revered memory of two noble priestly souls who, in different ways but in definite ways, had such an incalculable influence upon me—as upon many of us—Msgr. Reilly and Msgr. Crean, of blessed memory.

A litany most difficult to shorten will be terminated by an expression of thankfulness to the diocesan laity, who on the occasions I have had to serve them, have been so kind and considerate, and, in particular, to my beloved parishioners of St. Catharine's in Spring Lake for all they have done to make themselves my joy and consolation.

In conclusion, may I presume to note, as I do for myself, that beneath the pageantry of the sacred ritual, behind the ornamental brilliance of the Consecration ceremony, lie the *real* honor and burden, of the Episcopate—what His Holiness was pleased to call "the soul adorned with virtue." It is here that I most humbly beg your good prayers. While I pledge a renewed dedication of whatever energies God may grant to my Bishop, to the priests, sisters and faithful of the Diocese of Trenton, I entreat your prayers to the end that God, through the intercession of Our Blessed Lady, Queen of Apostles, will make me a

more fruitful instrument for His glory and for the welfare of Our Holy Mother the Church.

Following is the talk given by Msgr. McCorristin, speaker for the clergy, at the dinner.

Most Reverend Archbishop Boland, Most Reverend Bishop Ahr, Most Reverend Bishop Hogan, Most Reverend Bishops, Right Reverend and Very Reverend Monsignori; Very Reverend and Reverend Fathers:

It is a very great pleasure for me to represent the clergy of this diocese, on this great occasion, in offering greetings and felicitations to our newly consecrated Auxiliary Bishop Hogan. Naturally we are delighted to see the dawn of this day that gives our diocese the status of having an Auxiliary Bishop. We are happy, too, because this will lighten the heavy burden of our beloved Bishop Ahr, who has worked so energetically in this fast-growing area for the past 10 years in order that the people in every new development would be afforded spiritual care and given the opportunity to practice their holy religion.

It is not a difficult task to present the good wishes of our clergy to Bishop Hogan, for he is universally loved by his fellow priests, and rightly so, since he has always been more than generous in his service to us in the various positions he has held in the Chancery Office, since his ordination. Trained under the capable and gracious Msgr. Crean, whose 24-hour-a-day service is so well remembered, Bishop Hogan has always been the very essence of devoted service. His learned, kindly and useful advice and help have reduced the difficulties of our priestly ministry to a minimum. It is not surprising then that there has not been one dissenting voice on his selection as Auxiliary Bishop. Every priest was delighted on hearing the glad news of his appointment.

We are looking forward to happy years filled with great accomplishments for the Church, and for souls in this great Diocese of Trenton, with our energetic Bishop Ahr at the helm and Bishop Hogan as his right arm.

May God bless you, Bishop Hogan, with health and length of years in our midst, to continue and now to increase in your newly exalted state the wonderful work you have been doing for souls in Christ's vineyards—*ad multos annos.*

During the following decade came one of the most important and meaningful events of Bishop Ahr's episcopacy, the Second Vatican Council. Bishop Ahr participated in all four sessions of the Council in Rome—in 1962, 1963, 1964, and 1965—serving at the first session on a seven-member Committee on Faith and Morals. He interrupted his attendance only once, late in November of 1965 during the fourth session, to fly back to Trenton to attend a rally of diocesan campaign workers.

Before leaving for Rome to attend the first session, Bishop Ahr directed that in every parish of the diocese a Solemn Novena be celebrated in honor of the Holy Spirit to call down blessings on the Council Fathers in their deliberations. He further directed that a program be inaugurated in all the schools of the diocese to excite in the students a lively interest in the council and to induce them to a spiritual participation in

it. And he directed that, until the council officially ended, the Invocation, Versicle, Response, and Prayer to the Holy Spirit be recited after every Mass by the priest and the people.

Upon completion of the final session, Bishop Ahr returned to Trenton and immediately began implementing the liturgical and other changes that had been decided upon at the council. One of his first acts was to arrange a series of public meetings in the Community Room of the *Trenton Times* newspaper, at which he explained what had happened at the council and how it would affect the church in the Trenton diocese. At these sessions he presented experts on council documents, such as the one on ecumenism, who went into detail about the documents, their meaning, and their impact on the people of the diocese.

The enthusiasm with which Bishop Ahr embraced the results of the council un-

His Holiness, Pope John XXIII, with Bishop George W. Ahr at the Vatican.

doubtedly surprised many observers. He was regarded at the time as an arch-conservative in church matters and thus resistant to change. But in fact he was conservative only in the sense that he had no patience with those who would change or water down traditional Church teachings. His response to the council decrees made it clear that he was by no means opposed to change per se.

Msgr. William E. Maguire, who for several years was editor of *The Monitor,* observed many years later on the occasion of the 50th anniversary of Bishop Ahr's ordination to the priesthood that whether the bishop approved of the Vatican II changes was irrelevant to him.

"It mattered not whether the bishop personally favored a particular change," he commented. "If something now was the practice of the church, it now became the practice of the Diocese of Trenton. This is true also of optional practices. If the church has said it can be done, then he has shown no hesitation in permitting it to be done. That he himself might prefer to have it done otherwise has never been the issue."

Even before the final session of the council ended, Bishop Ahr had begun implementing its directives and recommendations. The Trenton diocese became one of the first in the country to witness the following changes.

— Attendance at Saturday evening Mass to satisfy the Sunday obligation.

— The use of English in the Mass and in the Sacraments.

— Participation in the Mass by the people.

— The use of folk music in the Mass.

— Celebration of Mass with the priest facing the people.

— Distribution of Communion by extraordinary ministers, that is, by laymen, laywomen, women religious, men religious, and seminarians.

— Reception of Communion in the hand.

The bishop also approved the formation of the Diocesan Council of Priests, an advisory body. And upon the recommendation of the council, he established a diocesan Office of Priest Personnel to assist him in making priest personnel assignments.

He created the diocesan Pastoral Council, a 300-member advisory and consultative group consisting of priests, sisters, brothers, and the laity. Francis X. Kennelly, a Jersey City attorney who served on the council for many years and as its chairman during its first two years, recalled that Bishop Ahr never missed a meeting of the panel and was always open to the problems of the people.

"He listened attentively to the items we requested him to consider," he said. The bishop never foreclosed dicussion of any matter affecting the diocese and the church, and he even intervened when members of the group wanted to cut off discussion because they felt an issue was not within the authority or competency of the board, Kennelly said. "He made it clear he wanted to know what the laity of the diocese were concerned with," he added.

Bishop Ahr established the diocesan Sisters' Senate. This organization was the result of an expressed wish of members of women religious congregations in the diocese, who wanted an opportunity to get to know one another and to collaborate actively in the life and work of the church. The bishop was most sympathetic, and he called the first meeting of the group in November 1969. Forty members of 40 congregations were present, and the bishop told them, "Because we are so intimately united in Christ and in the Apostolate, it seems we can best achieve this renewal by helping one another. So we create this new instrumentality . . . whereby we can more effectively and readily communicate as individuals and communities, sharing experiences with other communities, and all of us communicating with the diocese and its people."

One of the first major accomplishments of the Sisters' Senate was to draw up a job description for an associate vicar for religious in the diocese. Bishop Ahr approved the proposal, and Sr. M. Carita Pendergast, S.C., became the first associate vicar for religious in the Trenton diocese.

Sr. Cecilia King, first president of the Sisters' Senate, said she found Bishop Ahr to be "a true and valiant shepherd" to his people. "He internalized the council documents," she said. "To him, they were no mere words but a living challenge. He encouraged, initiated, and effected change with a quiet, indomitable personal power."

Sr. Eugene Marie Cavanaugh, the senate's first vice president, commented that "from that very first meeting it was clear to me that Bishop Ahr had a deep, passionate concern for the well-being of every

person in the Trenton diocese as it entered into the post–Vatican II era. Always evident was his concern for the doctrine of the church and how the implementation of that doctrine could bring people closer to God.

"Attributes aplenty can be ascribed to Bishop Ahr—he was understanding, compassionate, concerned, stern at times, agreeable at times, but in matters theological absolutely immutable, kind, generous, a melted heart when it comes to the elderly and the little ones, especially God's special children, the mentally and physically handicapped."

One of the Vatican Council documents to which Bishop Ahr responded most forcefully and effectively was its Document on Ecumenism—a call for outreach to other faiths. He established the diocesan Commission on Ecumenism, which under the direction of Msgr. John J. Endebrock and Msgr. Joseph C. Shenrock, made great strides in the months and years that followed in opening and continuing dialogue with other religious denominations.

He cooperated in the many programs arranged by the ecumenical commission, including a number of special seminars held at Princeton Theological Seminary, and "covenants" between Catholic and Protestant parishes.

In November 1974, Bishop Ahr participated in a special three-day seminar at Princeton Seminary, marking the 10th anniversary of the signing of the Vatican Council's Decree on Ecumenism by Pope Paul VI. Jan Cardinal Willebrands, president of the Secretariat for Promoting Christian Unity, was the principal celebrant

Jan Cardinal Willebrands assisted by
Fr. Joseph C. Shenrock on his left and
Fr. Charles Weiser on his right at
Princeton University Chapel.

and homilist in the Princeton University Chapel.

Bishop Ahr, one of the seminar speakers, told the gathering, "It is clearly recognized that the division that exists between those who profess to be followers of Christ openly contradicts the will of Christ, scandalizes the world, and damages the holy cause of spreading the Gospel to every creature.

"And moved by a desire for the restoration of unity among the followers of Christ, [the Vatican Council] 'wished to set before all Catholics the ways and means by which they can respond to the divine call for unity.' For this we are grateful."

The Trenton diocese and Princeton Theological Seminary, a Presbyterian institution, entered into an agreement for increased cooperation in the field of religious education. Many priests and sisters and lay-persons took advanced courses there in all areas of theology. This level of participation increased and deepened diocesan contacts with all of the neighboring non-Catholic communities.

Bishop Ahr's leadership in the ecumenical movement won him the admiration and gratitude of religious leaders throughout the area. In September 1976 representatives of many churches honored him at a dinner, and the presbyterate of New Brunswick presented to him a plaque for his efforts on behalf of interfaith understanding. The Rev. Dr. Andrew M. Sebben, pastor of the First Presbyterian Church of Trenton, who made the presentation, said that "under Bishop Ahr's leadership we have accomplished a miracle."

In 1978, the Trenton Ecumenical Area Ministry sponsored a dinner to honor Bishop Ahr on the Golden Jubilee of his ordination. United Methodist Bishop Prince A. Taylor, the principal speaker, described Bishop Ahr as "one of the finest Christian statesmen I've ever had the privilege to know."

Tracing the events of the previous half century, the problems facing church leaders, and Bishop Ahr's role in facing those problems, Bishop Taylor said, "We have here a success story in its purest sense and deepest meaning. That is what he has been. Success is a person who has chosen a way of life, committed himself to that way of life, and followed it through despite all the problems."

Dean Lloyd A. Chattin, of Trinity Episcopal Cathedral in Trenton, was master of ceremonies. A gold watch, inscribed for the

Prospect Presbyterian Church, Trenton, NJ, 1975.
Left to right: Fr. Joseph C. Shenrock;
Bishop George W. Ahr, speaker of service;
Rev. Dr. Douglas Davies, pastor.

jubilee occasion, was presented to Bishop Ahr by the Rev. Layton Anderson, executive director of the ministry team.

Bishop Taylor spoke specifically of Bishop Ahr's role in dealing with the turbulence and tensions which afflicted New Jersey's major cities during the 1960s. The Trenton bishop was a strong voice for calm and for action to cure the social ills at the root of the riots that took place in Trenton, Camden, Newark, and Paterson.

Following the assassination of civil rights leader Martin Luther King Jr. in 1968, Bishop Ahr took part in a memorial service for Dr. King in Trenton's Civic Center. In

his address, he declared that "Martin Luther King was not a political leader. He was a man of God and a preacher of the Gospel. It is not difficult for us Catholics to understand what he was saying and what he stood for and to respect him for it, for his principles and ideals are part of our Christian tradition and commitment."

He drew a comparison between the things Dr. King stood for and which the Second Vatican Council advocated: the dignity of the human person, reverence for humankind, brotherhood, antidiscrimination, and repudiation of violence.

A month later, he publicly supported a Poor People's March on Washington as it stopped in Trenton. And in July of that year, he joined, and assumed a leadership role in the New Jersey Religious Coalition to consider the "crisis in poverty, human rights and spiritual deprivation."

In June 1969, he joined in launching Project Equality of New Jersey with other dioceses and Protestant churches to promote equal opportunity in employment and housing for minority groups. "Every man, irrespective of his race, creed or color, has a God-given right to use his talents and skills to provide for himself and his family the necessities of life," he wrote in a statement to the faithful of the diocese. "Despite the clear teachings of our religion, and the laws which we have supported in our state and in our nation to protect these rights, discrimination continues to impose tremendous economic hardship on millions of our brothers."

In 1974, he issued a statement in support of the United Farm Workers of

America's efforts to seek justice for its workers through free and secret elections. That year he also chaired a statewide committee seeking approval of a $90-million bond issue for low- and middle-income housing.

In 1975, he established a Department of Social Concerns in the diocese, at the request of the Council of Priests, and in response to a document by the Synod of Priests, "Justice in the World." The department, headed first by Fr. Joseph C. Shenrock, attacked with the bishop's support certain social issues affecting the dignity of human life in the diocese. The new body was a leading factor in Project ECHO (Elderly Communication Help Outreach), a program that involved 11 Christian churches in Trenton in providing recreation, fellowship, travel, education, service, and help for senior citizens.

The department also arranged a course called Social Action in Catholic Perspective, which was given at Princeton Theological Seminary.

In 1976, Bishop Ahr was honored at a dinner for his efforts in providing manpower and money for the Mercer Opportunities Industrialization Center (OIC) of Trenton, a group dedicated to training the unemployed and helping them find jobs. The Rev. S. Howard Woodson Jr., chairman of the board of the organization, introduced the bishop at the affair, calling him "a great spiritual leader," not only of the diocese but of the nation. The Rev. Woodson was pastor of Shiloh Baptist Church, one of the largest black congregations in the Trenton area, and he also served as the first black speaker of the New Jersey Assembly.

He noted that Bishop Ahr had been a longtime supporter of the OIC, not only furnishing the services of two priests but making substantial financial contributions as well.

Bishop Ahr's concern for interracial harmony was manifested long before the crisis of the late 1960s. In 1963, he established the Diocesan Interracial Council as an educational and cooperative approach to interracial understanding in the diocese.

In 1977, after attending "Call to Action" hearings conducted by the National Conference of Catholic Bishops in Detroit, Bishop Ahr invited urban pastors in the diocese to hearings for discussion of their mutual problems. As a result, he formed the Diocesan Urban Committee. Later, he also established a diocesan office, Oficina de Ayuda al Imigrantes, to assist aliens regarding their status with the U.S. Department of Immigration and Naturalization.

As the numbers of Spanish- and Portuguese-speaking Catholics increased dramatically during the middle years of his episcopacy, Bishop Ahr created a diocesan office, that of coordinator for the Hispanic-American Apostolate, to minister to immigrants' needs and concerns. He demonstrated his interest in the Spanish-speaking faithful in many ways: by financial help and grants, by his personal involvement in the creation of new chapels and parishes, by his frequent visits to those places, and by celebrating Masses in Spanish whenever he visited a Spanish church.

Many Hispanic Catholic immigrants to Trenton settled in the area surrounding St. Mary's Cathedral, further enriching that historic congregation with their deep religious faith and their vibrant culture. Masses and services in both English and Spanish became part of the regular schedule in the diocese's spiritual center.

Again following the lead of the Second Vatican Council, Bishop Ahr in 1974 encouraged, approved, and restored the Permanent Diaconate, an order dating back to the beginnings of the church to help carry out its ministry. During the sixth century and for more than a thousand years thereafter, the diaconate fell into disuse and became strictly a stepping-stone to the priesthood. It was restored by the Vatican Council with the approval of Pope Paul VI in 1967.

In 1974, after an extensive period of study and planning, the Permanent Diaconate program was put into effect in the diocese under the direction of Fr. James P. McManimon, with headquarters at 1 Centre Street in Trenton, in the former Catholic Men's Club building. The first class of 46 candidates began a long period of training in preparation for ordination as permanent deacons. Once ordained, they began assisting pastors in many parish functions: officiating at weddings and baptisms, reading the Gospel and preaching, teaching and helping with education and charitable programs, and ministering to the sick. Permanent deacons soon came to be of tremendous assistance to pastors in most parishes of the diocese.

From the outset of Bishop Ahr's service in the diocese, the family was one of his principal concerns. He established the diocesan Family Life Bureau, a many-faceted organization, which concerns itself with every phase of family life, from the unborn to death. With the bishop's enthusiastic support, the bureau became one of the most successful groups of its kind in the United States.

The bureau carries on a ceaseless fight on behalf of the unborn and sponsors pre-Cana Conferences for those contemplating marriage and Cana Conferences for the married—a program for separated and divorced Catholics, as well as a speakers' bureau, whose members bring to organizations discussions of many informative subjects such as sex education for youth, parents, and teachers.

Beginning in 1963, the bureau sponsored one of Bishop Ahr's favorite programs, the Anniversary Hour for couples celebrating their 50th or 25th wedding anniversary. The bishop took great personal pleasure in presenting to each couple, at ceremonies in St. Mary's Cathedral, a signed scroll, shaking the hand of each person, and giving his blessing. During his 29 years as bishop, he congratulated some 25,000 jubilarians.

Nowhere was Bishop Ahr's concern for the family more evident than in his fervent support of the pro-life cause. Even before the U.S. Supreme Court's *Roe vs. Wade* decision, which legalized abortion, Bishop Ahr made the cause of defending the unborn his own. He was a pioneer in the development of the Respect Life Program in the United States.

In the late 1960s, he saw the handwriting on the wall concerning abortion liberalization, and under his guidance the Respect Life Committee was formed in 1968 for the Province of Newark (Archdiocese of Newark and the Dioceses of Camden, Paterson, and Trenton). This led to the formation of the New Jersey Right to Life Committee.

To organize pro-life personnel and speakers, Bishop Ahr presided at meetings of doctors, nurses, lawyers, the Knights of Columbus, and the Holy Name Society. When Valerie Vance Dillon of St. Matthias parish in Somerset put together the first handbook for pro-life content and organization, entitled "In Defense of Life," Bishop Ahr personally sent a copy to every bishop in the United States. Many pro-life organizations in the country owed their foundation to the book.

For the education of priests and religious of the diocese he brought in some of the top pro-life experts in the world, among them Jill Knight, Colin Clark, Frank Sheed, Charles Rice, Robert Byrne, and Fr. Charles Carroll.

He undertook the financing of Birthright, the volunteer organization that throughout the diocese assists women who have problem pregnancies.

When the Supreme Court announced its decision legalizing abortion on January 23, 1973, Bishop Ahr was quick to respond with a statement condemning the action.

The decision, he said, left unanswered many questions and created more problems than it solved.

"Our principal concern at the moment, however, is not a pastoral one," he declared. "The Supreme Court is not God. It cannot invalidate the moral law. Abortion is still a grave moral evil. Our Catholic people, lay and professional, have an obligation in conscience to accept the teaching of the church on abortion, most recently confirmed by the Second Vatican Council, and to 'obey God rather than men.'"

Bishop Ahr was in Chicago on January 23, 1973, to attend the first meeting of the Bishops' Committee for Pro-Life Activities, of which John Cardinal Cody of Chicago was chairman. The committee quickly issued a statement condemning the Supreme Court's action. Msgr. James T. McHugh, director of the committee, later recalled that Bishop Ahr's theological expertise enabled him to make valuable contributions to the body and that, for more than a decade, he had served on the committees of the National Conference of Catholic Bishops, which prepared statements on pro-life issues.

In 1975, when Terence Cardinal Cooke of New York succeeded Cardinal Cody as chairman of the committee, Bishop Ahr helped in the drafting of the Pastoral Plan for Pro-Life Activities, adopted by the bishops to give direction to pro-life efforts for many years to come.

Bishop Ahr was invited by the Holy See to be a member of the original Vatican Committee on the Family, established by Pope Paul VI in January 1973. For three years, he provided information and counsel as the only American on the committee.

That same year, he was one of the U.S. representatives to the Inter-American Bishops' meeting in Rio de Janeiro. The meeting focused on marriage and family life and involved bishops, priests, religious, and lay people from the United States, Canada, and South America.

For many years, Bishop Ahr was a strong voice in the National Conference of Catholic Bishops. He was a member, and served as chairman, of the conference's Committee on Doctrine.

On June 1, 1966, Auxiliary Bishop Hogan was appointed bishop of Altoona-Johnstown, Pennsylvania. He was installed on July 6, with Bishop Ahr assisting at the ceremonies.

On October 25, 1967, Pope Paul VI named Msgr. John C. Reiss to follow Bishop Hogan as auxiliary bishop in the Trenton diocese. At the time, Msgr. Reiss was pastor of St. Francis Church in downtown Trenton and officialis of the diocese. He previously had served as secretary and master of ceremonies to Bishop Ahr and as assistant chancellor and then vice-chancellor of the diocese.

The first native of the diocese to be elevated to the episcopacy, Msgr. Reiss was born in Red Bank, one of 11 children of Mr. and Mrs. Alfred Reiss. He graduated from St. James School and Red Bank Catholic High School, then attended Catholic University of America in Washington, D.C., until 1941, when he entered Immaculate Conception Seminary at Darlington. He completed the final year of his studies for the priesthood at Catholic University and was ordained May 31, 1947, in St. Mary's Cathedral by Bishop Griffin.

He served as assistant at Sacred Heart Church, Trenton; Holy Spirit, Perth Amboy; and St. Anthony's, Trenton, before returning to Catholic University to pursue studies in canon law. He received his doctorate in canon law in 1954. While attending the university, he served during the summer months at Our Lady of Perpetual Help Church, Highlands; St. Joseph's, Trenton; and St. Cecelia's, Iselin. He was administrator of St. Elizabeth's, Far Hills, and its mission, St. Brigid's, Peapack, until his appointment as Bishop Ahr's secretary and master of ceremonies on September 18, 1953. He was named by Pope John XXIII a domestic prelate with the title of right reverend monsignor in October 1963.

Farewell to Bishop Hogan, June 30, 1966.
Left to right: Rev. Msgr. Michael P. McCorristin, V.G.; Most Rev. James J. Hogan; Most Rev. George W. Ahr; Rev. Msgr. John C. Reiss.

On December 12, 1967, Msgr. Reiss was consecrated as titular bishop of Simidicca and auxiliary bishop to Bishop Ahr. In a modern, all-English ceremony in St. Mary's Cathedral, with more than a score of the hierarchy present, Bishop Ahr acted as the consecrator and principal celebrant of the Mass of the Blessed Virgin Mary of Guadalupe, whose feast day it was, with Bishop Hogan and Bishop Walter W. Curtis of Bridgewater, Connecticut, as co-consecrators.

Archbishop Thomas A. Boland of Newark, who was rector of Immaculate Conception Seminary during Bishop Reiss's student days, preached the sermon, in which he described the consecration as "an historic occasion." Every consecration of a bishop, he noted, "forms another link in the chain of apostolic succession." He called Bishop Reiss "a true pastor of souls, constantly in the midst of his flock," and said his years of parochial experience "will serve to keep him close to his people and enable him to understand fully their cares and problems."

During his episcopacy, Bishop Ahr witnessed a decline in the number of priests in the diocese while at the same time the Catholic population of the diocese was growing dramatically. In 1978, near the close of his episcopal service to the diocese, there were some 440 diocesan priests and 80 order priests to serve 850,000 Catholics. An increase in the number of vocations to the religious life was the bishop's constant prayer, and he never ceased to plead with the faithful to pray for vocations.

"I never feel more like a priest than when I am ordaining a priest," he said on one occasion. He established the diocesan Office of Vocations in Trenton, which became one of his prime concerns. In his efforts he had the assistance and support of the Serra Club of Trenton, a group of men dedicated to the promotion of priestly vocations.

On April 12, 1970, he presided at the first World Day of Prayer for Vocations ceremonies in St. Mary's Cathedral.

As a teacher, Bishop Ahr was acutely aware both of the importance of education in preparing young minds for life and of Catholic education in instilling in young Catholic minds the truths of their faith. So, from the first, he was fervently committed to a strong Catholic school system with the best facilities and well-trained teachers.

He communicated to pastors and the faithful the urgency of a faith-centered educational program. The baby boom of the late 1940s and the influx of Catholic families into the diocese necessitated the construction of scores of new schools throughout the eight diocesan counties. Schools and enrollments soon jumped by 80 percent.

In 1950, there were 29,276 pupils in 80 Catholic elementary schools and 4,795 students in high schools in the diocese. By 1978, the figures had jumped to 41,925 students in 116 elementary schools and 15,282 in 11 high schools. Proportionately enrollments had dropped slightly, due in part to a lack of teaching sisters.

At the beginning of Bishop Ahr's episcopacy, the vast majority of teachers in parish schools were nuns. But with the dropoff in religious vocations, more and more laypersons began to appear in classrooms. Bishop Ahr involved himself in teacher training programs, including the founding of an extension of Seton Hall University in Trenton. He also supported the establishment of programs for exceptional children.

On one occasion he told a group of parents, "We can all learn—it just takes some of us a little longer."

In December 1967, he appointed the diocesan Board of Catholic Education to advise him on school matters, and two days later he blessed the new diocesan Office of Education in Trenton.

In the 1970s, declining enrollments forced the closing of a number of parochial schools, and in 1972, the bishop appointed the diocesan Education Planning Commission, which joined other, similar units in other dioceses throughout the state to form the New Jersey Catholic Education Planning Commission in a common effort to implement realistically the teaching mission of the church.

Bishop Ahr frequently praised teachers for their dedication and their efforts in the classroom. "Let all teachers recognize that the Catholic school depends upon them almost entirely for the accomplishment of its goals and programs," he said in an address in 1977. "Many teachers, by their life as much as by their instruction, bear witness to Christ, the unique Teacher. The work of these teachers is in the real sense of the word an apostolate most suited to our times and at once a true service offered to society."

Msgr. Thomas J. Frain, who served as diocesan superintendent of schools for sev-eral years, once commented that Bishop Ahr's contribution to the diocese's educational system could not be measured solely in terms of a brick-and-mortar program. "Some men teach by their words, some men teach by their lives. Bishop Ahr is one of the latter," he said. "Some men build buildings, while others build faith communities. This ever remains the goal of Bishop Ahr."

If Bishop Ahr's parish work was at a minimum during his years in the priesthood, he more than made up for the lack after he became bishop. He identified himself closely with every aspect of parish life, showing keen interest in family life and social concerns.

He made it a point to personally visit parishes, to bless new buildings, and to let the people know he was aware of and appreciated the sacrifices they were making to promote the faith. Among the new parishes he established in the first decade of his episcopal service were St. Benedict's, Hazlet; St. John Vianney, Colonia; Guardian Angels, Edison; Holy Innocents, Neptune; and St. Bartholomew's, East Brunswick.

Among his hundreds of other blessings were those of the new St. Peter's Medical Center in New Brunswick, additions to St. Francis Medical Center in Trenton, the new St. Lawrence Rehabilitation Center in Lawrenceville, the refurbished Monastery of St. Clare in Bordentown, the Cenacle at Highland Park, and the new San Alfonso Retreat House in West End.

Bishop Ahr became involved on a daily basis with the hospitals in the diocese, the many phases of the Catholic Welfare Bureau, youth projects, evangelization, and numerous other organizations in the diocese such as the PTA, St. Vincent de Paul Society, Holy Name Society, Marriage Encounter, Catholic Charismatic Movement, and Cursillo. He continually promoted and attended the Nocturnal Adoration Society's all-night vigils on the first Friday of every month in the cathedral.

During his 29 years as bishop, he led numerous religious pilgrimages of the faithful and emphasized special occasions and events whose benefits redounded spiritually to the people. There were the pilgrimages to the National Shrine of the Immaculate Conception in Washington, D.C., diocesan participation in the Year of Faith proclaimed by Pope Paul VI in 1967, the Masses he celebrated in St. Mary's Cathedral every Sunday in 1966 to enable the people to receive the indulgences of the Extraordinary Jubilee proclaimed by Pope Paul commemorating the Second Vatican Council, and the Communal Penitential Rite he conducted and Mass he celebrated on the first Sunday of each month in 1974 as a preparation for the Holy Year of 1975.

In 1969, he led a delegation from the diocese to a consistory in Rome at which Pope Paul VI created 33 new cardinals, including John Cardinal Carberry, Archbishop of St. Louis, his close friend who had been stationed in Trenton as secretary to then Bishop Kiley. On that occasion, the Pope asked Bishop Ahr to join him in blessing the diocesan delegation.

When asked about his wide-ranging interests, the bishop replied, "I consider it part of my responsibility to be interested in all things, so that the presence and message of the church may be brought into all spheres of activity, and our people through these activities may have close direction and sacramental help in fulfilling their responsibilities."

So crowded was his daily routine that he had no time for hobbies or diversions. Once asked about this, he replied with a chuckle, "I do not think that anything I do could be dignified by the name of a hobby." How does a bishop relax after a busy day? "If he can find time, he sleeps."

In the area of evangelization, Bishop Ahr formed the diocesan Office of Evangelization, originally headed by Fr. Richard C. Brietske and Sister Mary Charitas. At first, its work was focused on nonpracticing Catholics, then on the coordination of evangelization programs in every parish of the diocese.

Establishment of *The Monitor,* the diocesen newspaper, soon after his installation was one of the bishop's most significant efforts in the evangelization field. Later he created the diocesan Office of Communications as a means of serving the communications media—newspapers, magazines, radio, and television—by making available before the public Catholic news and features of general interest.

With the other bishops of the state, Bishop Ahr joined in forming the New Jersey Catholic Conference (NJCC), the bishops' action arm whose purpose was to represent the Catholic Christian viewpoint before all branches of government, as well as other agencies in the private

Bishop George W. Ahr speaking with Pope Paul VI.

sector and religious groups. The conference on many occasions has made the Catholic position known on important issues to the legislature, the governor, and public bodies.

The bishop served as episcopal chairman of the conference, which also was charged with researching and identifying the needs of citizens of New Jersey in areas of human concern, such as civil rights, education,

employment, health and welfare, housing, and public morality.

Edward J. Leedom, who served as the first NJCC executive director, noted that Bishop Ahr's expertise on both the state and federal constitutions and his advice and counsel were invaluable assets during his many years of leadership of the conference.

Bishop Ahr was a proud member of the Knights of Columbus, and during a K of C membership recruiting campaign, he issued a statement declaring:

"The more I hear of the public and official acts of the Knights of Columbus, the more deeply I become familiar with the principles exemplified in your degrees," he declared, "and the more I am convinced that you are men of our times!

"On the one hand, I hear a resounding, unabashed acceptance and defense of the fundamental doctrines of faith and morals, and a loyal and devoted pledge of allegiance to our Holy Father and the bishops of the Church. On the other hand, I am made aware of a genuine willingness to accept the challenge of the Second Vatican Council even when this means adaptation and change, and to engage enthusiastically and whole-heartedly in the works of the apostolate, including programs of social action and ecumenical interest."

Tragedy again struck Bishop Ahr and the diocese when, on December 17, 1971, Fr. John P. Wessel, the 32-year-old associate pastor of St. Joseph's Church, Toms River, was mortally wounded by a shotgun blast fired by a distraught Vietnam veteran whom the young priest had gone to counsel. Nine days later, Fr. Wessel died of his wounds in Community Memorial Hospital, Toms River.

Bishop Ahr, who had ordained Fr. Wessel to the priesthood, was joined by nearly two score priests in celebrating a Mass of the Resurrection in St. Joseph's Church. Fr. Lawrence Donovan, then pastor of St. Joseph's, announced that an annual scholarship had been established in Fr. Wessel's

memory for any student who could not afford to attend St. Joseph's High School. Parishioners of Blessed Sacrament Church, Trenton, where Fr. Wessel had served his first and only other assignment, made plans for a continuing Crusade of Prayer for the eventual beatification and canonization of Fr. Wessel.

The final decade of Bishop Ahr's episcopate was marked by two joyful anniversaries. On March 20, 1975, he celebrated the Silver Jubilee of his episcopal ordination and installation as ordinary of the diocese. Congratulations and tributes poured in. Pope Paul VI bestowed on the jubilarian his Apostolic Blessing. The Apostolic Delegate to the United States Jean Jadot noted in a message that the past 25 years had been ones "truly devoted to the service of Christ and his Church in many and varied ways."

There were felicitations, too, from Archbishop Peter L. Gerety of Newark; from retired Archibishop Boland; Bishop Lawrence B. Casey of Paterson; Bishop George H. Guilfoyle of Camden; Bishop James J. Hogan; Bishop Michael J. Dudick of Passaic, Byzantine-Ruthenian Rite; and Archbishop Ambrose Senyshyn of Philadelphia, Byzantine-Ukrainian Rite.

Non-Catholic religious leaders joined in the celebration as well. Bishop Albert W. Van Duzer of the Episcopal Diocese of New Jersey pointed out that Bishop Ahr had been "widely acclaimed for having promoted understanding and goodwill among religious bodies of every denomination and creed. For his efforts he has been recognized as one of the outstanding leaders in ecumenism far beyond the boundaries of his diocese." Bishop Van Duzer continued, "Furthermore, by his life and personal example, this good man has won the recognition of his brothers and sisters as being a 'doer of the word.'"

Paul L. Stagg, general secretary of the New Jersey Council of Churches, spoke in a like vein. "In both my official and informal relationships, I have noted with joy the stirring of the ecumenical spirit within your diocese among the parishes, among both the priests and the laity, and the ties many of the parishes have established with local councils of churches. As a colleague in the coalition of religious leaders, I appreciate the opportunity to know you personally and to engage in serious discussion and relevant action in the mission of the Lord in 'setting the captives free,'" he concluded.

Rabbi Bernard Perelmuter of Har Sinai Temple, Trenton, speaking for the New Jersey Board of Rabbis, pointed to Bishop Ahr's "meaningful service" as chief shepherd of the diocese and added, "Your leadership has manifested itself in so many significant ways in the community. Those of us in the Jewish community appreciate particularly the strong bond of friendship that you have extended to us. Because of your efforts we have come to see the church as a stabilizing influence in our community, seeking to do the greatest good for the greatest number of people."

On the anniversary itself, March 20, 1975, Bishop Ahr celebrated privately a Mass of Thanksgiving. On April 13, the people of the diocese celebrated the jubilee in prayerful and festive ways. Nearly 1,200 people crowded into St. Mary's Cathedral for a Mass of Thanksgiving, and later in the day, more than 2,600 filled the Trenton Civic Center for a jubilee dinner.

Actually the bishop had turned thumbs down on any public celebration of the jubilee when he was approached by representatives of the Council of Priests, whose idea it was, and was asked to set a date. He was playfully told by the priests, "You have nothing to say in this matter, this is our affair." Whereupon he reluctantly agreed to go along with the plans.

Bishop Ahr was the celebrant of the Mass in the afternoon, with Bishop Hogan and Bishop Reiss, episcopal vicars, and representatives of the Council of Priests as concelebrants. Among those present were Cardinal Carberry of St. Louis, John Cardinal Krol of Philadelphia, retired Archbiship Boland, Archbishop Gerety of Newark, Coadjutor Archbishop John J. Maguire of the Archdiocese of New York, Byzantine Rite Bishop Dudick, Bishop Guilfoyle of Camden, and Bishop Casey of Paterson. Many representatives of other faiths also graced the colorful and solemn procession into the cathedral, including Bishop Van Duzer, Dean Chattin, and Canon Joseph Hall of the Episcopal Diocese of New Jersey; Bishop Prince Taylor of the United Methodist Church of New Jersey; the New Jersey Council of Churches' Rev. Paul Stagg; and the Rev. Dr. Jack Cooper of Princeton Theological Seminary.

Bishop Hogan was the homilist, noting the many memories, joyful and sorrowful, that must crowd Bishop Ahr's mind on this day. "Be assured of this," he said. "No joy for which he thanks God this day is comparable to that stemming from awareness of loyal, dedicated collaborators—priestly and religious."

In the evening, a tremendous round of applause resounded through the huge civic center as Bishop Ahr admitted he was happy that the anniversary had not passed unmarked as he had originally wished. He told the gathering, "I am glad we celebrated the jubilee because I am convinced that the celebration has brought the diocese closer together as a unit of the Family of God. Certainly because of the outpouring of prayer and love I have experienced, I feel closer to all of you than ever before." The jubilee, he said, while being observed in the present, was built on the past and looks to the future.

Bishop Reiss, the principal speaker, injected a lighthearted note into the evening as he recalled his student days at the Darlington seminary when Bishop Ahr was the rector. Pointing to the many changes that had taken place in the diocese during the past quarter century, he said that Bishop Ahr had "made the adjustments, but only after bringing to bear on each topic his vast knowledge, which could pull out the weeds and leave the essentials. He set the example by his words and deeds, holding fast to the basic truths and teachings, letting go the secretions and accumulations of nonessentials."

Msgr. Fitzgerald, chancellor of the diocese and master of ceremonies, gave the invocation and introduced Bishop Ahr. "Almighty God," he told the bishop, "must have been pleased at the way you, like Moses of old, have steadfastly led the priests, religious, and laity of our diocese through periods of terrible tragedy, constant development, tremendous growth, and unexpected change, keeping before them always by your life, your example, and your words the Promised Land and the Maker of us all."

In 1978, the priests, religious, and laity of the diocese saluted Bishop Ahr on the Golden Jubilee of his ordination to the priesthood. On June 22, a record-breaking 270 priests concelebrated a Mass of Thanksgiving in the cathedral. Following the Mass a dinner was held in the cathedral dining hall.

Three days later, on June 25, the women religious and the laity of the diocese filled the cathedral for a second celebration. This Mass was followed by a reception in the cathedral dining hall.

Cardinal Carberry, the bishop's friend from his seminary days in Rome, was the homilist at the June 22 Mass. He spoke of the three principal characteristics of the priesthood—one is called by Jesus, called to be with Jesus, and sent in the name of Jesus to proclaim the Gospel. "Unlike the Old Testament priesthood which was by right of birth," he said, "our priesthood is based on the loving invitation of the one priest, Jesus the Lord. It is a special grace, a unique gift, a privileged call. What is needed is our response. As we joyfully celebrate Bishop Ahr's 50 years of loving, faithful response to this call, the grace is offered to us priests to renew, to ratify, to intensify that 'yes' which we gave at our ordination to the gracious call of Jesus."

Auxiliary Bishop Reiss was the toastmaster at the dinner that followed the Mass. The speakers included Archbishop Boland and Bishop Hogan. And messages of congratulation were read, including one from President Jimmy Carter, a proclamation from Governor Brendan Byrne, and a resolution from the New Jersey Senate.

The senate resolution was sponsored by Senator Joseph P. Merlino, a member of Blessed Sacrament parish in Trenton, and pointed out that Bishop Ahr had "left an indelible mark upon all who have been fortunate to have served with him, to have learned from him, and, therefore, to have loved him." The resolution called the bishop "a man of God whose life has been an inspiration and whose example has set a magnificent standard for men and women of all faiths and creeds in their search for truth, peace and goodness."

Bishop Reiss delivered the homily at the June 25 Mass. He told the gathering that Bishop Ahr had been "teacher, preacher, and shepherd" during the 50 years of his priesthood. "A shepherd's celebration is really a celebration of the flock," he said. "We come to share in it and to rejoice in God's goodness to him and to us."

The Offertory gifts were presented by members of Bishop Ahr's family: his sister, Miss Eleanor Ahr, and brother, Wilbur, both of Irvington, and three of Wilbur Ahr's five sons and their wives: Peter and

Mary of South Orange; Paul and Deirdre of Bonair, Virginia; and Dennis and Barbara of Elizabeth.

Just before the conclusion of the Mass, Msgr. George A. Ardos, diocesan director of religious education, read a formal proclamation from Trenton Mayor Arthur J. Holland designating Sunday, June 25, as Bishop George W. Ahr Day in Trenton. Sister M. Jane Veldof, president of the diocesan Sisters' Senate, read from a spiritual bouquet to the bishop from the people of the diocese.

Bishop Ahr spoke briefly at both Masses, expressing gratitude to God; to his parents, who had encouraged him in his vocation; and to the priests, sisters, and laity of the diocese for their prayers and cooperation over the years. Again there was an outpouring of felicitations and tributes to Bishop Ahr from throughout the diocese, the community, and the Catholic world. Pope Paul VI sent his Apostolic Blessing and, recalling that he had done so three years earlier on the Silver Jubilee of Bishop Ahr's installation, added these words: "It appears that this auspicious event of your life adds an even greater measure of merit, because it not only underscores the duration of your sacred work in the daily ministry of the church— namely, half a century—but also clearly indicates the innermost and abundant source of your long-term pastoral zeal and also the source of all your manifold efforts initiated for the eternal salvation of man and for the welfare and prosperity of your ecclesial communities, namely, the sacerdotal grace of

Jesus Christ, which in a special manner, has inflamed and sustained in you a constant priestly fervor."

Messages came from Apostolic Delegate Arcbishop Jadot, Cardinal Carberry, Cardinal Cooke, Cardinal Krol, Archbishop Gerety, retired Archbishop Boland, Archbishop John Quinn of San Francisco and president of the National Conference of Catholic Bishops, Bishop Hogan, Bishop Dudick, Bishop Guilfoyle of Camden, and Bishop Rodimer of Paterson.

Archbishop Joseph L. Bernardin, former president of the National Conference of Bishops, noted that Bishop Ahr had served the conference in many capacities, including as chairman of the Doctrine Committee and as a member of numerous other committees. He said, "Bishop Ahr is what I would call a straight shooter. He never talks around a topic. He never speaks in an ambiguous way. Instead, he candidly tells everyone exactly where he stands on any subject under discussion. And he does it with both vigor and humor. At any meeting at which Bishop Ahr is present, you cannot help but know that he is there!"

Archbishop Bernardin added that he had tremendous respect for Bishop Ahr and his dedication to the church. "In addition to his work as a diocesan bishop, he has been most generous in the time and effort he has given to the Episcopal Conference. He has been a source of inspiration to me personally, and I consider him a friend."

Leaders of other faiths once more congratulated Bishop Ahr, repeating their praise for his ecumenical efforts over the years.

Pope John Paul I greets Bishop George W. Ahr following a papal audience granted to a group of American bishops in Rome for their five-year ad limina *visit.*

Expressions of brotherhood and respect came from Resident Bishop C. Dale White, of the United Methodist Church of the New Jersey area; Bishop Taylor, now retired bishop of the United Methodist Church of the New Jersey area; the Rev. Paul Stagg, general secretary of the New Jersey Council of Churches; Rabbi David H. Panitz, of Temple Emanuel, Paterson; Bishop Van Duzer; and retired Bishop Alfred L. Banyard, of the Episcopal Diocese of New Jersey.

Church policy established by Pope Paul VI and continued by Pope John Paul II called for a bishop to submit his resignation to the Pope when he reached the age of 75, although the Holy Father did not necessarily have to acccept it. Bishop Ahr let it be known as he neared his 75th birthday that he planned to retire on that milestone, and in the spring of 1979 he presented his resignation to Pope John Paul II.

On June 29, he annnounced that His Holiness had accepted the resignation effective June 23, his birthday, and that the Pope had appointed him as apostolic administrator pending the appointment of his successor.

In September 1979, Bishop Ahr underwent abdominal surgery in St. Francis Medical Center in Trenton. His recuperation went smoothly but it extended over several weeks and prevented him from taking an active part in the historic visit to the United States on October 3, 1979, by Pope John Paul II.

Msgr. Fitzgerald, chancellor of the diocese, coordinated the diocese's participation in the Pontiff's visit to Philadelphia on October 3. Tickets were provided for 23,000 people from the diocese to attend the Mass celebrated by the Pope on Philadelphia's Logan Circle. Auxiliary Bishop Reiss was among the hierarchy assisting at the Holy Father's Mass, and Msgr. Edward U. Kmiec, vice-chancellor of the diocese and secretary to Bishop Ahr, was selected to represent the clergy of the Diocese of Trenton as a concelebrant of the Mass.

Msgr. Fitzgerald was one of five priests of the diocese who were among those selected to receive Holy Communion from the hand of the Pope. The others were Msgr. Michael P. McCorristin, former vicar-general of the diocese and pastor of St. Anthony's Church; Fr. Walter A. French, pastor emeritus of St. Thomas the Apostle, Old Bridge, and liaison for the Council of Priests with the retired clergy of the diocese; Fr. Gabriel Ivascu, pastor of St. Basil's Romanian Byzantine Rite Church, Trenton; and Fr. Martin M. Komosinski, pastor of All Saints Church, Burlington, who had been chairman of an earlier fund drive among Polish churches for the Shrine of Our Lady of Czestochowa at Doylestown, Pennsylvania.

The Trenton delegation had seats in the front row of priests at Philadelphia's Civic Center ceremonies.

Later that month, Bishop Ahr approved for use by the faithful of the diocese a prayer for the selection of his successor. The prayer, prepared by Fr. John F. Campoli, director of the diocesan Liturgy Office, asked God to "give us the joy of receiving a shepherd who will be an example of goodness to your people and will fill our hearts and minds with the trust of the Gospel." The prayer also offered thanks for Bishop Ahr's many years of priestly leadership and asked that he be given many more years of peace and joy in the priesthood.

On March 5, 1980, Pope John Paul II named Auxiliary Bishop John C. Reiss to be the eighth bishop of the Diocese of Trenton.

Bishop Ahr welcomed the appointment, declaring, "I extend to Bishop Reiss my warmest congratulations upon being named the eighth bishop of the Diocese of Trenton. And I wish for him and the people of the diocese many years of growth, blessed by the peace and joy of Our Lord, inspired by his Holy Spirit.

"Bishop Reiss has been a faithful priest of the Diocese of Trenton for nearly 33 years. As the first priest of the diocese to assume the role of bishop of Trenton, Bishop Reiss begins his office with a real sense of familiarity and care for the people of central New Jersey. I believe that with the grace of God, Bishop Reiss will be a strong leader and a strong shepherd in the diocesan family of Trenton."

Upon turning over the episcopacy to Bishop Reiss, Bishop Ahr moved to a residence he had acquired in Bucks County, Pennsylvania, across the Delaware River from Trenton. It was his wish, he had said earlier, not to reside in the diocese he had led for almost three decades. "I do not wish to be an obstacle in the path of my successor," he explained.

On August 11, 1981, the retired bishop was a homilist at a Mass of Thanksgiving at the Garden State Arts Center in Holmdel, New Jersey, marking the centenary of the diocese. He said the history of the diocese was a source of great pride, "for this is an institution that has known adversity and survived opposition."

"What faith there was!" he said. "What loyalty! What courage in those who have gone before us! These are the things which make our hearts swell with pride—and our minds pause in sober self-examination."

"The history should be read and pondered," he continued. "It would be well if the noble qualities of our forebears found continued expression in our lives."

"But now," he said, "the diocese must look to the future. What will they say when they write the history of the next 100 years? The opposition has gone. But materialism and secularism constitute more formidable adversaries even than physical violence. Can we meet and overcome these difficulties as our forebears did theirs?

"Although the material needs of the diocese have for the most part been met, the spiritual needs still endure and have become more urgent. For in the last analysis it is for this that the diocese really exists: the glory of God and the salvation of souls. All else is secondary; all else is but the means to an end."

In June 1988, nearing his 84th birthday and with the growing infirmities of his advancing years, Bishop Ahr took up residence at the Morris Hall Home for the Aged in Lawrenceville. There he was given loving care and constant assurance that his long service and his contributions to the spiritual and material well-being of the diocese were not forgotten. Anniversaries were observed at Masses that he concelebrated in the chapel, including in 1988 the 60th anniversary of his ordination and in 1990 the 40th anniversary of his installation as bishop. Bishop Reiss concelebrated on these occasions.

Much of the success Bishop Ahr enjoyed in dealing with the unprecedented problems of his episcopacy undoubtedly can be credited to his strong, decisive personality, which was forged during his years as a seminary teacher. A tall, solidly built man with dark, piercing eyes, he projected an image of studious sternness, which was not relieved by his portraits that appeared on the walls of rectories, convents, and schools.

Msgr. William E. Maguire, editor of *The Monitor* for several years, noted that Bishop Ahr was inclined to be reticent at informal gatherings of priests, and at more formal priests' meetings, he gave the impression that he thought himself still in the classroom. He issued directives in clear and unequivocal terms. He left no doubt that he was in charge.

To strangers, Bishop Ahr could be intimidating and seemingly cold and aloof, and more than one news reporter who approached him unannounced received a frosty reception. But those who knew him were aware that that was a facade masking a warm, human person. Countless priests, religious, and laypersons could relate inci-

dents that demonstrated his innate kindness, caring, and consideration, and despite his natural stoicism, he could never completely hide his grief when tragedy struck or he lost a family member or friend to death.

He was especially fond of children and delighted in being with them. He took particular pleasure in the give-and-take of the question-and-answer periods at Confirmations and during his visits to schools. He was deeply interested in the work of such organizations as the Holy Innocents Society, a group dedicated to special children, and the former St. Michael's Home for Children in Hopewell. He visited the home frequently, talked with the youngsters, and eventually closed the home because he believed that for children, family living was preferable to institutional life.

A sister who cared for the St. Michael's children recalled that the bishop became a father figure for one small boy who was heartbroken because his natural father never visited him and whom the bishop took pains to comfort. The boy thereafter talked incessantly about "my daddy, the bishop," and included him in his prayers at night.

Bishop Ahr's visits to the Sister Georgine Learning Center, a school for mentally retarded children in Trenton, were exciting times for the youngsters. Sister Barbara Furst, who directed the center, recalled that the bishop always referred to them as his special children. They called him "Bishop George" because they had a hard time with last names, and the younger ones sat on his lap and played with the crucifix he wore.

Fr. Terrence McAlinden, who served as director of the diocesan Catholic Youth Organization (CYO), recalled many occasions when Bishop Ahr reached out to teenagers and enjoyed being with them. On one occasion, while planning to celebrate Mass for the young people and staff in a special program, he became involved in a serious discussion before the Mass with a girl who was in some trouble. During the Mass, when the girl had to leave for an appointment, Bishop Ahr stopped, waved, and sent someone to her with the message that he would return and confirm her when she was ready, Fr. McAlinden said.

On another occasion, Bishop Ahr was present for a CYO workshop at Notre Dame High School when he became involved with a hitchhiker who apparently had invited himself in for the program and was sounding off to the bishop, with some complaints about the institutional church. When the program was over, Bishop Ahr himself took the young man to the railroad station in Trenton to catch a train.

Bishop Ahr's concern was not limited to the young. He often also visited the elderly in hospitals and nursing homes.

Those who knew Bishop Ahr well were struck by the role that prayer played in his priestly life. Msgr. Maguire, who worked closely with Bishop Ahr during the years when he was editor of *The Monitor*, noted this in a tribute printed in the diocesan newspaper at the time of the bishop's Golden Jubilee.

"In addition to his own prayer life, which was intense, he shared in the prayer life of others," Msgr. Maguire said. "He participated in the monthly priests' day of recollection and the yearly priests' retreats. Each First Friday evening found him at the cathedral kneeling with the Holy Name men for an hour of Nocturnal Adoration. As he drove to some function or other, he invited companions in the car to join him in reciting the Rosary."

Vincent Weiss, longtime managing editor of *The Monitor*, said Bishop Ahr's outstanding attribute over the many years he had known His Excellency was "his absolute recognition of the power of prayer. Throughout his episcopacy, Bishop Ahr has never let an opportunity go by to let his people know that he has been praying for them, at the same time asking for their prayers."

"As the years passed," Msgr. Maguire added, "it became clear that the unknown quantity who in 1950 had been named the seventh bishop of Trenton was someone very special. And the diocese had reason to consider itself singularly blessed. He has always been a bishop of his times."

Bishop Ahr died in his sleep on Monday evening, May 3, 1993, at Morris Hall in Lawrenceville, New Jersey. His body lay in state at St. Mary's Cathedral, Trenton, on Monday, May 10, and the Office of the Dead was recited on Monday evening, at 7:30 p.m. The Mass of Christian Burial was held on Tuesday, May 11, at 11 a.m. in St. Mary's Cathedral, with Bishop John C. Reiss as the principal celebrant and homilist. The Most Rev. Theodore E. McCarrick presided in his capacity as archbishop of Newark and metropolitan of the ecclesiastical Province of Newark, of which Trenton is a suffragan see, and gave the final commendation.

Bishop Reiss's homily at the Funeral Mass was as follows:

I express my gratitude and the thanks of our diocese to His Eminence Cardinal Krol, to our metropolitan, Archbishop McCarrick, to my brother bishops from near and far, and to the priests of Trenton, Metuchen, Newark, and other dioceses. Your presence is a sign of your connection with and esteem of Bishop Ahr. I am also grateful to the deacons, religious, and laity who have come to memorialize Bishop Ahr.

I offer my prayerful sympathy, and that of the diocese, to Eleanor, Bishop's sister, and to his nephews and their children and relatives. I assure you that all of us will pray that God strengthen and console you in this time of sorrow. The loss of your brother and uncle is a loss to his beloved diocese and to me personally.

The selection of the Gospel reading for this Mass was made a few days ago, and by coincidence it appeared in the liturgy twice since then. Thus, strong emphasis is placed on the words of Christ: "I am the way, and the truth, and the life" (Jn 14:6). This short passage, addressed to the apostles, is the blueprint and key for all Christians who struggle on this pilgrimage to God, but it is especially applicable to priests and bishops as the shepherds of the flock committed to their care. These few words are not proclaimed merely to be admired, but to be lived if one is to enter the dwelling place prepared and promised by Christ. I wish to use this passage to describe Bishop Ahr's life.

"I am the way…" In order to follow "the way" there first had to be knowledge. The initial lessons came from his family, then from the schools. This basic acquaintance with Christ was expanded by theological study in the seminary and finally lived in the priesthood.

From the Gospels we learn how Jesus acted as "the way." In His public life He revealed and proclaimed the message of salvation and of the fulfillment of the promised Redeemer. Furthermore, the New Testament recounts the multiple activities of Christ as He journeyed through Israel and by His teaching with authority and by His actions to convince His followers of the truth, to strengthen them in their belief, to encourage them, and to inspire them even to the point of suffering.

Bishop Ahr followed "this way." He proclaimed the Word constantly to many different audiences, imitating Jesus as a teacher. He spent many years as a seminary professor of dogmatic theology, and several of us here present learned from him. In his role as priest and more so as bishop, he taught the faithful and clergy of this diocese. After his return from the Second Vatican Council, he conducted a series of lectures on the decrees of the council in order to explain their theological basis, their correct interpretation, and their practical application. During the council he was the chairman of the Committee on Dogma for the bishops from the United States—so he also taught bishops. In addition, Bishop Ahr served as the chairman of the Committee on Doctrine for the National Conference of Bishops. Another important role as teacher was his activity with the Committee on Family Life—both here in the United States and in Rome.

Bishop Ahr's following of "the way" as

teacher, and perhaps his greatest achievement as bishop of Trenton, lies in how he implemented the decrees of the Second Vatican Council and the subsequent decrees and instructions from the Holy See. His interpretation did not embrace either liberal or conservative extremes, but rather the mind of the Holy See. His stance was always *"sentire cum ecclesia"*—to think with the church.

Jesus "the way" not only proclaimed but was also active—so too was Bishop Ahr. During his years of service as diocesan bishop of Trenton from 1950 to 1980, the diocese, then composed of eight counties, more than doubled in population. This substantial increase of Catholics required the establishment of many new parishes, the building or expansion of churches, and the construction of elementary and secondary schools. Consequently, Bishop Ahr's activities were multiple and varied. They extended from decisions to establish, review blueprints, finance, and build to the blessing of completed churches, schools, and convents.

Bishop Ahr's activities were not confined to the material but included the spiritual. It was under his aegis that the diocesan diaconate program was introduced and fostered and the Family Life Bureau—a much needed program to defend and to promote family life—was established.

Bishop Ahr's activities, as in Christ "the way," embraced the sacramental life of the church in the diocese. As a bishop, he ordained many to the priesthood to serve here, as well as two auxiliary bishops. It would take a computer to count the throngs Bishop Ahr confirmed. He conferred this sacrament during his thirty years as ordinary and during five more years in retirement.

Finally, Bishop Ahr's activities included ecumenical affairs, particularly his work in organizing the statewide coalition of religious leaders. Within the state, there was his work with both the New Jersey Catholic Conference and the New Jersey Council of Bishops; within the nation, his service on many committees of the National Conference of Bishops; and internationally, his contributions to the Papal Committee on Family Life.

Remember that just as Jesus, "the way," had sorrows, so did Bishop Ahr. No doubt the greatest sorrow was the 1956 fire, which destroyed the cathedral, the rectory, and the Chancery Office, but most of all were the deaths of Msgr. Richard Crean and two housekeepers, in addition to the serious injury to four priests. This cathedral is the work of his hands.

In brief, we say that all of Bishop Ahr's activities were carried out in his efforts to follow Christ, "the way."

Jesus is also "the truth," and Bishop Ahr's focus was always on the truth. As a trained theologian and a teacher of theology, he applied himself to seek the truth in the Scriptures and in Tradition, the twofold source of revelation. Once he obtained it, he would ponder the truth, cultivate it in his own thinking, and then apply it to present-day culture and life. As stated before, his governing rule was *"sentire cum ecclesia"*—to think with the church, and then to believe with the church and to teach with the church. Thus our bishop did not embrace or fall victim to theologians who might concoct their own theories that might run counter to defined doctrine or to the official teachings of the church. In one sense, he was a true conservative—that is, preserving, protecting, and holding the teachings of the magisterium. We have already mentioned Bishop Ahr's activities in this vein as he taught in the seminary and in the diocese by his lectures, letters, and preaching.

An extraordinary gift Bishop Ahr had was his ability to examine and then critique a theological text. He was able to detect errors that might appear in even a single word. His own conclusions were based on the Scriptures, the documents of the Ecumenical Councils, and the official teachings of the church. Truly, he was a defender of the faith. He imitated "Christ...the truth."

Jesus said, "I am...the life." This "life" is the spiritual life here on earth and the everlasting life in heaven. The former must be practiced as a means to inherit the latter. Having served under Bishop Ahr for twenty-seven years and having lived with him for nine of those years, I can attest that he was a spiritual man molded after the Lord Jesus. His personal prayer life was quiet and unpretentious but strong and steady. The Mass was his principal prayer—a joyful celebration; then, the Breviary and his evident devotion to our Blessed Mother. This devotion is succinctly expressed in his episcopal motto: "Mary is my hope." As a matter of practice, we recited the Rosary together in our travels to or from a ceremony or meeting. He had a great interest in and exerted much influence on the Shrine of the Blue Army in Washington, New Jersey.

Bishop Ahr also demonstrated his following of Christ "the life" in public. This he did through his presence at and participation in conferences and by his spiritual remarks. In the public arena, he showed that he followed Christ "the life" by promoting various devotions and programs to enrich the spirituality of the clergy, religious, and laity of the diocese.

Jesus, in His public life on several occasions, had to confront error and evil. Following this example, Bishop Ahr would fearlessly enter the fray against dogmatic and moral errors or evils. He would point out the mistake but invite the person to reform.

From this quick review of Bishop Ahr's life, we can clearly see that he heard the words of Jesus, "I am the way, and the truth, and the life." He assimilated them into his own thinking and practice and he faithfully exemplified them in his prayers and actions. He gave his all for Christ, the High Priest.

In following Jesus, he made many personal sacrifices to complete his mission as a shepherd. Completing one's life on earth entails sacrifices or "giving up." Little by little, pieces of Bishop Ahr's sacerdotal living were removed: no longer bishop of the diocese, age eventually curtailed his administration of Confirmation; soon, it was not possible for him to celebrate Mass—a tremendous sacrifice for a priest.

Last, the thread that tied our good bishop to this earthly life was severed, thereby permitting him to enter the place prepared for him in accord with the promise of Christ. I am sure that this believing theologian had no reluctance to answer the Lord's call: "Come."

So, as we admire, praise, and esteem Bishop George W. Ahr, we do not say "farewell," but "till we meet again" in the abode prepared by Christ for those who embrace His statement, "I am the way, and the truth, and the life."

APPENDIX 1

Parishes Established by Bishop George W. Ahr

1953	St. Gregory the Great, Hamilton Square St. Mark, Sea Girt St. Vincent de Paul, Yardville
1954	Nativity, Fair Haven
1958	St. Leo the Great, Lincroft
1959	St. Benedict, Holmdel Holy Innocents, Neptune Corpus Christi, Willingboro
1961	St. Pius X, Forked River St. Joan of Arc, Marlton St. Charles Borromeo, Cinnaminson
1962	St. Veronica, Howell St. Dominic, Brick
1964	St. Aloysius, Jackson
1965	St. Clement, Matawan
1966	St. Jerome, West Long Branch
1971	St. Thomas More, Manalapan St. Robert Bellarmine, Freehold St. Francis of Assisi, Brant Beach
1972	St. Martha, Point Pleasant St. Justin, Toms River St. Anselm, Wayside Holy Name, Delran
1973	Epiphany, Bricktown
1976	St. Elizabeth Ann Seton, Whiting
1978	Jesus the Lord, Keyport St. John Neumann, Mount Laurel
1979	Our Lady of Peace, Normandy Beach

APPENDIX 2

A REMEMBRANCE
Address given by His Excellency, Bishop George W. Ahr, on the occasion of the dedication of Crean Hall at St. Francis Hospital, Trenton, on August 10, 1957

The building which we have dedicated today bears the name Crean Hall. It was the happy thought of the Sisters of St. Francis thus to perpetuate the memory of Rt. Rev. Msgr. Richard T. Crean, the late beloved rector of St. Mary's Cathedral and vicar-general of the Diocese of Trenton, whose tragic death we will not cease to mourn. And although I knew how utterly adverse Monsignor was during life to anything that savored of personal praise or recognition, yet I gladly assented to their request because I am determined that in death he shall not be forgotten, for I am convinced that his memory can be an inspiration for us all.

It is indeed a well-merited tribute which the sisters pay Msgr. Crean by enshrining his name in enduring stone over the portals of the building. As we go through life we are privileged, from time to time, to meet a person who by his talents, personality, attainments and character stands apart.

Such a person was Msgr. Crean. He was a man among men, a priest among priests. He was endowed with extraordinary talent and he extended it to an astonishing variety of fields. He had an amazing capacity for work and he used it with complete disregard for self and entire dedication to his calling.

He would have been outstanding in whatever vocation he had embraced. Fortunately for us, he became an outstanding priest of God. And hundreds, yes thousands, are the better for having known and loved him. There was in his bearing a great dignity and in his appearance something even of austerity. Yet, there was that in his eyes and in his smile which showed forth a heart that loved with the love of Christ for

souls, a heart that bled with the pain of Christ for the weaknesses and sufferings of men.

And men and women of all walks of life, and children, too, knew instinctively, it seemed, that in him they would find wise counsel in their problems and sympathetic understanding and paternal help in their need.

From the earliest days of his priesthood, Msgr. Crean manifested a special devotion in the care of the sick. It was this that brought him into contact with St. Francis Hospital. Over the years the sisters had come to know that they could rely on his interest and his help. To him they went frequently with many of the problems that arise in the administration of a hospital, confident that from him they would receive prudent guidance and efficient help.

When the time came to construct the latest splendid addition to the hospital, it was natural that the sisters should turn to Msgr. Crean for advice and assistance. He studied the drawings and specifications; he evaluated the plans for the fund-raising campaign; he gave vigorous leadership to the parish phase of that campaign; he arranged meetings to ensure participation in the federal aid program; he made contacts that guaranteed adequate financing during construction. Without taking one iota of credit from anyone else, I think it can be fairly said that without his help, the greater St. Francis Hospital would not have come into being.

He gave the same care and attention to the nurses' home. Fittingly does it bear his name, for there is much of his thought and planning in it. And this very auditorium and gymnasium is here because he kept urging and insisting that it was necessary for the physical and moral well-being of the students that they have facilities for exercise and recreation.

And let it not be forgotten as far as the nursing school is concerned that Msgr. Crean was not merely an interested outsider. He was a part of the nursing school, in effect a part of its staff as a member of the Nursing School Council. It is fitting then that the Sisters of St. Francis should have chosen to express their gratitude by constituting this building as a perpetual memorial of that great benefactor of St. Francis Hospital and School of Nursing, Msgr. Crean.

But there is another and more efficacious sense in which the naming of this building is singularly appropriate. The profession of nursing is a noble one indeed, but it is likewise one that makes great demands upon those who aspire to it and those who practice it. It requires qualities of character and virtues of a high order. And it is precisely here that the memory of Msgr. Crean will serve as a profound inspiration to those who will pass through these halls into the profession of nursing, for in his life he exemplified in a high degree the qualities and virtues which should adorn their own.

No one can be a successful nurse who has not a deep and abiding conviction of the dignity and nobility of that calling. Without this, one will not even try to develop the qualities that will create and maintain that dignity and nobility in oneself. In Msgr. Crean the student can find this basic quality exemplified, for Monsignor had a profound conviction of the dignity of his calling. He was like St. Paul—all things to all men—but he was always and everywhere the priest of the Most High God.

No one can be a successful nurse who does not have complete dedication to duty—for here we are dealing not with ordinary services where lack of attention to duty might lead to the displeasure of an employer or loss of a position. In a nurse, the price of carelessness or neglect of duty can be the life of a patient. From Msgr.

Crean the student can learn what devotion to duty really means. After a busy day in the office of diocesan administration, his evenings would be filled with pastoral activities, parish meetings, instructions, and personal counseling. And the early hours of the morning would find him often enough at the deathbed of a faithful parishioner.

No one can be a successful nurse who is not endowed with a lively spirit of sacrifice. It is the essence of the vocation of nurses that they spend themselves and are spent in the care of their patients. They must be willing to sacrifice their convenience and comfort, and even at times risk their health and their life in the line of duty.

This too the student can learn from Msgr. Crean. His days and nights were not his own. His talents and his energies were at the service of others without regard for his own convenience and comfort. More than once his sacrificial selflessness brought him to the verge of collapse. And his heroic death was but the crown of a life spent in sacrificial service to others.

And so one might go on enumerating the virtues of the nurse and finding them in the inspirational life of Msgr. Crean. There are yet two others deserving of special mention—faith and love. The mysteries of life and death and the pain between which confront the nurse, are such as to try the very soul if they not be sustained by a firm and lasting faith. As a priest, Msgr. Crean was likewise confronted with these, as well as the added mystery of sin. Yet his strong soul never wavered, for it was lifted up beyond the mist of human ignorance by a living faith in the Infinite Wisdom of God and in His Infinite Love for men.

And there remaineth charity, love of God, and love of neighbor. This is the crowning virtue of nurses, for it gives meaning and merit to all the others. It is the well-spring of their tenderness, the source of their strength, the guarantee of their fidelity. For only if they consider the fulfillment of their vocation as a manifestation of love of God will they have an enduring motive for a dedicated life, and only if they see God in their patients will they be able to love them as they ought and make the sacrifices that their calling demands.

Charity was also a crowning virtue of Msgr. Crean. He loved God with his whole heart and so was able to dedicate his life completely to His service. He loved all men for the love of God and so was able to sacrifice his life so unselfishly in the all too few years of his priesthood and so heroically in his death.

And so it is that the Sisters of St. Francis, in giving lasting expression of their gratitude to Msgr. Crean, have given to all future generations of St. Francis nurses the inspiration of all that is good and noble and desirable in their own lives.

I do not hesitate to say I am confident that Msgr. Crean, who had their interests so much to heart during life, will continue to exercise a beneficent influence upon this school of nursing and its students by his intercession before the throne of God. And I am certain that the young people who pass through these portals will be a brilliant credit to their profession, their school, and themselves if they accept the inspiring challenge of his dedicated life and walk unwaveringly in the footsteps of this humble, self-sacrificing, and noble priest of God.

Bishop Reiss entering St. Mary Cathedral for Bishop Ahr's funeral Mass on May 3, 1993. Shown in the photo from left to right are: Bishop Edward U. Kmiec, Bishop of Nashville; Bishop James J. Hogan, retired Bishop of Altoona-Johnstown; Bishop John C. Reiss; Archbishop Theodore E. McCarrick, Archbishop of the Archdiocese of Newark; and Father Edward Arnister.

APPENDIX 3

Letters of Bishop George W. Ahr

BISHOP'S HOUSE
901 WEST STATE STREET
TRENTON, NEW JERSEY

April 20, 1950.

REVEREND DEAR FATHER:

Through the foresight and zeal of my illustrious predecessor, Bishop Griffin of happy memory, the Diocese of Trenton has been blessed by the recent establishment of a foundation of Discalced Carmelite Nuns in New Brunswick.

The building has now been renovated so as to conform to the requirements of Canon Law for a Papal Cloister of Sisters with solemn vows. On Sunday, April 23, at 9 A. M., I shall celebrate Mass in the Chapel and thereafter canonically establish the Papal Cloister.

The Sisters of The Carmel engage in no gainful employment, but depend entirely upon alms for even the necessities of life. They would be grateful if the people of this Diocese were informed of the establishment of this foundation and invited to visit them to seek the benefits of their prayers and sacrifices.

Realizing the blessings that will accrue to the Diocese from the existence among us of these heroic women, I would be grateful to you if you would call to the attention of your people, either by reading this letter or by some other suitable announcement, this new foundation of Carmel and would invite them to exercise their characteristic generosity in behalf of these consecrated souls.

The address of The Carmel is Landing Lane, New Brunswick.

Sincerely yours in Christ,

✠ GEORGE W. AHR,

Bishop of Trenton.

October 24, 1950

Reverend dear Father:

The announcement that our Holy Father, Pope Pius XII, will solemnly define the doctrine of the Assumption of our Blessed Lady into Heaven has brought great joy to the hearts of Catholics everywhere.

The doctrine of the corporal assumption of our Lady is not new. It has been enshrined in art, in the Liturgy and in the hearts of the faithful for centuries. That the virginal body of our sinless Mother was not permitted to suffer the corruption of the grave but was reunited to her spotless soul and assumed into Heaven is a truth which takes its origin not from natural scientific investigation or from purely human testimony. It is a truth which has been made known to mankind by the revelation of God.

This is the meaning of the solemn action of our Holy Father soon to take place. For when he defines the doctrine of the Assumption he will be declaring with infallible accuracy that this truth was made known to the Church in the beginning by a revelation from God. So it is that we can and, after the definition, we must accept the doctrine of our Mother's Assumption on the authority of God Himself who can neither deceive nor be deceived and thus pay Him the worship of unquestioning Divine Faith in this as in all matters which He has revealed.

In order to celebrate in a fitting manner this solemn and unusual event in the life of the Church, I direct that on November 1, the day on which the doctrine will be defined, sermons be preached explaining the meaning of the doctrine and of the action of our Holy Father, and that suitable ceremonies of thanksgiving be held in all the Churches of the Diocese.

Blessing you and your people, I remain,

Sincerely yours in Christ,

✠ George W. Ahr

Bishop of Trenton.

December 17, 1950

Dearly Beloved of the Clergy, Religious and Laity:

The paternal voice of our Holy Father, Pope Pius XII, has been raised again in an earnest and urgent plea to his faithful children throughout the world to unite in a Crusade of Prayer to avert the ravages of another World War.

With a heart filled with foreboding he points out, once again, the futility of war and the horror and desolation that must inevitably follow in its wake. The mad sacrifice of countless lives by new weapons of unparalleled frightfulness; the useless slaughter of untold thousands of innocent victims — the young, the aged, the sick; the wanton destruction of towns and cities, and the incalcuable waste of natural and economic resources - all that and more are the gloomy prospects should we be engulfed in another world conflict.

The peoples of the world long for peace — a just and lasting peace. They have had enough of slaughter and mutilation, enough of destruction, enough of poverty, enough of gnawing uncertainty and constant dread of what is to come. Long and hopefully have they looked to the statesmen of the world to provide them with the peace their aching hearts so ardently desire, but they have looked to them in vain. With every passing hour the clouds grow darker and more menacing; the situation becomes more critical. With every fleeting moment it becomes more and more apparent that human means are inadequate for the task that lies before us, and it is to God that we must turn. From Him we must implore the just and lasting peace so long and so intensely desired.

It is in this grave hour, then, that our Holy Father has called upon us to unite in a Crusade of Prayer for peace. Particularly in the days that remain before the Feast of the Nativity does he ask us to implore from the Divine Child, the Prince of Peace, that peace which the world cannot give.

In compliance with the desires of our Holy Father, I direct that beginning today and continuing every day until Sunday, December 24, in every Parish and Mission Church in the Diocese of Trenton, the rosary of our Blessed Lady, the prayer to St. Joseph and prayers for peace be recited before the Blessed Sacrament exposed, and that these prayers be concluded with Benediction of the Blessed Sacrament.

And I urgently request that the practice of the Family Rosary be introduced into all the homes in the Diocese, and that prayers for peace be made part of the daily family prayers.

Confident that you will heed the voice of our Holy Father with generous and filial obedience, I bless you all from my heart and I wish to all a blessed Christmas and a peaceful New Year.

Sincerely yours in Christ,

✝ George W. Ahr,

Bishop of Trenton.

P.S. This letter is to be read at all the Masses in all the Churches of the Diocese on Sunday, December 17.
G.W.A.

Diocese of Trenton
Chancery Office
153 NORTH WARREN STREET
TRENTON 8, NEW JERSEY

February 23, 1951.

Reverend dear Father:

The enclosed statement with reference to the "Holy Year Jubilee Indulgences" is to be publicized to the people of your parish in the manner that you deem best, and at the earliest possible moment, so that all will have the opportunity of gaining the Indulgences as soon and as often as time and opportunity permits.

I am likewise enclosing for your *personal* and *confidential* information a transcript of the faculties granted to confessors during the Jubilee period, which terminates December 31, 1951. You are to acquaint yourself with these faculties in order that you might better administer to the spiritual needs of those who might approach you in Sacramental Confession with the view of gaining the Jubilee Indulgence.

In order to stimulate the desire of those entrusted to your spiritual care to take advantage of the great favor of the Jubilee Indulgence, it is my wish that a Parish Mission be conducted in those parishes that have not had such spiritual exercises during the year 1950, or to date during the current year. In the parishes that have had missions, it is suggested that a Retreat or Novena be conducted for the same purposes.

It is my hope, if it be possible, that a program as indicated above be conducted in each parish during the year so that Christ's faithful may be prepared in all propriety and holiness to obtain the remission of their sins and to gain a plenary indulgence of the punishment due to them.

With a blessing upon you and those committed to your care, I am,

Sincerely yours in Christ,

✝ George W. Ahr,
Bishop of Trenton.

Enc.

Diocese of Trenton
Chancery Office
153 NORTH WARREN STREET
TRENTON 8, NEW JERSEY

December 26, 1951

Reverend dear Father:

Sunday, December 30, has been selected as a Day of Prayer and Reparation in which we may bring to the attention of all our people in America the plight and needs of the persecuted faithful in countries behind the Iron Curtain and in the Orient.

I am enclosing a copy of the resolution of sympathy for these victims of persecution which was adopted at the Annual Meeting of the Bishops in Washington. I direct that this resolution be read at all the Masses on Sunday, December 30th.

On that day also Solemn Exposition of the Most Blessed Sacrament may be held during the afternoon and evening, to give to our people an opportunity to unite in prayer and reparation for the alleviation of the sufferings of our persecuted brethren.

I urgently request your whole-hearted cooperation in fostering and promoting this National Day of Prayer and Mourning to the end that Almighty God may soften the hearts of His enemies, grant the grace of perseverance to their victims, and bring to a timely end the persecution of the members of the Mystical Body of His Son.

Sincerely yours in Christ,

GEORGE W. AHR

Bishop of Trenton

Enc.

MARIA SPES MEA

DIOCESE OF TRENTON
153 NORTH WARREN STREET
TRENTON 8, NEW JERSEY

January 4, 1954

My dearly beloved in Christ:

On or about February 5, 1954, we propose to publish the first edition of the Diocesan Weekly Newspaper, THE MONITOR, the official publication of the Diocese of Trenton.

Were it possible for me to visit with you personally, I should be happy to do so but since time and pressure of duties will not permit, I must resort to this approach and ask your indulgence while I place before you the need for your support in this new Diocesan venture. In doing so I have complete confidence in your fidelity, loyalty and cooperation and feel certain that you share with me the desire and hope that this project will prove not only successful but fruitful and effective for the greater honor and glory of God's kingdom on earth.

The importance of the Press was graphically described by Pius XI, of happy memory, when he stated that "The printed word is ruler of the world." While this is not the objective of the Catholic Press, it does, nevertheless, indicate the potent force for good that such a paper could have upon our own Diocese. For us it will provide a means of publicizing news of Parochial and Diocesan interest, not omitting those matters on a National and International basis that have a direct bearing on the well-being of the Church; it will further serve to spread and disseminate the truth in the hope of enlightening the uninformed and leading them out of the valley of confusion and doubt into the light and friendship of God.

With the view that you will wish to join with me in this avowed purpose, I humbly submit my request for your subscription to THE MONITOR. Enclosed you will find a subscription envelope on which you may inscribe (by printing) your name and address and return it to your Pastor by January 10. You will note from the enclosure that the subscription price for one year will be $4.00. Payment is to be made directly to your Pastor, and may be made on an annual, semi-annual or quarterly basis, whichever suits your convenience. If for any reason you do not find it possible to return the subscription as indicated above by January 10, I am sure that duly appointed solicitors of your parish will arrange to visit you and secure your subscription.

May God look with favor upon these our humble efforts, and may He bless you for your cooperation.

Wishing you all the joys of this Holy Season, I remain

Sincerely yours,

+ George W. Ahr,
Bishop of Trenton

Diocese of Trenton
Chancery Office
701 LAWRENCEVILLE ROAD
TRENTON 8, NEW JERSEY

July 30, 1958

Dearly Beloved in Christ:

As you have heard, our Holy Father Pope Pius XII has recently called upon Catholics throughout the world to raise up public prayers particularly for the Church which in certain areas is sorely vexed and afflicted.

The Sovereign Pontiff recalls to our minds our responsibility as members of the Mystical Body of Christ to assist by our prayers and sacrifices the victims of persecution. He details the perilous state of the world where a just peace still does not reign. He describes the vexations by which the Church is oppressed in many countries. And while he is confident of the indefectibility and ultimate victory of the Church, his fatherly heart is grieved by the sufferings of so many of his children.

And so the Holy Father pleads with us to join our voices in public prayer, in accordance with the intentions which he lists in his Encyclical, during the nine days before the Feast of the Assumption of our Blessed Lady, that through her intercession her Divine Son will pour out many graces upon the Church and the world.

In response to this plea of our Common Father I hereby direct that in all the Churches of the Diocese there be celebrated a Solemn Novena from August 6 to August 14, consisting of a short exhortation on the intentions of the Holy Father, the recitation of the Rosary and Benediction with the Most Blessed Sacrament. And I urge our Catholic people with true charity to unite their prayers and their penances in the Novena that through the intercession of the Queen of Heaven a torrent of grace may fall upon this suffering earth.

With a grateful blessing, I remain

Devotedly yours in Christ,

+ George W. Ahr

Bishop of Trenton

P.S. Please read this letter at all the Masses on Sunday, August 3.
        G.W.A.

OFFICE OF THE BISHOP

October 9, 1958

Dearly Beloved of the Clergy, the Religious and the Laity:

     The death of our Holy Father, Pope Pius XII, has touched our hearts with sorrow.

     With filial love we have asked of Almighty God that we his children might continue to be blessed with the wise and gentle presence of our Father. But exhausted by his self-sacrificing efforts on behalf of the world, his frail body could no longer obey the commands of his indomitable will and, his providential mission accomplished, his great soul took its flight to God.

     Future generations will doubtless assign to Pope Pius XII an outstanding place in the history of the Church and of the world, but we his children are bowed down with present grief as we strive to offer a parting proof of love for our Father.

     In every parish there shall be celebrated a Requiem High Mass for the repose of the soul of Pius XII, at the earliest convenient date possible. The date and time of this Mass is to be announced to the faithful with an invitation to be present.

     I pray that his name will be held in lasting, loving, prayerful remembrance by the Clergy, Religious and laity of this Diocese, and that as he poured out his life so generously for the salvation of our souls we may by our prayers speed the moment of his everlasting reward.

               Sincerely yours in Christ,

                 + George W. Ahr

                 Bishop of Trenton

N.B. The Collect "Pro Eligendo Summo Pontifice, Sede Vacante" shall be added as an Oratio Imperata pro re gravi in all Masses when the rubrics permit, until the new Pope is elected.

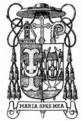

DIOCESE OF TRENTON

701 LAWRENCEVILLE ROAD

TRENTON 8, NEW JERSEY

OFFICE OF THE BISHOP

March 6, 1959

Reverend dear Father:

In accordance with the announcement made at the recent Clergy Conference, I am enclosing two tickets to the Solemn Blessing of our new Cathedral on Saturday, March 14, 1959.

I am deeply conscious of the part played by the Priests and people of the entire Diocese in making this happy day possible by their prayers and generosity. And I consider it most appropriate that every parish participate in the ceremonies in the person of its Priests and lay representatives, so that together we may share in the joy of the occasion and offer our thanksgiving to God for His goodness to us.

May I ask you then to select two persons to represent your parish at the Blessing of the Cathedral, and give to them the enclosed tickets.

The Procession will start at 9:45 A.M. The Blessing will begin at 10 o'clock and the Pontifical Mass at 10:30.

Bearers of tickets will be admitted to the Cathedral immediately upon their arrival.

With a grateful blessing, I remain

Sincerely yours in Christ,

+ George W. Ahr

Bishop of Trenton

Enc.

Diocese of Trenton

701 LAWRENCEVILLE ROAD
TRENTON 8, NEW JERSEY

September 26, 1962

Dearly Beloved of the Clergy and the Laity:

In his encyclical letter dated July 1, our Holy Father, Pope John XXIII, wrote as follows:

"Following the example of Our predecessors, We also, ardently wish to invite the whole Catholic world, clergy and laity—to prepare for the great Council's celebration through prayer, good works and penance.

"For this purpose We exhort you, venerable brothers, to institute in every parish of the dioceses entrusted to each of you, **just before the opening of the Council**, a Solemn Novena in honor of the Holy Spirit, to invoke upon the Fathers of the Council the advantages of heavenly light and of divine graces."

In response to this exhortation of the Holy Father I direct that in **every** parish of the Diocese of Trenton there be celebrated a Solemn Novena in honor of the Holy Spirit, beginning on Tuesday, October 2, and ending on **Wednesday**, October 10, the eve of the opening of the Council.

And because the Holy Father has emphasized the necessity of penance to make our prayers acceptable in the sight of God, I direct that on **each night** of the novena during the services there be preached a sermon on some **phase** of Penance and Mortification—their nature and necessity and the **means of** practicing them.

It is to be noted that to all those who take part in this novena **there will** be granted a plenary indulgence **under** the usual conditions.

I further direct that in all the schools of the diocese there be inaugurated a program, along lines suggested by the superintendent of schools, **to** excite in the students a lively interest in the Council and to induce **them** to a spiritual participation in it.

Finally, since the help of the Holy Spirit will be needed throughout **the** Council, I direct that after every Mass celebrated in this diocese, until **the** Council is officially ended, there be recited publicly by priest and people **the** Invocation, Versicle and Response and Prayer to the Holy Spirit, to call **down** abundant blessings on the Fathers of the Council, on their labors, on the **Church** and on the world.

With a blessing on those who heed this invitation of the Holy **Father,** I remain

Devotedly yours in **Christ,**
✠ George W. Ahr
Bishop of Trenton

N. B. Please read this letter at all the Masses on Sunday, September 30.

MARIA SPES MEA

OFFICE OF THE BISHOP

DIOCESE OF TRENTON

701 LAWRENCEVILLE ROAD

TRENTON 8, NEW JERSEY

June 4, 1963

Dearly Beloved of the Clergy, the Religious and the Laity:

The great heart of our Holy Father, Pope John XXIII, has been stilled by death and our hearts are heavy with sorrow. With filial love we have petitioned Almighty God to sustain our Father in his last illness, but we bow to the gentle dispositions of Providence which has relieved him of his agony and invited him to his reward.

John XXIII has captivated the hearts of mankind, and already he is being assigned an outstanding and even unique place in the history of the Church and of the world. We his children wish to offer a parting proof of love for our Father.

In every parish there shall be celebrated a Requiem High Mass for the repose of the soul of John XXIII at the earliest convenient date possible. The date and time of this Mass is to be announced to the faithful with an invitation to be present.

I shall offer a Pontifical Mass of Requiem for the repose of the soul of our Holy Father in St. Mary's Cathedral, Trenton, on Monday morning, June 10, at ten o'clock, and I invite the Priests, Religious and laity to be present.

May the name of Pope John XXIII be held in loving, prayerful remembrance by the Clergy, Religious and laity of this Diocese, and may we by our prayers speed the moment of his everlasting reward.

Devotedly yours in Christ,

+ George W. Ahr

Bishop of Trenton

N.B. 1) For this Mass cf. New Rubrics Nos. 394, 410, 411, 413. Permission is granted for an evening Mass, if it is judged more convenient for your people.
2) The Collect "Pro Eligendo Summo Pontifice, Sede Vacante" shall be added as an Oratio Imperata in all Masses when the rubrics permit, until the new Pope is elected. (Cf. New Rubrics No. 457.)
3) The Prayer for the Success of the Council is to be omitted until further notice.

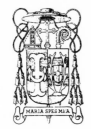

DIOCESE OF TRENTON
701 LAWRENCEVILLE ROAD
TRENTON, NEW JERSEY 08607

September 8, 1965

OFFICE OF THE BISHOP

Reverend dear Father:

        Our Holy Father, as you know, has recently called for prayer and penance
for the success of the last session of the Second Vatican Council. After stress-
ing the importance of the forthcoming Conciliar deliberations and emphasizing the
necessity of the guidance of the Holy Spirit, the Supreme Pontiff announced the
program of prayer and penance with which the Council Fathers themselves will
prepare for the session. Then he appealed to all in the following words:

                "And so, as a chorus of prayer and of penance which goes
        up from all five continents — wherever the Church is present,...
        we desire that in every parish, in every church of the Catholic
        world, there be held a ceremony of penance."

        In response to this plea of the Holy Father may I request that you arrange
in your parish a ceremony of prayer and penance for the success of the Council, to
be held on or before September 14.

        With a blessing for all who participate, I remain

                            Devotedly yours in Christ,

                            + George W. Ahr

                            Bishop of Trenton

N.B.

1. The ceremony might be the Stations of the Cross or the Penitential Psalms.

2. The Oratio de Spiritu Sancto is to be said as the Oratio Imperata in all
    Masses according to the Rubrics, until the end of the Council.

3. Please remind your people frequently to pray and do penance for the success
    of the Council.

DIOCESE OF TRENTON

701 LAWRENCEVILLE ROAD

TRENTON 8, NEW JERSEY

Rome, November 15, 1965

Dearly Beloved,

In his Apostolic Exhortation issued on November 6, 1965, in anticipation of the imminent closing of the Second Vatican Council, our Holy Father, Pope Paul VI has commanded that a solemn triduum of prayer be observed in all the dioceses, parishes and religious institutes of the entire Church.

The purpose of this triduum is to give thanks to Almighty God for His blessings upon the work of the Council as evidenced by the successful formulation and promulgation of an astonishing number of doctrinal and disciplinary documents, and by the respectful and favorable attention with which the world at large has followed the work of the Council.

A second, and not less important purpose of the triduum is to implore still more abundant graces upon the work of renewal in the Church that must begin at the Council's close. We are to beseech the Holy Spirit to pour out in abundance His grace upon the Bishops, Priests, Religious and faithful, that all may work together to implement the salutary decrees of the Council and in a new Pentecost renew the face of the earth.

In accordance with the command of the Holy Father, I direct that a triduum of prayer to the Holy Spirit be observed in every parish and religious institute in the Diocese of Trenton on the three days immediately preceding the Feast of the Immaculate Conception. On these three days, as the Holy Father suggests, occasion should be taken to instruct the faithful in their responsibilities regarding the Decrees of the Council, and to exhort them to embrace them in a spirit of faith promptly and wholeheartedly.

Finally, at all Masses on December 8, the day on which the Council will be officially closed, after the Creed of the Mass the customary invocation and prayer to the Holy Spirit shall be recited in common.

With a blessing, I remain

Devotedly yours in Christ,

✝George W. Ahr
Bishop of Trenton

N.B. Please read this letter at all the Masses in the Parish and Mission Churches of the Diocese on Sunday, November 28, and again on Sunday, December 5.

DIOCESE OF TRENTON
701 LAWRENCEVILLE ROAD
TRENTON, NEW JERSEY 08607

October 1, 1969

OFFICE OF THE BISHOP

TO THE PRIESTS, RELIGIOUS AND LAITY OF THE DIOCESE OF TRENTON

Dearly Beloved in Christ:

The Second Vatican Council has repeatedly emphasized the benefits which can accrue to the Church from the cooperation of all its elements. To achieve some of these benefits it urged the establishment in the dioceses of a Council of Priests, to assist the bishop by their advice in the fulfillment of his apostolic mandate. Similarly, in the "Decree on Bishops" it recommended the establishment of a Pastoral Council consisting of priests, religious and lay people to advise the bishop on "matters which bear on pastoral activity." In this Diocese of Trenton there have been established both a Council of Priests and a Pastoral Council with notable fruit.

The Pastoral Council has recommended to me the establishment of a similar consultative body to be known as a Parish Council, to serve with and to assist the pastor in each parish and mission in the Diocese. The Council of Priests has endorsed this proposal and recommended "that the Parish Council be an advisory body to the pastor, in the same manner as the Pastoral Council and the Council of Priests are advisory to the bishop." Both Councils concurred in the suggestion that, if in a particular case, a pastor has established a deliberative Council, he might continue such a Council with the understanding that his decision in this matter would not be binding on his successor. The same provision would hold if a particular pastor wished to establish such a Parish Council now.

I have accepted the recommendation of the Pastoral Council and the Council of Priests in this matter as being in harmony with the Decrees of the Second Vatican Council. Consequently, I direct that steps be taken promptly to inaugurate a Parish Council in each parish and mission of the Diocese.

There is a Committee of the Council of Priests which stands ready to assist the pastors in the establishment of a Parish Council. A similar Committee of the Pastoral Council is prepared to cooperate.

I pray that this important work may go forward in the spirit of faith and with the charity of Christ so that we may realize the hoped for benefits that we anticipate from this new pastoral instrumentality, and I bless all who cooperate in its realization.

Devotedly yours in Christ,

+George W. Ahr
Bishop of Trenton

N.B. This letter is to be read in all our parish and mission churches on Sunday, October 5.

OFFICE OF THE BISHOP

DIOCESE OF TRENTON
701 LAWRENCEVILLE ROAD
TRENTON, NEW JERSEY 08638

May 20, 1970

Reverend dear Father:

Our Holy Father, Pope Paul VI, will observe the 50th anniversary of his Ordination to the Holy Priesthood on May 29, 1970. On Sunday, May 31, I shall be the concelebrant of a Pontifical Mass at 10:30 A.M. in our Cathedral.

I suggest that during the days immediately preceding or following May 29, a Mass be celebrated also in each parish church in the Diocese for the intentions and for the well-being of the Sovereign Pontiff; that your parishioners be urged to attend this Mass, and that they be asked to offer for the Holy Father a generous Spiritual Bouquet of prayers, sacrifices and good works.

Since I have been requested to make a report of the participation of this Diocese in this significant event, I would appreciate having word from you concerning the part played by your parish. Therefore, a sample of a Spiritual Bouquet form is enclosed which you might prepare for distribution among your people. The results might be tabulated and a report of the total offerings in the several categories sent to me by June 5.

With a grateful blessing, I remain

Sincerely yours in Christ,

+George H. Ahr
Bishop of Trenton

Enc.

CHAPTER ELEVEN

EIGHTH BISHOP: JOHN C. REISS 1980~PRESENT

◆

BY MSGR. JOSEPH C. SHENROCK

HISTORIANS WARN US against attempting to write history until fifty years after the event; they are even more cautious about biographical work on a living person, let alone one who is still in office. This hesitancy arises from the well-founded conviction that when one is too close to the circumstances, objectivity is difficult, if not impossible. In other words, distance creates perspective.

With this in mind and assured of the wisdom of the position, we had to make a decision about the incorporation of the life and ministry of the Most Reverend John C. Reiss, the eighth bishop of Trenton, into the present volume. While we are intent on heeding the counsel of the historians, we are equally intent on giving Bishop Reiss a place in this work, lest the injustice of exclusion be committed. Thus did we settle on a middle course, which we trust will be accepted by all. This chapter contains historical documents relating to the present bishop's priestly vocation and episcopal service, offered without comment. In this way, the material is entered into the historical record, without effort at evaluation, leaving that to the next generation of Trenton diocesan historians.

On March 11, 1980, Archbishop Jean Jadot, apostolic delegate of the United States, announced the appointment of the eighth bishop of the Diocese of Trenton, Bishop John C. Reiss, J.C.D.

EARLY LIFE

Bishop John C. Reiss was born on May 13, 1922, in Red Bank, New Jersey. He was one of eleven children of Alfred and Sophia Reiss. Bishop Reiss had five brothers—George, Henry, Charles, Edward, and Alfred—and five sisters—Carolyn, Mary, Margaret, Eva, and Bertha.

ST. JAMES RECTORY
94 BROAD STREET
RED BANK, N. J.

June 9, 1939

Dear Father Crean:

The applicant for adoption to the diocese of Trenton, Mr. John Charles Reiss, has been in our school from first grade. And therefore is well known to me. In addition to this he has been serving Mass for the past eight years. He is what I would call a 100% boy. I believe he has a vocation and I trust he perseveres in that thought. He has my best recommendation.

Sincerely yours in Xt.,

Bishop Reiss attended and graduated from St. James School and Red Bank Catholic High School in Red Bank, New Jersey, and upon high school graduation, approached the Diocese of Trenton to study for the priesthood.

Little did Sister M. Angelica, principal of Red Bank Catholic High School, or Msgr. John B. McCloskey, pastor of St. James Church in Red Bank, realize, when they wrote their letters of recommendation to the Rev. Richard T. Crean for John C. Reiss to study for the priesthood in the Diocese of Trenton, that they were writing on behalf of the eighth bishop of Trenton.

John Reiss studied two years at the Catholic University of America in Washing-ton, D.C. (1939–41), and then entered Immaculate Conception Seminary in Darlington, N.J. (1941–46), returning for his last year of theology to the Catholic University (1946–47). He was recom-mended for ordination to the priesthood in May 1947 by the Rev. L. P. McDonald, rector of the Theological College in Wash-ington, D.C., with a letter to the Most Rev. William Griffin, then bishop of Trenton.

ORDINATION TO PRIESTHOOD

John Charles Reiss was ordained a priest on May 31, 1947, in Old Saint Mary's Cathe-

RED BANK, N. J., June 24, 1939

Rev. Richard T. Crean, Chancellor
153 North Warren St.
Trenton, New Jersey

My dear Father Crean:

John Reiss, one of our boys, who
was graduated on Sunday evening, June 18, desires
to study for the priesthood.

This young man has been in the
first quarter of his class since his entrance into
our High School four years ago. Previous to that he
was an honor student in our Grammar School.

His conduct has always been exemplary
and his family background excellent. He has faithfully served on the Altar for the past eight years.
Not once to the best of my knowledge, has he been
late for an assignment, nor has he ever failed to
keep one. He has showed every indication, in many
other ways of devoting his life to God's service.

I shall appreciate your considering
his application.

Sincerely yours in Xt.,

Sister M. Angelica
Principal

SA/A

Theological College

401 Michigan Ave., N. E.   Washington 17, D. C.

<u>John C. Reiss</u>

Candidate for Priesthood

Opinion of the Rector and Faculty

Mr. Reiss has been only one year with us but in that
time he has impressed us very favorably.

He has a good mind and works hard. He seems interested
in priestly studies.

His character is fine. He is docile, obedient, humble,
regular in his duties, and has a fine manly piety.

He mixes well and seems to be liked by others. He is quiet
but not shy. We feel that he gives good promise for the
priesthood. We testify to the sincerity of his faith.

L. P. McDonald
Rector

John J. Jepson
Vice-Rector

dral in Trenton by Bishop William A. Griffin, the sixth bishop of the Diocese of Trenton; he celebrated his first Mass at St. James Church in Red Bank and was assigned as a curate on June 10, 1947, to Sacred Heart Church in Trenton.

On April 12, 1949, the Rev. John C. Reiss was transferred to Holy Spirit Parish in Perth Amboy, and on February 16, 1950, was transferred to St. Anthony Parish in Trenton.

In the fall of 1950, Father John C. Reiss was assigned by the Most Rev. George W. Ahr to continue his studies at the Catholic University in Washington in the field of canon law. During the summer months, Father Reiss returned to the diocese and had summer assignments, first to Our Lady of Perpetual Help, Highlands (1951), then to St. Joseph's, Trenton (1952), then to St. Cecilia, Iselin (1953), and as administrator of St. Elizabeth, Far Hills, during August and September 1953.

On September 11, 1953, Father Reiss received a letter from Bishop Ahr appointing him secretary–master of ceremonies to the bishop of Trenton. Father Reiss was to hold this position for the next nine years until he was appointed administrator of St. Francis Parish in Trenton on June 29, 1962, and also continued as vice-chancellor of the diocese. On July 19, 1963, Father Reiss was appointed officialis of the Diocese of Trenton and on October 5, 1963, was honored by Pope Paul VI, who made him a domestic prelate, with the title of monsignor.

On February 3, 1965, Monsignor Reiss was appointed pastor of St. Francis Parish in Trenton. On November 29, 1965, Bishop Ahr announced to the diocese that a Diocesan Campaign would begin, to raise $16,500,000 to establish a new seminary, to renovate Catholic high schools, and to build new Catholic high schools. Monsignor Reiss was appointed by Bishop Ahr as coordinator of that Diocesan Campaign. The campaign was very successful, but the new seminary was never built because vocations to the priesthood had declined and there was no need for another seminary in New Jersey. The new high schools were built, and the old high schools were renovated.

CONSECRATION TO THE EPISCOPATE

On Wednesday, October 25, 1967, at 9 a.m., Pope Paul VI named Monsignor Reiss titular bishop of Simidicca and auxiliary bishop to Bishop Ahr. The announcement was made by Archbishop Luigi Raimondi, apostolic delegate of the United States. Reiss thus became the second auxiliary bishop that the Diocese of Trenton had (the Most Rev. Bishop James J. Hogan was the first auxiliary bishop, until he was transferred to become bishop of Altoona-Johnstown, Pennsylvania, on July 17, 1966).

Monsignor Reiss was consecrated a bishop on December 12, 1967, at St. Mary's Cathedral in Trenton. Bishop Ahr was the ordaining prelate, assisted by the Most Revs. Walter W. Curtis, bishop of Bridgeport, Connecticut, and James J. Hogan, Bishop of Altoona-Johnstown, as co-consecrators.

The master of ceremonies for the event was the Rev. Edward U. Kmiec, vice-chancellor of the Diocese of Trenton, who was destined to be the third auxiliary bishop of Trenton. The homilist for the occasion was the Most Rev. Thomas A. Boland, archbishop of Newark, delivered the following homily:

"All power is given to me in heaven and on earth. Go, therefore, and teach all nations; baptizing them in the name of the Father, and of the Son, and of the Holy Spirit. Teaching them to observe all things whatsoever I have commanded you. Behold, I am with you all days, unto the consummation of the world." (Matt. 28:18)

The white clouds of Mount Olivet were soon to envelop the form of the Savior. The sorrowing apostles were about to catch the last glimpse of His ascending figure. Before leaving them, however, He constituted them into a separate body of men—into His "Teaching Church"—to continue His own work for the salvation of mankind until the end of time.

We know from Sacred Scripture that Our Lord singled out twelve men from the multitude of His followers. For St. Luke tells us that "He called unto Himself His disciples and He chose twelve of them whom He named apostles." These he formed into a corporate or collegiate body, formally appointed to a definite office. He empowered them with jurisdiction to offer sacrifice, to loose and to bind, to teach and to govern in His name and with His authority. They and they alone were the exclusive depositories of His commission. On them alone He breathed His power; them alone He sent to teach all nations, promising the indwelling of His Holy Spirit to guide, to inspire, and to protect them and their successors until the end of the world. On these twelve He founded His church.

Today, then, is an historic occasion. For every consecration of a bishop forms another line in the chain of apostolic succession. The solemnity of the day is enhanced by the great gathering of priests and prelates, of religious and laity who throng this beautiful cathedral dedicated to the Glorious Mother of God, whose feast under the title of Our Lady of Guadalupe is celebrated today. The cordial interest of so many of the dignitaries, civil and ecclesiastical, emphasizes further the unique importance to the church and to the community of this sacred event.

This is, of course, an occasion of great honor to Bishop Reiss and of proud rejoicing on the part of his friends and loved ones. To him and to them we offer our cordial congratulations and pledge our prayers that God may accomplish through this bishop the highest and holiest hopes for him.

Even as the appointment of Bishop Reiss is a mark of affection and a paternal salute from the Holy Father to the Diocese of Trenton, to its distinguished bishop-ordinary, and all its clergy, so it is an accolade of praise to his beloved parents, now with us in spirit, and to the devout Christian family which reared this son so worthy of the priesthood and gave to the Church a priest so worthy of the episcopal dignity.

A providential arrangement of circumstances extending back to his eminently Catholic home has prepared the way for the unfolding of the talents and the development of the virtues of Bishop Reiss and the duties of the Episcopate which he has assumed today. He is a true pastor of souls, constantly in the midst of his flock. His years of parochial experience will serve to keep him close to his people and will enable him to fully understand their cares and problems. From his contact with his parishioners he has learned to "become all things to all men." His keen sense of justice and his complete grasp of canon law found expression in exactness of procedure as vice-chancellor and later as the officialis of the diocesan tribunal. This manifold experience further qualifies Bishop Reiss to render valuable assistance in these important branches of diocesan work. His many other assignments similarly proclaim the trust that his superiors placed in him. This day, then, bespeaks two acts of high approval—one on the part of the Holy Father, whose brief of appointment we heard read this morning, and the other on the part of his beloved superior, Bishop Ahr, whom we congratulate in a very special way today because he has been chosen again as a sacred living vehicle by which the fullness of priestly power has been conferred upon one of the clergy over whom he rules.

What does it mean to be a bishop? It means the acquisition of a new and special relationship to Christ, the Good Shepherd of souls. It means the possession of the fullness of the priesthood and incorporation into the College of the Apostles. It means to possess a new and special relationship with the Vicar of Christ, the Supreme Pontiff. For all bishops exercise their office, their orders, and their jurisdiction under the authority of the Chief of the Apostles and with due submission to his primacy. It means the exercise of new and wonderful powers in the Mystical Body of Christ which is His Church—powers, for example, of transmitting the priesthood from generation to generation; powers of guiding and consecration which are proper to the office of bishop alone and which are vital to the church.

Pope Pius XII, of happy memory, when a great assemblage of bishops was in Rome for the canonization of Pope St. Pius X, took the occasion to explain the duties of a bishop under the head of teaching, sanctifying, and governing. In summary, he said, "Christ Our Lord entrusted the truth which He has brought from heaven to the apostles, and through them to their successors. The apostles are therefore, by divine right, the true doctors and teachers in the church. And besides lawful successors of the apostles, namely, the Roman Pontiff for the Universal Church and the bishops for the faithful entrusted to their care, there are no other teachers divinely constituted in the Church of Christ." The Supreme Shepherd and the bishops may associate others with them in their work as teachers, but these do not act in their own names, nor by reason of their superior theological knowledge, but by reason of the mandate which they have received from the lawful teaching authority. The faculty always remains subject to that authority and is never exercised in their own right or independently.

History knows that to be a bishop of the Catholic church means to join that mighty company of those men of God who in every Christian century and in all the names of Christendom have transmitted from Jerusalem to the ends of the earth the apostolic succession which, like a golden chain, links every Catholic altar to Calvary, and every baptized Catholic to Christ. It means also to be one with such great high priests as St. Cyprian, the eloquent exponent of episcopal dignity, and of every pontifex of the ancient sees in the days of the fathers of the church. He should be one with St. Ambrose and St. Augustine and St. Boniface, St.

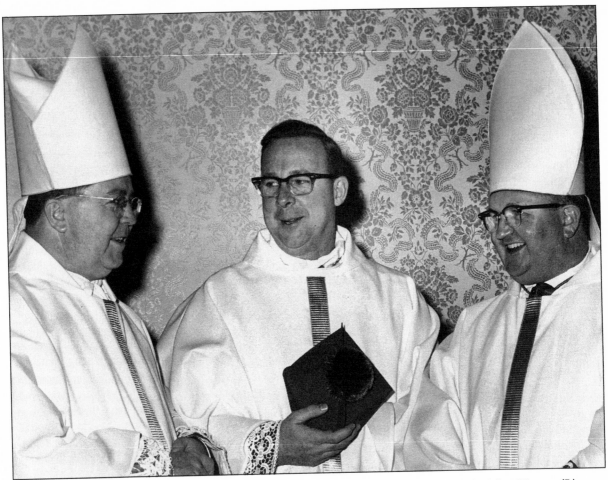

Consecration of Bishop John C. Reiss, December 12, 1967. Bishop Curtis (R) and Bishop Hogan (L).

DEARLY BELOVED OF THE TRENTON CLERGY, RELIGIOUS AND LAITY:

I APPRECIATE DEEPLY THE OPPORTUNITY AFFORDED ME TO ADDRESS A BRIEF MESSAGE . . . IN THIS MONITOR SUPPLEMENT MARKING THE CONSECRATION OF YOUR NEW AUXILIARY BISHOP . . . .

ONE CAN SCARCELY SPEAK TO THE FLOCK OF TRENTON CONCERNING THE GIFTS, LABORS AND ACCOMPLISHMENTS OF BISHOP REISS—THESE ARE WELL KNOWN AND APPRECIATED. MAY I JOIN YOU, HOWEVER, IN THANKING GOD FOR THE GRAND TRIBUTE ON THE PART OF THE HOLY SEE TO THE DIOCESE, TO ITS ZEALOUS SHEPHERD, BISHOP AHR, AND TO ITS PRIESTS, RELIGIOUS AND FAITHFUL IN THE APPOINTMENT OF BISHOP REISS . . . .

WITH ALL IN THE DIOCESE, I PRAY THAT GOD WILL BLESS YOUR NEW AUXILIARY BISHOP WITH CONTINUED HEALTH AND LENGTH OF YEARS . . . . YOU NEED NOT BE ASSURED, I AM CONFIDENT, THAT ONE OF THE GREAT JOYS OF MY LIFE IS THIS PRESENT OPPORTUNITY TO REVISIT THE DIOCESE AND FLOCK OF TRENTON AND, IN PARTICULAR, TO BE A CO-CONSECRATOR FOR BISHOP REISS. MAY I PRESUME TO ASK THAT YOU KEEP ME IN YOUR PRAYERS, AS YOU WILL NEVER CEASE TO BE IN MINE.

+JAMES J. HOGAN, BISHOP OF ALTOONA-JOHNSTOWN

Consecration of Bishop John C. Reiss, December 12, 1967.
Left to right: Msgr. Emmet Monhan, Msgr. George Ardos, Msgr. Joseph O'Connor, Bishop Curtis,
Bishop Reiss, Bishop Hogan.

◆

As we congratulate Bishop John C. Reiss upon the dignity and awesome responsibility assigned to him as Bishop, we remind ourselves of the reverence in which we should hold a Bishop . . . .

Marked with the fullness of the Sacrament of Orders, Bishop Reiss will be a steward of the grace of the Supreme Priesthood . . . . By praying and laboring for his people, he will channel the fullness of Christ's holiness in many ways and abundantly . . . .

The spirited and growing Diocese of Trenton will find in Bishop Reiss one who will sincerely model himself by the requirements of a Bishop in the Church.

To our long esteemed Bishop Ahr, I express my personal happiness that the Holy Father has given to him . . . the youthful and experienced Bishop Reiss as his new Auxiliary.

I express to Bishop Reiss my congratulations and my thanks for the distinct and appreciated privilege to serve as one of his Co-Consecrators.

+Walter W. Curtis, Bishop of Bridgeport

Consecration of Bishop John C. Reiss, December 12, 1967.
Anointing of his head with oil by Bishop Ahr.

THE NEWS THAT MSGR. JOHN REISS HAS BEEN ELEVATED TO THE EPISCOPATE BY HIS HOLINESS POPE PAUL VI TO SERVE AS AUXILIARY TO HIS BELOVED ORDINARY, BISHOP AHR, WAS RECEIVED WITH JOYFUL ACCLAIM BY HIS MANY FRIENDS IN THE ARCHDIOCESE OF NEWARK. IT WAS WITH DEEP PERSONAL GRATIFICATION I LEARNED THAT THE QUIET, SCHOLARLY, EFFICIENT SEMINARIAN WHOM WE KNEW IN HIS STUDENT DAYS AT DARLINGTON HAD MERITED BY HIS ZEALOUS APOSTOLIC ACCOMPLISHMENTS THE DISTINGUISHED HONOR OF THE FULLNESS OF THE PRIESTHOOD.

AS WE CONGRATULATE BISHOP-ELECT REISS IN THIS HIGH RECOGNITION FROM THE VICAR OF CHRIST, WE ASSURE HIM OF OUR CONTINUED PRAYERS THAT THE GRACES NECESSARY FOR HIS RESPONSIBLE OFFICE WILL BE GIVEN TO HIM IN EVER INCREASING ABUNDANCE.

+THOMAS A. BOLAND, ARCHBISHOP OF NEWARK

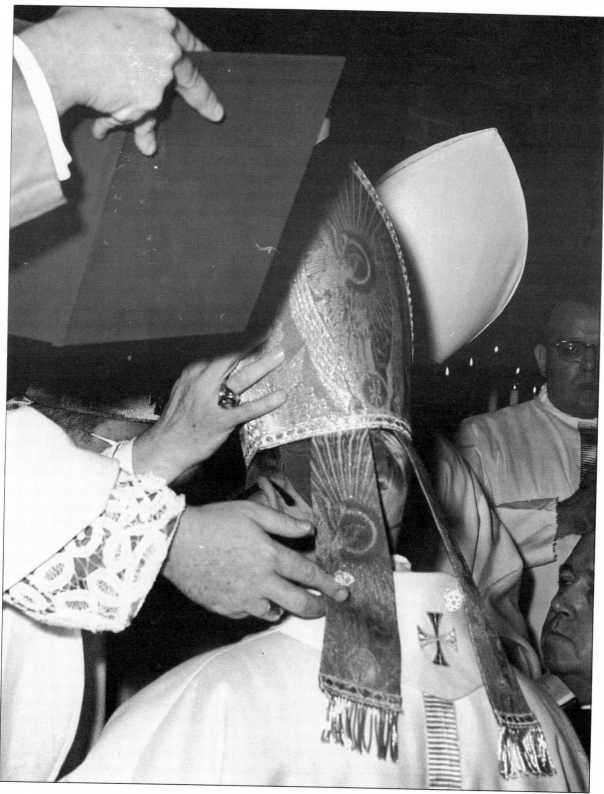

Consecration of Bishop John C. Reiss, December 12, 1967.
Bishop Ahr putting miter on Bishop John C. Reiss's head.

Bishop Ahr assisting Bishop Reiss down steps after his consecration on December 12, 1967, at St. Mary's Cathedral.

Following the consecration—left to right: Fr. John McDonald; Bishop George Ahr; Bishop John C. Reiss; his sister, Sr. Charitina Reiss, R.S.M.; Msgr. Emmet Monahan.

Patrick of Ireland and St. John Fisher of England. A priest who is called to serve as bishop in our own country takes his place in the glorious line of the American hierarchy, which includes such ecclesiastical giants as John Carroll, John England, John Hughes, James Roosevelt Bayley, Blessed John Neumann, James Gibbons, and John Spalding. I do not think there have been greater bishops in modern times than these or even others whom you may recall to mind. There certainly have been no greater Americans in our national history than these outstanding ecclesiastics in the Catholic church.

But Bishop Reiss, I am confident, does not look upon this high office as something which exalts him in the eyes of others, but rather as a means that makes it possible for him to sacrifice himself more completely for men and to espouse more thoroughly the interests of God and His church. He is thinking more of his responsibilities than of the honor which is his today.

We congratulate Bishop Reiss once again on the great honor which has come to him and beg Our Lady, Mother of the Church and Queen of the Apostles, to watch over him and guide him in all his work for the salvation of souls and the honor of her Divine Son.

PASTOR OF SACRED HEART, SOUTH PLAINFIELD

On February 5, 1969, Bishop Reiss was transferred from pastor of St. Francis Parish in Trenton to pastor of Sacred Heart Parish, South Plainfield, and appointed at the same time episcopal vicar for Middlesex County and vicar-general of the diocese in charge of

Most Rev. John C. Reiss, auxiliary bishop of Trenton.

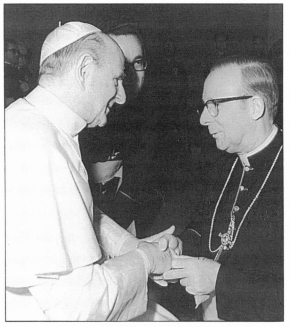

Bishop Reiss speaks to Pope Paul VI.

spiritual matters. He also continued as officialis of the Diocese of Trenton. Because of the distance from the office in Trenton, Bishop Ahr reassigned Bishop Reiss back to the Pastorate of St. Francis in Trenton on June 20, 1969. Bishop Reiss was to assist Bishop Ahr with Confirmations and other episcopal ceremonies for the next eleven years. On May 28, 1972, Bishop Reiss celebrated the Silver Jubilee of his ordination to the priesthood with a Mass at St. Francis Church in Trenton; his classmate, the Rev. Msgr. Joseph A. O'Connor, pastor of St. Denis Church, Manasquan, was the homilist at this Mass of Thanksgiving.

Bishop John C. Reiss (right), newly appointed as bishop of the Diocese of Trenton, chats with Bishop George W. Ahr, who was bishop of the diocese for twenty-nine years until his retirement.

EIGHTH BISHOP OF DIOCESE OF TRENTON

On March 11, 1980, the Most Rev. Jean Jadot, the apostolic delegate in Washington, D.C., announced that Bishop John C. Reiss had been appointed the eighth bishop of Trenton, succeeding Bishop Ahr, who had resigned in June 1979, when he reached the age of 75.

On the occasion of this announcement, Archbishop Peter L. Gerety of Newark, metropolitan of the Province of New Jersey, made the following statement:

> It was with great joy that I learned of your appointment as Bishop of Trenton to succeed Bishop Ahr. To carry forward Christ's work among your people building on the solid foundation of your predecessor is a tremendous challenge. I join the vast numbers of your admirers in asking God to grant

> you good health and all the graces necessary for the task.
>
> We live in one of the most exciting times in the history of the Catholic Church. It is a period of great changes, of multitudinous difficulties and problems and yet at the same time of profound spiritual growth and deepening sacramental and prayer life.
>
> May the Lord Jesus bless your efforts with abundant fruit, and may He give you many happy years of service in the position of high responsibility to which He has now called you.

On the occasion of his appointment as the eighth bishop of Trenton, Bishop John C. Reiss reflected with the press on his life and his vocation:

> With feelings of trepidation, but with firm faith in God, I have given willing acceptance to the office of bishop of Trenton with its attending duties and burdens.
>
> I thank the Holy Father Pope John Paul II for his confidence in bestowing this office. At the same time, I express my

personal gratitude and esteem, as well as that of the entire diocese, to Bishop Ahr, who is completing thirty years as the shepherd of Trenton and who presided over the extensive growth in the diocese during a troublesome period of change in the church.

I pledge myself to the service of all in Christ's Name. I am fully aware that further progress cannot be made by one person, but needs the help of the entire community. Therefore, I prayerfully seek the continued cooperation of the laity, religious sisters and brothers, and clergy and beg your assistance and your own prayers.

Let us place ourselves under the patronage of our Blessed Mother, seeking her intercession with her Divine Son, Whose Spirit will lead us all to the Father.

Let us love one another.

On April 21, 1980, the official welcoming ceremony was held for Bishop Reiss in

Bishop Reiss's coat-of-arms.

St. Mary's Cathedral. The priests, deacons, and religious of the Diocese of Trenton were invited to attend, and the cathedral was filled to capacity. At that welcoming ceremony, Bishop Reiss delivered his first official talk to the priests, deacons, and religious of the diocese:

My sisters and brothers in Christ, my chief coworkers in the vineyard of God, Greetings in the Lord Jesus, the Son of the Most High.

The search is over, and a new ordinary of Trenton has arrived.

I am delighted that so many of you could be present today to witness my canonical possession of the diocese and to share in this event. I can remember thirty years ago, when Bishop Ahr was consecrated and installed. We younger priests were in the procession, and our part consisted in walking up the center aisle, down the side aisle, and back outside—there was just no room. And this was in the days before closed-circuit television. Since the same circumstances still exist with regard to size, I decided to experiment with the present arrangement, in order to see more of the clergy and religious.

I deeply appreciate the confidence of the Holy Father, Pope John Paul, in appointing me as the eighth bishop of Trenton. I solemnly pledge my loyalty and fidelity to him and Holy Mother Church, and beg God to help me by His grace to fulfill this promise.

We are all taking part in a new experience—the transfer of the diocese with the former ordinary still very much alive, in good health (to a degree), and most active. I myself, and in your name, thank Bishop Ahr for the leadership which he has exer-

expansion of the diocese and during the period of Vatican II. It was not easy. I thank him also for the witness of his service to God, to the church and to the diocese. I can verify from close association that Bishop Ahr sought only the good of souls and never any personal praise or reward. His work has been to minister to others in the example of Christ with total dedication and total selflessness. May I be able to do the same.

Bishop, you will always be welcomed by me in the diocese, your home. I will count on your help in Confirmation seasons and maybe even by attending some meetings. The priests and sisters and deacons are free to invite you to whatever program or celebrations they may have. I know this may interfere with your planned and delayed retirement, but after a few months you might welcome the company of your priests and sisters—and perhaps a good meal.

In the hectic days which have intervened between the announcement of the appointment and today, I have been questioned by reporters and people many times. What are your plans? I replied to one that even during the search period I never indulged the fancy of thinking what I would do if I were bishop. Thus, I can honestly say that I have not evolved as yet any specific program. But I do have some general plans, and will tell you a few of them. The execution of these proposals will take time, especially in view of this time of year, when the spring schedule of Confirmations is in full swing, and the activities of May and June already listed.

First of all, it is my desire to meet and talk to all the priests in an informal way. Thus, I shall be able to get to see everyone and to listen to you. Remember—I cannot do everything, but I shall listen. I will do this on a vicarial basis and as soon as possible.

I propose also to examine and to activate some decentralization. The details are not even discussed. In broad outline, it means the strengthening of the vicariate system. What faculties or power to grant permissions remains to be determined. The first step in this direction will be the choice of my vicar-general. Thus, I name Msgr. George E. Everitt to this position, effective immediately. He is outside of Trenton and, I know, highly respected as a dedicated priest, wise counselor, and approachable.

That brings me to another debt of gratitude, one which we all owe to Monsignor McCorristin, who has served so nobly as vicar-general. Monsignor Michael is another complete servant of God and the church, without personal ambition or desire for praise or reward, except the reward of Christ. We are all indebted to you, Monsignor. I know I can continue to count on your counsel.

Another proposal will be the visitation of parishes. The method is undetermined. I do, however, envision a less formal type than previously employed. It will embrace a weekend, in order to meet the people during an evening session, and celebrating Mass with the parishioners. You realize that this is a long-range project with over 200 parishes.

I shall also in the near future establish a commission to review all the offices of the diocese and make recommendations. Our hope is to avoid duplication of services or, if necessary, to institute a service that may be lacking.

I feel that is enough plans for now.

I do, however, want to make some other important announcements which affect the work of the diocese. The bishop's power includes the judicial, which is exercised by the Tribunal under the officialis.

Thus, I appoint Father John Dermond as the officialis. The Tribunal predominantly handles marriage cases. Father Dermond has both the intellectual background and the practical experience to work in this hidden, highly technical, and frequently unrewarding apostolate.

I shall continue in office Monsignor Fitzgerald as chancellor and Monsignor Kmiec as vice-chancellor and my secretary. Both have the experience and willingness to serve. Father Romeo will be my master of ceremonies. All other offices will remain as they are for the time being. I hope to meet all department heads as soon as possible.

The Council of Priests is hereby reactivated, after its many months in limbo. It will continue in its former constitution for the present, and the normal election time will take place as usually scheduled. I hope that all priests will participate in the deliberations of the council, as that is the only way to obtain a really general consensus to form the basis for adequate advice to the bishop. I have in mind a few topics for study and consultation.

You deacons are not forgotten. It is interesting to note that in the early discussions about the revival of the Permanent Diaconate, the emphasis was on its importance for mission countries, yet the United States has the largest number of ordained deacons. This program will continue. I feel that the deacons will help to alleviate some of the difficulties due to the scarcity of priests.

Not to be overlooked are the sisters and brothers. It is impossible to evaluate the contribution of your services to the spreading of the Word. As the pastors and priests are the extension of the bishop in the parish, so are you the extension of the pastor; or if engaged in diocesan or nonparochial work, you are an extension of the bishop. You have the opportunity to reach and to touch personally with a religious witness more people. I do not want to lessen any ministry, but I only want to highlight and to encourage that important ministry of forming the minds and souls of youth through education. As difficult as this burden is, the results are permanent.

We have work to do. We have serious responsibilities to God and our fellow Christians. We must do this together.

Therefore, I appeal to my motto, which is now my goal for the diocese: "Let us love one another." Our aim is to make the Gospel message known, loved, and followed. We may differ in how this ought to be done, but let us respect other opinions and realize that at times the bishop must make a decision. I promise that my decisions will be made prayerfully and in accord with the command of Jesus: "Love one another, as I have loved you." I ask your cooperation; I ask your patience, because things cannot be done yesterday; above all I ask your prayers—in season and out of season—so that our work—mine and yours—may proceed to the greater glory of God.

Let us love one another.

INSTALLATION OF BISHOP REISS

On April 22, 1980, Archbishop Peter L. Gerety of Newark, metropolitan of the Province of New Jersey, solemnly installed Bishop John C. Reiss as the eighth bishop of Trenton in St. Mary's Cathedral in Trenton. Two cardinals attended this beautiful installation: John Cardinal Carberry, retired archbishop of St. Louis, and John Cardinal Krol, archbishop of Philadelphia. Many bishops, priests, deacons, leaders of the other Christian communities, rabbis, and laity attended this Installation Mass. At that Mass, Bishop John C. Reiss gave the following homily.

I begin by expressing inadequately my gratitude to Almighty God for the myriad graces, favors, and blessings which He has show-

Bishop Reiss speaking to Monsignor Kmiec prior to the bishop's installation on April 22, 1980.

ered upon me during my lifetime. It is He who brought me to this station. I can never repay Him.

I wish to state before this august assembly my appreciation to our Holy Father Pope John Paul II for his confidence in appointing me the eighth bishop of Trenton. Before you bishops, priests, sisters, deacons, and laity, I solemnly pledge my loyalty and fidelity, as well as that of the entire diocese, to the Bishop of Rome. I shall adhere to the teachings, dogmatic, moral, and social, of the Holy Father and the Holy See. These teachings are our sure and safe road to eternal happiness.

What can I say to Bishop Ahr? Thank you for the Christ-like example of priestly service and unselfish giving to the task of ordinary of Trenton for thirty years. That record will not be surpassed. You realize that I have been under his tutelage longer than that—as his student in theology at Immaculate Conception Seminary, then as master of ceremonies, and over the years in various capacities. Bishop, your advice will be sought. You are always welcome in the diocese, and you may—and I hope you will—accept whatever invitations are extended to you. Naturally, mine will be the first. I expect you to help with the Confirmation schedule in the fall. May God grant you an enjoyable and restful retirement from your labors.

I am pleased by the presence of my brother bishops, who also had to juggle their calendars to be here. Your attendance is a sign of solidarity and a pledge of assistance. Thank you.

I am also happy with the sign of friendship which is expressed by the coming of the religious leaders from the state of New Jersey and the confines of this diocese. I look forward to further meetings and mu-

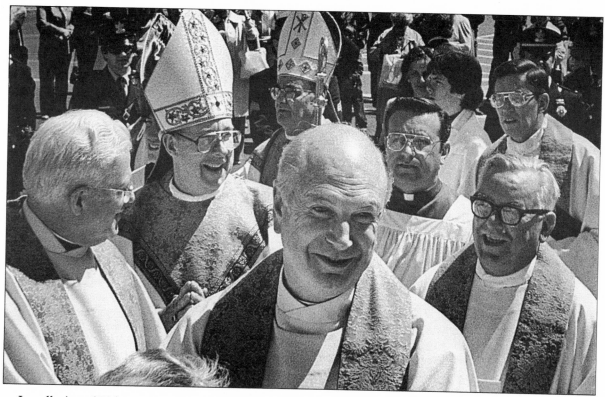

Installation of Bishop Reiss as eighth bishop of the Diocese of Trenton. Procession leading into the church—left to right: Msgr. John Torney, Bishop Reiss, Bishop Ahr, Msgr. George Everitt, Msgr. Edward Kmiec, Msgr. Joseph Brzozowski, Msgr. William Fitzgerald.

look forward to further meetings and mutual undertakings in an ecumenical spirit to promote the work of the Lord.

My thanks is due to the senators, congressmen, state senators, assemblymen, and all other civil officials. You honor the Diocese of Trenton. It is anticipated that I shall be working with you in matters which will promote the temporal and social well-being of the people of the diocese and the state of New Jersey.

Also, I am grateful to the priests of the diocese who are here and who have renewed, in the name of all the priests, their obedience and service to their new ordinary. I welcome my priest friends from outside the diocese, especially my classmates, who know me well. To the sisters,

sharers in the burdens of diocesan labors, I say thanks. And to all my friends, from near and far, I am happy that you can share my joy.

Finally, in this litany of gratitude, thanks to my family. I owe an overwhelming debt to my parents. They set for me the first and indelible example of love for God and His holy will—in both good times and bad. They, together with my brothers and sisters, encouraged by prayer and assistance my vocation to the priesthood. Without such loving concern I would not have made it.

As you know, when in 1967 I was ordained a bishop, I selected as my motto the words of my patron, St. John the Evangelist, found in his first epistle. "Let us love one another" (Jn 4:7). This letter was written in the latter part of his life after he had witnessed to the events of Christ's ministry on earth and to the spread of the infant church. His letter and these words, you could say, are the summary of his observations. Actually the Apostle of Love, in a softer tone, is merely repeating the command of the Divine Master found in the Gospel of John (15:12), "Love one another." This command is no blind, undirected order, but in the statement of Jesus it is most precise—"As I have loved you" (v.12). We, and that means all of us, must strive to follow Christ's example, which is selfless service and total sacrifice.

Our Blessed Savior gave us the clue to test our love for Him—"He who obeys the commandments he has from me, is the man who loves me" (Jn 14:21). These are the same commandments revealed by God to Moses on Mount Sinai; these are the same commandments which our Lord reiterated during His public life in the questioning of the rich young man (Mk 10:19); these are the same commandments we must follow today to fulfill our obligation to love God and to love our neighbor.

Furthermore, in demonstrating how we are to love, Jesus Himself set the priorities when He cried out in His own bloody agony, "Not my will but your will be done" (Mt 26:39), and when teaching the disciples how to pray: "Our Father . . . Thy will be done on earth as it is in Heaven." This will of God is synthesized by the Scriptures in the two great commandments "You shall love the Lord your God with all your heart, with all your soul, and with all your mind . . . you shall love your neighbor as yourself" (Mt 22:37–39).

Sometimes it is difficult to find this will of God. It may be discovered only by prayer and by listening to the church.

Consequently, my motto, "Let us love one another," is my ideal, and it is my goal as bishop of Trenton.

My goal, then, can have practical applications. It is impossible to list them all, so I shall treat only a few. It will be necessary for the diocese to reach out to others with love. First of all to the active members, so that they will be encouraged to expand their love by their own personal growth in spirituality and in their concerned service to others. This love must seek to aid and soothe the wounds of the hurting members of the diocese—to provide solutions, if they exist, but at least to encourage by prayer, word, and action.

The ideal of loving one another must go beyond the limits of the Catholic Diocese of Trenton and include those who profess other beliefs in a genuine spirit of ecumenical understanding and cooperation. Attentive listening in dialogue and in prayer must always be present.

"To love one another" includes within the Catholic Church of Trenton the fostering of programs for proclaiming the teachings of the church and for a fuller understanding of them. This education will, for the young, be accomplished through the Catholic school system and the Religious Education Office. But, also, it must touch adults of all ages.

"To love one another" must embrace the entire gamut of the social teachings of the church, especially as they affect the poor and the suffering. Thus, it is necessary to concentrate on various minority groups who have been victims of past and even present injustices—the large number of Hispanics throughout the diocese, the black communities, and other ethnic

The Diocese of Trenton, 1881–1993

"To love one another" certainly will include activity in the civil sphere. There must be efforts to initiate and to foster laws and branches of government to right wrongs and to promote the temporal well-being of all citizens in their quest for a share in earthly happiness.

We all know that these problems exist, and we all know that solutions are elusive. I admit I do not have the cures. I resolve, however, to work for solutions. I shall seek the collaboration of others. First of all with my priestly advisers—the diocesan consultors, the vicars, and the Priests' Council. I shall likewise seek assistance in the quest for answers from the Diocesan Pastoral Council and the Sisters' Senate. Such advice may call for the more learned opinions of experts—religious and lay, church and civil.

At any rate, there will not be any solving of problems unless there is the prayerful help of everyone in the diocese. Nor will these solutions come overnight; they cannot be done yesterday. It will demand a spirit of goodwill on the part of bishop, clergy, and laity. Above all, it will require constant, humble prayer for the guidance of the Holy Spirit.

The diocese, and I, personally, have another powerful ally. I have studied under the patronage of our Blessed Mother Mary at Catholic University on three occasions and at the Immaculate Conception Seminary in Darlington, and the diocese itself has Mary as its patron under the title of her Assumption into heaven. We must certainly enlist her assistance and her prayers with her Divine Son to carry out the works of the church in Trenton.

Finally, only in this spirit can we hope to achieve our ideal and goal: Let us love one another.

HONORARY DOCTOR OF LAWS CONFERRAL

On December 1, 1980, Bishop John C. Reiss received an honorary Doctor of Laws degree from St. John's University in Jamaica, New York. The degree was awarded at the university's annual St. Vincent de Paul Convocation and was conferred by Fr. Joseph T. Cahill, president of St. John's University. Following the conferral, Bishop Reiss gave the following lecture.

Through friends and personal contacts I have had an awareness of St. Vincent de Paul. I have shared the knowledge that he was the founder of the Vincentians, the Daughters of Charity, and the Ladies of Charity. I have even, on practically a daily basis, uttered frequently the aspiration "St. Vincent de Paul, pray for me" so that I may become a lover of the poor and a server to the poor. Yet, this awareness remained just on the surface until I was called upon to speak at this convocation. Things will be changed from now on.

Charity, in the sense of providing any kind of service to persons in need, has always been practiced. It can be exercised in both a public and a private manner. Here I take "public" to be synonymous with government. Past history shows that official government charity was very limited. Even Scripture depicts only a harsh exile and a total shunning of the lepers by officialdom. We can recall the description of "charity" as found in the Middle Ages and at the beginning of the Industrial Revolution. Remember the poorhouses and the orphanages in the works of Dickens, where unfeeling cruelty was the norm. Only in modern times do we see, and you might say, a total invasion of government into charity—in child care, in hospitals, and in other health facilities, to mention a few.

During these same periods, but in quite a different way, there is the opposite to public charity—private charity. I use this term to designate charity as performed by persons or institutions other than governments. The words of Christ Himself invite this charity, for example, when He spoke to the rich young man: "Go sell what you have, give to the poor and come follow me." The Acts of the apostles detail the common concern of the young Christians who shared their belongings to help one another. It is the church, especially after its civil emergence under Constantine, which is the mainstay of private charity. The lives of many saints through the centuries are filled with their charitable acts, especially to the poor and to the sick. Religious, clergy, and lay, even kings and queens, practiced heroic virtue and obtained sanctity through their Christian concern for the unfortunate. It remained for the genius of St. Vincent, after his personal spiritual journey, to organize *private* charity and to crystallize in word and action the foundation of such private charity. Not only do we consider him as an apostle of charity, but also we can classify him as a revolutionary. As an aside, and to stimulate one's imagination, we may speculate how St. Vincent would have weathered the changes of the past two decades.

I recall from my high school days a pep rally in which the priest moderator told us in Latin, "Vox, vox est nihil," which he immediately translated: "Talk, talk is nothing!" Unless talk is translated into action, it is just hot air. Such is not the case with St. Vincent and his activity in private charity.

Yet, to stimulate action, he had to preach and enunciate the firm spiritual foundation for charity. His convictions, gleaned from the Gospels and solidified by his spiritual reflection and contemplation, were already enunciated in his own day and in such a way as to form the basis for charitable actions in every age. The doctrine of the Mystical Body, whereby every person is an actual or potential member of Christ's Body, is the vibrant vital basis of his private charity. This truth, plus the expression "The love of Christ urges us," translated his words into action. These same two elements constitute the primary difference between public and private charity, as understood in this talk.

We see today that "public" charity has grown into a colossal giant. There are enormously large health care centers, which are supported by an equally large bureaucracy, which thereby demands a large supply of funds. The germ idea is good, but the result has its failures. For example, I have read that through government ("public charity"), a housing unit to be built to help the poor might cost, directly and indirectly, as much as $100,000 per unit. On the other hand, "private" charity is able to secure four units for the same price. This raises an unanswered question—Is this real charity for the poor? I am sure St. Vincent would have some pertinent comment and directives.

At the same time, there are also dangers for our own charitable institutions—"private" charity. These, too, have grown into great complexes of buildings with varied services and vast personnel. It is so simple just to go along with the times and to imitate the public sector. This is especially true of the danger of depersonalization, which can affect even private charity.

Here, I would like to shift gears and treat "private" in another sense. Now, let us use "private" to mean "personal." Personal charity is *the* distinct characteristic of true Christian charity. Personal charity is the trademark of the charity so evident in St. Vincent de Paul.

Once again, I like to make a distinction in personal charity with regard to its object and its subject. For us, for St. Vincent, the object of private or personal charity is a "person"—made in the image and likeness of God; a "person" who is baptized is a member of Christ's Mystical Body, and, if not baptized, a potential member. The object of his and our private-personal charity is a person who reflects, who represents, who is Christ to be ministered to here and now. St. Vincent believed this truth, he practiced this truth, he preached this truth. This teaching, portrayed by word and action, was made by St. Vincent the cornerstone of the charity to be practiced by his followers—the Vincentians and the Daughters of Charity.

As mentioned, personal charity has a subject. Private-personal charity must be practiced *in person*. St. Vincent de Paul did this precisely! I read about an incident in his life that graphically conveys this idea. Riding in his carriage, he heard a child crying. Immediately he stopped and investigated, finding an urchin with a cut hand. He personally took the child to a druggist, helped to dress the wound, and paid for the supplies. It would have been easy for him to let some other passerby take care of the matter. But he was alertly aware of the needs of others, and each chance to care for them was another opportunity to show his love for God in the person of the poor. This incident is merely one in the constant practice of charity by St. Vincent—he did such things all the time. It is this personal service which he enjoined upon his priests and sisters and even the laity who supported and shared in his works of charity. It is this personal service which St. Vincent wanted to be practiced in his institutions always. And it is this personal service which makes private charity continue to live in our world today.

This example of the private charity of St. Vincent, that is, charity exercised in person for persons, is one lesson we can all practice. We do not have to be professed Vincentians or Daughters of Charity to do so. We do not have to be in a hospital, home for the aged or other such institution. We are surrounded with opportunities to engage in private charity personally. These opportunities exist in our own home, in our parishes, and in our place of work. The sick at home afford a chance to become involved personally. We can all personally visit the sick in the neighborhood or in a hospital. We can provide food for a needy neighbor or clean house for a neighbor in mourning. St. Vincent did not always do great things. Generally, his private personal charity consisted of the little acts of kindnesses which are within the grasp of us all.

I conclude by presenting for your imitation St. Vincent de Paul—private charity

Pope John Paul II greets Bishop John C. Reiss, newly appointed bishop of the Trenton diocese.

in accordance with his insistence that the love of Christ urges us to see and serve Him in all persons personally.

St. Vincent de Paul, pray for us!

100TH ANNIVERSARY OF THE DIOCESE

On Ash Wednesday, the beginning of Lent, on March 4, 1981, Bishop John C. Reiss opened the Centennial year of the Diocese of Trenton by calling for a time of preparation through prayer, enrichment, and reconciliation. He celebrated Mass on Ash Wednesday in St. Thomas the Apostle Church, Old Bridge, New Jersey, and said, "For our Centennial, we have chosen the theme 'Alive in Faith.' As we pray and become reconciled and share during this Lent, I am sure that our diocese will be more than ever Alive in Faith. The theme for Phase I is 'An Invitation to Come Back Home.'"

The second phase of the Centennial celebration of the diocese was to give to the people of the diocese a chance to dialogue with Bishop John C. Reiss concerning their dreams, hopes, concerns, and expectations for their parish and church in the Diocese of Trenton. Each county in the diocese did have one of these dialogues with the bishop.

HOLY FATHER WOUNDED

On May 13, 1981, Pope John Paul II was shot in St. Peter's Square, and Bishop Reiss urged the people of the diocese to pray for his speedy recovery. "At this early date, without further information, I can only urge everyone to pray that the injury to our Holy Father is slight and that he will have a speedy and complete recovery. I trust that such a flagrant act of violence will alert everyone to strive to put an end to such acts."

CENTENNIAL CELEBRATION II

On Sunday, June 7, 1981, the Solemnity of Pentecost, Phase II of the Trenton diocese Centennial celebration, reached its culmination, "Call to Commitment—the New Pentecost," which included a special Mass in every church in the eight-county diocese. Bishop Reiss participated in all eight vicariate meetings, greeting the people with warmth and interest in what they had to say.

The diocese commissioned well-known artist Mrs. Peggy Peplow-Gummere to produce a commemorative piece for the Centennial: a beautiful pen-and-ink sketch of the Madonna holding the Infant Jesus.

FINAL PHASE OF CENTENNIAL

The third and final phase of the Centennial celebration of the diocese was the Centenary Festival and the Mass of Thanksgiving on August 9, 1981, at the Garden State Arts Center in Holmdel. This event was a festival of joy, with singing, dancing, praise, prayer, and historical displays. Some 5,000 people attended this Mass. In addition to Bishop

Reiss and Bishop Ahr, 175 priests concelebrated the Mass. At this Centennial Mass of Thanksgiving, Bishop Reiss preached the following homily.

BISHOP REISS'S HOMILY AT THE MASS OF THANKSGIVING

"Eternal life is this: to know You, Who are the only true God, and Him Whom You have sent, Jesus Christ" (Jn 17:3).

Happy anniversary to us! From every corner of the diocese, from every age group, from every state in life, from every background, we have assembled to celebrate spiritually and temporally the 100th anniversary of the establishment of the Diocese of Trenton. We commemorate the formal existence of Christ's church in that portion of the people of God as found within the territory of this diocese. We are marking as individuals our own personal religious history because all of us, united with the Pope and bishops and joined with Christ our Head are church.

The term "church," since it has so many applications, can seem to have a very impersonal meaning. "Church" can indicate all the buildings which have sprung up during the past 100 years and which are scattered in our 214 parishes. Definitely, "church" can signify that wonderful institution which was founded by the Lord Jesus on St. Peter and the Apostles, and which has spread over the whole world and thus, in a sense, due to its vastness, is in danger of losing its significance for the individual.

"Church" receives a more personal identification when we take it to equal people—the people of God—you and the hierarchy joined with Christ constitute the visible, living church here in Trenton. Therefore, in highlighting our 100th anniversary, we look to and recall people from the past; we consider people in the present; and we contemplate people in the future.

I am not going to give any detailed story of the diocese, but feel that we could mention a few circumstances which affected the pioneers of Trenton.

In addition to the hardships of the times associated with making a living in this "land of plenty," our predecessors in the faith had to overcome the added burden of religious persecution, not by being fed to the lions or put to death, but in the obstacles encountered as they tried to follow their religion and its customs. The principle of freedom of religion had been established in the Bill of Rights. Reducing principle to fact took many years and afflicted Catholics with many extra problems. The state of New Jersey was slow in guaranteeing this religious freedom, and the citizens, even slower. Traces of religious bigotry remain latent even today and occasionally appear in subtle form.

As Catholics grew in number, due to the ever constant wave of immigration to the United States and to New Jersey from the various countries of Europe, they gathered together in distinct enclaves. These Catholics brought with them their languages and particular rich religious customs, which certainly helped to solidify and preserve their Catholic heritage. Finally, coming close to our own day, there is the emergence and acceptance of the Catholic population.

Each of the preceding eras had its special problems which demanded wisdom and courage to overcome them. Our ancestors did just that—they faced the difficulties and overcame them. The people, under the leadership of local pastor and bishop, were eventually the victors. Consequently, and today, at this moment, it is the time to do so, and we must express deep in our hearts and through the Eucharist our overwhelming debt of gratitude to our religious forebears for preserving, building up, and passing on to us the faith of our fathers. We acknowledge in thanksgiving the sacrifices which they made for us, the Diocese of Trenton.

The way to demonstrate our thanks and at the same time pass on the light of faith is to imitate those who have served us. Briefly, we must reproduce and build up in ourselves the basic belief which they professed in the teachings of the Catholic Church. Their belief led them to personal commitment to the church in this diocese. This dedication was not in theory or in word only, but was a giving of self and of resources. Every parish represented here today can verify this in its history. All of us can recall examples which we possess from firsthand knowledge of the commitment of parents and of the prior generations, and of a commitment, even to the point of suffering and self-sacrifice.

Today, we are the inheritors of this legacy, and we are entrusted to keep it alive and well, so that we may pass on to succeeding generations a faith which is alive. As in the past, we too are faced with problems—some old, some new. Some of the new challenges center on nuclear power and its use and on genetic engineering as it affects persons. Some of the old challenges remain in the present, such as poverty, injustice, materialism, and an increasing acceptance of immorality.

As we move to consider people in the present, I would like to mention a few of the pressing problems. I list only a few and am aware that there are many others.

First, there is the leakage of membership, which can be noted from the decreased attendance at Mass and from the small number receiving the Sacraments. The dropping out has a peculiar characteristic in that it does not result in joining another religion, but entails just a cessation of practice. We cannot survey all of the reasons—real or imagined—but we can admit that there is work to be done. We must evangelize—evangelize in its total meaning. Therefore, we must renew our own faith and love for the church and the teachings of Christ. We must let these teachings take hold of our lives and transform us into concrete portrayers of God's love. Then, we must reach and call back to the fold those who have drifted away. Our experience recently in the program *Come Back Home* has indicated that for many, only a sincere invitation will move them into a renewed active practice. To those who labor under particular burdens, we must show the sympathy and comfort of Jesus, so as to lighten and share with them their hurts and pains.

Allied to a loss of members is an attitude which rejects the teaching authority of the church's magisterium. It appears that some wish to make their own judgments about religious truths or their feelings the norm for acceptance by God, rather than adhere to God's revelation. Since the church is obliged to proclaim the message of salvation as revealed by Jesus, often the church has to raise its teaching voice in opposition to the conclusions of a secularistic society filled with hedonism. Thus we must remember that the Son of God brought the Good News of salvation and entrusted it to His church. We can mistrust our own conclusions, but certainly can never doubt the church's teaching authority—the magisterium—which has the Holy Spirit as the preserver and protector of truth.

Finally, an urgent current problem in the Diocese of Trenton is vocations—the call to the priesthood, diaconate, sisterhood, and brotherhood. To evangelize, to teach, and to sanctify require that there be special ministers. In particular, without priests, the church in a given area can wither and die. Our priest personnel is at a dangerous level. It is incumbent upon each one of us "to pray that the Lord of Harvests will send laborers into His harvests." Thus, I call upon the clergy, religious, and laity to make vocations a priority. Vocations are to be fostered from the pulpit, in the schools, in the religious education programs, and, especially, in the family. Vocations are to be praised and exalted, so that our generous and brave youth may answer the call.

As we turn now to contemplate the people of the future and the problems we shall have to face, we can do no better than to imitate our predecessors in the Diocese of Trenton. We are, therefore, to walk in their footsteps by developing the same total commitment and to ensure that same personal dedication and firm resolve by a deepening of faith in our daily life.

It is good for us, then, to recall the verse from the Gospel which was proclaimed in the Liturgy of the Word, because it recalls the very purpose of the diocese and of our religion: "Eternal life is this: to know You, Who are the only true God, and Him Whom You have sent, Jesus Christ." In these few words we have placed before us not only our essential mission—to know God and Jesus—but also the reward for carrying out this task in our life and in the diocese, namely, "eternal life."

Through the fulfillment of this commission by each one of us in his or her individual life and by all of us as a diocese, we continue the work of Jesus our Head. Christ, as related by St. John, commended to the apostles and to us, the same message the Father gave to Him, the Son, and we are to receive it as did the Son.

To accomplish this purpose in the light of pressing obstacles, we need a vibrant hope. Here we look to that prayer of Solomon retold in the First Reading and make it our own: ". . . Just as the Lord has promised . . . May the Lord our God be with us as He was with our fathers . . . May He draw our hearts to Himself that we may follow Him in everything and keep the commands which He enjoined . . . that all the peoples of the earth may know the Lord is God" (1 Kings 8:55–61).

With St. Paul, let us rejoice in the proud heritage of our diocese and in that totally unmerited gift of faith which is ours today. "God chose us in Him (Christ) before the world began to be holy and blameless in His sight, to be full of love . . . In him (Christ) you too were chosen; when you heard the glad tidings of salvation, the word of truth, and believed in it, you were sealed with the Holy Spirit Who had been promised."

Faith in the Lord Jesus is ours. It is actually this faith which we celebrate today in the observance of the Centennial of the Diocese of Trenton. In view of what we mentioned earlier about the problem concerning vocations, in view of the fact that you are a constituent element of the church, it follows that we can look forward to an increased role for the laity in the future progress of the diocese. This role can be accepted and fulfilled by every person, insofar as each one gives personal example and witness of the acceptance of Jesus by living day after day a full Christian life. At the same time, the way will be opened to some to embrace specialized ministries after appropriate training and spiritual formation. The laity—the people—as in the past, will make and ensure the continual growth of the Diocese of Trenton.

Therefore, by our unselfish and prayerful working together—clergy, religious, and laity—the church in Trenton will continue to advance in the holiness of Christian life and thereby attain its essential goal.

And so, as we reflect upon the past, as we now rededicate ourselves and renew our commitment to the Lord as a diocese, we call upon Mary, the Patroness of the Diocese of Trenton under the title of her Assumption, to intercede for us, so that we may have the divine assistance of her Son, the guidance and strength of the Holy Spirit to lead us all to the Father.

MASS OF COMMEMORATION: AUGUST 11, 1981

A Mass of Commemoration was held at St. Mary's Cathedral in Trenton on August 11, 1981, the actual date of the 100th anniversary of the establishment of the diocese by Pope Leo XIII on August 11, 1881. But because of limited seating accommodations in the cathedral, admission to the cathedral Mass was by invitation only. Participating in this Mass were John Cardinal Krol of Philadelphia, Terence Cardinal Cooke of New York, and the Most Rev. Peter L. Gerety of Newark, the metropolitan of the Province of New Jersey. Bishop John C. Reiss was the principal celebrant of this Mass, and retired Bishop George W. Ahr gave the following homily.

"Behold, I am with you all days, even to the consummation of the world."

To celebrate, as we do today, the 100th anniversary of well nigh any event is an occasion giving rise to many and varied emotions. When, however, the event so signalized has had profound meaning for an entire community, its jubilee observance has broader impact. And when that event has produced effects that will outlast the ravages of time, the observance of its 100th Jubilee assumes a transcending significance.

We observe today the 100th anniversary of the founding of the Diocese of Trenton, an event which has profound meaning for the entire diocese and the surrounding area, and even for the entire church of Christ and the world—an event the results of which are to be calculated not in terms of time, but in the expectations of eternity.

We speak of today's celebration in terms of Jubilee. And, for us at least, this means heartfelt rejoicing. We are glad that the Diocese of Trenton was founded. We are happy that it has endured to this day. We rejoice in the incomparable and everlasting fruits it has produced.

And when we read the history of this diocese, we are filled with pride, for this is an institution that has known adversity and survived opposition.

What faith there was, what loyalty, what tenacity, what courage in those who have gone before us. These are the things which make our hearts swell with pride—and our minds pause in sober self-examination.

It is not our purpose to recount the history of the hundred years we celebrate. But it would be well if this history were read and pondered. It would be well if the noble qualities of our forebears found continued expression in our own lives.

Certainly that which has been accomplished, that which exists all about us, calls for the most generous and sincere thanksgiving. First of all, to Almighty God Who has raised up such men and women, such priests and religious; to God Who has sustained and strengthened them, and crowned their efforts with abundant spiritual fruit.

And then a prayerful, grateful remembrance is due to the founders of the diocese and to all the bishops, priests, religious, and faithful who followed and gave stability and permanence to the diocese.

As we celebrate the accomplishments of 100 years, we may indeed gaze into the past, but we must also look about us, for not a little of that accomplishment has been achieved in the memory and with the help of many of the living. There are many here today who have played an important part in these accomplishments, and in these they may take personal pride.

The visible history of a diocese can be written in terms of land and buildings or in terms of men and women, and most of this is familiar to you. But there is an invisible history that is known to God alone. How much good has been done by the Diocese of Trenton, how many souls saved, how much glory to God!

This part of our history we accept in faith, and in faith for this, too, we give thanks.

And now there remains tomorrow. Those who have gone before have received their reward. We of the present have our moment of glory and of pride. But what will they say when they write the history of the next 100 years?

The opposition has gone. But materialism and secularism constitute more formidable adversaries even than physical violence. Can we meet and overcome these difficulties as our forebears did theirs?

With some exceptions the material needs of the diocese have been met. Shall we have the determination to meet those that will continue to arise?

But overall, the spiritual needs still endure and become more urgent. And if the diocese will be faithful to these needs, then the others, I am confident, will be met, too. For in the last analysis, it is for this that the diocese really exists: the glory of God and the salvation of souls. All else is secondary; all else is but the means to the end.

As we round out the century of the Diocese of Trenton, we stand at the beginning of what may be the most challenging period in the history of the church. It is a challenge that is given to us by the Holy Spirit Himself in the Second Vatican Council.

The first part of the challenge was given in the constitution on the Liturgy. Perhaps it would be best to let the council speak for itself in the very words of the constitution:

The bishop is to be considered as the high priest of his flock from whom the life in Christ of his faithful is in some way derived and dependent. Therefore all should hold in great esteem the liturgical life of the diocese centered around the bishop, especially in his cathedral church; they must be convinced that the preeminent manifestation of the church consists in the full, active participation of all God's holy people in the liturgical celebrations;

especially in the same eucharist, in a single prayer, at one altar at which presides the bishop surrounded by his college of priests and by his ministers.

But because it is impossible for the bishop always and everywhere to preside over the whole flock of his church, he cannot do other than establish lesser groupings of the faithful.

Among these, the parishes, set up locally under a pastor who takes the place of the bishop, are most important, for in some manner they represent the visible church constituted throughout the world.

And therefore the liturgical life of the parish and its relationship to the bishop must be fostered theoretically and practically among the faithful and clergy; efforts must also be made to encourage a sense of community within the parish, above all in the common celebration of the Sunday Mass.

This is the program outlined by the Holy Spirit for the future of the Diocese of Trenton. From such holy united worship will issue the graces of the redemption that will give meaning to your lives and will add many jeweled pages to the resplendent history of the Diocese of Trenton.

Through the use of these graces will be fulfilled the hope expressed by the Second Vatican Council in the Decree on the Church in the Modern World:

Mindful of the words of the Lord: "By this all men will know that you are my disciples, if you have love for one another" (Jn 13:35). Christians can yearn for nothing more ardently than to serve the men of this age with an ever-growing generosity and success. Holding loyally to the Gospel, enriched by its resources, and joining forces with all who love and practice justice, they have shouldered a weighty task here on earth, and they must render an account of it to Him Who will judge all men on the last day. Not everyone who says, "Lord, Lord," will enter the kingdom of heaven but those who do the will of the Father and who manfully put their hands to the work. It is the Father's will that we should recognize Christ our brother in the person of all men and love them with an effective love, in word and in deed, thus bearing witness to the truth; and it is His will that we should share with others the mystery of His heavenly love. In this way, men all over the world will awaken to a lively hope (the gift of the Holy Spirit) that they will one day be admitted to the haven of surpassing peace and happiness in their homeland radiant with the glory of the Lord.

ECUMENICAL SERVICE

Two other religious events celebrated the 100th anniversary of the diocese. One was an Ecumenical Vespers Service on November 1, 1981, at St. Mary's Cathedral attended by a large number of non-Catholics in the Trenton area. Rev. Dr. James I. McCord, president of Princeton Theological Seminary, was the homilist at this service. Dr. McCord spoke on the theme Come, Creator Spirit. In his homily, Dr. McCord said, "The spirit of God gives unity and cohesiveness and draws to fulfillment, and today we want Him to draw us together and up into the mind of Christ. Talks between the different churches in recent years have revealed what they have in common and have helped to clear away the underbrush of history." Following the service, a reception was held in the cathedral dining hall.

The other service was held with the Jewish community, at Har Sinai Temple in Trenton on November 6, 1981, at the invitation of Rabbi Bernard Perelmuter. Bishop John C. Reiss preached at the Sabbath Eve service in the temple. An editorial in the diocesan *Monitor* on November 19, 1981, indicated the importance of this service.

An Event in Interfaith History

The participation of Bishop John C. Reiss as preacher at a November 19, 1981, Sabbath Eve service at Har Sinai Temple in Trenton was an inspiring as well as a history-making event. The several hundred Catholics and Jews who attended the service—believed to have been the first Jewish Sabbath service in a synagogue anywhere in the country in which a Catholic bishop has been invited to speak—came away with the warmest of feelings and with a reawakened awareness of the common roots which the two faiths share.

Bishop Reiss focused on those common roots in his talk, and pointed out that Catholics have learned much from their Jewish forebears. Those ancestors taught us, he said, to respect tradition—"not any whimsical tradition but a tradition that has evolved from wisdom and experience"; how to pray; how to "cry out in pain, to seek forgiveness for straying from God's plan"; how to rejoice; how to praise God; and how to suffer "in patience and in mystical silence, yet calling out for divine help."

A major point which Bishop Reiss stressed was that despite present differences, our common roots make it possible for Jews and Catholics to work together to find solutions for such present-day social problems as discrimination, defamation, unemployment, poverty and the plight of the elderly.

This significant and unprecedented service, which the Har Sinai Temple graciously dedicated as a commemoration of the 100th anniversary of the Diocese of Trenton, happily has opened the door for further expressions of mutual understanding, goodwill and cooperation among Catholics and Jews in communities within our diocese and elsewhere.

NEW DIOCESE OF METUCHEN

After the celebrations of the 100th anniversary of the diocese, life in the diocese went back to day-to-day operations, but not for long. On November 24, 1981, shortly after 8 a.m., the National Catholic News Service made the following announcement: "Pope John Paul II has established a new Diocese of Metuchen, New Jersey, and names Auxiliary Bishop Theodore McCarrick of New York to head it." With these few words, the rumors that had been around the Diocese of Trenton for years became a reality. The new Diocese of Metuchen took four counties away from the Diocese of Trenton, namely, Middlesex, Hunterdon, Somerset, and Warren, leaving Trenton with Mercer, Monmouth, Burlington, and Ocean counties.

Bishop John C. Reiss made the following statement on this announcement: "I assure Bishop McCarrick of a warm welcome by everyone in his new diocese. At the same time, I promise him my personal cooperation and the cooperation of my staff in connection with the difficult task of organizing the Diocese of Metuchen. Since I know the people of the area and have worked with them, I can also guarantee that the clergy, religious, and laity of his diocese will give him prayerful and loyal assistance."

The new bishop of Metuchen, Bishop Theodore E. McCarrick, also made a statement: "I look forward with joy and anticipation to the building up of the new Diocese of Metuchen and to collaborating with its priests, its religious, and its laypeople. From now on, in the Lord Jesus, you are my family and I pledge you my love."

On November 30, 1981, Bishop John C. Reiss wrote a letter to all the priests in Trenton and Metuchen:

Reverend dear Father:
The news has broken, and the new Diocese of Metuchen has arisen, with the Most Reverend Theodore E. McCarrick as its first ordinary. I have welcomed Bishop McCarrick in your name and have pledged him your known loyalty and cooperation.

Naturally, there are those pangs of loss and separation, both on my part and on the part of the priests who remain in Trenton. The bonds of friendship will certainly continue as contacts are maintained. To those in Metuchen, I encourage you to cooperate fully with Bishop McCarrick in helping to establish the new diocese. Those of us in Trenton will have to reassess many policies and adjust accordingly.

There is and there will be some confusion as details are worked out. However, as regards the Diocese of Metuchen, until the decree is formally signed, as bishop of Trenton, I retain full jurisdiction. Consequently, the usual correspondence relative to dispensations, parish resolutions, collections, and assessments will continue as is. Of course, you (in Metuchen) are free to contact Bishop McCarrick at any time and on any matter. Personnel, in accord with canon law, are now frozen, i.e., you belong to the diocese where you are currently assigned.

Let's pray together for the new diocese and its clergy so that a firm allegiance will develop.

I recommend all to the High Priest, Jesus Christ.

Fraternally yours in Christ,
/s/ + John C. Reiss
Bishop of Trenton

The Rev. Msgr. Dominic A. Turtora, chairperson for the installation of the new bishop of Metuchen, announced that the installation of Bishop Theodore E. McCarrick would be held on January 31, 1982, in the new Cathedral of St. Francis in Metuchen. Special celebrations for sisters, priests, deacons, and the laity of the diocese would precede the formal installation.

At the formal installation naming Bishop Theodore E. McCarrick as the first bishop of the new diocese, Bishop McCarrick gave the following homily:

Your Eminence, Cardinal Cooke, through your most welcome presence here we salute the church of New York which planted the first seeds of Catholicism in our four counties, and I salute Your Eminence in a personal way. The number of your kindnesses to me is infinite, and your friendship has been so great a grace.

Your Excellency, Archbishop Gerety, you come to us today as metropolitan archbishop of this ecclesiastical Province of Newark in which the Diocese of Metuchen now happily finds its place. You come as bishop of a diocese which more than 100 years ago cared for the people in the territory which now is Metuchen. On a personal note, may I say that no one could have been more thoughtful or gracious to me as I came to New Jersey. I am grateful for your leadership and your inspiration.

Your Excellency, Bishop Reiss, I pray that the people of the Diocese of Metuchen will find in their new bishop even half the priestly gentleman they had in their former bishop. I thank you for all your personal kindnesses to me during these past few weeks. The faith and the vitality of the Church of Metuchen are due to you and to your revered predecessor, Bishop Ahr, and to the devoted care of the faithful that marked your ministry. With all my heart I thank you on behalf of our priests, religious, and laity.

Msgr. Faccani, we are all most grateful for your presence here today in representation of our dear friend Archbishop Laghi, the apostolic delegate. Please bring him our own greetings. We miss him, but we understand his immense responsibilities and we all feel blessed to have him as the delegate from our beloved Holy Father. Your own presence here gives me and our priests, deacons, religious, and laity the opportunity once again to thank His Holiness Pope John Paul II for the gift to the Church of America of this new diocese and to pledge once more to the Holy Father our affectionate loyalty and our obedient love.

My brother bishops, welcome to the Church of Metuchen! This is the most beautiful diocese in America and most probably the best in the entire world. We don't have too many priests, but each one is a giant, and I have come to know their goodness, their dedication, and their faithfulness to the Gospel of Jesus Christ. Furthermore, Your Excellencies, we have the finest women religious in the whole country, the best brothers, and the best deacons. As you look around you to see the faces of God's people from all the parishes of this diocese, you will understand how blessed is the bishop of Metuchen and how much I thank our divine Lord for the faith and the grace-filled lives of the people of this lovely corner of the Kingdom of God.

My dear brother priests and deacons; dear sisters and brothers in consecrated life; your honors, the mayors, and other distinguished civic officials; my dear friends, the representatives of other churches and religious bodies; my aunts and uncle, representatives of my own family; and my brothers and sisters in my new family of the Diocese of Metuchen:

And so we begin!

This new ship of the Church of Metuchen now casts off its moorings from the safe harbor of the Diocese of Trenton, where with loving care it has been made seaworthy and given a secure berth for more than 100 years. We set out, all of us together, with Christ as our captain, His Gospel as our compass, and His Holy Mother Mary as our guiding star. We do not yet see the shoals that lie ahead of us, nor the squalls that will test the fiber of our sails, but we know that they are out there and that all of us have many leagues to journey on this pilgrim voyage that will one day bring us home to God.

We give thanks to our Heavenly Father that Jesus is truly in the boat with us and that, even more, it is His Hand on the tiller and His Spirit in the gentle breeze that blows us where He will. I am glad that all of us are in this boat together—priests and deacons, religious and laity, young and old, sinners and saints, wise and not so wise—with all our hopes and all our fears, but united in one Lord, one Faith, one Baptism, one God and Father of us all.

If I may hold on to this metaphor a little longer, I rejoice that there is room in this boat for the young people on whose energy and vitality—and on whose generosity in listening to God's call to service in priestly and religious life—we are now counting so much. There is room in this boat for the elderly, both for the frail to whose loving care we commit ourselves both as people and as Church and for those who are blessed by good health and now have the time to reach out to others in helpful service. In a special way, there is room in this bark of the Church of Metuchen for the poor and the needy, for the homeless and the unemployed, for the sick and the handicapped, for the lonely and the confused, for proud ethnic communities, and for those sisters and brothers of ours who suffer discrimination because of race or color or language. For all whose dreams have been shipwrecked by troubles and sorrows, let the bright lights of this new vessel call them all to a haven of safety, to a place of refreshment, light, and peace.

There is room for families in this boat of ours, for family life is the real strength of this diocese. To our parents in this new local church, I pledge my own wholehearted support as they strive to live out the Gospel message in the ebb and tide of today's swirling currents of pressures and problems. And as they accept the momentous responsibility of the religious education of their children, both through our truly miraculous Catholic school system and through essential parish programs of religious instruction, they can be sure of my own immediate concern, interest, and cooperation.

Likewise, the single men and women in this diocese should know that they can count on the church as their own family and on all of us as brothers and sisters in Jesus, so that no one need ever feel alone and that the talents of each may be used for the welfare of all. And there is a place too in this boat of ours for the divorced and separated among us who must come to understand that God's concern for them has never been greater than at that moment when He sometimes seems to let them drift a little distance from His love.

And so we set out. With trust in the Divine Providence and secure in the protection of the Living God. The banner high on the mast above witnesses our faith; it sings out in the fluttering wind with the proclamation that Jesus Christ is Lord. On that foundation then, let our journey begin.

And what are our sailing orders? Where are the charts on which to plot out the voyage that begins this day? Are they not to be found in the very Word of God and indeed in the message which He proposes to us today in the readings of this Mass?

The First Reading speaks of the prophet whom the Lord will appoint to take the place of Moses in the guidance of God's beloved people. The Gospel text shows Jesus in that role, teaching with authority, spellbinding His listeners, effecting miraculous cures of wonder and power. And we too are called, each in our own way, to teach with authority. Some of us are charged with a special care of God's people, with a special command from the Lord Himself to speak to them in His Name. Oh, pray for me, my friends, that I may never stray from a perfect faithfulness to that message, nor from its courageous proclamation, without fear or human respect.

Courage, fidelity, authority, truth, authenticity—all these virtues are required in the prophet who will speak in the Name of the Lord, and today the whole church is called upon to fulfill that role in union with the Holy Father, John Paul our Pope, and in faithfulness to the Gospel message. What an awesome challenge this is for all of us! What an impossible burden for men and women like ourselves!

But St. Paul reassures us as he reassured the Corinthians 2,000 years ago. In the Second Reading of today's Mass he meditates on the personal abilities of those who serve. With our brothers and sisters of the early Church of Corinth, we recognize that few of us are really noble or truly wise or influential. God knows the weakness of the instrument He prepares to use. But once He takes it in His hand, then in Him and through Him and with Him, there is really nothing that you and I cannot do!

Then let us set our sails this day, dear friends in Christ. The winds of Providence are at our back! The sun and the stars are in place to guide us! The Master of this vessel Who is Christ calls us to set out on this pilgrimage of faith, this journey into grace as a new church and a new family. Together we cry out in joyful response: Come, Lord Jesus, come with us as we go! The watchfires have been lighted, the night is driven off, and Lord, if You are with us, this light will never end. Amen.

Following the beautiful Mass of Installation, a reception was held for Bishop McCarrick at St. Thomas Aquinas High School in Edison. The new bishop was on hand at the reception to greet his well-wishers and stayed until the last person had been received.

This was the second time in the history of the Diocese of Trenton that a division occurred; the first had taken place on December 9, 1937, when Pope Pius XI created the Diocese of Camden from the southern counties of New Jersey.

EMMAUS PROGRAM

On January 22, 1982, Bishop John C. Reiss informed his priests by letter that the Emmaus Program would begin in the spring for all the priests in the diocese. The bishop indicated that the program had two goals: first, to assist each priest whether diocesan or religious, in his own spiritual renewal, and, second, to aid priests and their bishop in a renewal of their communal spirituality. Bishop Reiss appointed the Rev. Charles B. Weiser as chairperson of the Planning Committee for the Emmaus Program.

The following is a report in *The Monitor* of an interview with Bishop Reiss concerning the Emmaus Program.

Bishop John C. Reiss is excited about the possibilities of the Emmaus Program of priestly spirituality now under way in the Diocese of Trenton.

In an interview several days before the first overnight exercise in the program, he said the response of the priests of the diocese has been much better than he had expected. "They have a tremendous interest in it and I think they have a tremendous expectation. They, too, feel the need for themselves and they feel the need for building up our own closeness.

"I'm very happy. I'm delighted with the response."

The program is designed to increase the spirituality of the priests of the diocese and bring them closer together around their bishop through an initial overnight meeting (May 25 and 26) and a series of five-day retreats, which will accommodate all of the priests in the fall, and six monthly overnight meetings with smaller groups of priests.

"There is always a necessity for everybody, and I include the clergy, to increase their spirituality, and I felt that it is important for the clergy of the Diocese of Trenton to do something on this order.

"There are many programs that were presented and discussed and looked at, and this came out to be the one that was more tailored to the way our diocese should be. We don't have to leave the diocese. We can get together nearby, and it will give us an ongoing spiritual uplift whereby we can go through the retreats as they come along, take part in the small-group discussions and, praying together, move on to the final conclusion.

"In this way we can not only build up the individual's spirituality but also try to build up a really cohesive presbyterate of the Trenton diocese. And we're looking forward to the fact that we will have a better support system for one another.

"I feel that only a priest really understands the problems of a priest, and if a brother priest can step in and care, and be counted on for assistance, it should make for a much more relaxed atmosphere between one another to share our burdens."

Bishop Reiss said he looks upon the priests of the diocese as collaborators in his own responsibility to spread the Word of God.

There was a definite change of position in his relationship with the priests of the diocese two years ago when he went from serving as auxiliary bishop to ordinary in the diocese. "In one sense I am their ordinary—superior—in giving orders and making plans, so it does create a new relationship. But as the ordinary I am also charged with being vitally interested in what will affect their lives. I must depend on the priests to carry out my mandate to bring the Word of God to everyone, so we are collaborators. I look on them as collaborators.

"Thus I hope I can give them support, understanding, and leadership . . . In the Emmaus Program it is vital that the bishop take part in it, and be one with the priests as we go through the various steps.

"I am there as one of their brother priests . . ."

In preparing for a talk he was to give to the priests during the Emmaus Program May 26, Bishop Reiss said he took serious note of a statement from St. Augustine in which he said: "For you I am a bishop, with you I am a priest."

"That epitomizes my role and why I am in the program too—as a brother priest and as a bishop to set the example.

"My primary hope is for a deepening of each priest's own personal spiritual life, then, to move on and also increase his own temporal life and his own individual personality, and finally that there will be this mutual esteem, better communication, and support in connection with the duties and burdens attached to the priesthood.

"Of course, this will also trickle down. If the priests do this, they will set the example for the laity, and their own spirituality of the priesthood will affect the diocese. Since the people will be praying, it's going to be kind of a circle, one helping the other, with understanding and a realization that the priests need prayers and appreciation and understanding."

The whole issue with the Emmaus Program is not a matter of just being good, said Bishop Reiss, "but of being better and making the effort to seek perfection. There is no special reason why now, except just coincidentally with the split of the diocese it does create a very nice opportunity for the 'new' Diocese of Trenton to build up its own cohesiveness.

"And it can only be an outgrowth, too, of the fact that there is a need for spirituality throughout the church and in the world itself, which has turned away from God too much.

"The priests live the same kind of life with the obligations attached to it. First of all, the celibate life, the obligation of being spiritual leaders, both through the administration of the sacraments and through a personal prayer life. And only a priest with these duties would understand the particular type of difficulties that they have to face.

"For example, the idea of loneliness. The idea of demands made on the priests which at times could be excessive, which expect him to be master of everything—so unless you live the life, you wouldn't really understand it, so that's why only a priest can understand another priest."

While there is much potential in the Emmaus Program, Bishop Reiss said he does not know where it is leading.

"With some of the things going on in the church and, you might say, the almost excessive demands for the priest, it almost dictates that something has to be done by other people. Going back to the original church, when the apostles could not be taken from their primary duty of preaching and praying, they had to get the deacons to wait on tables. In other words, they had to get help. I don't want to insult our deacons, but it shows how we're in a situation where we need help too . . .

"The first spill-over effect might be as we used to say: If you have a saintly priest, you have a holy people; if you have a holy priest, you have a good people; if you have a good priest, you have a mediocre people. So if we have excellent, holy priests, as a by-product we should have fine, excellent, holy laity."

Overwork and tension are not so much part of the Emmaus Program, but are a part of the life of a priest and part of the modern world, said Bishop Reiss. "It goes back again to what is expected of a priest. As he puts himself into it completely, he can be absorbed with the externals . . . However, that is not so much connected with the Emmaus Program as it is with the life of the priest and the modern times.

"There are fellows really putting out— with a lot of meetings and programs, taking care of the old, taking care of the middle-aged, taking care of the married . . . so many demands. If he tries to do it all himself, he will overextend and that leads to everything else: tiredness, overwork, tension, and maybe the loss of enthusiasm for his work, but if the spiritual is put in its proper place, then all of these things will work out. One of those old axioms comes back to mind: You pray hard, you work hard, and you play hard.

"As you look at yourself as a priest and all that it entails from our theology, and from experience, and from Scripture, it should enhance the reason why I decided to become a priest and then spur me on to be a better priest.

"I feel confident that the priests will pursue it to the end and share in the fruits of their efforts by an increased spiritual life and service to the people of God.

"The whole program is going to ask the laity to pray for the priests. This should build up closer relationships, with the people of the parish praying for their pastor and their associates, and in turn, the priests, knowing that they are praying for them, will be praying for their people at home, so it should build up better love and appreciation and a desire to work together."

Through the Emmaus Program, the reality of the priest as spiritual leader should be enhanced for both himself and his people, said Bishop Reiss.

RCIA PROGRAM

In March 1982, the diocese began to study and implement the Rite of Christian Initiation for Adults with a special meeting held at St. Anthony of Padua parish in Hightstown with the Rev. Joseph F. McHugh as chairperson of this task force.

DELEGATE AT PRINCETON

In April 1982, the Most Rev. Archbishop Pio Laghi, apostolic delegate to the United States, spoke at the noonday chapel service at Princeton Theological Seminary in Princeton and gave an address at that same seminary at 2:30 p.m. in the lounge of the Campus Center. In his talks, Archbishop Laghi described the church in the United States as "a very fertile, dynamic, prophetic church. It's ahead and jumping ahead with new ways of ministry."

PASTORAL LETTER

On April 15, 1982, Bishop John C. Reiss issued a pastoral letter to all in the diocese in response to the needs expressed by the people of the diocese in the Call to Dialogue meetings, as part of the centennial celebration in 1981. In the pastoral letter, the bishop summed up the Call to Dialogue meetings by saying, "The local parish is the single most important part of the church. This is where, for our people, the mission of Christ continues. Our people have shown in their meetings that they do care for one another and are eager to accept the challenge of transforming their parish into a more graced fellowship." The bishop closed this pastoral letter by saying, "I am pleased that since the Call to Dialogue, many parishes, pastors, and people have worked hard to fulfill some of the dreams which were expressed. A goodly number of their desires can be implemented in the parishes in accord with existing directives and permissions. The diocesan offices stand ready to assist. New programs are under study."

On a few occasions there were openly expressed the eagerness and readiness of the laity to assist the pastor with all available talents and to do so in such a way as to recognize fully the pastor's position as shepherd. It is this harmonious dual effort which will make the parish the center of all efforts to serve the Lord. We can do this if we "love one another."

ECUMENISM

On May 29, 1982, Pope John Paul II made a historic trip to meet the archbishop of Canterbury—Archbishop Robert Runcie—and while in Canterbury celebrated an ecumenical service at ancient Canterbury Cathedral.

To commemorate this great ecumenical event in the life of the church, Bishop John C. Reiss and the Right Rev. Albert W. Van Duzer, bishop of the Episcopal Diocese of New Jersey, issued a joint pastoral letter to the clergy and people of their dioceses:

May 1982

Brothers and Sisters in Christ,
The Spirit of God brooded over the waters, and from chaos came creation. The Spirit of the Risen Christ transformed the confusion of Babel into an event of communication, understanding, and witness celebrated by the church as the Feast of Pentecost. The confusion of our own day, brought on by believers who have lost hope in Christ as the answer and by secularists who never had reason to hope, makes this time an ideal moment for God's Holy Spirit to work anew his miracle of unifying the family of man and, most especially, the family of Jesus' disciples.

Episcopalians and Roman Catholics rejoice that years of dialogue and study have met with success as the theologians of our respective Communions produced the documents of the Anglican–Roman Catholic International Commission. These documents deal with the Eucharist, the ministry, authority in the church, and papal primacy. Nothing short of a miracle as impressive as the first Pentecost could have wrought this agreement. Centuries of divi-

sion are being undone, and this is cause for rejoicing.

On Saturday, May 29, 1982, Canterbury and Rome will meet in the persons of the Most Reverend and Right Honourable Robert Alexander Kennedy Runcie and His Holiness Pope John Paul II. They will embrace as brothers, and at that moment each of us will be represented by them. As they lead our Communions in the renewal of our baptismal promises, the Spirit will be there, ushering in Pentecost 1982 in a manner reminiscent of that mighty wind which first blew the infant church to the farthest reaches of the globe.

Episcopalians and Roman Catholics of our dioceses need to celebrate this day. At noon on that day, Saturday, May 29, in Trinity Episcopal Cathedral, the Right Reverend Albert W. Van Duzer, Episcopal bishop of New Jersey, will preside at a Service of Thanksgiving; the Most Reverend John C. Reiss, Roman Catholic bishop of Trenton, will preach. Clergy and laity of every parish should be there. In a world of hatred, bigotry, and violence, God is doing a new and exciting thing with us and for us. In Christ's name, we have been chosen to be signs of reconciliation to the world. For Christ's sake, we respond with gratitude, hope and joy.

Sincerely yours in Christ,
/s/ The Rt. Rev. Albert W. Van Duzer
Diocese of New Jersey
/s/ The Most Rev. John C. Reiss
Diocese of Trenton

NEW AUXILIARY BISHOP

On August 31, 1982, Archbishop Pio Laghi announced that Msgr. Edward U. Kmiec had been appointed auxiliary bishop of Trenton by Pope John Paul II. Monsignor Kmiec, who was 46 years of age at the time of his appointment, had served as pastor of St. Francis Church in Trenton, vice-chancellor of the Diocese of Trenton, and secretary to Bishop John C. Reiss. The appointment by Pope John Paul II is "the cause of rejoicing in the entire diocese for this distinct honor," said Bishop Reiss in a statement released after the announcement.

At the same time, Bishop-Elect Kmiec issued a statement in which he expressed his gratitude to the Holy Father and pledged to Bishop Reiss "to devote myself wholeheartedly to the task of assisting him in pastorally ministering to all in our diocese."

"I humbly beg the prayers of all," said the bishop-elect, "that God may grant me the graces necessary to fulfill faithfully the obligations and expectations of this new dimension of priestly ministry which has been bestowed upon me, that thereby I may be a worthy servant of all."

Retired Bishop George W. Ahr, for whom Monsignor Kmiec had served as secretary and master of ceremonies for fifteen years, expressed "happiness" at the news and said he was "very pleased" to learn of the appointment.

Among the countless telephone calls the bishop-elect made after the formal announcement was one to Bishop Ahr.

"I told Bishop Ahr that if I prove worthy of the appointment it will be the result of the wonderful lessons I learned over the years I served with him," the young prelate said.

While both Bishop Reiss and Monsignor Kmiec knew of the appointment five days earlier, they were bound to secrecy by the Holy See until the formal announcement at 8 a.m., Tuesday, August 31, by Archbishop Laghi, Pope John Paul's representative in the United States.

From 8:01 a.m. through the rest of the day, the bishop-elect was busy making calls or answering the phone, accepting the congratulations of his many friends among the clergy, religious, and laity.

The first calls he made from St. Francis Rectory in downtown Trenton were to his brothers Joseph and Henry in Trenton and John in Langhorne, Pennsylvania.

"They were amazed," said Monsignor Kmiec. "They, like myself, just couldn't realize that their brother is a bishop."

Then, with a touch of sadness in his voice, the young prelate said: "Would that my parents and sister were here to hear the news."

Monsignor Kmiec's parents, John and Thecla Czupta Kmiec, and his sister, Mrs. Helen Jarkowski, were already deceased. Mr. and Mrs. Kmiec had been natives of Poland and had been born only a few miles from the hometown of Pope John Paul II.

"And that is what I told the Holy Father in my letter to him." said the bishop-elect.

As auxiliary bishop, Bishop-Elect Kmiec assisted Bishop Reiss in pastorally ministering to the spiritual needs of the nearly 550,000 Catholics in 124 parishes in the four counties that make up the Diocese of Trenton—Burlington, Mercer, Monmouth, and Ocean.

His Episcopal ministry included administering the Sacrament of Confirmation, in which Bishop Reiss has been assisted by Bishop Ahr as well as Msgr. George E. Everitt, vicar-general, and Msgr. Leonard R. Toomey, episcopal vicar for Mercer County.

The bishop-elect was born in Trenton June 4, 1936. The Kmiec family resided at 1416 Princeton Avenue in North Trenton and were parishioners of St. Hedwig's Church, one of the three Polish parishes in Trenton.

Educated at St. Hedwig's School and a 1954 graduate of Trenton Catholic Boys High School, the future bishop prepared for the priesthood at St. Charles Seminary, Catonsville, Maryland; St. Mary's Seminary, Baltimore; and the North American College in Rome, where he earned a licentiate in sacred theology at the Gregorian University.

He was ordained in St. Peter's Basilica in Rome on December 20, 1961, by the Most Rev. Martin J. O'Connor, rector of the North American College.

Returning to the United States in 1962, Father Kmiec was assigned briefly as associate pastor of St. Mary's Cathedral and on August 3 of that year was named associate pastor of St. Rose, Belmar.

Three years later, on June 11, 1965, Bishop Ahr appointed Father Kmiec an assistant chancellor of the diocese and at the same time made him his secretary and master of ceremonies; the latter two positions Father Kmiec filled for the next fifteen years.

Then on July 5, 1966, Bishop Ahr promoted Father Kmiec to vice-chancellor.

Among other diocesan posts the busy prelate filled were secretary to the diocesan Committee on Educational and Economic Opportunity Programs, secretary to the diocesan Liturgical Commission, pro-synodal judge of the diocesan Tribunal, and member of the diocesan Board of Consultors.

In recognition of his dedicated work for the church, Pope Paul VI, on the recommendation of Bishop Ahr, named Father Kmiec a prelate of honor on September 15, 1977, with the title of monsignor.

Following the retirement of Bishop Ahr in June 1979, and the subsequent appointment of Auxiliary Bishop Reiss as his successor, Monsignor Kmiec was appointed by Bishop Reiss as pastor of St. Francis Church and also as his secretary.

Bishop-Elect Kmiec is the third auxiliary bishop of Trenton in the diocese's history. The first was the Most Rev. James J. Hogan, who was appointed auxiliary bishop to Bishop Ahr on November 27, 1959, serving until his elevation to bishop of Altoona-Johnstown May 23, 1966, from which position he is now retired.

Bishop Reiss was appointed auxiliary bishop to Bishop Ahr October 21, 1967, serving in that capacity until he was named ordinary of the diocese on March 4, 1980.

Monsignor Kmiec and Bishop Reiss recalled a conversation they had at the Chancery Office on August 26, when the bishop called him into his office.

It went something like this:

"You'd better close the door," said the bishop. The door was closed. "How do you feel about serving the church?"

"Fine," said Monsignor Kmiec. "But what's this all about?"

With a smile on his face, Bishop Reiss replied, "They want you to be auxiliary bishop!"

Recalling the incident, Monsignor Kmiec says, "My whole life passed before me. I just couldn't believe it."

There followed his acceptance of "the offer" in a letter from Archbishop Laghi.

Later, speaking with the apostolic delegate, Bishop Reiss said he began to laugh and the archbishop asked him why. He explained: While he was auxiliary bishop, he also was titular bishop of Simidicca in Tunisia, a title vacated when he became ordinary of the diocese. It had been vacant until Pope John Paul II named Monsignor Kmiec an auxiliary bishop of Trenton and titular bishop of Simidicca!

Bishop Edward U. Kmiec was ordained a bishop on November 3, 1982, at St. Mary's Cathedral with Bishop John C. Reiss as the principal consecrator; the co-consecrators were Bishop George W. Ahr and Bishop James J. Hogan. Bishop Reiss gave the following homily:

"This is the day the Lord has made; let us rejoice and be glad in it."

How aptly this statement epitomizes our feelings today, as it applies to Bishop Kmiec—his day of receiving the fullness of Sacred Orders; to the entire Diocese of Trenton—clergy, religious, and laity—and to myself as we welcome his additional assistance. We all realize that the more difficult the goal, the greater is the joy. Our joy is very great, because it is not easy now to secure an auxiliary, for it entails many

Bishop Kmiec in procession before his episcopal ordination at St. Mary's Cathedral, November 3, 1982. At his right is Msgr. Francis L. Zgliczynski, who baptized Bishop Kmiec as a child.

letters of explanation regarding the size of the territory, the number of faithful, and the spiritual needs of the diocese.

First, I heartily express my profound gratitude to our Holy Father, Pope John Paul II, for granting this distinct favor to our diocese. I feel that this is another sign of the Pontiff's deep concern for the spiritual welfare of the people of God in this area. I am grateful for the invaluable assistance of the apostolic delegate, Archbishop Pio Laghi, in processing the request for an auxiliary bishop. I wish to thank the many bishops who have honored us with their presence, especially during this extremely busy season. To all the civic officials, I extend my appreciation for your attendance. I am delighted to have with us the representatives of other faiths in this concrete display of ecumenism. My thanks to the clergy of the Diocese of Trenton and, as of now, our "separated" brothers from Metuchen, and to the clergy from other dioceses who have come to welcome so warmly the new bishop. In the same way, I thank the religious delegates, the laity, and the friends and family of Bishop Kmiec.

There are two interesting items I would like to share with you. As you know, an auxiliary bishop is assigned a titular see—that is, the name of a diocese which no longer exists. By a coincidence, Bishop Kmiec has the titular see of Simidicca, which previously had been my own. Secondly, you have before you a few generations of Trenton Bishops—Bishop Ahr, who served here for thirty years; Bishop Hogan, who was the first auxiliary in Trenton; myself, the first native born to be bishop of Trenton; and now, Bishop Kmiec, the first native son of the city of Trenton, for the office of bishop.

The office of bishop begins with Christ. The Savior called His twelve apostles, trained them, instructed them, and finally commissioned them to proclaim the good news of salvation. Fully aware that the first chosen would not live forever, our Blessed Lord intended that there be successors and that their essential powers be passed on in the church. We have been assured frequently by the church, and even in the Second Vatican Council, that the bishops are the successors of the apostles and that the bishops possess the essential apostolic powers and functions.

Quite often in the New Testament, both by His disciples and by His enemies, Jesus is called "Teacher." Christ Himself, after His resurrection, commanded His apostles, "Go, and make disciples of all nations . . . teaching them to observe all that I have commanded you" (Mt 28:19–20). Thus, one of the most serious duties of a bishop is to teach—to proclaim "all that I have commanded you." This includes the revelations made by the Son of God concerning His Father's will for our salvation, the church, the commandments, the sacraments, and the basic law of love of God and neighbor. The bishop's obligation is to teach everyone the Deposit of Faith as it has been preserved and interpreted through the centuries by the church. The fulfillment of this charge is not always easy, especially when Christian teaching is so opposed to the prevalent spirit of secularism, hedonism, and selfishness. From time to time, the bishop must recall St. Paul's words to Timothy, ". . . be urgent in season and out of season; reprove, entreat, rebuke with all patience and teaching" (II Tim 4:2).

Primarily, the bishop assumes his role of teacher by preaching. Thus, as he goes about the diocese and appears in parishes or assemblies, the bishop must be ever mindful that he is to proclaim the Word of God, explain its meaning, and apply it to the circumstances of our modern world. Perhaps the greatest example today of such preaching is found in the person of Pope John Paul II, the bishop of Rome. We know this from his visit to our United States and from his visits to other countries.

The bishop, as the apostles, must also rule. "To rule" has a bad connotation nowadays. More acceptable is the term "to lead." The bishop as shepherd, then, is to set the example and to direct everyone on the road to salvation. To correct at times, to encourage, to heal, to cajole are all aspects of a bishop's leadership. It is true that an auxiliary bishop does not have a specific territory, but he does share in the institute of collegiality, so clearly enunciated in the

Second Vatican Council. Every bishop has to be concerned with whatever affects the church on a local basis, in the nation, and throughout the world.

Furthermore, there is the charge to sanctify, to make holy. With the fullness of the priesthood, the bishop becomes the ordinary minister of the Sacrament of Confirmation and is able to confer Sacred Orders. In his ministry to others, the bishop is bound to offer sacrifice and to pray both for himself and for the people. The sanctification of others will flow from his own personal holiness and example, as well as from the administration of the sacraments and from other liturgical activity.

The Gospel which has just been read summarizes the many obligations of a bishop in the term "service." "I have come not to be served, but to serve." Jesus' words reflect His actions—He healed the lame and the blind; He fed the multitude not only with bread but also with food for the soul; He closely associated Himself with the poor ("Even the poor have the gospel preached to them"); and, finally, He suffered and died for all. The bishop must serve others in imitation of Christ and hence will be required frequently to make personal sacrifice, even to the point of suffering. All of this service is not for an earthly reward, but only to follow Christ, Who told us He came not to do His own will, but the will of His heavenly Father—"I came to do the will of Him Who sent Me."

I might observe that as we briefly contemplate the office of bishop, we also look to the other side of the coin. There is a duty on the part of the faithful—clergy, religious, and laity—to respect the bishop. There is a duty to listen to him as teacher and to follow him as leader in the quest for eternal life.

As the ceremony unfolds, you will see that in the process of interrogation, Bishop Kmiec is fully aware of the serious obligations he is called upon to accept and perform. Just to recount these duties demonstrates how fearsome they are. I say that Bishop Kmiec knows these tasks when I recall the scene that occurred in the Chancery Office on August 26th. A telephone call had come from the apostolic delegate indicating that our bishop had been nominated an auxiliary and that his consent was being sought. I had him come to my office and asked, "How would you like to be a bishop?" My usually talkative coworker visibly blanched and temporarily—only temporarily—lost his tongue. In a brief instant, from his theology and training, he was conscious of the awesome responsibilities of a bishop. Recovering slowly, he asked a moment to pray, to reflect, and to discuss his decision. His "fiat" came quickly and has led to this day.

Bishop Ed has spent many years in the Chancery Office working closely with Bishop Ahr as his secretary and master of ceremonies and with Bishop Hogan and myself as assistant chancellor, and later as vice-chancellor. Thus, he is well acquainted with the working of the diocese. In his several capacities, he has been in close contact with priests, deacons, seminarians, sisters, brothers, and laity. He has listened to them, advised them, and helped them. In other words, Bishop Ed has given of himself in service to others. The service which he has rendered has never been for personal gain, but rather to show his love for God, for the church, and for people. He has acted out of Christian love. No wonder then, as you may have observed in the booklet, he has chosen for his motto "Charity and Service"—love leads to service. In his position as auxiliary bishop, Bishop Ed will continue in this fashion, fully cognizant of the burdens attached to his new office, being mindful though of the words in the First Reading from the Prophet Jeremiah: "Have no fear . . . because I am with you . . . says the Lord." He is further encouraged by the advice which St. Paul gave to Timothy: ". . . stir into flame the gift of God bestowed when my hands were laid upon you. The Spirit God has given us is no cowardly spirit, but rather, one that makes us strong" (2 Tim 1:6–8).

Bishop Ed, have no fear of the future performance of your duties—you are not alone. The Lord is with you through the graces of the Sacrament of Orders. Your family—so proud this very hour—will assist with their prayers, and, I am certain, your deceased mother, father, and sister are your heavenly advocates. Your fellow bishops will advise and cooperate with you. All the people of the diocese will offer their prayers for you, especially during the Eucharistic Sacrifice when you will be given special mention.

With these short reflections, let us prayerfully begin the ceremony of ordination, aware of God's presence among us, conscious of our filial devotion to Christ the High Priest and His Blessed Mother, confident of your expressed desire for charity and service, and rejoicing in the goodness of the Lord to the Diocese of Trenton.

BISHOP KMIEC'S REMARKS

At the end of the ordination ceremony, the new Bishop Edward U. Kmiec made the following remarks.

In the Epistle to the Romans, it is written: "How inscrutable are God's judgments, how unsearchable His ways . . . Who has given Him anything so as to deserve any-

After ordination, Bishops Kmiec, Ahr, and Reiss enter reception at Cedar Gardens restaurant.

thing? For from Him and through Him and for Him all things are. To Him be glory forever." This quotation aptly summarizes my feelings at this moment. I feel the "inscrutability" of God's providence as I blink in amazement and wonder at the realization that I stand here as a bishop, an authentic successor of the apostles in the fullness of the priesthood. It both humbles and elates, and it makes me aware of a great debt of gratitude I owe to so many, both in heaven and on earth.

Of course, first and foremost, I am grateful to God, Who has filled my life with countless blessings and now with this one. Indeed, "to Him be glory forever." I feel also a great sense of gratitude to our Blessed Mother. I am not one to give undue import to events of life or to see hidden meaning in them, but I cannot ignore, or simply dismiss as coincidence, that I chose to honor Mary by saying my first Mass at the altar of Our Lady of Czestochowa in the crypt of St. Peter's Basilica in Rome, and then 21 years later received notification of my nomination as bishop on August 26, the 600th anniversary of the Czestochowa icon. I simply conclude that I have been a beneficiary of her exceptional patronage all through my life.

Still in the heavenly realms, I call to mind my deceased parents, John and Thecla, present not in body here today but certainly in spirit. How could I ever repay or thank them adequately for all they gave me, never counting their own hardships and sacrifices and always pouring out their open-hearted love. From them I received life itself, the nourishment of my Faith, the home atmosphere that cradled a vocation to the priesthood, and so much more. In heaven, where their joy is already complete and full, I nevertheless still feel this has to be a special day for them, as it is for me. All I can say is, thank you, Mom and Dad!

Getting down to earth, an expression of gratitude is so much more difficult, because there are just so many to thank. I do single out our Holy Father, Pope John Paul II, and thank him for the great honor he has lavished upon me and the confidence shown in me by a call to this exalted ministry as bishop. And may I add to those with suspicious minds, I assure you, as I have been assured, that there is no "Polish Connection" here! I also single out Bishop Reiss, Bishop Ahr, and Bishop Hogan, to thank them for uncountable kindnesses and friendship and especially for their service today as principal consecrator and co-consecrators. And Bishop Reiss, the homily was just simply beautiful and inspirational.

By now, you might be getting the feeling: "My God, is he going to thank everyone individually in a litany of thanksgiving?" I certainly would like to do so, for you are

Bishop Kmiec gives his first bishop's blessing in St. Mary's Cathedral, after his ordination.

all special people to me. However, prudence and discretion dictate otherwise, for it has already been a long and warm and beautiful ceremony, and bishops should be prudent and discreet. Besides, I'll get another shot at you at dinner. For now, may I therefore just say a collective thank-you to you all for all the kindness and love you have shown me and for your presence here today to share in my joy. I say this now, particularly to those who will not be able to join us at dinner.

Prime among these are the bishops who have graced this occasion with their presence but who have to leave shortly due to the exigencies of their schedules and duties. I thank them all for their part in my ordination, for their wonderful witness to the fraternity and holy order of bishop, and for the great honor their presence has given to me, to my family, and to the Diocese of Trenton itself. Their welcome of me to the episcopacy has been most cordial and full of encouragement.

Similarly, I thank the distinguished churchmen of other faiths, for the ecumenical sign of fraternity and friendship we share in our mutual service to God, which your presence today has demonstrated.

Dear friends, St. Augustine was a bishop, and he had some beautiful reflections on his ministry. "The episcopacy," he said, "is the name of a work, not of any honor, and a bishop is not one who likes to hold sway but one who wants to be of help." Pope Paul VI echoed this sentiment in an allocution in which he said, "The episcopacy is not an honor that stands by itself. It is in the nature of a special ministry, which means it is a dignity that goes with and sustains a service for the benefit of others. We know well that such an elevation is not a goal unto itself but that it takes place for the good of the church." It is in that spirit and with those ideals that I assume my new ministry as bishop. I pray that everyone will find in me an open heart, a good listener, and an attentive observer. I do not pretend to be able to satisfy the needs of everybody, but I will make every effort to bring Christ to all His people, in the words of my motto, with Charity and Service. Thank you very much and God bless you!

After his episcopal ordination, Bishop Kmiec took up residence in St. Catharine Parish, Spring Lake, and devoted his time to assisting Bishop Reiss in confirmations and administering the Diocese of Trenton.

AD LIMINA VISIT TO ROME

In September 1983, Bishop John C. Reiss spent the month in Rome at the North American College on theological consultation studies. During that month, Bishop Reiss made his first ad limina visit to Pope John Paul II. Every five years each Catholic bishop in the world makes a personal visit to the Pope in Rome and gives a report on the work in the diocese. On his return from the ad limina visit, Bishop Reiss gave the following report to the people of the diocese.

"Many of the problems the Holy Father faces have no apparent solution," Bishop Reiss said in an interview, "and it is incumbent upon all of us to pray to the Holy Spirit to help him."

How did it feel to meet the Pope for the first time?

"There was a feeling of anxiety, of apprehension as I waited my turn in the Pope's summer home in Castelgandolfo," the bishop recalled, adding that he also was anxious to meet the Holy Father.

His introduction to Pope John Paul had a rather humorous twist.

Preceding him were the Hurley brothers—Archbishop Francis T. Hurley of Anchorage, Alaska, and Bishop Mark J. Hurley of Santa Rosa, California.

When Archbishop Jacques Martin, head of the papal household, ushered Bishop

Reiss into Pope John Paul's study, he introduced him as "Bishop Reiss of Trenton, California," apparently still having in mind the bishop of Santa Rosa.

Pope John Paul, said Bishop Reiss, had a map of the United States on his desk and, having met "Bishop Reiss of Trenton, California," immediately went to the map and was looking for Trenton, California, when Bishop Reiss said: "Holy Father, turn to the eastern United States; I'm sure you will find Trenton!" The Pope did and the audience began.

Then, waxing serious, Bishop Reiss described the next 15 minutes with Pope John Paul as probably one of the most impressive quarter-hours in his life.

Bishop Reiss said he spoke with him regarding his five-year report on the status of the Diocese of Trenton, with the Pope deeply interested in the statistics, asking in particular about the clergy and the women religious.

A favorable report was given by Bishop Reiss on both the priests and sisters, and when asked in the interview about the permanent deacons, he replied, "They are included in the clergy."

"It was tremendous to meet the Pope during those brief 15 minutes." Bishop Reiss observed. "He was so reassuring; one grasps immediately that he knows what he has to do. An example: the teaching of Catholic doctrine; the Pope impresses upon us that we, too, must adhere to Catholic doctrine—and teach it, even if it is not popular."

As the 15 minutes wound down, Bishop Reiss said he thanked Pope John Paul for having appointed an auxiliary bishop for him.

"And who is he?" asked the Holy Father.

"Bishop Edward U. Kmiec," Bishop Reiss replied, pronouncing the young auxiliary bishop's name with a Polish inflection, *Kim-ech*.

"The Holy Father's eyes lit up as he recognized the Polish name," Bishop Reiss recalled. "He had already given me a rosary, among other mementos, and then handed me a rosary for Bishop Kmiec." Bishop Reiss was in the company of the Holy Father three times: the 15-minute personal audience, luncheon with the Pope, and a meeting during which His Holiness addressed the group.

Bishop Reiss's personal audience wound up at 12:30 p.m., and he and the Hurley brothers had an opportunity to see Pope John Paul graciously take the time to address some 5,000 pilgrims from northern Italy who had crowded into a courtyard of his summer home.

Promptly at 1:30, the 14 bishops invited that day sat down to a luncheon with Pope John Paul, who, said Bishop Reiss, was a most pleasant host, inviting all his guests to speak freely about any subject. And they did!

In their conversation, Bishop Reiss noted, there were numerous Americanisms that the Pope did not understand but that were explained to him. As for slang, he said,

Pope John Paul neither uses nor understands it.

ECUMENISM—LUTHERAN ANNIVERSARY

The head of the conference of the Bishops' Committee for Ecumenical and Interreligious Affairs, the Most Rev. John F. Whealon, encouraged the bishops of the United States to observe the 500th anniversary of the birth of Martin Luther in "an ecumenical spirit."

"It is significant that this anniversary is being observed not in a unilateral, Reformation spirit, but in an ecumenical spirit that does not overlook the Catholicism of Luther" and gives "hope that in God's mysterious designs, Martin Luther may guide both our churches to unity in Christ," the archbishop said.

"If the climate in the diocese is favorable, a joint Catholic-Lutheran observance of this anniversary would be a constructive step in the ecumenical endeavor."

Bishop Reiss responded to the invitation with a letter about the anniversary to all the priests of the diocese.

October 17, 1983

Dear Brother in Christ:
This fall marks the 500th anniversary of the birth of Martin Luther. Pope John Paul II is commemorating the event by having accepted an invitation from the Lutherans in Rome to preach to that congregation for the occasion. I have accepted a similar invitation for Sunday, November 20, 1983; Bishop Herluf M. Jensen of the Lutheran Synod of New Jersey will preside at the Ecumenical Vespers Service to be held at 4:30 p.m. at the Lutheran Church of the Redeemer, 189 South Broad Street, Trenton, New Jersey.

Why should Roman Catholics celebrate this event? For a variety of reasons—first of all, distance creates perspective; that is, we Catholics now realize that Luther was not all wrong and did not intend all that resulted from his actions; Lutherans now realize that Luther was not all right. The goal of our gathering together on November 20th is to celebrate the unity we already share, to hail the progress we have made toward oneness, and to pledge ourselves to the hard work that remains before full communion is achieved.

Please take this as my personal invitation for you to participate in this celebration. I would ask each priest to attend with four laypeople from your parish; please return the enclosed reply card to the diocesan Commission on Ecumenical and Interreligious Affairs. Liturgical dress for the occasion will be cassock and surplice.

Of all the ecclesial communities with whom we have entered into dialogue, the Lutheran–Roman Catholic Dialogue is among the most satisfying, as we both operate from firm doctrinal bases, maintain firm moral positions, reverence the Word of God, and celebrate a lively liturgical life. Martin Luther was a pastor, theologian, and reformer. Let us pray that the very best of such qualities will exist in Lutheran and Catholic clergy alike, so that unity may be restored to the once seamless garment of Christ. Let that be the intention of our coming together on Sunday, November 20th.

Fraternally yours in Christ,
/s/ + John C. Reiss
Bishop of Trenton

At the Ecumenical Vespers Service on November 20, 1983, at the Lutheran Church of the Redeemer in Trenton, Bishop Reiss gave the homily. In *The Monitor* of November 24, 1983, a summary of the homily appeared.

Noting that the advancements made by the Joint Roman Catholic–Lutheran commission are "the results of calm, prayerful dialogue and they give firm hope for future success," nevertheless, Bishop Reiss said "dialogue must be brought down to the local level."

Observing that "it may be helpful in promoting such dialogue or conversations to mention some vital characteristics for fruitful success," Bishop Reiss offered the following.

"First, such communications must have the mark of *clearness*. Thus, we must review every angle of our language to guarantee that it be understandable, acceptable and well chosen.

"Second, there is to be *meekness*, for dialogue is not proud; it is not bitter; it is not offensive. Its authority is intrinsic to the truth it explains, to the charity it communicates, and to the example it proposes; it is not a command; it is not an imposition. It is peaceful; it avoids violent methods; it is patient; it is generous.

"Third, there must be *trust*. This trust must not be only in the power of one's words and in an attitude of welcoming the trust of the other speaker. Trust promotes confidence and friendship. It binds hearts in mutual adherence to the good which excludes all self-seeking.

"Fourth, there is to be *prudence*. This is the prudence which esteems the psychological and moral circumstances of the other. It strives to learn the sensitivities of the hearer and requires that we adapt ourselves in a reasonable way lest we be displeasing. In the dialogue conducted in this matter, the union of truth and charity and of understanding and love is achieved."

With those characteristics—clearness, meekness, trust, and prudence—present, Bishop Reiss emphasized, "the dialogue will make us discover elements of truth also in the opinions of others and it will force us to express our teaching with fairness."

However, Bishop Reiss added, there is another characteristic in dialogue: "Before speaking we must listen.

"How often we hear," Bishop Reiss pointed out, "but we do not listen! We hear the Gospel read week after week, but seldom do we really listen.

"We must learn to listen, not only to the other person's voice but also to the heart," said Bishop Reiss. "The other must first be understood, and where merited, agreed with. In trying to make ourselves understood, we must make ourselves their brothers or sisters. The spirit of dialogue is friendship."

Bishop Reiss asserted "we shall succeed," if bishops, pastors, and laity continue to dialogue in the manner he described, "provided we have one other element—prayer for the guidance of the Holy Spirit."

Earlier in his remarks, Bishop Reiss had referred to the "avalanche" of material about Martin Luther, his own prolific writings, the vast number of books, essays, and articles about him and his teachings, and his influence on religion and society, then noted that in a recent biography, the author wrote that Luther's final words probably were: "The truth is, we are beggars," words that Bishop Reiss said well might have referred to the blind beggar in Luke's Gospel account, who told Jesus, "Lord that I may see."

"Is this not what we want in our prayer—to see?" asked Bishop Reiss. "Not in the physical sense but in the intellectual sense—to see, to understand the light which shines forth from the Scriptures, showing us the truth of the Lord which leads us together to the Father.

"Today, as we commemorate in the Roman Catholic tradition the Feast of Christ the King—Son of David, today as we recall the birthday of Martin Luther and his teachings on faith, we can join together in asking Jesus that we might see. For in truth, we are beggars!"

RENEW IN THE DIOCESE

One of the results of the dialogue with Bishop Reiss during the centenary of the diocese in 1981 was to have a spiritual program for all the people of God in the diocese to renew their faith. Bishop Reiss, after consulting the Priests' Council, Sisters' Council, and Pastoral Council, announced a spiritual program for the diocese, called RENEW. The purpose of the RENEW program was to have a spiritual growth and development of the people of God in the diocese. The Rev. Michael Walsh was appointed the director of the RENEW program in the diocese.

Bishop Reiss sent the following letter to all the priests of the diocese on June 15, 1984.

All of us in the Diocese of Trenton are eager to promote the growth of our spiritual lives. We are given different opportunities to make this happen with greater intensity at various times. I believe that RENEW is such an opportunity for us and I urge you to give it your wholehearted support.

RENEW has as its goal helping every member of the parish to become a holier person. It challenges us to develop in our local church communities the kind of intensity of effort that will help all on our spiritual journey. It gives us priests and people a vehicle to help us in our quest for nearness to God.

The process of RENEW is basically in three phases. First is the *Information Phase*, which has already begun. Monsignor Kleissler's presentation to the presbyteral council and to the presbyteral assembly signaled the beginning of this process. Since then, the department heads of the diocese have been informed of the role that the diocesan offices will have in this process, and Father Walsh has addressed the Executive Board of the Sisters' Senate and also the Pastoral Council Representatives.

The next element is the *Information Nights*, which will be held in all of the clusters of the diocese. I urge you to put the *Information Night* for your cluster in your calendar now. Please seek to have your pastor and the other members of the parish who are in leadership roles attend with you. The people of the Diocese of Trenton have been requesting that a spiritual growth process be initiated in our diocese, and it is imperative that we provide the leadership for them at this critical time in our history.

The second phase is the *Training Phase*. The leadership of RENEW in each parish will be trained to facilitate the experience in the parish. All of the training will be provided through the diocesan office of RENEW.

The third and most important phase will be the actual process itself, extending over five 6-week seasons beginning in October 1985 and ending Thanksgiving 1987.

With this letter I introduce you to RENEW and call upon you to participate with your parish. I also request that you pray for the success of this effort in our diocese. It is only when we all cooperate with one another that Christ will truly be present in the Church of Trenton.

Sincerely yours in Christ,
/s/ + John C. Reiss
Bishop of Trenton

The program was to have five sessions beginning in 1985 and ending in 1987. Each session had a theme: Session I, 1985, The Lord's Call; Session II, 1986, Our Response; Session III, 1987, Empowerment; Session IV, 1987, Discipleship; and Session V, 1987, Evangelization.

On September 19, 1985, Bishop Reiss wrote another letter to all the people of God in the diocese and again urged them to participate in RENEW.

My dear Catholic Family:
I hope that each one of you had an opportunity to get some rest and relaxation during the summer months. As you all know, RENEW will begin in our diocese in a couple of weeks. Each one of us is called to be a holy person. In our effort to respond to that call, we are all invited to participate in RENEW. Pope John Paul II, speaking to the Canadian bishops last fall, said that "the graces of renewal and conversion would only be given to a church that prays." RENEW calls us to prayer as individuals and parishes. I ask that you work daily at developing your relationship with God in prayer.

RENEW offers all of us four different ways to experience the themes of the Gospel—Sunday Mass, take-home materials, large-group parish activities, and small sharing groups. This weekend in your parish you will have an opportunity to sign up to participate in the small-group phase of RENEW. Over the next day or two, give prayerful consideration to your participation in the small groups, and on the weekend when your parish offers you the formal invitation, give a positive response to it.

RENEW will direct us to become more prayerful and to achieve a greater understanding of God's Word, a keener sense of belonging to the parish, and a stronger commitment to the promotion of justice. It is an opportunity for everyone in our diocese to work at becoming a holier person. I look forward to experiencing it myself, and I invite all of you to participate enthusiastically with your parish. If you have any further questions about RENEW, do not hesitate to contact the staff of your parish or the diocesan RENEW office.

MISSION STATEMENT

Another result of the centenary celebration in 1981 after dialoguing with the bishop was the idea of a Mission Statement for the Diocese of Trenton. On November 28, 1984, at the diocesan Pastoral Board meeting of the Pastoral Council held at St. Joseph Parish in Keyport, work was begun on this Mission Statement. The Rev. Richard C. Brietske, pastor of Nativity parish in Fairhaven, was appointed chairperson of the committee to work on the Mission Statement.

The proposed Mission Statement was published in the diocesan newspaper, *The Monitor*, on August 1, 1985. This gave all in the diocese the opportunity to comment on the statement before it was finalized.

At the solemn opening of the second phase of the RENEW program on February 6, 1986, in St. Mary's Cathedral in Trenton, Father Brietske presented Bishop Reiss with the final edition of the Mission Statement for the diocese. Bishop Reiss wrote an introductory letter for the Mission Statement:

February 1986

Dearly Beloved in Christ:

"Jesus went into Galilee. There He proclaimed the Good News from God. 'The time has come,' he said, 'and the Kingdom of God is close at hand. Repent, and believe the Good News'" (Mk 1:14–15).

The diocesan Mission Statement is a proclamation of faith in the Good News of the Kingdom of God and a statement of challenge and hope for its advancement in our diocese. It represents a common vision of faith by our laity, religious, and clergy.

The process of forming the Mission Statement began five years ago in the Call to Dialogue during our centennial celebration. As your bishop, I was pleased and inspired to hear your hopes and expectations for our diocese as we began our second one hundred years. Subsequently,

various diocesan groups and organizations requested that our hopes and expectations be written in a Mission Statement. That process took two years to complete. Many were consulted, and all had an opportunity to express their ideas.

With joy I present our Mission Statement, its goals and objectives, to all the people of the Diocese of Trenton. I invite all to assist in its continual implementation. This statement is not chiseled in granite. Rather, it is open to change and development as we all grow in faith and in the awareness of God's will for us under the guidance of the Holy Spirit.

We commend our Mission Statement to the prayers of the faithful living and to the intercession of the holy men and women who have gone before us. We especially place our words of hope in the caring heart of our Patroness, Mary of the Assumption. And, above all, we face the future with confidence and peace because we know that the Lord Jesus is with us until the end of time.

My gratitude to all who participated in the formation of our Mission Statement. Together, let us continue to build up the Kingdom of God.

> With a blessing, I remain
> Sincerely yours in Christ,
> /s/ + John C. Reiss
> Bishop of Trenton

The Preface of the Mission Statement outlines the content of the statement:

"Where there is no vision, the people perish." "Where there is no vision, the people get out of hand." (Prov 29:18) These are two different biblical translations, but they convey the same message: vision promotes unity, and lack of vision diffuses purpose and strains the bonds that hold a people together.

The Mission Statement of the Diocese of Trenton with its goals and objectives is a statement of vision for all the people of our diocese. Its purpose is to keep alive and active the vision of the Father for us in this place and at this time so that we will move forward in faith as one people of God.

The vision of the Father is well stated in the prayer of Jesus at the Last Supper: "I have given them the glory you gave me that they may be one, as we are one; I living in them, you living in me, that their unity may be complete" (Jn 17:22–23). Jesus came to lift up all things to Himself, to restore unity to creation, and to lead everyone from exile into the Father's heavenly Kingdom (from Christmas Preface II).

The establishment of the Kingdom of God was the mission of Jesus. The proclamation and advancement of that Kingdom is the mission of the church. Our Mission Statement expresses the way we will proclaim and advance the Kingdom in our part of the church, the Diocese of Trenton.

The Mission Statement was born in 1981, our centennial year. In the Call to Dialogue, parishioners met in each parish to share and express their hopes and dreams for the church. Subsequently, these statements were presented to Bishop John C. Reiss at county gatherings. The hopes, dreams, and expectations written in those documents formed the basis of our Mission Statement. The Mission Statement Committee took two years to formulate the final document. During that time, people in the diocese had opportunities to express their ideas and critique the several drafts of the Mission Statement with its goals and objectives.

The Mission Statement Committee received ideas and suggestions from the Council of Priests, Council of Sisters, Council of Deacons, diocesan Pastoral Council, chancery staff, and heads of diocesan departments, agencies, and institutions. Through *The Monitor* the people of the diocese had two opportunities to review the drafts of the Mission Statement and to suggest changes. Bishop Reiss supported the process at every step and approved the final draft of the Mission Statement with its goals and objectives.

As our statement of mission is presented to the people, we recall that time when Jesus stated His mission in the synagogue of Nazareth, "Unrolling the scroll He found the place where it is written: 'He has sent me to bring good news to the poor, to proclaim liberty to captives and to the blind new sight'. . . . Then He began to speak to them; this text is being fulfilled today even as you listen" (Luke 4:17,18,21).

Even as we read this Mission Statement, we believe that the Kingdom of God is here and the mission of Jesus and His church is being fulfilled in our midst. However, we pray that the vision of our Mission Statement will unite us more deeply to the Lord and to one another as we proclaim and advance the Kingdom of God with renewed fervor and zeal in the Diocese of Trenton.

The preamble of the Mission Statement of the Diocese of Trenton is as follows.

MISSION STATEMENT: THE DIOCESE OF TRENTON

". . . Thy Will Be Done . . ."
Our Hope and Our Promises
In the Name of the Father and of the Son and of the Holy Spirit, we, the people of the

Catholic church of Trenton, are called to proclaim and advance the Kingdom of God in the New Jersey counties of Burlington, Mercer, Monmouth, and Ocean.

Within the diversity of our ages, races, classes, ministries, and conditions of life, we are made one by our baptism in Christ.

United with Jesus, the eternal shepherd, with our Holy Father, the universal shepherd, and with our bishop, the local shepherd, we form a community of faith, called to worship God, celebrate the Sacraments, and teach the Good News.

Responding to our call to discipleship, we reach out in love and service to all, ever striving to advance the cause of peace and justice in the Name of our Lord Jesus. As pilgrims conscious of our sinfulness and need for reconciliation, we seek renewal always in the Light of Christ.

Inspired by our Patroness, Mary of the Assumption, we joyfully wait in hope to hear the Lord's words: "Come, you have My Father's blessing. Inherit the Kingdom prepared for you from the creation of the world."

VICARIATE SYSTEM FOR THE DIOCESE

In January 1986, Bishop Reiss commissioned Bishop Kmiec to begin the work of restructuring the diocese and reorganizing the offices to conform to the new Code of Canon Law that had been promulgated in March 1983 and to fulfill the mandate given in the new Mission Statement.

With the approval of Bishop Reiss, Bishop Kmiec selected a committee to undertake the assignment of reorganizing the diocesan offices and appointed as chairperson of the new committee the Rev. Msgr. George A. Ardos, pastor of St. George's Church, Washington Crossing, and director of the Office of Religious Education.

On May 2, 1986, Bishop Reiss approved the new structure for the Diocese of Trenton and announced this new structure on June 5, 1986, in *The Monitor*. The new structure consisted of five vicariates, with five vicars appointed by Bishop Reiss. The new vicariates and vicars were as follows: Vicariate for Catholic Education Services, the Rev. Edward D. Strano; Vicariate for Christian Life Services, the Rev. William J. Dailey; Vicariate for Organizational Services, the Rev. Msgr. William F. Fitzgerald; Vicariate for Personnel Services, the Rev. Msgr. James P. McManimon; and Vicariate for Social Services, the Rev. Msgr. Joseph C. Shenrock.

At the same time as the vicariate system was established, Bishop Reiss created an Office of Planning and named Msgr. George A. Ardos as director. The director of planning is directly responsible to Bishop Reiss and works with the moderator of the Curia. A new diocesan *Pastoral Manual* was compiled and distributed in the fall by the Office of Planning. Monsignor Ardos said that the new manual would define and describe in length each vicariate and contain the policies and guidelines of the various offices and agencies within each vicariate.

With the new structure effective July 1, the bishop approved the recommendation of the restructuring committee that all diocesan offices and parishes in the four-county diocese—Burlington, Mercer, Monmouth, and Ocean—be on a July 1 to June 30 fiscal year.

One of the new titles in the new Code of Canon Law is moderator of the Curia, and Bishop Reiss appointed Bishop Kmiec to that position. Bishop Kmiec, also a vicar-general of the diocese with Msgr. George E. Everitt, pastor of St. Mary of the Lake Church, Lakewood, in the new structure served directly under Bishop Reiss as moderator of the Curia.

By way of explanation, the word "Curia" as it applies to the Trenton diocese can be compared with the Roman Curia, that group of executive, judicial, and official bodies through which Pope John Paul II governs the church. Bishop Kmiec was moderator of the Trenton diocesan Curia, that group of offices and agencies through which Bishop Reiss governs the Diocese of Trenton.

In the structural setup, continuing as consultative bodies to Bishop Reiss are the College of Consultors, Council of Priests, Council of Deacons, Sisters' Senate, Pastoral Council, Finance Council, and the *censor librorum*. Continuing also are the two vicars-general and the Tribunal, headed by Msgr. John K. Dermond, pastor of St. Francis Church, Trenton, as judicial vicar.

With the new vicariate structure, new office space was needed, and on September 11, 1986, Bishop Reiss announced that a new building was leased for this purpose. The following account appeared in *The Monitor* concerning the new facilities.

The recent restructuring and reorganization of the offices, services and ministries of the Diocese of Trenton have led Bishop John C. Reiss to relocate several key offices, five of them in new facilities in Ewing Township.

The new building, named Trenton Diocesan Pastoral Offices–Whitehead Road Building, is located at 1018 Whitehead Road, Trenton 08638. It was formerly occupied by Burroughs Corporation.

A second building, the former headquarters of the education office, is located in Lawrence Township. It has been redesignated the Trenton Diocesan Pastoral Offices–Brunswick Avenue Building. Its address is 1931 Brunswick Avenue, Trenton 08648.

Located in the Trenton diocesan Pastoral Offices' Whitehead Road Building are:

— Office of Catholic Education, headed by Sister of Charity Mary Louise Moran; includes the religious education office; the education office had been located on Brunswick Avenue and the religious education office at 33 West Front Street, Trenton.

— Office of Evangelization and Department of Liturgy, directed by Fr. John P. Czahur, relocated from 33 West Front Street.

— Pontifical Mission Aid Societies (Propagation of the Faith), headed by Fr. Richard L. Tofani, relocated from the Chancery building, 701 Lawrence Road.

— Diocesan Commission on Ecumenical and Interreligious Affairs, formerly headed by Msgr. Joseph C. Shenrock from his pastorate at Blessed Sacrament Church, 716 Bellevue Avenue, Trenton, now directed by Fr. Francis M. McGrath, associate pastor of St. Anthony's Church, Trenton.

—Office of Catholic Persons with Disabilities, formerly Apostolate for the Deaf, relocated from 1942 Pennington Road, headed by Fr. Paul S. Rimassa, associate pastor of St. James, Pennington.

MORE ON RENEW

One of the most successful programs in the diocese was the RENEW program. Rev. Michael J. Walsh and Sr. Jean Vogel, G.N.S.H., were interviewed about the program in the diocese on February 12, 1987, for *The Monitor*.

As we approach Season IV, are more participating in RENEW? Is it gaining popularity as the seasons continue? How many are involved now?

Father Walsh: I don't know how many people are in it and I don't want to know. But the people I'm involved with personally who are in it are experiencing more and more their being Catholic and their being believers and belonging to the church and their sense of what they should do as church people and their being more consistently responsible people.

I think most of the stories and the impact of RENEW we will never know about.

Sister Vogel: Or if they tell us, we can't repeat it because people in the parish could be identified. That's happened time and time again. People will tell me these moving things about people's lives and how their small-group support has helped them, but they'll also say don't put it in the *Update* [RENEW newsletter].

Father Walsh: Around here the level of involvement of parishes in social services activities over Christmas was phenom-

enal relative to what I had experienced previously.

Just seeing what the kids at Anchor House got, what Sister Regina [Griffin, director of Catholic Haitian Center] received, what I know was taken to St. Joseph's and Martin House [in Trenton]. There have always been people involved in that but there were more people involved in it this year. I think that is one sort of public indicator.

There have been situations where parishioners have invited inactive Catholics to come for coffee and chat. People are saying to their neighbors, "Let's talk about God." They never did that before, and it's because they've had the opportunity to talk about it for two years now so they're getting more comfortable with it and believing in it a little bit more strongly.

Sister Vogel: People have really wanted to do good. They have that urge to help their neighbors, but I think through RENEW they're making connections with other people and finding ways of doing it in their own parishes and neighborhoods. The goodwill has always been there but they're finding ways of challenging themselves.

Is it what you expected it to be?

Father Walsh: I really didn't have expectations. When I started it, I really didn't know. It was very much an act of faith, I guess. You know, "Let's give the opportunity to people and see how many are going to respond." People have responded enthusiastically. What we need to do now is maintain an attitude of providing the opportunity for people.

And to continue to invite those not involved to become involved.

Sister Vogel: It's showing up now in the level of commitment of the pastor and support of the priests. It is showing up more and more in the vitality of RENEW in the parishes.

There is a need for parish leadership to be supportive of one another in order to maintain the impetus.

If you had the chance to do it all again, would you?

Father Walsh: I would love to.

Sister Vogel: Absolutely. The faith, the insight I've gotten out of it: The faith of the people is just unbelievable. It is so inspiring. People who have great crosses and things you just cannot imagine and they can survive and they come through with this positive, almost brilliant, faith. It's been such an enriching experience for us.

Father Walsh: It also has heightened my sense of responsibility to people. Just having the opportunity to be in a small group . . . that has helped me tremendously. I learn every minute. I can't say I respond every minute, but I learn.

I know of people who see someone from their small group in church and they'll go sit beside that person in order to be with somebody they know and somebody they feel has a common commitment to church. I say that's the way they should feel about everybody in church. We should have that sense of belonging to one another.

Sister Vogel: Another inspiring thing has been the young adult activity that has surfaced in the diocese.

Father Walsh: People feel empowered by other people. One believer might have a sense of "well, I'd like to do this" but might not be able to do it without another ten people.

We hear a lot about how effective the small-group aspect of RENEW is, but what about the other areas?

Father Walsh: People sometimes ask, What good are the take-home materials? We can never measure the influence the material has when it gets into people's homes. You never know what influence that's going to have. We cannot measure that good by the number of people who come back to us with positive comments.

The very fact that we get material into people's homes—and we have the opportunity to do that—is giving them the chance to read it, pray it, study it.

Which aspect has been most successful?

Father Walsh: I don't want to tell you. It has four vehicles for sharing, and each of those four is valuable. Obviously the most important in any parish is Sunday Mass, and we encourage parishes to put the most possible energy and resources into that Mass.

We really can't measure the success of RENEW at all. I can't get inside everybody's heart. All we can do is continue to provide the opportunity for people.

This interview with Father Walsh and Sister Vogel indicates how successful this renewal program was among the priests and laity in the diocese. The final year of the RENEW program opened on Sunday, February 22, 1987, at St. Mary's Cathedral with a Mass celebrated by Msgr. Leonard R. Toomey, pastor of Sacred Heart Church, Trenton, and Fr. Michael J. Walsh, diocesan codirector of RENEW as the homilist. Over one thousand people and clergy from throughout the diocese attended this Mass.

BLACK APOSTOLATE OFFICE

On May 7, 1987, the first office for black Catholics was opened in the Trenton diocese, and Bishop Reiss appointed Oblate Sister of Providence Sr. M. Loretto Evans as the first director of the office. Sister Evans's plans for the office were as follows:

— To culturally and spiritually nourish black Catholics and the black community in general.
— To provide material, programs, events, and other resources for blacks as a means of updating their faith.
— To present changes in the church, both local and national, as they relate to blacks and existing black organizations.
— To meet the needs of many unchurched blacks through evangelization.
— To foster and support black leadership in the diocese.

According to Sister Evans, who had been in the diocese for a year, there were many unchurched blacks and many who were not informed on changes in the faith.

The previous year, she had organized a revival—true to the black tradition, with hand clapping, Gospel singing, testifying, and praising—in Our Lady of Divine Shepherd Church.

Everyone in the parish said, "This is the first time I've ever heard of a revival in the Catholic church." Sister Evans added that the church was so packed that people were standing in the aisles. She added, "People are still asking me when we are going to have another."

MARIAN YEAR, 1987

On June 7, 1987, the Solemnity of Pentecost, Bishop Reiss opened the Marian Year with a Mass at St. Mary's Cathedral. In his homily at that opening Mass, Bishop Reiss urged the people of the diocese to spend the months of the Marian Year as a kind of study period of the life of the Blessed Virgin Mary, who, in spite of many sufferings, at all times was always ready to help others. At the parish level, Bishop Reiss called on each parish over the course of the year to arrange a pilgrimage to one of four designated churches, which are:

Burlington County
Our Lady of Perpetual Help, Maple Shade

Mercer County
St. Mary's Cathedral, Trenton

Monmouth County
Our Lady Star of the Sea, Long Branch

Ocean County
St. Mary of the Lake, Lakewood

"The pastor or delegate should contact the pastor of a designated church to schedule a day and time," Bishop Reiss suggested. "The visiting parish clergy will be responsible for conducting whatever service is planned."

Each parish named in honor of Mary should have a "special" parish celebration on or near its feast day, Bishop Reiss stated.

"Parishes not so named should select a Marian feast from the liturgical year for a special celebration," Bishop Reiss said, adding, "Ethnic parishes should celebrate their special feast, with particular devotion to Mary."

Bishop Reiss also suggested that each parish choose a prayer card and distribute copies to all parishioners, encouraging family and individual recitation.

At the county level, Bishop Reiss called for Bible study, proposing a program during Advent on the infancy narratives, arranged on a cluster, or regional, level with the collaboration of the presbyteral and pastoral councils.

As another county-level program, Bishop Reiss suggested that an ecumenical prayer service with a Marian theme be arranged during Church Unity Week in January.

Plenary indulgences for the Marian Year could be gained, Bishop Reiss pointed out, at the following events, subject to the usual conditions of confession, Communion, and prayers for the intentions of the Holy Father:

— Participating in the June 7 official Marian Year opening.
— Taking part in a Marian celebration on a Saturday or a Marian feast day during the year.
— Attending Marian celebrations at designated churches with an organized pilgrimage.
— Communal recitation of the Rosary in a church or a special religious place.

HOUSING PROJECT IN TRENTON

On August 19, 1987, Bishop John C. Reiss and civil officials broke ground for Cathedral Square Housing Project, a 100-unit housing project for senior citizens, next to St. Mary's Cathedral in downtown Trenton.

Bishop Reiss credited Representative Christopher H. Smith (R–4th District) with being responsible for making the project possible.

"Three people are to be especially commended for their work on this project," said the bishop.

"Number one is Representative Smith, whose assistance and direction were most valuable for the planning of this project. Without him, we do not know whether or not we would be breaking ground today.

"Number two is James Waldron, whose assistance and attention to detail were so necessary to overcome the many obstacles we met.

"Finally, Monsignor [William F.] Fitzgerald, who has worked for three to four years and coordinated the effort of all involved to bring about Cathedral Square.

"I feel Cathedral Square will be of benefit to the city of Trenton, especially the inner city, to have people living in the area, near the various businesses. They will add new life to the area," the bishop concluded.

Congressman Smith, expressing satisfaction with the project to "achieve better housing and care for our elderly Americans," said the ground breaking marked the end "of a long and tough battle to win the federal dollars to help house properly our city's senior citizens.

"The sponsor of this project, the Diocese of Trenton," he said, "represents a most suitable host and guardian of our area's needy and aging residents. The Cathedral Square Project adds just one more layer of Christian outreach and service in Trenton and the entire diocese.

"I am pleased to have played a part in the establishment of the Cathedral Square complex," he concluded, "and I take great comfort in knowing that federal, city, and diocesan cooperation will achieve better housing and care for our elderly Americans."

Trenton Mayor Arthur J. Holland also gave high praise to the diocese for sponsoring the project.

"With the growing elderly population," he said, "I am confident that Cathedral Square will meet a real housing need. It is my hope that while this housing will be open to all, it may be a means of reattracting to the city and especially to Cathedral Parish those who may have, for whatever reason over the years, left the city.

"I want to commend the Diocese of Trenton for sponsoring this project. I think religiously based sponsorship makes for the highest possible level of public-private partnership."

The six-story, 99-apartment building contains both one-bedroom apartments and apartments with a large living area and no bedroom. Ten of the apartments were adapted for the handicapped.

NATIONAL MODERATOR OF HOLY NAME SOCIETY

On September 17, 1987, Bishop John C. Reiss was asked to be the national moderator of the National Association of the Holy Name Society, for a five-year term. He accepted. Bishop Reiss sent a message to the National Association of the Holy Name Society annual convention, which was held in Buffalo September 16-20, 1987.

The New Testament is filled with the praise and honor due to the Name of God, Father, Son and Holy Spirit. There were many miracles performed just by the invocation of Christ's Name.

How this marvelous practice of the early Christians and of subsequent generations has been grossly eroded! Sad to say, our modern media has fallen into the trap, has let down its former barriers and given way to careless use, disrespect and blasphemy. There is certainly a need for the Holy Name Society, and the task is not easy!

The strength we require to overcome this horrible tendency lies in our persistent effort to call upon the sacred Name of Jesus, and to personally display our love and devotion to His Name.

I am pleased to become your Episcopal Moderator. I deeply regret that I shall not be with you during your convention due mostly to the meeting of the bishops with our Holy Father. I look forward to future meetings and working with you.

MARIAN YEAR 1987

On September 26, 1987, Bishop John C. Reiss led a special pilgrimage of clergy and lay people to the Shrine of the Immaculate Conception in Washington, D.C. Since it was the Marian Year, thousands of clergy and laity joined the bishop in this pilgrimage to the national shrine. At the Mass in the shrine, the bishop gave the following homily.

"I am the Maidservant of the Lord; let it be done to me as you say" (Lk 1:38).

In this magnificent shrine, a center of our nation's devotion to the Blessed Mother of God, we come together to express and offer our honor to her. "Thou art all fair, O Mary, and the stain of original sin is not in thee." This proclamation has been said and sung through the centuries in recognition of Mary's Immaculate Conception! Thus, our purpose in making our pilgrimage to Washington is to publicly offer our collective praise to the Mother of God.

Our praise is based on her unique position in the history of salvation whereby she has by her intercession won many favors for the people of God. Praise leads us to thanksgiving both for the personal gifts we have received and for those bestowed on the universal church and the world at large. This action of thanksgiving makes us realize that we still stand in need of her continued intercession. And so, we once more with confidence lay our requests at Mary's feet.

We can pour out our respect to our Blessed Lady under any one of her numerous titles, or of her preeminent and extraordinary gifts: The Immaculate Conception; the virgin birth of Jesus; Mother of God; her sinlessness or total spiritual purity; her Assumption; her coronation; and on and on through the invocations of the Litany of Loretto.

If we examine these salutations, we shall see one basic thread in all of them: namely, the total union of Mary's will to the Will of God. This union is expressed in the Gospel just read: "Let it be done to me as you say." This submission was complete and not just for the joyful and glorious events, but equally for the sorrowful. The liturgy commemorates the seven major sorrows of the humble maidservant who mirrored her Son's prayer in the Garden of Gethsemane: "'. . . yet not my will but yours be done'" (Lk 22:42).

Mary's unity with the Father's plan graphically exemplifies a mark of the church that her Son founded. We recall these four marks or identifiable characteristics of the church as *One, Holy, Catholic, and Apostolic*. These marks were placed in the church by its divine Founder so that His church could be recognized. These marks are also needed to preserve the church and to protect it from attacks from without and even from within. For today I intend to center my attention on the initial mark—the church is One.

That the church is one means that there is a oneness or unity of faith or belief. *All* of its members are to accept *all* of the truths that Christ taught, and His church is infallibly protected against errors. That the church is one means that in its government or discipline Christ placed *one* in supreme authority over His whole church with full power to rule. "Thou art Peter and upon this rock I will build my church" (Mt 16:18). "'Full authority has been given to me. Go therefore and make disciples . . . teach them to carry out everything I have commanded you'" (Mt 28:18–20). "'Feed my lambs . . . feed my sheep'" (Jn 21:15–17). That one person today is the Holy Father, the successor of Peter and the visible head of the church.

The recently completed visit of Pope John Paul II to our part of the country brings to our attention in a concrete manner the *oneness* of the Catholic church. In the numerous talks, homilies, and addresses the Pontiff gave to various groups, he was exercising his prerogative as the chief teacher of the church and unequivocally setting forth the church's official teachings. It will take some time to reread, to ponder, and to absorb these teachings and their application to our lives.

Despite all the time and energy of the Holy Father in stating or restating our beliefs and morals, there are so many who reject them either completely or partially and who endeavor to put their own private opinions on the same level as the papal pronouncements. Sad to say, many of those who dissent, mostly without any theological reasoning, are from inside the church and who claim to be Catholic and, even worse, theologians.

Last month there came across my desk a magazine with an article about a survey that was conducted among more than 5,000 alumni of a Catholic university in another part of the country. This survey was a repeat of one given ten years ago. Among the findings from the later graduates were the results that today these persons who claim to be Catholic are less apt to avail themselves of confession, less inclined to accept the church's teaching on birth control and abortion, and less willing to align themselves with the church's stand on clerical celibacy, the male priesthood, and remarriage after divorce.

Many other similar polls and surveys during the past two weeks were published in newspapers or expanded via radio or television. The most startling reply reported was that only half agreed with the statement, "The Pope is infallible when he speaks ex cathedra on faith and morals." It is this particular finding which has affected me most deeply, as in the final analysis it attacks the very foundation of the church, namely, the mark of being *one*—the unity of faith.

When we look at the church today, we notice quickly that it is beset with many difficulties and problems. Some of these problems are in matters of church discipline, but the majority can be classified or reduced to problems that flow from a denial or misunderstanding of fundamental theology. This branch of theology deals with those truths which regard the establishment of the church and the nature of the church as Jesus wanted it to be.

As mentioned before and as seen in the references from the Gospels, our Divine Savior endowed His church with His own teaching authority. In addition, Christ sent the Holy Spirit to His church so that the church would be preserved from error in matters of faith or morals. In other words and briefly, the church teaches infallibly either through the Pope or through the college of bishops joined with the Pope.

The danger in this discussion is that if a person or persons reject or destroy the dogma of infallibility, a basic teaching of our church, the church itself will be threatened with disintegration and destruction. This will not happen, as Christ is with the church until the end of time. But, it is an evident danger today! The threat can grow if more and more turn from the official teachings of the church as they choose and pick only those teachings that please them.

There is a need then to return to some basic theology and discover the Will of Christ the God-Man, Who established the church with a hierarchy, with the Pope as the visible head of the church and its chief teacher; a church which is infallible in matters of faith and morals.

I have not forgotten Mary, the Mother of God and Mother of the church. Go back over the history of the church, and you will find that there were many attacks on the oneness or unity of the church. These attacks were not just persecutions, but also denials of belief. As each crisis arose, the faithful turned to the Blessed Virgin, pleading for her intercession with Jesus and the Father. In time, clarifications were made, and the truth was reestablished, accepted, and followed.

It is imperative that we do the same today. "Mary, Help of Christians, pray for us." With confidence, we can offer our prayers and sacrifices for the strengthening of the unity of faith. After all, "never was it known that anyone who fled to her protection was left unaided" (Memorare). As we pray, we should also examine our own status to see if there is any weakening or rejection of the church's teachings, and then correct them. "Not my will, but your will be done," as Jesus said, and "Let it be done to me as you say," as Mary stated. It is most important for us to follow this path of humble submission to the Father and give our respect and internal consent to the church's teachings as enunciated by the Pope, the head of the church. This action is for all—clergy, religious, and laity—no matter what their position in the church.

We should not become discouraged, but rather, courageously embark on prayer. "O Lord, I believe, help my unbelief." Pray Jesus' prayer to His Father. "'I pray also for those who will believe in me through their [i.e., the apostles'] word, that all may be one, as you Father are in me, and I in you; I pray that they may be one in us, that the world may believe that you sent me'" (Jn 17:20–21). Finally, call upon Mary, the patroness of the church in the United States under the title of her Immaculate Conception.

PASTORAL LETTER ON CATHOLIC EDUCATION 1988

Throughout the diocese we are celebrating the beginning of Catholic Schools Week. While this celebration has taken place every year, I believe, for reasons I shall mention later, this year marks a new era in Catholic education.

From the very beginnings of our country's history, the bishops of the United States have recognized the necessity of a Catholic school system as the best means at their disposal of handing down Catholic principles and values for our young. As early as 1829, the First Provincial Council of Baltimore mandated that "near each church, where it does not exist, a parochial school is to be erected and maintained in perpetuum."

It is for this reason that Catholic immigrants from every nation scraped up their nickels and dimes to build and support a Catholic school system, which soon became second to none in all the world. By the mid-1960s and early 1970s, 50 percent of all children from Catholic homes were educated in parochial schools.

Within the past 25 years, however, the school system has undergone many rapid and radical changes. There has been a vast reduction of sisters and religious brothers in the classroom.

The escalating cost of maintaining school buildings, reaching fair salaries for lay teachers, and providing high-tech equipment for classrooms has proved to be an overwhelming burden for parishes, leading to the closing of many schools throughout the nation and a prevailing attitude that the Catholic school system has reached its peak, is in a state of decline, has lost its value, and will soon disappear from the American scene.

Nothing could be further from the truth! The bishops of the United States today, echoing the sentiments of their predecessors of old, declare the absolute necessity of maintaining a Catholic school system, available not only to children of Catholic families but, in today's society, to non-Catholic children as well.

As far as the value of our schools is concerned, while you will not hear it as item one on the 11 o'clock news, or written in headlines across the front page of our newspapers, let me quote from Malcolm S. Forbes, editor of the prestigious *Forbes* magazine, in the December 12, 1988, issue, in which he says, "Catholic schools provide hugely consequential oases of impact and hope. Their value is, literally as well as figuratively, beyond measure. These indispensable Catholic schools are in an increasingly tough financial bind. They have to look to corporations and those in the business community with sufficient vision to recognize the vast non-parochial, signifi-

cant contributions this parochial system makes to America."

This increasing financial bind and the challenge of meeting it represent the reason why I said this year marks a new era in Catholic education.

Last September, I established a task force to recommend solutions to the financial bind with which we are faced.

Last November, I attended the New Jersey Conference on Catholic School Futures, where I met with fellow bishops, priests, major superiors, religious, school administrators, principals, teachers, and concerned lay persons, to map out directions for the road we must travel.

We have under discussion the possibility of our own diocesan miniconference, to be held this year to provide impetus for educational planning and development. In this planning, let me rush to assure you that the enhancement of the religious education of children not attending parochial schools, that is, students in the parish religious education programs, will not be considered secondary but will hold equal priority with plans for Catholic schools. As for today, and in celebration of Catholic Schools Week, let me send greetings and words of gratitude to all you Catholic laity whose financial support has allowed us to fulfill Christ's first mandate, "Go and teach." To you educators, religious, and lay alike, whose tireless dedication is the very thing that makes Catholic schools what they are, and finally to you, the most unrecognized educational facilitators . . . you pastors, whose many sleepless nights will assure you of the Master's reward, "Well done, good and faithful servant."

To you all, I extend my episcopal blessing!

BISHOP REISS ANNOUNCES 1991 DIOCESAN SYNOD

On May 11, 1989, Bishop Reiss announced to the clergy and laity of the diocese that a diocesan synod would be held.

My dear Brothers and Sisters in Christ,
As we celebrate the coming of the Holy Spirit to the church on Pentecost, we recall that the same Spirit was poured out upon each of us in baptism and strengthened in confirmation. Among the gifts of the Spirit we each have received are wisdom and counsel, knowledge and understanding. I would like to invite you to share these gifts with me and with the rest of the people of the Diocese of Trenton in a special way during the next two years.

I am now formally announcing that the Diocese of Trenton will be celebrating its Fourth Diocesan Synod in 1991 as we celebrate the 110th anniversary of the establishment of the diocese. This synod will be a group of clergy, religious, and laity called together to assist me in my pastoral leadership. I will be asking them to offer a unified vision of how we can effectively continue the spread of the Gospel in the four counties of Monmouth, Mercer, Ocean, and Burlington as we prepare to enter the twenty-first century. Since our life as a church is lived in our parish communities, I will be asking this synod body to center its attention on the life of our parishes.

During the next two years, we will be preparing for this synod in several ways. First of all, I ask you to join me in praying that the Holy Spirit will guide us as we prepare to renew our understanding of our fundamental mission to spread the Gospel.

Second, with the assistance of our diocesan advisory bodies and the cooperation of our parishes, I will be seeking input from you. Third, special groups will be formed to study important issues in depth, in order to help the synod members understand the issues and offer sound advice.

As these preparations continue, I thank you for your continued prayer and support as we strive together to fulfill the command of Christ to preach the Gospel to every nation.

> With a blessing I remain,
> Sincerely yours in Christ,
> /s/ + John C. Reiss
> Bishop of Trenton

THE FOURTH SYNOD

On January 13, 1991, Bishop John C. Reiss solemnly opened the Fourth Synod with a special Mass at St. Mary's Cathedral in Trenton and gave the following homily.

My dear friends, today is an historical occasion, as with this Mass, we open the Fourth Synod of the Diocese of Trenton. The Third Synod was held in 1931. In the intervening years, many ecclesial events have transpired to change the functioning of the church universal and the local or diocesan church. In addition to the upheavals in society, there has been held the Second Vatican Council, which issued various fundamental documents in its own name and commissioned revisions of the Liturgy and of the code of canon law. It is apparent, then, that this, our Fourth Synod, is of great importance for the life and worship of the church in Trenton.

This Mass marks the official opening of our synod, but a tremendous amount of work has already been completed over an extended period of months. The Presbyteral Council has been consulted and has recommended the synod; a central Steering Committee has given direction, counsel, and guidance; special working commissions have been formed with chairpersons and members; and documents have been collected and copied for the necessary study.

I am grateful to Bishop Kmiec, who chairs the Steering Committee, and to Father Troiano, who is the executive coordinator. My gratitude goes to the members of the Steering Committee, to everyone who has agreed to serve as a commission member, and to those who will be the voting representatives from the clergy, religious, and laity. You are generous in accepting the challenge to forge the synod and to offer your service and time to study, to advise, to formulate, and to recommend new norms.

Perhaps it will help you to appreciate the synod if we recall its purpose by seeing "what it is not," and then "what it is." On other occasions, there have been broad consultations throughout the diocese for producing a mission statement or to set forth goals and objectives for various offices and departments of the diocese. A synod is not either of these, although these may be by-products. Nor is the synod a wish list, that is, an enumeration of how some would like things to be without reference to what they must be.

The clearest way to describe a diocesan synod is to quote the appropriate canon 460: "A diocesan synod is a group of selected priests and other Christian faithful of a particular church, which offers assistance to the diocesan Bishop for the good of the entire community . . . " In other words,

this chosen assembly of priests, deacons, religious sisters, religious brothers, and laity will dedicate themselves to aid the diocesan bishop in his role as teacher, sanctifier, and ruler. Their objective is not any private agenda nor private goal, but rather whatever is good for everyone in the diocesan community. Their task will demand objectivity, vision, and prudence for the spiritual and even temporal well-being of everyone in the church of Trenton.

In their consultations and deliberations, they will strive to tailor the general law of the universal church to the specific needs of our local culture and traditions. It is clear that the synod cannot change the dogmatic or moral teachings of the church. This select group will also seek the best avenues to construct norms for the public conduct of the local church, for example, times and places for liturgical celebrations, meaning the handling of temporal affairs.

I anticipate a number of positive and helpful results and will mention a few. There should be as an outcome a more uniform way of action throughout the diocese. Now, this does not mean a strict uniformity, but rather staying within the established universal guidelines and the approved options. The synodal decrees will form the basis for objective accountability, as in financial matters and in reporting to diocesan offices. Another positive result of the enacted norms will be the guidance for clergy and laity and religious in seeking our common spiritual aim of service to God, to His church, and to His people.

As we speak about norms, canons, and law, there are some who begin to feel uneasy. Yet "law" has been with us from the very beginning of salvation history. God gave a clear norm or guideline or law to Adam and Eve: "'You are free to eat from any of the trees of the garden, except the tree of knowledge of good and bad'" (Gn 2:16–17). Later, God gave the Ten Commandments to Moses and the chosen people (Ex 20:2–17). These same commandments were reinforced by Jesus in His discussion with the young man who sought salvation. "'Good Teacher, what must I do to share in everlasting life?'" "'You have the commandments,'" Jesus replied (Mk 10:17, 19).

The power to enact binding laws for the church was given by our Divine Lord to Peter when He said, "'Whatever you declare bound on earth shall be bound in heaven; whatever you declare loosed on earth shall be loosed in heaven'" (Mt 16:19). This power entrusted to Peter as the visible head of the church and the vicar of Christ has been employed throughout the history of the church by popes and by ecumenical councils, and shared in by local councils and synods. These laws, then, do have a binding force. It must be remembered that these ecclesiastical laws, as a reflection of the Divine Law, are to assist us in our pilgrimage of salvation.

In discussing law, there are two extremes to be avoided. The first is "legalism," which is too much preoccupation with the letter of the law to the neglect of the spirit and purpose of the law. The other extreme is to see law as useless or something to be lightly regarded. Laws, ideally, state those things that are in the best interests of everyone and make sure the rights of all are safeguarded. Listen to a quote from Sirach: "He who hates law is without wisdom and is tossed about like a boat in a storm" (Sir 33:2).

As the Fourth Synod will result in certain norms (laws), it will serve us well to have a model to follow. This model is none other than Jesus, Whose baptism by John is commemorated today. The Gospels are filled with His examples of following the Judaic laws: His submitting to circumcision, paying the temple tax, and many others. His humble obedience is eminently found in His personal confession. "I always do the Will of my Heavenly Father" (Jn 6:38), and "Not my Will, but Yours be done" (Mt 14:36). Jesus' example is fully mirrored in the life of His Blessed Mother, even to the piercing of Her own heart with the sword of sorrows.

And so, we open the Fourth Synod of the Diocese of Trenton. I encourage the priests, deacons, religious, and laity to undertake this assigned duty with the courage necessary to promote the spiritual growth of the entire diocesan community. Be proud of your assignment: Be confident that with the guidance of the Holy Spirit, your labors will contribute enormously to the spiritual life of the church in Trenton as we move forward on our journey to the Father.

Finally, I beg every member of the diocese—clergy, religious, and laity—to pray fervently for the success of this, our Fourth Synod:

God, our Heavenly Father, hear our prayer!

We, your people, ask your guidance and inspiration as the Catholic church of Trenton gathers for a diocesan synod. Give us patience to listen, the wisdom to know Your will, the humility to serve, and the courage to act in Your Holy Name. Grant that our work, based upon the teachings of Your Son, will help to build a church that proclaims with confidence and joy our Catholic tradition of faith, hope, and charity. May we come to know the truth more fully and grow in holiness. We make our prayer through Christ, Our Lord. Amen.

Mary, assumed into Heaven, pray for us.

The synod came to a close on December 8, 1991, with a Mass at St. Mary's Cathedral, in Trenton. Bishop Reiss gave the following homily at that Mass.

"In every prayer I utter, I rejoice, as I plead on your behalf, at the way you have all continually helped promote the Gospel" (Phil 1:4–5). These words of St. Paul, read in our second Scripture passage, fittingly describe my feelings today as we conclude the Fourth Synod of the Diocese of Trenton. I rejoice and am amazed at the accomplishments of this synod. Everyone who has in any way participated should stand back in admiration and rejoice. The joy is compounded with the realization that our guiding principle throughout the time of preparation, the time of study, and the time in plenary sessions has always been "how best to proclaim and to promote the Gospel in the Diocese of Trenton." This primary objective underlay the abundant sacrifices of clergy, religious, and laity as they labored to formulate proposed statutes.

The formal opening of the Fourth Synod was on January 13, 1991, but preliminary plans and preparations began many months prior to that date. Very often the behind-the-scenes activities are missed or forgotten, but they must be acknowledged in light of the functioning of the three plenary sessions. These activities were monumental, as were the energy, work, and deliberations during the actual lengthy sessions.

I hardly know where to begin to express my gratitude. Part of the hesitation lies in the fact that there were hundreds who participated on the local level—in parishes or county meetings—who were not official and voting delegates, but nevertheless expressed their opinions in word and in writing. To all of them I say thanks.

To those who constituted the almost mysterious but vital Steering Committee, to the chairpersons of the seven major committees, to the subcommittee members, I say thanks.

To the excellent canonical experts, whose guidance was so essential, I say thanks.

To the committee and its members who coordinated arrangements for our meetings, hospitality, and Liturgies, I say thanks.

To the staff of the Chancery, whose heroic efforts to prepare and provide the materials and booklets for the deliberations under the added pressure of time, I say thanks, or, as the French say, "Merci mille fois," thanks a thousand times.

My words of gratitude seem so puny as I express them to Bishop Edward Kmiec as the chairman and to Father Leonard Troiano, the executive coordinator, for providing the leadership and coordination so necessary for the success of the Fourth Synod. Thanks to our absent priest, Father Joseph R. Punderson, for his guidance from a distance.

To everyone in the diocese who worked and who prayed, I say thank you. Rejoice, rejoice in a job well done! For what? The proposed statutes were prepared with the various amendments, either additions or deletions, and were presented to me in "draft form" following the third session. I have examined them all very carefully and made my decision. Most were accepted; some were rewritten; some were edited; some were joined to others; some were put under a different heading; some were eliminated because of duplication or because they were not statute material but rather guidelines or recommendations; and a small number were rejected. Time did not permit an actual count, but a well-founded estimate is that 350 statutes have been officially promulgated as synodal law for the Diocese of Trenton. This total represents a sign of the hard work of all the participants. Therefore, "Rejoice."

More work lies ahead. These approved statutes must be read again and edited for style, accuracy, and clarity. They must be numbered. A table of contents and an index must be prepared and appendixes added prior to having all the material printed and distributed. There is the pressure of time, for these must be done by Pentecost of 1992, the effective date of the new statutes. Presently, we have accomplished the first objective of the synod—the application of the general law of the church to the needs of this local church, the Diocese of Trenton. Our statutes are tailored for the diocese as a means to promote the Gospel.

As the final preparations for printing and dissemination proceed, we move on to the next objective—the implementation of the Fourth Synod. In the very near future, a new committee will be constituted to plan for this implementation. This task will be one of education and information— for the clergy, religious, and laity—so that all members of the diocese can put the statutes into practice. The details are yet to be established as to how this phase will be carried out. It must include our diocesan offices and directors, who will be responsible to follow recommendations and to institute or revise guidelines. This activity will take time but will begin almost immediately.

Another major objective of the Fourth Synod will flow from the dissemination and education, and that is accountability. Now there is an objective standard that can regulate the affairs of the diocese in an impartial manner and bring a uniform approach to the affairs of the diocese.

I offer one caution: just because the effective date for the Fourth Synodal Statutes is not until Pentecost, it does not mean that the diocese is without law, regulations, or guidelines. All of these continue in effect unless contrary to the promulgated statutes.

Let us return to the text of St. Paul to remind ourselves of the ultimate purpose underlying the Fourth Synod—and that is to promote the Gospel. Our statutes are to help us and to guide us on our journey to the Kingdom. These statutes will be for the guidance of clergy, religious, and laity in seeking our common spiritual aim of service to God, to His church, and to His people. As I proposed in the homily on January 13th, I place before you as a model Jesus, the obedient Son of God, Who said, "'I always do the will of My heavenly Father'" (Jn 6:38), and also our Patroness, the Blessed Mother, who stated, "'Be it done to me according to Your Word'" (Lk 1:37).

Since our labors are not yet finished, we must continue to pray for the ultimate success of this Fourth Synod, and we can do so with confidence in accord with St. Paul's message: "'I am sure of this much: that He who has begun the good work in you will carry it through to completion'" (Phil 1:6).

With thanksgiving in our hearts for the help given us by God in the important work of the Fourth Synod, with confident prayer for the true success of the Fourth Synod, let us proceed. Rejoice, again, I say, rejoice.

Mary, assumed into Heaven, "Pray for us!"

DIOCESAN CAMPAIGN: FAITH IN SERVICE

As the Fourth Synod of the diocese was under way, with much dialogue and discussion among the clergy and laity, it became evident to Bishop Reiss and his staff that once the synod ended, there would be a great need for funds to implement the decrees of the synod.

In April 1991, Bishop Reiss, with advice from his Steering Committee, made up of clergy and laity, engaged Community Counselling Service, a professional fund-raising organization from New York City, to undertake a major fund drive for the diocese. Bishop Reiss appointed Bishop Kmiec as the general chairperson for the drive.

After much study and discussion, Community Counselling Service came up with a case statement and logo.

In May 1991, Bishop Reiss sent a letter to all the priests concerning the drive.

Reverend dear Father:
As you are aware, our Fourth Diocesan Synod is under way and expected to be completed by the end of this year. At the very same time, we continue to study our fiscal situation and the challenges that we face as we move as a diocesan family into the 21st century. Indeed, our ability to respond to the recommendations that grow out of our synod will be measured, in part, by the financial resources available to us.

Among our many financial challenges will be to care for our retired and infirm priests, to respond to the ever-growing call for our Catholic Works of Mercy, and to continue our commitment to Catholic education in our schools, in our religious education programs, and in our special educational services to all ages.

In order to be prepared to address these financial challenges, plans are being put in motion for a special diocesan-wide fund-

raising campaign next year. Before embarking upon such an extraordinary effort, our first in over 25 years, it will be important to consult with our priests and our laity and to complete our synod.

To this end, I am pleased to announce that the diocese has retained Community Counselling Service Co., Inc. (CCS), a professional fund-raising firm, to undertake a special planning and consultative process this fall.

Upon the completion of this planning step, we will provide a special report for you in January 1992. It is anticipated that the campaign will be conducted throughout 1992 with an intensive campaign in all the parishes in September–December 1992. It is envisioned that this special campaign will be a three-year effort with an opportunity for parishes to raise funds for their own needs as well as for the diocese.

I will be providing you with more specific information with regard to the consultative process in August. I look forward to your input and our continued progress in planning together the future of our diocese.

Fraternally yours in Christ,
/s/ + John C. Reiss
Bishop of Trenton

Finally, on June 30, 1992, Bishop Reiss called a press conference at St. Gregory the Great Parish Center, Hamilton Township, to open the campaign for the diocese officially. Bishop Reiss made the following statement at the press conference.

Good morning and welcome to St. Gregory the Great Parish, one of the 124 parishes that compose the Catholic church in the Diocese of Trenton.

The history of each of our 124 parishes, as well as that of the diocese itself, is one of vision and progress. The first Mass in our diocese was celebrated in Burlington 85 years before the founding of our country. The first church, St. John (now Sacred Heart), was built in Trenton under the direction of a layman named John Sartori in 1814. Shortly thereafter, the great influx of European Catholic immigrants prompted the establishment of the Diocese of Trenton in the year 1881.

The people of God in the Diocese of Trenton have inherited a proud Catholic legacy, and we continue to build on that tradition. Today, our diocese encompasses four counties and provides spiritual and charitable service for the more than 215,000 Catholic families registered here. We educate approximately 29,000 young men and women every year in our 59 diocesan and parish elementary schools and 8 diocesan secondary schools. Through the auspices of Catholic Charities, a network of professional charitable services and programs that address a broad range of human needs, over 45,000 Catholics and non-Catholics are ministered to every year.

For more than 100 years, the Diocese of Trenton, through its parishes, schools, religious education programs, and charitable services, has served the laity by addressing the spiritual needs of the day and by anticipating future needs. Today, I am introducing a major initiative that will help to secure the stability of current diocesan programs and provide a solid financial base for our church as we move into the next century. After much prayer, careful deliberation, and consultation with our priests, religious, and laity during our Fourth Diocesan Synod, I wish to announce that the Diocese of Trenton is embarking on a capital fund campaign to raise $32 million. We have named the campaign Faith in Service.

Our diocese, through the Faith in Service program, will establish a $10-million Endowment Fund for Catholic education to ensure that the teaching mission of our schools remains strong. A Catholic education instills in our children faith and values of integrity, discipline, and responsibility to others. Our Catholic schools provide a primary focus for evangelization and are a leading source for vocations. As our church works to meet the issues confronting our society, we must strengthen our Catholic schools, which have a tradition of preparing young men and women to live Christ-centered lives and to be positive influences on the world around them. Direct subsidies to schools for operational, capital, and administrative expenses will assist in keeping Catholic education affordable and will encourage more families to send their children to Catholic schools. A diocesan committee will be formed to decide the allocation of these subsidies each year. In addition to aid to our schools, a portion of this income will support religious education programs.

As we prepare for our future by planning for Catholic educational needs, our diocese is also committed to providing a spiritual and caring environment for an increasing elderly lay population. We also have a particular obligation to provide for our retired priests, who have dedicated their lives to the pastoral work of our church. For these elderly, $14 million of the funds raised by Faith in Service will be used to build a comprehensive adult care campus that will connect St. Lawrence Rehabilitation Center in Lawrenceville with Morris Hall Home for the Aged and will incorporate a 120-bed skilled nursing care center, which will provide 24-hour medical and nursing care for lay people and priests, a new chapel, and retirement quarters for priests.

Also, a segment of funds raised by Faith in Service will be used to assist in the development of a Catholic-sponsored nursing home in Ocean County.

The Gospels and traditional teachings of Christ direct us to dedicate ourselves selflessly to others. Catholic Charities, a network of charitable and social welfare programs, last year assisted thousands of people across the diocese through a host of programs, including counseling for the physically, sexually, and emotionally abused, family and community services, maternity and adoption programs, and services for the elderly, the homeless, our children and battered women, those with serious mental illnesses, people suffering from chemical addictions, and HIV victims. A $5-million Endowment Fund for Catholic Charities will ensure the continuation of our current charitable and social services now facing severe governmental cutbacks and will assist with the development of new programs.

As we undertake this effort to prepare financially for our future, we are considering plans for a new diocesan pastoral center. Faith in Service will provide $3 million for partial funding of this project. A new pastoral center would centralize diocesan offices in one core location and provide for a more streamlined operation of all diocesan services. This would allow us to serve more effectively those in our care, many of whom compose our parishes, which are at the heart of all the projects we have undertaken.

Through our parishes, our faith is nurtured daily, and our families are provided with a solid base of support and encouragement. Every parish in the diocese will share and participate in our Faith in Service campaign and will be assigned a specific financial goal. Each parish that exceeds its goal will receive back 75 percent of all the over-goal

funds raised, which it may use for its own local parish concerns. The other 25 percent of the over-goal funds will be applied to the Endowment Fund for Catholic Education.

For Faith in Service to succeed, we need strong leadership! That is why I have asked Bishop Kmiec to serve as chairman of Faith in Service. Bishop Kmiec is an outstanding leader, and he possesses a keen sensitivity and vision for the mission of our diocese. I am confident that under his direction, Faith in Service will be a great success.

We entrust the successful outcome of this campaign to the Blessed Mother, who is the Patroness of our diocese. We ask for the prayers of all the faithful as we prepare our church for the 2,000th year marking the birth of our Lord and Savior, Jesus Christ.

Thank you. I would now like to introduce Bishop Kmiec, who will share some brief thoughts with you concerning the campaign and will discuss the manner in which we will raise the necessary funds.

Following Bishop Reiss's statement, Bishop Kmiec made these remarks.

Thank you, Bishop Reiss, for the introduction. I am very pleased to assist the bishop with this most important endeavor, and I am happy to accept the position of chairman of the Faith in Service campaign.

I am sure many of you are wondering exactly how we plan to raise the $32 million necessary to provide for the special needs of our diocese. I would like to take a moment to explain that to you.

Faith in Service will be conducted in two phases: a Major Gift phase and a Parish Fund-Raising phase. Right now, we are conducting the Major Gift phase. In July, the Parish Fund-Raising phase will begin.

During the parish phase, every parish in our diocese will be given the opportunity to participate in the campaign by conducting its own Faith in Service campaign with a specific financial goal.

Faith in Service is an opportunity for our diocese to work together as a family. The Diocese of Trenton is blessed with strong, committed, and faithful laity. Each year, thousands of volunteers take part in the many programs and activities of the church. The extraordinary nature of Faith in Service will help enlist the renowned cooperative spirit of our laity and clergy.

Christ has challenged us to fulfill His mission here on earth. He has provided many treasures that facilitate the ability of our diocese to fulfill that commission: outstanding clergy and religious, vibrant parishes, wonderful schools and health care facilities, and a dedicated laity. We are thankful to God for these many blessings, due in large part to the labor of those who came before us. With limited resources and unlimited vision, our Catholic ancestors sacrificed to build a dynamic church, which has for over a century ministered to the myriad needs of the people of God in the Diocese of Trenton. Building upon this heritage, we seek to secure, through Faith in Service, the resources necessary to serve each other now and to prepare our diocese to care for future generations.

BISHOP KMIEC APPOINTED BISHOP OF NASHVILLE, TENNESSEE

Shortly after 8 o'clock on the morning of October 7, 1992, Bishop Kmiec received a phone call from Archbishop Agostino Cacciavillan, papal pro-nuncio to the United States, informing Bishop Kmiec that the Holy Father had in mind to appoint him as bishop of Nashville, Tennessee.

On October 13, 1992, a public announcement was made in Trenton and Nashville, that the Holy Father, Pope John Paul II, had appointed Bishop Edward U. Kmiec to be bishop of Nashville, Tennessee.

Bishop Kmiec gave the following statement to the people of the Diocese of Trenton on his new appointment.

Dear Friends in Christ,
At this time, I trust that you have been made aware that our Holy Father, Pope John Paul II, has called me to serve the people of God as bishop of the Diocese of Nashville in Tennessee. Our Holy Father's representative in our country, the pro-nuncio, Archbishop Agostino Cacciavillan, telephoned me from Washington last week on the Feast of Our Lady of the Rosary to inform me that His Holiness had bestowed upon me this honor and privilege.

I first thank God for this and all his many blessings, but am keenly aware that this nomination implies an awesome responsibility of pastoral ministry. I therefore prayerfully and trustingly place myself in the hands of God, seeking his divine assistance as I assume this new office. I am thankful also to our Holy Father for the confidence and trust placed in me. I have pledged to him my loyalty and fidelity and will endeavor with all that is in me to serve faithfully and zealously as a worthy pastor and shepherd of the people of the Diocese of Nashville.

While I look forward eagerly to this new pastoral responsibility, I do so with mixed emotions, for it removes me from the Diocese of Trenton. For 30 years, as priest and auxiliary bishop, it has been my great joy and privilege to serve the people of our diocese. My ministry here, wherever and whenever I went, has been nourished by your faith, love, and affirmation. I thank you all, clergy, religious, and faithful, for the wonderful association we have had and for your many kindnesses.

I am especially grateful for the example and friendship I have received, first in time from Bishop Ahr, and more recently from Bishop Reiss, who graciously involved me fully in the whole range of administrative and pastoral ministry in our diocese as his auxiliary bishop. It has been a wonderful experience, and the lessons of faith, holiness, love, and service that I have learned from our bishops and all of you will serve me well as I go to minister to the church of Nashville. I will miss you and ever remember you with prayer-filled gratitude.

Though I have received much from you, I now ask even more. And that is your special remembrance of me in your prayers. I will need and depend on your prayerful support as I journey to a new venue of pastoral service. Thank you and God bless you!

BISHOP REISS'S CONGRATULATIONS

On October 13, 1992, Bishop Reiss issued this statement to the diocese on Bishop Kmiec's appointment.

I offer my congratulations to Bishop Kmiec and rejoice with him for the honor of being named by His Holiness, Pope John Paul II, as the diocesan bishop of the Diocese of Nashville. I am certain that this important ministry in the church is in recognition of the many years of devoted service which Bishop Kmiec has given to the church and the Diocese of Trenton.

He has distinguished himself in performing many important posts—master of ceremonies, secretary to Bishop Ahr, vice-chancellor, moderator of the Curia, vicar-general, and auxiliary bishop. In addition, there have been the specialized tasks of coordinator for the Fourth Synod of Trenton and now as the diocesan director for the Faith in Service campaign.

In all of his duties, Bishop Kmiec has shown a solid commitment to the church and to her teachings and a great rapport with people—clergy, religious, and laity, both old and young. He has also served with distinction on various committees of the National Conference of Bishops.

Finally, Bishop Kmiec has been a confidant, an adviser, and a loyal friend to me. I ask everyone to join me in praying that the Holy Spirit will enlighten and guide him as the shepherd to the people of God in Nashville. I shall miss him.

NEW APPOINTMENTS

On November 5, 1992, Bishop Reiss named Msgr. William F. Fitzgerald, pastor of Our Lady of Good Counsel Church, West Trenton, to be moderator of the Curia, succeeding Bishop Kmiec, who had been transferred as bishop of Nashville, Tennessee. Bishop Reiss also announced that Msgr. Joseph C. Shenrock, pastor of St. Elizabeth Ann Seton Church, Whiting, had been appointed chairman of the Faith in Service campaign, succeeding Bishop Kmiec, who had served as chairman of this diocesan campaign.

BISHOP KMIEC'S FAREWELL

On Monday, November 23, 1992, the clergy and laity gathered at St. Mary's Cathedral in Trenton to bid farewell to Bishop Kmiec as he celebrated his final Mass in the cathedral as the auxiliary bishop of Trenton. In his final homily at Mass he stated, "This is an end, just as my service here in the diocese is coming to an end."

A second coincidence is the start of Advent on November 29, which marks the opening of the new liturgical year. Bishop Kmiec pointed out that his new ministry in Nashville is a new beginning for him.

A third comparison the bishop noted is Thanksgiving Day, November 26. Bishop Kmiec said he is thankful for the time he served in the Diocese of Trenton.

Bishop Kmiec paid tribute to the two Trenton bishops with whom he worked closely, Bishop George W. Ahr and Bishop John C. Reiss, saying that he had learned a great deal from them.

"Bishop Ahr and Bishop Reiss have been a great gift to me. They are both outstanding leaders in the church of Trenton, and I have been privileged to have served with them."

To his brother priests, the deacons, the religious, and the faithful of the diocese, Bishop Kmiec gave thanks for their affirmation and support during his years of service in the diocese. He assured them that all of them would be remembered in his prayers, and he asked them in turn to pray for him.

"My departure is coming quickly. I leave for Nashville on Saturday," Bishop Kmiec said.

With his wonderful sense of humor, Bishop Kmiec joked about his trip to Nashville as a "one-way trip," for it was the one time in his life he did not have to buy a round-trip ticket. Nevertheless, Bishop Kmiec assured the congregation that he intends to return for visits to the Trenton diocese whenever time permits.

"My heart is filled with a great sense of gratitude for all the support I have been given during my years of service here. The Diocese of Trenton has a great community of faith. I leave you in body but my heart stays with you."

After the Communion of the Mass, Bishop Reiss extended to Bishop Kmiec prayerful thanks and best wishes. He said he was happy for Bishop Kmiec and pointed out that in being named bishop of Nashville, he is being recognized for his talents.

"I consider Bishop Kmiec not only a coworker but a friend. He will be missed," Bishop Reiss said. "Trenton's loss will most definitely be Nashville's gain."

On December 2, 1992, at noon, a chartered plane left Mercer Airport in Trenton bound for Nashville, Tennessee, for the installation of Bishop Kmiec. Bishop Reiss led the delegation of bishops, priests, deacons, religious, and laity to the installation ceremony that took place on December 3, 1992, at 3 p.m. at the Nashville Convention Center. The Most Rev. Thomas C. Kelly, O.P., archbishop of Louisville and metropolitan for the Nashville diocese, was the installing bishop. Over 3,000 bishops, priests, deacons, religious, and laity jammed the Nashville Convention Center for the installation Mass. At the Mass, Bishop Kmiec gave the following homily.

My Brothers and Sisters in Christ:

What a wondrous and dramatic moment our Gospel evokes for our reflection on this auspicious day as we gather here to celebrate: Our Lord Jesus commissions and sends his apostles to "go and make disciples of all the nations." It was the culmination of their life and time with Jesus. Soon, they would be imbued with the Holy Spirit and venture out as evangelizers, bearing the good news to all the world. It was their principal task, and it continues into our times as the principal task and the essential mission of the church. Pope Paul VI wrote, "To evangelize is the grace and vocation proper to the church, her most profound identity." More recently, Pope John Paul II affirms the same by declaring, "The entire mission of the church is concentrated and manifested in evangelization. Through evangelization, the church is built up into a community of faith, more precisely, into a community that confesses the faith in full adherence to the Word of God, which is celebrated in the sacraments and lived in charity, the principle of Christian moral existence."

Just as the work of evangelization has been the basic mission of the church over the world through the passage of history, so has it been in its time for this local church of Nashville. For 155 years, this diocese has been faithfully engaged in that mission. By virtue of his consecration, a bishop is a "successor of the apostles," providing a continuity of the mandate to evangelize given by Christ to the original apostles and bearing it into the life of a local faith community. Over the years of its existence, the Diocese of Nashville has had a succession of nine bishops as its spiritual leaders, who dutifully put into practice the instruction of Saint Paul to Timothy on the duties of a bishop, namely, "Do the work of an evangelist." This is evidenced by the ever-enlarging community of faith, vibrantly alive in the spirit, that is the church of Nashville today.

Into this context and tradition, it is my great privilege to come to you in the providence of God as your tenth bishop. I come humbly with hope and prayer to seek to continue God's good work done here in the past and to build upon it as we proceed into the future, accomplished through faithful loving service rendered to God and all of you. Mindful of that, I pledge to God, "Here I am, Lord; I come to do your will." To you, I pledge, "Here I am; I come to you as one who serves." I make this entrance into your midst and into your lives with a sense of great joy, excitement, enthusiasm, and anticipation, with a commitment to serve you with all the spirit, strength, and ability within me, and with a sense of hope and confidence springing from a trust in God and in all of you. I thank God for this opportunity to serve you, and I also thank our Holy Father, Pope John Paul II, who called me to the office of bishop ten years ago and who now places new trust and confidence in me by calling me to serve you as bishop of Nashville.

A few days ago, I received a congratulatory note from one of my brother bishops, which I would like to share with you now. Speaking of you, he offered these very assuring words. "You enter a great diocese, a truly Christian community. I just marvel at the Nashville people of God, a lone bishop, a handful of dedicated priests and deacons, holy and visionary sisters, and a most active laity. You have inherited a precious jewel of Catholicity in the South. They love Bishop Niedergeses but will welcome you with open arms." He was not the only one offering such complimentary sentiments, and my brief acquaintance with you leads me to believe that all he said is very true. And may I add that among the many arms extended in welcome, none have been more welcoming than those of Bishop Niedergeses. Within a few minutes of my learning of this appointment to Nashville, he was on the phone long distance to offer me his welcome and good wishes. Since then, he has been my tour guide in Nashville and has generously assisted in every aspect of making and facilitating the transition. In his book *The Catholic Church in Tennessee,* Thomas Stritch writes, "If pastoral solicitude is the first mark of a good bishop, as many say, Bishop Niedergeses is a nearly perfect specimen of the species. Problems we have always with us. We need more of Bishop Niedergeses' overflowing faith and abounding love." Bishop, you not only pass on to me a marvelous diocese but also offer me a high pastoral standard to emulate. With God's grace, I shall endeavor to do so. Thank you for all you have done in service to Nashville and for your generous personal kindness to me. On behalf of us all, I welcome you to continue to grace us with your priestly presence and new pastoral ministry as our cherished and beloved bishop emeritus.

A short time ago in the installation rite at our Eucharistic celebration this afternoon, the pastoral staff of spiritual leadership for the Diocese of Nashville was placed in my hands. Since a bishop's role is one of service, whatever satisfaction one could derive from its honor is quickly absorbed in consciousness of the awesome responsibil-

ity and accountability before God that this office implies. In a classic passage, Saint Augustine, himself a bishop with keen insight into his apostolic role, wrote this reflection: "What I am for you terrifies me; what I am with you consoles me. For you I am a bishop; but with you I am a Christian. The former is a duty; the latter, a grace. The former is a danger; the latter, salvation."

As I begin today my ministry to you and for you, I take those cautionary words to heart. I recall a Holy Thursday message from our Holy Father sent to the priests of the world a few years ago. It answers the question of how one is to serve, and I paraphrase our Holy Father's words. Following Jesus' example, a bishop, "the steward of the mysteries of God," is truly himself when he is "for others." A bishop needs a special sensitivity to these "others," making him attentive to their lives and destiny. A bishop needs to recognize those whom the "Father has given to him." These are, in the first place, those whom the Good Shepherd has placed in the path of his pastoral ministry and care. They are children, adults, and the aged. They are the youth, married couples, and families but also those who are alone. They are the poor, the homeless, and the hungry. They are the sick, the suffering, and the dying. They are those who are spiritually close and willing to collaborate in the apostolate but also those who are distant and those who are alienated or indifferent, though many of them may be searching and reflecting. They are those who for different reasons are negatively disposed, those who find themselves in difficulties of various sorts, those who are struggling against addiction to vices and sins, those who desperately fight for faith and hope, those who seek help and those who reject it, those who accept us and those who reject us. How can a bishop be "for" all of these people, and "for" each of them, according to the model of Christ? How can we be "for" those whom "the Father has given us" committing them to our trust? The answer is through love, rendering service in true, generous Christian charity.

Over the past thirty years, it has been my good fortune to have in the path of my pastoral ministry the people of the Diocese of Trenton in New Jersey. It has been a time of grace and blessing, certainly for me and hopefully for them. Now, in his providence, God has placed you in the path of my pastoral ministry as your bishop. I am grateful to God for that privilege, and, true to my episcopal motto, "Charity and Service," I mean to serve you as I served others before you: with love, the way by which I can be "for" all of you and "for" each of you. I humbly ask you all—clergy, religious, and laity—first of all for your prayers, and I invite you to be with me collaborators in ministry and Christian service. The church of today, local or universal, has a broad agenda in doing God's work on earth and in our communities, and we need your partnership in accomplishing it, joined together in solidarity of faith and purpose. There are good and new initiatives. For instance, a little over a week ago, at our national meeting in Washington, the bishops approved a national plan and strategy for Catholic evangelization in the United States: "Go and Make Disciples." By way of three stated goals, the plan seeks to rekindle in Catholics an enthusiasm for their faith, to invite all to hear the message of salvation in Jesus Christ, and to foster values in our society promoting the dignity of the human person and the common good of all. At this time of a new beginning for our church of Nashville and middle Tennessee, this document provides a plan and an incentive for reevangelization in order to continue our essential mission as

church on our pilgrimage of faith. A prime instrument for this task will also be shortly forthcoming, the long-awaited "Catechism of the Catholic Church," a compendium of the tenets of our faith, which will provide a basis for new religious education for the young and for adults as well.

In the months and years ahead, as I lead you as bishop, I will seek also your input and cooperation to discern how best to fulfill our mission as church and grow in virtue and holiness, so that we might be a light and leaven to all about us. I ask your patience and understanding, for as you are well aware, I am new to this area, its people, and its ways, but I hope to be a perceptive listener, a good student, and a quick learner, so as not to inhibit our progress together on our path of building God's Kingdom. Our trust is in the Holy Spirit and in the wisdom and guidance He will bestow on us to show us the way.

I look forward to meeting all of you. Getting to know you will be one of my priorities, and over the course of time I hope to accomplish that on a personal basis. For now, thank you from the bottom of my heart for your most warm welcome and gracious kindness. May God reward you for your goodness and for this wonderful demonstration of true Southern and Christian hospitality.

Often, new bishops are asked what is their vision of the diocese they come to serve. In response, I would say that my vision for Nashville is what Saint Paul expressed in his epistle for the Christian community at Ephesus: "I pray that [God] will bestow on you gifts in keeping with the riches of his glory. May he strengthen you inwardly through the working of his Spirit. May Christ dwell in your hearts through faith, and may charity be the root and foundation of your life. Thus you will be able to grasp fully, with all the holy ones, the breadth and length and height and depth of Christ's love and experience this love which surpasses all knowledge so that you may attain to the fullness of God himself."

Over the past weeks, I have received hundreds of letters. Among them were letters from second graders at Overbrook School in Nashville. They were very welcoming, offering prayers, sacrifices, and the willingness to show me the city, including a stop at Chuck E. Cheese for pizza. Another offered a sure formula for success: It came from a young lady in New Jersey—Melissa by name—a third grader in Our Lady of Good Counsel School in the town of Moorestown. May I read what she wrote to me?

> Dear Bishop Kmiec:
> I hope you have good luck in Nashville, Tennessee. Thank you for being our bishop here in Moorestown. I hope you have a beautiful house.
> You have to remember three things. One is to pray before you go to sleep. Two is to say grace before your meals. And three is to come visit us. And also make nice friends.
>
> Sincerely,
> Melissa

Melissa, I have a nice house; I will pray as you suggest; and I have already found a lot of nice friends in Nashville. God bless you!

The diocesan campaign, Faith in Service, continued until the spring of 1993. On February 12, 1993, Bishop Reiss announced that the $32 million goal had been reached; on June 2, 1993, the drive exceeded $40 million.

The diocesan family, both clergy and laity, prepared to celebrate on December 12, 1992, Bishop John C. Reiss's 25th anniversary of his ordination as a bishop—13 years as auxiliary bishop of the diocese and 12 years as the ordinary of the diocese. The diocesan celebrations of this anniversary were held on Sunday, April 18, 1993, with a Mass of Thanksgiving in St. Mary's Cathedral, followed by a reception at the Hyatt Regency Princeton.

As we bring this chapter to a close, we conclude this section of the history on the bishops of the Diocese of Trenton. The eight bishops have surely lived up to the mandate of the Second Vatican Council decree on the pastoral office of bishop in the church.

> Bishops should devote themselves to their apostolic office as witnesses of Christ to all people. They should not limit themselves to those who already acknowledge the Prince of Pastors but should also devote their energies wholeheartedly to those who have strayed in any way from the path of truth or who have no knowledge of the Gospel of Christ and of his saving mercy, so that ultimately all people may walk "in all goodness, justice and truth" (Eph 5:9).

SOURCES

1. Archives of the Diocese of Trenton.
2. Interviews with Bishop John C. Reiss, Rev. Msgr. Joseph A. O'Connor, and Rev. Msgr. William F. Fitzgerald.
3. *The Monitor*, 1981–89, bound volumes 28–36.
4. *The Monitor*, 1990–93, unbound issues, volumes 37–39.

PART THREE

FAITH IN ACTION IN THE DIOCESE OF TRENTON

CHAPTER TWELVE

PARISHES

◆

BY JAMES F. O'NEILL JR.

BRIEF HISTORIES OF the 124 independent parishes and two of the older missions are contained in this chapter. More extensive histories of parish high schools currently in operation appear with the private high schools of the diocese in the chapter on institutions.

We thank all of the people within each parish for providing us with substantial historical information and answers to our questions. We also thank the many people who provided photographs of their churches. Additional historical details have been extracted from a variety of sources, the most important of which was Rev. Walter T. Leahy's book on the history of the Diocese of Trenton, published in 1906. Emphasis in this chapter is on the foundations of each parish, that is, the celebration of first masses, arrivals of first resident pastors, and building of the parish plants. We have attempted to include particulars of parish elementary schools, unique characteristics of the parishes, and highlights of other parish events and functions. As Leahy did, we ask for the

reader's kind indulgence for any imperfections contained in these sketches.

PARISHES WITHIN THE CITY OF TRENTON

Saint Mary's Cathedral

In 1865, Rev. Anthony Smith, pastor of old St. John's in Trenton, purchased property in the northern section of Trenton. Ground was broken on April 23, 1866, for St. Mary's Church, then a mission of St. John's. The Most Rev. James Roosevelt Bayley, bishop of Newark, laid the cornerstone on July 15, 1866. Bishop Bayley returned nearly five years later, on New Year's Day, 1871, to bless and dedicate the church under the patronage of the Blessed Virgin with the title St. Mary's of the Assumption. Father Smith resigned his pastorate at St. John's and became St. Mary's first rector.

Even before the completion of the church, Father Smith planned for the development of a school, and he purchased ground for it in 1868. Shortly after Bishop Bayley dedicated the church, the school was finished. The Sisters of Charity from Convent Station opened the school for classes on October 2, 1871. By July 1875, the growth of the parish prompted Father Smith to buy land for a school addition.

In December 1876, Father Smith purchased land in Hopewell for the construction of St. Alphonsus Church. By 1882, Father Smith had built a combination church/school in the eastern section of Trenton, establishing St. Joseph's Parish. Father Smith was also responsible for building St. Mary's rectory and purchasing land for a cemetery in 1872. On July 15, 1881, Trenton was recognized as the episcopal city of a new diocese for southern New Jersey, and St. Mary's was selected as the diocesan cathedral. By 1883, Father Smith had constructed the episcopal residence for the Most Rev. Michael J. O'Farrell. Bishop O'Farrell appointed Father Smith as the first vicar-general of the Diocese of Trenton.

Upon Father Smith's death, Bishop O'Farrell assumed the pastorship of St. Mary's Cathedral. Before he appointed a permanent rector, Rev. J. Joseph Smith and Rev. John M. McCloskey served as acting rectors. Rev. James A. McFaul arrived as rector in October 1890, was named vicar-general on November 1, 1890, and became Trenton's second bishop on July 20, 1894.

The Most Rev. James A. McFaul appointed Rev. John H. Fox as pastor of St. Mary's Cathedral on February 1, 1895. Father Fox was appointed vicar-general in November 1900 and was elevated to domestic prelate in 1904. Monsignor Fox increased the size of the school, built a convent, and improved the church building.

The Sisters of Charity were recalled from Trenton to the Newark diocese in 1906. The Sisters of Mercy from North Plainfield continued operation of the school. Though some high school classes had been offered previously, the state department of education placed St. Mary Cathedral High School on its list of approved secondary schools. The Most Rev. Thomas J. Walsh named Cathedral High School as one of the central high schools to welcome students outside its parish. In 1920, Sr. Mary Concepta, R.S.M., developed the first parochial parent-teacher organization east of Chicago.

Msgr. Maurice R. Spillane, soon after his arrival, renovated the church building. He served as administrator of the diocese during the interim between the episcopates of the Most Rev. John J. McMahon and the Most Rev. Moses E. Kiley. Bishop Kiley redistributed the high school students by sending the boys to Trenton Catholic High School and the girls to St. Mary Cathedral High School. In 1940, Cathedral High School and Cathedral Grammar School received separate principals. In 1963, Cathedral High School became coeducational again. However, the facilities had become increasingly inadequate, and safety was a grave concern. After consideration of numerous options, Cathedral High School was closed in 1972. The students were absorbed by Notre Dame High School, St. Anthony High School, and public high schools.

On March 14, 1956, a tragic fire destroyed the cathedral and took the lives of the rector, Msgr. Richard T. Crean, and two housekeepers, Miss Mary Brennan and Miss Mary Donnellan. On the day after the fire, 4-year-old Joseph Molyneux from Eatontown asked his mother to send his only penny to the bishop for the construction of a new church. Within two months after the fire, a formal fund drive started.

On Friday, March 13, 1959, at the laying of the new St. Mary's Cathedral cornerstone, the Most Rev. George W. Ahr placed in the cornerstone box many contemporary mementos, artifacts from the original St. Mary's cornerstone, and Joseph Molyneux's penny. Bishop Ahr solemnly blessed the cathedral on Saturday, March 14, 1959. The first mass in the new cathedral, a Pontifical Mass of Thanksgiving, was celebrated by the Most Rev. Thomas A. Boland, archbishop of Newark; Bishop Ahr assisted. The following bishops were present in the sanctuary: James A. McNulty of Paterson; Justin J. McCarthy of Camden; John J. Carberry of Lafayette, Indiana; Martin W. Stanton and Walter W. Curtis, auxiliaries to the archbishop of Newark; and Stephen J. Kocisko, auxiliary to the apostolic exarch of the Byzantine Diocese of Pittsburgh.

The number of cathedral parishioners diminished over the years to as few as 100, leaving the cathedral buildings underutilized, while Our Lady of Mount Carmel Church was becoming too small for its large Hispanic community. As a result, the Most Rev. John C. Reiss announced the consolidation of St. Mary's Cathedral and Our Lady of Mount Carmel. Rev. Joseph F. Lupo, O.Ss.T., was appointed rector of the cathe-

Cathedral of Saint Mary, Trenton

dral on October 9, 1981. Masses are offered in Spanish as well as English.

Pastors: Rev. Anthony Smith, 1871–88; Most Rev. Michael J. O'Farrell, 1888–90; Rev. James A. McFaul, 1890–95; Msgr. John H. Fox, 1895–1928; Msgr. Maurice R. Spillane, 1929–34; Msgr. Richard T. Crean, 1934–56; Msgr. John E. Grimes, 1956–66; Msgr. Alfred D. Smith, 1967–75; Rev. Paul T. Gluth, 1975–81; Rev. Joseph F. Lupo, O.Ss.T., 1981; Rev. Armand Iavarone, O.Ss.T., 1982–84; Rev. Aaron Dowdell, O.Ss.T., 1984–85; Rev. Raymond S. Bianchi, C.M.F., 1986–present.

Principals of St. Mary Cathedral School: Sr. Cornelia, S.C., c1871; Sr. Mary Genevieve, S.C.; Sr. Mary Gonzaga Thompson, R.S.M., 1906–14; Sr. Mary Consilio Brennan, R.S.M., 1914–17; Sr. Mary Concepta Smith, R.S.M., 1917–40.

Principals of St. Mary Cathedral Grammar School: Sr. Maria Conlain, R.S.M., 1940–52; Sr. Mary Hubert Huley, R.S.M., 1952–53; Sr. Mary Benita Lyons, R.S.M., 1953–55; Sr. Mary Nicholas Farley, R.S.M., 1955–61; Sr. Mary Fidelis McLaughlin, R.S.M., 1961–67; Sr. Gertrude Conway, R.S.M., 1967–73; Sr. Mary Vincent de Paul Giamarese, R.S.M., 1973–76; Sr. Irene Nebus, R.S.M., 1976–79; Sr. Mary Lou Miller, R.S.M., 1979–82; Sr. Lee Ann Amico, R.S.M., 1982–85; Sr. Ruth Morgan, R.S.M., 1985–90; Mrs. Ruth Ferrer, 1990–91; Ms. Mary O'Donnell, 1991–present.

Principals of St. Mary Cathedral High School: Sr. Mary Barbara O'Malley, R.S.M., 1940–57; Sr. Mary Charitas Marcotte, R.S.M., 1957–68; Sr. Mary Albert Cottrell, R.S.M., 1968–69; Sr. Alice Kelsey, R.S.M., 1969–72.

Trenton, Blessed Sacrament

With permission of the Trenton Public Schools, Blessed Sacrament's first mass was celebrated on October 13, 1912, in the Gregory Public School. Masses were held in the school until a small wooden church was built on parish land near the present rectory. Rev. Martin F. Casey had acquired a site for the rectory, the church-school building, and the convent. On January 3, 1922,

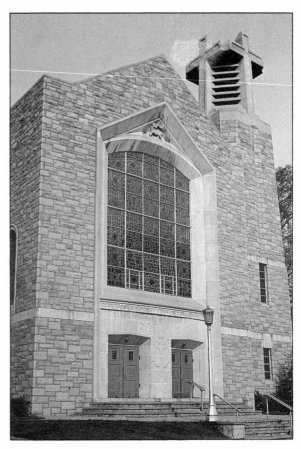

Church of the Blessed Sacrament, Trenton

Blessed Sacrament School opened, staffed by the Sisters of the Immaculate Heart of Mary from West Chester, Pennsylvania. Five years later they were succeeded by 7 of the Sisters of St. Francis from Glen Riddle, Pennsylvania. Despite losing nearly half of the parish families to the newly established Church of the Incarnation in 1947, Rev. J. Arthur Hayes initiated construction of a larger church, dedicated on November 10, 1951. Father Hayes also enlarged the school and the rectory. Rev. Eugene V. Davis renovated the sanctuary of the church in 1968, and he modernized the school. Msgr. Joseph C. Shenrock continued the excellent education programs of the school with the addition of a kindergarten in 1976 and a nursery school in 1978. The Sisters of St. Francis left the school in 1989.

Pastors: Rev. Michael H. Callahan, 1912–15; Rev. Martin F. Casey, 1915–33; Rev. Thomas A. Kearney, 1934–41; Rev. J. Arthur Hayes, 1942–66; Rev. Eugene V. Davis, 1966–71; Msgr. Joseph C. Shenrock, 1971–87; Rev. Richard J. Gallagher, 1987–89; Rev. James A. O'Brien, 1989–present.

Principals: Sr. Jacoba, O.S.F., c1927; Sr. Bertilda, O.S.F., c1943; Mother Lorenzo, O.S.F., 1947–50; Sr. Antonita Donahue, O.S.F., 1950–55; Sr. Irmengard, O.S.F., 1955–56; Sr. Berchmans Knapp, O.S.F., 1956–62; Sr. Miriam Wanda Binkowski, O.S.F., 1962–65; Sr. Catherine Georgine Portner, O.S.F., 1965–71; Sr. Kathryn Miller, O.S.F., 1971–73; Sr. Margaret Christine Sullivan, O.S.F., 1973–75; Sr. Margaret Appell, O.S.F., 1975–83; Sr. Alice Klein, O.S.F., 1983–84; Sr. Maria Gross, O.S.F., 1984–89; Mr. Kenneth A. Figgs, 1989–present.

Trenton, Holy Angels

Holy Angels Parish began in 1912 as a mission of St. Francis of Assisium, Trenton. In 1918, the Most Rev. Thomas J. Walsh placed the mission under the jurisdiction of Sacred Heart, Trenton. Rev. Peter J. Hart, pastor of Sacred Heart, erected a church/school building in the spring of 1921. The first mass in the new building was celebrated on October 9, 1921. A few days later, Bishop Walsh established Holy Angels

as an independent parish with Rev. John F. Walsh as first resident pastor. At the same time, Holy Angels was given the responsibility for St. Raphael's Mission in Trenton. The parish school formally began in August 1922. Three Sisters of St. Francis from Glen Riddle, Pennsylvania, took charge of the school. In 1926, Father Walsh constructed a new church with the first mass celebrated on Christmas Eve of the same year. Msgr. Michael P. McCorristin built a larger school on the original site of the old school in 1951. The larger school required more teachers, which necessitated a convent. In 1953, Rev. Thomas E. Carney completed the new rectory begun by Monsignor McCorristin. The church was remodeled in

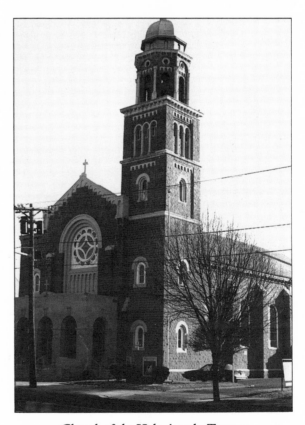

Church of the Holy Angels, Trenton

1957, and a combination parish center/school was finished in 1963.

Pastors: Rev. John F. Walsh, 1921–39; Rev. Joseph A. Mulligan, 1939–40; Msgr. Michael P. McCorristin, 1940–52; Rev. Thomas E. Carney, 1952–71; Rev. Francis P. Gunner, 1971–76; Rev. Peter J. Mooney, 1976–85; Rev. Anthony L. Capitani, 1985–86; Rev. Frank J. Iazzetta, 1986; Rev. Michael J. Walsh, 1987–present.

Principals: Sr. Mary Ruperta, O.S.F., 1922–25; Sr. Mary Callista, O.S.F., 1925–26; Sr. Mary Sincletica, O.S.F., 1926–32; Sr. Mary Friedberta, O.S.F., 1932–35; Sr. Mary Norbertina, O.S.F., 1935–38; Sr. Mary Elizabeth Gannon, O.S.F., 1938–43; Sr. Mary Ursula Warga, O.S.F., 1943–46; Sr. Mary Ambrose Booth, O.S.F., 1946–52; Sr. Mary Eutropia Quinn, O.S.F., 1952–57; Sr. Mary John Gabriel Jonansky, O.S.F., 1957–61; Sr. Mary Joseph Catherine, O.S.F., 1961–66; Sr. Manetto Ruocchio, O.S.F., 1966–71; Sr. Mauritia Konicki, O.S.F., 1971–75; Sr. Marie Anthony Heiss, O.S.F., 1975–81; Sr. Caroline Sweeney, O.S.F., 1981–88; Sr. Elizabeth Anne, O.S.F., 1988–present.

Trenton, Holy Cross

In 1891, Holy Cross was established by a small group of Polish immigrants from southeastern Poland. Led by founding pastor Rev. Valentine Swinarski, the parish bought a house and converted it into a rectory, chapel, and school. Land was purchased for a cemetery and a future parish plant. A school began operations in 1891 with Mr. Vincent Sieniewicz as the first teacher; the Felician Sisters from Buffalo, New York, arrived to teach in 1901. The present church was consecrated and dedicated in the autumn of 1911 by the Most Rev. Paul Rhode, the first bishop of Polish descent in the United States. In 1919, a three-story school building was constructed next to the church, and shortly after his arrival in 1967, Rev. Thaddeus J. Wojciehowski began a series of renovations to the parish buildings. The Holy Cross Community Center was dedicated on December 10, 1979, for all social gatherings and major parish events. The Church of the Holy Cross is located in South Trenton, a mecca of twenty-two ethnic churches.

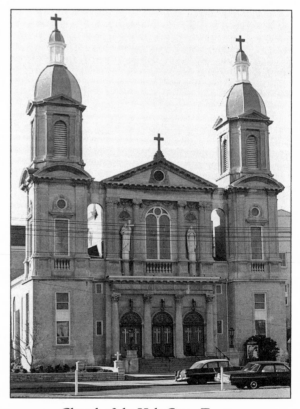

Church of the Holy Cross, Trenton

Pastors: Rev. Valentine Swinarski, 1891–95; Rev. Dr. John Ciemniewski, 1895; Rev. Francis Czernecki, 1896–1902; Rev. Francis Wojtanowski, 1902–04; Rev. Dr. Joseph Dziadosz, 1904–16; Rev. John Budziak, 1916–23; Msgr. Martin Lipinski, 1923–34; Msgr. Francis Kasprowicz, 1934–67; Msgr. Thaddeus J. Wojciehowski, 1967–91; Rev. Casimir Milewski, 1991–present.

Principals: Sr. Mary Felixsa, C.S.S.F., 1901–03; Sr. Mary Ignatius, C.S.S.F., 1903–05; Sr. Mary Veronica, C.S.S.F., 1905–07; Sr. Mary Beatrix, C.S.S.F., 1907–10; Sr. Mary Josephine, C.S.S.F., 1910–12; Sr. Mary Hedwig, C.S.S.F., 1912–15; Sr. Mary Anatolia, C.S.S.F., 1915–21; Sr. Mary Sigismunda, C.S.S.F., 1921–27; Sr. Mary Fabolia, C.S.S.F., 1927–30; Sr. Mary Emilia, C.S.S.F., 1930–33; Sr. Mary Juvenalia, C.S.S.F., 1933–36; Sr. Mary Callista, C.S.S.F., 1936–39; Sr. Mary Alice, C.S.S.F., 1939–42; Sr. Mary Othilia, C.S.S.F., 1942–48; Sr. Mary Felicianna, C.S.S.F., 1948–51; Sr. Mary Sabina, C.S.S.F., 1951–54; Sr. Mary Eulogia, C.S.S.F., 1954–57; Sr. Mary Scholastica, C.S.S.F., 1957–60; Sr. Mary Jerome, C.S.S.F., 1960–63; Sr. Mary Irma, C.S.S.F., 1963–64; Sr. Mary Wenceslaus, C.S.S.F., 1964–65; Sr. Mary Adelia, C.S.S.F., 1965–68; Sr. Joseph Marie, C.S.S.F., 1968–69; Sr. Marie Barbara, C.S.S.F., 1969–74; Sr. Mary Elvine, C.S.S.F., 1974–80; Sr. Mary Victoria, C.S.S.F., 1980–81; Mrs. Patricia Palinczar, 1981–present.

Trenton, Immaculate Conception

In 1874 the Conventual Franciscans, led by Rev. Peter Jachetti, O.F.M. Conv., bought a baseball lot in the borough of Chambersburg as a site for their theological seminary. Residents of the area attended mass in the seminary chapel, but they soon requested a separate place of worship. Father Jachetti, former pastor of St. Francis of Assisium Parish in Trenton, received permission from the Most Rev. Michael A. Corrigan, bishop of Newark, to develop a parish. On April 25, 1875, the erection of Our Lady of Lourdes Chapel commenced with Father Jachetti as pastor. In 1884, Father Jachetti purchased ground for a cemetery. The growth of the parish prompted the construction of the present, larger church, starting in 1887. On October 5, 1890, a beautiful church of Old World Gothic design was dedicated as Immaculate Conception Church.

The parish embraced German Catholics in Trenton, Hightstown, Perrineville,

Church of the Immaculate Conception, Trenton

Manasquan, Point Pleasant, and Seaside Park, a territory extending as much as fifty miles from Our Lady of Lourdes Chapel. The parish also served as the parent church for other ethnic groups. Gradually, parishes developed throughout the city of Trenton and the entire diocese. Ultimately, Immaculate Conception was designated as a territorial parish for the Chambersburg section of Trenton.

In 1875, four rooms in the friary basement were used for the first classes of a grammar school, staffed by the Sisters of St. Francis of Philadelphia. By 1880, a building of frame construction housed the grammar school classes. In 1906, the grammar school moved to a large stone building. The cornerstone of the new school, a gift from Pope Pius X, was laid by the Most Rev. Dominic Rauter, O.F.M. Conv., minister general of the Franciscans. The school also houses the Sister Georgine Learning Center, started in 1969 to educate exceptional children. In 1898, St. Francis Minor Seminary and College opened, but in 1914 it closed, having been replaced by a seminary in Floyd Knobs, Indiana. In 1921, transformation of the college building began, resulting in Immaculate Conception High School, also staffed by the Sisters of St. Francis. The high school was expanded in 1925 with the construction of Austin Hall. In 1936, the Most Rev. Moses E. Kiley invited the Conventual Franciscan Fathers to conduct a boys' high school. While the girls attended St. Mary Cathedral High School, Immaculate Conception High School evolved into Trenton Catholic Boys High School. Friars and lay

teachers taught the boys. One of the most distinguished students was Edward U. Kmiec, who graduated in 1954 and became the third auxiliary bishop of Trenton in 1982 and the tenth bishop of Nashville, Tennessee in 1992. Trenton Catholic Boys High School closed in June 1962 but contributed much to the people of Trenton and became nationally known for great basketball and high academic standards. Today, the grammar school occupies the high school facilities. Trenton Catholic high school students now attend McCorristin High School, run by St. Anthony's Parish, or Notre Dame High School in Lawrenceville, run by the Sisters of Mercy from North Plainfield.

The Conventual Friars served as chaplains of New Jersey State Prison, Trenton, for many years and of St. Francis Hospital, Trenton, until 1989. In 1874, Father Jachetti and the Sisters of St. Francis of Philadelphia established St. Francis Hospital, now St. Francis Medical Center. The Sisters of St. Francis first resided in St. Francis Hospital; then, a small, rented home; next, the former St. Francis College; and finally, a beautiful convent of their own, since 1949. Father Jachetti helped to establish several parishes during his priesthood, including: Immaculate Conception; St. Stanislaus, Trenton; St. Clare, Florence; Assumption, New Egypt; St. Joseph, Toms River; and St. Peter, Point Pleasant Beach. The Sisters of the Holy Infancy of Jesus came with the Conventual Franciscans to the "burg" in order to serve wherever needed, especially as visiting nurses. They also sheltered unwed mothers. These dedicated German sisters left Chambersburg in 1963.

Rev. Daniel Lyons, O.F.M. Conv., directed the rebuilding of the church's interior in 1960–61. The people of Immaculate began an extensive athletic program for the youth in the 1960's. In 1970, under the guidance of Rev. Timothy Lyons, O.F.M. Conv., further alterations were made to adjust the church for a post Vatican II liturgy. A supplemental food pantry was started in 1972, and a pre-kindergarten program was initiated in the elementary school in 1989.

Pastors: Rev. Peter Jachetti, O.F.M. Conv., 1874–81, 1882–92; Rev. Anselm Auling, O.F.M. Conv.; Rev. Francis Lehner, O.F.M. Conv., 1892–95; Rev. Bonaventure Zoller, O.F.M. Conv., c1896; Rev. Dominic Reuter, O.F.M. Conv.; Rev. Bernardine Ludwig, O.F.M. Conv., c1906; Rev. Peter Scharoun, O.F.M. Conv.; Rev. Alphonse Lehrscholl, O.F.M. Conv., c1921; Rev. Raphael Hubor, O.F.M. Conv.; Rev. Austin Fox, O.F.M. Conv., c1921; Rev. Stephen Korthas, O.F.M. Conv.; Rev. Adolph Bernholz, O.F.M. Conv., 1935–42; Rev. Engelbert Eichenlaub, O.F.M. Conv., 1942–48; Rev. Dominic Rapp, O.F.M. Conv., 1948–51; Rev. Joachim Dunn, O.F.M. Conv., 1951–54; Rev. Alexander Sheridan, O.F.M. Conv., 1954-57; Rev. Daniel Lyons, O.F.M. Conv., 1957–63; Rev. Roger Nelipowitz, O.F.M. Conv., 1963–64; Rev. Timothy Lyons, O.F.M. Conv., 1963–76; Rev. John Larity, O.F.M. Conv., 1976–79; Rev. Casimir Sabol, O.F.M. Conv., 1979–82; Rev. Ernest

Ruede, O.F.M. Conv., 1982–88; Rev. Emmett Carroll, O.F.M. Conv., 1988–91; Rev. Dominic McGee, O.F.M. Conv., 1991–present.

Principals of Immaculate Conception Grammar School: Sr. Ermelina, O.S.F., 1938–41; Sr. Jacoba, O.S.F., 1941–44; Sr. Eutrapin, O.S.F., 1944–50; Sr. Bertilda, O.S.F., 1950–55; Sr. Antonita, O.S.F., 1955–56; Sr. Flacitta Joseph, O.S.F., 1956–63; Sr. Marie Anthony, O.S.F., 1963–72; Sr. Catherine Therese, O.S.F., 1972–75; Sr. Margaret Patrice, O.S.F., 1975–78; Sr. Ann Forrest, O.S.F., 1978–89; Sr. Margaret Appell, O.S.F., 1989–present.

Principals of Immaculate Conception High School: Sr. Mary Ceciliana, O.S.F., 1921–26; Sr. Mary Clavdia, O.S.F., 1926–31; Sr. Mary Calista, O.S.F., 1931–36.

Principals of Trenton Catholic Boys High School: Rev. Roland Gross, O.F.M. Conv., 1936–37; Rev. Francis Edic, O.F.M. Conv., 1937–39; Rev. Dominic Rapp, O.F.M. Conv., 1939–48; Rev. Jerome Dukette, O.F.M. Conv., 1948–49; Rev. Robert Yudin, O.F.M. Conv., 1949–62.

Trenton, Incarnation

Incarnation Parish was established as an independent parish on November 14, 1947. The parish first celebrated mass on June 20, 1948, at the site of the present church in a relocatable steel structure. The church was dedicated in the fall of 1951. The steel building became the Catholic Youth Organization building, serving as a parish center for the next 25 years. Incarnation School was opened in 1956, staffed by the Sisters,

Church of the Incarnation, Trenton

Servants of the Immaculate Heart of Mary, from Immaculata, Pennsylvania. During the school's first year, the freshmen from Cathedral High School attended Incarnation School. A convent and rectory were built in 1960. The church was renovated in 1986 and the school in 1989.

Pastors: Rev. Edward A. McAndrews, 1947–50; Msgr. John J. Endebrock, 1950–65; Msgr. Bernard C. DeCoste, 1965–81; Rev. Hugh F. Ronan, 1981–present.

Principals: Mother Alfreda Hannigan, I.H.M., 1956–63; Sr. Mary Vincentia, I.H.M., 1963–69; Sr. Maria Consilia, I.H.M., 1969–72; Sr. Sponsa Christi, I.H.M., 1972–77; Sr. Miriam Vincent, I.H.M., 1977–81; Sr. Marita Rose, I.H.M., 1981–84; Sr. Marita Celine, I.H.M., 1984–86; Sr. Elizabeth Thomas, I.H.M., 1986–

92; Sr. Rosemary Varra, I.H.M., 1992–present.

Trenton, Our Lady of the Divine Shepherd

In 1941, the Most Rev. William A. Griffin invited the Divine Word Missionaries to staff a Trenton church and specialize in the apostolate to blacks. Very Rev. Francis Humel, S.V.D., provincial of the Eastern Province, assigned Rev. Joseph Ford, S.V.D., to inaugurate the work. A three-story building had been purchased by the diocese. After renovations, Bishop Griffin celebrated Our Lady of the Divine Shepherd's first mass on June 15, 1941. Four sisters of the Third Order of St. Francis arrived on October 22, 1941. A school officially opened in September 1943. The Oblate Sisters of Providence from Baltimore, Maryland, currently staff the school. The Most Rev. George W. Ahr strongly supported the parish over the years. In 1963, Bishop Ahr defended the parish's right to have a school and appointed Rev. Bernard Kowalski, S.V.D., to represent him as spokesman in a civil rights "March on Trenton."

Pastors: Rev. Joseph Ford, S.V.D., 1941–44; Rev. Vincent Smith, S.V.D., 1944–48; Rev. Alexander Leedie, S.V.D., 1948–52; Rev. Peter Heyer, S.V.D., 1952–61; Rev. Bernard Kowalski, S.V.D., 1961–70; Rev. Victor Butler, S.V.D., 1970–78; Rev. Edward McGuinn, S.V.D., 1978–86; Rev. William Hegarty, S.V.D., 1986–92; Rev. Timothy M. Donnelly, S.V.D., 1992–present.

Church of Our Lady of Sorrows, Trenton

Principals: Mrs. Annamarie C. Reilly, present.

Trenton, Our Lady of Sorrows

On Christmas in 1938, Rev. Peter J. Teston from St. Anthony's, Trenton, offered mass at the Mercerville Fire House. A church was completed and the cornerstone was laid by the Most Rev. William A. Griffin on October 18, 1942. Rev. John P. McKeon became pastor of Our Lady of Sorrows Parish when the parish was raised to independent status on June 19, 1943. The priests lived in a rented house until the completion of a rectory in January 1950. Our Lady of Sorrows served both Mercerville and Hamilton Square until the latter formed a parish of its own, St. Gregory the Great, in 1953.

Our Lady of Sorrows School was completed and opened in September 1955. Two houses had been purchased the previous year for the Marianite Sisters of Holy Cross. In 1963, a new convent was finished. The Marianite Sisters of Holy Cross staffed the school from its opening until 1990.

Pastors: Rev. John P. McKeon, 1943–48; Rev. James McGraff, 1948; Rev. Paul Grieco, 1948–67; Msgr. Edward O'Keefe, 1967–86; Rev. Daniel Sullivan, 1986–90; Rev. Ralph Stansley, 1990–93; Rev. Paul Rimassa, 1993–present.

Principals: Sr. Mary Hugh Kelly, M.S.C., 1955–58; Sr. Immaculata Conception O'Dowd, M.S.C., 1958–60, 1962–63; Sr. Mary Carolan, M.S.C., 1960–62; Sr. Anne Therese Keating, M.S.C., 1963–73; Sr. Patricia Schladebeck, M.S.C., 1973–86; Mrs. Mary Henk, 1986–88; Mr. John Flammer, 1988–90; Ms. Mary Helen Ward, 1990–present.

Trenton, Sacred Heart

In 1729, a Jesuit priest, Rev. Joseph Greaton, S.J., arrived in Philadelphia, where he built a chapel, old St. Joseph's, about 1732. He took charge of the West Jersey Mission, extending from Trenton to Cape May. Although the date of the first mass celebrated in Trenton is uncertain, at least by about 1797, priests from Philadelphia were attending to the Catholics of Trenton. In 1803, the Most Rev. John Carroll, bishop of Baltimore, wrote in a letter that he was called to Trenton to settle a disturbance in the congregation. In the following year, services were held in the printing office of Isaac Collins, a Quaker. From 1811 to 1814, mass was celebrated in the home of Mr. John Baptist Sartori (Giovanni Battista

Church of the Sacred Heart, Trenton

Sartori), a consul from the Papal States.

In 1814, Mr. Sartori and Captain John Hargous were instrumental in building New Jersey's first Catholic church, old St. John's, in the city of Trenton. The Most Rev. Michael Egan, bishop of Philadelphia, conducted the dedication ceremony on June 12, 1814. Priests from Philadelphia, especially from St. Augustine's and St. Philip's and occasionally from Holy Trinity, attended to the West Jersey Mission. The Jesuits of old St. Joseph's in Philadelphia cared for the parish from 1833 until 1837, when Rev. Daniel Magorien became resident pastor.

Rev. John P. Mackin, appointed pastor in 1844, erected a larger St. John's Church. The Most Rev. Francis P. Kenrick, bishop of Philadelphia, laid the cornerstone on June 27, 1847. The church was opened for mass on Christmas 1847 and was dedicated on August 27, 1848. In 1851, the older church building was sold to Mr. Peter A. Hargous, son of Captain Hargous, and became the German Catholics' place of worship, St. Francis of Assisium Church. Rev. Anthony Smith opened an asylum for orphaned children, who were cared for by the Sisters of Charity from Convent Station, then part of Madison. In 1866, Father Smith planned for another church, St. Mary's, which he would move to in 1871.

On Sunday evening, September 30, 1883, a devastating fire destroyed the newer St. John's. Rev. Thaddeus Hogan erected in its place the parish's third church, to be called Sacred Heart Church. The cornerstone was laid on August 3, 1884, by the Most Rev. Jeremiah F. Shanahan, bishop of Harrisburg, Pennsylvania, and the church was dedicated on June 30, 1889, by the Most Rev. Michael J. O'Farrell. A rectory and a clubhouse were also constructed about 1889.

During the pastorate of Rev. Frederick J. Halloran from 1934 to 1952, the priests of the parish began serving as chaplains to the Trenton State Prison and the Trenton Fire Department. One of Father Halloran's associates was a newly ordained priest, Rev. John C. Reiss. Father Reiss served the parish from June 10, 1947, until April 12, 1949, and would eventually become the eighth bishop of Trenton. Between 1959 and 1961, Rev. William A. Barron refurbished the school, convent, and rectory.

Additional land was purchased in 1972 from the city of Trenton through an Urban Renewal Program and was transformed into a landscaped parking yard. In 1975, the church's stained glass windows were repaired. Sacred Heart Church was designated as a historic site in 1976. A complete restoration of the church interior began in 1977, and scaffolding filled the church for almost two years. Msgr. Leonard R. Toomey discussed the progress of improvements with a step-by-step description each week. The church hall was renovated in 1985, and the exterior of the church was improved in 1987.

Father Mackin had started a tradition of Catholic education in 1854, opening St. John's School, with Miss Mary Scanlon and Miss Anna McCaffrey as teachers. In 1874, Rev. Patrick Byrne built a new school, and, in 1924, Rev. Peter J. Hart built another new school and a convent. In 1981, ten additional feet of land was purchased to extend the school play yard and driveway, and the windows in the school and convent were replaced in 1982. Sacred Heart School was designated by William Bennett, U.S. secretary of education, as a National School of Excellence in 1988. The Sisters of Charity of Saint Elizabeth from Convent Station have taught in the schools since 1864.

Pastors: Rev. Daniel Magorien, 1837–40; Rev. John C. Gilligan, 1840–44; Rev. John P. Mackin, 1844–59, 1871–73; Rev. James John Joseph O'Donnell, 1859–60; Rev. Alfred Young, 1860–61; Rev. Anthony Smith, 1861–71; Rev. Patrick Byrne, 1873–78; Msgr. Thaddeus Hogan, 1878–1918; Rev. Peter J. Hart, 1918–28; Rev. John H. Sheedy, 1928–34; Rev. Frederick J. Halloran, 1934–52; Rev. John H. Horan, 1952–57; Rev. William A. Barron, 1957–63; Msgr. Maurice P. Griffin, 1963–66; Msgr. Leonard R. Toomey, 1966–92; Rev. Dennis A. Apoldite, 1992–present.

Principals: Sr. Mary Vincent Daly, S.C.; Sr. Mary Gonzaga Carroll, S.C.; Sr. Mary Blanche Donahue, S.C.; Sr. Mary Demetria Callahan, S.C.; Sr. Mary Veronica Johnston, S.C.; Sr. Mary Emeliana McCrudden, S.C.; Sr. Mary Grata Mullaney, S.C.; Sr. Joseph Leo Monahan, S.C.; Sr. Cecilia Dolores O'Rourke, S.C.; Sr. Marie Eustelle Schroth, S.C.; Sr. Grace Carmella Keenan, S.C.; Sr. Mary Miles Sweeney, S.C.; Sr. Helen Aloysius Tracy, S.C.; Sr. Honora Marie Kelley, S.C.; Sr. Agnes Bernadette Morley, S.C.; Sr. Margaret Austina Casey; Sr. Anne Cecilia McGarigle, S.C., 1967–92; Sr. Ruth Edward Durfee, S.C., 1992–present.

Trenton, Saint Anthony

Catholic families of northeast Trenton petitioned the Most Rev. Thomas J. Walsh to establish a parish. On April 15, 1921, St. Anthony's was incorporated and established as an independent parish. Rev. Alphonse Lehrscholl, first pastor, constructed a parish hall in 1921. A combination church/school was built; St. Anthony's Grammar School was opened on November 28, 1921. The Sisters of St. Francis of Philadelphia served the school and later the high school. They moved into a convent in November 1923. Within three years, increasing Catholic popu-

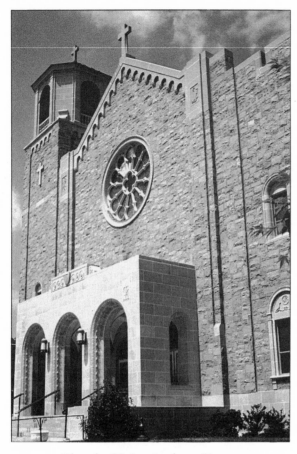

Church of Saint Anthony, Trenton

school was renamed in honor of Msgr. Michael P. McCorristin.

Pastors: Rev. Alphonse Lehrscholl, O.F.M. Conv., 1921–26; Rev. Sylvester Ahlhaus, O.F.M. Conv., 1926–32; Rev. Raymond Werdge, O.F.M. Conv., 1932–35; Msgr. Linus A. Schwarze, 1935–52; Msgr. Michael P. McCorristin, 1952–88; Msgr. James P. McManimon, 1988–92; Rev. Joseph L. Ferrante, 1992–present.

Principals of St. Anthony's Grammar School: Sr. Emily, O.S.F., 1921–31; Sr. Mary Andrew, O.S.F., 1931–32; Sr. Mary Pius, O.S.F., 1932–38; Sr. Mary Lauriana, O.S.F., 1938–44; Sr. Mary Bertilda, O.S.F., 1944–50; Sr. Frumentia, O.S.F., 1950–55; Sr. Adelinda, O.S.F., 1955–61; Sr. John Gabriel, O.S.F., 1961–63; Sr. Manetto, O.S.F., 1963–66; Sr. Gerald Eileen, O.S.F., 1966–72; Sr. Loretta Marie, O.S.F., 1972–80; Sr. Marie Angela Presenza, O.S.F., 1980–present.

Trenton, Saint Francis of Assisium

Rev. John P. Mackin moved the Trenton congregation from the older St. John's Church, built in 1814, to the newer St. John's Church, which opened for mass on Christmas of 1847. Sacred Heart Parish developed from the newer St. John's, while the older St. John's became the place of worship for St. Francis of Assisium Parish.

The older St. John's Church was eventually closed, but Mr. Peter A. Hargous purchased the church building in 1851. The Diocese of Philadelphia, under the direction of the Most Rev. John N. Neumann,

lation required the school to occupy the church section of the building. Under the pastorate of Rev. Sylvester Ahlhaus, O.F.M. Conv., a rectory was built and completed in November 1927. Our Lady of Sorrows Mission was founded in 1938; it separated from St. Anthony's as an independent parish in 1943. The Depression of the 1930s and World War II in the 1940s delayed the erection of a new church building. Finally, the Most Rev. George W. Ahr blessed a new church on June 24, 1951. St. Anthony's High School opened in September of 1962. A convent was constructed by the men of the parish. The grammar school entered a new building in 1968. In 1979, the high

Church of Saint Francis of Assisium, Trenton

The rectory was built in 1867. The present St. Francis Church, which had formerly been used as the Dutch Reformed Church and the Front Street Methodist Church, was acquired in 1869. The exterior of the church was made more imposing with the addition of a tower. In the late 1880s, Rev. Joseph Thurnes improved the interior of the church, including lowering the floor several feet. The church was also refurbished in the early 1930s and in 1967. St. Francis Cemetery was consecrated on October 9, 1870. The parish also cares for Holy Sepulchre Cemetery.

Father Gmeiner purchased two lots and erected a school in 1856. He placed the Sisters of Notre Dame in charge, but they were recalled in 1869. St. Francis Grammar School was started in 1869 in the basement of the second church. The Sisters of St. Francis from Glen Riddle, Pennsylvania, staffed the school until 1879, when the Franciscan Sisters of Syracuse, New York, took charge. A school building was erected in 1876 with a wing used as the convent. About 1910, the Wheeler Home was purchased for use as a convent and was enlarged in 1930. St. Francis School was closed in 1975 because of diminished enrollment.

Pastors: Rev. Joseph Gmeiner, 1853–56, 1859–65; Rev. Anton Muller, 1856–59; Rev. Joseph Storr, 1865–66; Rev. Francis Gerber, 1866–69; Rev. Peter Jachetti, O.F.M. Conv., 1869–74; Rev. Andrew Avellino Szabo, O.F.M. Conv., 1874–82; Rev. Conrad Elison, O.F.M. Conv., 1882–83; Rev. Joseph Thurnes, 1883–1902; Rev. Joseph Rathner, D.D., 1902–26; Rev.

C.Ss.R., and Mr. Hargous agreed to have the celebration of mass in the church building. The Redemptorists of St. Peter's in Philadelphia held services for the mostly German congregation from 1851 until the establishment of the Diocese of Newark in 1853. Rev. Joseph Gmeiner was appointed first pastor on June 21, 1853. Mr. Hargous then presented the building for the sum of one dollar to the Most Rev. James Roosevelt Bayley, first bishop of Newark. King Louis of Bavaria presented a painting of St. Francis to the parish in 1856. Documents verify that the parish name of St. Francis was in use at least as early as 1859. St. Francis of Assisium Parish was incorporated on September 20, 1864.

Bartholomew B. Doyle, 1926–30; Rev. Linus A. Schwarze, 1930–36; Msgr. Francis J. Yunger, 1936–62; Msgr. John C. Reiss, 1962–68; Rev. Frank Porazzo, 1968; Most Rev. John C. Reiss, 1968–80; Most Rev. Edward U. Kmiec, 1980–83; Msgr. John K. Dermond, 1983–present.

Principals: Sr. Mary Hyacintha, O.S.F., c1869; Sr. Mary Josepha, O.S.F., c1879; Sr. Francis Marie, O.S.F., c1910; Sr. Marise, c1975.

Trenton, Saint Hedwig

During the end of the nineteenth century, the first influx of Polish Americans settled in southern Trenton and attended mass at St. Stanislaus Church. As the number of Polish immigrants increased in the northern section of Trenton, the need for a new Polish national parish arose. A petition to the bishop was denied in 1900, but to prove their dedication, Polish Americans in northern Trenton started four different organizations. The Casimir Pulaski Society organized a school and hired a lay teacher. Masses were celebrated in the school by priests from Holy Cross, Trenton. Funds were raised. In 1904, the Most Rev. James A. McFaul accepted a second petition and established the independent parish of St. Hedwig on July 16, 1904. Rev. John Supinski came from Poland to be the first resident pastor. He constructed a church/school and a rectory. Rev. Joseph Urban appealed to have the Felician Sisters staff the school and then added two classrooms to the school. Rev. Julian Zielinski added two more classrooms during his pastorate. He also constructed a school in 1922 and a church in 1924. Rev.

Arthur J. Strenski acquired two homes for use as a new convent. Msgr. Martin J. Lipinski's 35-year pastorate included many accomplishments such as an assessment of the parish's spiritual life, renovations to parish buildings, a new convent in 1941, an increase to the cemetery, and payment of the long-standing debt. Msgr. Francis L. Zgliczynski also improved and renovated parish buildings. In 1987, the youth center was renovated to house the Felician Sisters. A preschool opened in 1989. Recently, a chapel in honor of Our Lady of Czestochowa was constructed in the convent on Indiana Avenue.

Pastors: Rev. John Supinski, 1904–07; Rev. Joseph Regorowicz, 1907–11; Rev.

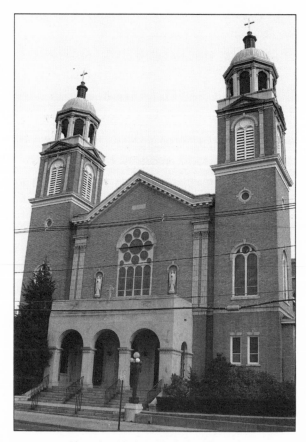

Church of Saint Hedwig, Trenton

Joseph Urban, 1911–13; Rev. Anthony Lechert, 1913–15; Rev. Julian Zielinski, 1915–24; Msgr. Arthur J. Strenski, 1925–34; Msgr. Martin J. Lipinski, 1934–69; Msgr. Francis L. Zgliczynski, 1969–86; Rev. Henry F. Schabowski, 1986–present.

Principals: Sr. Mary Floriana, C.S.S.F., 1911–14; Sr. Mary Pius, C.S.S.F., 1914–17; Sr. Mary Adjuta, C.S.S.F., 1917–20; Sr. Mary Alfreda, C.S.S.F., 1920–21; Sr. Mary Cezarja, C.S.S.F., 1921–24; Sr. Mary Cantalicia, C.S.S.F., 1924–30; Sr. Mary Esperance, C.S.S.F., 1930–33; Sr. Mary Anastasia, C.S.S.F., 1933–35; Sr. Mary Pontia, C.S.S.F., 1935–38; Sr. Mary Lucille, C.S.S.F., 1938–40; Sr. Mary Bogumila, C.S.S.F., 1940–42; Sr. Mary Clara, C.S.S.F., 1942–47; Sr. Mary Agnes, C.S.S.F., 1947–50; Sr. Mary Salesiana, C.S.S.F., 1950–53; Sr. Mary Azelle, C.S.S.F., 1953–59; Sr. Mary Aniela, C.S.S.F., 1959–62; Sr. Mary Joanette, C.S.S.F., 1962–64; Sr. Mary Zephyrine, C.S.S.F., 1964–67; Sr. Mary Antoinette, C.S.S.F., 1967–70; Sr. Mary Lucille, C.S.S.F., 1970–75; Sr. Mary Colette, C.S.S.F., 1976–82; Sr. Mary Alphonse, C.S.S.F., 1982–85; Sr. Mary Theresa Marie, C.S.S.F., 1985–86; Mrs. Sally B. Hammerstone, 1986–present.

Trenton, Saint James

The pastor of St. Joachim's in Trenton, Rev. Edward C. Griffin, took on the responsibility of the Holy Family Mission in 1916. The Most Rev. Thomas J. Walsh, in response to Father Griffin's request for a north Trenton spiritual center, had purchased a former moviehouse to be utilized as a chapel.

Church of Saint James, Trenton

The mission received an administrator early in 1919 and its first pastor, Rev. Louis Guzzardi, on July 3, 1919, thus making Holy Family an independent parish. The necessary funds for the construction of a church building were donated by Mr. and Mrs. Frank Curran. The name of the parish was changed to honor St. James and the Currans' son, James, lost in World War I. The first mass in the church was celebrated on March 19, 1921. A parochial grammar school was dedicated on June 3, 1923, with the Religious Teachers Filippini staffing the school. Father Guzzardi purchased a house for the sisters, converting it into a convent by May 1924. In 1937, the Most Rev. Moses E. Kiley engaged the Trinitarian Fathers to administer to the people. During Rev. Thomas Rocca's pastorate, the parish plant was renovated and the debt reduced.

Also, a new church was dedicated on October 11, 1959. Rev. Peter Pinci renovated the parish buildings without a campaign.

Pastors: Rev. Louis Guzzardi, 1919–28; Rev. Joseph Monaco, 1928–30; Rev. John Prosseda, C.M., 1930–31; Rev. Vincent Fucci, 1931–37; Rev. Thomas Rocca, O.Ss.T., 1937–68; Rev. Peter Pinci, O.Ss.T., 1968–71; Rev. Luke Mennella, O.Ss.T., 1971–74; Rev. Philip Cordisco, O.Ss.T., 1974–85; Rev. Boniface Ruzich, O.Ss.T., 1985–present.

Principals: Sr. Matilde Blasi, M.P.F., 1923–29; Sr. Edvige DeCurtis, M.P.F., 1929–31, 1955–56; Sr. Ines Forchi, M.P.F., 1931–35; Sr. Marietta Rossi, M.P.F., 1935–36; Sr. Rose Melchiorre, M.P.F., 1936–39; Sr. Antoiniette Boccardi, M.P.F., 1939–45; Sr. Pierina Valeriani, M.P.F., 1945–46; Sr. Colombina Musi, M.P.F., 1946–48; Sr. Virginia Bellegia, M.P.F., 1948–49; Sr. Mary Santoro, M.P.F., 1949–55; Sr. Angelina Pecoraro, M.P.F., 1956–61; Sr. Antoinette DiIorio, M.P.F., 1961–64; Sr. Josephine Longo, M.P.F., 1964–66; Sr. Theresa Costantini, M.P.F., 1966–72; Sr. Mary Pezzino, M.P.F., 1972–78; Sr. Veronica Corbet, M.P.F., 1978–81; Sr. Nancy DeAngelo, M.P.F., 1981–present.

Trenton, Saint Joachim

In order to serve the early Italian immigrants moving into Trenton, the Most Rev. Michael J. O'Farrell and the Most Rev. James A. McFaul authorized the establishment of St. Joachim's. In 1901, Rev. Aloysius Pozzi was given the task of founding the first Italian parish in Trenton, and mass was

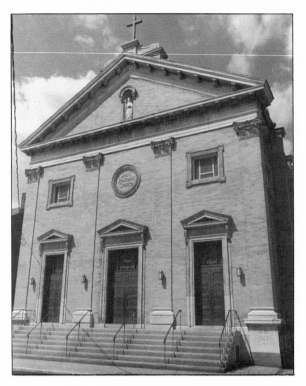

Church of Saint Joachim, Trenton

first celebrated in Centennial Hall. St. Joachim's Church was dedicated on July 16, 1904. Through Monsignor Pozzi's efforts and requests to Pope Pius X, five sisters from the Maestre Pie Filippini in Italy arrived to staff the parish school in September 1910. Starting in 1919, the Most Rev. Thomas J. Walsh assisted in the establishment of an American province of the Religious Teachers Filippini. Rev. Edward C. Griffin, in 1916, initiated a mission in North Trenton that would become St. James. In 1941, the parish's first vocation to the priesthood, Rev. Emilio A. Cardelia, was assigned as St. Joachim's fifth pastor and served for 40 years. A Catholic Lending Library opened in 1943. Major renovations to the church were completed in 1957.

Pastors: Msgr. Aloysius Pozzi, 1901–13; Rev. Edward C. Griffin, 1913–18; Rev. Michael Dilelsi, 1918–19; Rev. Alfonso Palombi, 1920–41; Msgr. Emilio A. Cardelia, 1941–81; Rev. James J. Sauchelli, 1981–present.

Principals: 1910–34: Sr. Concetta Loreti, M.P.F.; Sr. Maria Figliamonti, M.P.F.; Sr. Ninetta Ionata, M.P.F.; Sr. Antonina Belli, M.P.F.; Sr. Assunta Crocenzi, M.P.F.; Sr. Virginia Belleggia, M.P.F., 1934–36, 1944–45, 1964–66; Sr. Teresa Saccucci, M.P.F., 1936–39; Sr. Mary Brenna, M.P.F., 1939–42; Sr. Antoinette Boccardi, M.P.F., 1942–44; Sr. Gilda DalCorso, M.P.F., 1945–47; Sr. Rose Melchiorre, M.P.F., 1947–48; Sr. Assunta Crocenzi, M.P.F., 1948–51; Sr. Ernestine Arcangeli, M.P.F., 1951–57; Sr. Esther DelDuca, M.P.F., 1957–63; Sr. Mary Rotante, M.P.F., 1963–64; Sr. Josephine Longo, M.P.F., 1966–70; Sr. Domenica Troina, M.P.F., 1970–79; Sr. Ginetta Andriola, M.P.F., 1979–84; Sr. Alma Blume, M.P.F., 1984–88; Sr. Roseann Fernandez, M.P.F., 1988–present.

Trenton, Saint Joseph

Rev. Anthony Smith, pastor of St. Mary's Cathedral, recognized the need for a parish in the eastern section of Trenton. In 1881, St. Joseph's Parish began its life under the guidance of Father Smith as a mission of St. Mary's Cathedral. A small school was built in 1881 for the children of the growing number of factory and pottery workers in East Trenton. The Sisters of Charity staffed the school until 1899, when the Sisters of Mercy from North Plainfield took charge and remained until the school closed in 1982.

St. Joseph's was raised to parish status on September 23, 1891, with the appointment of its first resident pastor, Rev. James A. McFaul, later bishop of Trenton. The present church was erected in 1904 and the rectory in 1907. The parish flourished in the first half of the twentieth century, but after World War II, a period of slow decline began as many of the core parishioners moved to the suburbs.

Church of Saint Joseph, Trenton

In recent years, the parish has experienced a marvelous rebirth with the influx of a large number of Hispanic parishioners and the commencement of mass and services in Spanish. St. Joseph's, today, is involved in many outreach efforts for the disadvantaged people of East Trenton, especially in the areas of housing, food distribution, and youth programs. The convent is now the home of some thirty troubled teenagers in a state-sponsored program of rehabilitation. The school is used on weekdays for children with learning disabilities.

Pastors: Rev. James A. McFaul, 1891–93; Rev. John H. Fox, 1893–95; Rev. Michael A. O'Reilly, 1895–98; Msgr. Henry A. Ward, 1898–1934; Rev. Joseph M. Sutliff, 1935–53; Rev. Patrick F. Larkin, 1953–56; Rev. Bernard C. DeCoste, 1956–65; Rev. John L. Callahan, 1965–67; Msgr. William F. Fitzgerald, 1967–73; Rev. William J. Dailey, 1973–present.

Principals: 1881–99: Sr. Mary Celestine, S.C.; Sr. Marietta, S.C.; Sr. Agnes DeSales, S.C.; Sr. Frances Clare, S.C.; Sr. Anina, S.C.; Sr. Mary Baptist Meehan, R.S.M., 1899–1900; Sr. Mary Anthony McNamara, R.S.M., 1900–09, 1915–21; Sr. Mary Veronica Magee, R.S.M., 1909–15; Sr. Mary Helena McHale, R.S.M., 1921–27; Sr. Mary Neri Carroll, R.S.M., 1927–35, 1951–57; Sr. Mary Florian Bloomer, R.S.M., 1935–39; Sr. Mary Hilda Sullivan, R.S.M., 1939–45; Sr. Mary Christopher Ray, R.S.M., 1945–51; Sr. Mary Cosmas Purcell, R.S.M., 1957–60; Sr. Mary Damasa Cosgrove, R.S.M., 1960–66; Sr. Mary Irene Connolly, R.S.M., 1966–69; Sr. Mary Ann Liddy,

Church of Saint Michael, Trenton

R.S.M., 1969–75; Sr. Mary Karina Haywood, R.S.M., 1975–80; Sr. Lee Ann Amico, R.S.M., 1980–82.

Trenton, Saint Michael

The Slovak Catholics of northern Trenton established St. Michael's Society on September 20, 1908. A committee formed in 1919 to petition the bishop for permission to build a church. The Most Rev. Thomas J. Walsh agreed and blessed a completed church in 1921. Several administrators, including pastors from St. Stanislaus and St. Hedwig, both in Trenton, cared for St. Michael's Mission.

The parish received its first pastor, Rev. Ladislas Rakvica, on December 3, 1936. In thanksgiving for his recovery from a near fatal illness, Father Rakvica started the first St. Jude Novena on October 20, 1939. The St. Jude Thaddeus Novena has become a major parish function. The present pastor, Rev. James G. Innocenzi, served as administrator from 1982 until his promotion to pastor on June 6, 1986. Father Innocenzi has focused on improving the liturgy. After renovation of the sanctuary, the Most Rev. John C. Reiss solemnly rededicated St. Michael's Parish on July 12, 1987.

Pastors: Rev. Ladislas Rakvica, 1936–72; Rev. William J. Capik, 1972–74; Rev. Louis W. Kralovich, 1974–82; Rev. James G. Innocenzi, 1986–present.

Church of Saints Peter and Paul, Trenton

Trenton, Saints Peter and Paul

Ss. Peter and Paul Slavonic Catholic Church was established in January 1896 with a temporary church and a rented hall. Rev. Ladislav Neuwirth, first pastor, supervised the building of a new church, completed in 1901. A rectory was built in 1904, and land for a burial ground was purchased in 1906. During his 43-year pastorate, Msgr. Coloman Tomchany contributed greatly to the growth of the parish in terms of improvements and additions to the parish plant. A parish school was organized in 1912, with the Sisters of St. Dominic from Newburgh, New York, as the teaching staff. A new convent was built in 1962, but the school closed in 1975. The present, larger church was finished in 1927, at which time the original church was converted into a parish hall.

Pastors: Rev. Ladislav Neuwirth, 1896–1901; Rev. John Gurecky, 1901–03; Rev. Alexander Kovacs, 1903–05; Msgr. Coloman Tomchany, 1905–48; Rev. Andrew Sakson, 1948–59; Rev. Ladislaus Petrick, 1959–67; Rev. John Spisak, 1968–73; Rev. John Churak, 1973–91; Rev. Andrew Cervenak, 1991–present.

Trenton, Saint Raphael

In 1915, Miss Marian Taylor obtained permission from the Most Rev. James A. McFaul to establish a Sunday school for the children of White Horse, a section of Trenton. Because the room used was unheated, classes taught by Miss Maisie Kolb were discontinued with the advent of cold weather. The

Church of Saint Raphael, Trenton

Sunday school, a discussion meeting in September 1916, and fund-raising resulted in the incorporation of a parish in October 1917. The Rosary-Altar Society (originally Altar Society) formed in August 1917 and started another Sunday school in cooperation with the Mount Carmel Guild. St. Francis, Trenton, and then Sacred Heart, Trenton, attended to the spiritual needs of St. Raphael's until April 1921, when the parish was made a mission of Holy Angels, Trenton. Mass was celebrated in the newly constructed church in October 1921. Finally, on June 18, 1943, the Most Rev. William A. Griffin appointed Rev. Wilfrid B. Emmons as first pastor.

Four Sisters of St. Francis from Glen Riddle, Pennsylvania, started teaching in the parish hall in September 1950. The church/school building opened the following September and was dedicated in December 1951. A house was remodeled in 1950 for use as a convent. The small size of the house necessitated the construction of a larger convent by 1958. A new rectory was completed in 1964, and a parish center was dedicated in June 1974. The church/school building was improved and enlarged in 1984, including the addition of a meeting room, music room, and storage room. The decline in school enrollment and number of teaching Sisters of St. Francis prompted the three sisters to move to a private home. In 1986, the convent was leased to the Contemplative Sisters of the Good Shepherd.

Pastors: Rev. Wilfrid B. Emmons, 1943–71; Msgr. William E. Maguire, 1971–78; Rev. John V. Bowden, 1978–80; Rev. Ernest J. Siska, 1980–present.

Principals: Sr. Mary Rosita, O.S.F., 1951–52; Sr. Mary Ambrose, O.S.F., 1953–69; Sr. Thomas Marie, O.S.F., 1969–70; Sr. Virginia McNiff, O.S.F., 1970–71; Sr. John Agnes, O.S.F., 1971–79; Sr. Mary Louise, O.S.F., 1979–81; Sr. Mary Kennedy, O.S.F., 1981–87; Mr. Joseph McCormack, 1987–90; Sr. Rosemary Bucchi, O.S.F., 1990–present.

Trenton, Saint Stanislaus

The Conventual Franciscan Friars in Trenton began to organize the Polish people at the Immaculate Conception Church between 1888 and 1890. Under the guidance of Rev. Peter Jachetti, O.F.M. Conv., and Rev. Leopold Moczygemba, O.F.M. Conv., St. Stanislaus Bishop and Martyr Church was founded on November 9, 1890. The parish church was dedicated in August 1893. St. Stanislaus's parish school opened in September 1895. St. Stanislaus Parish School is staffed by the Franciscan Sisters of St. Joseph from Hamburg, New York, who have taught in the parish school continuously since 1911. The friars and parishioners have enjoyed a long and harmonious relationship in both building their own parish community and assisting the Conventual Franciscan order. The parish built a pleasant, sisters' convent in 1921 and a new school in 1928. In addition, the parish maintains a cemetery to serve the parish and two homes to serve as organizational meeting places. Polish traditions are still fostered within the life of the parish even though their active expression is limited.

Pastors: Rev. Stanislaus Czelusniak, O.F.M. Conv., 1890–93, 1914–20; Rev. Felix Baran, O.F.M. Conv., 1893–96; Rev. Stanislaus Tarnowski, O.F.M. Conv., 1896–97; Rev. Julian Zielinski, 1897–99; Rev. Matthias Tarnowski, 1899–1901; Rev. Thomas Misicki, 1901–02; Rev. Giles Block, O.F.M. Conv., 1902–11; Rev. Adalbert Topolinski, O.F.M. Conv., 1911–14; Rev. Ignatius Kusz, O.F.M. Conv., 1920–38; Rev. Celement Kacprzynski, O.F.M. Conv., 1938–66; Rev. Peter Bucki, O.F.M. Conv., 1966–73; Rev. Robert Grzybowksi, O.F.M. Conv., 1973–79; Rev. David Stopyra, O.F.M. Conv., 1979–82; Rev. Victor Maksimowicz, O.F.M. Conv., 1982–85; Rev. Raymond Borkowski, O.F.M. Conv., 1985–88; Rev. James Elliott, O.F.M. Conv., 1988; Rev. Blase Wegierski, O.F.M. Conv., 1989–91; Rev. Bonaventure Jezierski, O.F.M. Conv., 1991–present.

Principals: Sr. Mary Colette Hilbert, F.S.S.J., 1895–98; Sisters of St. Francis from Alverno, Pennsylvania, 1898–1903; Sr. Mary Ezra, F.S.C.C., 1903–11; Sr. Mary Elizabeth, F.S.S.J., 1911–19; Sr. Mary Cecelia, F.S.S.J., 1919–32; Sr. Mary Anselma, F.S.S.J., 1932–38; Sr. Mary Ignatia, F.S.S.J., 1938–41; Sr. Mary Salome, F.S.S.J., 1941–43; Sr. Mary Joseph, F.S.S.J., 1943–45; Sr. Mary Sebastian, F.S.S.J., 1945–48; Sr. Mary Seraphine, F.S.S.J., 1948–51; Sr. Mary Margaret, F.S.S.J., 1951–56; Sr. Mary Jean Marie, F.S.S.J., 1956–57; Sr. Mary Susan, F.S.S.J., 1957–64; Sr. Mary Maurice, F.S.S.J., 1964–67; Sr. Mary Angelis, F.S.S.J., 1967–72; Sr. Mary Loretta, F.S.S.J., 1972–76; Sr. Mary Marietta, F.S.S.J., 1976–78; Sr. Mary Barbara Ann, F.S.S.J., 1978–81; Sr. Mary Clementine, F.S.S.J., 1981–87; Sr. Mary Pauline, F.S.S.J., 1987–90; Sr. Mary Rosetta, F.S.S.J., 1990–present.

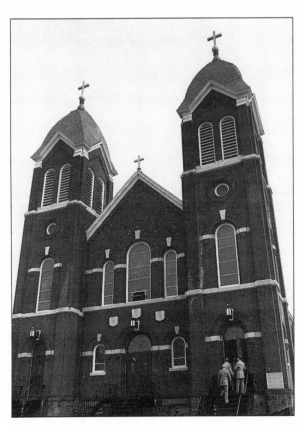

Church of Saint Stanislaus, Trenton

Trenton, Saint Stephen the King

In the nineteenth century, Hungarian immigrants settled in the Trenton area and in 1895 formed the St. Stephen Sick Benefit Society, from which St. Stephen Parish is an outgrowth. St. Stephen's became an independent, national parish by receiving its first pastor, Rev. Francis Eller, on Christmas in 1903. A building was rented to serve as church and rectory. Father Eller initiated construction of a church that would be blessed on May 31, 1905, by the Most Rev. James A. McFaul. Rev. Charles Radoczy purchased the first rectory, a convent, and a clubhouse for the Knights of Columbus. He was transferred before the school was completed. The Daughters of Divine Charity began their labors among the children in September 1914. While Rev. John Szabo was pastor, he bought three buildings for the parish.

During the pastorate of Rev. Julius A. Kish, several significant changes occurred. The old rectory was demolished and rebuilt; a convent was constructed; and a chapel was added to the cemetery. The school, church, convent, and rectory were renovated, repaired, remodeled, or expanded at various times. A parish center was purchased. Several lots were bought in order to expand the parking lot and playground. The houses on the lots were razed.

Rev. Anthony J. Huber purchased more lots for the playground and the construction of a garage. In June 1971, the school closed when the Daughters of Divine Charity left the parish. As a result, many families with children attended territorial parishes

Church of Saint Stephen the King, Trenton

with schools. Remodeling and renovations to parish buildings continued. The cemetery chapel was demolished due to vandalism and disrepair. A suitable memorial to Father Kish was established on its site. In May 1987, the Hungarian Franciscans took over the jurisdiction of St. Stephen's Parish. The school was razed in 1987, and a beautiful prayer garden was created in its place.

Pastors: Rev. Francis Eller, 1903–05; Rev. Charles Radoczy, 1905–20; Rev. John Szabo, 1920–34; Rev. Ladislaus C. Chanyi, 1934–37; Rev. Julius A. Kish, 1937–64; Rev. Anthony J. Huber, 1964–75; Rev.

Ernest J. Siska, 1975–80; Rev. Stephen Getlik, 1980–84; Rev. Kalman Miskolczy, Sch.P., 1984–87; Rev. Dominic L. Csorba, O.F.M., 1987–89; Rev. Eugene A. Lenner, O.F.M., 1989–90; Rev. Ivan J. Paldeak, O.F.M., 1990–92; Rev. Francis Zalewski, 1992–present.

PARISHES OUTSIDE THE CITY OF TRENTON

Allentown, Saint John the Baptist

Masses were celebrated in the Greater Allentown area by Rev. Joseph Biggio, pastor of St. Mary's in Bordentown, as early as 1857. In 1869, Rev. Patrick Leonard purchased Christ Episcopal Church, which would serve as St. John the Baptist's Church for 87 years. Established as an independent parish on July 26, 1878, St. John's received its first pastor, Rev. Joseph Borghese. By 1885, the parish had its own cemetery. Rev. James Hendricks moved the church building adjacent to the rectory during his pastorate. Despite additions and renovations, a new church became needed, was constructed, and was blessed on January 22, 1956. While Rev. Edward Atzert was pastor, he constructed a library and convent.

Several religious communities of women have served the people of Allentown. For a few years, parishioners weekly brought two Sisters of Mercy from St. Mary's Cathedral to teach catechism to the children. From 1948 to 1973, the Daughters of the Heart

Church of Saint John the Baptist, Allentown

of Mary staffed a Regional Catechetical Center in Allentown that provided religious instruction for nearby parishes without parochial schools. The Missionary Sisters of Verona, now called the Comboni Sisters, taught the children from 1974 to 1982. The library is now the center of religious instruction, and the convent houses the Sisters of St. Francis of Philadelphia, who have taught the children since 1982.

Pastors: Rev. Joseph Borghese, 1878–79; Rev. Stanislaus Danielou, 1879–85; Rev. Thomas McCormack, 1885–86; Rev. Michael O'Donnell, 1886–89; Rev. William Lynch, 1889–95; Rev. Thomas McLaughlin, 1895–98; Rev. James Hendricks, 1898–99; Rev. John A. Lawrence, 1899–1904; Rev. Peter Kelly,

1904–05; Rev. Thomas Blake, 1905–14; Rev. John Sheedy, 1914–19; Rev. John Walsh, 1919–21; Rev. Joseph McCorristin, 1921–26; Rev. John McGrath, 1926–29; Rev. Leo Cox, 1929–34; Rev. Thomas Gribbon, 1934–42; Rev. Daniel Sullivan, 1942–47; Rev. Thomas Ridge, 1947–52; Rev. John Callahan, 1952–65; Rev. James Coley, 1965–67; Rev. Thomas Ryan, 1967–69; Rev. Edward Atzert, 1969–82; Rev. Joseph Procaccini, 1982–present.

Asbury Park, Holy Spirit

In 1870, Asbury Park's few Catholics walked or rode in a stage coach six miles to Long Branch if they were to hear Sunday mass. Mr. James A. Bradley, founder of Asbury Park, donated land to the Catholic community. In 1879, Rev. James A. Walsh, pastor of Our Lady Star of the Sea in Long Branch, started construction of a small wooden church, which was dedicated on April 28, 1880.

Rev. Michael Glennon, pastor of St. Catharine's in Holmdel, was transferred to Holy Spirit in 1880, becoming the parish's first resident pastor. As a result, St. Catharine's became a mission of Holy Spirit. From 1880 through 1882, Father Glennon or his assistants celebrated mass in Sea Girt. Successive masses were offered in Spring Lake until 1897, when a resident pastor was assigned to that town. The enormous summer population required several Sunday masses in the old casino, the educational hall, and the old auditorium. In addition, Rev. Thomas Roche started the Bradley Beach Mission in 1907. Father Roche served

Church of the Holy Spirit, Asbury Park

the mission until 1909, when Ascension Mission became an independent parish with a resident pastor. Ground was broken in 1909 for a much larger Church of the Holy Spirit in order to accommodate the growing parish. The church dedication took place July 28, 1912.

A school existed from 1922 through 1980. The Immaculate Heart Sisters from Scranton, Pennsylvania, taught the children until 1928. During the greater portion of the school's history, the Dominican Sisters of Caldwell educated the children.

Pastors: Rev. Michael Glennon, 1880–1900; Rev. Thomas Roche, 1900–41; Rev. John C. Farrell, 1941–53; Rev. Joseph M.

Sutliff, 1953–56; Rev. Francis L. Nolan, 1956–71; Rev. John J. Connelly, 1971–78; Rev. John J. Meehan, 1978–86; Rev. Jerome M. Nolan, 1986–92; Rev. Leonard P. Lang 1992–present.

Principals: 1922–80: Sr. Thomas, Sr. Terisita, Sr. Adele, Sr. Anna Daniel, Sr. Incarnata, Sr. Marjorie, Sr. Elizabeth Mary, Sr. Elizabeth Abernathy, S.S.C.

Asbury Park, Our Lady of Mount Carmel

Our Lady of Mount Carmel Parish's beginning is intimately linked to the influx of Italian Catholic immigrants to the Asbury Park area during the twentieth century's first decade. In 1904, Italians first gathered for worship in a hall belonging to Mr. Dominic Musto. In the following year, a wood-frame church, Whittier Chapel, was purchased and moved to a section west of the railroad known as West Park. Our Lady of Mount Carmel Church achieved parish status on June 25, 1905. The first pastor, Rev. Nicola Leone, and his successors were chosen from among diocesan priests until 1912. Then the Most Rev. James A. McFaul entrusted the parish to the priests of the Trinitarian order, who continue to minister to Our Lady of Mount Carmel Parish to this day. A parochial school was built in 1923, with the Religious Teachers Filippini serving until 1931. Then the Missionary Sisters of the Sacred Heart conducted education at the school through 1934. The school system was operated from 1934 through 1990 by the Sisters, Servants of the Immaculate Heart of Mary. The basement of the school doubled as a place of worship from 1923 until completion of a new church in 1951. The old Whittier Chapel became the church for the parish of St. Peter Claver in 1943. Construction continued around the new Our Lady of Mount Carmel Church, with the present rectory finished in 1956; the new school and convent completed in 1963; and a parish center, housing a gymnasium/auditorium, built in 1969. Marianites of the Holy Cross arrived to assist the parish in 1990, specializing in religious education and remedial studies. The parish, originally categorized as a national parish for Italians, is now composed of persons with a variety of ethnic backgrounds.

Pastors: Rev. Nicola Leone, 1905–06; Rev. Thomas Fusco, 1906–07; Rev. Nicola Rosapepe, 1907–08; Rev. Vincent Pieroni, 1908–12; Rev. Anthony Giovannini, O.Ss.T., 1912–38; Rev. Marcellino Romagno,

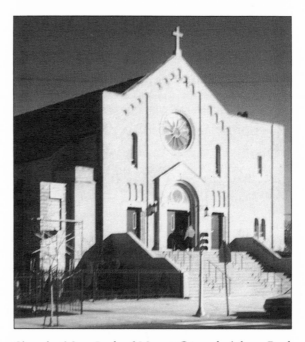

Church of Our Lady of Mount Carmel, Asbury Park

O.Ss.T., 1938–71; Rev. Philip Cordisco, O.Ss.T., 1971–74; Rev. Peter Pinci, O.Ss.T., 1974–78; Rev. David Colella, O.Ss.T., 1978–81; Rev. Gerard Lynch, O.Ss.T., 1981–present.

Principals: Sr. Mary Neuman, I.H.M., 1934–38; Sr. Felix, I.H.M., 1938–40; Sr. Vincentia, I.H.M., 1940–50; Mother Mary Beata, I.H.M., 1950–53; Sr. Georgina, I.H.M., 1953–60; Sr. Daniella, I.H.M., 1960–62; Sr. Catherine Patricia, I.H.M., 1962–67; Sr. John Berchmans, I.H.M., 1967–69; Sr. Rita Halligan, I.H.M., 1969–75; Sr. Anita Brotherton, I.H.M., 1975–83; Sr. Rosemary Casey, I.H.M., 1983–86; Sr. Dolores Banick, I.H.M., 1986–87; Sr. Mary Rita Smith, I.H.M., 1987–90; Mrs. Joyce Brennan, 1990–present.

Asbury Park, Saint Peter Claver

At the beginning of the twentieth century, African-American Catholics who had migrated from Maryland formed a group named the St. Benedict Society. They met in their homes once a week to praise the Lord in prayer and song, to pray the rosary, and to discuss their problems. As the families grew and more black Catholics moved into the area, it was evident that they needed a church. The Most Rev. William A. Griffin invited the Society of the Divine Word to minister to this community. Whittier Chapel, once used by Our Lady of Mount Carmel for mass, became St. Peter Claver Church. The first mass at St. Peter Claver's was celebrated on April 11, 1943, by an African-American priest, Rev. Vincent Smith,

Church of Saint Peter Claver, Asbury Park

S.V.D. The parish was formally established on October 22, 1943. Since its beginning, St. Peter Claver Parish has had a reputation of reaching out to all those in need in the community, feeding the hungry, clothing the naked, and proclaiming the Good News.

Pastors: Rev. John Buys, S.V.D., 1943–50; Rev. Vincent Smith, S.V.D., 1950–52; Rev. Bernard Kowalski, S.V.D., 1952–62; Rev. William Hagen, S.V.D., 1962–64; Rev. Joseph Gunning, S.V.D., 1964–74; Rev. August Langenkamp, S.V.D., 1974–84; Rev. Anthony Hemphill, S.V.D., 1984–86; Rev. John Wadeson, S.V.D., 1986–present.

Atlantic Highlands, Saint Agnes

In 1885, Rev. John J. F. O'Connor, pastor of St. Mary's in New Monmouth, celebrated

Atlantic Highlands's first mass in the Women's Christian Temperance Union. The pastor of Holy Cross in Rumson, Rev. John H. Fox, purchased land for the original church on October 25, 1889. The cornerstone was laid on November 30, 1890, and the church was dedicated on May 31, 1891. Rev. Thomas Roche was assigned as first pastor of St. Agnes Church on October 8, 1891. Our Lady of Perpetual Help, Highlands, was under Father Roche's care until 1898. Father Roche built the first rectory, which would in 1924 become the parish convent, and Rev. William P. Tighe constructed a school, which opened in 1924. Then, as now, the school was staffed by the

Sisters of St. Francis from Stella Niagara, New York. Father Tighe also built the new rectory, but in 1925 he died before inhabiting it. Rev. John P. McKeon built an addition to the convent and set in motion plans for a new church. After Father McKeon's death, the new pastor, Rev. Francis L. Nolan, completed in 1954 the process of erecting the present imposing church. Having outgrown the original structure and other acquired buildings, a new school was constructed and opened for students on November 27, 1967. Renovations to the rectory were completed in April 1986.

Pastors: Rev. Thomas Roche, 1891–1900; Rev. William J. O'Farrell, 1900–1906; Rev. James F. Morrison, 1906–16; Rev. William P. Tighe, 1916–25; Msgr. Michael A. Callahan, 1925–47; Rev. John P. McKeon, 1947–51; Rev. Francis L. Nolan, 1951–56; Msgr. Michael J. Lease, 1956–86; Rev. Joseph J. Farrell, 1986–present.

Principals: Mother Mary Laurissa, O.S.F., 1924–30; Mother Mary Lucille, O.S.F., 1930–36; Mother Mary Rose, O.S.F., 1936–38; Sr. Euphemia, O.S.F., 1938–43; Sr. Christine, O.S.F., 1943–49; Sr. Longina, O.S.F., 1949–55; Sr. Gerald Cleary, O.S.F., 1955–61; Sr. Agnese, O.S.F., 1961–62; Sr. Louis Fahey, O.S.F., 1962–65; Sr. Margaret Mary, O.S.F., 1965–67; Sr. Dolores, O.S.F., 1967–72; Sr. Clement, O.S.F., 1972–74; Sr. Philip, O.S.F., 1974–76; Sr. Joanne Fogarty, O.S.F., 1976–89; Sr. Regina Snyder, O.S.F., 1989–92; Sr. Teresa A. Bruno, S.C., 1992–present.

Church of Saint Agnes, Atlantic Highlands

Avon-by-the-Sea, Saint Elizabeth

Prior to having a church of their own, Catholics of the Avon area attended St. Rose Church in Belmar. St. Rose's pastor, Rev. William J. McConnell, proposed to the Most Rev. James A. McFaul that a mission church be erected in Avon. In the late 1920s, St. Elizabeth's Mission was transferred to Ascension Church, Bradley Beach. In 1930, Rev. Thomas F. Hennessey was appointed St. Elizabeth's first resident pastor. After Father Hennessey built the rectory, the incurred debt engulfed the parish during the Great Depression. The church was taken by the bank because the final payment was not made. Matters worsened when Father Hennessey's failing health required his transfer, and Ascension Church again assumed administration of the parish. The second resident pastor, Rev. Leo Dineen, was appointed on June 7, 1936. On August 22, 1986, a fire destroyed the church interior. The renovated church with a new addition was blessed on August 18, 1988, by the Most Rev. John C. Reiss.

Pastors: Rev. Thomas F. Hennessey, 1930–33; Rev. Leo Dineen, 1936–40; Msgr. Joseph A. Mulligan, 1941–72; Rev. John W. McMullin, 1972–79; Rev. Joseph A. Radomski, 1979–present.

Barnegat, Saint Mary

At the beginning of Rev. Thomas J. Whalen's pastorate at St. Thomas Aquinas, Beach Haven, a mission of that parish began in Barnegat. In 1907, a one-room schoolhouse was purchased for use as a church.

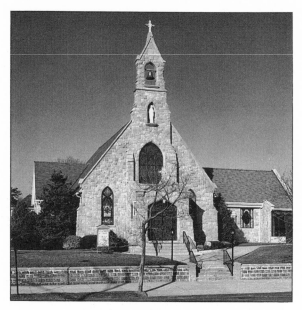

Church of Saint Elizabeth, Avon-by-the-Sea

The mission was named St. Mary's under the title of the Assumption.

Ironically, St. Thomas Aquinas would become a mission of St. Francis of Assisi in Brant Beach, while on November 14, 1947, the Most Rev. William A. Griffin established St. Mary's as an independent parish. Rev. Peter J. Teston was assigned as first resident pastor with the added duties of St. Theresa's Mission in Tuckerton. In 1950, the second pastor, Rev. Alexander A. Burant, was given the responsibility of the Forked River mission, St. Mary's in the Pines. In 1954, St. Theresa's received her own pastor, and in 1961, Father Burant was transferred to the Forked River parish, renamed after St. Pius X.

Rev. Frank J. Janos built the parish center in nearby Manahawkin, dedicated by the Most Rev. George W. Ahr on August 21, 1977. During the pastorate of Rev.

Gerard J. McCarron, a parish cemetery and mausoleum were opened, and a new church and a rectory were erected. The Most Rev. John C. Reiss dedicated the cemetery on October 25, 1985, the church and the rectory on September 8, 1987, and the mausoleum on August 14, 1988.

Pastors: Rev. Peter J. Teston, 1947–50; Rev. Alexander A. Burant, 1950–61; Rev. Casimir J. Przechacki, 1961–66; Rev. Frank J. Janos, 1966–82; Rev. Gerard J. McCarron, 1983–90; Rev. Leonard P. Lang, 1990–92; Rev. Kenard Tuzenear, 1992–present.

Bay Head, Sacred Heart

Before the erection of Sacred Heart Church in 1914, Catholics in Bay Head and Mantoloking traveled by foot, carriage, or trolley to St. Peter's, Point Pleasant Beach. Those in Mantoloking had to sail to Bay Head. The Conventual Franciscans administered to the congregation of Sacred Heart first from St. Peter's and then from St. Catharine's, Seaside Park. However, between 1915 and 1921, the Franciscans did reside in Bay Head, especially during the summer. In April 1927, the church building was moved to its present location. Establishment as an independent parish was achieved on June 11, 1942, with diocesan pastor Rev. William Brennan. Simultaneously, Our Lady of Perpetual Help in Seaside Heights became a mission of Sacred Heart Parish. In 1944, Father Brennan purchased a rectory. Msgr. Joseph T. Casey constructed the parish social hall in 1959. A two-story, six-classroom religious education building was added to the hall in 1976.

Church of the Sacred Heart, Bay Head

Pastors: Rev. William Brennan, 1942–46; Rev. Patrick Larkin, 1946–53; Msgr. Joseph T. Casey, 1953–69; Msgr. James S. Foley, 1969–77; Msgr. William E. Maguire, 1977–present.

Bayville, Saint Barnabas

The rapid growth of St. Joseph's, Toms River, necessitated the creation of a new parish, which now encompasses Bayville, Beachwood, Ocean Gate, Pine Beach, and South Toms River. Rev. Julian C. Rucki arrived as first pastor shortly after St. Barnabas's establishment on September 27, 1966. In October 1969, a parish complex consisting of a church, parish center, and rectory was completed on a 54-acre parcel

Church of Saint Barnabas, Bayville

of land. The Dominican Sisters of New-burgh, New York, stationed at St. Joseph's, educated the parish children weekly between October 1969 and 1980. Sisters of St. Francis and lay volunteers have continued the religious education program. Rev. Thomas Brennan became St. Barnabas's second pastor on October 19, 1979, and immediately initiated development of a multipurpose Spiritual Center. St. Joseph's Parish had started Our Lady of Victory Mission, Ocean Gate, in 1953. St. Barnabas Parish continued the mission until 1987.

Pastors: Rev. Julian C. Rucki, 1966–79; Rev. Thomas Brennan, 1979–present.

Belmar, Saint Rose

Rev. Michael Glennon, pastor of Holy Spirit Church in Asbury Park, started a summer mission for Belmar in 1888. The responsibility for St. Rose Mission was transferred in 1897 to St. Catharine's, Spring Lake. Meanwhile, the chapel was slowly replaced by a frame church. In 1902, Rev. Thomas B.

Nolan was appointed first pastor, making St. Rose's an independent parish. The present rectory was finished in 1905 and a church next to it in 1906.

Rev. William J. McConnell realized his dream for a school as a redbrick building opened for classes on November 13, 1921. A convent for the school's instructors, the Sisters of St. Joseph from Chestnut Hill, Pennsylvania, was occupied late in 1923. High school freshmen were added to the school in 1923, and by 1927, classes at all four levels of high school were made available. A high school building opened in 1957 and a new grammar school building four years later. The grammar school received a principal of its own in 1964; Sr. Marie Emily Smith, S.S.J., remained as principal of the high school.

Church of Saint Rose, Belmar

Father McConnell built the present church of Gothic design in 1926 in order to celebrate mass for the growing parish. With an ever-increasing population, extra masses were offered in McCann's Hotel until the school gymnasium could be used for them.

Pastors: Rev. Thomas B. Nolan, 1902–06; Rev. William J. McConnell, 1906–32; Rev. Frederick S. Kimball, 1932–34; Rev. John F. Welsh, 1934–37; Rev. James P. O'Sullivan, 1937–50; Msgr. Peter J. Teston, 1950–75; Msgr. Alfred D. Smith, 1975–present.

Principals of both St. Rose schools: Sr. Roberta Gleason, S.S.J., 1921–26; Sr. Mary Leo McGlashen, S.S.J., 1927–29; Sr. Vincentia Novoceltzoff, S.S.J., 1929–32; Sr. Davidica, S.S.J., 1933–36; Sr. John Evangelist Meehan, S.S.J., 1937–43, 1949–51; Sr. Lucia Flynn, S.S.J., 1943–49; Sr. Mary of Mercy Seipel, S.S.J., 1951–57; Sr. Joseph Bernard McGoldrick, S.S.J., 1957–63; Sr. Marie Emily Smith, S.S.J., 1963–64.

Principals of St. Rose Grammar School: Mother Theresa Maria, S.S.J., 1964–70; Sr. Helen Miller, S.S.J., 1970–77; Sr. Joseph Eleanor Motzenbacher, S.S.J., 1977–83; Sr. Madeline Franz, S.S.J., 1983–87; Sr. Ann Marian Voloshin, S.S.J., 1987–89; Sr. Dorothy Payne, S.S.J., 1989–present.

Principals of St. Rose High School: Sr. Marie Emily Smith, S.S.J., 1964–65; Sr. Teresa Maria Rudden, S.S.J., 1965–70; Sr. Saint Xavier Roth, S.S.J., 1970–73; Sr. Adele Solari, S.S.J., 1973–79; Sr. Joan Immaculate O'Donnell, S.S.J., 1979–87; Sr. Kathleen Letts, S.S.J., 1987–present.

Berkeley Township, Saint Maximilian Kolbe

The Most Rev. John C. Reiss established St. Maximilian Kolbe Parish on August 16, 1985. A few days later, Rev. Francis E. Santitoro was installed as the founding pastor. Masses were first celebrated at clubhouses in the nine adult communities within the parish boundaries. On June 22, 1987, the parish purchased a 23-acre tract of land for the parish facilities. A building campaign was initiated to raise $6.1 million for a church, chapel, and parish center. Construction began in January 1990. The parish auditorium was completed in August 1991. Masses were celebrated in the parish auditorium until the church was dedicated on October 10, 1992. Plans for a rectory are in progress. The parish also offers weekly mass and other religious services to a 180-bed care center.

Pastor: Rev. Francis E. Santitoro, 1985–present.

Church of Saint Maximilian Kolbe, Berkeley Township

Beverly, Saint Joseph

In the 1840s and 1850s, the Beverly area received an influx of Irish Catholic immigrants, many of whom worked as hired farmhands and day laborers. They had to walk four to five miles to St. Paul's in Burlington for the comfort of mass and the sacraments. In 1856, at Mr. James Cain's invitation, Rev. Joseph D. Bowles, pastor of St. Paul's, celebrated the first mass in Beverly. In a building purchased from the Baptist congregation, a mission of St. Paul's started on May 28, 1857. From 1874 through 1883, the Franciscan Friars of Trenton carried out the functions of St. Joseph's Mission. A plot of land was purchased in 1881, and a new church was erected by Christmas 1882. On October 25, 1883, the Most Rev. Michael J. O'Farrell raised St. Joseph's to parish status and installed Rev. Matthew Gibson as first pastor. A one-room school run by one nun operated between 1867 and 1883. On September 4, 1963, another school began, with the Sisters of St. Joseph of Peace from Englewood Cliffs teaching. On April 5, 1964, the Most Rev. George W. Ahr celebrated the first mass in a new church. A new school was completed in August 1967, and the old church was razed during the same year.

Pastors: Rev. Matthew Gibson, 1883–88; Rev. James McKernan, 1888–91; Rev. Thomas Degnan, 1891; Rev. John M. McCloskey, 1891–94; Rev. Simon B. Walsh, 1895–1902; Rev. Peter Dernis, 1902–16; Rev. James J. McKeever, 1916–30; Rev. William J. Fahey, 1930–34; Rev. Walter T. Doyle, 1934–48; Rev. James A. McKenzie,

Church of Saint Joseph, Beverly

1948–49; Rev. James B. Coyle, 1949–56; Rev. James F. Murphy, 1956–69; Rev. Francis Porazzo, 1969; Rev. John E. Sullivan, 1969–72; Rev. William E. Barna, 1972–86; Rev. Joseph McHugh, 1987–90; Rev. G. William Evans, 1990–present.

Principals: Sr. Regina Agnes, C.S.J.P., 1963–65; Sr. Declan, C.S.J.P., 1965–67; Sr. Michael James, C.S.J.P., 1967–68; Sr. Mary, C.S.J.P., 1968–69; Sr. Margaret Ann, C.S.J.P., 1969–70; Sr. Kathleen Flynn, C.S.J.P., 1970–76; Miss Carol Cuccilo, 1976–79; Mr. Robert Cunningham, 1979–81; Sr. Kathleen Doyle, C.S.J.P., 1981–85; Mr. James Field, 1985–86; Miss Florence M. Morton, 1986–89; Miss Joan Simpson, 1989–92; Mr. Robert DiGiacomo, 1992–present.

Bordentown, Saint Mary

Originally, the Catholics of Bordentown and White Hill traveled to Trenton for the celebration of mass. Joseph Bonaparte, ex-king of Spain, came to Bordentown in 1818, purchased 1,400 acres of woodlands and clearing, and built a mansion upon a hilltop. The Bonapartes occasionally received priests who offered mass in the mansion's chapel. Mass was also said for a number of years in the homes of Mr. John P. Flynn and Mr. Daniel Graham, who both lived in White Hill.

Starting in October 1837, Rev. Daniel Magorien, pastor of old St. John's in Trenton, regularly offered mass in Bordentown

Church of Saint Mary, Bordentown

and White Hill homes. The pastors of St. John's continued to care for the mission. Bordentown's first Catholic church was erected in 1842 and received several additions to accommodate the increasing population. The pastors of St. Paul's in Burlington cared for St. Mary's Mission from 1845 until the establishment of St. Mary's as an independent parish in 1854, with Rev. Joseph D. Bowles as first resident pastor.

Prior to 1862, Rev. Joseph Biggio had built the first school, originally staffed by lay teachers. The Sisters of Mercy, originally from Manchester, New Hampshire, arrived on September 24, 1873, to educate the children. A new church was dedicated in October 1872 by the Most Rev. William O'Hara, bishop of Scranton, Pennsylvania. A new rectory was built close to the church. The old church became a school, and the old rectory became a convent for the sisters. During his pastorate, Rev. Patrick F. Connolly enlarged the convent. He erected for the parish the Academy of St. Joseph, finished in 1885. The sisters moved into a new convent in 1886; the Poor Clare's inhabited the old convent in 1908. Father Connolly constructed a new parochial school in 1888. The parish school, like the parish, is currently named in honor of St. Mary.

During his pastorate, Rev. John Sweeney renovated the church, including installation of side altars and painting of the church for the first time in fifty years. Rev. James F. McGrath purchased new properties and acquired buildings for conversion into classrooms. Plans were made and carried out during Rev. Gerald T. Celentana's pastorate to refurbish the school and auditorium. In 1969, Rev. Edward D. Strano came to St. Mary's as associate pastor. He organized the youth of the parish, initiating Catholic Youth Organization activities. Priests from Divine Word Seminary have assisted St. Mary's with masses and youth activities. Parishioners are currently in the midst of a major project to renovate their beloved church.

Pastors: Rev. Joseph D. Bowles, 1854–56; Rev. Joseph Biggio, 1857–66; Rev. John P. Mackin, 1866–69; Rev. Patrick Leonard, 1869–76; Rev. Patrick F. Connolly, 1876–97; Rev. Robert E. Burke, 1897–98; Rev. Dennis J. Duggan, 1898–1914; Rev. John Sweeney, 1915–29; Rev. Edward J. Whalen, 1929–44; Rev. Francis Lyons, 1944–49; Rev. John Horan, 1949–53; Rev. James F. McGrath, 1953–67; Rev. Richard J. McEwan, 1968; Rev. Gerald T. Celentana, 1969–90; Rev. Michael J. Burns, 1990–present.

Principals: Mother Mary Joseph, R.S.M., c1873; Sr. Mary Ursala, R.S.M., c1904; Sr. Mary Thecla, R.S.M.; Sr. Mary Lawrence Sweeney, R.S.M., 1908–c1914; Sr. Mary Assisium Thompson, R.S.M., c1914–20; Sr. Mary Bernardine Kirk, R.S.M., 1920–21; Sr. Berchmans Mary O'Neill, R.S.M., 1925–31; Sr. Mary Ligouri Daley, R.S.M., 1931–37; Sr. Mary Cyprian O'Connor, R.S.M., 1937–38; Sr. Mary Lucille Cairns, R.S.M., 1938–44; Sr. Mary Thomasina Brennan, R.S.M., 1944–48; Sr. Mary Laurentine Bracken, R.S.M., 1948–54; Sr. Mary Michaeli Burns, R.S.M., 1954–57; Sr. Mary Mechtilde Bulfin, R.S.M., 1957–63; Sr. Mary Cordelia Kelly, R.S.M., 1963–69;

Sr. Mary Hedwig Grudziecka, R.S.M., 1969–73; Sr. Mary Peter Damian Mitchell, R.S.M., 1973–76; Sr. Helen Miller, R.S.M., 1976–89; Mrs. Patricia McEwan, 1989–90; Sr. Joyce Marie Riley, R.S.M., 1990–present.

Bradley Beach, Ascension

Rev. Thomas Roche, pastor of Holy Spirit Church in Asbury Park, formed Ascension Mission in 1907. The church property was donated by Mr. James Bradley, founder of Bradley Beach. On August 2, 1909, when Ascension Church was established, Rev. John O'Hara was appointed pastor. He

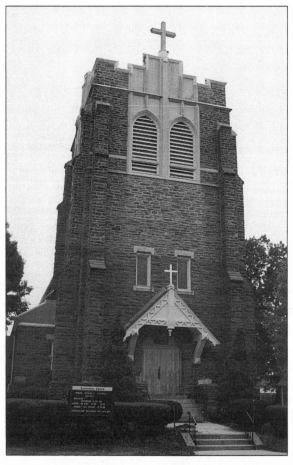

Church of the Ascension, Bradley Beach

Faith in Action in the Diocese of Trenton

served in that capacity for 62 years, retiring at age 92. Father O'Hara also administered to St. Elizabeth's in Avon-by-the-Sea for seventeen years.

A church was dedicated in 1911 and a rectory constructed in 1913. In 1915, the church basement was converted to a recreation hall. Then, in 1943, the recreation hall was converted into a chapel to accommodate the great number of people attending mass, especially during the summer. It served as a chapel until 1986. In 1989, the church basement was restored to its original purpose as a recreation hall.

With the completion of a parish center, social activities resumed in 1963. On November 8, 1967, the church was gutted by fire. Many worried about 87-year-old Msgr. John O'Hara's reaction. Two days later, in its second article on the fire, the *Asbury Park Press* quoted Monsignor O'Hara's response: "I will restore it." Mass was celebrated in the parish center until April 19, 1969, when restoration was finished. Rev. Samuel C. Constance, as second pastor, almost immediately began improvements to the parish's buildings. In 1989, Rev. James J. Brady had the church painted and returned to its original beauty.

Pastors: Msgr. John O'Hara, 1909–72; Rev. Samuel C. Constance, 1972–84; Rev. Michael S. Vona, 1984–87; Rev. James J. Brady, 1987–present.

Brant Beach, Saint Francis of Assisi

As early as 1885, masses were celebrated in private homes in Beach Haven by priests from the Camden/Philadelphia area. Rev.

Church of Saint Francis of Assisi, Brant Beach

Thomas Healy, pastor of St. Mary of the Lake in Lakewood, assumed charge of St. Thomas Aquinas Mission on July 9, 1893. Several priests from various parishes cared for the mission until the appointment of Rev. William A. Gilfillan as first resident pastor in June 1905. St. Thomas Aquinas Parish included missions in Surf City, Barnegat, and, later, Tuckerton. Increasing summer populations necessitated the offering of masses in theaters in Beach Haven and Brant Beach. St. Thomas Aquinas Parish was transferred to the care of the Franciscans of Holy Name Province in June 1928. Extensive building and expansion occurred during Rev. Terence McNally's pastorate. In 1958, St. Francis of Assisi Church was constructed in Brant Beach. A new friary was finished in 1962. In 1965, new churches were completed for St. Thomas Aquinas, Beach Haven, and St. Thomas of Villanova, Surf City. A pastoral team, led by coordinators, administered to the parish from 1970 to 1990. In 1971, St. Francis of Assisi Church and St. Thomas Aquinas

Church of the Epiphany, Bricktown

Church switched roles. St. Francis of Assisi was established as the main, independent parish, and St. Thomas Aquinas became one of the missions. St. Francis Community Center opened in 1972, and St. Clare's Mission in Loveladies was founded in 1978.

Pastors: Rev. William A. Gilfillan, 1905–06; Rev. Thomas J. Whelan, 1907–13; Rev. Francis J. Quinn, 1913–16; Rev. Simon B. Walsh, 1916; Rev. Michael DiIelsi, 1917–19; Rev. Joseph Verheyes, 1919–20; Rev. Neil A. Mooney, 1920–25; Rev. Cornelius B. Reagan, 1925–28; Rev. Seraphin Geegan, O.F.M., 1928–34; Rev. Paul Neville, O.F.M., 1934–41; Rev. James Keenan, O.F.M., 1941–44; Rev. Ivo McElroy, O.F.M., 1944–49; Rev. Bonaventure McIntyre, O.F.M., 1949–55; Rev. Terence McNally, O.F.M., 1955–67; Rev. Edward Sullivan, O.F.M., 1967–70; Rev. Donnon McNally, O.F.M., 1970–85; Br. Christopher Coccia, O.F.M., 1985–88; Rev. Vincent Licursi, O.F.M., 1988–89; Br. Alan A. Thomas, O.F.M., 1989–90; Rev. Theodore Cavanaugh, O.F.M., 1990–present.

Bricktown, Epiphany

On November 9, 1973, the Most Rev. George W. Ahr established a new parish and purchased a site for the construction of a parish center. Saturday masses were celebrated in St. Paul's United Methodist Church, the first mass on December 4, 1973. Lanes Mill School was the location for Sunday masses and preschool religious instruction. A home was purchased in March 1974 for the pastor, parish offices, confessions, and daily mass. Religious education classes began in October 1974 at Veteran's Elementary School. In 1977, religious instruction took place in parishioners' homes for groups of ten. Construction of a church started in September 1980, with a dedication ceremony held on January 3, 1982. In September 1989, religious education classes were moved to Veteran's Memorial Middle School.

Pastors: Msgr. Edward A. Reissner 1973–81; Rev. Robert J. Schecker, 1981–92; Rev. John V. Bowden, 1993–present.

Bricktown, Saint Dominic

Tremendous population growth in Bricktown and Point Pleasant prompted the Most Rev. George W. Ahr to establish St. Dominic's Parish on June 18, 1962. St. Mary's Academy, Lakewood, accommodated the first pastor, Rev. John Ozarowski, until the rental of a house in Point Pleasant. The house served as living quarters, chapel, parish offices, and meeting place. The first mass was celebrated in 88 Bowling Lanes, Point Pleasant. Thereafter, mass was offered at 88 Bowling Lanes, Point Pleasant Boro

Church of Saint Dominic, Bricktown

Firehouse #2, or Midstreams School in Bricktown. A large church, a 16-classroom school, an all-purpose room, and a rectory were blessed and dedicated in 1965. The Bernardine Sisters from Villanova, Pennsylvania, lived in the school's second floor until a home was purchased. A kindergarten wing and a new parish center were built in 1983. The school has expanded from grades 1 through 3 to kindergarten through grade 8. Construction of a five-classroom addition was dedicated on January 29, 1992. The Bernardine Sisters withdrew from the school in 1992 and were replaced by the Sisters of Mercy from North Plainfield. Because of continued growth, St. Martha's Church, Point Pleasant, was separated from St. Dominic's in 1972, and Epiphany Church of Bricktown was established in 1973.

Pastors: Rev. John Ozarowski, 1962–71; Rev. Edward Bumbera, 1972–77; Rev. John J. Gibbons, 1977–present.

Principals: Sr. Marianne Paczura, O.S.F., 1965–71; Sr. Mary Amandine Chytrowski,

O.S.F., 1971–77; Sr. Mark Ann Florkiewicz, O.S.F., 1977–80; Sr. Joan Eileen Christian, O.S.F., 1980–83; Sr. David Ann Niski, O.S.F., 1983–87; Sr. Maria James Riedel, O.S.F., 1987–92; Sr. Mary Jane Veldof, R.S.M., 1992–present.

Bricktown, Visitation

In the 1930s, Rev. John F. Baldwin, pastor of St. Mary of the Lake in Lakewood, sent priests to celebrate mass in Bricktown, first in an area store and later in the Cedarwood Park Country Club House. A chapel was dedicated in June 1938. Rev. Charles A. Bulla was appointed first pastor when Visitation was established on June 17, 1948. The basement was used for larger congregations, and in 1960, a huge circus tent was purchased for summer crowds. The first mass in the present church was celebrated on June 28, 1964. The old church became

Church of the Visitation, Bricktown

the Catholic Youth Organization Center. Rev. Francis V. Piccolella secured use of Emma Havens Young School for Confraternity of Christian Doctrine classes for the more than 1,000 children attending public schools. Rectories have been located in Kingfisher Cove, Cedarwood Park, and Metedeconk Pines. The present rectory, dedicated in 1970, is adjacent to the church.

In 1985, a group of high school students and a couple of advisers discussed enhancements to the religion classes. In September, after extensive planning, Visitation A.C.T. was formed. Many related groups have developed, including a junior high group, a young adult group, a separate music ministry, a youth and family mass, and a central governing body: IMPACT Ministries. Fund-raisers for the needy, service to the suffering, retreats, and seminars are among the many youth activities.

Rev. William M. Dunlap has renovated the parish plant during his pastorate, including adding a library.

Pastors: Rev. Charles A. Bulla, 1948–57; Rev. John A. Spisak, 1957–67; Rev. Francis V. Piccolella, 1967–90; Rev. William M. Dunlap, 1990–present.

Browns Mills, Saint Ann

In November 1905, Rev. William A. Gilfillan, pastor of St. Thomas Aquinas Church in Beach Haven, founded St. Ann's as a mission church. Land was purchased in October 1934 for the first church of frame construction. Sacred Heart in Mount Holly and St. Mary's of the Lakes in Medford

Church of Saint Ann, Browns Mills

cared for the mission church. However, in September 1947, St. Ann's was established as an independent parish, with Rev. Eugene B. Kelly as first resident pastor. In 1950, the church was moved to Trenton Road with a rectory built alongside it. The original church became the parish center upon completion of a new church in 1986. Originally known as St. Ann's in the Pines, Rev. Harry E. Cenefeldt changed the parish name in 1979.

Pastors: Rev. Eugene B. Kelly, 1947–48; Rev. Thomas A. Kane, 1948–51; Rev. Walter J. Radziwon, 1951–59; Rev. Joseph A. Rucinski, 1959–65; Rev. Thomas B. Dennen, 1965–69; Rev. Vincent J. Nebus, 1969–78; Rev. Harry E. Cenefeldt, 1978–81; Rev. John V. Bowden, 1981–89; Rev. Daniel G. Cahill, 1989–present.

Burlington, All Saints

On March 10, 1910, the Most Rev. James A. McFaul transferred Rev. Andrew Szostakowski to Burlington, establishing

Church of All Saints, Burlington

All Saints Parish. Two days later, on Palm Sunday, Father Szostakowski offered the Polish parish's first mass in St. Paul's Church, Burlington. A Quaker meetinghouse was rented for the celebration of mass from April 9, 1910, until it was purchased on September 10, 1910. After the completion of additions in 1911, the Most Rev. James A. McFaul blessed and dedicated the church on November 29, 1911. A house adjacent to the church was purchased on December 2, 1912, and the present rectory was bought on June 9, 1917. A two-story combination church and school was built between July 1924 and June 1927. The Bernardine Sisters of Reading, Pennsylvania, opened the school on September 12, 1927, and staffed the school until 1990. A house was purchased on May 10, 1936, for use as a convent. Extensive repairs were conducted by the fourth pastor, Rev. Stephen A. Buszka. For the growing congregation, Father Buszka constructed a larger church, solemnly blessed and dedicated by the Most Rev. George W. Ahr on March 8, 1959. The school annex opened on September 6, 1978, providing separate classrooms for each grade.

Pastors: Rev. Andrew Szostakowski, 1910–29; Rev. Walter Urbanik 1929–35; Rev. Matthew Konopka, 1935–44; Rev. Stephen A. Buszka, 1944–73; Rev. Martin M. Komosinski, 1973–present.

Principals: Sr. Bufemia, O.S.F., 1927–28; Sr. Clara, O.S.F., 1928–29; Sr. Narcisa, O.S.F., 1929–32; Sr. Cajetana, O.S.F., 1932–36; Sr. Valeria, O.S.F., 1936–37; Sr. Bogumila, O.S.F., 1937–39; Sr. Ludwina, O.S.F., 1939–45; Sr. Lauretta, O.S.F., 1945–49; Sr. Rita, O.S.F., 1949–50; Sr. Edward, O.S.F., 1950–52; Sr. DePaul, O.S.F., 1952–55; Sr. Antoinette, O.S.F., 1956–62, 1966–67; Sr. Bertrand, O.S.F., 1962–63; Sr. Cecilian, O.S.F., 1963–64; Sr. Rose Viterbia, O.S.F., 1964–66; Sr. Symphronia, O.S.F., 1967–68; Sr. Francis Solaine, O.S.F., 1968–70; Sr. Floria, O.S.F., 1970–76; Sr. Mary Francis, O.S.F., 1976–77; Sr. Anne, O.S.F., 1977–83; Sr. Steven Marie, O.S.F., 1983–86; Sr. Marie Janeen, O.S.F., 1986–87; Sr. Roseangela, O.S.F., 1987–90; Mrs. Joann Tier, 1990–present.

Burlington, Saint Paul

Mr. John Tatham, a resident of the city of Burlington, was appointed governor of West Jersey shortly after the death of his predecessor, Mr. Barclay, on October 3, 1690. Mr. Tatham's mansion was known as a resting stop for Catholic priests traveling along their route between Baltimore and New York City. Mass was probably celebrated in his mansion in secret, to avoid confrontation.

Rev. John Ury was very cautious about not being publicly seen in priestly garb. Yet, in 1741 in New York City, the several-month-long, so-called Negro Plot resulted in Rev. Ury's hanging, primarily for being a priest. For a year, starting on June 18, 1739, he had resided in Burlington as a teacher. Whether or not John Ury was a priest has been disputed. Nevertheless, his death illustrates the severity of anti-Catholicism during the time period.

In 1771, Rev. Ferdinand Steinmeyer, S.J. (Father Farmer), a Jesuit priest from St. Joseph's in Philadelphia, visited Burlington. His baptismal register indicates that he ministered to the scattered Catholics there.

The Revolutionary War Barracks, location of the original church, was the site of a few English military barracks, including a hospital. In 1778, Rev. Lotbinier, a Canadian priest, was brought from Canada as chaplain for the king's Catholic soldiers. In 1787, Rev. William O'Brien visited Burlington, and, in 1798, Rev. La Grange also visited the city.

In 1798, the Augustinian Fathers from St. Augustine's in Philadelphia attended to the Catholics in the West Jersey Mission, including Burlington. The Augustinians probably retained charge of Burlington until 1833, when the Jesuits of St. Joseph's in Philadelphia attended to both Trenton and Burlington.

Church of Saint Paul, Burlington

Secular clergy claimed Burlington in 1837 when Rev. Daniel Magorien assumed the pastorate of old St. John's in Trenton and the care of the West Jersey Mission. Rev. John P. Mackin, appointed pastor of old St. John's in 1844, was assisted the following year, when Rev. Jeremiah Ahearn was appointed the first resident pastor of St. Paul's in Burlington. Father Ahearn purchased the Revolutionary War Barracks, using the old English military buildings as a church and rectory. On August 26, 1849, the Most Rev. Francis P. Kenrick, bishop of Philadelphia, confirmed twenty in the church of St. Paul.

Rev. Joseph D. Bowles, pastor of St. Mary's in Bordentown, moved to Burlington in June 1856 to become pastor of St. Paul's. During his pastorate, Father Bowles purchased the Humphrey property for a rectory and remodeled the barracks into the original church. One wall of the original church, still standing, was part of one of the barracks. In 1856, land for St. Paul Cemetery was acquired, and, in 1883, ground was obtained for Laurel Hill Cemetery.

In 1870, Rev. Michael Kirwan opened a Catholic school in the basement of the church. The first teacher was Mr. Patrick P. Cantwell. Lay teachers staffed the school until the arrival of the Sisters of St. Francis. In 1886, the Sisters of Mercy from North Plainfield came to teach religion. They have served the parish ever since. Rev. John J. Griffin improved the school in 1892. Rev. Henri Russi constructed a school in 1904 and purchased the Binnoy homestead for use as a convent in 1916. Rev. Joseph B. Miller built a new, modern school complex in 1960.

In 1916, Father Russi purchased the Budd mansion for use as a rectory. A church of medieval style and granite construction was erected in 1925. Rev. Bernard C. DeCoste renovated the church in 1952. During Rev. Joseph B. Miller's pastorate, an auditorium was constructed shortly after the erection of the school. The old convent was sold, and a new, smaller convent was built. Father Miller's devotion to the Blessed Mother was revealed in the practice of saying the rosary every evening in the church at seven o'clock. The present pastor, Rev. James H. Dubell, bought the old convent back and converted it into meeting rooms for the senior citizens of the parish. He also completely renovated the rectory, the former Budd mansion.

Pastors: Rev. Jeremiah Ahearn, 1845–49; Rev. Hugh Lane, 1849–53; Rev. Hugh Kenny, 1853–55; Rev. Benjamin F. Allaire, 1855–56; Rev. Joseph D. Bowles, 1856–67; Rev. James J. McGahan, 1867–68; Rev. Michael Kirwan, 1868–76; Rev. Secundinus Pattle, 1876–85; Rev. Patrick Treacy, 1885–92; Rev. John J. Griffin, 1892–99; Rev. Henri Russi, 1899–1934; Rev. Francis Sullivan, 1934–41; Rev. William Margerum, 1941–42; Rev. Lewis B. Hayes, 1942–51; Rev. Bernard C. DeCoste, 1951–56; Rev. Joseph B. Miller, 1956–87; Rev. James H. Dubell, 1987–present.

Principals: Sr. Mary Xavier Burke, O.S.F., 1884–86; Sr. Mary Patricia Dullea, R.S.M., 1886–89; Sr. Mary Stanislaus Dillon, R.S.M., 1893–98; Mother Mary Joseph O'Donohoe, R.S.M., 1898–1900; Sr. Mary Emmanuel McNamara, R.S.M., 1900–1907, 1913–19; 1925–31; Sr. Mary Thomas Hogan, R.S.M., 1907–13, 1919–25, 1931–34; Sr. Mary Helena McHale, R.S.M., 1934–37; Sr. Mary Hildegarde McHale, R.S.M., 1937–40; Sr. Mary Ligouri Daley, R.S.M., 1940–45; Sr. Mary Berenice McKinnon, R.S.M., 1945–51; Sr. Mary Fidelis McLaughlin, R.S.M., 1951–57; Sr. Mary Madelon McCrea, R.S.M., 1957–63; Sr. Mary Rosario Coyle, R.S.M., 1963–70; Sr. Mary Margo Kavanaugh, R.S.M., 1970–76; Sr. Marianne Chorba, R.S.M., 1976–79; Sr. Mary Laboure Cramer, R.S.M., 1979–89; Sr. Mary Peter Damian Mitchell, R.S.M., 1989–present.

Cinnaminson, Saint Charles Borromeo

Cinnaminson Catholics were a part of Sacred Heart Parish, Riverton, until September 22, 1961, when the Most Rev. George W. Ahr established the territorial parish of St. Charles Borromeo. The all-purpose room of Cinnaminson Memorial School was the site for St. Charles Borromeo Parish's first mass, on October 8, 1961. The first pastor, Rev. Francis V. McCusker, moved into the rectory on November 11, 1961, and constructed a combination church, school, and auditorium. The T-shaped building was blessed in November 1963. The following September, just after four Sisters of Mercy from North Plainfield arrived in August, St. Charles Borromeo School opened. In 1981, Marsh Hall was erected to handle some of the many parish organizations' meetings.

Pastors: Rev. Francis V. McCusker, 1961–70; Rev. Robert P. Murray, 1970; Msgr. Carl A. Wagner, 1970–87; Rev. Gregory D. Vaughan, 1987–92; Rev. Thomas J. Triggs, 1992–present.

Principals: Sr. Mary Wendelin, R.S.M., 1964–70; Sr. Joyce Buscku, R.S.M., 1970–71; Sr. Mary Lucy, R.S.M., 1971; Sr. Margaret Russell, R.S.M., 1971–88; Sr. Eileen McNamee, R.S.M., 1988–89; Mrs. Geraldine Murphy, 1989–present.

Colts Neck, Saint Mary

Catholics of Colts Neck were served by clergy from St. Paul's in Princeton during the 1850s and 1860s. Priests from St. James in Red Bank visited Colts Neck for several

Church of Saint Charles Borromeo, Cinnaminson

months prior to the establishment of St. Rose of Lima Church in Freehold. During three different periods between 1871 and 1930, Msgr. Frederick Kivelitz, first pastor of St. Rose's, was in charge of St. Mary's Mission. St. Mary's was an independent parish for a few months when Rev. Thomas Roche was resident pastor. Starting in 1905 and for eleven years, St. Mary's was cared for by St. Dorothea's, Eatontown. Monsignor Kivelitz had built the original church in

Church of Saint Mary, Colts Neck

1879. St. Rose's second pastor administered to St. Mary's Mission during the 1930s. From 1939 to 1972, St. Catherine of Siena in Farmingdale was responsible for St. Mary's.

In February 1972, Rev. Raymond Griffin, former pastor of St. Catherine's, was transferred to St. Mary's as second resident pastor. He had initiated construction of the church that stands today while still pastor of St. Catherine's. Father Griffin's successor, Rev. William J. Bausch, has continued to expand St. Mary's, with new offices, a parish house, a Spiritual Center, and a meditation garden and grotto.

Pastors: Rev. Thomas Roche, 1890–91; Rev. Raymond Griffin, 1972–73; Rev. William J. Bausch, 1973–present.

Deal, Saint Mary of the Assumption

Prior to having a church in Deal, Catholics traveled to St. Michael's in Long Branch or Holy Spirit in Asbury Park for mass. A committee of summer residents in the late summer of 1900 approached Rev. Michael Glennon, pastor of Holy Spirit, to arrange for the celebration of Sunday mass in Deal. Father Glennon referred the committee to the Most Rev. James A. McFaul. Bishop McFaul appointed Rev. Richard A. Crean, pastor of St. Michael's, to attend to the matter during the following summer.

Known as the Canvas Church, masses were celebrated under a canvas tent during the summers of 1901 and 1902. The parish of St. Mary's was formed to serve the Catholics of Deal, Allenhurst, Loch Arbour, Interlaken, and the adjoining section of

Church of Saint Mary of the Assumption, Deal

Ocean Township. Msgr. John W. Norris, first pastor, started developing a church in 1903 to be completed in 1905. A rectory was constructed in 1906. The Ivy Hedge estate was purchased on September 16, 1959, and was opened for classes as a school in 1961. The present school building was constructed and opened in 1964, with the Dominican Sisters of Newburgh, New York, staffing the school until 1990. The present principal is Sr. Anne Claytor, S.C., a Sister of Charity from Convent Station.

Pastors: Msgr. John W. Norris, 1903–19; Rev. William Lynch, 1919–22; Rev. Walter Leahy, 1922–38; Rev. Joseph Mahoney, 1938–49; Msgr. George Welsh, 1949–56; Msgr. William Lannary, 1957–70; Rev. John MacDonald, 1970–74; Rev. William J. Carton, 1974–present.

Principals: Sr. Mary Paula, O.P., 1960–65; Sr. Claretta, O.P., 1965–68; Sr. Kathellen, O.P., 1968–70; Sr. Lois Dee,

O.P., 1970–73; Sr. Margaret Scott, O.P., 1973–75; Sr. Patricia Flynn, O.P., 1975–81; Sr. Ann Cecilia, O.P., 1981–90; Sr. Anne Claytor, S.C., 1990–present.

Delran, Holy Name

Before a church was built in Delran, Catholics traveled to St. Peter's and St. Casimir's in Riverside and Our Lady of Good Counsel in Moorestown for mass and spiritual needs. On June 12, 1972, the Most Rev. George W. Ahr established the Church of the Holy Name in Delran and appointed Rev. Donald J. Reilly as pastor. With permission from the Delran Board of Education, the first mass, on June 25, 1972, and subsequent masses were celebrated at Millbridge School until a church could be used. Bishop Ahr laid the church cornerstone on October 5, 1974, and celebrated the first mass in the church.

Pastors: Rev. Donald J. Reilly, 1972–84; Rev. Michael J. O'Connor, 1985–present.

East Keansburg, Saint Catherine

St. Catherine's Church was originally a barn and carousel. Priests from St. Ann's in Keansburg celebrated mass in East Keansburg from August 1937 to 1948 during the summer months. In September 1948, Rev. Francis P. Gunner was appointed first resident pastor. Father Gunner remodeled the church building and acquired most of the church furniture from other churches. The second pastor, Rev. Thaddeus J. Wojciehowski, purchased property, moved the rectory,

Church of the Holy Name, Delran

renovated the church, and acquired beautiful hand-painted murals for the church. At the same time, he bought a tavern and converted it into the parish hall. He also erected the school and the convent. The school, opened in September 1964, has been staffed by the Religious Sisters of Mercy from North Plainfield. Rev. John B. Cook added a gymnasium and two kindergarten trailers to the school. In addition, he built a new rectory and refurbished the church.

Pastors: Rev. Francis P. Gunner, 1948–55; Rev. Thaddeus J. Wojciehowski, 1955–67; Rev. John B. Cook, 1967–92; Rev. James A. Conover, 1992–present.

Principals: Sr. Margaret Bulfin, R.S.M., 1964–69; Sr. Anne Powers, R.S.M., 1969–present.

Eatontown, Immaculate Conception

On March 24, 1984, Rev. Augustine C. Park celebrated the first mass for Immaculate Conception Korean Church in Eatontown. The church had been the spiritual

Church of the Immaculate Conception, Eatontown

home of St. Dorothea's, Eatontown, prior to 1965 and had served Spanish-speaking parishioners from 1965 until the completion of a new church, St. John the Baptist, in Long Branch, in 1984. Immaculate Conception conducts two masses in Korean and one children's mass in English. Two missions, in Princeton and Browns Mills, are served by Immaculate Conception, the only Korean church in the diocese. One mass in Korean is offered at each mission on Sundays. With the diocese's general subsidy, Immaculate Conception is able to work with one student priest, Rev. John J. Kim, who serves the church and the two missions. An American priest, Rev. Robert Pearson, teaches catechism and celebrates the children's mass in English in Eatontown.

Pastors: Rev. Augustine C. Park, 1984; Rev. James B. Choi, 1984; Rev. Barnabas Park, 1984; Rev. Paul Holt, 1985–88; Rev. Joseph T. Kim, 1989–90; Rev. Joseph C. Kim, 1990–present.

Eatontown, Saint Dorothea

St. Dorothea's parish was established on November 11, 1905. St. Mary's in Colts Neck and St. Catherine of Siena in Farmingdale became missions of St. Dorothea's. A church was completed by the end of 1906. The Church of the Precious Blood in Monmouth Beach also was a mission between 1912 and 1947. In 1929, St. Catherine of Siena became an independent parish, with St. Mary's as its mission. In between the third and fourth pastorates of St. Dorothea's, Msgr. John B. McCloskey, pastor of St. James in Red Bank, was administrator. During the 1950s, 10 acres of land was purchased. A Family Center was built on this land and dedicated on May 9, 1965. In the spring of 1965, the parish sold the

Church of Saint Dorothea, Eatontown

church to the Diocese of Trenton, which used it for Spanish-speaking people in the region. The church was renamed Immaculate Conception Church, and it currently serves as the main church for Korean Catholics of the diocese. St. Dorothea's moved all of its masses and activities to the Family Center until a church and rectory were built. The Most Rev. George W. Ahr dedicated the new church on Trinity Sunday, June 9, 1968.

Pastors: Rev. Aloysius S. Quinlan, 1905–14; Rev. Peter B. Corr, 1914–24; Rev. Charles J. Farran, 1914–36; Rev. Michael F. O'Keefe, 1939–44; Rev. Francis J. Dwyer, 1944–47; Rev. Frederick Child, 1947–60; Rev. James B. Coyle, 1960–90; Rev. Sean P. Flynn, 1990–present.

Englishtown, Our Lady of Mercy

Our Lady of Mercy was declared an independent parish on November 14, 1947. Rev. Thomas F. Nolan, first pastor, celebrated mass the following day in the home of Mr. and Mrs. Joseph Noce. When their home became inadequate, the pastor moved to the Englishtown firehouse. A church was erected in 1948. Father Nolan resided at St. Rose of Lima Rectory, Freehold. Rev. Albert Tomaszewski, second pastor, purchased a rectory in March 1952. The growth of the parish necessitated the establishment of St. Thomas More Church in Manalapan. Our Lady of Mercy's third pastor, Rev. John Petri, was assigned to the newly formed St. Thomas More's in 1971. The pastors of Our Lady of Mercy have been given the

Church of Our Lady of Mercy, Englishtown

additional duty of attending to St. Joseph's Mission, Perrineville, since 1948.

Pastors: Rev. Thomas F. Nolan, 1947–50; Rev. Albert Tomaszewski, 1950–60; Rev. John Petri, 1960–71; Rev. Charles R. Valentine, 1971–present.

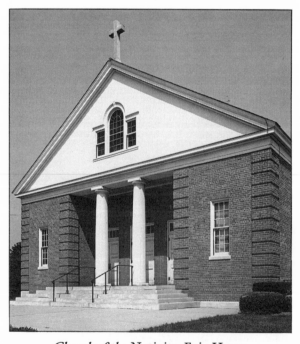

Church of the Nativity, Fair Haven

Fair Haven, Nativity

Established on October 26, 1953, Nativity parish was formed entirely from the parish of St. James, Red Bank. The first pastor, Rev. Donald E. Hickey, was appointed in June 1954. A rectory and church were constructed. The church was opened and blessed on February 13, 1955. A parish center containing classrooms, meeting rooms, workrooms, staff offices, a reception and secretarial area, and a chapel was dedicated in October 1990. Social Concerns ministers provide for basic needs of the poor, bereaved, homebound, and hospitalized.

Pastors: Rev. Donald E. Hickey 1954–82; Rev. Richard C. Brietske, 1982–92; Rev. Jerome M. Nolan, 1992–present.

Farmingdale, Saint Catherine of Siena

St. Catherine of Siena was founded in 1872 as a mission of St. Rose of Lima, Freehold, by Rev. Frederick Kivelitz. Masses were celebrated at Mr. Daniel Mahoney's home until 1892. For the next twenty years, masses were offered in Red Men's Hall. Jurisdiction of St. Catherine's was given to St. Dorothea's, Eatontown, in 1904. Through the efforts of Rev. Aloysius S. Quinlan and many parishioners, the present church was built in 1912 with available funds only. Rev. Joseph A. Sullivan was appointed first pastor when St. Catherine's was established as an independent parish in July 1939. A house was rented and later purchased to be used as the rectory. St. Mary's Church in Colts Neck, the Allenwood Tubercular Sanatorium, and the Tuberculosis Preventorium

Church of Saint Catherine of Siena, Farmingdale

for Children were attached as missions. From 1950 through 1962, St. Mary of the Assumption in the Freewood Acres section of Howell was a mission of St. Catherine's. St. Veronica's Church, Howell, developed out of this mission. The Most Rev. John C. Reiss divided the parish again by establishing St. William the Abbot Parish, Howell Township, on August 30, 1985.

Pastors: Rev. Joseph A. Sullivan, 1939–41; Rev. Joseph J. Donnelly, 1941–47; Rev. Joseph R. Brzozowski, 1947–56; Rev. James B. Coyle, 1956–58; Rev. Myron P. Gayda, 1958–60; Rev. Warren W. Abrams, 1960–62; Rev. Mitchell J. Cetkowski, 1962; Rev. Stephen A. Bielen, 1962–68; Rev. Raymond Griffin, 1968–72; Rev. John

Church of Saint Clare, Florence

Bordentown. In 1886, St. Clare's became a separate parish, with Rev. Thomas J. Degnan as first resident pastor. Rev. Neil McMenamin, second pastor, purchased property for St. Clare's Calvary Cemetery. In 1900, due to economic hardship, St. Clare's returned to mission status under St. Mary's. Constructed in 1904, the present church embraces all nationalities. Resident pastors have been assigned to St. Clare's since September 28, 1908. A large home was purchased in 1920 adjacent to the church. It was first rented to a parishioner and later used as the rectory by Rev. Michael J. Bacso. Rev. Francis J. Porazzo enacted a massive program of renovation and refurbishing of the church before 1974.

Pastors: Rev. Thomas J. Degnan, 1886–91; Rev. Neil McMenamin, 1891–94; Rev. Cornelius F. Phelan, 1894–1900; Rev. John A. Caulfield, 1908–11; Msgr. William I. McKean, 1911–14; Rev. Thomas F. Hennessy, 1914–17; Msgr. Edward A. Cahill, 1917–30; Rev. John E. Caton, 1930–44; Rev. Walter H. Greene, 1945; Rev. Michael J. Bacso, 1946–69; Rev. Francis J. Porazzo, 1969–88; Rev. Felix F. Venza, 1988–present.

Grabowski, 1972; Rev. Michael F. Venutolo, 1972–87; Rev. Michael S. Vona, 1987–present.

Florence, Saint Clare

Irish Catholics immigrated to Florence starting in 1857. They traveled to Mount Holly, Burlington, and Bordentown for mass. Priests from these parishes began to offer mass in the village of Florence, first in the home of Mr. Robert Mullen. By 1873, the Conventual Franciscan Fathers of Trenton had initiated a mission with Rev. Peter Jachetti, O.F.M. Conv., administrating. A small wooden structure was erected in 1874 as the original St. Clare Church. In 1883, the mission was transferred to St. Mary's,

Forked River, Saint Pius X

In 1950, Rev. Alexander A. Burant, pastor of St. Mary's in Barnegat, started a Forked River mission, originally St. Mary's in the Pines. Masses were celebrated in the Lacey Township Community Hall. When Pope Pius X was canonized a saint in 1954, the name of the mission was changed to St. Pius X. A church was completed in 1954, with

Church of Saint Pius X, Forked River

the basement used as a parish hall. On June 15, 1961, St. Pius X became a parish in its own right, with Father Burant as pastor. Administrators cared for the church from February 1970 through June 1972, when a second pastor was appointed. Across the street from the church, a parish center was constructed in 1973. A rectory was built in 1962 and enlarged in 1984. A chapel and four classrooms were added to the parish center in 1986.

Pastors: Rev. Alexander A. Burant, 1961–70; Rev. William C. Eelman, 1972–82; Rev. George E. Deutsch, 1982–present.

Freehold, Saint Robert Bellarmine

On June 18, 1971, the Most Rev. George W. Ahr founded the new parish of St. Rob-

ert Bellarmine, with Rev. Thomas F. Dentici as its pastor. The parish covered an area that had been the southwest corner of St. Rose Parish, Freehold. A rectory and a convent were purchased. Four Religious Sisters of Mercy from North Plainfield joined Father Dentici. Rev. Leo Kelty was also in residence. Masses were held in local public schools from 1971 to 1975. On September 14, 1975, Bishop Ahr presided at the blessing and dedication of St. Robert Bellarmine Parish Family Center. In 1978, an accord for Christian fellowship and joint activity was signed with Hope Lutheran Church. Classes for the religious education program are held in private homes in groups of eight to ten students.

Pastors: Msgr. Thomas F. Dentici, 1971–78; Rev. Francis Kaspar and Rev. John Butler, 1978–79; Rev. John W. Ryan, 1979–84; Rev. Robert A. Wozniak, 1984–87; Rev. Thomas J. O'Connor, 1988–present.

Church of Saint Robert Bellarmine, Freehold

Freehold, Saint Rose of Lima

Sent to St. Paul's, Princeton, in 1850, Rev. John Scollard traveled to the Freehold area to celebrate mass. On November 10, 1851, a piece of land was purchased for the erection of a frame church. Rev. Alfred Young, pastor of St. Paul's in Princeton, served the parish between 1857 and 1860. Father Young purchased a plot of land to serve as a cemetery. After several mission priests, the Most Rev. James Roosevelt Bayley, bishop of Newark, assigned Rev. Frederick Kivelitz as first resident pastor on January 9, 1871. Father Kivelitz traveled by saddle horse to serve the congregations of St. Rose and its missions that were scattered over an area of 125 square miles. Father Kivelitz purchased a parsonage and built many churches for the missions of St. Rose. St. Rose of Lima Church was blessed in August 1882. The present rectory was completed in October 1931. Many renovations to the church were accomplished during the 1930s.

St. Rose of Lima School has developed through four phases: Orchard Street School (1875–1911); McLean Street School (1911–57); Lincoln Street School, blessed in 1957; and the South Street addition, blessed in 1966. The Sisters of St. Francis of Philadelphia have served the first parochial school in Monmouth County since 1878.

The size of the congregation required the celebration of extra masses in the school gymnasium. The difficulties associated with holding mass in a gymnasium were eliminated when Msgr. Thomas A. Coffey constructed a new church. In November 1980, the Most Rev. John C. Reiss blessed the new

Chapel of Saint Rose of Lima, Freehold

church building, capable of seating 750 people and known as St. Rose of Lima Chapel. The old church, St. Rose of Lima Church, is still standing and in use.

Pastors: Msgr. Frederick Kivelitz, 1871–1930; Msgr. John A. Kucker, 1930–63; Rev. Thomas P. Ridge, 1964–71; Msgr. Thomas A. Coffey, 1971–90; Rev. Gerard McCarron, 1990–present.

Principals: Sr. Mary Helena, O.S.F., 1878–80; Sr. Mary Hildegarde, O.S.F., 1880–83; Sr. Mary Jerome, O.S.F., 1883–84; Sr. Mary DeSales, O.S.F., 1884–87; Sr. Mary Theodore, O.S.F., 1887–1908; Sr. Mary Climaca, O.S.F., 1908; Sr. Mary Gregory, O.S.F., 1908–11; Sr. Mary Victoria, O.S.F., 1911–14; Sr. Mary Agatha, O.S.F., 1914–15; Sr. Mary Leonora, O.S.F., 1915–17; Sr. Sincletica, O.S.F., 1917–23, 1932–36; Sr. Mary Jacoba, O.S.F., 1923–27; Sr. Stephen, O.S.F., 1927–32; Sr. Narcissus, O.S.F., 1936; Sr. Mary Rosaline, O.S.F., 1936–38; Sr. Mary Sabina, O.S.F., 1938–39; Sr. Mary Ellen, O.S.F., 1939–44; Sr. Mary Rosita, O.S.F., 1944–51; Sr. Mary

Church of Our Lady Queen of Peace, Hainesport

Eutropia, O.S.F., 1951–52; Sr. Mary John Gabriel, O.S.F., 1952–56; Sr. Loretta Marie, O.S.F., 1956–60, 1966–72; Sr. Laureen Francis, O.S.F., 1960–66; Sr. Martina Therese, O.S.F., 1972–81; Sr. Marie Agnes, O.S.F., 1981–present.

Hainesport, Our Lady Queen of Peace

Early in 1943, Rev. George E. Duff, pastor of Sacred Heart in Mount Holly, started investigating Hainesport as the possible site of a mission church. Masses were celebrated during the summer on the lawn at the home of Mr. and Mrs. Alexander Polkowski. In January 1944, Father Duff purchased a building for mass; the building now serves as the rectory. On June 15, 1944, the Most Rev. William A. Griffin established Our Lady Queen of Peace as an independent parish, with Rev. Michael J. Lease as first pastor. Father Lease involved himself with the es-

tablishment of Mount Holly Regional Catholic School, run by Sacred Heart Parish. Rev. Edward P. Blaszka purchased land in June 1948 upon which Rev. Michael F. Bakaisa would construct a church in 1951. Father Bakaisa also purchased a school bus to transport the children to the regional grammar school. In 1985, Rev. William J. McKeone began a pledge campaign to purchase a ranch-style dwelling to provide living quarters for Sr. Mary Grata, R.S.M., and additional classroom space for the religious education program. A ramp for the increased number of handicapped was added to the church in November 1991.

Pastors: Rev. Michael J. Lease, 1944–48; Rev. Edward P. Blaska, 1948–49; Rev. Michael F. Bakaisa, 1949–57; Rev. Francis J. Klimkiewicz, 1957–61; Rev. Frederick J. Clancy, 1961–67; Rev. Mario A. Fralliciardi, 1967–83; Rev. William J. McKeone, 1983–89; Rev. Richard J. Gallagher, 1989–present.

Hamilton Square, Saint Gregory the Great

Early Catholics of Nottingham, now Hamilton Square, journeyed to Assumption Church in New Egypt or St. John's, now Sacred Heart, in Trenton. In 1938, residents of Hamilton Square were able to attend mass at what would become, in 1943, Our Lady of Sorrows Parish, Trenton. Population growth in Hamilton Square necessitated the founding of a parish on November 24, 1953. Rev. Edward J. Draus was appointed pastor in June 1954. He was simultaneously appointed managing editor of the newly formed diocesan newspaper, *The*

*Church of Saint Gregory the Great,
Hamilton Square*

Monitor. A newly erected church was blessed on February 27, 1955.

Rev. Joseph T. Wade's plans for education of the children came to fruition in September 1965 with the opening of a school and convent. The Bernardine Sisters staffed the school until 1978; the Sisters of St. Francis of Philadelphia continued educating the parish children thereafter.

St. Gregory's was the first parish in the diocese to participate in the RENEW program from May 28, 1982, to Pentecost Sunday, May 30. Starting in 1986, Rev. Joseph L. Ferrante renovated the church. On November 4, 1990, the Most Rev. John C. Reiss blessed the new St. Gregory the Great Parish Community Center.

Pastors: Rev. Edward J. Draus, 1954–57; Rev. Joseph T. Wade, 1957–73; Rev. Joseph A. Bischoff, 1973–78; Msgr. James P. McManimon, 1978–86; Rev. Joseph L. Ferrante, 1986–92; Rev. Richard C. Brietske, 1992–present.

Principals: Sr. Mary Dulcine, O.S.F., 1965–67; Sr. Mary Vitalia, O.S.F., 1967–68; Sr. Mary Nazaria, O.S.F., 1968–74; Sr. Mark Ann, O.S.F., 1974–77; Sr. Mary Albertine, O.S.F., 1977–78; Sr. Nora Nash, O.S.F., 1978–present.

Highlands, Our Lady of Perpetual Help

In 1863, Rev. Thomas M. Killeen, pastor of St. James in Red Bank, celebrated Highland's first mass. Priests from Red Bank continued to administer to the community until 1879, when Rev. John J. O'Connor took up residence in Highlands. Father O'Connor assumed the pastorate of St. Mary's Parish, which then consisted of New Monmouth and Highlands. In 1883, when Father O'Connor moved nearer to St. Mary's Church in New Monmouth, Rev. John H. Fox, pastor of Holy Cross in Rumson, took responsibility for the Catholics of Highlands. In 1888 Father Fox built Highland's first church. Rev. Thomas Roche, pastor of St. Agnes in Atlantic Highlands, took charge of Highlands in 1891.

Our Lady of Perpetual Help's first pastor, Rev. John T. Sweeney, arrived in 1898, thus establishing an independent parish. Father Sweeney constructed a parish hall and the present rectory in 1901. Rev. Thom-

Church of Our Lady of Perpetual Help, Highlands

as Kearns completed a larger church by 1932. In 1951, Rev. Joseph J. Donnelly started a school in the basement of the church. A building for the Sisters of St. Francis from Stella Niagara, New York, was purchased in 1951. The present, more convenient convent was purchased and renovated in 1957. Rev. James A. Thompson constructed a school building in 1963, and about 1978, the Franciscan Missionary Sisters of the Infant Jesus from Woodbury assumed the teaching duties of the school.

Pastors: Rev. John T. Sweeney, 1898–1906; Rev. Joseph A. Rigney, 1906–14; Rev. Thomas Kearns, 1914–33; Rev. John J. Henry, 1933–34; Rev. James A. Bulfin, 1934–35; Rev. John C. Farrell, 1935–38; Rev. Neil Mooney, 1938–42; Rev. Thomas A. Gribbin, 1942–46; Rev. Eugene Kelly, 1946–47; Rev. Joseph J. Donnelly, 1947–62; Rev. James A. Thompson, 1962–68;

Rev. Raymond L. Szulecki, 1968; Rev. David G. Delzell, 1968–present.

Principals: Mother Benecita, O.S.F., 1963–68; Mother Clara, O.S.F.; Mother Karen, O.S.F.; Sr. Gabriel, O.S.F.; Sr. Hilda, O.S.F.; Sr. Clara Joseph Leonardi, F.M.I.J., 1978–81; Sr. Gloria Louise, F.M.I.J., 1981–84; Sr. Theresa May, F.M.I.J., 1984–88; Sr. Carmelisa Dragoni, F.M.I.J., 1988–present.

Hightstown, Saint Anthony of Padua

The earliest known mass in Hightstown was celebrated in 1852. Until the 1880s, visiting priests offered mass, or Hightstown Catholics traveled to neighboring towns. Then, in the latter half of the 1880s, Hightstown was served by St. Joseph's in Perrineville. Shortly after the parish's incorporation in 1885, a church was erected. However, the parish struggled financially and had to close in 1890. Under the direction of the Most Rev. Michael J. O'Farrell,

Church of Saint Anthony of Padua, Hightstown

the Franciscan Fathers from Trenton re-opened the church in 1892. They served the parish until the appointment of a resident pastor in 1906, thus making St. Anthony of Padua an independent parish. The congregation's growth, starting in the late 1940s, required a larger church and other facilities. A ten-year building program was initiated in 1960. A parish hall was finished in 1961; the present church and the Confraternity of Christian Doctrine classroom building, in 1969; and the present rectory, in 1973.

Pastors: Rev. John B. McCloskey, 1906–08; Rev. John B. Conway, 1908–18; Rev. Edward Whalen, 1918–29; Rev. Aloysius McCue, 1929–30; Rev. Francis J. Sullivan, 1930–34; Rev. William Quinn, 1934–41; Rev. Louis Cogan, 1941–66; Rev. William J. Haughney, 1966–75; Rev. Russell E. Loughman, 1975–78; Rev. John H. MacDonald, 1978–80; Rev. Francis E. Santitoro, 1980–85; Rev. Patrick J. Castles, 1985–present.

Holmdel, Saint Benedict

St. Benedict Parish was established on July 6, 1959, to meet the spiritual needs of the families moving to this "rural" community of Holmdel in northern Monmouth County. Rev. Edward P. Blaska was assigned the challenge of organizing the new parish. He arrived at his rectory, the former farmhouse of Mr. Edwin Peseux, on June 12, 1959. Masses were celebrated at the rectory and the Indian Hill School, Holmdel. Confraternity of Christian Doctrine classes were taught by volunteers and Sisters of Mercy

Church of Saint Benedict, Holmdel

from St. Joseph, Keyport. On September 23, 1962, the Most Rev. George W. Ahr blessed a church/school building. The school began operation in 1962, staffed by lay teachers and the Marianites of Holy Cross from Our Lady of Princeton Convent in Princeton. The Marianites left in 1974, and only lay teachers remain. St. Benedict is operated with a pastor, a parish council, a pastoral assistant, a social ministries coordinator, and a business administrator.

Pastors: Rev. Edward P. Blaska, 1959–69; Rev. William C. Anderson, 1969–present.

Principals: Sr. Margaret Mary, M.S.C., 1962; Sr. Mary of the Sacred Heart, M.S.C., 1962–64; Sr. Mary Delores Dolan, M.S.C., 1964–69; Sr. Ann Gillard, M.S.C., 1969–71; Sr. Monica O'Keefe, M.S.C., 1971–72; Miss Ann Bicolla, 1972–73; Mrs. Carolyn Cattani, 1973–74; Mrs. Constance Cholowenski, 1974–89; Mrs. Nancy Ronayne, 1989–present.

Holmdel, Saint Catharine

The area of Monmouth County known as Morrisville, later as Everett, and finally as

Holmdel, was originally served by a visiting priest, Rev. John A. Kelly, pastor of St. Mary's in South Amboy. Father Kelly came on horseback every few months to celebrate mass and perform baptisms and weddings. The few Catholics, mostly of Irish and German descent, gathered in one of the largest of the area farmhouses, after a fire, lit atop a hill, signaled the arrival of a priest. About four or five times a year, the people from this area would walk to Red Bank for mass. Also during this period, the "Confession Tree" became quite popular. When the visiting priest came, he would walk into the woods and sit down on one side of a large tree. Anyone wishing to receive the sacrament would then come to the tree and kneel down on the opposite side. During the 1870s, the pastors or assistants of St. James in Red Bank visited Morrisville about once a month.

The first resident pastor, Rev. Michael Glennon, arrived early in 1879. The Most Rev. Michael A. Corrigan, bishop of Newark, dedicated the church building on No-

vember 25, 1879. Father Glennon was named pastor of a new parish, Holy Spirit in Asbury Park, and St. Catharine's became a mission of that parish. On June 1, 1883, St. Catharine's was transferred to the care of St. Mary's in New Monmouth. St. Gabriel's of Marlboro administered the parish from August 24, 1885, until October 1, 1982.

A new structure was needed for the rapidly increasing population. On September 4, 1971, the first mass in a new St. Catharine's Church was celebrated. In 1982, St. Catharine's was reestablished as an independent parish with its second resident pastor, Rev. Eugene R. Scheg. By 1983, another new church was needed, and work was begun under the direction of Father Scheg. The present pastor, Rev. Eugene M. Rebeck, broke ground for the building on December 1, 1985, and celebrated the first mass in April 1987. The Most Rev. John C. Reiss conducted the solemn blessing and dedication of the newest St. Catharine's Church on April 27, 1987.

Pastors: Rev. Michael Glennon, 1879–80; Rev. Eugene R. Scheg, 1982–84; Rev. Eugene M. Rebeck, 1985–present.

Hopewell, Saint Alphonsus

Early Columbia Catholics attended mass at either St. Paul's in Princeton or St. John's in Lambertville. Starting in 1874, Rev. Thomas R. Moran from St. Paul's offered two masses per year in Columbia, renamed Hopewell in 1891. By December 1876 the growing number of Catholics allowed for a new parish. Rev. Anthony Smith, pastor of St. Mary's in Trenton, purchased land and

Church of Saint Catharine, Holmdel

Church of Saint Alphonsus, Hopewell

initiated the construction of a church. A covered basement was finished by the summer of 1877, with the first mass said on July 11. Rev. Michael Holland, an assistant from St. Mary's, took charge of the mission. The mission was cared for at various times by St. Mary's Cathedral, St. John the Evangelist in Dunellen, and St. Joseph's in Bound Brook.

Finally, on January 21, 1894, St. Alphonsus became an independent parish, receiving its first resident pastor, Rev. Joseph Keuper. In 1921, Rev. John J. West installed stained-glass windows in the church. Rev. Edward J. O'Connell renovated the church during his pastorate. An institution formerly served by the parish was the New Jersey Neuro-Psychiatric Institute in Skillman, now a part of the Diocese of Metuchen.

The pastors of St. Alphonsus served as chaplains of St. Michael's Home during its activity from the time of the Most Rev. James A. McFaul's dedication on May 30, 1898, to its closing on June 29, 1973. Before the addition of a rectory in 1940, the pastors resided at St. Michael's. The Franciscan Sisters from Glen Riddle, Pennsylvania, brought 80 children from St. Mary's Home in New Brunswick to what was then called St. Michael's Orphan Asylum and Industrial School. The primary purpose of St. Michael's was to house orphans. However, after 1940, children from broken homes also stayed at St. Michael's. The Franciscan Sisters operated a school for the "home kids" and some of St. Alphonsus Parish's "town kids."

Pastors: Rev. Joseph Keuper, 1894; Rev. John M. Murphy, 1894–96; Rev. Michael J. Hagerty, 1896; Rev. Thomas J. O'Hanlon, 1896–99; Rev. William Dunphy, 1899–1901; Rev. Thomas A. Maloney, O.S.A. 1901–02; Rev. Peter J. Clune, 1902–03; Rev. William Reddan, 1903–05; Rev. James J. Powers, 1905–11; Rev. Edward C. Manion, 1911–14; Rev. Peter B. Corr, 1914–15; Rev. John A. Caulfield, 1915–17; Rev. Hugh L. Massey, 1917–19; Rev. John J. West, 1919–26; Rev. Michael A. Dalton, 1926–35; Rev. Salvatore DiLorenzo, 1935; Rev. Edward A. McKenna, 1935–37; Rev. James F. McGrath, 1937; Rev. John F. Thompson, 1937–60; Rev. Edward J. O'Connell, 1962–69; Rev. Joseph M. Krysztofik, 1969–71; Rev. Eugene V. Davis, 1971–75; Rev. Frederick J. Clancy, 1975–85; Msgr.

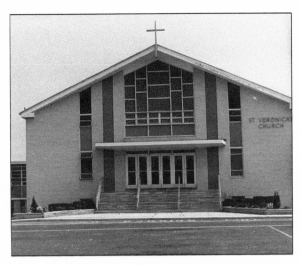

Church of Saint Veronica, Howell

Thomas A. Luebking, 1986–89; Rev. John V. Bowden, 1989–1992; Rev. Ralph Stansley, 1993–present.

Howell, Saint Veronica

Catholics of Howell Township first attended mass at either St. Mary of the Lake, Lakewood, or St. Rose of Lima, Freehold. In 1950, a mission parish, St. Mary of the Assumption, was founded and assigned to St. Catherine of Siena, Farmingdale. With Mr. Henry E. Beretta's $45,000 and the community's $5,000, a church was constructed by May 1951.

On June 1, 1962, the Most Rev. George W. Ahr established a territorial parish of St. Veronica. Rev. Mitchell J. Cetkowski, pastor of St. Catherine of Siena, was transferred to St. Veronica's. St. Mary of the Assumption then became a mission of St. Veronica's. Under Father Cetkowski's pastorate, a rectory, church, school, and convent were constructed. The school, staffed by the Sisters

of Resurrection, opened September 8, 1965. The fifth pastor, Rev. H. Brendan Williams, began Parish Renewal and Renew as tools for spiritual growth. Father Williams has also undertaken another addition to the school, providing ample room for the parish activities to expand.

Pastors: Rev. Mitchell J. Cetkowski, 1962–69; Rev. Dominic Turtora, 1969–75; Rev. Michael Clark, 1975–76; Rev. William Roos, 1976–79; Rev. H. Brendan Williams, 1979–present.

Principals: Sr. Angelica, C.R., 1965–71; Sr. Mary Rosaria, C.R., 1971–72; Sr. Mary Lucille, C.R., 1972–73; Sr. Mary Christopher, C.R., 1973–81; Sr. Alexandra Jazwinski, C.R., 1981–92; Sr. Cherree Ann Power, C.R., 1992–present.

Howell Township, Saint William the Abbot

The first Saturday and Sunday liturgies were celebrated at the Ramtown Elementary School, in the southeasternmost section of Howell Township. Prior to the establishment of the parish on August 30, 1985, most of the Catholic population of Ramtown attended mass at St. Mary's of the Lake or Holy Family, both in Lakewood. Weekday masses are celebrated at the parish house, located in Allenwood, in the southern section of Wall Township. Weekend masses are celebrated in Ramtown Elementary School and Holy Family Church. The site of the new parish complex, now in the planning stages, will be in the center of Ramtown.

Pastor: Msgr. Leo A. Kelty, S.T.L., 1985–present.

Jackson Township, Saint Aloysius

The Parish of St. Aloysius was established on June 12, 1964, by the Most Rev. George W. Ahr. Rev. Amedeo L. Morello was assigned as founding pastor. The first parish mass was offered at the Switlik School Auditorium on Sunday, July 5, 1964. Father Morello purchased a tract of land with two buildings on it in November 1964. One building became the rectory, and the other became a chapel for daily mass and small services. Mass was celebrated in a new church building starting December 18, 1966. In 1985, six full classrooms and a gymnasium were added to the parish complex to provide better religious education and recreational facilities for the parish.

Pastor: Msgr. Amedeo L. Morello, 1964–present.

Jobstown, Saint Andrew

During the Great Famine in Ireland, Irish Catholics emigrated to the United States, some landing in Burlington, a few settling in the village of Jobstown. Mr. Thomas Beakey, one of those immigrants, and his friends worked with Rev. Hugh J. McManus, pastor of Sacred Heart in Mount Holly, for the foundation of a mission church in Jobstown. The Most Rev. Michael A. Corrigan ordered incorporation of the mission under the patronage of St. Andrew, which officially took place on February 23, 1880. A church was built during that year and dedicated by Bishop Corrigan on September 19, 1880.

Ten families that founded St. Andrew's were the Harts, Engles, Rahillys, Cochrans,

Church of Saint Aloysius, Jackson Township

Tuteks, Koenigs, O'Connors, Durrs, Sheedys, and Connors. From the Hart family came a vocation to the priesthood, Rev. Peter J. Hart, who served as pastor of Sacred Heart from 1900 to 1914. Father Hart attended to St. Andrew's Mission until 1908, when the parish received its first and only resident pastor, Rev. Edward A. Cahill. Father Cahill was also in charge of St. Ann's Mission, Browns Mills. Sacred Heart has attended to St. Andrew's Mission during most of its existence, receiving permanent charge of the mission on September 8, 1944. St. Mary's in Bordentown cared for St. Andrew's between 1885 and 1901, and from 1912 until 1944.

On October 24, 1982, the Akins property, adjacent to the church, was acquired. Mrs. Jennie Akins, though not Catholic, had acted as the unofficial "watchdog" of the church property. After she passed away, her grandson Earl Akins sold the property to St. Andrew's. With many years' worth of contributions and the assistance of a loan, construction began in March 1988 for an addition to the church. On September 9, 1990, the Most Rev. John C. Reiss dedi-

Church of Saint Andrew, Jobstown

6, 1917. The Most Rev. Thomas J. Walsh established St. Ann's as an independent parish on January 8, 1924, and appointed Rev. John A. Carroll first resident pastor. Rev. Thomas A. Kearney constructed St. Ann's School. The Sisters of Mercy from North Plainfield have staffed the school since its inception in September 1931. A mission church was founded in 1935 in East Keansburg by Rev. John J. Lucitt, St. Ann's fourth pastor. In 1942, Holy Family, Union Beach, was founded from territory formerly belonging to St. Ann's. St. Catherine's, East Keansburg, became an independent parish in 1948. Rev. Edward A. Corrigan constructed a new playground and an addition to the school in 1961. St. Ann's Bayshore

cated the new expansion, which serves as extra space for masses and as a place to hold Confraternity of Christian Doctrine classes and social events.

Pastor: Rev. Edward A. Cahill, 1908–12.

Keansburg, Saint Ann

Beginning in 1910, Keansburg was served by St. Mary's, New Monmouth. Rev. John E. Murray, pastor of St. Mary's, celebrated mass at McDonald's Hotel. Father Murray purchased land in 1916 for a mission church in which the first mass was offered on May

Church of Saint Ann, Keansburg

Senior Day Center opened in July 1975 under Rev. Frederick A. Valentino's pastorate. In July 1980, Rev. Edward D. Strano opened Project P.A.U.L. (Poor, Alienated, Unemployed, Lonely) for the needy. St. Ann's Childcare Center was established in August 1982.

Pastors: Rev. John A. Carroll, 1924; Rev. Thomas A. Kearney, 1924–34; Rev. Thomas F. Maher, 1934; Rev. John J. Lucitt, 1934–44; Rev. Edward A. Corrigan, 1945–71; Rev. Frederick A. Valentino, 1971–76; Rev. Edward D. Strano, 1976–86; Rev. Rocco A. Cuomo, 1986–90; Rev. Joseph A. Halpin, 1990–present.

Principals: Sr. Mary Philomena, R.S.M., 1931–35; Sr. Mary Angela, R.S.M., 1935–36; Sr. Mary Damasa, R.S.M., 1936–42; Sr. Mary Florian, R.S.M., 1942–48; Sr. Mary Theodora, R.S.M., 1948–54; Sr. Mary Charitina, R.S.M., 1954–60; Sr. Marie Jeanne, R.S.M., 1960–66; Sr. Mary Elizabeth, R.S.M., 1966–72; Sr. Kathleen Curnyn, R.S.M., 1972–80; Sr. Mary Charlene, R.S.M., 1980–83; Sr. Mary Irene, R.S.M., 1983–85; Sr. Mary Dora, R.S.M., 1985–present.

Keyport, Jesus the Lord

For Spanish-speaking Catholics of upper Monmouth County, a garage was rented for services in 1966, and a first-aid building was purchased as a place of worship in 1970. Rev. Paul W. Robb, the first resident priest, resided at St. Joseph's rectory in Keyport. A rectory was bought in 1974. On February 24, 1977, the Chapel of the Immaculate

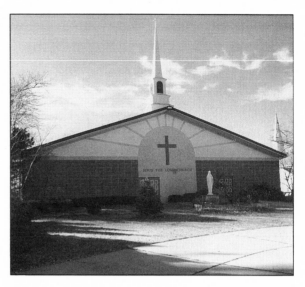

Church of Jesus the Lord, Keyport

Conception was elevated to parish status. The name was changed to Jesus the Lord in March 1978. A parish center was erected in 1979 at the site of the old first-aid building.

Pastors: Rev. Paul W. Robb, 1972–73; Rev. Nicholas Lodo, I.M.C., 1973–1993.

Keyport, Saint Joseph

A little brick church was completed and dedicated in 1854 despite antagonism toward Keyport area Catholics. Rev. John A. Kelly, pastor of St. Mary's in South Amboy, cared for the parish until 1876. St. Joseph's then received its first resident pastor, Rev. Patrick McGovern. Under the guidance of Rev. Augustine G. Spierings, a larger, Gothic church was erected and dedicated on June 27, 1879. During Father Spierings's pastorate, the original church was converted into a two-room school, and the original rectory was built. Ground was obtained for a cemetery through a non-Catholic intermediary, Captain Cornelius Britton.

Church of Saint Joseph, Keyport

Three Sisters of St. Francis of Philadelphia ran the school from 1882 until 1890, when the Sisters of Mercy from North Plainfield assumed the teaching duties. Rev. Joseph A. Linnane received permission to build a six-classroom school to house the increasing school population. The new school opened in 1924 and also provided facilities for the parish organizations that had developed under Rev. Michael C. O'Donnell. In 1928, a convent was constructed. During Rev. Cornelius J. Kane's pastorate, the school was remodeled and enlarged to accommodate more than a thousand students. The school was dedicated on September 13, 1953.

The parish was divided several times due to a population boom. St. Benedict's in Hazlet and St. Clement's in Matawan were founded. Parishioners also transferred to Holy Family, Union Beach. Due to structural weakness of the 94-year-old St. Joseph's

Church, masses were celebrated only in the school auditorium as of April 1972. A more modern church was constructed, with the first mass celebrated on December 8, 1976.

Pastors: Rev. Patrick McGovern, 1876–77; Rev. Augustine G. Spierings, 1877–90; Rev. Michael C. O'Donnell, 1890–1923; Rev. Joseph A. Linnane, 1923–29; Msgr. John P. Burke, 1929–50; Rev. Cornelius J. Kane, 1950–71; Rev. John Dzema, 1971–72; Rev. Vincent A. Lloyd, 1972–81; Rev. Ronald Bacovin, 1981–89; Rev. Ronald J. Cioffi, 1989–present.

Principals: Sr. Constance Gleason, R.S.M., 1970–present.

Lakehurst, Saint John

In 1868, the Most Rev. James Roosevelt Bayley, bishop of Newark, established the Manchester Mission, forerunner of St. John's, Lakehurst. Rev. John A. Kelly, pas-

Church of Saint John, Lakehurst

tor of St. Mary's in South Amboy, celebrated the first several masses in the home of Mr. Patrick Gratton.

Rev. John F. Salaun, pastor of St. James in Red Bank, took charge of the Manchester Mission, especially between 1868 and 1871. Despite anti-Catholicism, prevalent during that time, Father Salaun obtained land from Mr. William A. Torrey Sr., an ex-Presbyterian minister. According to page 50 of the *Diocesan Journal of Michael Augustine Corrigan, Bishop of Newark, 1872–1880*:

> Father Salaun having asked for a donation was upbraided for his audacity in requesting what he himself would most assuredly not do for a Protestant Church. Father S. explained the difference between Catholic & Protestant principles, and received the following reply by note, 'As I despair of bringing you (Catholics) to the true faith, and as any religion is better than none, I donate ground for church and Cemetery.'

Construction of a church proceeded slowly, with the first mass in the church celebrated on May 3, 1874.

The Conventual Franciscans of Trenton offered mass for the congregation from 1871 until 1874. Rev. Patrick Delaney, O.F.M. Conv., served the congregation in 1874 until the end of September. From then until 1879, Rev. Stanislaus Danielou, assistant pastor at St. James in Red Bank, took charge of the mission. Rev. Joseph Esser, pastor of St. Nicholas in Egg Harbor City, seems to have attended to St. John's for a few months in 1879. Rev. Michael Glennon, pastor of Holy Spirit in Asbury Park, then assumed responsibility for the

mission from October 1879 to May 1880. From 1880 to 1884 or even through 1890, the Franciscans again offered mass for the Manchester Mission, especially Rev. Peter Jachetti, O.F.M. Conv., and Rev. Angelus Goessmann, O.F.M. Conv. Several different priests from various places visited the Manchester Mission between 1868 and 1886. For most of that time, diocesan priests from Red Bank and the Franciscans from Trenton seem to have shared responsibility for the mission.

The first resident pastor in Ocean County was probably Rev. Joseph F. Flanagan, who appears to have served St. John's Parish from January to September 1886. The areas of Manchester, Bricksburg (now Lakewood), and Toms River were within his territory. Father Flanagan continued construction of the parish's second church, started by the Franciscans.

Upon Father Flanagan's departure, St. John's Parish was without a resident pastor. Rev. John A. Lawrence, assistant pastor of St. Mary's in South Amboy, served the parish and finished building the church during his short tenure. Rev. Michael Hosey served the parish until December 1887, when Rev. Michael A. Dolan took over. From 1889 to 1899, St. John's was a mission of St. Mary's in Lakewood. From 1899 to 1902, Rev. Joseph A. Egan, pastor of St. Joseph's in Toms River, attended to the Catholics of St. John's Mission. Rev. James A. Moroney may have visited the congregation between 1902 and 1915. He was pastor at St. Mary's in Sandy Hook until 1905, when he was transferred to St. Ann's in

Holly Beach. The priests from St. Joseph's did continue to serve St. John's throughout the early part of the twentieth century, and, in 1915, St. Joseph's clergy assumed complete control of St. John's Mission.

In the mid-1960s, the construction of adult communities in Manchester Township resulted in growing attendance at Sunday masses. Three masses were held in the old church building while two masses were celebrated across the street in the Lakehurst Firehouse. Finally on November 21, 1969, St. John's Parish received its second resident pastor, Rev. Philip T. Matera. To serve better the growing parish, Father Matera constructed an all-purpose building, with ground-breaking ceremonies on July 31, 1972, and with mass first celebrated in the church on May 26, 1973. A rectory was erected adjacent to the parish center/church building. Father Matera also recognized the need of a church in the Whiting section of Manchester Township, and in December 1976, Rev. John J. McGovern was appointed to serve the Whiting area.

Pastors: Rev. Joseph F. Flanagan, 1886; Rev. Philip T. Matera, 1969–82; Rev. James A. Thompson, 1982–89; Rev. Ronald J. Bacovin, 1989–present.

Lakewood, Saint Anthony Claret

The influx of Hispanics to Ocean County in the 1950s prompted the Claretians from Our Lady of Fatima in Perth Amboy to visit on weekends. Mass was first celebrated at a chicken farm in Lakehurst. In the early summer of 1957, Father Martin from Our Lady of Fatima moved the mission to the Cassville section of Jackson Township. A chapel was built and named after St. Anthony Claret, founder of the Claretians in Spain in 1849. In the 1960s, many of the chicken farms, a major source of employment for Hispanics, were moved to southern states. As a result, Hispanics moved to the more industrial centers of Ocean County, including Lakewood, Howell, and Toms River. In 1971, a bus was used to transport the faithful from Lakewood to Jackson for mass.

By 1974, inadequate bus transportation necessitated the purchase of property in Lakewood. Of the two buildings that were already on the 5-acre parcel of land, one was immediately converted into a rectory. A parish center was constructed in 1976, with the first mass celebrated on Christmas of 1976. The Most Rev. George W. Ahr inaugurated the parish center on January 16, 1977, and later that year designated St.

Church of Saint Anthony Claret, Lakewood

Anthony Claret Parish as a national Hispanic parish. Bishop Ahr assigned Rev. Richard Bartlett, C.M.F., as first resident pastor at Lakewood, with missions in Jackson and Toms River. Additional property was purchased in 1980 for the expansion of St. Anthony Claret Parish. The Hispanic population of Ocean County is now concentrated in Lakewood, Howell, Toms River, and Freehold. As a result, in 1990, the Jackson mission church was returned to the diocese and became St. Monica's Church, a mission of Assumption Parish in New Egypt.

Three religious communities of women have served the parish, including the Missionary Servants of the Most Blessed Trinity (1983–84), the Missionary Catechists of the Sacred Hearts of Jesus and Mary (1985–86), and the Caldwell Dominicans (1991–present).

Pastors: Rev. Richard Bartlett, C.M.F., 1977–78; Rev. Wayne J. Barron, C.M.F., 1978–79; Rev. Raymond S. Bianchi, C.M.F., 1979–86; Rev. Robert J. Billett, C.M.F., 1986–87; Rev. Benjamin Martinez, C.M.F., 1987–90; Rev. Richard S. White, C.M.F., 1990–present.

Lakewood, Saint Mary of the Lake

The first mass in Ocean County may have been celebrated in 1850 between the lakes of Lakewood in the home of Mr. Larry Reilly. Shortly thereafter, a small wooden mission chapel was constructed. Priests from Manchester (now Lakehurst), Freehold, Red Bank, and Trenton served the Catholics of Lakewood. Rev. James E. Sheehy, S.P.M., erected the second chapel in 1889. A short

Church of Saint Mary of the Lake, Lakewood

time later, on November 1, 1889, the Most Rev. Michael J. O'Farrell assigned Rev. Thomas B. Healy as first resident pastor. Father Healy raised money for a church to replace the chapel. On April 19, 1891, with thirty-five priests in attendance, the church was dedicated by Bishop O'Farrell. Father Healy also built a rectory and organized a cemetery. Of the cemetery's 55 acres, 40 were purchased in 1964.

Originally a temporary substitute for a parish school, St. Mary's Academy was founded in 1898. Rev. Maurice R. Spillane was instrumental in the 1924 purchase of George J. Gould's 200-acre estate by North Plainfield's Sisters of Mercy. The estate became the new home of Mount Saint Mary's College, which became known as Georgian Court College. A new St. Mary's Church was dedicated on May 17, 1925. On April 3, 1928, Monsignor Spillane, promoted to domestic prelate in 1926, moved the old church onto the grounds of Georgian Court College. The awesome undertaking was reported in *Ripley's Believe It or Not.*

In response to growth in Cedarwood Park, Rev. John F. Baldwin erected the Church of the Visitation, Bricktown, by 1938. The parish was divided again in 1962, with portions of St. Mary's Parish transferred to St. Veronica's in Howell and St. Dominic's in Bricktown. In 1964, St. Aloysius, Jackson, also received some of St. Mary's parishioners.

Rev. George E. Everitt renewed the parish plant. He razed the old rectory, parish hall, and Holy Name Hall and constructed a new rectory. He also acquired the former Methodist church property and established the Holy Family Mission. The Parish Center was completed in 1970 near Holy Family Church. Father Everitt felt the need for a parish school and opened Holy Family School in September 1975. The Religious Teachers Filippini staff the school. Monsignor Everitt, promoted in 1977, planned the construction of a new Holy Family Church, dedicated on February 15, 1987. Committed to the education of the children, Monsignor Everitt added to the school three classrooms, a library, a cafeteria, and an art room. In addition, in 1990, Holy Family Pre-School opened. Another

seven classrooms were added to the school in 1992. St. Mary's Mausoleum was dedicated on September 27, 1986, and the second phase of the mausoleum, Chapel of Our Lady, was built in 1992.

Pastors: Rev. Thomas B. Healy, 1889–1910; Rev. James J. Powers, 1911–18; Msgr. Maurice R. Spillane, 1918–29; Msgr. John F. Baldwin, 1929–64; Msgr. George E. Everitt, 1964–present.

Principal of Holy Family School: Sr. Laura Longo, M.P.F., 1975–present.

Lavallette, Saint Bonaventure

Before 1905, Catholics of Lavallette attended mass at St. Peter's in Point Pleasant Beach and until 1918, at St. Catharine's in Seaside Park. During the year 1918, a group of Lavallette Catholics petitioned Rev. Bede Hess, O.F.M. Conv., pastor of St.

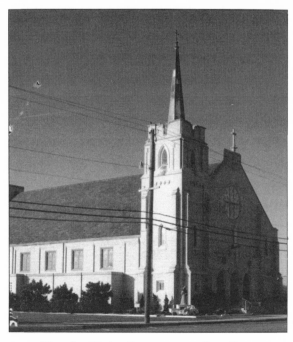

Church of Saint Bonaventure, Lavallette

Catharine's Parish, to send a priest to Lavallette for the celebration of Sunday mass. Father Hess referred the request to the Franciscan provincial Very Rev. Leo Greulick, O.F.M. Conv., and to the Most Rev. Thomas J. Walsh. The request was granted. Rev. Martin Weitekamp, O.F.M. Conv., of Syracuse, New York, offered the first mass in Lavallette on July 6, 1919, in the Union Church of Lavallette. On August 23, 1921, the mission of Lavallette was incorporated as the Church of St. Bonaventure. In 1922, land was acquired upon which the original church was completed by the spring of 1924. On June 29, 1924, a solemn high mass, the first mass in the church, was celebrated by Father Hess. The church was dedicated by Msgr. John H. Fox, vicar-general, on August 3, 1924. A parish Catholic Youth Organization hall was erected and opened for extra Sunday masses on June 29, 1947. The mission was cared for by St. Catharine's until 1942, when Rev. William J. Brennan was appointed founding pastor of Our Lady of Perpetual Help in Seaside Heights and given the duty of St. Bonaventure Mission.

On June 15, 1950, St. Bonaventure was established as an independent parish, with Rev. Joseph S. Keefe as first resident pastor. In 1951, a rectory was constructed. A second church was dedicated on May 22, 1966.

Pastors: Rev. Joseph S. Keefe, 1950–57; Rev. Stephen I. Buividas, 1957–62; Rev. Michael F. Bakaisa, 1962–77; Rev. Joseph A. Doino, 1977–79; Rev. George M. Albano, 1979–90; Msgr. Frederick A. Valentino, 1990–present.

Lawrenceville, Saint Ann

In 1891, a small group gathered in the Burke residence for Lawrenceville's first mass, celebrated by Rev. John M. McCloskey. Priests from St. Mary's Cathedral continued to offer mass for the township until 1898, when residents took the new trolley or walked to St. Mary's Cathedral or St. Joseph's, Trenton. A home for the aged, Morris Hall, was erected in Lawrenceville in 1904. Masses were celebrated by the chaplains in Morris Hall's Our Lady of the Rosary Chapel.

Rev. Michael P. McCorristin arrived as Morris Hall chaplain in late 1933. An independent parish was established on August 9, 1937, with Father McCorristin as pastor. Through the efforts of Father McCorristin and the parishioners, including volunteers and contractors, a church was erected and

Church of Saint Ann, Lawrenceville

was dedicated on June 26, 1938. St. Ann's first five pastors maintained their residence at Morris Hall. Rev. Joseph M. Kurtz purchased the rectory on December 4, 1951. After a fire destroyed the original church on January 2, 1982, the congregation voted to replace it. The new, larger church opened for mass on December 21, 1985.

During Rev. Joseph S. Keenan's pastorate, a school was constructed by the 1964–65 school year, and a convent was completed in 1965. The Sisters of St. Joseph of Newark staffed the school until 1974. Lay people ran the school until the Sisters of the Resurrection from Castleton-on-Hudson, New York, arrived in 1979. The Sisters of the Resurrection left in 1989.

Pastors: Rev. Michael P. McCorristin, 1937–39; Rev. Edward A. McAndrews, 1940–42; Rev. James G. Harding, 1943; Rev. Joseph F. Ketter, 1944; Rev. Thomas T. Barry, 1945–51; Rev. Joseph M. Kurtz, 1951–54; Rev. Joseph S. Keenan, 1955–67; Msgr. Thomas J. Frain, Ph.D., 1967–present.

Principals: Sr. Mary Agnes, C.S.J., 1964–68; Sr. Kathleen Doyle, C.S.J., 1968–77; Rev. William J. Lynch, S.J., 1977–79; Sr. Christine Marie Bykowski, C.R., 1979–81; Sr. Mary Daniel Colembiewski, C.R., 1981–85; Sr. Eva Marie Zajkowski, C.R., 1985–89; Mrs. Paulette Bearer, 1989–present.

Lincroft, Saint Leo the Great

The Most Rev. George W. Ahr established St. Leo the Great Parish in June 1958 and named Rev. Arthur J. St. Laurent founding

Church of Saint Leo the Great, Lincroft

pastor. The parish's first mass, on July 26, and subsequent masses were celebrated in the Lincroft Public School until the church was completed in June 1960. Because the plans included a building complex suitable for both a church and school, at the completion of the school building, the Sisters of St. Francis of Glen Riddle, Pennsylvania, provided teaching sisters for the September 1960 school year. A parish house was built in December 1963, and a convent for the nuns was completed in June 1965. In August 1980, upon the death of Father St. Laurent, Rev. William J. Bohnsack, then associate, was promoted to pastor. The church was renovated in 1982. The Sisters of St. Francis left the school in 1983. With the phenomenal growth in families and programs, the Arts and Athletic Center was constructed to benefit the parish community. It opened in June 1986 and combines a stage, gymnasium, and classrooms.

Pastors: Rev. Arthur J. St. Laurent, 1958–80; Rev. William J. Bohnsack, 1980–85; Rev. James M. Clark, 1985–present.

Principals: Sr. Loretta Marie, O.S.F., 1960–65; Sr. Laureen Francis, O.S.F., 1965–72; Sr. Adele, O.S.F., 1972–73; Sr. Maria Gross, O.S.F., 1973–83; Mrs. Elena A. Torregrossa, 1983–present.

Long Branch, Holy Trinity

At the beginning of the twentieth century, Msgr. William P. Cantwell, pastor of Our Lady Star of the Sea in Long Branch, realized that Italian immigrants would be better served by priests who spoke Italian. The Trinitarian Fathers visited the community at stated intervals to celebrate mass. Then, Italian-speaking Rev. John O'Connor was assigned to Star of the Sea as curate. In May 1904, an Italian priest, Rev. Isidor Cortesi, started traveling from Asbury Park on weekends to serve the needs of Italian Catholics in Long Branch. Monsignor Cantwell granted Father Cortesi full use of Star of the Sea Lyceum's auditorium for the celebration of mass.

In 1906, the Most Rev. James A. McFaul formed Holy Trinity as a national parish for Italian-speaking Catholics. Similar national parishes had already been erected in Red Bank and Asbury Park. Rev. John Prosseda, C.M., first pastor, oversaw construction of a basement church and a rectory. The church, a covered basement, was finished on May 5, 1908. Rev. Francis Fisher, O.Ss.T., completed the entire church in 1917.

During the administration of Rev. Emilio Cardelia, 1938–41, the Religious Teach-

Church of the Holy Trinity, Long Branch

ers Filippini were invited to teach catechism to the children of the parish. Rev. Gerald T. Celentana became pastor in June 1941, and, before the end of the year, the men of the parish had converted the church basement into a parish hall. Father Celentana made it possible for the house that had been acquired in 1941 to be used as a convent starting in September 1942. Sr. Josephine Palmeggiano, M.P.F., together with two other sisters labored in the vineyards of the faithful by establishing the school with a kindergarten class. In 1953, a first grade was added, and each subsequent year, a new grade was added. In 1957, classes were transferred to St. Jerome's in West Long Branch until Holy Trinity Parish built a school of its own. In July 1961, ground was broken for the new school, which opened in September 1962. It accommodated eight grades and a kindergarten. A new convent was also finished in 1962.

Between 1974 and 1979, Rev. Salvatore Livigni served as administrator. To the church he added Saints Chapel, which was dedicated in 1976. Father Livigni also purchased an organ. Rev. Frank Iazzetta renovated the parish complex and revived the annual festival in honor of Our Lady of Mount Carmel. Under Rev. John F. Campoli's direction, a preschool, Trinity Treasures, was founded. In August 1991, Rev. Thomas Gervasio was appointed administrator.

Pastors: Rev. John Prosseda, C.M., 1906–10; Rev. Alex Petrone, O.Ss.T., 1910–12; Rev. Francis Fisher, O.Ss.T., 1912–21; Rev. Gerardo Cristiani, 1921–38; Rev. Gerald T. Celentana, 1941–59; Rev. George Albano, 1959–70; Rev. Joseph Doino, 1971–74; Rev. Frank Iazzetta, 1979–82; Rev. John F. Campoli, 1982–91.

Principals: Sr. Josephine Palmeggiano, M.P.F., 1942–48; Sr. Matilde Blasi, M.P.F., c1948; Sr. Catherine Girgenti, M.P.F.; Sr. Adele Venezia, M.P.F.; Sr. Louise Del Carpine, M.P.F.; Sr. Norma Garbaccio, M.P.F.; Sr. Victoria Dal Corso, M.P.F.; Sr. Josephine Longo, M.P.F.; Sr. Claire Grieco, M.P.F.; Sr. Domenica Troina, M.P.F.; Sr. Elizabeth Dalessio, M.P.F., present.

Long Branch, Our Lady Star of the Sea

The Most Rev. Joseph J. Hughes, bishop of New York, celebrated mass in Long Branch as early as September 1, 1848. In 1854, Rev. John A. Kelly, the young pastor of St. Mary's in South Amboy, built Long Branch's first Catholic church. In 1871, Rev. John F.

Church of Our Lady Star of the Sea, Long Branch

Salaun, the new pastor of St. James in Red Bank, erected the second church, and on July 1, 1876, he became Our Lady Star of the Sea's first resident pastor. In 1879, Rev. James A. Walsh began construction of Holy Spirit Church in Asbury Park, which would receive a resident pastor of its own during the following year. Rev. James A. McFaul convinced the Sisters of Charity from Convent Station to open an academy, separate from the parish, in 1885. In 1890, he initiated the construction of two mission churches, Precious Blood in Monmouth Beach and Saint Michael's in the West End section of Long Branch.

By 1900, the parish school, Star of the Sea Lyceum, was educating its first youngsters. Rev. Isidor Cortesi started ministering to Italian-speaking Catholics in the school in 1904, and by 1906, Rev. John Prosseda was serving them as the Holy Trinity Parish.

The present rectory was provided in 1916 by Rev. Michael C. McCorristin. At 5 a.m., Sunday, December 5, 1926, a tragic fire destroyed the church. A new church opened with a First Holy Communion mass on May 12, 1929. The parish was divided in 1956 with the establishment of St. Jerome in West Long Branch. The Sisters of Charity, Convent Station, staffed the parish school from 1900 to 1979. The Newburgh Dominicans and the Congregation of the Marianites of the Holy Cross successively served the school until its closing in 1986. The parish ministers to the sick at Monmouth Medical Center and three nursing homes.

Pastors: Rev. John F. Salaun, 1876–77; Rev. James A. Walsh, 1877–83; Rev. James A. McFaul, 1883–90; Msgr. William P. Cantwell, 1890–1915; Rev. Michael C. McCorristin, 1915–31; Rev. William J. McConnell, 1932–35; Rev. Leo M. Cox, 1935–57; Rev. John Horan, 1957–77; Rev. M. Joseph Mokrzycki, 1977–present.

Principals: Sr. Mary Digna Lacey, S.C., 1900–1915; Sr. Clara Teresa Valentine, S.C., 1915–22, 1928–38; Sr. Maria de Sales Smith, S.C., 1922–28; Sr. Mary Rachel Blacker, S.C., 1938–44; Sr. Dolores Marie Burke, S.C., 1944–45; Sr. Anna Margaret Schwarz, S.C., 1945–51; Sr. Rita Gabriel Carney, S.C., 1951–57; Sr. Catherine Edward Nieuzytek, S.C., 1957–63; Sr. Rose Celeste McCaffrey, S.C., 1963–69; Sr. Agnes Maureen Iveson, S.C., 1969–72; Sr. Virginia Margaret Lunau, S.C., 1972–78; Sr. Michael Vincent Dailey, O.P., 1978–85; Sr. Patricia Schladebeck, M.S.C., 1985–86.

Long Branch, Saint John the Baptist

In June 1965, the Most Rev. George W. Ahr designated the old St. Dorothea's Church, Eatontown, as the spiritual center for Monmouth County's Spanish-speaking people. The church was renamed Immaculate Conception Church. Due to the growing population of Spanish-speaking people in Monmouth County, Immaculate Conception was divided into the following churches: Our Lady of Providence, Neptune; Jesus the Lord, Keyport; and St. John the Baptist, Long Branch. Immaculate Con-

Church of Saint John the Baptist, Long Branch

ception Church is now a Korean national parish.

In 1977, a garment factory was purchased and remodeled into the present St. John the Baptist Church. Bishop Ahr dedicated the church on September 18, 1978, as a mission of Immaculate Conception. On October 24, 1984, St. John the Baptist was established as an independent parish, with Rev. Manuel Fernandez as first pastor. Services are conducted in Spanish, Portuguese, and English.

Pastor: Rev. Manuel Fernandez, 1984–present.

Long Branch, Saint Michael

Long Branch was a popular seaside resort as early as the 1830s. Five U.S. presidents have conducted their affairs of state during the summer months within the confines of St. Michael's Parish, as follows: Ulysses S. Grant, 1868; Rutherford B. Hayes, 1877; James A. Garfield, who died in Elberon, September 19, 1881; Chester A. Arthur, 1882; and Woodrow Wilson, 1916. Although none of them were Catholic, the many Catholics in their entourages were responsible for bringing attention to the need for a church in the West End section of Long Branch.

St. Michael's was named after the first bishop of Trenton, the Most Rev. Michael J. O'Farrell, who started the parish and construction of a church in 1886. Bishop O'Farrell regularly visited during the church's construction and dedicated the building on August 1, 1891. In the summer of 1892, Bishop O'Farrell appointed Rev. Richard A. Crean as first resident pastor, establishing St. Michael's as an independent parish.

The main altar of the church was given in memory of Mr. Francis Anthony Drexel, banker and philanthropist of Philadelphia. Mr. Drexel was most generous in aiding charities and left a great part of his estate to the Catholic Church. He died in 1885, but his daughter who summered at West End became the founder of the Sisters of the Blessed Sacrament. Mother Katherine Drexel labored among the Indians and Negroes of the United States until her death at age 97 on March 3, 1955.

In 1907, the private casino and theater of Mrs. Norman Monro's estate were purchased and moved across the street on Norwood Avenue. This became the Norwood Mission, where mass was celebrated during the summers until 1924. With the assistance of a buggy and his horse, Duffy, Father Crean attended to the missions and the sick. He did eventually purchase a Ford automobile for his travels. Despite being in bed with a heavy cold, Father Crean rallied to celebrate two masses each on Christmas of 1928 and on the Sunday before Christmas. However, he developed pneumonia and passed to his eternal reward on December 27, 1928.

The second pastor, Msgr. John J. Sweeney, always kept the parish plant in good repair. With a wooden floor and plaster walls, the basement of the church was finished for parish socials and meetings. Monsignor Sweeney modernized the heating facilities of the church and rectory by installing oil burners. He even convinced city officials to plant cherry trees around the lovely Lake Takanesse that borders the church.

The proximity to Lake Takanesse and the Atlantic Ocean caused the church and rectory to deteriorate. Rev. Lewis A. Hayes practically rebuilt the rectory. With the assistance of some good engineering advice, he had the basement of the church waterproofed and turned into a very attractive parish hall with a stage and kitchen. In addition, Father Hayes had the church repaired, painted, and renovated.

Pastors: Rev. Richard A. Crean, 1892–1928; Msgr. John J. Sweeney, 1929–42; Rev. Charles J. Farran, 1942–51; Rev. Lewis A. Hayes, 1951–69; Msgr. Paul F. Bradley, 1969–89; Rev. Charles B. Weiser, 1989–present.

Manalapan, Saint Thomas More

St. Thomas More Parish was formed out of Our Lady of Mercy, Englishtown, in 1970. The pastor of Our Lady of Mercy, Rev. John C. Petri, recognized that the new housing developments along the Route 9 corridor would initiate a major population expansion in the Manalapan area. The new parish grew around Yorktowne, the first housing development in the area, upon land donated by the developer to the Diocese of Trenton. In June 1971, Father Petri was transferred to St. Thomas More as first resident pastor. Eventually a parish hall was built for Sunday worship. Later, a classroom wing was added for the more than 1,100

Church of Saint Thomas More, Manalapan

students in the religious education program. Finally, a church was completed in 1979.

Pastors: Rev. John C. Petri, 1971–89; Rev. Paul A. Scaglione, 1989–present.

Manasquan, Saint Denis

In the 1900s, Rev. Daniel Lutz, O.F.M. Conv., pastor of St. Peter's in Point Pleasant Beach, was assigned to minister to Catholics of Manasquan, Brielle, and Sea Girt. He celebrated the area's first recorded mass on Sunday, February 3, 1907, in the home of Mr. John Mealey. Local Catholics formalized plans to organize St. Denis Parish. The Most Rev. James A. McFaul officially approved the parish establishment on June 22, 1909. The first mass celebrated in the completed church took place on October 11, 1911. Rev. Hubert Osterman, O.F.M.

Conv., from St. Francis College in Trenton, served the congregation between 1912 and 1914.

Rev. James A. Healy was assigned as first resident pastor in 1914. However, after a short time, Father Healy switched positions with Rev. James A. Gough, pastor of St. Gabriel's in Marlboro. During the pastorate of Rev. John F. Welsh, an expansion and development program was initiated. The original church was expanded to accommodate 750 people. During the late 1940s, Father Welsh bought a prefabricated Quonset hut to serve the needs of the Catholic Youth Organization and parish societies. Construction of a school and convent began in 1958. From the fall of 1959,

the Religious Congregation Sisters of St. Joseph from Chestnut Hill, Pennsylvania, ran the school until 1982, when the Dominican Sisters from Caldwell took over. Under Msgr. James A. Harding's guidance, a beach chapel was constructed for summer visitors and was appropriately called Star of the Sea Chapel. Msgr. Joseph A. O'Connor renovated the parish plant and built the Father John F. Welsh Parish Center, with gymnasium and classrooms, in 1984.

Pastors: Rev. James A. Healy, 1914; Rev. James A. Gough, 1915–23; Rev. Thomas M. Healy, 1923–40; Rev. John F. Welsh, 1941–64; Msgr. James A. Harding, 1964–70; Msgr. Joseph A. O'Connor, 1970–92; Rev. Robert J. Parenti, 1992–present.

Principals: Sr. Joseph Andrew, S.S.J., 1959–62; Sr. Winifred, S.S.J., 1962–68; Sr. Rosine, S.S.J., 1968–73; Sr. John Eudes, S.S.J., 1973–76; Sr. Mary McKenna, S.S.J., 1976–82; Sr. Patricia O'Donnell, O.P., 1982–92; Sr. Christine Coakley, O.P., 1992–present.

Maple Shade, Our Lady of Perpetual Help

In 1919, Rev. Leo Dineen, assistant pastor at Our Lady of Good Counsel in Moorestown, celebrated Maple Shade's first mass, in a silk mill. Mass was offered in the Poplar Avenue Grammar School auditorium for the first time on March 14, 1920. The Most Rev. Thomas J. Walsh laid the cornerstone for Our Lady of Perpetual Help's original church on April 24, 1921. The Sisters of St. Joseph from Chestnut Hill,

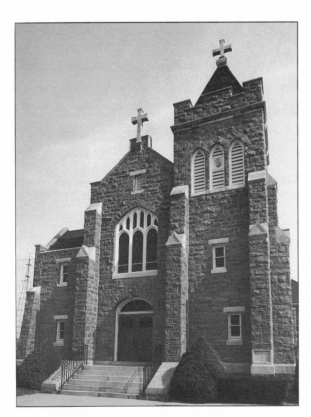

Church of Saint Denis, Manasquan

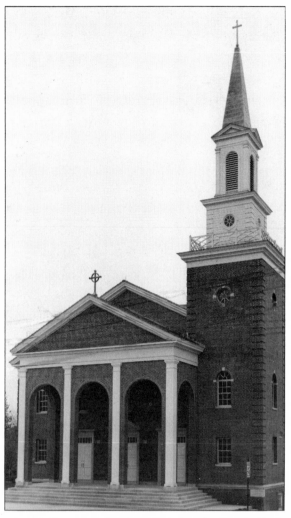

Church of Our Lady of Perpetual Help, Maple Shade

Pastors: Rev. Leo Dineen, 1929–30; Rev. John Farrell, 1930–35; Rev. George E. Duff, 1935–42; Rev. James McGrath, 1942–48; Msgr. Edward C. Henry, 1948–50; Rev. Thomas F. Nolan, 1950–69; Rev. James E. Coley, 1969–73; Rev. John J. Meehan, 1973–77; Rev. Eugene M. Rebeck, 1977–85; Rev. Bernard J. Keigher, 1985–present.

Principals: Sr. Albertine, S.S.J., 1928–36; Sr. Thomas Marie, S.S.J., 1936–41; Sr. Mary Conception, S.S.J., 1941–43; Sr. Miriam Alacoque, S.S.J., 1943–48; Sr. Saint Leo, S.S.J., 1948–53; Sr. Rose Mercedes, S.S.J., 1953–59; Sr. Maria Pace, S.S.J., 1959–64; Sr. Rose Eileen, S.S.J., 1964–71; Sr. John Raymond, S.S.J., 1971–73; Sr. Marie Williams, S.S.J., 1973–75; Sr. Kathryn Davis, S.S.J., 1975–82; Sr. Mary Beth Hamm, S.S.J., 1982–90; Mrs. Mary Ann Figura, 1990–present.

Marlboro, Saint Gabriel

In 1871, Rev. Frederick Kivelitz, pastor of St. Rose of Lima in Freehold, traveled to

Pennsylvania, have staffed the parish school since its inception in 1928, first teaching in the original church building. The cornerstone for the school building was laid by the Most Rev. John J. McMahon on November 23, 1929. Our Lady of Good Counsel continued to care for Our Lady of Perpetual Help until Father Dineen was transferred to Maple Shade as resident pastor on May 14, 1929. Growth of the parish necessitated Rev. Thomas Nolan's breaking ground for a larger church on April 18, 1955.

Church of Saint Gabriel, Marlboro

Marlboro via horsecart and later by bicycle to offer mass and help the congregation of Marlboro and vicinity. St. Gabriel's Mission developed with a church dedicated on November 4, 1878, by the Most Rev. Michael A. Corrigan, bishop of Newark. By August 1885, St. Gabriel's was clear of debt and as a result received its first resident pastor, Rev. John M. O'Leary. Established as an independent parish, St. Gabriel's received a mission of its own, St. Catharine's of Holmdel. St. Catharine's became a parish in its own right in 1982. St. John's Church, a second mission of St. Gabriel's, was built in the hamlet of Marlboro in 1922 but was sold in 1983 and converted to a professional office. St. Gabriel's Church was plagued by several fires during the early 1900s that damaged the church, rectory, and bell tower. The church hall, formerly two barracks donated by the Good Shepherd Sisters of Wickatunk, was destroyed by fire in 1967. However, St. Gabriel's continued to flourish. In 1972, during Msgr. James T. Connell's pastorate, a larger church, hall, and rectory were completed. The original church and rectory still function as places for meetings and mass. A new parish center with classrooms for religious instruction was erected in 1988 under the guidance of Rev. Ralph W. Stansley.

Pastors: Rev. John M. O'Leary, 1885–88; Rev. James A. Lawrence, 1888–1906; Rev. John E. Caton, 1906–09; Rev. James F. Gough, 1909–14; Rev. James A. Healy, 1914–19; Rev. John P. Grady, 1919–24; Rev. Francis J. Sullivan, 1924–30; Rev. John J. Lucitt, 1930–34; Rev. Louis F. Cogan, 1934–36; Rev. Thomas A. Daly, 1936–37; Rev. A. C. Hamel, 1937–41; Rev. John J. Horan, 1941–48; Rev. John J. Nowack, 1948–60; Rev. Vincent A. Lloyd, 1960–66; Msgr. James T. Connell, 1966–83; Rev. Ralph W. Stansley, 1983–90; Rev. Eugene J. Roberts, 1990–present.

Marlton, Saint Joan of Arc

St. Joan of Arc Parish was established on June 16, 1961, and Sunday masses were then celebrated at the Florence V. Evans School in Marlton. The first church was dedicated in October 1963. The school was opened in September 1965, and to this day the school is staffed by the Sisters of St. Joseph of Chestnut Hill, Pennsylvania. Significant growth over the next twenty years impelled planning for a larger church. A new, 1,200-seat church was dedicated in July 1988. The structure included additional classrooms and an all-purpose room. Concurrently, the old church was converted into a gymnasium and is used regularly by the parish youth. St. Joan of Arc Parish also provides the necessary pastoral care for the West Jersey Hospital–Marlton Division.

Church of Saint Joan of Arc, Marlton

Church of Saint Clement, Matawan

Pastors: Rev. William J. Kokoszka, 1961–73; Msgr. Armand A. Pedata, 1973–present.

Principals: Sr. Joseph Andrew, S.S.J., 1965–71; Sr. Ann Christopher, S.S.J., 1971–75; Sr. Sandra Kessler, S.S.J., 1975–81; Sr. Anne Cook, S.S.J., 1981–89; Sr. Patricia Pycik, S.S.J., 1989–present.

Matawan, Saint Clement

On June 3, 1965, the Most Rev. George W. Ahr established the parish of St. Clement and appointed Rev. Joseph Rucinski as founding pastor. Initial Sunday masses, including the first, on June 13, 1965, were held in the Matawan High School auditorium. Within six months, Father Rucinski purchased a home, converting it into a rectory and chapel. Ground breaking at a 24.5-acre lot occurred on April 19, 1969. A catechetical center and gymnasium were completed and opened for masses in October 1970. The church was finished on March 13, 1971. A rectory was built in 1981, and tennis courts and a baseball field were completed in 1983. Shortly before Father Rucinski's retirement, the Parish Banquet Hall was finished in September 1986.

During his pastorate, Rev. Edward D. Strano, second pastor, has developed many activities, including Pre-Cana, R.C.I.A., Adolescent Catechesis, ministry to the sick, Hospital Committee, and ministry to the bereaved. He also reactivated the Holy Name Society and Confraternity of Christian Doctrine. Father Strano established the children's choir, basketball and volleyball teams for the youth, and the Social Concerns Committee, which reaches out to the poor and needy of the community.

Pastors: Rev. Joseph Rucinski, 1965–86; Rev. Edward D. Strano, 1986–present.

Medford, Saint Mary of the Lakes

Before 1931, mass was celebrated in Medford in a pavilion during the summer months only. In 1931, a small log cabin church was erected. The Most Rev. William A. Griffin established St. Mary of the Lakes as an independent parish on June 25, 1943, with Rev. Paul A. Grieco as first pastor. For the next several years, the log cabin church was renovated to make it usable all year. In June 1961, the diocese split the parish, establishing St. Joan of Arc, Marlton. Construction of a new church was begun in 1965 and completed the following year. In October 1982, the diocese again split the parish, establishing Holy Eucharist, Tabernacle.

The Sisters, Servants of the Immaculate Heart of Mary, Scranton, Pennsylvania, came to Medford Lakes to teach catechetical

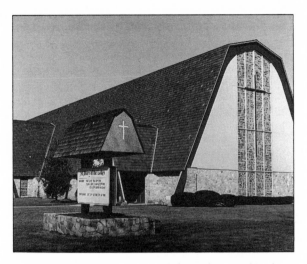

Church of Saint Mary of the Lakes, Medford

classes. In 1947, a convent was purchased. Three Sisters of St. Joseph of Peace from Newark came to continue religious instruction and later staffed St. Joseph's School, now named after St. Mary of the Lakes. The school opened in 1953 for the Medford area. Since 1969, the Sisters of St. Francis of Philadelphia have taught in the school. In 1985, an addition to the school allowed for double the enrollment and provided Confraternity of Christian Doctrine offices, a school library, and needed office space.

Pastors: Rev. Paul A. Grieco, 1943–48; Rev. Raymond T. Hurley, 1948–59; Rev. William J. Campbell, 1959–80; Rev. John F. Campoli, 1980–82; Rev. Joseph M. LaForge, 1982–92; Rev. Joseph A. Tedesco, 1992–present.

Principals: Sr. Mary Eucharista, C.S.J.P., 1953–55; Sr. Teresa Catherine, C.S.J.P., 1955–57; Sr. Teresa Rose, C.S.J.P., 1957–58; Sr. Eileen Joseph O'Donoghue, C.S.J.P., 1958–59; Sr. Ann Fox, C.S.J.P., 1959–62; Sr. Laurence Marie, C.S.J.P., 1962–63; Sr. Elizabeth Ann, C.S.J.P., 1963–67; Sr. Elenor Maragliano, C.S.J.P., 1967–69; Sr. Euthalia, O.S.F., 1969–70; Sr. Antonita Donahue, O.S.F., 1970–73; Sr. Lorraine Joubert, O.S.F., 1973–74; Sr. Marie Agnes, O.S.F., 1974–81; Sr. Justina Marie Miller, O.S.F., 1981–present.

Monmouth Beach, Precious Blood

Affluent summer home owners in Monmouth Beach along with two large hotels employed numerous people, including many Catholics. Eventually, Monmouth Beach was made a mission of Our Lady Star of the Sea in Long Branch, the nearest church at which Monmouth Beach Catholics had been attending mass. During the summers, the few permanent residents and the summer employees raised funds through card parties, raffles, and dances. Mr. John Maney donated property to Rev. James A. McFaul, then pastor of Our Lady Star of the Sea, for the erection of a church. The Most Rev. Michael J. O'Farrell dedicated the church building on June 21, 1891. A recreation hall was also constructed and used during the summer months for fund-raising social events.

Precious Blood Parish remained a mission of Our Lady Star of the Sea until 1910, when the Most Rev. James A. McFaul appointed Rev. Patrick J. Powers as first resident pastor. In 1916, after Rev. William Tighe's transfer to St. Agnes in Atlantic Highlands, the parish became a mission of St. Dorothea's, Eatontown. The congregation dwindled, and the church closed during the winters due to the lack of central heating. In the early 1930s, central heating was installed, allowing for year-round celebrations of the mass.

Finally, in 1947, the Most Rev. William A. Griffin reestablished Precious Blood Parish and reassigned Rev. Francis J. Dwyer, then pastor of St. Dorothea's, to the pastorate of Precious Blood. Father Dwyer used the Burns Cottage as a rectory. Rev. Walter H. Greene built a rectory and purchased additional land for future needs. Msgr. Maurice P. Griffin temporarily used the borough hall and public school for religious instruction. On November 5, 1961, the Most Rev. William A. Griffin dedicated the catechetical center, the first building of its kind in the diocese.

Pastors: Rev. Patrick J. Powers, c1910; Rev. William Tighe, c1916; Rev. Francis J. Dwyer, 1947–c1952; Rev. Walter H. Greene, c1952; Msgr. Maurice P. Griffin, c1963; Rev. Earl A. Gannon, c1964; Rev. Ronald Becker, c1989; Rev. John T. Kielb, 1989–present.

Moorestown, Our Lady of Good Counsel

In 1832, James and Fannie Laverty, recent emigrants from Ireland, settled on a farm in Fellowship, now occupied by Exit 4 of the New Jersey Turnpike. The Laverty home soon became one of the regular stops for itinerant missionary priests, who served scattered Catholic families of the West Jersey area. This gathering of the faithful soon outgrew the Laverty home. One of the outbuildings was turned into the Chapel of Our Lady and St. Patrick, ministered to by the priests from Immaculate Conception, Camden. So rapid was the growth of the Catholic community that in 1852, the Most Rev. John N. Neumann, C.Ss.R., bishop of Philadelphia, directed that mass be said at Our Lady and St. Patrick once a month. In February 1867, a fire destroyed the chapel.

The community acquired a parcel of land on the main street of Moorestown. Because of strong antipathy toward Catholics at the time, a third party had to be engaged in the person of Mr. Peter Verga of Camden to negotiate the transaction. When asked what use he had for the land, he responded that he was acting as an agent for

Church of Our Lady of Good Counsel, Moorestown

one who would open a business of repairing souls. Thinking only in terms of a shoe repair shop, the seller readily signed over the deed. A brick church was built in the heart of the village of Moorestown, completed by 1870.

On February 27, 1879, the Most Rev. Michael A. Corrigan, bishop of Newark, raised the status of Our Lady and St. Patrick from a mission church to an independent parish with a resident pastor. Sometime in the early 1890s, the building sustained extensive damage from a windstorm, necessitating a new and larger church. On July 14, 1895, the cornerstone was laid, and sixteen months later, the present church was dedicated under the title of Our Lady of Good Counsel.

On June 15, 1924, the cornerstone of a school was laid. In September 1927, classes began, taught by the Sisters of St. Joseph from Chestnut Hill, Pennsylvania. The school received additions, including one larger than the school itself in 1962. The Sisters of St. Joseph left the school in 1985. The present principal, Sr. Michael Vincent Dailey, O.P., is a Dominican sister.

Pastors: Rev. James McKernan, 1880–86; Rev. Peter Dernis, 1886–90; Rev. John W. Murphy, 1890–1914; Rev. James F. Hendrick, 1914–28; Rev. Thomas F. Rudden, 1928–37; Msgr. Edward A. Cahill, 1937–49; Rev. Michael F. O'Keefe, 1949–66; Msgr. Edmund W. Kreger, 1966–69; Rev. James F. Murphy, 1969–81; Rev. James J. McGovern, 1981–present.

Principals: Mother Mary Albertine, S.S.J., 1927–33; Mother Agnes Josephine, S.S.J., 1933–39; Sr. Mary Andrew, S.S.J., 1939–43; Sr. Saint Eugene, S.S.J., 1943–49; Sr. Irma Magdalen, S.S.J., 1949–51; Sr. Helen Augustine, S.S.J., 1951–59; Sr. Ethel de Sales, S.S.J., 1959–64; Sr. Rose Amadeus, S.S.J., 1964–65; Sr. Agnes Angela, S.S.J., 1965–71; Sr. Francis Patrice, S.S.J., 1971–75; Sr. Ann Regina Lannon, S.S.J., 1975–77; Sr. Clare Madeleine, S.S.J., c1977; Sr. Michael Vincent Dailey, O.P., present.

Mount Holly, Christ the Redeemer

On October 1, 1974, Rev. Alex Ducci gathered a large group of Hispanics and celebrated, in Spanish, the mission's first mass at St. Joseph's in Beverly. Subsequent masses were offered at both St. Joseph's, Beverly, and Sacred Heart, Mount Holly.

Church of Christ the Redeemer, Mount Holly

The original name of the mission church, signifying its purpose and nationalities, was El Centro Católico Hispánico, or the Catholic Hispanic Center. The congregation consisted of numerous Hispanics from Puerto Rico, Latin America, and Spain, wishing to attend services conducted in their native language.

On October 3, 1975, the first mass was celebrated in the newly purchased Mount Holly church, previously a Protestant church and then a bank. On June 12, 1976, the Most Rev. George W. Ahr dedicated and blessed the church. On February 24, 1977, Bishop Ahr transformed the center into the new parish, Iglesia Cristo Redentor, or Christ the Redeemer Church. Father Ducci purchased a rectory. In September 1982, the parish added a day care center known as Busy Corner Learning Center.

Pastors: Rev. Alex Ducci, I.M.C., 1976–77; Rev. Victoriano F. Sandoval, O.S.A., 1977–present.

Mount Holly, Sacred Heart

On November 19, 1843, a sailing vessel from Ireland arrived at Burlington. A number of the Catholics on board settled in Mount Holly and traveled seven miles on foot to Burlington to hear mass. In 1848, Rev. John P. Mackin, pastor of old St. John's in Trenton, began to offer mass in Mount Holly.

Later in 1848, the Mount Holly faithful became a mission of St. Paul's, Burlington. The first Catholic church in Mount Holly, under the patronage of St. Mary, was erected in 1852 by Rev. Hugh Lane,

pastor of St. Paul's. Land was purchased for a cemetery in 1857. Apparently, a school with lay teachers existed between 1868 and 1876. On October 27, 1871, Rev. Thaddeus Hogan was assigned as Mount Holly's resident pastor, establishing St. Mary's as an independent parish. Father Hogan began construction of the second St. Mary's Church in May 1872. During the pastorate of Rev. Hugh J. McManus, the church was completed, and a rectory was built and furnished.

Priests from Mount Holly and St. Mary's, Bordentown, alternately served a mission in the village of Jobstown. Early in 1880, the Most Rev. Michael A. Corrigan, bishop of Newark, ordered the mission to be incorporated under the patronage of St. Andrew. Permanent responsibility of the mission was given to Sacred Heart Parish in 1945.

On January 16, 1881, while Rev. Robert E. Burke was pastor, the name of the parish was changed to Sacred Heart. Rev. Peter J. Hart made a lasting contribution to the church by a complete interior improve-

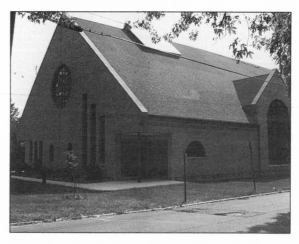

Church of the Sacred Heart, Mount Holly

ment and beautification. Rev. J. Arthur Hayes, known as the "improvement priest," reconditioned the church, including applying a new slate roof to the church. In 1935, he built St. Ann's Church in Browns Mills. In January 1956, during Rev. Joseph Kozak's pastorate, the cornerstone was laid for an all-purpose auditorium, which was blessed and dedicated at the same time. Rev. Francis P. Gunner is responsible for adding 25 acres to the parish cemetery. In 1983, the church was recognized as in dire need of repair. However, the church was later deemed unsafe. Ground was broken on December 18, 1988, for the erection of a new church dedicated on October 6, 1991.

The Most Rev. William A. Griffin took an unusual interest in the education of Mount Holly children. He requested Rev. George E. Duff to find suitable quarters for the nuns he was sending to Mount Holly. In September 1943, four Sisters, Servants of the Immaculate Heart of Mary, from Scranton, Pennsylvania, took up residence within the parish and taught catechetical classes. The success of the classes prompted Bishop Griffin to purchase the Johnson mansion on June 1, 1944. Extensive remodeling during the summer allowed for the opening of the Mount Holly Regional Catholic School for the 1944–45 school year. On October 15, 1944, Bishop Griffin dedicated the school and convent. After additions and increased enrollment, the regional school became the sole responsibility of Sacred Heart Parish in 1953. Additions to the school continued, including a large auditorium in 1956.

Pastors: Rev. Thaddeus Hogan, 1871–74; Rev. Samuel J. Walsh, 1874–75; Rev. Hugh J. McManus, 1875–80; Rev. Robert E. Burke, 1880–84; Rev. Dennis J. Duggan, 1884–86; Rev. James A. Reynolds, 1886–91; Rev. John M. O'Leary, 1891–92; Rev. Michael J. Brennan, 1892–94; Rev. Joseph Keuper, 1894–96; Rev. William J. Fitzgerald, 1896; Rev. Stephen M. Lyons, 1896–1900; Rev. Peter J. Hart, 1900–1914; Rev. Peter J. Kelly, 1914–26; Rev. Michael A. Dolan, 1926–28; Rev. John J. Foley, 1928–30; Rev. Aloysius D. McCue, 1930–34; Rev. J. Arthur Hayes, 1934–43; Rev. George E. Duff, 1943–45; Msgr. James S. Foley, 1946–50; Rev. Joseph Kozak, 1950–57; Rev. Francis P. Gunner, 1957–59; Rev. Gerald T. Celentana, 1959–67; Rev. James A. Thompson, 1969; Rev. Michael J. Clark, 1969–73; Rev. Justin J. Herbst, 1973–92; Rev. Robert J. Schecker, 1992–present.

Principals: Mother Mary Alphonsus, I.H.M., 1944–46; Mother Mary Brigida, I.H.M., 1946–52; Mother Raymond, I.H.M., 1952–58; Sr. Cecily, I.H.M., 1958–64; Sr. Saint Mark, I.H.M., 1964–70; Sr. Robert Mary, I.H.M., 1970–71; Sr. Daniel Mary, I.H.M., 1971–74; Sr. Virgine, I.H.M., 1974–78; Sr. Fidelis, I.H.M., 1978–88; Sr. Ann Monica Bubser, I.H.M., 1988–91; Sr. Jean Louise Bachetti, I.H.M., 1991–present.

Mount Laurel, Saint John Neumann

In June 1978, the first parish in the diocese named in honor of St. John Neumann was established. The Most Rev. George W. Ahr

Church of Saint John Neumann, Mount Laurel

appointed the prior of the Cistercian Monastery of Our Lady of Fatima, Rev. Vittorino Zanni, O. Cist., as the parish's first pastor. Father Zanni was assisted by the other Cistercian priests of the monastery. The rural parish is set in the farmlands of Mount Laurel on the beautiful grounds of the Cistercian Monastery. Initially, the monastery facilities were used in order to accommodate the parish. However, more families in attendance necessitated construction of a parish center, blessed on November 23, 1980. In 1988, a parish hall was built for meetings, socials, activities, and parish offices.

Pastors: Rev. Vittorino Zanni, O. Cist., 1978–89; Rev. Lino S. Parente, O. Cist., 1989–present.

Neptune, Holy Innocents

In the mid-1950s, the western section of Neptune Township grew rapidly. A large percentage of these new residents were Catholics who attended six different surrounding churches. In 1959, the Most Rev. George W. Ahr gave them a parish of their own. Mass was celebrated in Wilson School, Neptune City, until the first building of the parish plant was completed in August 1960. The building consisted of a gymnasium, cafeteria/auditorium, office, and small living quarters for the pastor. Mass was celebrated in the gymnasium. In 1964, a rectory was built, and a convent was added the following year. A classroom was attached to the original structure in time for the start of school in September 1965. The Religious Teachers Filippini have staffed the school since its inception. A new church building was dedicated on November 8, 1992.

Pastors: Rev. James A. Reilly, 1959–82; Rev. John J. Scully, 1982–present.

Principals: Sr. Adele Venezia, M.P.F., 1965–67; Sr. Anne Marie Cervasio, M.P.F., 1967–70; Sr. Angelina Pelliccia, M.P.F., 1970–76; Sr. Elizabeth Dena, M.P.F., 1976–78; Sr. Catherine Paone, M.P.F., 1978–83; Sr. Elsa Donati, M.P.F., 1983–90; Sr. Betty Jean Takacs, M.P.F., 1990–present.

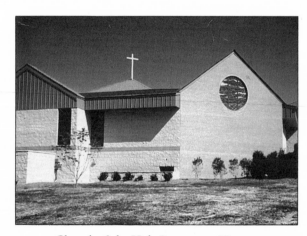

Church of the Holy Innocents, Neptune

Neptune, Our Lady of Providence

As his first assignment as a priest, Rev. Pedro L. Bou, S.V.D., arrived at St. Peter Claver in Asbury Park in January 1976. Father Bou took over ministry to the Hispanic community, and the church developed a new identity. A committee was formed to search for a church location. A Spanish-speaking parish was established on August 20, 1981, in Neptune, with Father Bou as founding pastor. The patroness, under the title Our Lady, Mother of Divine Providence, corresponds to the patron saint of the island of Puerto Rico. The former Assemblies of God Church, after repairs, became Our Lady of Providence Church. An adjacent, small school building was remodeled as the rectory. The Most Rev. John C. Reiss dedicated and blessed the church on July 18, 1982.

Pastor: Rev. Pedro L. Bou, S.V.D., 1981–92; Rev. James Vorwerk, S.V.D., 1992–present.

Church of Our Lady of Providence, Neptune

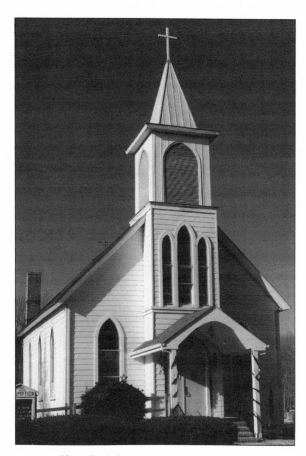

Church of the Assumption, New Egypt

New Egypt, Assumption

In 1853, Catholic services were held in nearby Hornerstown. It is believed that priests from St. Mary's, Bordentown, cared for area Catholics. In 1866, Rev. John P. Mackin, pastor of St. Mary's, purchased the Mormon church in Hornerstown. In 1871, the Most Rev. James Roosevelt Bayley transferred care of the Hornerstown Mission to the Conventual Franciscan Fathers of Trenton. Rev. Peter Jachetti, O.F.M. Conv., pastor of St. Francis of Assisium in Trenton, built a church in New Egypt in 1873.

The Most Rev. Michael A. Corrigan, bishop of Newark, wrote a short passage in his diary about his visit to New Egypt. He stated that the Mormon church had been moved from Hornerstown to a sand bank about two miles distant. The more central location was chosen to serve better the scattered Catholics of the neighborhood. Bishop Corrigan was present on that Tuesday, December 15, 1874, to bless the new church in New Egypt. Eventually, the parish's first church was razed.

In 1879, Assumption Parish became a mission of St. John's Church, Allentown. Land was purchased in 1907 and 1920. The first parcel became the site for a rectory, and the second parcel became part of the cemetery.

It was not until November 14, 1947, that the Most Rev. William A. Griffin made a separate and independent parish of Assumption. In 1948, the first pastor, Rev. William A. Barron, undertook a construction program including a new rectory, a parish hall, and renovations to the church.

A parish census taken in 1951 and 1952 revealed a number of Catholics in the Cassville section of Jackson Township. A mission under the patronage of St. Monica was proposed. Masses were celebrated in the Cassville Firehouse from November 2, 1952, until April 28, 1957. In the early summer of 1957, Father Martin from Our Lady of Fatima, Perth Amboy, started a mission under the patronage of St. Anthony Claret for the area's Spanish-speaking Catholics. St. Anthony Claret Church was ministered to by the Claretian Missionaries until the summer of 1990, when the church building was transferred to Assumption Parish. The church was renamed upon reinstitution of St. Monica's Mission and rededicated on August 25, 1991, by the Most Rev. John C. Reiss.

Rev. Francis J. Porazzo twice purchased land for the possibility of a school and an extension of the cemetery. Rev. Raymond L. Szulecki, Rev. Thomas P. Ridge, and Rev Anthony M. Carotenuto all accomplished renovations to parish buildings.

Pastors: Rev. William A. Barron, 1947–51; Rev. Francis J. Coan, 1951–55; Rev. Stephen G. Horvath, 1955–57; Rev. Francis J. Porazzo, 1957–69; Rev. Raymond L. Szulecki, 1969–71; Rev. Thomas P. Ridge, 1971–81; Msgr. Maurice P. Griffin, 1981–82; Rev. Philip T. Matera, 1982–85; Rev. Anthony M. Carotenuto, 1985–present.

New Monmouth, Saint Mary

In 1853, Rev. John Callan, pastor of St. Mary's in Dover, offered mass in Dr. Edwin Taylor's barn. Father Callan continued to care for New Monmouth Catholics until 1855. From 1855 to 1863, Rev. John A. Kelly, pastor of St. Mary's in South Amboy, served New Monmouth. The first three pastors from St. James in Red Bank were in charge of the New Monmouth mission from 1863 until 1879. However, in 1874, Rev. Stanislaus Danielou was named Red Bank's assistant pastor. He took primary responsibility for several missions, including New Monmouth. During his tenure at Red Bank, from 1874 to 1879, Father Danielou offered mass once a month in the New Monmouth area.

In 1863, Mr. George P. Fox offered land for a church to the Most Rev. James Roosevelt Bayley, bishop of Newark. This offer was turned down because the United States was in the middle of the Civil War. Mr. Fox's second offer, in 1875, was accepted by the Most Rev. Michael A. Corrigan, bishop of Newark. In 1878, plans were made for the establishment of a parish to cover Highlands, New Monmouth, and the adjacent countryside. Rev. John J. F. O'Connor arrived in the area on July 28, 1879, residing in Highlands. During the following year, Father O'Connor constructed a church in New Monmouth, which was blessed on September 12, 1880, by Bishop Corrigan under the patronage of the Blessed Virgin Mary, Mother of God.

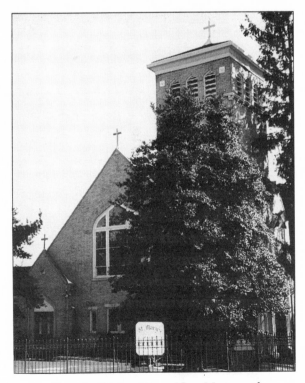

Church of Saint Mary, New Monmouth

Rev. John R. O'Connor, third pastor, constructed the present rectory and the church, modeled after a church he viewed in a small Italian village. Rev. John E. Murray developed the mission church of St. Ann in Keansburg. The first superintendent of schools in the Diocese of Trenton, Msgr. William J. McConnell, arrived as pastor in 1935. Rev. Robert T. Bulman, ordained in July 1940, was assigned as assistant pastor and served as administrator for seven years during Monsignor McConnell's long illness. Father Bulman succeeded as pastor and erected a grade school and high school. St. Mary's School opened in September 1953 and received structural or property additions three times through 1960. A 90-year-old red barn was purchased and transformed into St. Mary's Convent. Another major construction project resulted in Mater Dei High School, which was dedicated on March 28, 1965. (A separate entry for the high school appears in the chapter on institutions.) High school classes had started in September 1961 in the grade school, conducted in four tractor trailers. The Franciscan Sisters of Stella Niagara, New York, teach in the grade school and high school to this day. In 1983, the Dominican Sisters of Newburgh, New York, joined the Franciscans in the grade school.

Pastors: Rev. John J. F. O'Connor, 1879–94; Rev. Daniel P. Geoghegan, 1894–95; Rev. John R. O'Connor, 1895–1906; Rev. John E. Murray, 1907–24; Rev. Joseph R. Hughes, 1924–28; Rev. Robert F. Maron, 1928; Rev. J. A. Sullivan, 1929; Rev. Thomas F. Maher, 1929–34; Rev. Leo

M. Cox, 1934–35; Msgr. William J. McConnell, 1935–50; Msgr. Robert T. Bulman, 1950–92; Rev. Gregory D. Vaughan, 1992–present.

Principals of St. Mary's School: Mother Euphemia Nash, O.S.F., 1953–61; Mother Mary Bede Loob, O.S.F., 1961–63; Sr. Rosemarie, O.S.F., 1963–68; Sr. Nancy Grassia, O.S.F., 1968–72; Sr. Mary Ann, O.S.F., 1972–75; Sr. Helen Marie Schumacher, O.S.F., 1975–77; Sr. Patricia McMahon, O.S.F., 1977–83; Sr. Louise Cababe, O.P., 1983–present.

Normandy Beach, Our Lady of Peace

In 1945, the Most Rev. William A. Griffin established a mission parish in Normandy Beach, cared for by St. Bonaventure, Lavallette. The Most Rev. George W. Ahr dedicated a church in June 1953. Masses were celebrated only during the summer until 1975, when they were offered year-round by Army chaplains. On July 13, 1979,

Our Lady of Peace was established as an independent parish, with Msgr. Edmund W. Kreger as first permanent pastor. Repairs and renovations to the parish plant have occurred throughout the parish's history, including remodeling of the sanctuary in 1988.

Pastors: Msgr. Edmund W. Kreger, 1979–81; Rev. Vincent A. Lloyd, 1981–86; Rev. Laszlo Rauch 1986–present.

Pennington, Saint James

Prior to 1895, the small group of Pennington Catholics, mostly recent Irish immigrants, attended mass at St. Mary's Cathedral or St. Alphonsus in Hopewell. In 1895, Pennington's first mass was celebrated in the home of Mr. and Mrs. Patrick Tyman. On June 11, 1899, the cornerstone was laid for a church, which would be dedicated by the Most Rev. James A. McFaul on October 1, 1899. The pastors of St. Alphonsus were in charge of St. James Mission until 1898. Rev. Henry A. Ward, pastor of St. Joseph's in Trenton, took charge of the mission for a

Church of Our Lady of Peace, Normandy Beach

Church of Saint James, Pennington

Faith in Action in the Diocese of Trenton

month. Then, Rev. Joseph Thurnes, pastor of St. Francis of Assisium in Trenton, cared for the parish until 1900, when the priests from St. Mary's Cathedral took over. In 1905, care of the parish was transferred to Rev. John M. Gammell, chaplain of Morris Hall in Lawrenceville.

Finally on June 18, 1943, St. James Parish was established as an independent parish, with Rev. Francis Zgliczynski as first resident pastor. In 1966, a parish center was built, and during Msgr. Thomas C. Ryan's pastorate, a rectory was purchased and renovated. The present pastor, Rev. James J. McConnell, constructed a new church, dedicated in October 1987, for the growing congregation. Among the programs Father McConnell has added to the parish are a weekly 6:30 a.m. prayer group and an active social concerns group that reaches out to those within and outside the parish.

Pastors: Msgr. Francis Zgliczynski, 1943–69; Msgr. Thomas Ryan, 1969–77; Rev. James J. McConnell, 1977–present.

Perrineville, Saint Joseph

The pastors of St. Paul's in Princeton attended to Catholics of Freehold and Perrineville from 1850 through 1871. Rev. Frederick Kivelitz, first pastor of St. Rose of Lima in Freehold, then took care of the Catholics in Perrineville. On December 28, 1879, the Most Rev. Michael A. Corrigan, bishop of Newark, blessed a small brick terra cotta mission church under the patronage of St. Joseph in the town of Perrineville. Father Kivelitz celebrated the first mass in the church. A year later, St. Joseph's became

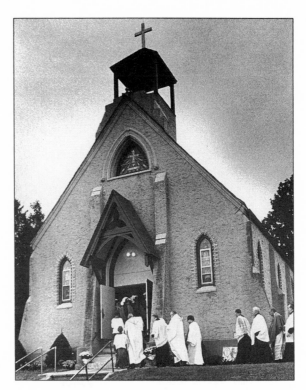

Church of Saint Joseph, Perrineville

a mission of St. James Church, Jamesburg. In 1886, 2 acres of ground was donated north of the church for a cemetery. From 1885 through 1891, St. Joseph's was attended to by its only resident pastor ever, Rev. Bartholomew Carey. Father Kivelitz again took charge of the parish until 1906, when St. Joseph's became a mission of St. Anthony of Padua, Hightstown. Since 1948, Our Lady of Mercy in Englishtown has served the needs of St. Joseph's Mission.

Pastor: Rev. Bartholomew Carey, 1885–91.

Point Pleasant, Saint Martha

The Borough of Point Pleasant was part of the parish territory of St. Peter's in Point Pleasant Beach until 1962, when it became attached to St. Dominic's in Bricktown.

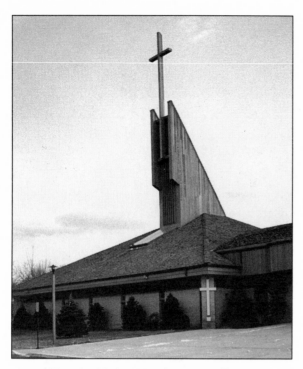

Church of Saint Martha, Point Pleasant

After having been assigned to various parishes for many years, Catholics of Point Pleasant joyously became an independent parish in 1972. The Most Rev. George W. Ahr chose the patron, St. Martha, for the newly established parish because he was ordained on July 29, the feast of St. Martha. The founding pastor, Rev. Henry A. Murphy, celebrated the parish's first mass on June 18, 1972, in the Nellie Bennett School. A house was soon purchased and converted into a rectory and chapel. The Nellie Bennett School and Kings Grant Inn were used for mass until March 17, 1976, when mass was first celebrated in the new combination church and parish center. In 1991, part of the parish center became a permanent church and was blessed on July 29, 1992.

Pastors: Rev. Henry A. Murphy, 1972–80; Rev. Joseph M. LaForge, 1980–82; Rev. Patrick F. Magee, 1982–present.

Point Pleasant Beach, Saint Peter

Early in the year 1881, Rev. Peter Jachetti, O.F.M. Conv., set out from Trenton to establish a mission in Lakehurst, then part of Manchester Township. Father Jachetti received the blessing of the Diocese of Newark, his provincial superior having instructed him to serve the needs of shore area Catholics and to provide a summer rest home for invalid and convalescent members of the order. According to one story, Father Jachetti fell asleep on the train and missed his transfer point in Farmingdale, alighting in Manasquan. There he met Mr. Patrick McElhinney, who convinced him that Point Pleasant was more favorably situated and showed greater promise for growth.

Church of Saint Peter, Point Pleasant Beach

On April 28, 1881, land was purchased for the original St. Peter's Church. By the summer of 1882, the church and rectory were completed. While attending to his primary duties in Trenton, Father Jachetti remained in charge of St. Peter's. If he did not travel to Point Pleasant to celebrate mass, then he sent Franciscans in his place, at least during the summer. The following Franciscans resided in Point Pleasant during the summers to serve the summer population: Rev. Angelus Goessmann, Rev. Fidelis Voigt, Rev. Peter Scharoun, and Rev. Roger Kexel. Father Kexel assumed responsibility of St. Peter's from 1890 to 1897. Then, Rev. Daniel Lutz, O.F.M. Conv., a professor at St. Francis College in Trenton, succeeded Father Kexel, residing in Point Pleasant during the summers. He celebrated mass during the rest of the year more and more often until he was offering mass every Sunday. In the year 1908, Father Lutz was relieved of his duties at St. Francis College. He became St. Peter's first permanent, year-round, resident pastor.

The addition of a tower and the renovation of the church in 1899 and 1900 transformed the building into a more suitable place of worship. However, on January 14, 1901, a fire destroyed the church and rectory. At a more central location, the parish built a new church, completed in the early summer of 1902. The Conventual Franciscan Friars have not only served St. Peter's Parish throughout its history but have also founded St. Catharine's in Seaside Park, St. Denis's in Manasquan, Sacred Heart in Bay Head, and a mission in Mantoloking.

By 1923, St. Peter's Parish had undertaken construction of the first parochial school in Ocean County, which opened in September 1924. Larger enrollment necessitated erection of a new school, which opened in September 1957. Three religious congregations have staffed the school: Dominican Sisters of Philadelphia, 1924–48; Sisters of the Holy Union, Sacred Heart Province from Fall River, Massachusetts, 1948–70; and Sisters of St. Joseph from Chestnut Hill, Pennsylvania, 1970–present. In 1962, an auditorium and gymnasium were dedicated. The building doubles as a place of worship during the summer to alleviate crowded conditions.

Pastors: Rev. Daniel Lutz, O.F.M. Conv., 1908–12; Rev. Berard Schweitzer, O.F.M. Conv., 1912–23; Rev. Felician Fehlner, O.F.M. Conv., 1923–29; Rev. Adolph Bernholz, O.F.M. Conv., 1929–35; Rev. Gerard Stauble, O.F.M. Conv., 1935–36; Rev. Cornelius Richartz, O.F.M. Conv., 1936–42, 1948–54; Rev. Callistus Scheid, O.F.M. Conv., 1942–48; Rev. Roger Nelipowitz, O.F.M. Conv., 1954–60; Rev. Bernardine Golden, O.F.M. Conv., 1960–66; Rev. Herbert Baloga, O.F.M. Conv., 1966–70; Rev. Sebastian Weber, O.F.M. Conv., 1970–76; Rev. Timothy Lyons, O.F.M. Conv., 1976–82; Rev. Henry Madigan, O.F.M. Conv., 1982–88; Rev. Kevin Kenny, O.F.M. Conv., 1988–present.

Principals: Sr. Mary Dominic, O.P., 1924–35; Sr. Mary Aquinas, O.P., 1935–

49; Sr. Paul Elizabeth, S.U.S.C., 1949–58; Mother John Francis, S.U.S.C., 1958–70; Sr. Francis Gervase, S.S.J., 1970–76; Sr. Agnes Mercedes, S.S.J., 1976–82; Sr. Josephine Wade, S.S.J., 1982–88; Sr. Karen Washabaugh, S.S.J., 1988–present.

Princeton, Saint Paul

As early as 1795, a French priest Rev. La Grange, ministered to Catholics of Princeton. In 1843, Rev. Hugh McGuire of St. Patrick's (now St. Peter's) in New Brunswick was directed by the Most Rev. Joseph J. Hughes, bishop of New York, to begin a mission parish in Princeton. Father McGuire celebrated mass on a regular basis in the Boyle home. In 1845, Rev. John Rogers succeeded Father McGuire and visited Princeton twice per month. A church was erected in 1849. Rev. John Scollard came to live in Princeton in 1850. The mission was formally established as Immaculate Conception. Sometime between 1850 and 1857, it was renamed St. Paul's Church. Rev. Alfred Young built a new church and opened the present cemetery. In 1867, another church was planned by Rev. James John Joseph O'Donnell and was opened two years later. Msgr. Thomas Moran invited the Sisters of Mercy from Manchester, New Hampshire, to start a school in September 1878. The school was initially called St. Scholastica's Seminary for young ladies. St. James Mission at Rocky Hill, opened in 1911, was transferred in 1982 to the care of St. Charles Borromeo Parish in Skillman, part of the Metuchen diocese. The present school building was built in 1931 under the direction of

Church of Saint Paul, Princeton

Rev. Patrick Clune. The present church, convent, and rectory were constructed in 1957.

Pastors: Rev. John Scollard, 1850–57; Rev. Alfred Young, 1857–61; Rev. James John Joseph O'Donnell, 1861–67; Msgr. Thomas Moran, 1867–1900; Rev. Robert E. Burke, 1900–1904; Rev. Walter Leahy, 1904–14; Rev. William Fitzgerald, 1914–20; Rev. Dennis S. Kelly, 1920–24; Rev. Michael Callahan, 1924–25; Rev. Patrick J. Clune, 1925–35; Rev. John Leo Meerwald, 1935–39; Rev. John F. Walsh, 1939–48; Msgr. Edward C. Henry, 1950–70; Msgr. John J. Endebrock, 1970–79; Rev. Evasio DeMarcellis, 1979–present.

Principals: Sr. Gabriel Redigan, R.S.M., 1878; Mother Mary Regis, R.S.M., 1879; Sr. Mary Stanislaus, R.S.M.; Sr. Mary Xavier,

R.S.M.; Sr. Mary Baptiste, R.S.M., 1924–26; Sr. Mary William, R.S.M., 1926–31; Sr. Mary Bernadette, R.S.M., 1931–34; Sr. Mary Roberta, R.S.M., 1934–37; Sr. Mary Theodora, R.S.M., 1937–40; Sr. Mary Anne, R.S.M., 1940–46; Sr. Mary Marcelline, R.S.M., 1946–52; Sr. Maria, R.S.M., 1952–58; Sr. Carolyn Haas, R.S.M., 1958–64; Sr. Mary Sienna Geller, R.S.M., 1964–66; Sr. Mary Gabriella McCausland, R.S.M., 1966–72; Sr. Janice Smith, R.S.M., 1972–75; Sr. Mary Valerie Balbach, R.S.M., 1975–84; Sr. Mary Karina, R.S.M., 1984–87; Sr. Teresa Bruno, S.C., 1987–91; Ms. Judith McBride, 1991–present.

Red Bank, Saint Anthony

Rev. Umberto Bacigalupi offered mass for Italians in the old St. James School, Red Bank, during 1911–12. Factories had attracted many Italians to Red Bank, and the first committee meeting to organize an Italian parish was held in a clothing factory on March 4, 1917. In April 1918, the committee purchased property in anticipation of the Most Rev. Thomas J. Walsh's establishment of an Italian national parish on November 3, 1920. Rev. Nicholas Soriano was appointed St. Anthony's first pastor. He promptly erected a church, opened for worship on January 30, 1921. A building on the property became the rectory. However, a new rectory was finished on March 6, 1930, and the old one was sold and moved off parish land. During 1936, Father Soriano extensively renovated the church, including adding two chapels to the auditorium of the church. A parish hall was built in 1938. The

Church of Saint Anthony, Red Bank

second pastor, Rev. Salvatore R. DiLorenzo, served the parish for more than fifty years. Father DiLorenzo started many parish organizations during his early years. In September 1942, he opened a convent for the Religious Teachers Filippini from Morristown, who had been secured to begin Confraternity of Christian Doctrine classes for the children of the parish.

Pastors: Rev. Nicholas Soriano, 1920–39; Msgr. Salvatore R. DiLorenzo, 1939–90; Rev. Joseph J. Miele, 1991–present.

Red Bank, Saint James

The first known Catholic mass in Red Bank was celebrated about 1849, because Mr. Francis Leonard had carried his infant son to St. Peter's, Jersey City, for baptism and informed the pastor, Rev. John Kelly, that there were Catholics in Red Bank. A mission was formed and later transferred to St. Mary's, South Amboy. Prior to 1856, baptized children received education at the home of Mrs. Ann O'Reilly.

Rev. Thomas M. Killeen arrived in April 1863 as St. James's first resident pastor. Father Killeen erected the first church and the first rectory. The transfer of the site of St. James Parish began in August 1887. Construction of the second St. James Church started in the autumn of 1893, and the Most Rev. James A. McFaul performed the dedication on August 11, 1895. During his pastorate, Msgr. John B. McCloskey extensively renovated the church. The seventh pastor, Msgr. Joseph T. Casey, made repairs to the church and school.

Rev. John F. Salaun, second pastor, initiated a Catholic school in the church basement. Miss Thompson was in charge during the school's tenure, from 1867 to 1869. During Rev. Michael E. Kane's pastorate, a school building was constructed. Lay persons helped Father Kane from 1880 until 1888, when three Sisters of Mercy came from Bordentown. A new grammar school and a four-year high school building were dedicated in 1927. The ninth and tenth grades had already existed at the site of the old grammar school. To make room for the school, the rectory had been moved

Church of Saint James, Red Bank

behind the church and been converted into a convent. During the interim between pastors, 1945 to 1946, significant repairs to the school and the erection of a central heating plant/garage building were done under administrator Rev. James Duffy.

The school system had been served by one principal. However, in 1946, Sr. Mary Benigna assumed responsibility of the grammar school while Sr. Mary Eleanor continued to run the high school. The Most Rev. William A. Griffin decided to erect a temporary grammar school building. It was not replaced until 1960. The temporary school building was enlarged, and two properties were purchased and converted into classrooms. The high school was renovated in the early 1960s and extended in 1967. A new convent was blessed in 1968.

In 1920, St. Anthony's Parish was established in Red Bank to serve Italian Catholics. St. James School was used for St. Anthony's masses. Baptisms, marriages, and funerals were held at St. James until St. Anthony's Church was built in 1921. The parish split twice more with the establishment of Nativity Parish, Fair Haven, in 1954 and St. Leo the Great Parish, Lincroft, in 1958.

The parish owns and is responsible for the care of Mount Olivet Cemetery. The cemetery serves numerous area parishes. Its first parcel of land was purchased in 1863, a mausoleum was constructed in 1978, and an office building/garage was built in 1980.

Born in Red Bank on May 13, 1922, the Most Rev. John Charles Reiss is St. James's most famous native son. He attended St. James Grammar School and Red Bank Catholic High School. Ordained on May 31, 1947, Bishop Reiss was installed as Trenton's eighth bishop on April 22, 1980.

Pastors: Rev. Thomas M. Killeen, 1863–67; Rev. John F. Salaun, 1867–76; Rev. Michael E. Kane, 1876–91; Rev. James A. Reynolds, 1891–1914; Msgr. Dennis J. Duggan, 1914–25; Msgr. John B. McCloskey, 1925–45; Msgr. Joseph T. Casey, 1946–53; Msgr. Emmett A. Monahan, 1953–75; Msgr. Fredrick A. Valentino, 1976–90; Rev. Philip A. Lowery, 1990–present.

Principals of St. James Grammar School: Sr. Mary Scholastica, R.S.M., 1888–1919; Sr. Mary Elizabeth, R.S.M., 1919–25; Sr. Mary Eugene, R.S.M., 1925–27; Sr. Mary Wilfred, R.S.M., 1927–34; Sr. Mary Angelica, R.S.M., 1934–44; Sr. Mary Eleanor, R.S.M., 1944–46; Sr. Mary Benigna, R.S.M., 1946–52; Sr. Mary Marcelline, R.S.M., 1952–54; Sr. Mary Lilian, R.S.M., 1954–55; Sr. Mary Benita, R.S.M., 1955–59; Sr. Mary Laetitia, R.S.M., 1959–65; Sr. Mary Matilda, R.S.M., 1965–71; Sr. Mary Jane Veldof, R.S.M., 1971–75; Sr. Mary Labouré, R.S.M., 1975–78; Sr. Mary Denise, R.S.M., 1978–83; Mrs. Maureen Hintlemann, 1983–present.

Riverside, Saint Casimir

In 1913, Polish-speaking Catholics of the Riverside area gathered at Riverside's first Catholic church, St. Peter's, for Sunday services under the leadership of Rev. Andrew Szostakiewicz of All Saints Parish, Burlington. One year later, the Parish of St. Casimir was established, with Rev. Julian Zielinski as its first resident pastor. Worship

Church of Saint Casimir, Riverside

was conducted in a small two-story building until 1919, when the first permanent church, a building in the Spanish style, was completed. Children attended school in the church basement starting in 1922. The following year, care of the students was assumed by the Bernardine Sisters of the Third Order of St. Francis of Reading, Pennsylvania. The Bernardine Sisters from Stamford, Connecticut, continue current teaching duties in the school. The school building, whose foundations were dug by the parishioners themselves, was opened in 1927. In 1936, care of the parish was entrusted to the Conventual Franciscan Friars of St. Anthony of Padua Province, with Rev. Hubert Konieczny, O.F.M. Conv., as the first Franciscan pastor. The friars continue their life of community and service at St. Casimir today. To serve better the parish's expanding needs, a social hall was built in 1969. A new church, whose art and architecture reflect the faith of the community, was blessed in April 1980.

Pastors: Rev. Julian Zielinski, 1914–15; Rev. Peter Wieczorek, 1915–25; Rev. Ignatius Bembenek, 1925–30; Rev. Louis Andler, 1930–36; Rev. Hubert Konieczny, O.F.M. Conv., 1936–37; Rev. Michael Drzewucki, O.F.M. Conv., 1937–39; Rev. Gregory Zablonski, O.F.M. Conv., 1939–40; Rev. Fabian Zator, O.F.M. Conv., 1940–60; Rev. Chester Kicia, O.F.M. Conv., 1960–64; Rev. Stanley Wlodyka, O.F.M. Conv., 1964–76; Rev. Edmund Szymkiewicz, O.F.M. Conv., 1976–82; Rev. Martin Dombrowski, O.F.M. Conv., 1982–85; Rev. Robert Grzybowski, O.F.M.

Conv., 1985–91; Rev. Herman Czaster, O.F.M. Conv., 1991–present.

Principals: Sr. Mary Ambrose, O.S.F., 1923–24; Sr. Mary Edward, O.S.F., 1924; Mother Mary Edmund, O.S.F., 1925; Sr. Mary Dominic, O.S.F., 1925–26; Sr. Mary Raphael, O.S.F., 1926–27; Sr. Mary Berchmans, O.S.F., 1927–30; Sr. Mary Bonaventure, O.S.F., 1930–33; Mother Mary Jerome, O.S.F., 1933–34; Sr. Mary Ignatia, O.S.F., 1934–35; Mother Mary Clare, O.S.F., 1935–38; Sr. Mary Paul, O.S.F., 1938–44, 1961–63; Sr. Mary Julianna, O.S.F., 1944–45; Sr. Mary Bridget, O.S.F., 1945–46; Sr. Mary Joachim, O.S.F., 1946–49; Sr. Mary Cornelia, O.S.F., 1949–55; Sr. Mary Nazaria, O.S.F., 1955–61; Sr. Mary Edwardine, O.S.F., 1963–66; Sr. Rose Viterbia, O.S.F., 1966–70; Sr. Mary Victorette, O.S.F., 1970–73; Sr. Mary Vincent, O.S.F., 1973–79; Sr. Mary Josene, O.S.F., 1979–87; Sr. Marie John, O.S.F., 1987–88; Sr. Mary Maureen, O.S.F., 1988–89; Sr. Linn Marie, O.S.F., 1989–92; Sr. Belgrace Villamil Gonzalez, O.S.F., 1992–present.

Riverside, Saint Peter

In the year 1853, the Most Rev. John N. Neumann, C.Ss.R., bishop of Philadelphia, visited the town of Progress, later called Riverside, and received a plot of ground from Mr. Samuel Bechtold. After the construction of a church, the Redemptorist Fathers from St. Peter's, Philadelphia, ministered to the congregation. In May 1870, care of the mission was transferred to Ss. Peter and Paul, Camden. The Conventual

Church of Saint Peter, Riverside

Franciscan Friars of Trenton took responsibility for the parish in 1872. Also in 1872, a school was established and staffed by the Sisters of St. Francis from Syracuse, New York. Because the church was deemed unsafe, a new church and a school were constructed by 1879. Fire destroyed the church in 1882, but a larger church was built by the end of the same year. When the Franciscans withdrew in 1897, Rev. Theodosius Goth, O.S.B., was appointed first pastor. The Conventual Franciscans returned in 1936, and Rev. Daniel Lyons, O.F.M. Conv., erected the present church in 1954. The first mass in the present church was celebrated on May 22, 1955.

Pastors: Rev. Theodosius Goth, O.S.B., 1897–1914; Rev. Joseph Keuper, 1914–19; Rev. John Caton, 1919–30; Rev. Anthony Shuvlin, 1930–36; Rev. Raymond Werdge, O.F.M. Conv., 1936–42, 1948–51; Rev. Adolph Bernholz, O.F.M. Conv., 1942–48; Rev. Daniel Lyons, O.F.M. Conv., 1951–57; Rev. Matthias Manley, O.F.M. Conv., 1957–63; Rev. Eric Fenner, O.F.M. Conv., 1963–70; Rev. Giles Van Wormer, O.F.M. Conv., 1970–76; Rev. Crispin Fuino, O.F.M. Conv., 1976–82; Rev. Conall McHugh, O.F.M. Conv., 1982–85; Rev. Lawrence McGoldrick, O.F.M. Conv., 1985–89; Rev. Julius Toth, O.F.M. Conv., 1990–present.

Principals: Sr. Mary Ludovica, O.S.F., 1872–75; Sr. Mary Aloysius, O.S.F., 1875–77; Sr. Mary Angela, O.S.F., 1877–78; Sr. Mary Matilda, O.S.F., 1878–81; Sr. Mary Catherine, O.S.F., 1881–85; Sr. Mary Scholastica, O.S.F., 1885–88; Sr. Mary Josepha, O.S.F., 1888–92; Sr. Mary Philomena, O.S.F., 1892–95; Sr. Mary Theresa, O.S.F., 1895–98; Sr. Mary Lucy, O.S.F., 1898–99; Sr. Mary Walburga, O.S.F., 1899–1902; Sr. Mary Cecilia, O.S.F., 1902–10; Sr. Mary Callista, O.S.F., 1910–14; Sr. Mary Adelaide, O.S.F., 1914–18; Sr. Mary Nazarene, O.S.F., 1918–21; Sr. Mary Barbara, O.S.F., 1921–23; Sr. Mary Adalberta, O.S.F., 1923–25; Sr. Mary Ferdinand, O.S.F., 1925–28; Sr. Mary Martha, O.S.F., 1928–31; Sr. Mary Loretta, O.S.F., 1931–37; Sr. Mary Afra, O.S.F., 1937–43, 1944–50; Sr. Mary Damian, O.S.F., 1943–44; Sr. Mary Prudentia, O.S.F., 1950–53; Sr. Mary Alexia, O.S.F., 1953–59; Sr. Mary Leo, O.S.F., 1959–63; Sr. Mary Joanna, O.S.F., 1963–69; Sr. Mary

Benedicta, O.S.F., 1969–75; Sr. Eleanor Grace, O.S.F., 1975–76; Sr. Elizabeth John, O.S.F., 1976–82; Sr. Marise, O.S.F., 1982–85; Sr. Grace Ann, O.S.F., 1985–87; Sr. Mary Edwin, O.S.F., 1987–91; Mr. Joseph Chinnici, 1992–present.

Riverton, Sacred Heart

Prior to 1874, Riverton Catholics attended mass in Riverside, Moorestown, Camden, and Philadelphia. In 1874, a group of Riverton Catholics visited Riverside to ask Rev. Peter Jachetti, O.F.M. Conv., pastor of St. Francis in Trenton, to have mass occasionally said in Riverton. Mass was offered in private homes between 1874 and 1879. The cornerstone for the original church was laid on May 31, 1879, and mass was celebrated in the parish's first church on July 6, 1879. In February 1888, Sacred Heart was declared a mission parish of St. Joseph's, Beverly. A frame church was built in 1893.

The first resident pastor, Rev. John J. Hendrick, was appointed on May 28, 1901, thus making Sacred Heart an independent parish. In 1931, the parish school, now the religious education center, opened. A new school opened in 1957 but closed in 1976. The Sisters of Charity of Halifax, Nova Scotia, Canada, staffed the school while it operated. The Palmyra School District now occupies the newer school building. In December 1963, the old frame church closed. Construction of a new church was finished in 1965, in time for worship at Easter.

Pastors: Rev. John J. Hendrick, 1901–14; Rev. Joseph A. Rigney, 1914–34; Rev.

Church of the Sacred Heart, Riverton

John J. McGrath, 1934–37; Rev. John F. Welsh, 1937–41; Rev. William F. Quinn, 1941–62; Rev. Joseph R. Hughes, 1963–80; Rev. James E. Coley, 1981–90; Rev. John P. Czahur, 1990–present.

Principals: Sr. Frances Gerard, S.C.H., 1938–39; Sr. Maria Winifred, S.C.H., 1939–41; Sr. Mary Angelus, S.C.H., 1941–45; Sr. Mary Justa, S.C.H., 1945–49; Sr. Rita Angela, S.C.H., 1949–55; Sr. Francis Magdalen, S.C.H., 1955–57; Sr. Louise Claudia, S.C.H., 1957–58; Sr. Mary Rosaire, S.C.H., 1958–64; Sr. Christopher Marie, S.C.H., 1964–67; Sr. Agnes Carmella, S.C.H., 1967–69; Sr. Alfred Marie, S.C.H., 1969–71; Sr. Joan McGuire, S.C.H., 1971–75; Sr. Carol Cuccolo, S.C.H., 1975–76.

Roebling, Holy Assumption

In April 1913, four Hungarian women from Roebling were successful in convincing the

Most Rev. James A. McFaul to send a priest to celebrate mass. These four women also obtained permission from Mr. Anderson, vice president of John A. Roebling's Sons Company, to use the boarding house for mass. Rev. Paul Csizmadia from South River offered the parish's first mass, on Pentecost Sunday, June 11, 1913. The parish was incorporated on June 18, 1913, as St. Emericus Hungarian Parish.

In 1916, Rev. Albert Szmoliga was appointed the first pastor. The name of the parish was changed in 1919 to Holy Assumption. In 1919, Father Szmoliga purchased land upon which Rev. Francis Grosz constructed a church in 1922. In 1939, the parish was placed under the care of the Franciscan Friars of the Custody of St. John Capistran. Holy Assumption became a territorial parish in 1940. Construction started in May 1948 to significantly expand the size of the church.

The parish school was founded in 1923 under the guidance of the Daughters of Divine Charity from Arrochar, Staten Island, New York. Classes were first held in the basement of the church. In 1943, larger enrollments were handled by using the basement of the newly built friary, and later the library and refectory were also utilized. Finally, in 1957, a new school building was erected and was blessed by the Most Rev. George W. Ahr on October 17, 1957.

Pastors: Rev. Albert Szmoliga, 1916–21; Rev. Rudolf Hudecz, 1921; Rev. Francis Grosz, 1921–25; Rev. Barnabas Blihar, O.F.M., 1925–28; Rev. Bela Andrassy, O.F.M., 1928–32; Rev. Romuald Raffinsky, O.F.M., 1932–33, 1936–41; Rev. Jerome Hedly, O.F.M., 1933–34; Rev. Zeno Hajnal, O.F.M., 1934–36; Rev. Tarcisius Gerencser, O.F.M., 1941–46; Rev. Capistran Petrie, O.F.M., 1946–50; Rev. Julian Fuzer, O.F.M., 1950–60; Rev. Alipius Forro, O.F.M., 1960–63; Rev. Edmund Ellis, O.F.M., 1963–65; Rev. Eugene A. Lenner, O.F.M., 1965–79; Rev. Capistran Polgar, O.F.M., 1979–present.

Principals: Sr. Mary Erzilia, F.D.C., 1923–27; Sr. Mary Charitas, F.D.C., 1929–32; Sr. Mary Stanislaus, F.D.C., 1932–36, 1938–41; Sr. Mary Amanda, F.D.C., 1936–38; Sr. Mary Gabriella, F.D.C., 1941–49; Sr. Mary Laetitia, F.D.C., 1949–50; Sr. Mary Eleanor, F.D.C., 1950–55; Sr. Mary Dorothy, F.D.C., 1955–58; Sr. Mary Donata, F.D.C., 1958–61; Sr. Mary Gregory, F.D.C., 1961–64; Sr. Mary Dolora, F.D.C., 1964–67; Sr. Mary Philomena, F.D.C., 1967–70; Sr. Mary Virginia, F.D.C., 1970–73; Sr. Mary Benigna, F.D.C., 1973–76; Sr. Mary Bridget, F.D.C., 1976–79, 1986–90; Sr. Mary Jude, F.D.C., 1979–86; Sr. Lydia Etter, O.S.F., 1990–present.

Rumson, Holy Cross

In May 1883, the Most Rev. Michael J. O'Farrell commissioned Rev. John H. Fox from St. Joseph's in Bound Brook to establish a parish in Sea Bright. On June 17, the first mass was celebrated in the River Side Hotel. The parish was incorporated on March 3, 1884, as "The Church of the Holy Cross, Sea Bright, N.J." On August 30, 1885, the cornerstone of the new church was laid in neighboring Rumson. Bishop

Church of the Holy Cross, Rumson

O'Farrell dedicated the church on June 27, 1886. A parish hall, built in 1893, housed a one-room school between 1894 and 1898. It was demolished in 1967. The second Holy Cross school, dedicated in 1941, held classes in a former private home, which also served as a convent. A new school building was constructed in 1953. Additional classrooms and a new convent were built in 1962. Sisters of Mercy from North Plainfield staffed the school between 1941 and 1979. The Franciscan Missionary Sisters of the Infant Jesus operated the school between 1979 and 1990. Our Lady of Perpetual Help in Highlands, St. Agnes in Atlantic Highlands, and St. Mary's Chapel at Fort Hancock in Sandy Hook were all missions of Holy Cross at one time. Holy Rosary Church, Rumson, constructed in 1923, is a

mission of Holy Cross. In 1977, a new rectory was built for Holy Cross.

Pastors: Rev. John H. Fox, 1883–93; Rev. Edward J. Egan, 1893–1915; Rev. Michael H. Callahan, 1915–23; Rev. John W. Murray, 1923–40; Msgr. Patrick J. Clune, 1940–47; Msgr. Joseph A. Sullivan, 1947–73; Rev. William J. Kokoszka, 1973–88; Rev. Joseph W. Hughes, 1988–present.

Principals: Miss McCarthy, 1894–96; Miss Jackson, 1896–98; Sr. Marie Jeanne, R.S.M., 1941–47, 1953–59; Sr. Mary Margaret, R.S.M., 1947–53; Sr. Mary Arthur, R.S.M., 1959–65; Sr. Mary Noel, R.S.M., 1965–71; Sr. Mary Clarita, R.S.M., 1971–78; Sr. Mary Margo, R.S.M., 1978–79; Sr. Carmelisa Dragoni, F.S.I.J., 1979–88; Sr. Isabel Piunti, F.S.I.J., 1988–90; Mrs. Janet Wood, 1990–92; Mr. Thomas Bugliaro, 1992–present.

Sea Girt, Saint Mark

Prior to the erection of a church in Sea Girt, area Catholics attended mass at St. Denis in Manasquan, St. Catherine of Siena in Farmingdale, or St. Catharine in Spring Lake. The Diocese of Trenton purchased land in 1945 to be used for a parish in Sea Girt. Msgr. Richard T. Crean, pastor of St. Mary's Cathedral, organized St. Mark's after its incorporation on October 31, 1952. He initiated construction of a church with a basement containing a parish hall and kitchen. In November 1953, Msgr. Francis M. J. Thornton was appointed St. Mark's first resident pastor, establishing St. Mark's as an independent parish. On November 22, 1953, the Most Rev. George W. Ahr

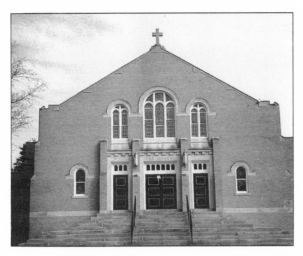

Church of Saint Mark, Sea Girt

blessed the church and laid the cornerstone together with the recently appointed pastor. During his pastorate, Rev. J. Frederick Child renovated the church, including a complete refurbishing of the sanctuary in 1970.

During 1977, the parish resolved a problem that had been a concern for some time. The rectory and church were fully occupying all of the property owned by the parish, and the lack of space on any side was alleviated when a lot east of the rectory became available for purchase. The parish bought the land in 1977 and rented the single-family house that was on the lot.

Pastors: Msgr. Francis M. J. Thornton, 1953–60; Rev. J. Frederick Child, 1960–75; Msgr. Emmett A. Monahan, 1975–80; Rev. William J. Campbell, 1980–84; Rev. Samuel C. Constance, 1984–present.

Seaside Heights, Our Lady of Perpetual Help

On September 22, 1942, Our Lady of Perpetual Help was incorporated as a separate parish. Catholics in Seaside Heights had been cared for by the Conventual Franciscans from St. Catharine of Siena, Seaside Park. The pastor of Sacred Heart in Bay Head, Rev. William J. Brennan, assumed responsibility for the Seaside Heights mission. Father Brennan and his associates offered mass for the growing congregation in a former butcher shop for several years.

In January 1946, Father Brennan moved to Seaside Heights, becoming Our Lady of Perpetual Help's first resident pastor. He purchased a Quonset hut for the celebration of mass in February 1947. A church was constructed and the first mass was celebrated by the second pastor, Rev. Thomas T. Barry, on July 6, 1952. During the pastorate of Rev. Bernard Coen, significant renovations to the parish plant took place. Rev. Joseph J. Miele added a prayer garden between the rectory and church. The original statue of the Blessed Mother was replaced after being

Church of Our Lady of Perpetual Help, Seaside Heights

destroyed by vandalism during the July 4th weekend in 1989. By the summer of 1990, the prayer garden was finished and could be enjoyed by parishioners.

Pastors: Rev. William J. Brennan, 1946–51; Rev. Thomas T. Barry, 1951–67; Rev. Daniel Sullivan, 1967–71; Rev. Bernard Coen, 1972–84; Rev. Joseph J. Miele, 1984–91; Rev. Phillip Pfleger, 1991–present.

Seaside Park, Saint Catharine of Siena

Church of Saint Catharine of Siena, Seaside Park

While vacationing in Seaside Park, Rev. Gregory Scheuermann, O.F.M. Conv., professor of mathematics at St. Francis College in Trenton, noticed a small summer community of Catholics eager for the celebration of mass nearby. Father Scheuermann accommodated them, particularly during the summers, from the day of the first mass, on July 16, 1905, until 1913. After the offering of the first mass in a cottage, masses were celebrated in the nonsectarian Union Church of Seaside Park. In 1912, a permanent church was built on land donated by Mr. Francis P. Larkin, Sr. Rev. Fridolin Stauble, O.F.M. Conv., offered mass during the summers of 1913, 1914, and 1916, and he lived in the sacristy in 1916. Rev. Daniel Lutz, O.F.M. Conv., lived in Seaside Park during the 1915 summer season. By the winter of 1915, masses were being celebrated on a regular basis year-round by the Conventual Franciscans, who usually resided in Bay Head or Seaside Park during the summers and in Trenton during the rest of the year. From September 16, 1917, through April 18, 1918, Rev. Hubert Osterman, O.F.M. Conv., traveled from Washington, D.C., every two weeks to offer mass. He was a professor at the Catholic University of America in Washington, D.C.

On October 15, 1918, Rev. Bede Hess, O.F.M. Conv., was relieved of his teaching duties at St. Francis College, Trenton. Father Hess and the Conventual Franciscans resided year-round in Bay Head. In 1920, the Conventual Franciscans requested and received permission to build a rectory in Seaside Park. They rented cottages in Seaside Heights and Seaside Park from October 21, 1921, until they moved into the rectory on December 22, 1922. The parish of St. Catharine covered the territory of Seaside Park, Seaside Heights, and Lavallette. Permission was granted by the Most Rev. John J. McMahon to build a parish hall in 1930. Father Hess was promoted in 1932 to the position of minister provincial of the Immaculate Conception Province. In 1936, he was elected to the highest position in the Franciscan order—minister general—becoming the 112th successor of St. Francis of Assisi.

In 1919, a mission was started in Lavallette under the patronage of St. Bonaventure. In 1942, diocesan priests were assigned to care for the congregations of Lavallette, Bay Head, and Seaside Heights, all formerly in the charge of the Conventual Franciscans. As a result, St. Catharine of Siena Parish was reduced in size to cover the area of Seaside Park and South Seaside Park.

The inadequacy of the old small church and parish hall became evident by 1953, when Rev. Gebhard Braungart, O.F.M. Conv., announced plans for a new church to seat 1,200 people, a response to the rising summer population and increasing number of year-round residents. On April 17, 1955, the new church was dedicated by the Most Rev. George W. Ahr, assisted by Very Rev. William D'Arcy, minister provincial of the Immaculate Conception Province.

From 1918 through 1979, the Franciscan Mission Band was active and made important contributions to parishes in New Jersey and neighboring states. In 1918, Father Hess invited a few Franciscans to join him in Bay Head for the founding of the Mission Band. Throughout the years, the Mission Band visited various churches, offering missions in order to foster the renewal of parishioners' spiritual lives.

Pastors: Rev. Bede Hess, O.F.M. Conv., 1921–32; Rev. John Murnane, O.F.M. Conv., 1932–33; Rev. Hubert Osterman, O.F.M. Conv., 1933–40; Rev. Godfrey Wolf, O.F.M. Conv., 1941–42, 1949–50; Rev. Raymond Werdge, O.F.M. Conv., 1942–45; Rev. Daniel Lyons, O.F.M. Conv., 1945–48; Rev. Gebhard Braungart, O.F.M. Conv., 1951–60; Rev. Luke Ziegler, O.F.M. Conv., 1960–63; Rev. Basil Corbett, O.F.M. Conv., 1963–64; Rev. Anthony Billy, O.F.M. Conv., 1964–67; Rev. Armand Sorento, O.F.M. Conv., 1970–76; Rev. Emmett Carroll, O.F.M. Conv., 1976–88, 1991–present; Rev. Neil Murphy, O.F.M. Conv., 1988–91.

Spring Lake, Saint Catharine

From 1880 through 1882, Rev. Michael Glennon, pastor of Holy Spirit in Asbury Park, or his assistants celebrated mass in Sea Girt. Masses were then offered in Mr. Thomas Devlin's Spring Lake cottage. Spring Lake's popularity as a summer resort together with its increasing Catholic popula-

Church of Saint Catharine, Spring Lake

tion prompted the erection of St. Ann's Church in 1884. A rectory was established in 1887 for the visiting priests. Rev. John W. Norris was assigned as St. Ann's first resident pastor in 1897.

Mr. Martin J. Maloney, a summer resident, was granted permission by the Most Rev. James A. McFaul to build a new church as a gift in memory of his deceased youngest daughter, Catharine. Bishop McFaul and the trustees of St. Ann's decided to change the parish's name in honor of St. Catharine as of January 11, 1901. The cornerstone was laid on March 17, 1901, and the church was dedicated on May 25, 1902. On the western shore of the lake and near the ocean, St. Catharine's Church, of Romanesque architecture, is in the shape of a Greek cross. The church has a massive octagonal dome, marble altars, and works of art, including paintings and windows depicting religious scenes and stories.

A new rectory was occupied in 1910. Land was donated by Mr. Maloney in 1910 for the construction of a convent. St. Catharine's cemetery began in 1917 with the purchase of a 3-acre parcel of land in Sea Girt. Thirty-six more acres were purchased later, and a mausoleum was erected in 1972.

Because of the large number of Catholics coming to Spring Lake for summer vacation, in 1930 a new church, St. Margaret's, was erected by Msgr. Thomas U. Reilly. St. Margaret's basement was first used as four classrooms for St. Catharine's School. The Sisters of St. Joseph from Chestnut Hill, Pennsylvania, took charge of educating the children until 1987. Two houses

were purchased to house the sisters. Later, a convent for all of the sisters was built. A brick school building opened in 1951, with a ten-classroom addition constructed in 1965. The seventh pastor, the Most Rev. James J. Hogan, transformed the basement of St. Catharine's Church into the Monsignor Thomas U. Reilly Chapel. The Sisters of St. Dominic of Caldwell currently staff the school. The Most Rev. Edward U. Kmiec, former auxiliary bishop of Trenton, was in residence at St. Catharine's Parish.

Pastors: Rev. John W. Norris, 1897–99; Rev. Thomas P. McLaughlin, 1899–1906; Rev. P. W. Morrissey, 1906–07; Rev. Stephen M. Lyons, 1907–13; Rev. Walter T. Leahy, 1913–22; Msgr. Thomas U. Reilly, 1923–53; Most Rev. James J. Hogan, 1954–66; Msgr. John E. Grimes, 1966–89; Msgr. Thomas A. Luebking, 1989–present.

Principals: Sr. Lena Picillo, O.P., c1991; Sr. Michael Maurice, O.P., 1992–present.

Tabernacle, Holy Eucharist

The parish of St. Mary of the Lakes in Medford began scheduling Sunday mass in the Tabernacle area in the late 1970s. The first location for mass was the Hampton Lakes Firehouse; then the mission moved to Tabernacle Middle School. Rev. Walter Norris, S.A.C., became a regular celebrant. The Most Rev. John C. Reiss established a new parish on September 17, 1982, named it in harmony with the locale, and appointed Rev. James J. Roche first pastor. Holy Eucharist Church was completed and dedicated on September 7, 1986. The parish territory covers the four townships of

Church of the Holy Eucharist, Tabernacle

Shamong, Southhampton, Tabernacle, and Woodland.

Pastor: Rev. James J. Roche, 1982–1993.

Toms River, Saint Joseph

Prior to 1873, the Most Rev. Michael A. Corrigan, bishop of Newark, recognized the needs of Toms River Catholics, sending priests to the small group on an irregular basis. Rev. John A. Kelly, pastor of St. Mary's in South Amboy, first visited the area. Another visitor was Rev. Stanislaus Danielou, who was assistant pastor of St. James in Red Bank from 1874 to 1879. He was given the responsibility of the Manchester Mission, precursor to St. John's in Lakehurst. That responsibility was extended to include offering mass for the small Toms River congregation.

The connection between the Manchester and Toms River missions continued. St. John's was first served by Rev. Joseph Esser, pastor of St. Nicholas in Egg Harbor City, and then by Rev. Michael Glennon, pastor of Holy Spirit in Asbury Park. Records indicate that the Franciscans served both St.

John's and St. Joseph's at least from 1880 until 1884, particularly Rev. Peter Jachetti in 1880–83, Rev. Angelus Goessmann in 1883–84, and Rev. Fidelis Voigt in 1884. Rev. Joseph Flanagan, pastor at St. John's, also served the Toms River and Lakewood congregations for a few months in 1886. Rev. Michael J. Hosey and Rev. Michael A. Dolan were in charge of St. Joseph's Mission until the establishment of St. Mary's of the Lake in Lakewood. St. Mary's pastor, Rev. Thomas B. Healy, assumed responsibility at St. Joseph's between 1893 and 1895 until Father Healy's curate, Rev. John J. McCullough, took over between 1896 and 1899. St. Joseph's first resident pastor, Rev. Joseph A. Egan, arrived in 1899.

Father Jachetti is the priest known for organizing the congregation. He first celebrated mass in Toms River on May 24, 1880. Subsequently, he offered mass twice per month during the summers and once per month during the winters. He was the first priest to provide Toms River Catholics with a regular schedule of masses. Father

Church of Saint Joseph, Toms River

Jachetti led construction of the first Catholic church in Toms River, a small wooden frame building. On June 28, 1882, the Most Rev. Michael J. O'Farrell dedicated the church, which would serve the congregation until 1904. St. Joseph's Parish was incorporated on October 30, 1883.

A larger church was built in 1904, and in 1909 the first rectory was finished. In 1932, a social hall was erected behind the church. This was later renovated to house the first school, which opened in September of the same year and graduated its first class of seven students in 1934. A school/church building was completed in 1952. Another classroom building and Holy Family Hall opened in 1959. History was made again, when in September 1962, St. Joseph's Parish opened the first and only Catholic high school in Ocean County. The high school was later renamed to honor Msgr. Lawrence W. Donovan's 38 years of service to St. Joseph's parish community. The Sisters of St. Dominic of Newburgh, New York, have operated St. Joseph Grade School and Monsignor Donovan High School since their inceptions. The parish recently constructed a new church, which was dedicated on January 9, 1993.

One of St. Joseph's former curates is a modern-day martyr. Rev. John Patrick Wessel, born on September 20, 1939, attended Sacred Heart Grammar School in Mount Holly. He was ordained in St. Mary's Cathedral on May 22, 1965, and was first assigned to Blessed Sacrament in Trenton. He was transferred to St. Joseph's on September 24, 1971. In his first sermon at St.

Joseph's, Father Wessel told the congregation, "If you ever need me, call the rectory and ask for Father John." Mrs. John Kelly Jr. called in behalf of her son, John Kelly III, who had received the Bronze Star Medal in 1968 for combat in Vietnam. He then sustained serious injuries in a noncombat accident and returned home in 1970 withdrawn and depressed. Fully aware that John Kelly required more assistance then he could provide, Father Wessel visited him on December 17, 1971. After their conversation, while walking back to his car, Father Wessel was shot in the back from a second-story window. His spinal cord was severed, and he never regained consciousness before his death on December 26, the feast day of St. Stephen the Martyr.

The population growth of the original territory of St. Joseph's Parish prompted the establishment of missions and new parishes. In 1908, St. Gertrude's of the Holy Spirit was started as a mission in Island Heights. Construction of a church for St. Gertrude's began the following year. Worship also began in 1953 in Ocean Gate, which became known as Our Lady of Victory Mission. The mission church was built with funds donated by private individuals who then turned the building over to the Diocese of Trenton, which then placed it under the care of St. Joseph's. Also during the summers, services were occasionally offered in Pine Beach's nondenominational chapel. From 1899, the priests of St. Joseph's were among the clergy serving St. John's Mission in Lakehurst. Eventually by 1915, St. Joseph's took complete control of St.

John's. In 1966, St. Barnabas Parish, Bayville, was formed and given charge of Our Lady of Victory Mission, Ocean Gate. In 1969, St. John's received a resident pastor. Two territorial parishes were founded in Toms River: St. Justin's in 1972 and St. Luke's in 1982. In 1985, St. Maximilian Kolbe Parish was founded in Berkeley Township.

Pastors: Rev. Joseph A. Egan, 1899–1902; Rev. John A. Caulfield, 1902–05; Rev. Patrick J. Powers, 1905–09; Rev. Joseph A. Linnane, 1909–23; Rev. Michael P. Waldron, 1923–26; Rev. George A. Welsh, 1926–49; Msgr. Lawrence W. Donovan, 1949–87; Msgr. Casimir H. Ladzinski, 1987–present.

Principals of St. Joseph Grade School: Sr. Dalmatia Finnegan, O.P., 1932–1934; Sr. Geraldine Herold, O.P., 1934–36; Sr. Grace Louise Jeckert, O.P., 1936–41; Sr. Carmelita Colahan, O.P., 1941–46; Sr. Marie Anthony Lynch, O.P., 1946–47; Sr. Eucharia Campbell, O.P., 1947–52; Sr. Anita Rosaire Fay, O.P., 1952–58; Mother Christina Marie McDonald, O.P., 1958–63; Sr. Edwardina Jung, O.P., 1963–65; Sr. Mary Daniel Shannon, O.P., 1965–71; Sr. Mary Juliana Naulty, O.P., 1971–present.

Toms River, Saint Justin

On November 10, 1972, the Most Rev. George W. Ahr established Toms River's second Catholic parish, St. Justin's. Rev. George E. Deutsch, first pastor, initially offered masses at the East Dover First Aid Building. Other pastoral services were offered at the rectory. Bishop Ahr approved a building campaign on March 11, 1973. The steel parish hall went up quickly, being first used for mass in April 1973. A second steel building was finished by October 1973, providing additional space for the religious education program, parish organizations, and parish activities. The church building was built in 1974 and was consecrated by Bishop Ahr on November 2, 1974. The first regular mass in the church was celebrated on December 19, 1974. A rectory was constructed on the parish's 10 acres of land in 1975. The current parish hall was completed in August 1978. The original parish hall was set apart for the youth of the parish as a meeting place and gymnasium. Despite the founding of a third Toms River parish—St. Luke, in 1982—the celebration of up to thirteen weekend masses warranted an addition to St. Justin's Church in 1987. Ground was broken on October 11, 1987, for the addition, and the Most Rev. John C. Reiss dedicated the newly enlarged church on June 1, 1989, the feast of St. Justin.

Pastors: Rev. George E. Deutsch, 1972–82; Rev. William J. Nolan, 1982–present.

Toms River, Saint Luke

The area of Toms River was growing so rapidly that it was necessary for the Diocese of Trenton to establish the new parish of St. Luke to assist the parishes of St. Joseph and St. Justin. St. Luke's Parish was founded on October 1, 1982, with the first pastor, Rev. Louis W. Kralovich, residing at St. Justin's rectory for a year. Masses were celebrated at the Silver Bay and North Dover grammar schools. The Most Rev. John C. Reiss then authorized a building campaign to generate money for construction of a parish center, which was dedicated in November 1985. Father Kralovich lived in a Silverton house from 1983 until the completion of the parish center, which includes a rectory. The parish center has become the focal point for celebrations, catechesis, and socials.

Pastor: Rev. Louis W. Kralovich, 1982–present.

Tuckerton, Saint Theresa

St. Theresa's was engendered as a mission of St. Thomas Aquinas Church, Beach Haven, during October 1934. For ten years, the Franciscans celebrated mass in a rented store on West Main Street. The Steelman home was purchased, and the first mass was celebrated there on October 22, 1944. St. Theresa's became a mission of the newly

Church of Saint Theresa, Tuckerton

established St. Mary's of Barnegat on November 14, 1947. A new building was constructed in the same place as the old St. Theresa's and dedicated on April 12, 1953. St. Theresa's became formally established as a parish in September 1954. To accommodate increased attendance, especially in the summer, St. Michael's Mission was started in Mystic Island during 1974–75. St. Theresa's Church underwent a structural addition in 1985.

Pastors: Rev. Arthur J. St. Laurent, 1954–58; Rev. James A. Thompson, 1958–62; Rev. Joseph Remias, 1962–65; Rev. Dominic Turtora, 1965–69; Rev. Thomas Dennen, 1969–72; Msgr. Maurice P. Griffin, 1972–81; Rev. Harry E. Cenefeldt, 1981–86; Msgr. James P. McManimon, 1986–88; Rev. Terence McAlinden, 1988–present.

Union Beach, Holy Family

Faithful Catholics in the Union Beach area initiated their mission church in 1923. Priests from nearby parishes celebrated mass in the Union Beach Fire House. A house and property were purchased in 1929, and the house was named "The Catholic Club House." After completion of the first Holy Family Church in 1942 and the arrival of Rev. Walter Slattery in June, Holy Family became an independent parish. A house near the church was purchased in 1943 as the rectory. Rev. Edward Sullivan began erecting a new church in 1954. After Father Sullivan's death, Rev. Joseph G. Fox completed the construction of the new church for the growing congregation. By Septem-

Church of the Holy Family, Union Beach

ber 1967, a parish elementary school in Hazlet was finished. Three orders of sisters have staffed the school: School Sisters of Notre Dame, Baltimore, Maryland; Carmelite Sisters of St. Teresa, Karala, India; and Religious Sisters of Mercy, North Plainfield.

Pastors: Rev. Walter Slattery, 1942–48; Rev. Edward Sullivan, 1948–54; Rev. Joseph G. Fox, 1954–79; Rev. Patrick G. Fitzpatrick, 1979–present.

Principals: Sr. Rosemary, S.S.N., 1967–72; Sr. Mary Jean, R.S.M., 1972–73; Sr. Mary Rosarita, C.S.S.T., 1973–80; Sr. Yvonne Marie, C.S.S.T., 1980–83; Sr. Mary Nadine, R.S.M., 1983–present.

Washington Crossing, Saint George

Shortly after a meeting with townspeople and summer vacationers, the Most Rev. Thomas J. Walsh declared the Washington Crossing area to be a vicinage of St. John's, Lambertville. In July of 1920, St. John's pastor, Rev. Joseph J. Mahoney, celebrated the community's first mass under a tent. The Washington Crossing Inn's dining room doubled as an altar until the construction of a church in 1921–22. St. George's Church, named partly in honor of General George Washington, was built upon land donated by Dr. Isador P. Stritmatter, M.D., a vacationer from Philadelphia. During the years 1924 to 1947, St. George's operated as a mission of St. James, Pennington. In 1936, St. George's was incorporated; year-round masses started in 1938. From 1947 through 1972, St. George's existed as a mission of Our Lady of Good Council, West Trenton.

Finally, after 52 years, St. George's Church was established as an independent parish on May 31, 1972. During his tenure, Rev. Nicholas Murphy, the first resident pastor, constructed the rectory alongside

Church of Saint George, Washington Crossing

the church. Having outgrown the original structure, also in need of repairs, the parish built a new church, dedicated on May 17, 1992.

For several years, beginning in 1966, St. George's welcomed, as a Sunday celebrant, Rev. Stanley Jaki, a lecturer and author, who holds doctorates in theology and physics. He is a professor of the history and philosophy of physics at Seton Hall University, South Orange, and a member of the Institute of Advanced Study, Princeton.

Pastors: Rev. Nicholas Murphy, 1972–79; Msgr. George A. Ardos, 1979–present.

Wayside, Saint Anselm

In June of 1972, the Church of St. Anselm first celebrated the Eucharist as a parish community in the Wayside School. The following year, a parish center with a learning center and worship area was dedicated. A parish council directs the activities of the parish and its outreach to the community at large. A major expansion of facilities is currently under way to accommodate these activities. Three of St. Anselm's special activities are Interfaith Neighbors, an organization serving the homeless; Stephen Ministry, a group serving community members in need; and Community Outreach, a pledge of 5 percent of parish income dedicated to needs outside the community.

Pastors: Rev. Joseph Miele, 1972–84; Rev. Robert F. Kaeding, 1984–present.

West Long Branch, Saint Jerome

On October 18, 1956, the Most Rev. George W. Ahr established the territorial parish of St. Jerome and appointed Rev. Francis X.

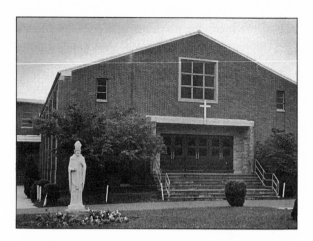

Church of Saint Jerome, West Long Branch

McGuinness as the first pastor. Staffed by the Religious Teachers Filippini, the school opened its classroom doors in September 1957. An existing home on the property served as a rectory; a convent was constructed to house the sisters. In 1984, the sisters were relocated by their motherhouse in an effort to provide a community spirit among the order of Religious Teachers Filippini in the immediate area. The sisters continued to serve the parish. Construction began on a new rectory and convent in 1986, and the buildings were inhabited the following year. Subsequently, the old rectory was destroyed. St. Jerome's Parish, located in a parklike setting, is near beaches and is witness to growth in West Long Branch and surrounding communities.

Pastors: Rev. Francis X. McGuinness, 1956–66; Rev. Henry M. Tracy, 1967; Rev. Gerald T. Celentana, 1967–68; Rev. Michael M. Garry, 1969–81; Rev. Paul T. Gluth, 1981–87; Rev. Frederick W. Jackiewicz, 1987–present.

Principals: Sr. Catherine Girenti, M.P.F., 1957–62; Sr. Mary Jerome Pezzino, M.P.F.,

1962–68; Sr. Laura Longo, M.P.F., 1968–74; Sr. Delores Callegher, M.P.F., 1974–79; Sr. Angelina Pelliccia, M.P.F., 1979–present.

West Trenton, Our Lady of Good Counsel

Rev. Alfonso Palombi, pastor of St. Joachim's in Trenton, celebrated the first mass on Palm Sunday, April 24, 1918, in West Trenton (then Trenton Junction). A Grand Avenue parcel of land, purchased in the mid-1920s, became the site for Our Lady of Good Counsel Church, dedicated on November 1, 1931. From the turn of the century to 1947, the spiritual needs of West Trenton were served by the following Trenton institutions: St. Joachim's Church, Blessed Sacrament Church, St. Francis Hospital, St. James Church, and Villa Victoria

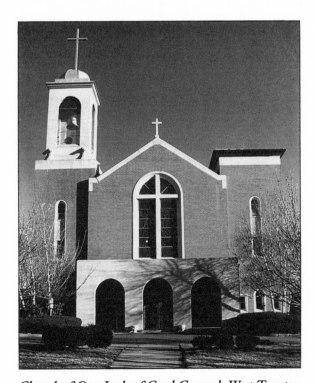

Church of Our Lady of Good Counsel, West Trenton

Academy. On November 14, 1947, the Most Rev. William A. Griffin established Our Lady of Good Counsel as a full-fledged parish, with St. George's of Washington Crossing as her mission. In 1949, Rev. Bernard C. DeCoste, first pastor, purchased a home across from the church as a rectory. Ground was broken on July 3, 1960, for a larger, brick church with a parish hall and rectory. The West Upper Ferry Road buildings were dedicated in December 1962. Assistant pastors have been regularly assigned to Our Lady of Good Counsel since 1966.

Pastors: Rev. Bernard C. DeCoste, 1947–51; Rev. Joseph W. McLaughlin, 1951–73; Msgr. William F. Fitzgerald, 1973–present.

West Windsor, Saint David the King

Early in 1981, St. David's started as a mission of St. Paul's, Princeton. Initially, mass and religious instruction classes were held in the West Windsor–Plainsboro High School. St. David's was established as a parish on January 8, 1988. Plans for building a church were soon begun under pastor Rev. John F. Wake. A building was purchased in June 1988 for use as a rectory. The church was dedicated on January 4, 1992, by the Most Rev. John C. Reiss.

Pastor: Rev. John F. Wake, 1988–present.

Whiting, Saint Elizabeth Ann Seton

Starting in 1965, the first Catholics who moved into the Whiting area villages, primarily adult villages, attended mass at St. John's in Lakehurst. In the middle of 1975,

Church of Saint David the King, West Windsor

Rev. Philip T. Matera, pastor of St. John's, met with the residents of Whiting, and all agreed on the need for the formation of a new parish in Whiting. A fund drive was initiated, and shortly thereafter on February 11, 1975, the first 5 acres of the present 10-acre parcel of land were purchased.

On December 3, 1976, the Most Rev. George W. Ahr appointed Rev. John J. McGovern as first pastor. The newly established parish was named in honor of St. Elizabeth Ann Seton, who was canonized a saint on September 14, 1975. Daily masses were celebrated in the Whiting Memorial Park chapel; weekend masses were offered in the Whiting Fire Department's auditorium. However, on Palm Sunday, April 3, 1977, use of the firehouse was given to another group, and the growing parish required large quarters for the celebration of mass. A gigantic tent was rented and placed at the shore of Harry Wright Lake in Whiting. The cold, rainy, and windy day kept the

ushers busy trying to keep the tent standing and the congregation as comfortable as possible. On subsequent weekends when the firehouse facilities were unavailable, the Crestwood Evangelical Congregational Church offered use of its church.

Ground was broken on September 25, 1977, for construction of the parish complex to include a parish center, church, and rectory. Mass was first celebrated in the parish center on June 24, 1978, and in the church on March 25, 1979. Bishop Ahr laid the cornerstone and blessed the completed church on June 10, 1979. The Most Rev. John C. Reiss solemnly dedicated the church and burned the mortgage on June 12, 1983. Monsignor McGovern, elevated to prelate of honor on March 10, 1984, was stricken with his final illness on February 24, 1986. Rev. Antony Poovakulam soon arrived as

Church of Saint Elizabeth Ann Seton, Whiting

parochial vicar, and Father Matera took over as administrator.

Monsignor McGovern resigned in November 1986, and Msgr. Joseph C. Shenrock arrived on January 2, 1987, as the parish's second pastor. On June 7, 1987, an ecumenical Pentecost service was held in the church to begin the Marian Year. All of the pews, designed to seat about 850 people, were filled. Numerous congregants were also standing inside and outside the church.

During her stay from July 1, 1987, until July 19, 1992, Sr. Adrienne Fallon, O.P., served as pastoral assistant. She restructured and improved the religious education and youth programs. Monsignor Shenrock constructed an addition to the parish center, including a library, bookstore, offices, meeting rooms, stage, and garage. On November 17, 1990, Bishop Reiss blessed the addition, which facilitates the growing number of parish activities. Monsignor Shenrock, who has also conducted renovations to the parish plant, is currently vicar for social services and diocesan archivist.

Pastors: Msgr. John J. McGovern, 1976–86; Msgr. Joseph C. Shenrock, 1987–present.

Willingboro, Corpus Christi

In June 1958, a number of young couples fled from the cities of Philadelphia and New York to newly built rural homes in Willingboro. The establishment of Corpus Christi parish on April 29, 1959, alleviated the stress on St. Joseph's Church in Beverly. Rev. Francis J. Coan, appointed pastor, arrived in the community during Easter

week to the joyous welcome of his flock. At Somerset Park School, Father Coan celebrated the new parish's first mass on May 3, 1959, and a ground-breaking ceremony for a church and school took place in November of the same year. The Most Rev. George W. Ahr officially blessed and dedicated the new church and school on October 16, 1960. The Sisters of St. Francis of Philadelphia began educating their first group of students on September 9, 1959. An eighteen-room convent was occupied on Thanksgiving Day, November 26, 1964.

Pastors: Rev. Francis J. Coan, 1959–64; Msgr. Charles E. McGee, 1964–68; Msgr. Henry S. Bogdan, 1968–present.

Principals: Sr. Edward Paul, O.S.F., 1959–65; Sr. Mary Regis, O.S.F., 1965–71; Sr. Justina Marie, O.S.F., 1971–81; Sr. Robert Marie, O.S.F., 1981–present.

Yardville, Saint Vincent de Paul

Prior to 1954, Catholics in Yardville attended mass at St. Raphael's Church in Trenton. In 1954, a church and parish hall

Church of Corpus Christi, Willingboro

were built, and a house was purchased as the first rectory. St. Vincent de Paul was established as an independent parish on March 15, 1955, with Rev. Francis J. Coan as first resident pastor. The parish included territory that had belonged to St. Raphael's and St. Gregory's, Hamilton Square. On March 17, 1980, religious education classes were transferred from the church auditorium to the new religious education building, and a new rectory was completed on May 6, 1980.

Pastors: Rev. Francis J. Coan, 1955–59; Rev. Francis Gunner, 1959–71; Rev. Arthur F. Conlon, 1971–present.

SOURCES

The parish histories were based on responses to questionnaires sent to the parishes at the beginning of this project. Additional information was obtained from the archives of the Trenton diocese. Many of the parish files contain pamphlets or reports written for various celebrations, including the centennial of the diocese in 1981. In addition, some of the records from the fire at St. Mary's Cathedral were salvaged. Information was also cross-referenced with histories of the religious communities and institutions serving the diocese. Rough drafts of the parish histories, with questions, were sent to the parishes, and their answers incorporated into the historical summaries. Many of the more recent issues of *The Monitor* (through at least January 1993) were consulted to update information on pastors and principals.

The sources listed below were quite valuable, especially the books by Rev. Walter T. Leahy and Rev. Joseph M. Flynn.

1. *Catholic Telephone Guide*. New Rochelle: The Catholic News Publishing Company, 1988, 1990, 1991, and 1992.
2. Connelly, James F., S.T.L., Hist. E.D., *The History of the Archdiocese of Philadelphia*. Philadelphia: Unigraphics Incorporated, 1976.
3. *Diary and Visitation Record of the Rt. Rev. Francis Patrick Kenrick*. Under the direction of the Most. Rev. Edmond F. Prendergast, Archbishop of Philadelphia. Lancaster, Pennsylvania: Wickersham Printing Co., 1916, p. 68.
4. Flynn, Joseph M. *The Catholic Church in New Jersey*, Morristown, New Jersey: The Publishers' Printing Co., 1904.
5. Fox, John H. *A Century of Catholicity in Trenton, N.J.* Trenton: Naar, Day & Naar, Printers, 1900.
6. *A History of Trenton 1679–1929*. Princeton: Princeton University Press, 1929, pp. 446–462.
7. Leahy, Rev. Walter T. *The Catholic Church of the Diocese of Trenton, N.J.* Princeton: Princeton University Press, 1906.
8. Mahoney, Joseph F., and Peter J. Wosh, eds. *The Diocesan Journal of Michael Augustine Corrigan, Bishop of Newark, 1872–1880*. Newark and South Orange: New Jersey Catholic Historical Records Commission, 1987.
9. *The Monitor*, March 20, 1959, Cathedral Blessing Commemorative Edition.
10. *The Official Catholic Directory*. P. J. Kenedy & Sons, 1991.
11. Shinn, Henry C. *The History of Mount Holly*. Mount Holly: *Mount Holly Herald*, 1957, pp. 87–88. (Published by the *Mount Holly Herald*; printed by Sleeper Publications, Inc., in Mount Holly.)

CHAPTER THIRTEEN

RELIGIOUS COMMUNITIES

◆

BY JAMES F. O'NEILL JR.

FORTY-TWO PROFILES of religious communities serving the Diocese of Trenton appear in this chapter. The majority of information was obtained from the communities themselves. Some additional information was obtained through research on the parishes and institutions. Each title line contains the name of the community. Subtitles, names of provinces, and locations of motherhouses may appear on successive lines before the beginning of a community's historical summary. The *1992 Catholic Telephone Guide* and *The Official Catholic Directory* of 1991 were valuable references for specific details such as location of motherhouses, territory of provinces, date of establishment, and complete name. We thank the religious communities for sending records of their progress since the beginning of their work in the diocese.

Benedictine Sisters of Elizabeth (O.S.B.)

Motherhouse: Elizabeth, New Jersey

In 1864, Rev. Henry Lemke requested that the prioress of St. Scholastica Convent, Newark, supply several sisters for St. Michael School in Elizabeth. Sr. Philomena Spiegel, O.S.B., and Sr. Walburga Hock, O.S.B., commenced classes. In 1868, Mother Walburga Hock established the Benedictine Sisters of Elizabeth as an independent monastic order whose charisma is community. The Benedictines are members of the Federation of St. Scholastica, one of four federations of Benedictine women in the United States. As disciples of St. Benedict, they follow a contemplative way of life characterized by liturgical and personal prayer, *lectio divina*, silence, and solitude. They find their expression in monastic stewardship, hospitality, and works on behalf of the people of God.

By 1868, Father Lemke had built St. Walburga Convent, which served as a motherhouse, church, parochial school, private academy, and orphanage. On the remainder of the twenty-two lots purchased by Father Lemke, the sisters cultivated fruit and vegetable gardens and raised chickens and cows. They were assisted in the marketing of milk, butter, eggs, and other farm products by Mr. Ives, one of the community's earliest benefactors. Until her death, Miss Eileen Sullivan, in her volunteer capacity, acted as sales agent, representing the sisters' handiwork to business concerns.

Over the course of years, missions were opened primarily in northern New Jersey but also in New Hampshire, Maryland, Ohio, the District of Columbia, and Ecuador. In the Trenton diocese, Sister Arline, O.S.B., is pastoral associate at St. Agnes Parish in Atlantic Highlands.

Bernardine Sisters of the Third Order of St. Francis (O.S.F.)
Heart of Mary Province
Provincial House:
Stamford, Connecticut

The Bernardine Sisters of the Third Order of St. Francis, popularly known as the Bernardine Franciscan Sisters, were founded in the United States in 1894. They constitute a pontifical institute and an active order, with simple vows. The origin of the community can be traced to the year 1453, when St. John Capistrano, a disciple of the newly canonized St. Bernardine of Siena, established the reformed branch of the Friars Minor in Krakow, Poland. A group of tertiaries, ladies of the Cracovian nobility, desiring to lead a life in common, formed an active community of the Third Order of St. Francis. Because these sisters attended services in a church dedicated to St. Bernardine of Siena, they became known as Bernardines.

St. Agnes, the name of the first convent of the Bernardine Sisters, erected in 1453, eventually gave rise to the Sacred Heart Convent at Zakliczyn, Poland, in 1883. It was from this convent that the Bernardine Sisters came to the United States when Mother Veronica Grzedowska and 3 companions arrived at the first American house in Mount Carmel, Pennsylvania, in 1894. The current generalate house is located in Villanova, Pennsylvania, and provincial houses are located in Reading, Pennsylvania; Stamford, Connecticut; and Farmington Hills, Michigan. The Bernardine Sisters came to help meet the educational needs of the growing church and expanding communities of the time, devoting themselves wholly at first to teaching in the elementary parochial schools.

In 1899, Rev. Matthias Tarnowski invited the Bernardine Sisters to staff the reopened school of St. Stanislaus, Trenton, their first mission in the Diocese of Trenton. The Bernardine Sisters left the school within a few years. The sixty-three-year-long presence of the sisters at All Saints School in Burlington ended in 1990, when the sisters handed over administration of the school to lay personnel. St. Dominic's School, Bricktown, was served by the Bernardine Franciscans from its opening in 1965 until 1992, when the Franciscans were replaced by the Sisters of Mercy. The Bernardine Franciscans also served St. Gregory the Great School, Hamilton Square, from 1965 to 1978. In the case of each of these withdrawals, shortage of teaching personnel was the cause.

Three Bernardine Sisters came to St. Casimir School, Riverside, in September 1923, with a starting enrollment of 97 pupils. Increasing enrollment necessitated the building of a new school in 1927. The sisters continue to minister in this school.

The sisters were involved not only in the teaching apostolate but also as organists, sacristans, and teachers of Confraternity of Christian Doctrine. From the 1930s to the 1970s, the cultural development of students was encouraged by a variety of programs, highlighted by operettas and plays.

Health care, nursing home facilities, and retreat houses are staffed by the Bernardine Franciscans. To meet the needs of today's church, the sisters are also engaged in parish and pastoral ministry, campus ministry, and spiritual direction. The Bernardine Franciscans remain faithful to their commitment of "continuing the mission in His Name."

Brothers of the Christian Schools (F.S.C.)

New York Province
La Salle Provincialate:
Lincroft, New Jersey

In 1680, Brothers of the Christian Schools, also known as de La Salle Christian Brothers, was founded by Rev. John Baptist de La Salle, a priest and canon of the Cathedral of Reims, France. Through a series of circumstances, he became involved with teachers in the local parish schools. The teachers, though religiously motivated, were largely ill trained, and de La Salle assisted in their training and their work in the "charity schools" for the poor. Eventually he took them into his home and became a part of their life and work. Formed into a religious community, 12 brothers took a vow of obedience in 1686. De La Salle wrote books on educational instruction and on operation of the schools, organizing teacher training schools and times for retreats. He died in 1719. In 1900 he was canonized and, in 1950, named the Patron of Teachers. The Institute of the Brothers of the Christian Schools has about 10,000 members, who work in more than eighty countries.

The Brothers of the Christian Schools entered the Diocese of Trenton in 1959 to staff a boys' high school in Lincroft, New Jersey. (Christian Brothers Academy, located on a 160-acre campus in Lincroft, appears as a separate entry in the next chapter.)

La Salle Provincialate in Lincroft has been the administrative headquarters of the New York/New Jersey Province of the Brothers of the Christian Schools since 1979. It contains the offices of the brother provincial—the head elected superior—who conducts personal interviews with the brothers twice a year, appoints the directors of the various communities, and pays visits to them and the communities in the brothers' mission schools. To aid him in these matters and in correspondence, he has auxiliary provincials, who deal with contracts, school visitations, retreats for the brothers, finances, and development.

Provincial John Martin urged the construction of a retirement home for Christian Brothers. The Board of Trustees of Christian Brothers Academy contributed 20 acres of land in Lincroft for the project. De La Salle Hall was built for the care of retired, elderly, and infirm Christian Brothers of the New York/New Jersey Province. On April 13, 1980, the Most Rev. John C. Reiss dedicated the twenty-four-bedroom retirement home.

Cistercian Congregation of Casamari (O. Cist.)

Cistercian Monastery of Our Lady of Fatima Mount Laurel, New Jersey

In September of 1957, two Cistercian monks—Rev. John Paolucci, O. Cist., and Rev. Julian Bruni, O. Cist.—from the abbey of Casamari, Italy, were sent as guests to the Cistercian Monastery of Our Lady of Spring Bank, in Oconomowoc, Wisconsin. On October 7, 1960, the two monks contacted the Most Rev. George W. Ahr, requesting permission to establish a Cistercian monastery in the Diocese of Trenton. In February 1961, abbot President Buttarazzi and Bishop Ahr met to arrange for the monks to reside in the diocese as guests of St. Anthony Rectory, Trenton. The pastor at St. Anthony's was Msgr. Michael P. McCorristin, vicar-general of the diocese, whose contributions were instrumental in the founding of the monastery.

A 97-acre property with a farmhouse, designated for a religious purpose in the will of Mr. Alexander Breger, was donated by Bishop George W. Ahr to the Cistercian Fathers. On September 23, 1961, remodeling of the farmhouse was begun with the financial and physical assistance of Monsignor McCorristin. In December 1961, Father Paolucci and Father Bruni moved into the farmhouse. In August 1965, Bishop Ahr blessed an addition to the farmhouse, donated by Mr. Blase Ravicchio, a contractor in Moorestown. In December 1972, Bishop Ahr dedicated the first wing of the regular monastery, built through the generosity of Mr. Roland Aristone, a contractor in Marlton. Meanwhile, other monks traveled back and forth from Casamari, Italy, allowing the monastic community to grow. Father Paolucci was assigned as the first prior of the Cistercian Monastery of Our Lady of Fatima, Mount Laurel, New Jersey.

The Cistercian order, founded in France in 1098, follows the Rule of St. Benedict. The main purpose is a contemplative life with emphasis on liturgical celebrations and with ministries compatible with the monastic life, such as parishes, retreats, preaching, and teaching, provided the exercise of such ministries comes within the limits of the monastery.

The monks of the Cistercian Monastery of Our Lady of Fatima built a rosary garden around their lake, a place where many people come for prayer and reflection. The monks began and developed the devotional practices of first Fridays and first Saturdays of the month. Occasionally, priests are accepted for private retreats; religious groups attend for evenings of recollection. From the beginning, the monks assisted the neighboring parishes of the Burlington County area in many ways.

On November 18, 1978, Bishop Ahr created the parish of St. John Neumann, Mount Laurel, entrusting the monks with the care of the new parish. Rev. Vittorino Zanni, O. Cist., who succeeded Father Paolucci as prior, was installed as the first pastor. On November 23, 1980, the Most Rev. John C. Reiss dedicated the parish church. The parish office complex and social hall were added later. On September 2, 1989, Rev. Lino Parente, O. Cist., was installed as second pastor, succeeding Father Zanni. He remains in that position today and is also prior of the Cistercian Monastery of Our Lady of Fatima.

Claretian Missionaries (C.M.F.)

Eastern Province
Provincial Headquarters:
Oak Park, Illinois

In 1849, the Missionary Sons of the Immaculate Heart of Mary, known as the Claretians, was founded in Catalonia, Spain, by Rev. Anthony Claret. The congregation's apostolate consisted of parish missions throughout Spain. The Claretians spread quickly to other countries, principally in South America but also in Africa and Europe. More recently the order has had success in Kerala, India, and has initiated work in Korea. There are approximately 3,000 Claretian priests and brothers worldwide.

In the United States, there are two provinces, Eastern and Western. In both, the apostolate has operated chiefly on the parish level among Hispanics. However, the Eastern Province also has a strong commitment to publications, with *U.S. Catholic* heading the list.

In the Diocese of Trenton, the Claretians first offered mass on a chicken farm in Lakehurst in 1955. In 1957, the mission was moved to the Cassville section of Jackson Township, where a small church was built. The church, St. Anthony Claret, at first the only one in Jackson Township, also received non-Hispanics for Sunday mass. At the end of the 1960s, local poultry farms started moving to southern states. As a consequence, many Hispanics also had to move in order to find employment in Lakewood, Howell, and Toms River.

In 1974, Rev. Richard Bartlett, C.M.F., then pastor, together with his parishioners, studied various options and finally decided to move to a location three quarters of a mile from the center of Lakewood. A parish center was built, consisting of office space and a large multipurpose hall with one side prepared as an altar. From 1975 to 1989, a small chapel was rented in South Toms River to minister to the Hispanics there who lacked transportation to Lakewood. More recently, under the pastorship of Rev. Raymond Bianchi, C.M.F., the community has built a spacious rectory, largely from funds gained from holding Bingo games. In 1990, the Jackson church was returned to the diocese for use as St. Monica's Church, a mission of Assumption Parish, New Egypt.

Consolata Society for Foreign Missions (I.M.C.)
Region of North America
Headquarters: Somerset, New Jersey

The Consolata Society takes its name from the famous Shrine of Our Lady of Consolation located in the northern Italian city of Turin. It was there that Rev. Joseph Allamano, a diocesan priest and rector of the shrine, received the inspiration to found a new missionary society. On January 29, 1901, Father Allamano established the Consolata Fathers and Brothers. In 1910, under instructions of Pope Pius X, he established the Consolata Sisters, who would assist in missionary activities. The founder died in 1926 and was beatified by Pope John Paul II on October 7, 1990.

By the end of 1991, there were 1,006 professed members of the Consolata Fathers and Brothers and 1,140 Consolata Sisters. They are serving in England, Italy, Portugal, Spain, Switzerland, Ethiopia, Kenya, Liberia, Mozambique, Somalia, South Africa, Tanzania, Uganda, Zaire, South Korea, Argentina, Brazil, Colombia, Venezuela, Canada, and the United States.

In 1947, the Consolata Missionaries came to the United States. With the help of generous benefactors, they developed quickly. They promote vocations and service to non-Christians. On September 4, 1963, Rev. Joseph Moncher, I.M.C., provincial superior in the United States, received written permission from the Most Rev. George W. Ahr to move the Consolata Missionaries' headquarters to the Diocese of Trenton. A 93-acre parcel of land in Somerset County was purchased from Mr. and Mrs. Morris Pivnik. The newly elected provincial, Rev. Ambrose Ravasi, with 6 fathers and, later, 1 brother, moved from Washington, D.C., to the new site in Somerset.

On May 10, 1975, a large mission center built on the Somerset property was dedicated by Bishop Ahr. It includes a private chapel, an audiovisual theater, a library, and a mission art exhibit. The facility enables people of central and southern New Jersey to come for spiritual, cultural, educational, and recreational activities related to the worldwide activities of the Consolata Missionaries.

With the creation of the Diocese of Metuchen in November 1981, the Consolata compound came under its jurisdiction. In June 1991, the Consolata Missionaries of the United States and Canada merged into one region of North America, with the residence in Somerset chosen as the headquarters.

In February 1974, the Diocese of Trenton entrusted to Rev. Nicholas Lodo, I.M.C., the administration of Immaculate Conception Chapel, serving Spanish-speaking people of Keyport. The chapel was replaced later by a new church, Jesus the Lord.

Conventual Franciscans (O.F.M. Conv.)

Immaculate Conception Province
Provincial House:
Union City, New Jersey

Saint Anthony of Padua Province
Provincial House:
Ellicott City, Maryland

The Conventual Franciscans, also known as the Friars Minor Conventual, were founded by the Poverello, Francis of Assisi, in 1209. The definite rule of the community calls for the friars to observe the Gospel of Jesus Christ by living in obedience, poverty, and chastity. The Conventual branch of the Franciscan family, identifiable already in the thirteenth century and distinct by the fifteenth century, has accented the communal call to witness as well as openness to the needs of the church. The Franciscans found their most extensive development in the great urban centers of the world.

The Conventual Franciscan Friars, responding to the nascent immigrant church in the United States, arrived in this country in 1852. After a brief stay in Texas, the community gradually migrated to the Northeast for work among the immigrant community, most particularly among German Catholics.

In 1858, the superior general of the Conventual Friars in the United States, the Very Rev. Bonaventure Keller, accepted the invitation of the Most Rev. John N. Neumann, C.Ss.R., bishop of Philadelphia, to care for St. Alphonsus Parish in Philadelphia. Circuit riding among the scattered German congregations between early establishments in Philadelphia and Brooklyn provided the first Conventual contacts in the state of New Jersey. In 1869, the Most Rev. James Roosevelt Bayley, first bishop of Newark, called upon the Conventual Franciscans to accept care of German immigrants living in the Trenton area. Old St. John's Church had been purchased and renamed in honor of St. Francis of Assisi. In 1883, the parish was turned over to diocesan clergy. The Most Rev. Michael J. O'Farrell, first bishop of Trenton, suggested the founding of the parish of Ss. Peter and Paul in Camden, then within the Trenton diocese.

In 1872, a large friary dedicated to St. Francis was built in the Chambersburg section of Trenton. At the same site, in 1874, the parish of Our Lady of Lourdes was established. This became the headquarters for the missionary activity of the friars in New Jersey from which parishes developed in New Egypt, Lakehurst, Lakewood, Riverside, Hightstown, Florence, Beverly, Riverton, and Toms River. St. Francis College in Chambersburg was the training center for future Conventual Franciscans for more than twenty-five years.

In 1890, a new church dedicated to the Immaculate Conception of the Blessed Virgin Mary was built to replace Our Lady of Lourdes Church. A large grammar school and parish high school were soon added. In 1936, at the request of the Most Rev. Moses E. Kiley, the latter became Trenton Catholic Boys High School, staffed almost entirely by friars. Thousands of students, many of whom became priests, passed through its doors before it closed in 1962.

Today, the Conventual Franciscans are represented by two provinces in Trenton. Founded in 1872, Immaculate Conception Province, the oldest Franciscan province in the United States, serves Immaculate Conception Parish, Trenton; St. Peter, Riverside; St. Peter, Point Pleasant Beach; and St. Catherine, Seaside Park. St. Anthony of Padua Province was founded in 1905. Rev. Stanislaus Czelusniak, O.F.M. Conv., formed in 1890 what was later to become the Polish parish of St. Stanislaus. The St. Anthony Province friars assumed the care St. Casimir Parish, Riverside, in 1936. St. Francis Medical Center, Trenton, is also served by the Conventual Franciscan Friars.

Daughters of Divine Charity (F.D.C.)

St. Joseph Province
Provincial House:
Staten Island, New York

The Daughters of Divine Charity were founded in Vienna, Austria, in 1868 by Bavarian-born Franciska Lechner. The original charisma, which is still continued, is twofold: to provide eduction for the young and to provide a residence, a home away from home, for young women who seek education or employment in large cities. Founded in the Austro-Hungarian Empire of Francis Joseph I, the congregation spread rapidly into the various parts of the empire. Hungary was one of the lands where the Daughters of Divine Charity quickly made a name for themselves as educators of the

first order and providers of spiritual and temporal assistance at their St. Mary's residences.

It was at St. Margaret's Institute in Budapest, Hungary, that the Most Rev. Joseph Schrembs, bishop of Toledo, Ohio, met the sisters in the summer of 1906. Impressed with their work, Bishop Schrembs requested that members of the congregation from the Hungarian province come to his diocese to care for the spiritual needs of the children of the many Hungarian immigrants who were settling in that area. In 1906, however, there were barely enough sisters to meet the commitments already made in Hungary. Thus, while no definite answer was given to Bishop Schrembs, the promise was made to keep the project under consideration.

In the early months of 1913, Mother Mary Ignacia Egger, superior general of the congregation, notified the Hungarian provincial, Mother Mary Valeria Morvay, that she could send sisters to the United States. The call was made for volunteers to leave home for the mission field, and the project was begun. Mother Mary Valeria Morvay and Sr. Mary Kostka Bauer, the novice mistress from Hungary, sailed from Hamburg, Germany, to the United States in 1913. On arrival, they learned that in the meantime, Bishop Schrembs had enlisted another congregation to care for the needs of the Hungarian children in his diocese.

Unwilling to return to Hungary to report failure, the two sisters asked for permission to settle in the Archdiocese of New York. His Eminence, James Cardinal

Farley, archbishop of New York, gladly gave his permission, especially for the establishment of a St. Mary's Residence for the hundreds of young women who were immigrating to the United States. Thus, New York City, with a residence established on East 72nd Street, became the base of operations for the Daughters of Divine Charity in the United States.

Pastors of Hungarian parishes in New Jersey immediately heard of the arrival of the sisters and requested their services. On September 2, 1914, two Daughters of Divine Charity arrived in Trenton to begin work with the children of St. Stephen the King Parish. Three days later, two sisters were accompanied to New Brunswick to begin their apostolic labors in St. Ladislaus Parish. At first, sisters kept coming from Hungary to fill the many demands that were being made for their services. However, beginning in 1915, the first Hungarian-American aspirants asked for admission into the congregation. Having only an elementary education thus far, these aspirants received their high school education at St. Peter's High School in New Brunswick.

In 1923, Daughters of Divine Charity began to staff the school established at Holy Assumption Parish in Roebling. The sisters are also engaged in ministry to the sick and aged members of the parish. With the razing of St. Stephen's School and the construction of the Diocese of Metuchen, the Daughters of Divine Charity currently serve only one parish in the Trenton diocese, Holy Assumption Parish.

In 1950, the Rutherford Estate in Allamuchy was acquired as a home for infirm and retired members of the province. This convent, Villa Madonna, subsequently became the novitiate of the province.

Dominican Sisters (O.P.)

Congregation of Our Lady of the Rosary
General Motherhouse:
Sparkill, New York

In 1876, the Dominican Congregation of Our Lady of the Rosary was founded as an independent Dominican Congregation of Diocesan Rite in New York City by Miss Alice Mary Thorpe, an Englishwoman who had been a member of the Anglican Church. After conversion to Roman Catholicism, Alice and her sister, Lucy, came to New York City in 1872 and began to minister to the sick and poor of the city.

In 1874, Alice came in contact with the provincial of the Dominican Fathers, Very Rev. J. A. Rochford. He wanted to establish a home for indigent women and sought her assistance. A generous benefactor offered them her home on Second Avenue, and thus work began at St. Joseph's Mission Home. Alice and her sister were joined by other women who, like themselves, wished to consecrate their life to the service of the needy. Father Rochford soon obtained permission from His Eminence John Cardinal McCloskey, archbishop of New York, to establish the congregation, which would adopt as its guides the Rule of St. Augustine and the Constitutions of the Third Order of St. Dominic. Alice took the name Mother Catherine Mary Antoninus and became superior of the community.

The beginning years held many difficulties for the sisters. With no financial resources, the struggling community took in washing, did needlework, and begged for alms. The first work of the congregation was the care of indigent women, but it soon added the care of the sick in their home. From this developed the necessity of caring for poor and destitute children. The difficulties undermined the health of Mother Antoninus, who died on March 2, 1879. Her sister, Lucy, who chose the name Sr. Mary Agnes, assumed the office of superior but relinquished it at the end of the year.

Sr. Mary Dominic Dowling, appointed superior in 1880, was given an ultimatum that if the community was not on a firm financial footing by the end of a year, it would be disbanded. Sister Mary formed a corporation and, with the help of a few generous benefactors, managed to purchase land and build a convent on East 63rd Street, where the sisters cared for over 150 orphan girls. Orphan boys were soon included in their program. In 1884, Sister Mary purchased a 26-acre farm in Sparkill to accommodate future expansion. In 1889, a complex of buildings was completed, and in 1895, the motherhouse and novitiate were moved from East 63rd Street to Sparkill.

In August 1899, a disastrous fire razed the buildings at Sparkill. Mother Dominic organized fund-raising efforts to rebuild, but she did not live to see this accomplished. Her successor, Mother Thomas Gargan, saw the return of the sisters and the children to Sparkill in 1902.

By 1900, the work of the congregation had been expanded to include teaching and other ministries, and subsequently the sisters moved into several other dioceses. Today within the Diocese of Trenton, the Sparkill Sisters operate Emmaus House in Elberon. It is a facility designed to provide effective therapy for sisters from religious congregations throughout the United States, Canada, Australia, and Europe who have developed alcoholic, chemical, or other addictions. Also, Sr. Mary Reynolds, O.P., is a chaplain at Riverview Medical Center Hospice, Red Bank.

Dominican Sisters of Newburgh (O.P.)

General Motherhouse: Newburgh, New York

The Dominican Sisters of the Congregation of the Most Holy Rosary, whose motherhouse is located at Mount Saint Mary, Newburgh, New York, have long been associated with the Diocese of Trenton. They arrived in South Jersey eight years before the Trenton diocese came into existence. In 1873, 4 sisters started Saint Mary School in Gloucester. The Newburgh Dominicans have taught in many schools in parishes now belonging to the Diocese of Camden or the Diocese of Metuchen.

The first foundation of the Dominican Sisters of Newburgh within the present boundaries of the Trenton diocese was in the city of Trenton itself. In September

1908, a school was opened in Ss. Peter and Paul Parish at the request of the late Msgr. Coloman Tomchany. The school began in the basement of the church and continued operating there until a new school was constructed several years later. The sisters left Ss. Peter and Paul Parish in 1973.

Under the direction of pastor Rev. George A. Welsh, St. Joseph School, Toms River, staffed by 4 Dominican sisters, opened in September 1932. Registration for grades 1–6 numbered about 80 students during that first year. The original school was formed from one large room. A vast educational complex serving 1,000 students exists today. In addition to conducting the school, the sisters were very active in catechetical work in the vast areas of Ocean County that were rapidly receiving people from New York and Pennsylvania. This work lasted for many years until new parishes and schools were formed to care for the increasing population.

Monsignor Donovan High School (formerly Saint Joseph High School) began in 1962. It is the only Catholic secondary school in Ocean County. In September 1962, 116 freshmen began classes in the grammar school; in 1963, they moved into the new, twelve-room high school section of the building. The Dominican Sisters have seen this grow into a building with an additional twenty-six rooms.

Newburgh Dominican Sisters currently minister to the parish grammar schools of St. Mary's, New Monmouth, and Our Lady of Good Counsel, Moorestown. They serve Ocean County Community College, Toms River, and the parishes of St. Elizabeth, Avon, and Epiphany, Bricktown. The sisters have also served in the parish schools of St. Mary's, Deal, and Our Lady Star of the Sea, Long Branch; in Mater Dei High School, New Monmouth, and Holy Cross High School, Delran; and in Georgian Court College, Lakewood. Their ministrations have extended to the parishes of Holy Cross, Rumson, and St. Dominic, Bricktown.

Felician Sisters (C.S.S.F.)

Immaculate Conception Province
Provincial House: Lodi, New Jersey

In 1855, the Congregation of the Sisters of St. Felix, known as the Felician Sisters, was founded in Warsaw, Poland, by Mother Angela Truszkowska. It was the first indigenous community of religious sisters in Poland, and the first there to break with the tradition that kept nuns cloistered. Mother Angela wanted her sisters to be contemplatives in action, women of prayer dedicated to the service of the poor. The Felician way of life is gospel living according to the Rule of St. Francis of Assisi.

Rev. Joseph Dabrowski, a pioneer Polish priest, settled in Wisconsin to aid his countrymen. He believed that education was the key to advancement and amalgamation into the American mainstream. He begged the Felician Sisters to assist him in his ministry. In 1874, 5 Felician Sisters came to the United States to assist Father Dabrowski in implementing the Polish parochial school system in the United States.

Since then, the Felicians have expanded to care for orphans and those needing health care.

In 1913, because of a large influx of Polish immigrants, the Felician Sisters established the Immaculate Conception Province in Lodi, New Jersey. In 1901, they were invited to staff Holy Cross School, Trenton, and in 1911, St. Hedwig's School, Trenton. The Felicians also taught in many other schools, which are now a part of the Metuchen diocese.

Another apostolate of the sisters was Holy House U.S.A. in Washington, New Jersey, now part of the Diocese of Metuchen. From 1971 to 1984, the sisters participated in activities of the Blue Army and conducted a house of prayer, where women religious could spend time in prayer or retreat. The Felicians also rendered spiritual service to the many pilgrims who visited the shrine there.

In addition to the original ministries of education and health care, the Felicians are engaged in social services, Confraternity of Christian Doctrine classes, and diocesan and pastoral ministry. They currently number about 300 in the Immaculate Conception Province. The Felician Sisters have seven provinces in the United States, three in Poland, one each in Canada and Brazil, and three missions and a native novitiate in Kenya, Africa.

Franciscan Missionary Sisters of the Infant Jesus (F.M.I.J.)

**United States Province
Provincial House:
Cherry Hill, New Jersey**

The form of life for the Franciscan Missionary Sisters of the Infant Jesus is to observe the Gospel of Jesus Christ in the spirit of St. Francis of Assisi. Founded on Christmas Day, 1879, by Barbara Micarelli, later known as Sr. Mary Joseph of the Infant Jesus, the religious family draws its specific identity from the mystery of Bethlehem. In imitation of Jesus, who became a child in order to be loved and not feared, they strive to live the virtues that characterized and surrounded Jesus in the stable in Bethlehem: humility, simplicity, docility, and charity. Through evangelization, catechetical and pastoral ministries, education, health care, and social assistance, they commit themselves to the betterment of the human condition in North America, South America, Europe, Asia, and Africa.

In 1961, their mission in the United States began. The first 3 sisters came from Assisi to the Diocese of Camden, following a request by the local ordinary, Archbishop Celestine J. Damiano. They were to help meet the educational needs of the diocese, which were mounting with the influx of population into the suburban area of Philadelphia. Since 1961, they have served in schools and in the catechetical, pastoral, and charitable ministries in St. Margaret, Woodbury Heights, and St. Joseph Pro-Cathedral, Camden. A novitiate was opened in 1965 in Woodbury Heights, and local vocations have since been received and formed to live the Franciscan life-style here in the United States. In 1983, the novitiate moved to a new location in Cherry Hill, and this same location also became the residence of the delegate superior.

In 1977, 3 sisters came to the Diocese of Trenton in response to a request by Rev. David Delzell to staff the parish school of Our Lady of Perpetual Help, Highlands. In 1980, 3 more sisters came to Holy Cross School in Rumson, in response to Rev. William Kokoszka's request. However, they no longer staff Holy Cross School.

Franciscan Sisters of Allegany, New York (O.S.F.)

General Motherhouse: Allegany, New York

The Franciscan Sisters of Allegany, New York, trace their beginnings to April 25, 1859, when, in the chapel of St. Bonaventure College and Seminary, Rev. Pamfilo da Magliano, O.S.F., gave the habit of the Third Order of St. Francis and the name Sister Mary Joseph to Mary Jane Todd. Father Pamfilo, the custos-provincial of the Friars Minor of the Immaculate Conception Custody, had come with 3 other friars to western New York State in 1855 at the invitation of the Most Rev. John Timon, C.M., bishop of Buffalo, New York, and Mr. Nicholas Devereux, a Catholic layman and landowner. Bishop Timon had also asked Father Pamfilo to "seek for Sisters of the Third Order" to provide education for the young women of the area. His search led

him to form a new congregation in Allegany, New York.

After the reception of Sr. Mary Joseph, Ellen Fallon was received on June 24, 1859, and took the name Sr. Mary Bridget. Several months later, these 2 sisters were joined by Mary Anne O'Neil, a 15-year-old girl from New Jersey who had been exhorted by Father Pamfilo to be generous with the Lord despite her young years. Mary Anne was received on December 8, 1859, and took the name Sr. Mary Teresa.

The 3 women formed the nucleus of the new community, which soon began to attract other young women from surrounding areas. From the beginning of the congregation, the sisters were under the jurisdiction of Father Pamfilo. He appointed the officers of the new community until 1865, when he presented the sisters with their first statutes, which had been adapted from those of the Franciscan Sisters in Glasgow, Scotland. That same year the sisters held their first chapter and elected Sr. Mary Teresa as their general superior. She was to serve in this capacity for fifty-five years (two by appointment, fifty-three by election) and give leadership and formative vision to the new community.

In 1860, St. Elizabeth Academy was opened in Allegany for the education of young women. From this beginning, the sisters branched out to open schools in Connecticut, New York, and other states along the eastern coast of the United States. In 1879, 3 sisters were sent to Jamaica, British West Indies. As a result, the Franciscan Sisters of Allegany became the first

U.S.-founded congregation of religious women to send sisters to foreign missions. Missions were opened in Brazil in 1946 and in Bolivia in 1965. Sisters also went to serve the poor in the southern United States.

The year 1883 marked the beginning of involvement with apostolates other than schools: hospital administration and health care, homes for the young and the elderly, pastoral and social work, and many more ministries, which continue, some in different forms, to this day.

The first Franciscan Sisters of Allegany arrived in New Jersey in 1924 at St. John's Parish in Dunellen, now in the Diocese of Metuchen. Members served in a number of ministries in the present dioceses of Camden and Metuchen before they separated from the Diocese of Trenton in 1937 and 1981, respectively. Their presence in the Diocese of Trenton is manifested in the Diocesan Vocation Office; the Medical Records Department at St. Lawrence Rehabilitation Center; the Religious Education Program at St. Alphonsus Parish, Hopewell; the parish ministry at St. Francis of Assisi, Brant Beach; the Diocesan Office of Evangelization and Parish Life; and the Chaplaincy in Deborah Hospital, Browns Mills.

Franciscan Sisters of Saint Joseph (F.S.S.J.)

General Motherhouse: Hamburg, New York

A memorial plaque in the entrance of St. Stanislaus Church in Trenton commemorates Mother Colette Hilbert, foundress of the Franciscan Sisters of St. Joseph. Engraved with her name and image is her motto: "In all things—Charity," left as a legacy for the congregation.

At St. Stanislaus Church in 1897, Sister Colette, a member of the Sisters of Charity of St. Charles Borromeo, with 4 novices received the Franciscan habit from Rev. Hyacinth Fudzinski, O.F.M. Conv., who obtained from Pope Leo XIII approval for the establishment of a new congregation. The Franciscan Sisters' mission was to collaborate in serving the needs of Polish immigrant families, particularly in the areas of education and charity.

Because the teaching apostolate terminated three years later at St. Stanislaus School, Mother Colette with her sisters accepted the invitation of Father Fudzinski to teach at Corpus Christi School in Buffalo, New York. The first motherhouse and novitiate were established near Corpus Christi Parish.

Once again, in 1911, the Franciscan Sisters of St. Joseph were asked to assume the direction of St. Stanislaus School in Trenton. In 1928, both the motherhouse and the novitiate were transferred from Buffalo to Hamburg, New York. The sisters were called to take charge of schools in New York, Massachusetts, Wisconsin, Michigan, Connecticut, Maryland, Pennsylvania, and Alabama. In 1926, the congregation initiated the care of the aging and the infirm, and, in 1940, it ventured into hospital work and higher education. A mission was established in Brazil in 1965. Recently, the congregation extended itself to social service work and other diverse ministries.

As the expansion of ministries continued, so also did the congregation's spiritual development. In 1936, final approbation was received from Pope Pius XI, erecting the Franciscan Sisters of St. Joseph as a pontifical institute. In 1982, the congregation assumed the revised Rule of the Third Order Regular of St. Francis. Three years later, the congregation's revised constitutions were approved by a special blessing of the church.

Among the new thrusts is the establishment of an Affiliate Program for those who desire to deepen their relationship with God and the Franciscan Sisters of St. Joseph Community. The hope is that the laity and the Franciscan Sisters become stronger partners in ministry for the church.

Currently in Trenton, 5 Franciscan Sisters of St. Joseph continue to administer and staff St. Stanislaus School; 160 children are enrolled. Through the years, the sisters have received nine vocations from St. Stanislaus Parish.

Grey Nuns of the Sacred Heart (G.N.S.H.)

**General Motherhouse:
Yardley, Pennsylvania**

In 1737, St. Marguerite d'Youville founded the Sisters of Charity of Montreal, also known as the Grey Nuns. In 1990, Sister Marguerite, considered one of the founders of the church in Canada, was canonized a saint. A religious congregation branched from the Sisters of Charity of Montreal in 1845. They were called the Grey Nuns of the Cross and are now known as the Sisters of Charity, at Ottawa. The Sulpicians were influential in the early development of the Grey Nuns, whose spiritual heritage is characterized by loving trust in Divine Providence. The Grey Nuns were initially committed to the care of the sick and poor, principally at the General Hospital in Montreal. They added education, particularly of girls and young women, to their official works.

The Grey Nuns of the Cross began staffing schools and hospitals in New England and northern New York State. In 1921, 150 Grey Nuns of the Cross from Ottawa, Canada, founded the U.S. congregation of the Grey Nuns of the Sacred Heart. The new congregation initially developed within the Diocese of Buffalo, New York. The Most Rev. Dennis J. Dougherty, bishop of Buffalo, between 1915 and 1918, was a crucial element in the foundation process. Many other bishops also supported the new foundation, including the Most Rev. Thomas J. Walsh, then bishop of Trenton. It is believed that Bishop Walsh invited the leadership of the new congregation to establish the motherhouse in the Trenton diocese. However, Cardinal Dougherty, who was promoted to the Archdiocese of Philadelphia in 1918 and created cardinal in 1921, invited the Grey Nuns to his diocese. Because of his prior support and influence, his offer was accepted, and the Grey Nuns of the Sacred Heart established their motherhouse in Yardley, Pennsylvania.

Shortly thereafter, in 1923, Rev. J. R. O'Connor, pastor of St. Joseph's Parish in Carteret, then in the Trenton diocese, invited 10 Grey Nuns, who staffed the parish school until 1934. Other invitations from parishes now in the Camden or Metuchen diocese were declined in order to allow time for formation of the young congregation. At its foundation, the new congregation became responsible for staffing a college for women and two hospitals in northern New York State as well as several parish schools.

Currently, Grey Nuns minister in the Trenton diocese at St. Francis Medical Center, St. Mary's Cathedral, Trenton State College, St. Raphael's School, and Our Lady of Sorrows Parish, all in Trenton. They serve St. Lawrence Rehabilitation Center and St. Ann's Parish, Lawrenceville; Georgian Court College, Lakewood; and Emmaus House, Elberon. Previously, Sr. Jean Vogel, G.N.S.H., served as codirector of RENEW from 1984 to 1988 and as associate director of the Office of Evangelization and Parish Life from 1989 to 1991. Other Grey Nuns have served in recent years at St. Alphonsus Parish, Hopewell, and Notre Dame High School, Lawrenceville.

Marianites of Holy Cross (M.S.C.)
**Province of North America
Headquarters: New Orleans, Louisiana**

Rev. Basil Moreau's life is one that speaks of courage, zeal, generosity, and trust; of strong belief in the Providence of God; and of human response to divine grace. In 1835, Father Moreau founded a society of auxiliary priests at Le Mans, France. In 1836, he was given the care of the Brothers of St. Joseph. The union of the two societies took place in 1837, becoming known as the Congregation of Holy Cross. Father Moreau's vision also included female members in the congregation. In 1841, 3 postulants began training given by the superior of Good Shepherd Convent. They were soon joined by Miss Leocadie Gascoin, a doctor's daughter, destined to be the first superior general of the Marianites, Mother May of the Seven Dolors.

Although its beginnings were poor and its sufferings many, the Congregation of the Marianites of Holy Cross grew in France, the United States, and Canada. In time the sisters in the Indiana and Canadian provinces separated from the motherhouse in France and became independent congregations. The sisters in Louisiana and New York remained attached to their roots in France.

On July 15, 1947, the Marianites took up residence in the Trenton diocese at Our Lady of Princeton Convent in Princeton. The Marianites, invited in 1955, staffed and administered Our Lady of Sorrows School in Trenton until 1990. From 1962 to 1974, St. Benedict's parochial school in Holmdel was entrusted to the Marianites. Another work confided to the Marianites was St. John Vianney Regional High School, Holmdel, in 1969. In 1980, the pastor of St. Mary of the Lakes, Medford, requested that the Marianites help him with parish ministry. In 1989, Our Lady of Mount Carmel Church, Asbury Park, graciously received the Marianites into its parish. During these years, individuals were also serving at St. Catharine's, Holmdel; Nativity, Fair

Haven; McCorristin High School, Trenton; Star of the Sea, Long Branch; St. Francis Medical Center, Trenton; St. Lawrence Rehabilitation Center, Lawrenceville; and Morris Hall, Lawrenceville.

In 1985, a new government structure was adopted by the Marianites to consolidate the congregation into only two provinces, one in France and the other in North America. In September 1991, the novitiate for the Marianites of the North American Province was established in Hazlet, a part of the Trenton diocese.

Missionary Catechists of the Sacred Hearts of Jesus and Mary (M.C.)

Motherhouse: Tlalpan, Mexico

United States Foundation: Victoria, Texas

The Missionary Catechists of the Sacred Hearts of Jesus and Mary is an institute of consecrated life for the work of evangelization and catechesis. The congregation was founded in 1928 by Madre Sofia Garduño Nava, originally from Mexico City.

The charisma of the Missionary Catechists is to make present the saving and compassionate love of the heart of Jesus, who generously gave Himself for the salvation of humanity. Special focus is placed upon the strengthening of family life.

Through their presence and work in the apostolic ministry in St. Mary's Cathedral, Trenton, the Missionary Catechists fulfill their vocation as consecrated women who are "sent." They visit homes in order to reach out to people in the Trenton area,

transmitting the love of God, especially to those who have experienced hurt. The Missionary Catechists coordinate the Confraternity of Christian Doctrine program. They also meet every night with a different group of families to meditate upon the Word of God.

Missionary Servants of the Most Blessed Trinity (M.S.B.T.)

Generalate: Philadelphia, Pennsylvania

In the year 1912, in Baltimore, Maryland, the earliest group of associates first occupied the same residence with a common apostolate. Father Judge was assigned by his Vincentian community to Opelika, Alabama, in 1915. Shortly thereafter, he "sent for" some of the "associates" to create a Catholic presence in his territory. Thus, three or four years after their initial foundation, the Missionary Servants of the Most Blessed Trinity was firmly established. The first mother general was Margaret Louise Keasey of Butler, Pennsylvania. Her religious name was Mary Boniface, and she served as mother general from 1919 until her death on November 22, 1931.

The congregation's first motherhouse was in Russell County, Alabama, at a place called then and now Holy Trinity, Alabama. In 1931, after the motherhouse was burned to the ground, the congregation moved to Philadelphia in response to an invitation by His Eminence Dennis Cardinal Dougherty.

The sisters are a part of a larger family working for the church. The other groups consist of priests and brothers (Missionary

Servants of the Most Holy Trinity), laity (Missionary Cenacle Apostolate [MCA]), and the beginnings of a pious union called the Blessed Trinity Missionary Institute (BTMI). The two religious congregations share a Common Rule of Life approved by Rome in 1985. MCA and BTMI have rules based on the Common Rule of the religious members of the family.

The charisma shared by all the branches is a missionary one. An excerpt from Rule of Life #4 follows:

> The missionary thought, the missionary idea, the missionary spirit should be dominant in our Missionary Cenacles. We meet the pressing needs of our day by undertaking works that the Church wants, that are good and necessary, and that have a note of abandonment about them. . . .

The statements about the charisma do not mention any specific apostolate. The desire of the founder, Father Judge, was for the congregation to meet the pressing needs of the day, whatever those needs may be, and wherever they may betake the congregation.

From a small group in Alabama at the beginning of the 1920s to missionary cenacles in Philadelphia; Pensacola, Florida; Tucker, Mississippi; Newark, New Jersey; Brooklyn, New York; and many other places, the congregation has expanded. Today it has cenacles in thirty-three dioceses and archdioceses throughout the continental United States, Puerto Rico, and Mexico.

The Most Rev. William A. Griffin and Rev. Francis M. J. Thornton, director of the Catholic Bureau, invited the congregation to serve in the Diocese of Trenton. Starting in 1943, Sr. Mary James and Sr. Mary Adel commuted from the motherhouse to begin the apostolate in the Diocesan Social Service program in Trenton. In October 1944, the congregation opened Our Lady of Light Missionary Cenacle at 55 North Clinton Avenue, in the Cathedral Parish, Trenton. In 1957, a branch office was opened in Fords and in 1961, one in Red Bank. Due to a shortage of personnel and changing social conditions, the sisters have withdrawn from these apostolates.

Other apostolates in the Diocese of Trenton have included Marion House, Belmar; St. Anthony Claret Parish, Lakewood; St. Francis Parish Community Center, Brant Beach; and Mt. Carmel Guild, Trenton. Currently, Sr. Susanne Thibault serves at St. Mary Parish, Colts Neck.

Oblate Sisters of Providence (O.S.P.)
General Motherhouse: Baltimore, Maryland

When a flood of black refugees from the Isle of Hispaniola–San Dominique, now known as Haiti, poured into Baltimore, Maryland, in the early 1800s, they found no schools for their children. One of them, Miss Elizabeth Lange, established a tiny free school in her home. In 1829, with 3 companions and under the direction of a French Sulpician priest, Rev. James Hector Joubert, S.S., she founded a teaching order to give permanence to their educational venture.

The Oblate Sisters' ministry of education exists at all levels and remains their primary focus. Today, Oblates serve in eight states, the District of Columbia, and Costa Rica. Their ministries are woven with threads of prayer and dependence on Providence as they strive to meet the daily needs of God's people.

In 1956, God called the Oblate Sisters to staff Our Lady of the Divine Shepherd School, Trenton. Through the years, Oblates have carried on the tradition handed down by their foundress and founder, that of educating and evangelizing people of African and Central American backgrounds.

Fifty-six Oblates have responded to the call to come and see Jesus Christ in the urban community of Trenton. The sisters have witnessed the rise and fall and rise again of school enrollment. They have experienced the cooperation and support of the Most Rev. George W. Ahr and the Most Rev. John C. Reiss. Oblate Sisters of Providence have shared a positive relationship with the Society of the Divine Word Fathers and Brothers in their service to the parish community of Our Lady of the Divine Shepherd.

Order of St. Clare (O.S.C.)
Monastery of St. Clare
Bordentown, New Jersey

The Order of St. Clare was founded in Assisi, Italy, in 1212 by Saint Clare under the inspiration and sponsorship of St. Francis. Thus was born the Second Franciscan Order: a cloistered, contemplative order with a simple gospel life-style that centers on the liturgical prayer of the church.

The chief apostolate is that of prayer—prayer for the church and the world.

In 1875, two Poor Clares, who were also blood sisters—Mother Maddalena and Mother Constance—of the noble Bentivoglio family, came from Italy to establish a Poor Clare monastery in the United States. After many rejections and hardships, they were successful in founding a monastery in Omaha, Nebraska, in 1878. From there the order spread to other parts of the country.

In February 1909, the Most Rev. James A. McFaul invited the Poor Clare nuns of Evansville, Indiana, to come to the Trenton diocese. He informed them that the Sisters of Mercy had vacated their former motherhouse and academy located in Bordentown and that it would be available on reasonable terms. The community at Evansville, having recently established a foundation in Boston, did not feel it could spare any sisters for a new foundation at that time. Therefore, it sent Bishop McFaul's invitation along to Mother Charitas Burns, foundress of the Boston Monastery. She agreed to supply the personnel for the venture.

On August 12, 1909, a pioneer group from Boston arrived in Bordentown. It consisted of Sr. Mary Immaculate McPyke, Sr. Mary Maddalena Burns, Sr. Mary Anthony Hebert, Sr. Mary Columba O'Donnell, and Sr. Mary Brigidae Daly. The formal dedication of the monastery, with Bishop McFaul officiating, took place on Thanksgiving Day, November 25, 1909.

Difficulties were many for the pioneer group, and the heavy debt was a cause of great concern to them. At first, their only source of income, other than alms, resulted from the sale of fine needlework. The sisters later started an altar bread business. This represented a much better source of profit to them and, at the same time, a help to the diocese. It continues to be the sisters' main work.

Because of the heavy debt that had to be paid off, Mother Mary Charitas Burns remained in charge of the Bordentown foundation until it was firmly established, although Sr. Mary Immaculate McPyke was delegated as the local superior. In 1920, the first canonical elections were held, and Mother Mary Maddalena Burns was elected abbess, an office she held for many years. Succeeding abbesses have been Sisters Mary Charitas Rogers, Mary Paschal Burke, Patricia Henry, Natalie Hayes, Mary McCourt, and the present abbess, Sr. Claire Andrew Gagliardi, elected in 1990.

The bishops of Trenton have always shown a fatherly solicitude and concern for the community. The Most Rev. George W. Ahr deserves special mention, because he has spent a great deal of time with the community, giving classes in theology and seeing sisters individually for spiritual direction. He also arranged for extensive remodeling of the monastery building in 1953.

Order of the Most Holy Trinity (O.Ss.T.)

U.S.A. Province, Province of the Immaculate Heart of Mary
Provincial House:
Baltimore, Maryland

The Order of the Most Holy Trinity (the Trinitarians) was founded in the area of Cerfroid, France, in the year 1198 by John de Matha and Philip of Valois. From the very outset, a special dedication to the mystery of the Holy Trinity has been a constituent element of the order's life. The founding intention for the order was the ransom of Christians held captive by nonbelievers during the time of the Crusades. Soon after papal approbation, the Trinitarian ministry to Christian captives was incorporated into the order's title: Order of the Holy Trinity and of Captives or Order of the Holy Trinity for the Ransom of Captives. In addition to the order's purpose of ransoming Christian captives, each local community of Trinitarians served the people of its area. And so, their ministries included hospitality, care of the sick and poor, churches, and education. Eventually, the Trinitarians also assumed the work of evangelization.

Brother John's founding intention expanded quickly into a considerable network of houses committed to the ransom of Christian captives and the mercy works of their locales. The first generation of Trinitarians could count some fifty foundations. The thirteenth century was a time of vitality and achievement. The following centuries, reflecting events in the church and in

European history, saw the order experience alternately times of difficulty and decline and times of growth and development. During the last decades of the nineteenth century, the Trinitarian order began to rise from its collapse in Italy and Spain. The members dedicated themselves to fostering and promoting devotion to the Holy Trinity, to evangelization of nonbelievers, to spiritual assistance for immigrants to the United States, to education, and to pastoral ministry in parishes.

When U.S. bishops appealed to Europe for missionary priests, such a mission fitted right in with the work traditionally done by the Order of the Most Holy Trinity. Used to facing the dangers of rescuing Christians enslaved by pagans, the mission would face a long and perilous journey into a new and hostile land to take up again the vital work of saving souls and strengthening a faith besieged not by physical torture but by suspicion, innuendo, and open hostility. Father Migliorini, O.Ss.T. came to the United States in 1906 but failing to organize any parish here, returned to Italy in 1909. He returned to the United States in 1911 with Rev. Anthony Giovanni, O.Ss.T.

Father Giovanni accepted calls in the New York area until January 1912, when the bishop of Trenton, the Most Rev. James A. McFaul, offered the Trinitarians the direction of a parish in Asbury Park. Father Giovanni was pastor of Our Lady of Mount Carmel Church, Asbury Park, for twenty-five years before returning to Italy. Trinitarians still serve the parish. The Italian immigrants at nearby Holy Trinity Parish, Long Branch, were served by the Trinitarians from 1912 to 1921.

Until 1937, diocesan clergy served the parish of St. James, Trenton. Under the Most Rev. Moses E. Kiley, the Trinitarians assumed the care of the parish, with Rev. Thomas Rocca, O.Ss.T., as administrator and Rev. August Pinci, O.Ss.T., as his assistant. Beginning in 1963, the order furnished chaplains for Our Lady of Mt. Carmel, Trenton, a Puerto Rican mission. The chaplains continued to serve the mission parish until 1981, when it merged with St. Mary's Cathedral Parish in Trenton. The Trinitarians served Cathedral Parish from 1981 to 1986.

Redemptorists (C.Ss.R.)
Province of Baltimore
Provincial Residence: Brooklyn, New York

The Congregation of the Holy Redeemer (Redemptorists) was founded by St. Alphonsus Liguori in 1732. Alphonsus had been a lawyer in the Kingdom of Naples. In his middle twenties, he heard the call of Christ: Come follow me. Alphonsus gave up a promising legal practice and was ordained to the priesthood at the age of 30. The Kingdom of Naples had an abundance of priests, but Alphonsus found that the poor in country areas were often spiritually neglected. So, in 1732, he and a number of companions founded a religious order "to follow the example of Jesus Christ the Redeemer by preaching the Gospel, especially to the most abandoned."

Rev. Alphonsus Liguori was also a prolific writer. For his efforts in successfully combating the rigorism of the times, which pictured Christ as a severe judge, he was made a doctor of the church and the official patron of confessors and moral theologians. Father Alphonsus stressed God's love and mercy to be had through prayer and the reception of the sacraments. God blessed Father Alphonsus's efforts to the extent that his Redemptorists have become the seventh-largest order of priests in the church, with more than 6,000 members in over sixty countries throughout the world.

In 1832, 6 stalwart Austrian Redemptorists braved a sixty-six-day ocean voyage to preach the Gospel to Native Americans. However, at the time, there were thousands of immigrants without priests. So the bishops insisted that they first serve the needs of these poor people lest they lose the faith. The Redemptorists did so by founding flourishing parishes in Baltimore, Boston, New York City, Philadelphia, Pittsburgh, and Rochester. They also preached missions to revitalize the faith of the people. Their first U.S. vocation was the Most Rev. John N. Neumann, C.Ss.R., fourth bishop of Philadelphia, who was later canonized a saint.

The Redemptorists have been in the Diocese of Trenton since 1893. At present in Long Branch, they staff San Alfonso Retreat House, established in 1925. All the early houses founded by St. Alphonsus were also retreat houses. Their main purpose was the development of groups of dedicated lay people who would bring Christ into the marketplace. The work of the retreat house has prospered with the active support of bishops and priests and through highly effective promotional efforts on the part of the Knights of Columbus and the members of the Retreat League.

The first two lay retreats in 1925 had a total attendance of 15 retreatants. In 1990, approximately 13,000 utilized the facilities. San Alfonso has room for 150 persons, a large chapel, spacious meeting rooms, a well-appointed dining room, and a religious article and book store. There is also a prayer garden on the grounds, and, along the Atlantic Ocean, are a boardwalk and benches.

The programs at San Alfonso include weekend retreats for men, women, and couples; Matt Talbot retreats; charismatic retreats; preached retreats for priests, brothers, and sisters; high school and young adult retreats; private and directed retreats; days of prayer and evenings of recollection; and meetings and conferences for diocesan, parish, and school groups and members of religious institutes.

Religious of the Sacred Heart of Mary (R.S.H.M.)

Eastern American Province
Provincial House:
Tarrytown, New York

The Religious of the Sacred Heart of Mary originated in 1849, in Beziers, a town within the Diocese of Montpellier in the south of France. The human force behind the foundation was a priest of that diocese, Rev. Pierre Jean Antoine Gailhac. As a young man, Father Gailhac had been chaplain of a local hospital, the Hôtel Dieu. There he assisted those in material need and gave spiritual direction to numerous people. Later, he aided women whose poverty and lack of education had made them victims of society. He opened a shelter for these women, some of whom would otherwise have had to resort to prostitution. Soon, Father Gailhac was also receiving abandoned children and orphans into the shelter. In these enterprises he was aided by sisters of various, already established, congregations.

His friendship with a former classmate and lawyer, Eugene Cure, and his wife, Apollonie Pelissier, constituted another source of advice and material help. For various reasons, the religious who worked at the shelter were withdrawn, and Father Gailhac was in grave difficulty. However, on the death of her husband, Madame Cure and 3 companions, joined by 2 more women at the shelter, known as the Refuge, resolved to commit themselves as religious sisters to a life of poverty, chastity, and obedience. After a period of probation, Father Gailhac, their spiritual guide, drew up for them a rule of life and formed them to the life they were to undertake: "whatever work would contribute to the glory of God and the salvation of souls." Soon other recruits joined them, and their works did multiply. A boarding school for girls was added to the existing orphanage, and the Refuge eventually closed. As the group expanded, so did the horizons. Houses were opened in Portugal, Ireland, England, and the United States. Madame Cure, known as

Mère St. Jean, and Father Gailhac visited and watched over the foundation.

Over the years, interest in education grew. Other works, particularly orphanages, also flourished. To meet existing needs, adult education was undertaken in Ireland. As changes occurred in society, new needs had to be met. The Good News still had to be spread. The sisters became active in Italy, Africa, Brazil, Colombia, Mexico, and Canada. True to the founder's vision, the sisters embraced any work that could contribute to the salvation of souls. Education on the primary, secondary, and post-secondary levels continued to be of great importance. In Brazil, the shortage of priests gave rise to the *comunidade de base*. Africa invited involvement in social work and nursing. In England, Ireland, and the United States, sisters have also become engaged in pastoral ministry, prison work, nursing, social work of various types, law, and retreat work. In addition, in the United States, the sisters have undertaken ministries in rural areas as well as suburban and urban regions.

In 1975, the Religious of the Sacred Heart of Mary first arrived in the Diocese of Trenton. Two sisters took up residence in Princeton and were engaged in education, public and private. In 1988, they moved to Lawrenceville, where they are currently living. In 1990, another sister took up parish work at St. Mary's in Deal.

Religious Teachers Filippini (M.P.F.)

Saint Lucy Filippini Province
Provincial House:
Morristown, New Jersey

The Pontifical Institute of the Religious Teachers Filippini (Maestre Pie Filippini) is one of the oldest teaching communities of sisters in Italy. It began in Montefiascone in 1692, when His Eminence Cardinal Mark Anthony Barbarigo asked Lucy Filippini to direct the schools he had established for the education of young girls. Twelve years later, he devised a set of rules to guide Lucy and her followers in the religious life. These Religious Teachers were to provide Christian training for the children of the common people. As the community grew, it attracted the attention of Pope Clement XI, who called Lucy to Rome in 1707 to begin schools that he placed under his special protection.

Lucy impressed her style and educational method onto her schools. The primary objective was the formation of women who would serve to strengthen family life, especially among the poorer classes. This educative and didactic adventure still continues today through the schools and social ministry started by the Religious Teachers. Their mission has spread beyond Italy into other parts of Europe, the United States, Brazil, Ethiopia, and India.

In 1910, a new era began for the Religious Teachers Filippini when, at the command of Pope Pius X, 5 sisters came to the United States. Their destination was St. Joachim Parish, Trenton, and their mission was to serve the needs of neglected Italian immigrants. The Religious Teachers spoke their language, understood their customs, and cherished their traditions. After these Italian immigrants achieved some social improvement and security, the Religious Teachers continued to staff schools for all children, regardless of race, nationality, or creed. In 1916, under the leadership of Sr. Ninetta Ionata, the new superior, administration of the first school improved. During the 1917–18 Spanish influenza epidemic, she challenged the sisters to assist the sick and the destitute. They served as nurses and provided hot meals. Soon after, they were recalled to Rome by the superior general. Only when Sister Ninetta appealed to the new bishop of Trenton, the Most Rev. Thomas J. Walsh, did their situation change.

In 1920, using a donation made by a benefactor, Bishop Walsh purchased the property now known as Villa Victoria on the banks of the Delaware River in Trenton to serve as a motherhouse and novitiate. Within a decade, when he was transferred to Newark, Villa Walsh, the former Gillespie estate on Tower Hill in Morristown, became the new motherhouse and the community's educational headquarters.

In March 1922, Sr. Teresa Saccucci arrived to become head of the first U.S. vicariate, which, under her leadership, became a province. Within four years, four schools had opened in the Diocese of Trenton. By 1927, Villa Victoria was granted its own Normal School Charter and was staffed by the Religious Teachers Filippini. An academy was opened there for young girls in grades kindergarten through 12. Other schools soon flourished in the Diocese of Trenton; some now form part of the Dioceses of Camden and Metuchen. In the United States, members of the Province of Saint Lucy also staff schools in New York, Ohio, Pennsylvania, and South Carolina, as well as New Jersey.

The present generation of Religious Teachers has inherited a style of life that gives testimony to a spirituality, a simplicity, and a hospitality that are truly evangelical. Their spirit consists appropriately in the union of consecration and mission and of contemplation and action. The motto of the Religious Teachers, which has been incorporated into the institute's coat of arms, is *Euntes Docete Verbum Domini* (Go and Teach the Word of God).

School Sisters of Notre Dame (S.S.N.D.)

Baltimore Province
Provincial House: Baltimore, Maryland

The School Sisters of Notre Dame traces its actual beginning to October 24, 1833, when Caroline Gerhardinger (later known as Mother Mary Theresa of Jesus) and 2 other women began a common religious life in Neunburg vorm Wald, Bavaria. Their action was inspired by an apostolic spirituality destined to shape their own lives and profoundly affect those of many others.

The sisters came to the Middle Atlantic States in response to a request to teach the neglected children of German immigrants. Soon after they arrived in this country,

Mother Theresa and 5 companions set out for the German colony of St. Mary in the backwoods of Pennsylvania. Mother Theresa was soon convinced of the unsuitability of this location for a motherhouse. She and several sisters traveled to Baltimore, where Rev. John N. Neumann, C.Ss.R. (later bishop of Philadelphia and now saint), offered to sell them the Redemptorist Novitiate at St. James in Baltimore, Maryland. The sisters lived there until they built their own convent on the adjoining properties in 1863. A few weeks later, the Redemptorist Fathers brought 2 orphans to the sisters to be cared for. Responding to this need, the sisters soon had orphanages in Pittsburgh and Philadelphia, Pennsylvania; Rochester, Yorkville, and New York, New York; and Newark, New Jersey.

At the time of Mother Theresa's death in 1879, more than 2,500 School Sisters of Notre Dame were living religious life according to her spirit. They met the needs of their time by educating girls, principally in elementary schools, but also in orphanages, day nurseries, and industrial schools. They trained future teachers and pioneered in the development of kindergartens. For girls who were factory workers, they established homes and provided night schools where these girls could receive basic education.

In the Diocese of Trenton, School Sisters of Notre Dame went to Holy Family Parish, Hazlet, in 1966 but withdrew in 1972. In 1984, Sr. Ann Marie Impink, S.S.N.D., worked in Spanish ministry at our Lady of Providence, Neptune. At this time also, Sr. Elizabeth Rosser, S.S.N.D., became house manager of St. Clare's Home for Children in Ocean Grove.

Servants of the Holy Infancy of Jesus (O.S.F.)

**Regional House:
North Plainfield, New Jersey**

It was in response to a request by the Conventual Franciscan Friars of the Immaculate Conception Province in 1934 that the community first established a convent in Trenton. The first 5 pioneer sisters had come from Germany to Staten Island, New York, in 1929 to perform domestic work in the seminaries of the friars. They were asked to assist them in other ministries as well. Their entrance into the Diocese of Trenton was supported and blessed by the Most Rev. Moses E. Kiley. Upon moving into Immaculate Conception Parish on August 5, 1935, the sisters worked in the rectory as cooks and laundresses. Expanding their ministry in 1941, they also worked in the school cafeteria and attended to the homebound sick and elderly of the parish as visiting nurses. St. Clare's Convent, a three-story house, served as headquarters for the American Region of the Servants of the Holy Infancy of Jesus until a larger, more suitable location was found in North Plainfield.

In July 1938, the sisters moved into the North Plainfield convent, Villa Maria, which was also to be used as a home for the aged, so it needed to be modernized. On October 6, 1938, the congregation received from the Apostolic See the right to establish a novitiate at Villa Maria. In 1941, a new chapel with adjoining enclosure was placed into service. Other wings were added in 1947 and 1953, and a new infirmary and laundry building were erected in 1976. Today, Villa Maria is thriving as a residence, nursing home, and headquarters of the American Region. In 1981, Villa Maria became part of the Diocese of Metuchen. Due to changing needs and the advancing age of the sisters, St. Clare's convent was closed in 1975.

As regional superior, Mother Mary Praxedis Zirkelbach, O.S.F., longed to establish a home for the original work and purpose of the congregation: the physical and spiritual welfare of wayward girls and women. Mother Praxedis and the Most Rev. William A. Griffin agreed to establish a home for unwed mothers and their infants. An ideal location was found in Yardville in 1943 and was greatly expanded in 1960. The legalization of abortion in 1973 and changing social attitudes decreased the home's population. By 1975, St. Elizabeth's Home had started serving mentally handicapped women. (More information about St. Elizabeth's Home can be found in the chapter on institutions.)

Sisters of Charity of Saint Elizabeth (S.C.)

**General Motherhouse:
Convent Station, New Jersey**

The Sisters of Charity of Saint Elizabeth, an apostolic congregation of pontifical right, follow the Rule of St. Vincent de Paul as approved by St. Elizabeth Ann Bayley Seton, foundress of the Sisters of Charity in the United States. Through her nephew, the Most Rev. James Roosevelt Bayley, bishop of Newark, they became linked to the motherhouse at Emmitsburg when Mother Margaret George of the Cincinnati foundation agreed in 1858 to train the first 5 novices from Newark. In 1859, Mother Jerome of the New York foundation lent Sisters Mary Xavier Mehegan and Mary Catherine Nevins to direct the young community. In 1860, 10 sisters, including Mother Mary Xavier Mehegan, moved to Convent Station, then part of Madison, into buildings formerly occupied by Seton Hall College.

The Sisters of Charity began work within the present boundaries of the Trenton diocese on March 27, 1862, to care for Civil War orphans. Rev. Anthony Smith, pastor of old St. John's in Trenton, had opened the orphan asylum, requesting the Sisters of Charity to care for the children. In 1864, the sisters began classes in the basement of St. John's Church. A separate St. John's Academy developed, but it closed in 1914. The parish school was renamed Sacred Heart School to reflect the new name of the parish. According to the community's archival records, 194 Sisters of Charity have taught at Sacred Heart School, and 58 girls from the school have become Sisters of Charity themselves. Seven girls became Sisters of Mercy, 6 became Franciscans, and 2 became Dominicans.

Within the present perimeter of the Diocese of Trenton, the Sisters of Charity have staffed the following schools: St. Mary Cathedral School, Trenton (1871–1906); St. Joseph School, Trenton (1881–99); Star of the Sea Academy, Long Branch (1885–1970); and Star of the Sea Parochial School, Long Branch (1900–1979). They operated Stella Maris Rest House for Sisters in Sea Girt from 1920 to 1927. They taught religious education at St. Mary Catechetical Center, Deal, from 1949 to 1953. For the Trenton diocese, a Sister of Charity served as director of religious from 1977 to 1988. The offices of assistant superintendent and superintendent of Catholic education were held by Sisters of Charity between 1978 and 1991. Social work with problem teenagers was performed at Triad House from 1983 to 1989. The sisters were involved with nurse-hospice programs from 1984 to 1992. Since 1985, they have worked for Mount Carmel Guild, with Sr. Marian Immaculate Gillen, S.C., as current executive director.

Sisters of Mercy of New Jersey (R.S.M.)

Generalate: Watchung, New Jersey

By the time the Diocese of Trenton was formed in 1881, the Sisters of Mercy had been laboring in its vineyard for eight years. The sisters came first to St. Mary's, Bordentown, in 1873, and then went to St. Paul's, Princeton, in 1878, remaining in both parishes to this day.

At the time of the formation of the Trenton diocese, the Mercy Congregation was only fifty years old, having been established in Ireland in 1831. Its foundress, Catherine McAuley, dedicated her sisters to the service of the poor, the sick, and the ignorant. To accomplish these ministries, she obtained pontifical approval for her group to be noncloistered, a revolutionary concept for religious women in her day.

The able women whom Catherine McAuley trained continued her good work not only in Ireland but also in other countries. One of these women, Frances Warde, brought the Sisters of Mercy to Pittsburgh, Pennsylvania, in 1843. From there, Mercy works spread to Chicago, Illinois; Providence, Rhode Island; Manchester, New Hampshire, and many other American cities. It was from Manchester, New Hampshire, that Frances Warde made her New Jersey foundations.

Soon after his appointment, the Most Rev. Michael J. O'Farrell, first bishop of Trenton, suggested that the Sisters of Mercy in Princeton and Bordentown become independent of Manchester by beginning their own motherhouse in Bordentown. By 1885, the sisters had built a substantial headquarters there on Crosswicks Street. By the turn of the century, however, they had already outgrown it. The second bishop of Trenton, the Most Rev. James A. McFaul, advised the sisters to relocate rather than expand their Bordentown residence. So the sisters sold their property to the Poor Clares and began building on 40 acres of lovely wooded land in the Watchung mountains, still within the area of the Trenton diocese at that time.

The sisters' original ministry in the Tren-ton diocese had been teaching. In more recent years, the sisters also have served in religious education, pastoral ministries, and social services. Besides working in diocesan offices and institutions, the Sisters of Mercy have ministered in twenty-six parishes of the diocese: St. Mary's Cathedral, Trenton; St. Joseph, Trenton; Sacred Heart, Bay Head; St. Mary, Bordentown; St. Dominic, Bricktown; St. Paul, Burlington; St. Charles Borromeo, Cinnaminson; St. Mary, Colts Neck; St. Catherine, East Keansburg; Nativity, Fair Haven; St. Robert Bellarmine, Freehold; Our Lady Queen of Peace, Hainesport; St. Anthony, Hightstown; St. Catharine, Holmdel; St. Ann, Keansburg; St. Joseph, Keyport; St. Mary of the Lake, Lakewood; St. Gabriel, Marlboro; St. Joan of Arc, Marlton; St. Clement, Matawan; Our Lady of Good Counsel, Moorestown; St. Paul, Princeton; St. James, Red Bank; Holy Cross, Rumson; Holy Family, Union Beach; and St. George, Washington Crossing.

Other educational facilities in the diocese currently or previously staffed by the Sisters of Mercy are St. Mary Academy, Lakewood (1898–1991); Notre Dame High School, Lawrenceville; and Georgian Court College, Lakewood, the only Catholic college in the diocese (since 1924). Social services are conducted at Mercy Center, Asbury Park; Mount Carmel Guild, Trenton; Spring House, Eatontown; and Epiphany House, Long Branch. Houses of Prayer include the Upper Room Spiritual Center, Neptune, and St. Francis House of Prayer, Mount Holly.

Sisters of St. Dominic of the American Congregation of the Sacred Heart of Jesus (O.P.)

Dominican Motherhouse: Caldwell, New Jersey

"To contemplate and give to others the fruits of contemplation," is the charisma of the Sisters of St. Dominic, an order founded over 700 years ago. St. Dominic conceived the idea of a contemplative lifestyle for women when he struggled with the Albigensian heretics in France. To these women he entrusted the care and education of children, especially young girls, in the hope of offsetting the ravages of heresy. Among the early monasteries was that of the Holy Cross in Ratisbon, Germany, founded in 1233 by Blessed Jordan of Saxony, the immediate successor of St. Dominic.

In 1853, sisters from Ratisbon emigrated to New York City. A central house was acquired for the group in 1881 and called the Convent of St. Dominic. In 1906, after much dialogue, the status of the group was changed from the Dominican Second Order to the Third Order Regular. By 1912, the Sisters of St. Dominic of the American Congregation of the Sacred Heart of Jesus was officially established in Caldwell, New Jersey. In 1939, Caldwell College, in the Archdiocese of Newark, opened its doors. Today it is a coed institution that attracts students from throughout the United States as well as from several foreign countries.

Like other religious, the Caldwell sisters have entered into ministries other than teaching. They participate in parish religious education programs, hospital ministry, pastoral ministry, the social justice apostolate, counseling services in diocesan religious education, vocation offices, and campus ministry.

The Caldwell Dominicans' ministry within the Trenton diocese began when they assumed the responsibility of teaching in Holy Spirit Parish, Asbury Park. They taught in the school from 1927 until its closing in 1980. From 1944 to 1957, a Religious Education Center was maintained at St. Peter Claver Parish, also in Asbury Park.

Currently, the congregation staffs the schools and participates in other ministries at St. Denis, Manasquan; St. Catharine, Spring Lake; and St. Anthony Claret, Lakewood. In the recent past the Caldwell Dominicans have served in St. Mary's, Colts Neck; St. Elizabeth Ann Seton, Whiting; the Spanish apostolate of the diocese; and the Monmouth County Library System.

Sisters of St. Francis of Penance and Christian Charity (O.S.F.)

Holy Name Province
Provincial House:
Stella Niagara, New York

The Sisters of St. Francis of Penance and Christian Charity (commonly called the Stella Niagara Franciscans) came to the Diocese of Trenton in 1924, when Mother Gerard accepted the invitation of the Most Rev. Thomas J. Walsh to start an elementary school in St. Agnes Parish in Atlantic Highlands. In September 1924, Sr. Laurissa Tierney, O.S.F., the appointed superior and principal, traveled with her companions, Srs. Clement Finkel, Laurentine Hensel, Euphemia Nash, and Inez Baierski, to Atlantic Highlands. They were warmly welcomed by the pastor, Rev. William P. Tighe. Since St. Agnes was the first parochial school in that part of New Jersey, pupils came not only from the home parish but also from the neighboring towns of Keansburg, Highlands, Monmouth, and Sea Bright. Initial enrollment totaled 180 youngsters, filling the classrooms beyond capacity.

The sisters from St. Agnes Convent in Atlantic Highlands conducted religious education classes and summer programs at Our Lady of Perpetual Help, Highlands, and St. Mary's, New Monmouth, for a number of years. In 1951, Rev. Patrick Donnelly, pastor of Our Lady of Perpetual Help, requested and received sisters to staff a school in his parish. Srs. Benecita Fasel and Clara Gallagher arrived in the area on August 21 of that year and were joined by Srs. Hyacinth Cullinan and Josephine Graci several days later. Seventy pupils registered in September for grades 1–7. Classes were held in the basement of the church. The sisters also gave religious instruction at nearby Fort Hancock in Sandy Hook.

Rev. Robert T. Bulman was the next to request sisters for a proposed school in St. Mary's Parish in New Monmouth. Father Bulman was promised 3 teachers for September 1953 on the condition that he had a school and convent ready for them. Father Bulman rushed to obtain the Most Rev. George W. Ahr's approval and to get construction of the school and convent under way. The school building was ready for occupancy in September, but the convent was not. In the meantime, the sisters were given temporary housing at Port Monmouth by Dr. and Mrs. Gerard Conlon. They were transported to and from school by the parishioners. Finally, in March, Bishop Ahr blessed the new convent, converted from a barn. On opening day, 287 pupils were registered for kindergarten through grade 6. Within three years, registration had doubled, and three additions to the structure were required in time. A new convent, too, eventually replaced the older one. However, Father Bulman's dream was not complete until he received permission to begin Mater Dei High School, which at first was conducted in the grade school building but moved to new quarters in 1965. Sr. Bede Loob, O.S.F., served as principal of the new high school.

At Bishop Ahr's request, 2 sisters of the Stella Niagara Franciscans acted as core members for the Franciscan House of Prayer in Mount Holly from 1974 to 1978.

Sisters of St. Francis of Philadelphia (O.S.F.)

St. Anthony Province
Provincial Residence:
Delran, New Jersey

The Sisters of St. Francis of Philadelphia (commonly known as the Glen Riddle Franciscans) were founded on April 9, 1855, by the Most Rev. John N. Neumann, C.Ss.R., bishop of Philadelphia. On that day, in St. Peter's Church, Philadelphia,

Bishop Neumann invested in the Franciscan order 3 women, 1 of whom was the foundress, Mother Francis Bachman, O.S.F., a widow with 4 children. "No risk—no gain" (a quote from the foundress), dependence on Divine Providence, openness to the Spirit, faith, and a genuine concern for all types of people with all kinds of needs characterize the Franciscan Sisters of Philadelphia, known now also as the "Aston Franciscans."

In 1869, the community entered the present boundaries of the Diocese of Trenton by teaching at St. Francis of Assisium's parochial school. In 1874, Rev. Peter Jachetti, O.F.M. Conv., and the Franciscan Sisters founded St. Francis Hospital (now St. Francis Medical Center) in Trenton. That commitment to health care is still present today.

The following are schools formerly or currently staffed by the sisters: Blessed Sacrament, Trenton (1927–89); Holy Angels, Trenton (1922–present); Immaculate Conception School (Our Lady of Lourdes), Trenton (1875–present); Immaculate Conception High School, Trenton (1921–36); St. Anthony Grade School, Trenton (1921–present); St. Anthony de Padua Coed High School, renamed McCorristin High School in 1979, Trenton (1962–present); St. Francis of Assisium, Trenton (1869–79); St. Raphael, Trenton (1950–present); St. Rose School, Freehold (1878–present); St. Gregory the Great, Hamilton Square (1986–present); St. Joseph, Keyport (1882–90); St. Leo, Lincroft (1966–83); St. Mary of the Lakes, Medford (1969–present); and Corpus Christi, Willingboro (1959–present).

Other apostolates of the Sisters of St. Francis of Philadelphia included Guardian Angel Day Nursery, Trenton (1918–26); St. Michael's Children's Home, Hopewell (1898–1973); and catechetical teaching at St. Alphonsus, Hopewell (1943–55). The sisters have performed pastoral work at Holy Angels, Trenton; St. John, Allentown; St. Barnabas, Bayville; St. Alphonsus, Hopewell; St. Leo, Lincroft; and Corpus Christi, Willingboro.

Various other ministries have included Sr. Georgine Learning Center for mentally retarded children, Trenton (1969–present); Morris Hall, Home for the Aged, Lawrenceville (1905–81); St. Lawrence Health and Rehabilitation Center, Lawrenceville (1971–80); St. Rose of Lima House of Prayer, Freehold (1978–82); and Juliann House, a residence for sisters in pastoral ministry, Ocean Grove (1983–88).

Individual sisters have been involved in ministry in Cathedral School, Trenton; St. Alphonsus Retreat House, Long Branch; the Trenton Diocesan Office for the Disabled; St. Gabriel, Marlboro; St. Denis, Manasquan; Holy Eucharist Church, Tabernacle; St. Joseph, Beverly; and Holy Assumption, Roebling.

Sisters of St. Joseph of Chestnut Hill, Philadelphia (S.S.J.)

Motherhouse: Chestnut Hill, Philadelphia, Pennsylvania

"Ready for any and every good work" describes the creative and vital spirit of the Sisters of St. Joseph of Philadelphia, whose heritage is rich and enduring, reaching from its foundation in seventeenth-century

France and the sisters' arrival in nineteenth-century America. They are called to an individual and corporate life of self-emptying concern, to be "all for the dear neighbor." Their service includes social, educational, and spiritual ministries.

In the late 1880s, lack of funds prevented the acceptance of land in Point Pleasant, offered with the condition that an academy be built there. However, in November 1969, the sisters were asked to go to St. Peter's, Point Pleasant Beach, to succeed the Sisters of Holy Union of the Sacred Hearts, who had begun their labors there in 1948. The Sisters of St. Joseph arrived in August 1970 to staff the school.

In 1921, Msgr. William J. McConnell, pastor of St. Rose in Belmar and superintendent of schools, opened an elementary school. In 1923, high school classes began with 14 freshmen. The Sisters of St. Joseph have staffed and continue to staff both schools. In 1931, St. Catharine's School, Spring Lake, opened with grades 1–4. By 1935, the school held grades 1–8. Until a convent opened in 1935, the sisters commuted from Belmar. Due to dwindling numbers in the congregation, the Sisters of St. Joseph withdrew from St. Catharine's in 1987.

The sisters taught at Our Lady of Good Counsel School, Moorestown, from 1927 to 1985. In 1927, 150 pupils from Maple Shade were transported to Moorestown. The first four grades of a school were started in Maple Shade in September 1928. The sisters commuted from Moorestown until 1936, when a convent in Maple Shade was dedicated.

From 1959 to 1983, the sisters labored at St. Denis School, Manasquan. Announcement of their withdrawal was made in 1982, at which time they were sharing the convent with 3 Caldwell Dominicans who had succeeded the Sisters of St. Joseph.

Sisters of St. Joseph of Peace (C.S.J.P.)

St. Joseph Province, Eastern Province Provincial House: Englewood Cliffs, New Jersey

In 1884, in Nottingham, England, under the inspiration of the Spirit, Margaret Anna Cusack founded a religious congregation of women ". . . to promote the peace of the Church both by word and work" (*Constitutions*, 1884). This congregation had its origin in the foundress's response to the social concerns and needs of the time. Deeply moved by the sufferings of poor and oppressed people, Margaret Anna Cusack, known as Mother Francis Clare, C.S.J.P., sought ways to share her gifts with them. Honoria Gaffney, later named Mother Evangelista, together with a few other women, joined the new community. From the beginning, the sisters involved themselves in ministries of social service, education, and health care. They worked with the poor and sick in their own home, and they provided housing and care for women, orphans, and blind children and adults. They established schools and hospitals. This development of ministry was accompanied by a geographical expansion to North America. The sisters set up three provinces—one in England, one in New Jersey, and a third in the Pacific Northwest and British Columbia, Canada. The congregation received a Decree of Praise as a pontifical religious institute in 1895, and its constitutions were approved in 1929.

Today, as sisters of St. Joseph of Peace, they build upon a rich heritage. Their founding spirit calls them to further the work of peace. In accord with their tradition, they commit themselves to promote peace in family life, in the church, and in society. They strive to respect the dignity of all persons, to value the gifts of creation, and to confront oppressive situations. They respond to God's people in need and promote social justice as a way to peace. Their charisma of peace challenges them to prophetic risk so that God's reign might be more fully realized. Confident of God's faithful love and collaborating with others who work for justice and peace, they face the future with gratitude and hope (*Constitutions*, revised September 15, 1990, pp. 3–6).

Since 1940, the Sisters of St. Joseph of Peace have served in a number of locations in the Diocese of Trenton, some of which now fall within the boundaries of the Diocese of Metuchen. Today, sisters are present at St. Joseph Elementary School, Beverly; Stella Maris Retreat and Vacation House, Elberon; and St. James Parish, Pennington.

The sisters believe that integral to their mission and spirituality as Sisters of St. Joseph of Peace is the promotion of peace through justice. "Action on behalf of justice and participation in the transformation of the world fully appear to us as a constitutive dimension of the preaching of the Gospel, or, in other words, of the Church's mission of the redemption of the human race and its liberation from every oppressive situation." (Roman Synod, 1971, *Justice in the World*, General Chapter, 1974)

Sisters of the Good Shepherd (R.G.S.)
Contemplative Sisters of the Good Shepherd (C.G.S.)
Province of New York
Provincial House: Jamaica, New York

In 1875, the Sisters of the Good Shepherd opened the first Good Shepherd home in Newark to serve girls and women. In 1927, Mrs. Robert Collier, of the Collier publishing family, turned over her summer estate on Conover Road, Wickatunk, New Jersey, to the New York Province of the Sisters of the Good Shepherd. Collier Services, named after the donor, directs its efforts toward those who are most in need: the poor, the disenfranchised, and the social outcasts. The people on the fringe are the choice of the Sisters of the Good Shepherd. (More information about Collier Services and Collier School, an alternative high school, appears in the chapter on institutions.)

The role of the contemplative branch of the congregation is to provide spiritual support for the apostolic sisters and their ministry. This they do by their quiet life of love, labor, and prayer. In 1986, the Contemplative Sisters of the Good Shepherd were invited to the Diocese of Trenton by the Most Rev. John C. Reiss. The contemplatives moved into St. Raphael's Convent in Trenton, where they continue their ministry of prayer. In addition to the three traditional vows, Sisters of the Good Shepherd take a special vow of zeal. This calls them forth to pray, work, and live for the salvation of others. While living apart in community, the sisters have a strong apostolic thrust in their prayer, striving to be present to the mystery of God as well as to the needs of all God's people.

Sisters of the Humility of Mary (H.M.)

Motherhouse:
Villa Maria, Pennsylvania

The Sisters of the Humility of Mary began in 1845 as an association of laywomen who felt called to revitalize Christian values in northeastern France. Marie-Antoinette Potier (Mother Magdalen) opened her home in Donmartin-sous-Amance to the small group. These women worked with their parish priest, Rev. John Joseph Begel, teaching and caring for the sick in poor villages. The arrangement was simple, practical, and innovative. Their plan was to live, for the sake of ministry and community, in small groups. The association was not structured like older religious communities, many of which were semicloistered and could not go into homes to minister.

In 1864, at the invitation of the Most Rev. Amadeus Rappe, bishop of Cleveland, Ohio, the entire community, led by Marie Tabourat (Mother Anna) and Father Begel, came to the United States. Although Mother Magdalen planned to leave France with her sisters, she died on March 7, 1864. Her property, the sale of which was to have financed the trip and the foundation, was retrieved by her family, and the sisters were left with no resources. The sisters had only enough funds to buy a $2,500 house on a farm in New Bedford, Pennsylvania, near the Ohio state line. Within eight years, the sisters were serving in parishes in the Dioceses of Cleveland; Pittsburgh, Pennsylvania; Erie, Pennsylvania; and St. Joseph, Missouri. As early as 1877, Mother Anna had seen to the incorporation of the congregation in Pennsylvania. In 1889, when the sisters opened a U.S. post office, Villa Maria became the official name of the motherhouse property.

During the building of the railroad in nearby Lowellville, Ohio, Mother Anna established St. Joseph Infirmary in 1879 on convent grounds to care for injured workers. This was the first hospital in the Mahoning Valley and was followed by expansion into other medical centers, schools of nursing, health education, and public health nursing.

In the Original Rule, the first sisters expressed their readiness to respond generously "in all the works of charity possible, rendering themselves competent and disposed to do all kinds of good works." This spirit has inspired present-day sisters to expand their traditional ministries to include social services, pastoral and campus ministry, action for peace and justice, retreats, and spiritual direction. The work of the sisters has spread to other parts of the United States, Mexico, and El Salvador.

The presence of the Sisters of the Humility of Mary in the Trenton diocese began September 1984, with one member in ministry at the Diocesan Office of Pastoral Ministry to the Deaf. This ministry included the use of sign language for the deaf, training of others in the use of this necessary skill, and specialized leadership training and education for deaf persons. In February 1990, the one member vacated this position to serve as pastoral minister at Garden State Reception and Correction Institute, Yardville.

Sisters of the Resurrection (C.R.)
Eastern Province
Provincial House:
Castleton-on-Hudson, New York

The congregation of the Sisters of the Resurrection was founded in Rome, Italy, in 1891, by a widow, Celine Borzecka, and her daughter, Hedwig. This was the first time in the history of the church that a religious community of women was founded by a mother and daughter.

Celine, daughter of a wealthy landowner, was born in eastern Poland. From her early childhood she fervently desired to dedicate herself entirely to God as a religious. However, in obedience to the wishes of her parents, she married Joseph Borzecki at the age of 21. She continued to grow as a woman of prayer and sacrifice, generously sharing herself and her resources on behalf of the poor of her country and her church.

Sixteen years following her marriage, her husband was stricken with paralysis. He died a few years later, leaving Celine with their two small children. In 1875, the young widow and her children went to Rome seeking the will of God in whatever way it would be manifested to them. Celine and her daughter Hedwig subsequently founded the congregation of the Sisters of the Resurrection on January 6, 1891.

Mother Celine's excellent education and knowledge of languages assisted her in establishing homes for the congregation in various countries almost simultaneously. The first apostolate of the sisters in Rome was a school for girls and a workshop aimed at raising the status of women in society. A foundation in Poland soon followed. A year later, a novitiate to train young sisters was opened in Kety, Poland. It is here that the bodies of Mother Celine and Mother Hedwig are interred; both were declared venerable by the church in 1982.

The Sisters of the Resurrection arrived in the United States on the second day of February 1900 and subsequently taught in several schools in the Chicago area. The sisters were requested to teach at St. Casimir School in Yonkers, New York, in 1910. They then moved into other cities in New York, Connecticut, New Jersey, and Massachusetts. As the number of sisters grew in this area, a second U.S. province was established in New York in 1928.

In September 1965, the Sisters of the Resurrection began their ministry at St. Veronica's Parish in Howell when Rev. Mitchell Cetkowski requested teachers for his newly established parish school. The sisters have been involved in the parish school, the religious education program, and recently the evangelization program. The sisters assumed responsibility of St. Ann School, Lawrenceville, in September 1979. They ministered in both the school and the religious education program until June 1989.

Sisters of the Third Franciscan Order (O.S.F.)

Generalate: Syracuse, New York

In 1855, the Sisters of the Third Franciscan Order were founded in Philadelphia by the Most Rev. John N. Neumann, C.Ss.R., bishop of Philadelphia. Three young women—Mrs. Anna Bachmann, her sister Barbara Boll, and Anna Dorn—made known to their spiritual director, Rev. John Hespelein, C.Ss.R., rector of St. Peter Church, Philadelphia, their desire to dedicate their lives to God in the spirit of St. Francis of Assisi. Bishop Neumann received the request while in Rome. He received permission from Pope Pius IX and from the minister general of the Friars Minor Conventual to invest and profess members of the Third Order of St. Francis. From this tiny nucleus, six Neumann communities have evolved.

In 1860, upon the request of the Franciscan provincial, 6 sisters were assigned to Assumption Parish in Syracuse, New York, and St. Joseph Parish in Utica, New York, to minister to the German immigrants there. The Most Rev. James F. Wood, Bishop Neumann's successor, did not approve of the sisters' working outside the diocese. He separated them from the Diocese of Philadelphia without consultation or explanation. The bishop of Albany was notified by letter they were in his jurisdiction.

The first ministries were teaching and nursing. In 1866, the sisters opened St. Elizabeth Hospital in Utica. In 1869, they opened St. Joseph Hospital in Syracuse. Later ministries included orphanages, day care centers, hospices for the terminally ill, pastoral care, parish ministries, and the administration and care of a leper colony in Hawaii.

Rev. Andrew Avellino Szabo, O.F.M. Conv., asked the Sisters of St. Francis of Syracuse to staff St. Francis School, Trenton. The sisters began work in the school in September 1879. Declining student enrollment and the consequent financial drain on the parish led to the sisters' departure and the school's closing in June 1975.

The Sisters of St. Francis have also labored in Beverly; at St. Paul's, Burlington; and at St. Lawrence Rehabilitation Center, Lawrenceville. They now minister at St. Raphael School, Trenton; St. Peter School, Riverside; and St. Mary School, Bordentown.

Sisters, Servants of the Immaculate Heart of Mary (I.H.M.)

General Motherhouse:
Immaculata, Pennsylvania

Two foundations of the Sisters, Servants of the Immaculate Heart of Mary, serve the Diocese of Trenton. Their motherhouses are located in Immaculata and Scranton, Pennsylvania. The congregations are pontifical, religious institutes whose members are committed to God and to the church by profession of the public vows of poverty, chastity, and obedience.

In 1845, Rev. Louis Florent Gillet, C.Ss.R., a Redemptorist priest, asked the Oblates of Providence in Baltimore to assist the young people of immigrant parents in Michigan. He envisioned an educational apostolate conducted by religious women who would give witness to prayerfulness, humility, simplicity, forgetfulness of self, and a deep love and respect for each individual soul. Thereafter, a band of 3 women entered a log cabin convent on the shores of the Raisin River in Monroe, Michigan. Father Gillet guided the group in basing its community on the spirit of St. Alphonsus Liguori.

Among the original 3 was Theresa Maxis Duchemin, an intelligent, well-educated young woman from Baltimore. Born of unwed parents and of mixed racial lineage into a society that held both conditions in contempt, she was one of the founding members of the Oblates of Providence in Baltimore. When the congregation seemed on the brink of dissolution, she was providentially called to help Father Gillet. She became the first superior general of the Sisters, Servants of the Immaculate Heart of Mary.

In 1858, in response to an invitation by the Most Rev. John N. Neumann, C.Ss.R., bishop of Philadelphia, the sisters agreed to staff St. Joseph School in Susquehanna, Pennsylvania. The community found it necessary to separate into two distinct branches, one in the Diocese of Detroit and the other in the Diocese of Philadelphia. The Sisters, Servants of the Immaculate Heart of Mary, chose to establish a motherhouse in West Chester, Pennsylvania. They eventually moved to Immaculata, Pennsylvania. The Diocese of Scranton was established in 1868. As a result, in 1871, the Pennsylvania congregation decided to form two separate branches, one in the Diocese of Philadelphia and one in the Diocese of Scranton.

As early as October 30, 1947, the Most Rev. William A. Griffin requested sisters from Immaculata for several schools in the Diocese of Trenton. Circumstances did not allow for consideration of this plan at the time, but the Most Rev. George W. Ahr kept the request in mind, and on August 13, 1956, circumstances made possible the fulfillment.

The sisters received a warm welcome from the administrator of Incarnation Parish, Trenton, who was likewise superintendent of Catholic schools. The convent was already complete in every detail except that the chapel was not dedicated until August 29, 1956. The first registration showed the necessity of double sessions for kindergarten (115), first grade (116), and second grade (110). Additional grades were added, contributing to larger enrollments. Catechetical classes were organized for children in upper grades, who could not immediately be received.

Sisters, Servants of the Immaculate Heart of Mary (I.H.M.)

General Motherhouse:
Marywood, Scranton, Pennsylvania

In 1871, the second congregation of the Sisters, Servants of the Immaculate Heart of Mary, in the commonwealth of Pennsylvania was founded in Scranton. This congregation and the one in Immaculata, Pennsylvania, developed from the original congregation established in 1845 in Monroe, Michigan.

The Scranton congregation serves schools, religious education programs, and campus ministry and is involved in the administration, nursing, therapy, and technology departments of hospitals. It cares for special children, unwed mothers, women in crisis, the aged, the poor, the imprisoned, and the oppressed in twenty-two dioceses in the United States; in Kelowna, British Columbia; and in Lima, Peru.

In the Diocese of Trenton, the Scranton sisters ministered in Our Lady of Mount Carmel Elementary and Catechetical School, Asbury Park, from 1934 to 1990. In 1943, the Most Rev. William A. Griffin invited the congregation to Sacred Heart Parish, Mount Holly, to begin a regional catechetical center for Mount Holly and nine other locales, namely, Hainesport, Medford Lakes, Rancocas, Masonville, Jobstown, Pine Grove, Red Lion, Browns Mills, and New Lisbon. The success of the catechetical center prompted the construction of Sacred Heart Regional Elementary School, which the sisters have staffed since 1944. Sr. Anne Fulwiler, I.H.M., serves as director of religious for the Trenton diocese. Sr. Joanne Campanini, I.H.M., is director of the Office of Migration and Refugee Services.

Society of the Divine Word (S.V.D.)

Chicago Province
Province of Blessed Joseph
Freinademetz, S.V.D.
Province Center: Techny, Illinois

In 1875, Blessed Arnold Janssen founded the Society of the Divine Word in Steyl, Holland. The order, also known as the Divine Word Missionaries, was established in the United States in 1895 by Brother Wendelin Meyer. In 1941, the Most Rev. William A. Griffin invited Very Rev. Francis Humel, S.V.D., provincial of the society's Eastern Province, to send priests and brothers to serve African-American Catholics, specifically at Our Lady of Divine Shepherd Parish in Trenton and a smaller parish to be founded in Asbury Park. Bishop Griffin also granted the society permission to establish a seminary in the Trenton diocese when feasible. In 1985, the Eastern Province amalgamated with the Northern Province; both territories are now served from Techny, Illinois.

Father Humel sent Rev. Joseph Ford, S.V.D., to serve as pastor of Our Lady of the Divine Shepherd. The diocese had acquired a three-story brick building originally erected in 1928 as a state lodge for Negro masons. After some renovations, Bishop Griffin celebrated the first mass in the church on June 15, 1941. In the 1960s, Rev. Bernard Kowalski, S.V.D., pastor, and Rev. Richard

Thibeau, S.V.D., associate pastor, clearly demonstrated the society's commitment to the poor. The parish hall is named in honor of Rev. Edward McGuinn, S.V.D.

In 1943, Rev. John Buys, S.V.D., from the Netherlands, and Rev. Vincent Smith, S.V.D., one of the first African Americans ordained in the United States, became the first Divine Word Missionaries to serve St. Peter Claver Parish, Asbury Park. The church, formerly Whittier Chapel, was situated in an old Quaker meetinghouse. The parish has developed lay leadership, initiated various programs aimed at youth, and provided assistance for families of the parish. In 1989, two families of the Neocatechumenate Way came to the parish to aid in evangelization.

In 1976, Rev. Pedro L. Bou, S.V.D., went to St. Peter Claver Parish to minister to Spanish-speaking Catholics. By 1980, as the number of Hispanics grew, it became evident that a new parish was needed. In December 1981, a renovated Assemblies of God building in Neptune was dedicated as Our Lady of Providence Church. In 1992, Rev. James Vorwerk, S.V.D., was promoted to pastor. Father Bou became pastoral vicar at Ss. Peter and Paul, Trenton, beginning a ministry among Hispanics there.

In 1941, the society purchased the former Joseph Bonaparte estate in Bordentown as the site for a seminary for men of junior college age or older interested in pursuing a missionary vocation. Rev. Peter Weyland, S.V.D., was the founding rector. In 1958, the seminary began welcoming high school students. Because the number of candidates increased, a new building was constructed in 1961, with classrooms, a dormitory, and a dining room. In 1968, a gymnasium and auditorium were added. By 1975, Divine Word Seminary was serving boys evidencing interest in the Society of the Divine Word, Montfort Missionaries, or the diocesan priesthood.

When a disastrous fire on February 2, 1983, destroyed the Bonaparte Mansion, the society decided not to rebuild but to close the seminary. Bordentown was made a residence for retired members and those engaged in various apostolates. The retired priests, as well as the active ones, continue both to offer pastoral services to the Poor Clares and to help out in parish assignments, retreat ministry, and prison chaplaincies.

Society of Mary (S.M.)
Province of New York
Provincial House: Baltimore, Maryland

The Family of Mary is made up of men and women, religious and laypersons, and single and married people, with varied cultural, economic, and ethnic backgrounds, who share the spirit of faith and service that characterizes the Marianist spirituality taught by Rev. William Joseph Chaminade and Sr. Adele de Trenquellon. The Family of Mary is composed of autonomous groups such as the Society of Mary, also known as the Marianists.

During the Reign of Terror in France, a courageous priest eluded hostile authorities to bring the sacraments to the rich and poor alike. This priest, Father Chaminade, was eventually forced to leave France for exile in Spain. When he returned to France in 1799, he became well-known for his spiritual direction, his gift of reconciliation, and his ability to bridge the gaps between sharply divided socioeconomic classes. Father Chaminade organized groups that included both professional and trade workers, bringing them together for prayer, sharing, and spiritual development. Through these adult sodalities, people lived their discipleship more strongly in such ministries as caring for the poor, visiting the imprisoned, helping unwed mothers, and teaching catechism classes.

In 1816, Father Chaminade, in cooperation with Adele de Trenquellon, established a religious community of women, now known as Marianist Sisters. One year later, at the request of 7 men, he started a religious community of men, the Marianists.

In the Diocese of Trenton, a community of 3 brothers now lives and works at Martin House in inner-city Trenton, where they practice the characteristics of Marianist spirituality: prayer, hospitality, and community, which constitute the mission to take the Gospel to all people by developing and forming communities of faith, always looking to Mary as model and mother.

Society of the Sacred Heart (R.S.C.J.)
United States Province
Provincial House: St. Louis, Missouri

The Society of the Sacred Heart, also known as the Religious of the Sacred Heart of Jesus, was founded in France in 1800 by Madeleine Sophie Barat and a small group of women to educate young girls. Later canonized a saint, Madeleine Sophie governed the society until her death in 1865. By that time there were more than one hundred schools in twelve countries carrying on the purpose of spreading the love of the Sacred Heart to children and their families. In Europe, each time an academy was founded, a free school was also opened. Missionary work spread to the New World in 1818, when Rose Philippine Duchesne and 4 companions opened schools in Missouri and Louisiana. Faithful to tradition, Rose Philippine, also canonized a saint, opened the first free school west of the Mississippi. Schools soon spread from coast to coast.

A request by parents for a Catholic, private school for girls in the Princeton area received a response from Mother Agnes Barry, R.S.C.J., then vicar for the Washington Province. The Most Rev. George W. Ahr and Msgr. Leonard R. Toomey were supportive in the undertaking, and the desire became a reality. In September 1963, the Religious of the Sacred Heart began their ministry in the Trenton diocese when Stuart Country Day School of the Sacred Heart opened for the education of girls. Boys and girls attend the preschool; only girls attend kindergarten through grade 12.

From 1963 through 1979, the Religious of the Sacred Heart lived and taught at Stuart. By 1979, the growth of the school and other ministries prompted the rental of a home in Belle Mead, now a part of the Diocese of Metuchen. Four of the religious continued to work at Stuart; 2 joined parish ministry. In 1983, the Catholic Youth Organization house in Lawrenceville was purchased, enabling a group to minister in Trenton more easily. Sr. Marian Miller, R.S.C.J., works at Morris Hall. Religious of the Sacred Heart have also been part of the chaplaincy at Princeton University. Sr. Lorette Piper, R.S.C.J., left Stuart to organize the Learning Center at Martin House in 1983. She continued there until 1989, when a staff of women, assisted by suburban coworkers and led by Brother Joseph Jansen, a Marianist, assumed leadership of the Learning Center. The students, faculty, and parents of Stuart and Martin House participate together in various service areas. Summer learning programs at Stuart have welcomed both parochial and public school children from Trenton since 1983.

Under the guidance of the Most Rev. John C. Reiss, another house was purchased in Lawrenceville in 1986 for the beginning of a new ministry in the Trenton diocese. Sr. Regina Griffin, R.S.C.J., one of the original members of the Belle Mead group, moved to Lawrenceville to serve the pastoral and social service needs of Haitian immigrants, a group suffering from poverty, social isolation, and lack of organized outreach by the Catholic Church. From a tiny one-room office in downtown Trenton, the center moved to larger quarters in St. Francis Parish, Trenton, in the summer of 1987. Linking with Martin House and other diocesan offices, the center established an English as a second language program and programs for community and leadership development.

Sr. Joan Magnetti, R.S.C.J., headmistress at Stuart from 1977 to 1990, served on the Bishop's Education Advisory Board. Sr. Lorette Piper served as a voting delegate to the Diocesan Synod of 1992. The growth of Stuart Country Day School and the service of the Religious of the Sacred Heart in the Trenton diocese were celebrated at a mass in St. Mary's Cathedral on the twenty-fifth anniversary in 1989.

CHAPTER FOURTEEN

INSTITUTIONS

BY JAMES F. O'NEILL JR.

HISTORICAL SUMmaries of a number of institutions serving the Diocese of Trenton have been included in this chapter. The first section contains the parish and private high schools currently in operation. Also included in the first section are an alternative school and two private schools that educate students from kindergarten through twelfth grade. Histories of Georgian Court College and Catholic campus ministries follow. The fourth section contains information about retreat houses and houses of prayer; other sections are dedicated to the histories of Catholic Charities and the permanent diaconate. The last section contains histories of other organizations performing valuable work for the diocese. Although closed, two institutions—St. Michael's Children's Home and the Newman School—have also been included in the last section. Most of the information within this chapter was provided by the institutions themselves. We thank these institutions for providing pictures and information. We hope that these short histories will convey some of the work occurring in the Trenton diocese, not necessarily on a parish level.

PARISH AND PRIVATE HIGH SCHOOLS AND PRIVATE ELEMENTARY SCHOOLS

Christian Brothers Academy, Lincroft

Christian Brothers Academy had an unusual beginning. A group of laymen felt the need for a Catholic college-preparatory boys' high school in Monmouth County. Mr. John Henderson, chairman of the group, was aided by Dr. George Sheehan, Mr. Peter Fleming, and Mr. John Higgins. They received from the Most Rev. George W. Ahr permission to found a school; then they approached the Brothers of the Christian Schools to staff the high school. They eventually convinced Brother John Halpin, F.S.C., provincial for the New York Prov-

Christian Brothers Academy, Lincroft

ince. Funds were raised to purchase the 160-acre Jaycee Horse Farm in Lincroft, owned by the Holsey family. The legal title for the property was given to the Christian Brothers.

In September 1959, a freshman class of 125 boys began classes in a converted horse barn. Dedication took place in October of that year. Christian Brothers Academy, staffed by 20 brothers and 40 lay teachers, currently has about 890 students, many of whom commute by buses provided by their local school boards. The academy offers college-preparatory courses with emphasis on science, mathematics, English, and foreign languages. CBA enjoys a high academic standing in the community, as well as the success of its interscholastic teams.

Collier School, Wickatunk

In 1927, as a result of the legacy of the Collier family, the Sisters of the Good Shepherd moved to the Collier estate in Wickatunk. Incorporated as the Collier School for the Care and Training of Girls, Sister Sebastian, R.G.S., served as first principal for 32 children.

Classes were held in what was then the Carriage House. By 1933, there were 100 children, too many for the convent, where they lived, and the Carriage House, where they attended school. In 1938, Smith Hall, a gift of Mr. and Mrs. John Thomas Smith, was dedicated. It provided a home for 125 young people and allowed for the creation of a separate school in the original Collier home. In 1939, the separate school was given its first name, St. Dorothy's, Mrs. Robert Collier's confirmation name. In addition to granting an elementary school diploma, the school offered an academic and vocational three-year high school education.

In 1965, the current Collier School building was constructed as a result of a bequest from Mrs. Robert Collier, who passed away in 1963. The newly named Collier School was accredited by the New Jersey Department of Education to award high school diplomas. Sr. Carol Beairsto, R.G.S., served as principal.

In 1977, the residential program closed, enabling the enlargement of the special education day treatment program for girls and, for the first time, for boys. Dr. Terrence P. Zeland was the director of this special education facility, serving until June 1987. Currently, Ms. Aideen Bugler is the director of the school, and Mr. Raymond Bock is principal. Collier School serves approximately 140 students per year from Monmouth, Middlesex, Ocean, Mercer, and Somerset counties. Collier School is funded both privately and by local public school districts. Students who have difficulty adapting to public schools are guided and supported in reaching their full potential through the use of Individual Education Plans; year-round individual, group, and family counseling; small classes with dedicated teachers; and active involvement by child-study teams from the public school systems.

Holy Cross High School, Delran

Thirty-seven years ago, the 90-acre campus that Holy Cross High School occupies today was a vast tract of open farmland. With vision and fortitude, the Most Rev. George W. Ahr and Rev. Paul A. Cartier transformed a former peach orchard into the site of the only Catholic secondary school in Burlington County. Their shared vision was for a facility that could eventually educate 2,000 students in the mostly rural, but rapidly developing, southern portion of the diocese.

The first parcel of land was purchased in 1953, and the cornerstone for the school was laid in 1956. The original building, a quadrangle with a partial second floor of classrooms, plus an auditorium, chapel, all-purpose room, library, and gym, opened its doors to its first freshman class in 1957 and graduated its first class in 1961. The school was designed for 1,100 students in grades 9 through 12. Enrollment soon grew to the point where expansion became necessary. Eight classrooms and a guidance wing were built in 1966, completing the second floor quadrangle. The Sisters of the Holy Cross assisted the principal, Father Cartier, through the period of tremendous growth.

Rev. William J. Capik's primary concern as second principal was the religious and intellectual growth of the students. He sought to make the daily schedule more flexible. Holy Cross experienced a marked increase in programs and sophistication of teaching techniques. The use of creative audiovisual instruction increased. More field trips were added, including educational trips abroad. Holy Cross became a serious athletic competitor in several sports. Largely because of Father Capik's efforts, the school entered the Burlington County Scholastic League in 1974. Holy Cross competes in twenty sports, fielding forty teams.

The third principal, Rev. Joseph M. LaForge, was known to teach courses and lessons in science, language, or religion. He began the practice of celebrating mass for different classes in the school chapel and gave fascinating and uplifting homilies and showed unmistakable exuberance at pep rallies and assemblies.

By 1980, enrollment once again reached the capacity of the building. Classes were meeting in the kitchen pantry, convent basement, coat check room, book closets, and orchestra pit. To ease the burden, a temporary, self-contained, two-classroom unit was installed by the principal, Father LaForge. Student population continued to swell during his administration and that of his successor, Rev. James Dubell. Father Dubell began the long, arduous process of obtaining legal permits for an addition.

The Sisters, Servants of the Immaculate Heart of Mary, continued the work of the Sisters of the Holy Cross in 1984. When current principal, Sr. Mary Persico, I.H.M., succeeded Father Dubell, expansion became a high priority. Sister Mary formed a study group, which developed a proposal to consolidate into an area of new construction certain key programs that require specialized instructional space, then renovate into academic classroom space the rooms these programs vacated. The project was announced to the general public in June of 1989 at a kickoff fund-raising dinner. The results of a feasibility study were overwhelmingly favorable, and campaign plans were laid. A full-time director of development and alumni relations was hired in August of 1990. The development committee volunteers began their efforts, and the first major gifts were pledged in September. Also started in 1990 were the professional production and publication of an Alumni Directory, the first alumni annual fund solicitation, the acquisition of a new computer system and development software, and the beginning of a massive donor research project.

During that same year, a significant effort was made to reestablish direct relations with the school's twenty-four sending parishes. Working with Episcopal Vicar and former Principal Father Dubell, Jim Lyons '69 presented a comprehensive proposal to the parishes. Currently, more than half of these parishes have made multiyear pledges and/or agreed to special collections for the $2.8-million building project. Parents were brought together and presented with the case for the campaign in a series of unique assemblies. Faculty and staff joined the campaign through a payroll deduction program. In addition, student organizations came forward with a major five-year pledge.

Ground was broken on April 1, 1992, with great ceremony. Sr. Loretta Hogan, C.S.J., and Sr. Shaun Kathleen Wilson, C.S.B., representatives of the Diocese of Trenton, and Sr. Redempta Sweeny, I.H.M., headed the list of dignitaries on hand. However, it was Holy Cross High School student Kelly Roman, a junior, representing the 1,450 students of the school, who turned the first spade of earth.

New construction should be completed by the fall of 1993, with occupancy by the second semester. The facility will house the Business and Related Arts Department on the lower floor, including three computer lab/classrooms, design and drafting, two art studios, a darkroom, a kiln room, a music/audiovisual studio, practice rooms, an art gallery, offices, and storage space. The main floor will house a practice gym, wrestling room, coed training room, girls' team room, office, and storage space.

Six or seven more academic classrooms will be made available through renovations in the present building, continuing into 1993. The school's oil-fired heating plant will be replaced by gas. Fire detection and suppression systems will be in place, and the school will also meet additional requirements set forth by the Americans with Disabilities Act.

Principals: Rev. Paul A. Cartier, 1957–67; Rev. William J. Capik, 1967–72; Rev. Joseph M. LaForge, 1972–80; Rev. James H. Dubell, 1980–87; Sr. Mary Persico, I.H.M., 1987–present.

Mater Dei High School, New Monmouth

On September 4, 1961, Mater Dei High School welcomed its first freshman class of 105 students, bringing to fruition the dreams of its founder, Msgr. Robert T. Bulman, former pastor of St. Mary's, New Monmouth. For over three decades, Mater Dei has instilled in its students a tradition of learning and faith that has enabled them to analyze and adapt to an ever changing environment by making choices and decisions grounded in the school's motto, "Fide et Fortitudine" (Faith and Fortitude).

After World War II, the extraordinary growth, residentially and commercially, in Middletown Township prompted Father Bulman (later Monsignor), under the aegis of the Most Rev. George W. Ahr, to direct the construction of a parochial high school. The first parcel of land was purchased in March 1961. The 32-acre tract of land known as Griggs farm was transformed, over the next four years, into a high school campus. The cornerstone for the two-story steel structure was laid in March 1965, with dedication taking place later that year.

The Sisters of St. Francis from Stella Niagara, New York, have staffed Mater Dei High School and St. Mary's Grammar School since their inceptions. Mother Mary Isabelle, O.S.F., then provincial superior, appointed Mother Mary Bede Loob, O.S.F., as principal for Mater Dei High School and St. Mary's Grammar School as well as superior of St. Mary's Convent. Mother Bede guided Mater Dei through its first six years, overseeing an increase in programs, faculty, and

Mater Dei High School, New Monmouth

student population. From 1961 to 1964, Mater Dei was housed in portable classrooms and a wing of St. Mary's Grammar School. Ground breaking for Mater Dei's permanent home took place on September 2, 1963. Classes were first conducted in the new building during the 1964–65 school year. Students, including the first senior class, received school rings, witnessed the laying of the cornerstone, and prayed together in retreats. They published the school's first yearbook, *Theotokos*, meaning "Mother of God."

With the new building came expansion of the curriculum and a variety of extracurricular activities, including intramural and interscholastic athletic programs. On September 26, 1966, Monsignor Bulman dedicated a new combined football/track/baseball complex, shared by the Mater Dei Booster Club. With the assistance of the athletic directors, including Rev. Paul Gluth and Rev. Charles Kelly, more athletic fields were added to the high school campus.

The outgoing personality and genuine concern of the second principal, Sr. Maryrose, O.S.F., was made evident by her engagement in almost every school activity. She sought to make the daily schedule more flexible, increase the number of programs, and raise the level of sophistication of teaching techniques. During Mr. Frank Outwater's term as athletic director, the number of teams proliferated, and Mater Dei became a serious athletic competitor.

Rev. William J. Lynch, S.J., third principal, implemented a new schedule, with more diversified course offerings. He accented academics, and plans were made to further develop Advanced Placement programs. When circumstances permitted, he entered classrooms to teach religion or just observe. Father Lynch began the practice of celebrating mass for different classes throughout the year. As director of the religion department, he developed a more intellectually challenging approach to religious education in order to strengthen students' personal faith.

During Mr. John V. Lonergan's tenure as principal, Mater Dei established an ROTC program, which offered students the opportunity to take courses in naval sciences. A student aide program was initiated by Sr. Lois, vice principal, to enable students interested in teaching careers to work in tutorial programs that served the local grade school. Senior courses in anthropology, philosophy, and Advanced Placement sciences were instituted. Under the direction of Mr. Frank Outwater, also vice principal, Mater Dei became an annual participant in the Model United Nations program held each year in the Netherlands. Mater Dei was one of only sixteen schools in the United States to be invited.

Miss Marie Deegan, former assistant superintendent for the Diocese of Syracuse, New York, succeeded Mr. Lonergan in 1978. The Deegan years were marked by an expansion of the curriculum, increased enrollment, and more direct involvement with the local Catholic grammar schools. Student programs and school assemblies became an integral part of school life. Miss Deegan encouraged greater involvement on the part of the student government. Mr. Robert Kitson, appointed athletic director in 1978, entered Mater Dei's sports programs into the Shore Conference. In 1983, Rev. Thomas Triggs was appointed full-time chaplain. He introduced class-level retreat programs and celebrated weekly liturgies.

Under the direction of its founder, Monsignor Bulman, Mater Dei prepared for the celebration of twenty-five years of Catholic education and service to the community. Mr. Thomas Murray established committees composed of faculty, students, parents, and alumni, who organized various gala events to commemorate the anniversary. The sixth principal and former vice principal, Sr. Mary Hugh Brady, O.P., implemented a master computer system and computer courses. The guidance department was expanded to include additional counselors and a computer-ready career resource room. Father Triggs started a peer counseling program that served as a model for other Catholic schools. He also initiated a freshman orientation program.

The seventh principal, Mr. Frank Poleski Jr., outlined an exacting three-year plan for Mater Dei: to increase enrollment and public relations, to acquire accreditation by the Middle States Association of Colleges and Schools, and to establish an ongoing development/scholarship program. In October 1989, Mater Dei began an extensive visitation program with local grammar schools. This, coupled with a revitalized Open House, led to an increase in enrollment. In 1991 and 1992, two new scholarships were established: the Frank Outwater Scholarship and the Monsignor Robert T. Bulman Scholarship. On April 18, 1992, Mr. Poleski was informed that Mater Dei was being given another ten-year accreditation by the Middle States Association. In 1991, Mater Dei's transition into an exciting, new era was evidenced by improved student publications, enhanced music and drama productions, extensive social activities, and the formation of academic clubs. Rev. Robert Tynski, the new chaplain, created service programs, which traveled to New York to work with Mother Teresa's sisters. Christian service programs were established within the parish, giving students a chance to effectively put their faith into action.

After fifty-two years of priestly dedication, Monsignor Bulman retired on April 14, 1992. At a mass of thanksgiving, he encouraged students to be thankful for the opportunities given them by their parents and Mater Dei and to be loyal to God and to themselves.

Principals: Mother Mary Bede Loob, O.S.F., 1961–67; Sr. Maryrose, O.S.F., 1967–71; Rev. William J. Lynch, S.J., 1971–74; Mr. John V. Lonergan, 1974–78; Miss Marie Deegan, 1978–84; Sr. Mary Hugh Brady, O.P., 1984–89; Mr. Frank Poleski Jr., 1989–present.

McCorristin High School, Trenton

In September 1961, Msgr. Michael P. McCorristin, pastor of St. Anthony's Parish in Trenton, initiated a Building Fund Campaign. He took this step to fill the gap in Catholic education created by the closing of Trenton Catholic Boys' High School. The new high school would be named after the parish's patron, St. Anthony of Padua.

Construction of the school began in March 1962. Classes began on September 5, 1962, with grades 9 and 10. Eight Glen Riddle Franciscans with three priests and eight lay teachers formed the first faculty. The Most Rev. George W. Ahr laid the cornerstone for the incomplete structure on September 5, 1962. An eleventh grade was added the following year. After seniors were added, construction began for an addition in the spring of 1965 to accommodate increased enrollment. The school chapel opened during the 1966–67 school year. Construction was completed during the summer of 1972 for the second story of the new wing in order to accommodate an influx of 400 students after the closing of Cathedral High School.

At the graduation ceremonies of June 1979, Bishop Ahr renamed the school in honor of Monsignor McCorristin. In June 1988, Monsignor McCorristin retired as pastor of St. Anthony's and director of McCorristin High School, and a scholarship was established in his name. During the same year, the Verro Scholarship was also instituted in the name of a deceased graduate. On December 5, 1990, Monsignor McCorristin passed to his eternal reward. A committee of school officials, parents, and alumni, under the auspices of the Development Office, met and outlined plans for an annual Founder's Day Celebration. The first celebration was held on Sunday, September 29, 1991, the Feast of St. Michael. As part of the celebration, the annual Founder's Day Award was presented for the first time. The award is to recognize a member of the community who has exhibited the same firm foundation of deep faith and commitment to education and youth that Monsignor McCorristin displayed in his life. The first recipient was the Honorable Richard J. Hughes, former governor and chief justice of the Supreme Court of New Jersey.

Principals: Sr. Mary Georgianna, O.S.F., 1962–67; Sr. Mary John Joseph, O.S.F., 1967–73; Sr. Elizabeth, O.S.F., 1973–81; Sr. Catherine, O.S.F., 1981–83; Sr. Marguerite O'Bierne, O.S.F., 1983–present.

Monsignor Donovan High School, Toms River

Prior to the 1960s, Ocean County students wishing to attend a Catholic high school could not do so within the boundaries of their county. Most of the Toms River area students attended either public schools or St. Rose High School in Belmar, 20 miles

away. Rev. Lawrence W. Donovan, pastor of St. Joseph's Parish in Toms River, already had in mind the founding of a Catholic high school. In September 1962, St. Joseph's Parish opened Ocean County's first and only Catholic high school, then named St. Joseph High School. The Sisters of St. Dominic of Newburgh, who operated St. Joseph Grade School, staffed the high school as well.

Ground for the high school was broken early in 1962. Despite an incomplete building, classes were offered temporarily in the grammar school for 116 freshmen that September. High school classes were moved to the finished high school building on March 4, 1963. The school's first graduation exercises were held in 1966. After a period of steadily increasing enrollment and the addition of twenty-six classrooms, the student population stabilized at about 1,000. The curriculum is mainly college preparatory, but career programs are also available. At least 85 percent of the graduates attend an institution of higher learning.

In honor of Monsignor Donovan's thirty-eight years of service to St. Joseph's parish community, the Most Rev. John C. Reiss announced at the parish's 100th Anniversary Mass that the high school would henceforth be called Monsignor Donovan High School.

Principals: Sr. Mary Joseph, O.P., 1962–65; Sr. Francis Joseph, O.P., 1965–67; Sr. Mary Janice, O.P., 1967–71; Sr. Carmella DiMatteo, O.P., 1971–88; Mr. Edward Gere, 1988–present.

Red Bank Catholic High School, Red Bank

In 1927, St. James Parish, Red Bank, constructed a new school building to house both the grammar school and the high school. The ninth and tenth grades had already existed since 1925 at the site of the old grammar school. In 1944, the grammar school was moved to a "temporary" structure that was not replaced until 1960. As a result of the move, the school that had been built in 1927 became used exclusively for Red Bank Catholic High School. In 1945 and 1946, under Rev. James Duffy's administration, significant repairs were made to the high school. Until 1946, the school system was served by one principal. In 1946, Sr. Mary Benigna, R.S.M., became principal of the grammar school, and Sr. Mary Eleanor, R.S.M., assumed responsibility for the high school. The Sisters of Mercy have staffed the high school since its beginning. During Sr. Mary Eleanor's tenure as principal, a student council was organized, and the first issues of the school newspaper, the *Signpost*, and yearbook, the *Emerald*, were printed.

In the early 1960s, renovations were made to the high school. On May 22, 1966, ground was broken by the Most Rev. James J. Hogan for an addition. In 1967, Red Bank Catholic opened nineteen more teaching areas. The Most Rev. George W. Ahr blessed and dedicated the finished structure on May 28, 1967.

John Charles Reiss graduated from St. James Grammar School in June 1935, and four years later, he graduated from Red

Red Bank Catholic High School, Red Bank

Bank Catholic High School. He was ordained to the priesthood on May 31, 1947, and installed as the eighth bishop of Trenton on April 22, 1980.

Principals: Sr. Mary Wilfred, R.S.M., 1927–34; Sr. Mary Angelica, R.S.M., 1934–44; Sr. Mary Eleanor, R.S.M., 1944–56; Sr. Mary Agnese, R.S.M., 1956–57; Sr. Mary Edith, R.S.M., 1957–58; Sr. Mary, R.S.M., 1958–70; Sr. Percy Lee Hart, R.S.M., 1970–80; Sr. Mary McAuley Ronan, R.S.M., 1980–present.

Saint John Vianney High School, Holmdel

Founded in 1969 at the direction of the Most Rev. George W. Ahr, St. John Vianney High School is a diocesan-owned, co-educational institution. The Marianite Sisters of Holy Cross and lay professionals staff St. John Vianney, which serves northern Monmouth and southern Middlesex counties.

In 1989, the school's booster club conducted an assessment of the school's ath-

Saint John Vianney High School, Holmdel

letic facilities. During the winters, six basketball teams, three wrestling teams, three competitive cheerleading squads, two indoor track teams, and an indoor color guard squad were all vying for practice time in the gymnasium. Students were staying at the school as late as 10 p.m. during the winter sports season. An addition was completed in February 1992, containing additional gymnasium space, a classroom for health education, and an area for weight training. On May 7, 1992, the Most Rev. John C. Reiss blessed the addition and also confirmed eight students at the ceremony.

Principals: Rev. William R. Capano, 1969–77; Rev. John P. Magdziak, 1977–85; Mr. Joseph F. Deroba, 1985–present.

Saint Rose High School, Belmar

Rev. William J. McConnell, former superintendent of schools for the Diocese of Trenton and pastor of St. Rose Parish in Belmar, built a grammar school that opened for classes on November 13, 1921. In 1923, a freshman class was added to the school, and by 1927 all four years of high school were represented. The Sisters of St. Joseph of Chestnut Hill, Pennsylvania, have administered both schools throughout their histories. The original school building continued to house all grades until 1957, when a new high school building opened. Until 1964, one principal assumed the responsibility for both elementary and secondary education. Sr. Marie Emily Smith, S.S.J., continued as principal of the high school when the grammar school received a principal of its own. In 1963, a science wing and library were added to the high school.

Although founded as a parish school, St. Rose High School draws its student population primarily from southern and western Monmouth County and northern Ocean County. It is a coed institution with a diverse student body comprising all races and creeds. Upon graduation, a majority of students continue their studies at four-year colleges. St. Rose also provides educational opportunity for those choosing technical school, the military, and the work force. Students can participate in a cooperative program with Monmouth County Vocational-Technical School. To enhance St. Rose's curriculum, Dessert Courses, focusing on current topics, provide unique cocurricular opportunity. A variety of interscholastic sports and intramural sports are offered to foster school spirit and sportsmanship.

As part of the religion curriculum, St. Rose requires students to participate in service to others, which encourages students to recognize their responsibility to the environment and to the entire human family. Several community and religious groups benefit from volunteer hours given by St. Rose students.

Principals: Sr. Roberta Gleason, S.S.J., 1923–26; Sr. Mary Leo McGlashen, S.S.J., 1927–29; Sr. Vincentia Novoceltzoff, S.S.J., 1929–32; Sr. Davidica, S.S.J., 1933–36; Sr. John Evangelist Meehan, S.S.J., 1937–43, 1949–51; Sr. Lucia Flynn, S.S.J., 1943–49; Sr. Mary of Mercy Seipel, S.S.J., 1951–57; Sr. Joseph Bernard McGoldrick, S.S.J., 1957–63; Sr. Marie Emily Smith, S.S.J., 1963–65; Sr. Teresa Maria Rudden, S.S.J., 1965–70; Sr. Saint Xavier Roth, S.S.J., 1970–73; Sr. Adele Solari, S.S.J., 1973–79; Sr. Joan Immaculate O'Donnell, S.S.J., 1979–87; Sr. Kathleen Letts, S.S.J., 1987–present.

Stuart Country Day School of the Sacred Heart, Princeton

Situated in a woodland section of Princeton, Stuart Country Day School of the Sacred Heart is an independent college-preparatory day school for girls from preschool through grade 12. Boys are admitted to the preschool only.

Stuart opened in the fall of 1963, as a result of the diligent efforts of a group of Catholic parents who dedicated themselves to founding for their children a school that would educate for informed, creative Christian living. Its dual role would be to model academic excellence and practical gospel values. The founders' initial concept of a lay-conducted coed enterprise became a school for girls when the parents invited the Society of the Sacred Heart, internationally known educators, to assume the school's direction.

The school's first student body was made up of 85 young people from preschool to grade 11. At present, Stuart enrolls 450 students. The school's reputation for the cultivation of critical thinking, its commitment to the spiritual development of the individual, and its atmosphere of personal attention and support have inspired families of many religions and races to send their daughters to Stuart from more than forty New Jersey and Pennsylvania communities.

Stuart's two-level building, set into a gentle slope on 55 acres, is a noted example of contemporary architecture. It is one of the few realized structures designed by the late renowned architectural academician Jean Labatut, past chairman and professor at the School of Architecture at Princeton University, who is considered the mentor of many of the country's best practicing architects. Labatut's poetic use of glazed brick, glass, concrete, and rocks has made the school seem part of its wooded setting. Especially of interest are the original renderings of the Madonna and the Crucifixion, two of many religious references indigenous to the structure.

The long, low building includes a spacious reception hall/art gallery, a small chapel, a little theater, two libraries, and a student dining room. Central to the design are three resource centers for the Upper, Middle, and Lower Schools. The resource centers are surrounded by respective classrooms and by science, computer, and art rooms. Numerous offices, seminar/work rooms, and a dining room accommodate the faculty and staff. A separate cluster of four classrooms and playgrounds houses the preschool. An adjacent gymnasium is equipped for tennis, volleyball, basketball, and dance. Outside are two playing fields, tennis courts, the Lower School playground, and an endowed nature trail.

In the summer of 1992, construction of a two-story science wing began. Added classroom and music space for the Lower School will be provided on the ground floor; state-of-the-art biology, chemistry, and physics laboratories for the Upper School will exist on the second floor.

Sixty-six faculty members, consisting of 5 religious and 61 lay women and men, teach at Stuart. Forty-five have advanced degrees. All continue to pursue professional advancement in their disciplines through faculty endowment for workshops, summer study, and sabbaticals. Faculty members commit themselves to the promulgated goals of Sacred Heart education as expressed in *Goals and Criteria,* published by the Network of Sacred Heart Schools in the United States. This network, of which Stuart is the youngest member, operates nineteen schools in fourteen states. It is part of the worldwide mission of the Society of the Sacred Heart, begun in France in 1800. Hundreds of educational institutions and other influential projects are directed by almost 6,000 Religious of the Sacred Heart on six continents.

Since its founding, Stuart has been dedicated to the concept of training its graduates to take their place in the world as responsible citizens. Participation in four years of community service is required for graduation. Students volunteer throughout the Princeton and Trenton area during the school year. In the summer, volunteers work in Appalachia and with Habitat for Humanity.

Stuart, committed to the value of an education for women, trains its students for leadership. Its 800 alumnae, active in business, medicine, law, the arts, education, science, the ministry, publishing, and government, testify to the success of its educational philosophy. Annual Upper School Career Days have proved to be an opportunity for Stuart students to learn from the Stuart women who have preceded them into the work of the world. Stuart is governed by a Board of Trustees of 24 men and women who oversee the direction of the school, its annual budget, and the investment of its $1.5-million dollar endowment.

Headmistresses: Sr. Joan Kirby, R.S.C.J., 1963–67; Sr. Mary Bush, R.S.C.J., 1967–73; Sr. Judith Garson, R.S.C.J., 1973–77;

Sr. Joan Magnetti, R.S.C.J., 1977–90; Sr. Sandra Theunick, R.S.C.J., 1990–93; Sr. Frances de la Chapelle, R.S.C.J., 1993–present.

Villa Victoria Academy, Trenton

Located on the banks of the scenic Delaware River, Villa Victoria Academy educates students from kindergarten through grade 12. On its land is the original home of Mr. John Scudder, for whom a segment of the region is named Scudders Falls. His home dates back to the year 1770.

In the 1860s, Mr. Harvey Fisk, an internationally known financier, purchased the land because it was near the childhood home of his wife, the former Miss Louise Green. On it he built Victorian Mansion, noted for its rare brownstone, and other buildings, which now serve as part of Villa Victoria's Lower School. The place was known as Riverside, and the land extending from the mansion was cited as Blooming Grove on early geographic charts.

After the death of Mr. Fisk in 1890, the estate was put up for sale. The Most Rev. Thomas J. Walsh found the property suitable for purchase in 1921. He had become protector to a group of 5 Religious Teachers Filippini who had been sent by Pope Pius X to work among Italian immigrants. These sisters had been housed in St. Joachim's Parish. In 1921, 20 other sisters were sent from Rome to share in the work of evangelization. Because St. Joachim's Convent could not accommodate them all, Bishop Walsh took it upon himself to find new

Villa Victoria Academy, Trenton

quarters for them. He approached Mr. James Cox Brady, a New York financier and benefactor of many Catholic institutions in New Jersey. Mr. Brady presented Bishop Walsh with a gift of $50,000 in memory of his deceased wife, Victoria Mary Perry Brady. Bishop Walsh used the money to purchase the Fisk Estate in the name of the Religious Teachers Filippini, who in gratitude to Mr. Brady named the property Villa Victoria, thus making it a lasting memorial to Mr. Brady's deceased wife.

For twelve years Villa Victoria served as a motherhouse and novitiate for the sisters. In 1933, Bishop Walsh was promoted to archbishop of Newark. He then suggested that the sisters move their motherhouse within the confines of his new diocese, and as a result of their transfer to Morristown, Villa Victoria began as a private academy.

In the school's first year, 1933, Sr. Florinda Martella registered 7 students. Two years later, the first elementary school graduation was held. In June 1937, 4 high school graduates received their diplomas. Within the next ten years, many structural changes took place as the school buildings were enlarged to accommodate an increasing number of students.

Progress in educational offerings kept pace with the external improvements. A course of study was designed to prepare students for admission to leading colleges in the country. The fine academic program won for the academy its state accreditation and acceptance into an affiliate program with the Catholic University of America. Students were exposed to the fine arts through studies in visual art and music. A student government was organized. Students in the Forum Club became participants in the Catholic Forensic League and the Forensic League of the State of New Jersey. Club members won many local and state awards and participated in national competitions. Dramatics played an important part in the school's activities, as did girls' sports. Villa Victoria had earned a prominent place in the front ranks of private schools.

In the early 1960s, Dr. Leonard Felix Fuld, a philanthropist interested in the nursing profession and the welfare of nursing students, began to take an interest in Villa Victoria. With his encouragement, a nursing preparatory program was initiated. The science program was expanded to include biochemistry, microbiology, anatomy, and physiology, and the course of study was reorganized so that eligible students might qualify to take such advanced courses in their senior year. Until his death in 1965, Dr. Fuld paid the tuition of the students accepted into this program.

With the development of the nursing program, there arose the need for more laboratory space and additional classrooms. These and other needs led to the construction of a new high school building. Groundbreaking ceremonies took place on February 8, 1963, and in the fall of 1965, faculty and students walked into a three-level structure of total masonry. Adjacent and attached to the high school building are the gymnasium and a large theater, equipped with professional lighting and sound systems.

To respond more effectively to the educational and career needs of its students, Villa Victoria Academy is divided into a Lower School and an Upper School. The Lower School is coeducational, comprising kindergarten through grade 6. Grades 7–12 constitute the Upper School, which is a college-preparatory school for girls. Each school has its own principal, faculty, and identity. Both operate under the direction of academy President Sr. Lillian Harrington, M.P.F., and a governing board consisting of clergy, sisters, and laity.

Principals of the entire academy: Sr. Florinda Martella, M.P.F., 1933–35; Sr. Carmelina Mugnano, M.P.F., 1936–47; Sr. Mary Brenna, M.P.F., 1948–54; Sr. Mary Carmela Pagano, M.P.F., 1954–61.

Principals of the Lower School: Sr. Gloria Caglioti, M.P.F., 1962–69; Sr. Louise DelCarpine, M.P.F., 1969–74; Sr. Elizabeth Jean Takacs, M.P.F., 1974–81; Sr. Patricia Martin, M.P.F., 1981–84; Sr. Mary Lou Shulas, M.P.F., 1984–88; Sr. Mary DeAngelis, M.P.F., 1988–91; Sr. Elizabeth Calello, M.P.F., 1991–present.

Principals of the Middle School: Sr. Margaret Pierro, M.P.F., 1979–82; Sr. Roseann Fernandez, M.P.F., 1982–85.

Principals of the Upper School: Sr. Concetta Latina, M.P.F., 1961–72; Sr. Clare Testa, M.P.F., 1972–76; Sr. Lillian Harrington, M.P.F., 1976–84; Sr. Dolores Potkay, M.P.F., 1984–85; Sr. Giacinta Basile, M.P.F., 1985–91; Sr. Helen Sanchez, M.P.F., 1991–present.

GEORGIAN COURT COLLEGE, LAKEWOOD

On December 8, 1905, the Sisters of Mercy of New Jersey signed an act of incorporation, establishing a college for women. In September of 1908, Mount Saint Mary's College opened its doors in North Plainfield, New Jersey. In 1911, the college was destroyed by fire, then immediately rebuilt. Four young women graduated from Mount Saint Mary's in 1912 from a total student body of 12. The North Plainfield site, in addition to the college, also contained a motherhouse, a novitiate, and an academy. Because of overcrowding, the Sisters of Mercy and the Most Rev. Thomas J. Walsh agreed that the college needed a separate location.

The sisters, Bishop Walsh, and Rev. Maurice R. Spillane, pastor of St. Mary of the Lake in Lakewood, were involved in purchasing the 200-acre Lakewood estate of Mr. George Jay Gould. They agreed that the estate with its buildings could be con-

verted into a women's college. In 1924, under Bishop Walsh's guidance, the Sisters of Mercy purchased the estate, bordering Lake Carasaljo, with funds raised through a diocesan campaign. At that time, the college was renamed Georgian Court College, retaining the name of the estate. The current president, Sr. Barbara Williams, R.S.M., said, "Throughout the years, the sisters completed payment on the mortgage and then repaid the loan they received from the diocese."

On April 3, 1928, Monsignor Spillane moved Lakewood's old church onto the grounds of Georgian Court College for use as the students' chapel. The awesome undertaking was reported in *Ripley's Believe It or Not*. Over the years, buildings were added to the campus and the curriculum expanded.

The original mansion of the George Gould estate is one of the main buildings of Georgian Court College, founded by the Sisters of Mercy.

In 1976, a graduate school opened with 114 men and women enrolled to begin academic work toward a Master of Arts degree in education. In 1978, the entire campus was entered into the National Register of Historic Places and the New Jersey Register, and, in 1985, the entire campus was designated as a National Historic Landmark. In 1979, a coeducational undergraduate evening division was instituted. A Master of Arts degree program in mathematics was initiated in 1988. Georgian Court College provides a liberal arts education in keeping with Roman Catholic tradition and cultivates scholarly study and dialogue, academic excellence, specific intellectual skills, a personal world view, and a sense of values.

Presidents: Mother Mary Cecilia Scully, R.S.M., 1908–29; Mother Mary John Considine, R.S.M., 1929–48; Mother Marie Anna Callahan, R.S.M., 1948–62; Sr. Mary Pierre Tirrell, R.S.M., 1962–68; Sr. Mary Stephanie Sloyan, R.S.M., 1968–74; Sr. Maria Cordis Richey, R.S.M., 1974–80; Sr. Barbara Williams, R.S.M., 1980–present.

CATHOLIC CAMPUS MINISTRY

Aquinas Institute, Princeton University, Princeton

In 1928, two Catholic professors, Hugh Scott Taylor and David A. McCabe, invited the first Catholic chaplain, Rev. Quitman Beckley, O.P., to Princeton University. Professor Taylor, born in Lancashire, England, became the David B. Jones Professor of Chemistry at Princeton; Professor McCabe was a professor of economics. These two professors are the true founders of the Catholic chaplaincy at Princeton University. Initially, meetings and the celebration of mass were held at St. Paul's Church, Princeton. For about twenty years, Father Beckley said mass on campus in Alexander Hall.

The tenure of the second chaplain, Rev. Hugh Halton, O.P., proved to be six stormy years for the faculty and students. Throughout them, the Most Rev. George W. Ahr supported Father Halton, refusing to remove him from the chaplaincy, despite a request made in the form of an ultimatum. Father Halton attacked the Department of Religion for failing to have a Catholic theologian on faculty and accused the faculty, in general, for distortion of truth and lack of godliness. He attacked Catholic professors, including Dr. Taylor, one of the founders of the Catholic chaplaincy, for failing to defend their faith. During the McCarthy era, Father Halton stated that he was the only non-Communist at Princeton. He was also an outspoken critic of the university's "abusive liberalism." In the fall of 1957, President Goheen withdrew official university recognition of Father Halton, declaring him, in effect, persona non grata. Finally, the master general of the Dominican order removed Father Halton from his post. During his tenure, Father Halton did acquire the current property, a house once lived in by Thomas Mann, the German novelist. The name of the club was also changed from the Catholic Club to the Aquinas Institute.

In 1964, Rev. Robert Murray discontinued mandatory attendance at chapel services. In 1966, Catholic Masses were allowed in the Princeton University Chapel, a building as large as a cathedral, with many historical figures represented in the stained glass windows. Apparently from all indications, Father Murray was well liked at Aquinas.

During the chaplaincy of Rev. Charles B. Weiser, Aquinas Institute developed and gained respect. Father Weiser hired associate chaplains and a nun. Opus Dei Society came to Princeton in 1985 to work with the priests of Aquinas Institute. However, within a few years, the society opened its own Opus Dei House at Princeton. Rev. Vincent E. Keane established the first Aquinas Council, composed of students and townspeople. He began renovations of Aquinas Building and hired a laywoman as associate chaplain. Currently, Catholics of Princeton University are served by 3 priests and 1 laywoman.

Chaplains: Rev. Quitman Beckley, O.P., 1928–52; Rev. Hugh Halton, O.P., 1952–58; Rev. Robert Murray, 1958–67; Rev. John Connolly, 1967–68; Rev. Christopher Reilly, 1968–70; Rev. Charles B. Weiser, 1970–88; Rev. Vincent E. Keane, 1988–present.

Bede House, Trenton State College, Trenton

The actual house that bears the name of St. Bede, the monk, priest, theologian, and Doctor of the Church, was built seventy-five years ago for the brother of the founder of Vernum Dairy Farm and his family. The double lot stands directly next to the dairy barn, which was the center of a large farm

Bede House, Trenton State College, Trenton

that has now been subdivided into housing developments. The Diocese of Trenton acquired the property more than twenty-five years ago to serve as a residence for the full-time chaplain, currently Rev. David A. Hillier. Bede House is less than two blocks from the main campus of Trenton State College and also serves as the offices for the student-run Newman Club. It is the place where Wednesday night Bede House dinners have fed the students of the college for as long as anyone can remember. In the true spirit of St. Bede, an extensive library has been maintained over the years to assist students in philosophy and religion courses. The library also serves as a general resource center for the quest of knowledge and deeper faith, characteristic of the college years. The house has in the past served as a residence for Catholic male students, but the practice was discontinued due to adequate housing that now exists on campus.

The physical plant allows for all retreats and evenings of renewal to be conducted at the house. Although mass is celebrated at the house on those occasions, the numbers attending daily and Sunday mass can be accommodated only in the on-campus Alumni Meditation Chapel and the Travers/Wolfe Residence Hall main lounge.

The space behind and above the sizable garage has for some years housed the Trenton chapter of Birthright. The special work accomplished by Birthright volunteers gives witness, help, and faith-filled inspiration to the student community.

A summary of what the Bede House is and why it exists is best expressed in the words of a recent graduate who said, "I think of the Bede House as a home away from home, where there is quiet, prayer, an attentive ear, an active community of faith, and some of the best food I have tasted this side of my mother's table."

Bethlehem Newman Center, Monmouth College, West Long Branch

On November 17, 1972, a house was purchased from Angeline Marcolini to be used as the Bethlehem Newman Center—Catholic center for Monmouth College students. The name Bethlehem was chosen because translated it means "House of Bread." The blessing and dedication were held on October 18, 1973, with the Most Rev. George W. Ahr presiding.

In addition to serving as a residence for the chaplain, Bethlehem Newman Center contains a chapel where the Blessed Sacrament is permanently reserved and where mass is celebrated. The Newman Club, a student organization, is dedicated to the constant improvement of campus spirit and the total welfare of the Monmouth College community. According to the second article of the club's constitution, these objectives are to be fostered through the intellectual, social, religious, and philosophical interests and efforts of club members.

Chaplains: Rev. M. Joseph Mokrzycki, 1972–77; Rev. Richard C. Brietske, 1977–86; Rev. John W. Russo, 1986–present.

Emmaus House, Rider College, Lawrenceville

The first Catholic mass at Rider College was celebrated on October 10, 1965, by Rev. Thomas A. Coffey in Gill Memorial Chapel. In the summer of 1970, the Diocese of

Emmaus House, Rider College, Lawrenceville

Faith in Action in the Diocese of Trenton

Trenton purchased a large redbrick house directly across from the main entrance to Rider College. After several months of renovation, it became the Catholic student center for Rider students, faculty, and staff. The renovated building consists of an all-purpose room, library, reading room, office, dining room, kitchen, and bathroom. The second floor provides living space for the chaplain.

The chaplain at the time, Rev. Jeremiah J. Cullinane, requested that the Most Rev. George W. Ahr name the new center Emmaus, for on their way to Emmaus the disciples had their faith strengthened. Referring to the Emmaus story in Luke's gospel, Father Jeremiah said, "We feel that our Center is an inn on the side of the road where, hopefully, the Lord will make himself manifest." In speaking at the dedication ceremony, Dr. Frank Ellicott, president of Rider College, said, "I hope that that which transpires across the street and the activities which will center on this building will sharpen our vision so that we may in Peter Marshall's great, if brief, prayer 'know thy will and do it.'"

Since its dedication on October 5, 1971, Emmaus House has provided the Rider community with a place to gather, to study the Catholic faith, to pray, to socialize, and to be challenged. The Catholic student center provides a strong base of support for the Catholic students of Rider and serves as a reminder of the Trenton diocese's commitment to college students.

Chaplains: Rev. George A. Ardos, Rev. Edward D. Strano, Rev. Jeremiah J. Cullinane, Rev. Walter E. Nolan, Rev. Phillip C. Pfleger, Rev. R. Vincent Gartland.

RETREAT HOUSES AND HOUSES OF PRAYER

Francis House of Prayer, Rancocas

Located on 125 acres of Mount Holly farmland, Francis House of Prayer has been a place of grace for the people of the Trenton diocese since its opening on June 29, 1974. The Most Rev. George W. Ahr celebrated the initial liturgy and appointed Sr. Clare Wilde, O.S.F., a Stella Niagara Franciscan, as the first director. The simple rustic charm of Francis House has attracted many people to attend liturgies, solitude and prayer, private and directed retreats, spiritual direction, days and evenings of recollection, and

Francis House of Prayer, Rancocas

programs on the spiritual life. Francis House has also been used as a shelter for homeless women and children as needed.

Sr. Vida O'Leary, R.S.M., was assisted by several Sisters of Mercy during her twelve years as director. For a year, Sr. Dominica di Francesco, R.S.M., and Sr. Pauline Carugno, R.S.M., codirected Francis House. A layman, Mr. Stephen Reichenbach, served as director until the arrival of codirectors Rev. Joseph Tedesco and Sr. Marcella Springer, S.S.J. They also operated the Upper Room Spiritual Center, Neptune, from July 1991 to July 1992. Sister Marcella, a Sister of St. Joseph of Philadelphia, is the present full-time director of Francis House. She is assisted by a volunteer staff.

Directors/Codirectors: Sr. Clare Wilde, O.S.F., 1974–76; Sr. Vida O'Leary, R.S.M., 1976–88; Sr. Dominica di Francesco, R.S.M., 1988–89; Sr. Pauline Carugno, R.S.M., 1988–89; Mr. Stephen Reichenbach, 1989–91; Rev. Joseph Tedesco, 1991–92; Sr. Marcella Springer, S.S.J., 1991–present.

Maris Stella, Harvey Cedars

Maris Stella is a summer vacation compound staffed by the Sisters of Charity of Saint Elizabeth, Convent Station. It serves primarily the Sisters of Charity from June to September but also welcomes sisters from all other communities as time and space permit.

Mother Ellen Marie McCauley, S.C., purchased the estate of Frederick Small in 1959. The building was revamped to suit the simple needs of the sisters. The property consists of six efficiency units, varying in size and capacity for occupants, and one main building on the oceanfront for sisters who prefer the larger community atmosphere. Meals are provided in the main building. The spacious grounds add a climate of peace and relaxation for all to enjoy on both the bay side and the ocean side of the property.

Administrators: Sr. Maria Clare Brosnahan, S.C., 1959–62; Sr. Francis Elise Byrne, S.C., 1962–68; Sr. Jude Miriam Hayden, S.C., 1968–74; Sr. Anne Philip Beggans, S.C., 1974–89; Sr. Audrey Boettcher, S.C., 1989–present.

Morning Star House of Prayer, Trenton

Founded and staffed by the Religious Teachers Filippini, Morning Star House of Prayer is an oasis of peace and harmony located in the deep recesses of Villa Victoria Academy grounds. The Province of St. Lucy Filippini is dedicated to the Christian transformation of the family, particularly women. From 1692 to 1732, St. Lucy Filippini gave parish missions and retreats for women because she believed that to sanctify womanhood was to sanctify the family. To continue this mission, the House of Prayer first opened its doors to the religious, clergy, and laity on October 7, 1974, in Monmouth Beach, with Sr. Geraldine Calabrese, M.P.F., and Sr. Josephine Aparo, M.P.F., as staff.

On May 17, 1978, after four years of ministry to the people of Monmouth County, the House of Prayer was moved to its present location situated between the Delaware River and the Delaware Raritan Canal. A prayer garden and hermitage were added in 1981. Places for quiet reflection along the brook were constructed in 1983. The grotto of Our Lady of Fatima was built and dedicated in 1985. Walkways and the Way of the Cross were also constructed in 1985. In 1986, a new aspect of the prayer ministry developed with the publication of original music from Morning Star.

Morning Star House of Prayer takes its name from Revelation 22:16: "I, Jesus . . . am of David's line, the root of David and the bright star of the morning." It is a place of prayerful confrontation with the mystery that gives meaning to life and where all activities are subordinated to this primary goal. Morning Star is a school of prayer where one may rediscover or deepen a relationship with the Lord and thus rediscover or deepen relationships with others.

Morning Star offers its guests a beautiful chapel, private rooms, a hermitage, and good food. There are beautiful grounds, landscaped and rustic; a running brook; a prayer garden for meditation; and a walking path along the canal and the Delaware River. Morning Star offers book and tape libraries, prayer experiences for both individuals and small groups, and spiritual direction for those requesting it.

Coordinator: Sr. Geraldine Calabrese, M.P.F., 1974–present.

Saint Joseph by the Sea Spiritual Center, South Mantoloking

St. Lucy Filippini, foundress of the Religious Teachers Filippini, dedicated her life to education, particularly among women.

She founded schools of Christian doctrine, gave Spiritual Exercises to women preparing for marriage, and taught the Word of God through instruction and retreat experiences. Her charismatic gift was "the wisdom of Word," and she made every effort to spread the Word of God to everyone. She was a contemplative in action; all her actions stemmed from her union with God.

It is this spirit that the Religious Teachers Filippini wish to create at St. Joseph by the Sea Spiritual Center, which opened on January 17, 1983. It is their aim to provide the atmosphere and means for the individual who goes there to "Let the word of Christ, rich as it is, dwell in you" (Col. 3:16). Having experienced quiet and solitude, one goes back out in the world renewed and refreshed to incarnate God's love and Word in loving response to the transforming power to the Father. Programs are offered to enrich, renew, and deepen one's interior communion with the Lord in an atmosphere of prayer, quiet, and solitude.

Directors: Sr. Frances Lauretti, M.P.F., c1983; Sr. Donna Gaglioti, M.P.F., present.

San Alfonso Retreat House, Long Branch

On July 9, 1922, the Congregation of the Most Holy Redeemer established a residence in the West End section of Long Branch to be used as a vacation house. With the consent of the Most Rev. Thomas J. Walsh, the house opened for retreats on September 25, 1925. By virtue of faculties granted by the Sacred Congregation for Religious and with the prior consent of the

Most Rev. William A. Griffin, the Redemptorists erected the residence as a canonical religious house on July 25, 1945.

San Alfonso Retreat House is a Redemptorist spiritual center situated on 8 beautiful acres along the Jersey coast. In 1925 there were two retreats with 15 retreatants. At present, the retreat house serves several thousand people each year. The dramatic increase in the number of retreatants is due in great measure to the efforts of the Knights of Columbus and of the Retreat League and its captains.

The retreat house contains rooms for 150 persons, a large chapel, spacious meeting rooms, a well-appointed dining room, and a religious article and book store. There is also a prayer garden on the grounds, and, along the Atlantic Ocean, are a boardwalk and benches. The programs at San Alfonso include weekend retreats for men, women, and couples; Matt Talbot retreats; charismatic retreats; private and directed retreats; and days of prayer and recollection. Meetings and conferences are held for diocesan, parish, and school groups and for members of religious institutes.

Superiors: Rev. Charles J. Becker, C.Ss.R., 1922–25; Rev. Charles F. Hoff, C.Ss.R., 1925–28; Rev. Joseph Turner, C.Ss.R., 1928–30; Rev. William V. Knell, C.Ss.R., 1930–33; Rev. Francis Fischer, C.Ss.R., 1933–37; Rev. John P. O'Connor, C.Ss.R., 1937–42; Rev. Thomas Sanderson, C.Ss.R., 1942–45; Rev. Thomas McCauley, C.Ss.R., 1945–47; Rev. Andrew L. Doran, C.Ss.R., 1947–50; Rev. John Driscoll, C.Ss.R., 1950–56; Rev. James Collins,

C.Ss.R., 1956–61; Rev. Richard F. O'Malley, C.Ss.R., 1962–64; Rev. Joseph G. McManus, C.Ss.R., 1964–69; Rev. Bernard Power, C.Ss.R., 1969–75; Rev. James H. Geiger, C.Ss.R., 1975–77; Rev. William Heanue, C.Ss.R., 1977–81; Rev. Thomas Schmitt, C.Ss.R., 1981–87; Rev. Paul V. Bryan, C.Ss.R., 1987–present.

Stella Maris Retreat House, Elberon

With the approval of the Most Rev. William A. Griffin, the Sisters of St. Joseph purchased a mansion in Elberon in September 1941. Bishop Griffin conducted the formal opening of the "summer home for sisters" in May 1942. In January 1965, the Most Rev. George W. Ahr granted permission to keep Stella Maris open year-round and to conduct weekend retreats. Since then, a full-time retreat ministry has developed.

Administrators: Sr. Philomena Cronin, C.S.J.P., 1942–50; Sr. Gerard Doyle, C.S.J.P., 1950–63; Sr. Jerome Fitzpatrick, C.S.J.P., 1963–84; Sr. Kathleen Connell, C.S.J.P., 1984–present.

The Upper Room Spiritual Center, Neptune

The mission of The Upper Room Spiritual Center is to serve the Diocese of Trenton through prayer, spiritual direction, charismatic renewal, associated programs for the development of spiritual directors, and education. In August 1977, Rev. James O'Brien was appointed as the first liaison for charismatic renewal of the diocese. Funding for the Office of Liaison coupled with the invi-

The Upper Room Spiritual Center, Neptune

tation of Msgr. Robert T. Bulman, pastor of St. Mary's, New Monmouth, to use the former convent allowed for a wider use of the Spiritual Center. The Most Rev. George W. Ahr gave his approval for the center on June 9, 1978. In July 1978, The Upper Room Spiritual Center opened with Father O'Brien as director, Sr. Janice Edwards, R.S.M., in ministry, and Linda Rover as administrator. Starting in the early 1980s, Mr. Edwin Voll and Mr. Ronald Novak were sponsored through the center to serve as deacons. The *Upper Room News,* the center's newsletter, began in 1980. In September 1982, the three-year program in Spiritual Direction was inaugurated. The center moved from New Monmouth to the former convent of Holy Innocents Parish, Neptune, in the summer of 1984. In 1988, Rev. Joseph Tedesco was named as liaison for charismatic renewal.

Directors/Codirectors: Rev. James O'Brien, 1977–88; Sr. Maureen Conroy, R.S.M., 1979–present; Sr. Janice Edwards, R.S.M., 1982–86; Sr. Carol Conly, R.S.M., 1986–present; Rev. Joseph Tedesco, 1988–1992.

CATHOLIC CHARITIES

St. Michael's Aid Society was incorporated on January 20, 1913, to provide child care services for the Diocese of Trenton. On April 1, 1943, the director of diocesan institutions and agencies was assigned as supervisor of the agency with instructions to coordinate the charitable activities from a central diocesan office. The name of the agency was legally changed on January 23, 1947, to Catholic Welfare Bureau, Diocese of Trenton. On October 19, 1988, the name was again changed, to Catholic Charities, Diocese of Trenton. Past directors include Mr. William Doherty, Mr. Michael Campbell, Ms. Elizabeth Ann Henry, Rev. Francis M. J. Thornton, and Msgr. Theodore A. Opdenaker. Currently, Mr. Francis E. Dolan directs Catholic Charities, which is the purview of the vicar for social services, Msgr. Joseph C. Shenrock.

Alcoholism/Addictions Program

The mission of the Alcoholism/Addictions Program is to reduce the prevalence of the disease of alcoholism and other drug dependence and to provide assessment and treatment for affected individuals and their families. The program, which strongly adheres to twelve-step principles, is staffed by certified alcohol and drug counselors and social workers.

Christopher House

Christopher House is a psychosocial and prevocational rehabilitation program in

Mercer County for adults recovering from persistent mental illness. The program helps its members to manage and stabilize their illness, to remain successfully in the community, to enhance family and social supports, and to make meaningful choices and set realistic goals.

Delaware House Mental Health Services

In 1971, a three-day-a-week program began, serving just 4 clients. Delaware House Mental Health Services now comprises six programs serving nearly 900 seriously mentally ill clients and their family members in Burlington County. In general, Delaware House attempts to prepare clients to live as independently as possible. Structured activities are offered for clients, including social, prevocational, and educational groups. Group counseling and follow-up services are also offered. In addition, Delaware House has residential, hospital liaison, and supported employment programs.

Emergency Services

In Burlington County, a 24-hour, seven-day-a-week program provides comprehensive assistance in response to people in need. Services include information and referral, recycled clothing and household goods, community education, advocacy, and case management. The program's housing component offers an alternative housing option, which includes permanent and transitional housing, prevention of homelessness, Project Home Share, and housing advocacy.

In Ocean County, Emergency Services concentrates on assisting homeless persons to locate affordable, suitable housing. The program networks with a myriad of community agencies, landlords, and businesses that share the common goal of alleviating the plight of the homeless and the hungry.

Family and Community Services

FACS, a major presence of Catholic Charities in each county of the diocese, offers help in solving a wide range of personal, premarital, marital, and family problems. A variety of treatment methods are implemented, including individual counseling, family therapy, couple counseling, group counseling, and mediation for family disputes. Also provided are prevention-oriented workshops, consultation, community education, information and referral, and advocacy services.

Family Growth Program

The Family Growth Program provides specialized treatment services for avoiding family violence in Burlington, Mercer, and Monmouth counties. Specific areas of intervention include child abuse and neglect, child sexual abuse and incest, spouse battering, and abuse of the elderly. While the program's focus is the entire family, counseling and therapy are offered to individuals and couples also. Specialized services are provided for adult and child victims, as well as adult and juvenile perpetrators.

All components of the Family Growth network of services deal with long waiting lists. The program treats the most serious abuse cases and frequently receives from other agencies and clinicians requests for consultation on the treatment of family violence. In 1991, Family Growth Program garnered national recognition by being included in the Program Exchange, a special project that identifies model programs sponsored by the Institute for the Advancement of Child Welfare Practice of the Child Welfare League of America.

Guidance Clinic

The Guidance Clinic provides outpatient mental health services for residents of Trenton, Ewing, and Lower Lawrence who experience severe emotional difficulties. Priority is given to those currently hospitalized for mental illness or at risk of psychiatric hospitalization. Among the goals of the clinic are to prevent psychiatric hospitalization and to educate the community about mental illness and mental health.

Maternity and Adoption Services

Maternity and Adoption Services offers a comprehensive psychotherapeutic program, adoption services, pregnancy testing, foster and permanent placement, supervision services, complaint investigations, and legal referrals. It also offers child-birthing classes, support groups for those involved in crisis pregnancy, referrals for physical relief, medical and residential care, and reunion services for adult adoptees and birth parents.

Providence House

A Providence House has operated in Burlington County since 1978, one in Ocean County since 1986. Both offer a comprehensive array of services to individuals and families suffering domestic violence. Services provided by one or both programs include 24-hour access to emergency shelter, 24-hour hotline services, supportive and therapeutic counseling, weekly support groups, men's programs, advocacy services, information and referral, court accompaniment, children's programs, follow-up services, and community education.

School Social Services Program

Established by Catholic Charities in 1980, the School Social Services Program is designed to provide unique pupil personnel service for parochial school students whose behavioral, social, emotional, physical, or learning difficulties interfere with success in academic performance. The program assists students, their families, teachers, and communities in all four counties in the Diocese of Trenton.

Services for the Elderly

Services for the Elderly provides needs assessment, information and referral services, and social services. It aids clients and their families who are having difficulty in social functioning or maintaining their independence. A strong point of this program is its ability to tailor services to the particular needs of a parish or other community group.

PERMANENT DIACONATE

The deacon of today can trace his roots to the earliest days of the Christian church. We read of the establishment of the diaconate in Acts 6:3, 6: "Therefore, brothers, choose seven men from among you who have a good reputation, and who are full of the Spirit and of wisdom . . . These they set before the apostles and placed their hands upon them." Throughout history the role of the deacon changed until it became a transitional state on the way to the priesthood. In the Dogmatic Constitution on the Church in the Second Vatican Council, the bishops decided to restore the diaconate as a permanent order of ministers in the church. In 1968, the U.S. bishops petitioned the Holy See for permission to restore the diaconate in their country. Permission was granted, and by the spring of 1971, thirteen programs were in operation.

In the Diocese of Trenton, Rev. James P. McManimon, then vocation director, performed an exhaustive study that indicated that the rate of priestly vocations was not keeping pace with the rapid growth of the Catholic population. The Most Rev. George W. Ahr gave his permission for the establishment of the Permanent Diaconate Program. In the fall of 1974, after a year of planning, the diaconate program was launched, with 46 men selected from 135 applicants. During the first year of formal training, the candidates traveled to the Archdiocese of Newark for their courses. On September 22, 1975, candidates were able to start attending classes at St. Stephen's Parish in Trenton. On May 14, 1977, Bishop Ahr ordained the first class of 41 permanent deacons for ministry in the Diocese of Trenton.

In October of 1977, the Diaconate Office and classes were moved to their current location at 1 Centre Street in Trenton, part of the Sacred Heart Parish complex. Since 1977, 269 men have been ordained as permanent deacons at St. Mary's Cathedral in Trenton. The creation of the Diocese of Metuchen on November 24, 1981, sent 83 men either ordained or in training to the new diocese. Today, the vicar of deacons for the Trenton diocese is Rev. Michael J. Walsh, who succeeded Monsignor McManimon in 1986.

The deacon is a person called to service as an ordained minister of the church. His life must be centered in Christ, whose words "I have come to serve" explain his own calling. The Bishops' Guidelines on the Permanent Diaconate note in this regard that the deacon is "in communion with the bishops and priests." The deacon, a person of faith and honor, a person called and enriched by sacramental grace, brings Jesus to the community through his presence and his charisma.

Most candidates for the permanent diaconate are initially sponsored by their parish's pastor. Even before making application for entry into the diaconate program, however, candidates are usually actively involved in various parish ministries of the Word, Eucharist, and charity. Deacons manifest their ministry of charity by meeting parishioners during the week to serve their spiritual needs. The ministry of charity opens for the deacon the other ministries of the Word and the Eucharist. The deacon proclaims the scriptures, preaches the gospel, baptizes, officiates at weddings, and leads funeral rites.

The majority of deacons are married. They and their wives give testimony to the sacrament of marriage. The formation programs for the diaconate in the United States seek to build a consciousness of the sacrament of marriage as a beautiful sign of God's presence in the world. The formation programs also invite deacons to celebrate the sacrament of marriage with new enthusiasm each day.

The future direction of the life of the deacon is still not clear. The diaconate has been restored in a historic era of great and rapid change. With guidance from the Holy Spirit, we hope the deacon will continue to be a strong witness to Christ and a faithful provider of pastoral care for those in need.

MISCELLANEOUS INSTITUTIONS

Anchor House, Trenton

Some youngsters are unable to cope with the pressures of growing up. Others, tragically, are the victims of physical, mental, or sexual abuse and are forced to take to the streets. The need for a safe place where teenagers could go for counseling, shelter, and medical services was becoming apparent to the staff of an evening teen center. A site was needed in the heart of the city of Trenton with easy access to bus routes and a large building able to house 10–12 children at reasonable cost or rent.

The staff found the ideal building, less than a quarter mile from the teen center. Ss. Peter and Paul's former convent was available as a result of the closing of the elementary school in 1975. Pastor John Churak listened attentively to the proposed shelter for teenagers and worked with parish members to gain support and establish a reasonable rent level. The tasks of gathering support from local officials, community leaders, neighbors, and the media and raising the initial money began. Many months of setbacks were encountered, from initial resistance by neighbors to hard-fought verbal confrontations before the city planning board. Finally, in February 1979, local teens and parents, giving emotional testimony, addressed the planning board and eventually gained its support.

On April 1, 1979, Anchor House opened its doors. Without a track record, government and private financial support was difficult to obtain. During the first two years, Anchor House survived totally on the generosity of the public. Expenses for rent, utilities, food, and other items were paid for with dollars raised by the Ride for Runaways program and other events. Because of the lack of funds, however, salaries were not paid to the full-time staff of 6. In time, the work of Anchor House attracted stable financial support, allowed salaries to develop further, and retained strong staff for expansion of critical area programs.

With twelve individual bedrooms, ten bathrooms, a full kitchen, a recreation room, and offices and smaller rooms for staff purposes, the building is suitable for Anchor House's mission. The property is owned by the Diocese of Trenton, yet Anchor House is not affiliated with the Roman Catholic Church. It was the recognition of the need for the facility that encouraged diocesan leadership to make the building available. Anchor House maintains a warm relationship with all segments of the religious community.

On a day-to-day basis, the children residing at Anchor House are responsible for various chores, such as sweeping and cleaning up after meals. Volunteers also play a key role in the upkeep of the house. The proper appearance of the building, in concert with respect for maintaining and contributing to the peace of the neighborhood, has contributed to the development of a strong appreciation for Anchor House by its Centre Street neighbors.

Anchor House provides food, clothing, shelter, and medical and psychological services as well as counseling for teenagers and their families. The counseling and volunteer staff members provide well-balanced, nutritious meals for their clients. Chores are assigned to each client so that a spirit of family sharing prevails. Thanks to the generosity of many area residents and community groups, clean used clothing is made available for children in need.

Within 72 hours, a new resident is scheduled for a complete physical at Delaware Valley Pediatric Associates. Vision and hearing tests, blood work, and tuberculosis and sickle cell anemia testing are performed, and a general medical history is taken. Recommendations and follow-up care are also provided. In the event of a medical emergency, staff may call the pediatric group at any time to express concerns or seek professional advice.

The efforts of Anchor House have been recognized by experts in the social service and judicial fields, government, and the media as constituting an effective means of coping with the tragic circumstances of these young people.

Collier Services, Wickatunk

In 1927, Mrs. Robert Collier, of the Collier publishing family, turned over her summer estate to the Sisters of the Good Shepherd. The institution opened on October 20, 1927, being incorporated as Collier School for the Care and Training of Girls on November 22, 1927. The original purpose of Collier was to provide a residential program for troubled adolescent girls whose family situation was such that they could not live at home.

Collier Services, Wickatunk

In 1966, in recognition of the changing needs of young people, a separate Department of Social Services was initiated. Counseling was made available to the adolescents in residence and to their families. In 1970, a summer day camp program for neighborhood children was initiated as a service project of the adolescents in residence.

For four years, starting in 1974, the Pelletier School operated in Trenton. It was a special education program for adolescents, the first program sponsored by Collier for both boys and girls. Starting in 1975, Collier offered a program called Juveniles in Need of Supervision, to meet Monmouth County's need for an adolescent shelter for teenage girls. The program lasted two years.

To reflect the growing number of coed programs, the Sisters of the Good Shepherd renamed the agency Collier Services in 1976. The closing of the residential program for adolescent girls in 1977 allowed for an enlarged special education day treatment program for girls and boys on the Collier estate. In 1985, Collier Services Foundation was incorporated to encourage private support for the growing needs of the Collier programs. The Shepherd Center for child care, a program for infants and toddlers, was opened in 1989 in the original Collier School.

In 1976, Kateri Camp Center was established in the old Collier carriage house to provide overnight group camping experiences for young people and families. The following year, Kateri Day Camp began for disadvantaged children of Monmouth County. A year-round environmental edu-cation center, nature trails, and museum were created in 1979 to complement the Kateri summer day camp program.

The Collier Group Home started in Red Bank in 1973 to provide an off-campus community living experience for adolescent girls. In 1988, a new Collier Group Home was purchased in Red Bank and enlarged by the foundation board. The new building, capable of housing 12 adolescent girls, was dedicated to the memory of Sr. Eileen Groogan. Partially funded by the Division of Youth and Family Services, the home is supervised around the clock by child-care staff, and daily by social workers and clinicians. The residence of peers with similar concerns creates unity. This, together with social and academic guidance from staff, offers each girl a supportive, disciplined, and encouraging environment. Participation in community service programs, household chores, part-time employment, and emphasis on school studies provide a balanced living situation. Social activities include the use of community resources, group participation activities, and day trips. Weekend family visits are encouraged. Collier's goal is to prepare these young people for a brighter future as they return to their family or to independent living.

Superiors: Sr. Mary Bernard Smith, R.G.S., 1927–33; Sr. Mary Norberta Carney, R.G.S., 1933–36; Sr. Mary Divine Heart Dargin, R.G.S., 1936–42; Sr. Mary of Margaret Mary Roche, R.G.S., 1942–47; Sr. Mary Claudentius Rutledge, R.G.S., 1947–53; Sr. Mary Benigia Aylward, R.G.S., 1953–59; Sr. Mary Loretto Dundala, R.G.S.,

1959–65, 1972–75; Sr. Mary Leo Mahoney, R.G.S., 1965–68; Sr. Mary William Hart, R.G.S., 1968–70; Sr. Mary Dorothy Ryan, R.G.S., 1970–72; Sr. Eileen Marie O'Carroll, R.G.S., 1975–79; Sr. Mary Catherine Bender, R.G.S., 1979–85; Sr. Regina Ahearn, R.G.S., 1985–88.

Coordinators: Sr. Mary Catherine Bender, R.G.S., and Sr. Ellen Kelly, R.G.S., 1988–present.

Martin House, Trenton

The priests' senate in 1968 suggested to the Most Rev. George W. Ahr that the diocese create a special ministry to deal with racism in society. In 1969, three priests—Rev. William Dailey, Rev. Samuel Lupica, and Rev. John Ryan—volunteered to undertake the ministry. The following year, two of the priests left, and Rev. Brian McCormick arrived. Father Dailey took up another ministry in 1974. In 1980, Rev. William McLaughlin, I.M.C., offered his services. The ministry developed as the group better understood its mission. In 1980, a building was rehabilitated to hold the growing ministry. Martin House Clothing Store, run by elderly women in the community, functions as a means to get good and warm clothing and furniture to people.

In 1984, Sr. Lorette Piper, R.S.C.J., arrived and created an approach to inner-city education. The program, Martin House Learning Center, was continued by Brothers Joseph Jansen, S.M., and Steven O'Neil, S.M., after Sister Lorrette's departure in 1989. In 1988, a fund-raising program was

Martin House, Trenton

initiated for new facilities. During 1989, a building was constructed to house members and to conduct all the Martin House programs. In 1990, in conjunction with Better Community Housing of Trenton, Martin House started a new program called Doorway to Hope. Better Community Housing of Trenton, Inc., is a housing development plan, with a program run by inner-city people. A fourteen-unit apartment complex was built to house homeless families for five months. Brother David Conrad, S.M., came in 1990 to help with the store and to work on furniture. Shortly thereafter, Brother James Fitzgibbons came to help further implement the shelter program. At the end of 1990, Dr. Jose Acuna from the Bronx, New York, worked with Martin House to initiate his inner-city health approach, Project Faith, Inc.

Morris Hall, Lawrenceville

In 1898, Colonel Daniel Morris of Atlantic City left a substantial bequest to the Diocese of Trenton with the stipulation that it be used for the construction of two charitable institutions: an orphanage and a home for the aged. Morris Hall Home for the Aged was established and completed in 1904. The cornerstone was laid by the Most Rev. James A. McFaul on Sunday, October 2, 1904. The Sisters of St. Francis of Philadelphia operated the home from its beginning until 1981.

Morris Hall began as a boarding home for the aged. In 1910, an addition was constructed to include Our Lady of the

Morris Hall, Lawrenceville

Rosary Chapel, a dining room, and kitchen facilities. The chapel was used for the celebration of mass for Lawrenceville Catholics until they built a church of their own in 1938. In 1937, two additional wings were constructed; they were blessed by the Most Rev. John J. McMahon. Currently, there are fifty-six beds for residential care. In 1976, a fifty-nine-bed skilled care nursing unit was established.

A short-term Respite Care program is available in the residential section for temporary stays when a resident's caregiver is sick or on vacation. Morris Hall also contains a convent for retired Sisters of St. Francis who continue to volunteer their services. The Most Rev. John C. Reiss recently announced a construction project to integrate Morris Hall and St. Lawrence Rehabilitation Center. The old building will be torn down and replaced by a larger residential home.

In the early days, residents were called inmates. They helped in the kitchen and worked on the farm that surrounded the facility. The sisters used horse and buggy to ride into Trenton to raise funds for the institution. Prospective residents now choose Morris Hall for security and for the company of others their own age. They are involved in many activities both within the home and within the community.

Administrators: Sr. Margaret Mary, O.S.F., c1945–75; Sr. Joseph Antoine, O.S.F., 1975–78; Sr. Beatrice Diamond, O.S.F., 1978–81; Mrs. Rosalie Danek, 1981–present.

Mount Carmel Guild, Trenton

Using limited resources, the people of Mount Carmel Guild of the Diocese of Trenton are called to serve God's people—the poor of Mercer County—in whatever way possible to meet their needs. Responding to a specific call to serve, they reach out in love and service to all needing their care through their Emergency Assistance, Home Health Nursing, and Preschool Day Care Services.

While chancellor of Buffalo, New York, the Most Rev. Thomas J. Walsh founded Mount Carmel Guild in the Diocese of Buffalo. His chance to establish the guild in the Diocese of Trenton came after World War I with the dissolution of the National Recreation Service. This dissolved group had been created to minister to the leisure time of servicemen. The group ended the war with a surplus, which was divided equally among the Jewish, Protestant, and Catholic faiths. The National Catholic War Council was appointed the clearinghouse as part of the Catholic share. Bishop Walsh applied for a grant and upon receiving the money, established and staffed a community house.

In January 1920, Bishop Walsh, a great organizer, invited women of the diocese who were interested in doing charitable work to a meeting held at the cathedral. He outlined for them the organization of Mount Carmel Guild and proposed that a local guild be established along the same lines.

The various activities were each designated a department of the guild with their own supervisors. The employment bureau found jobs in domestic services for those in need. The literature department distributed magazines and books to hospitals. The girls' club gave girls of all backgrounds access to social and educational programs. The motor corps transported patients and their families to hospitals. Institutional visitors made sure that patients without families had visitors. The colored mission worked within the black community. The USO cooperated with the guild. Services were also provided by the guild's visiting nurse, legal aid, and day nursery departments.

The Sisters of the Holy Infancy of Jesus staffed the Home Health Nursing Unit from 1941 to 1975. Sisters of Mercy of New Jersey were executive secretaries from 1969 to 1985. A Sister of Charity of Saint Elizabeth currently serves as executive secretary. A Dominican Sister of Amityville is a case worker. A Sister of Mercy is supervisor of the Emergency Assistance Program. Past moderators for Mount Carmel Guild have been Msgr. John H. Fox, Rev. Michael P. McCorristin, Rev. Thomas A. Kearney, Msgr. Richard T. Crean, and Rev. Theodore Opdenaker. Since 1987, the guild has been under the jurisdiction of the vicar for social services, Msgr. Joseph C. Shenrock. The guild is also a United Way agency.

On January 19, 1978, the guild's building was designated as a landmark by the Trenton Landmarks Commission by a resolution adopted by the city council. The building was chosen because it is one of Trenton's finest Italianate villas. The interior also contains some of Trenton's most elaborate mill and cabinet work.

Newman School, Lakewood

The Newman School had the distinction of being America's first preparatory school for boys under the patronage of the Roman Catholic Church but administered by laity. The school moved to Lakewood in 1920 and operated until 1942. At first it occupied two old Lakewood estates, those of Claflin and De Forest. Subsequently, the property was enhanced by contributions from wealthy Catholic lay people. To the older Locke Hall and Gibbons House were added MacDonald Hall, Kuser Hall, and the excellently equipped Raskob Gymnasium. The resident chaplain always celebrated daily mass in St. Cyril's Chapel when school was in session. The school's chaplains included Rev. Christopher Weldon, future bishop of Springfield, Massachusetts; Msgr. John Middleton, late pastor of Old St. Peter's in New York City; Scottish Benedictine Rev. Ninian MacDonald; and Rev. John Finnegan who had been trained at Louvain, Belgium.

Educationally, the school reached its apogee during the 1920s. Newman School had graduates living in thirty-eight states and nine foreign countries. Alumni performed successfully in such institutions of higher learning as Princeton, Harvard, Yale, MIT, Georgetown, Fordham, and Cambridge (England).

In Orange, New Jersey, the school's founder and first Catholic lay headmaster was Dr. Jesse A. Locke, formerly an Episcopalian. He was succeeded in Lakewood by Mr. Claude Delbos, who was responsible for the distinctly British flavor of Newman's pedagogical principles. Discipline was rigid, and high scholastic standards strictly enforced. Under Mr. W. Griffin Kelley, the school enjoyed a national reputation for excellence. During the brief incumbency of Mr. William Franklin, Coach Eddie Mahan, who had made football history at Harvard, arrived.

In September 1942, Newman School suddenly closed. Apparently, the Great Depression of the 1930s, the inability of the trustees to raise an endowment, and the advent of World War II were contributors. The building was then leased to the U.S. Navy.

Principals: Dr. Jesse A. Locke, Mr. Claude Delbos, Mr. W. Griffin Kelley, Mr. William Franklin, Dr. William M. Agar, Mr. Xavier Prum, Mr. Paul de Rosay, Mr. Henry MacDonald.

Saint Elizabeth Home, Yardville

As regional superior of the Servants of the Holy Infancy of Jesus, Mother Mary Praxedis Zirkelbach, O.S.F., longed to establish a home for the original work and purpose of the congregation: the physical and spiritual welfare of wayward girls and women. Mother Praxedis, a social worker by profession, saw a great need to establish a home for unmarried mothers and their infants. The Most Rev. William A. Griffin shared her vision, as there was a great need at that time for a place of refuge, a place to protect a young, unwed mother's reputation. Several miles outside of Trenton, an ideal location found in Yardville was purchased by the congrega-

Saint Elizabeth Home, Yardville

tion in 1943. This building served as a convent for 5 sisters and as a residence for 14 pregnant teens and young women. As the demand grew, it became necessary to build a larger residence in 1960. After being blessed by the Most Rev. George W. Ahr, the new St. Elizabeth's Home opened its doors, able to accommodate 40 mothers and their infants. This ministry flourished until 1973, when the Supreme Court legalized abortion, and the view of society changed regarding pregnant unmarried women. During those years, over 4,000 infants and more than 3,000 mothers had passed through St. Elizabeth's Home. About 1975, another ministry was sought. This coincided with government revamping of institutions for mentally handicapped adult women. The 9 sisters stationed there care for 30 adults and conduct a much needed and flourishing ministry.

Superiors: Sr. Mary Eulogia Durschang, O.S.F., 1943–48; Sr. Mary Febronia Fries, O.S.F., 1948–54; Sr. Mary Valentiana Hall,

O.S.F., 1954–64, 1966–71, 1977–84; Sr. Mary Regis Bauer, O.S.F., 1964–66; Sr. Mary Melitta Koeth, O.S.F., 1971–77; Sr. Mary Hortensia Schng, O.S.F., 1984–present.

Saint Francis Medical Center, Trenton

In 1869, 3 Sisters of St. Francis of Philadelphia—Sr. Mary Hyacintha, O.S.F.; Sr. Mary Veronica, O.S.F.; and Sr. Mary Pancratia, O.S.F.—arrived in Trenton to open a school for St. Francis of Assisium Parish. Shortly after their arrival, Sr. Hyacintha, the foundress, recognized the need for a hospital in the city. The sisters began a house-to-house appeal for funds. They acquired property at Hamilton Avenue and Chambers Street for the hospital.

The cornerstone was laid on October 15, 1871, and on May 31, 1874, the institution was opened with a dedication by the Most Rev. Michael A. Corrigan, bishop of Newark. The original building cost $38,000. In the first annual report, the hospital was described as "an imposing brick structure, 86 by 54 feet, with four stories and an attic." There were thirty-eight rooms with fifty to sixty beds. During the first year, 98 patients were admitted.

The first of many expansion programs began in 1879. In 1890, a new chapel was built and dedicated. On April 28, 1895, the cornerstone of a new wing was laid, and on September 17, 1896, the new annex was blessed by the Most Rev. James A. McFaul. The addition housed a dispensary, laboratory, pharmacy, operating room, X-ray room, and surgical wards and rooms for patients. On January 4, 1903, Mr. Charles G. Roebling purchased land on Chambers Street and St. Francis Avenue extending back to Bert Avenue. He gave the deed to St. Francis Hospital, and construction of another new wing began on June 13, 1903.

In April 1905, Mr. Roebling gave the hospital $20,000, the largest unsolicited gift it had ever received. The state of New Jersey issued a charter for the new St. Francis Hospital Training School for Nurses.

In 1921, with funds raised by Mrs. Rosalie Kuser; her daughter, Mrs. Joseph E. Ribsam; and the newly founded St. Francis

Saint Francis Medical Center, Trenton

Aid, another wing was built, bringing the bed capacity to 225. In 1925, as the number of patients admitted approached 5,000 per year, the hospital opened its first official fund drive. With Mrs. Ribsam, president of the Aid, spearheading the drive, $600,000 was raised, exceeding the goal by $100,000. The funds were used for construction of a four-story brick and tile structure, facing Hamilton Avenue. It contained four operating room suites, a pathology laboratory, a cystoscopy room, a cast room, a physiotherapy department, and what was called the accident department. The building also housed administrative offices and ancillary testing services.

Following World War II, the hospital looked again at the possibility of expansion; in 1954, the eight-story North Wing was opened. In 1957, the School of Nursing's Crean Hall opened. Growing still, the hospital added the South Wing in 1964, which provided more patient beds and established an intensive care unit.

Rapidly changing technology and expansion of services were the focus of hospital growth starting in the 1960s. In the late 1970s, a long-range-planning committee developed a comprehensive design for the future of St. Francis Medical Center. In 1979, the state commissioner of health approved a new building program. The additions included a five-level parking garage, which opened in 1981. The four-story Clinical Building was dedicated in 1982 and houses an extensive radiology department, outpatient clinics, an emergency department, a ten-suite operating room complex, and a new intensive care unit. Also in 1982, the Service Building was opened with a 360-seat cafeteria, a new kitchen, a general receiving area, an instrument decontamination room, general storage space, and a supply, processing, and distribution department.

Today, the 436-bed St. Francis Medical Center is Trenton's largest acute care teaching hospital. It is one of eleven Catholic health care facilities in the Franciscan Health System, a national holding company of the Sisters of St. Francis of Philadelphia. From two departments staffed by 4 physicians, St. Francis has grown to comprise a staff of more than 200 active members and thirty-four medical and surgical departments. Through its health ministry, St. Francis Medical Center continues the mission begun in 1874 to provide compassionate, high-quality, holistic care in the tradition of St. Francis of Assisi.

Saint Lawrence Rehabilitation Center, Lawrenceville

The center received its first patient on April 26, 1971, and was dedicated by the Most Rev. George W. Ahr on May 22, 1971. St. Lawrence Rehabilitation Center is a 152-bed, fully accredited specialty hospital providing comprehensive physical rehabilitation and short-term skilled nursing services to the central New Jersey area. Originally Morris Hall Health and Rehabilitation Center, the facility had a licensed capacity of 203 beds, 50 for rehabilitation and 153 for skilled nursing services (long-term care).

In 1983, because of increased demand for rehabilitation services, the center re-ceived permission for temporary conversion of twenty-six beds from long-term-care use to rehabilitation use. The center formally submitted a Certificate of Need to make these twenty-six beds permanent for rehabilitation. Consequently, St. Lawrence continued its operations, with seventy-six beds for comprehensive rehabilitation use and sixty-six beds for short-term skilled nursing. In November 1990, the department of health granted approval for an expansion of ten beds, bringing the total number of rehabilitation beds to eighty-six.

The center employs 395 full- and part-time staff members, who provide a wide range of inpatient and outpatient rehabilitation programs and services, including brain injury rehabilitation, chronic pain management, burn care services, and respite care.

Chief Executive Officers: Sr. Marie Cecilia Irwin, O.S.F., 1968–75; Mr. Thomas O'Malley, 1975–76; Sr. Joseph Antoine, 1977–79; Mr. Martin Idler, 1980–86; Sr. Janet Henry, R.S.M., 1986–91; Mr. Charles Brennan, 1991–present.

Saint Michael's Children's Home, Hopewell

The Most Rev. Michael J. O'Farrell opened St. Mary's Home in New Brunswick in 1892. However, the home became too small to accommodate the increasing number of dependent children in the diocese. Therefore, Bishop O'Farrell purchased the Van Dyke farm, 464 acres on the outskirts of Hopewell Borough. He had planned the erection of a diocesan children's home, but death claimed him on April 2, 1894. In his

Saint Michael's Children's Home, Hopewell

Mary de Sales, O.S.F., superior, arrived with 4 sisters and 80 children from St. Mary's Home, New Brunswick.

Because of the increasing population and the demand for child placement, Bishop McFaul organized St. Michael's Aid Society to undertake the work of supervising institutional and foster home placement. Several additions were made to the original building, including a chapel, erected in 1905 as a memorial to Bishop O'Farrell, who had planned St. Michael's. Bishop McFaul had a crypt installed in the sanctuary, and in July 1906, the remains of Bishop O'Farrell were placed there.

In 1914, the north wing, or baby building, was erected. A spacious gymnasium was erected in 1922. Under the direction of Rev. John J. West, chaplain between 1919 and 1926, St. Michael's Band became popular because of its high quality. In 1931, the Most Rev. John J. McMahon appealed to the diocese for funds for a separate building for boys. The building was constructed in that same year. In 1941, the Most Rev. William A. Griffin launched an extensive program for improvements. Soon after, Bishop Griffin reorganized St. Michael's Aid Society, creating the Catholic Welfare Bureau, which became the central agency for all diocesan charitable and welfare activities. It was renamed Catholic Charities in 1988.

St. Michael's Orphanage was also a grammar school. Both "home kids" from the orphanage and "town kids" from St. Alphonsus Parish, Hopewell, attended the school. The pastors of St. Alphonsus served

will he bequeathed $60,000 of his estate to form the nucleus of the fund that would build the institution. The building fund was increased by $50,000 through the generous contribution of Bishop O'Farrell's friend Colonel Daniel Morris, who died on December 2, 1898.

In 1897, the Most Rev. James A. McFaul decided there were sufficient funds to begin construction. He turned the first spadeful of earth on October 18, 1897. Bishop McFaul blessed the completed initial structure on May 20, 1898. The care of St. Michael's Orphan Asylum and Industrial Home was entrusted to the Sisters of St. Francis of Glen Riddle, Pennsylvania. On July 2, 1898, Sr.

as chaplains. In fact, they resided at St. Michael's until a rectory was completed in 1940.

On May 13, 1973, the Most Rev. George W. Ahr announced that St. Michael's Children's Home would close on June 29, 1973. He stated:

> Contrary to common belief, St. Michael's is not today a home for orphans. In fact, there have been no orphans at the home since 1955. Because of national trends in adoptions, as well as other factors, St. Michael's now accommodates 48 wards of the state, from 6 to 14 years of age, whose average stay is eighteen months. The Home has a capacity of 450. Its population has dropped from 418 in 1943 to 56 today.

Bishop Ahr indicated that the deficit created by running the home was increasing tremendously and that necessary, yet insufficient, renovations would cost a million dollars. Also, enrollment in the school had decreased to only a couple of dozen because most of the home kids required special education through the public school system. After considering all options, including discussions with state officials, it was deemed best to allocate the money more efficiently to other charitable causes in the diocese. Bishop Ahr expressed his deep gratitude to the Sisters of St. Francis and the volunteers who had served St. Michael's faithfully for so many years.

Superiors/Principals: Sr. Mary de Sales Hoffman, O.S.F., 1898–1913; Sr. Mary Edigna McGlinchey, O.S.F., 1913–28; Sr. Mary Benedict Labre Otterbach, O.S.F., three years between 1913 and 1929; Sr. Mary Gildara McHugh, O.S.F., 1929–31; Sr. Mary Cornelius Stanzel, O.S.F., 1931–37; Sr. Mary Amanda Post, O.S.F., 1938–41; Sr. Mary Cherubina Hyland, O.S.F., 1941–47; Sr. Mary Wilberta Klepsis, O.S.F., 1947–51; Sr. Mary Clarinda Golden, O.S.F., 1952–67; Sr. Mary Ulrich Marx, O.S.F., 1968–70; Sr. Anthony Marie Earls, O.S.F., 1971–73.

Sister Georgine Learning Center for Exceptional Children, Trenton

Sr. Georgine Wohnhaas, O.S.F., a Glen Riddle Franciscan, was for many years a teacher in elementary education. In 1965, at the request of the Most Rev. George W. Ahr, she ventured out to St. Coletta's in Milwaukee, Wisconsin, to begin training in the area of religious education of the mentally handicapped.

The first religious education class for the mentally handicapped in Trenton opened in 1966 in Immaculate Conception Parish, Trenton. Sister Georgine and many volunteers conducted Saturday religion classes. Students not only learned about God but also were enjoying music, art, storytelling, and printing. It was evident that the children were learning more in their Saturday classes than in the special classes they attended at the local public school.

With the encouragement and backing of the parents of these children, Sister Georgine proceeded to request that a day school be started to educate the mentally handicapped in a Catholic school setting. With the blessing of Bishop Ahr; Sr. Euthalia, O.S.F., Provincial; Rev. Timothy Lyons, pastor of

Immaculate Conception; and Msgr. Thomas J. Frain, superintendent of Catholic schools, Sister Georgine opened the first full-time day class for the mentally handicapped in Immaculate Conception Grammar School. Sr. Marie Anthony, O.S.F., principal of Immaculate, graciously found room in the grammar school to house the class.

The school, known as Diocesan Learning Center, opened with 7 students in September 1969. The dream of many parents of handicapped children had come true. Sister Georgine was determined that these special children were capable of learning and becoming active members of society. The students were using basic readers, doing math, singing, speaking French, conversing, acting, playing the organ, and learning about God and His goodness. At that particular time, such achievement in the education of the handicapped was rare. Sister Georgine, with patience, effort, and determination, made the Diocesan Learning Center a place where people came to observe the progress of these special children.

Due to the growth of the school to 12 students, a second class was started in 1971. Because of lack of space in the grammar school, Sister Georgine moved one class to St. Ann's Convent. Sr. Barbara Furst, O.S.F., became the new teacher of the class at Immaculate.

Early in the 1971–72 school year, Sister Georgine was stricken with leukemia. Both classes were combined at Immaculate. Sister recovered and felt positive. In 1972, through the graciousness of Monsignor Frain and the sisters of St. Ann's, the school was moved into the convent. The parents worked tirelessly in remodeling a part of the convent into classrooms. The school's population increased to 17.

In 1973, the first lay teacher was hired. There were now three classes and 19 students. However, Sister Georgine's health deteriorated, and she was confined to a hospital bed for most of the year. Still, she constantly planned for the children and encouraged all to strive to do their best. On August 31, 1974, Sister Georgine died from leukemia. The school continued, moving back to Immaculate Conception during the summer of 1975. Two sisters and 4 lay teachers staffed the school of 28 students. In honor of Sister Georgine, the name of the school was changed to Sister Georgine Learning Center for Exceptional Children.

The school was formally approved by the state of New Jersey in 1977 as a private school for the handicapped. This action allowed local public school districts to refer students to the school. Prior to the approval, parents had been completely responsible for tuition.

At present, classes at the center consist of 4–8 students each. Each class is staffed by a certified special education teacher and a full-time teaching assistant. The Learning Center includes support staff who are all state certified in their area of specialization. The low student-teacher ratio fosters individualized attention.

The center's curriculum is specifically designed to meet the special needs and interests of students. It places emphasis on the skills that are critical for personal independence and productive living. Areas of study and training include functional academics, fundamental processes, language/communication, independent living, community living, safety, family life, and prevocational training. The curriculum guide is evaluated annually and updated when innovations in programs warrant change. In an effort to assist students in achieving their maximum potential, the Learning Center also offers the following services: speech/language therapy, occupational therapy, health education, adapted physical education, woodshop, library education, recreational activities, training for Special Olympics, testing and evaluation, health services, and field trips.

The school is associated with Trenton State College in the training of student teachers. The Sister Georgine Learning Center continues to give students between the ages of 5 and 21 years the opportunity to become independent, self-sufficient, moral, and useful members of society according to their abilities. Sr. Barbara Furst, O.S.F., is the current principal.

SOURCES

A majority of the information was provided by the institutions themselves. Certain details were obtained from the parishes and religious communities. Rev. Walter T. Leahy's book *The Catholic Church of the Diocese of Trenton, N.J.,* published by Princeton University Press in 1906, was a minor source. The information about St. Michael's Children's Home was obtained from the file at *The Monitor*'s offices. The history of the Newman School appears in diocesan archives.

A P P E N D I X A

VICARS-GENERAL
OF THE DIOCESE
OF TRENTON

Very Rev. Anthony Smith, V.G. 1881–88

Very Rev. John A. Kelly, V.G. 1888–91

Very Rev. James A. McFaul, V.G. 1892–94

Rt. Rev. Msgr. John H. Fox, V.G., P.A. 1900–28

Rt. Rev. Msgr. Maurice Spillane, V.G., P.A. 1929–38

Rt. Rev. Msgr. Thomas U. Reilly, V.G., P.A. 1938–53

Rt. Rev. Msgr. Richard T. Crean, V.G., P.A. 1953–56

Rt. Rev. Msgr. Michael P. McCorristin, V.G., P.A. 1956–80

Most Rev. John C. Reiss, V.G., J.C.D. 1969–80

Most Rev. Edward U. Kmiec, V.G. 1982–92

Rev. Msgr. George E. Everitt, V.G. 1980–present

V.G. = Vicar-General
P.A. = Protonotary Apostolic
J.C.D. = Doctor of Canon Law

APPENDIX B

NECROLOGY OF PRIESTS OF THE DIOCESE OF TRENTON

Rev. James Carney	Sept. 8, 1860	Rev. Richard Kerr	May 24, 1902
Rev. Michael A. Madden	May 19, 1868	Rev. Joseph Thurnes	June 7, 1902
Rev. John P. Mackin	Mar. 27, 1873	Rev. Bartholomew Carey	Mar. 20, 1903
Rev. Peter P. Niederhauser	Aug. 16, 1873	Rev. Joseph Wust	July 27, 1905
Rev. John Betani	Oct. 14, 1882	Rev. Thomas B. Nolan	Sept. 21, 1905
Rev. John Rogers	July 10, 1887	Rev. William P. Treacy	Apr. 6, 1906
Rev. Anthony Smith	Aug. 11, 1888	Rev. William J. O'Farrell	Nov. 30, 1906
Rev. William H. Oranus	Apr. 15, 1889	Rev. Thomas J. McLaughlin	Jan. 30, 1907
Rev. Henry Martins	June 21, 1889	Rev. Michael J. Brennan	May 31, 1909
Rev. James A. Walsh	Dec. 22, 1889	Rev. Thomas B. Healy	Dec. 9, 1910
Rev. Msgr. John A. Kelly	Feb. 27, 1891	Rev. Patrick J. Powers	May 1, 1913
Rev. Michael E. Kane	Apr. 4, 1891	Rev. Edmond J. Gonch	Jan. 14, 1914
Rev. Thomas Degnan	Sept. 21, 1891	Rev. James J. Heaney	Mar. 4, 1914
Rev. Joseph Smith	Oct. 30, 1891	Rev. Stephen Lyons	Apr. 2, 1914
Most Rev. Michael J. O'Farrell	Apr. 2, 1894	Rev. James A. Reynolds	May 25, 1914
Rev. John J. O'Connor	Oct. 30, 1894	Rev. William H. Miller	Sept. 14, 1914
Rev. Nicholas Freeman	Sept. 9, 1895	Rev. Patrick Hanley	Nov. 7, 1914
Rev. Daniel P. Geoghan	Jan. 15, 1896	Rev. Msgr. Patrick F. Connolly	Jan. 4, 1915
Rev. John H. Kenny	Jan. 24, 1897	Rev. Martin van den Bogaard	July 20, 1915
Rev. Stanislaus Danielou	Apr. 2, 1897		
Rev. Secundino Pattle	May 1, 1897	Rev. Patrick J. Quinn	Aug. 9, 1916
Rev. Peter Dernis	Oct. 29, 1897	Rev. James F. Morrison	Aug. 26, 1916
Rev. John G. Murphy	Nov. 25, 1897	Rev. Msgr. Bernard T. O'Connell	Feb. 28, 1917
Rev. John M. McCloskey	Oct. 22, 1898		
Rev. Joseph F. Flanagan	Jan. 7, 1899	Most Rev. James A. McFaul	June 16, 1917
Rev. Msgr. Thomas R. Moran	Mar. 29, 1900	Rev. Msgr. John A. O'Grady	Jan. 15, 1918
Rev. Michael A. O'Reilly	Apr. 6, 1900	Rev. John A. Graham	Jan. 21, 1918
Rev. Michael E. Glennon	Oct. 15, 1900	Rev. Msgr. John F. Brady	Feb. 2, 1918
Rev. William F. Dunphy	Oct. 8, 1901		

Rev. John Supinski	Feb. 9, 1918	Rev. Michael Dolan	July 18, 1931
Rev. Msgr. Thaddeus Hogan	Mar. 18, 1918	Rev. Michael C. McCorristin	Nov. 30, 1931
Rev. James A. Healy	Mar. 24, 1918	Rev. John Gammell	Mar. 8, 1932
Rev. John A. Lawrence	Apr. 22, 1918	Rev. James E. Gough	July 26, 1932
Rev. James F. Divine	June 9, 1918	Rev. Richard J. O'Farrell	Oct. 5, 1932
Rev. John W. Murphy	June 12, 1918	Most Rev. John J. McMahon	Dec. 31, 1932
Rev. John J. Griffin	Sept. 30, 1918	Rev. Martin F. Casey	Apr. 23, 1933
Rev. James J. Powers	Oct. 24, 1918	Rev. Thomas F. Kearns	July 13, 1933
Rev. Joseph Keuper	Apr. 16, 1919	Rev. Columbino Galassi	Oct. 19, 1933
Rev. John J. Kerr	May 7, 1919	Rev. Louis Guzzardi	Nov. 26, 1933
Rev. Michael J. Hagerty	July 20, 1919	Rev. Msgr. Edward J. Egan	Dec. 10, 1933
Rev. John M. Szeneczey	Feb. 16, 1920	Rev. John H. Sheedy	Jan. 1, 1934
Rev. Peter Dermis	May 16, 1920	Rev. Msgr. Peter S. Petri	Mar. 12, 1934
Rev. Thomas J. O'Hanlon	Sept. 17, 1920	Rev. Henry W. Russi	July 7, 1934
Rev. Robert F. Burke	July 2, 1922	Rev. James A. Regney	Aug. 21, 1934
Rev. Michael C. O'Donnell	Feb. 3, 1923	Rev. John J. Leonard	Nov. 26, 1934
Rev. Felice Morelli	June 18, 1923	Rev. Thomas F. Maher	Dec. 27, 1934
Rev. Denis S. Kelly	Sept. 27, 1923	Rev. Msgr. Henry Ward	Dec. 31, 1934
Rev. Joseph J. Zimmer	Oct. 9, 1923	Rev. Msgr. Joseph C. Urban	Jan. 10, 1935
Rev. Aurelius Poli	Dec. 31, 1923	Rev. Andrew Szostakowski	Jan. 12, 1935
Rev. Louis A. Schneider	Aug. 16, 1924	Rev. Msgr. Joseph A. McGrath	Mar. 23, 1935
Rev. John J. Grady	Sept. 20, 1924	Rev. Francis X. Langan	Jan. 13, 1936
Rev. John A. Carroll	Oct. 1, 1924	Rev. Louis C. Andler	Mar. 25, 1936
Rev. B. A. Calewski	Oct. 3, 1924	Rev. Eugene P. Hunt	Nov. 12, 1936
Rev. Peter B. Carr	Oct. 10, 1924	Rev. Lawrence J. Travers	Dec. 31, 1936
Rev. Julian Zielinski	Nov. 24, 1924	Rev. Frederick Kimball	Jan. 5, 1937
Rev. William P. Tighe	May 3, 1925	Rev. Thomas F. Rudden	Feb. 13, 1937
Rev. Msgr. Denis J. Duggan	Oct. 25, 1925	Rev. Charles R. Prendegast	Feb. 21, 1937
Rev. Msgr. William P. Cantwell	Mar. 27, 1926	Rev. Matthew P. Waldron	Apr. 14, 1937
Rev. Neil McManamin	May 13, 1926	Rev. John J. McGrath	May 11, 1937
Rev. Joseph Rathner	Nov. 22, 1926	Rev. Msgr. Aloysius Pozzi	May 22, 1937
Rev. James F. Hendrick	Apr. 10, 1928	Rev. Joseph A. Leddy	Oct. 25, 1937
Rev. Msgr. John W. Norris	May 8, 1928	Rev. Richard T. Ryan	Nov. 18, 1937
Rev. Joseph F. Hughes	July 9, 1928	Rev. John R. O'Connor	Jan. 8, 1938
Rev. Aladar Kiss	July 26, 1928	Rev. Francis J. Quinn	Apr. 12, 1938
Rev. John Pawlowski	Nov. 2, 1928	Rev. Walter T. Leahy	June 4, 1938
Rev. Msgr. John H. Fox	Dec. 25, 1928	Rev. Msgr. William F. Dittrich	June 21, 1938
Rev. Richard A. Crean	Dec. 26, 1928	Rev. Alexius H. Rogovszky	Nov. 14, 1938
Rev. John A. Sullivan	Sept. 5, 1929	Rev. John L. Meerwald	Apr. 30, 1939
Rev. Joseph A. Linnane	Sept. 14, 1929	Rev. Leo E. Dineen	Feb. 5, 1940
Rev. Joseph A. Ryan	Sept. 19, 1929	Rev. Leopold Mosonyi	Mar. 29, 1940
Rev. James H. Farrington	Dec. 13, 1929	Rev. John E. Murray	Nov. 11, 1940
Rev. Msgr. Frederick Kivelitz	Apr. 24, 1930	Rev. Thomas M. Healy	Nov. 23, 1940
Rev. Anthony Klyanowicz	Apr. 2, 1931	Rev. Alfonso Palombi	Mar. 25, 1941

Rev. Msgr. Thomas A. Roche	May 7, 1941	Rev. Msgr. William J.	
Rev. Edward J. Heil	June 10, 1941	McConnell	Nov. 20, 1950
Rev. Msgr. Edward C. Griffin	June 11, 1941	Rev. William J. Brennan	Jan. 28, 1951
Rev. Leo S. Schwarze	June 30, 1941	Rev. John P. McKeon	Apr. 29, 1951
Rev. James J. Egan	July 13, 1941	Rev. Charles J. Farren	June 28, 1951
Rev. Francis Czernecki	Oct. 11, 1941	Rev. James G. Harding	July 8, 1951
Rev. Thomas A. Kearney	Nov. 6, 1941	Rev. Msgr. Linus A. Schwarze	May 3, 1952
Rev. Msgr. John F. Sweeney	Feb. 28, 1942	Most Rev. Thomas J. Walsh	June 6, 1952
Rev. George D. Quigley	June 18, 1942	Rev. Frederick J. Halloran	July 9, 1952
Rev. Neil A. Mooney	July 9, 1942	Rev. Edward McAndrews	Aug. 10, 1952
Rev. Peter J. Kelley	Oct. 5, 1942	Rev. Msgr. William I. McKean	Aug. 28, 1952
Rev. Victor Mylnarski	Jan. 17, 1943	Most Rev. Moses E. Kiley	Apr. 15, 1953
Rev. Joseph N. Szabo	June 15, 1943	Rev. John C. Farrell	July 28, 1953
Rev. Antony C. Shuvlin	Nov. 5, 1943	Rev. Thomas A. Kane	Aug. 18, 1953
Rev. Nicholas Soriano	Dec. 1, 1943	Rev. Msgr. Thomas U. Reilly	Sept. 26, 1953
Rev. Joseph Dziadosz	Feb. 11, 1944	Rev. Amedeo Russo	Oct. 28, 1953
Rev. Charles A. Dusten	Apr. 5, 1944	Rev. Edward R. Sullivan	Dec. 12, 1954
Rev. John B. Conway	Apr. 13, 1944	Rev. Jeremiah B. Murphy	Mar. 14, 1955
Rev. John E. Canton	July 10, 1944	Rev. Daniel F. Houlihan	Apr. 1, 1955
Rev. Edward J. Whalen	Aug. 18, 1944	Rev. Robert J. Graham	Mar. 5, 1956
Rev. Msgr. John B. McCloskey	May 8, 1945	Rev. Msgr. Richard T. Crean	Mar. 14, 1956
Rev. Msgr. William A.		Rev. Patrick F. Larkin	June 10, 1956
Gilfillan	Nov. 11, 1945	Rev. D. A. Simcoe	June 12, 1956
Rev. Francis X. Degnan	Mar. 29, 1946	Rev. Joseph M. Sutliff	June 29, 1956
Rev. Gerard Cristiano	Apr. 11, 1946	Rev. John F. Budziak	July 16, 1956
Rev. James A. Sheridan	May 5, 1947	Rev. John F. Walsh	Sept. 4, 1956
Rev. Thomas F. Hennessy	June 6, 1947	Rev. Msgr. George A. Welsh	Nov. 26, 1956
Rev. Msgr. Patrick J. Clune	Nov. 15, 1947	Rev. Leo M. Cox	Feb. 27, 1957
Rev. John J. West	Dec. 14, 1947	Rev. Peter Wieczorek	Mar. 12, 1957
Rev. Msgr. Coloman		Rev. Joseph F. Ketter	Aug. 17, 1957
Tomchany	Jan. 29, 1948	Rev. Lawrence Horvath	Sept. 13, 1957
Rev. Cornelius P. McGonigle	Apr. 4, 1948	Rev. Edward J. Draus	Oct. 15, 1957
Rev. Msgr. Edward J. Dunphy	May 3, 1948	Rev. Thomas H. Massey	Nov. 4, 1957
Rev. Msgr. Michael H.		Rev. Andrew J. Sakson	July 14, 1959
Callahan	May 14, 1948	Rev. Thomas A. Gribbin	Oct. 24, 1959
Rev. Alexander Bor	Feb. 4, 1949	Rev. Walter Greene	Jan. 8, 1960
Rev. Msgr. Edward A. Cahill	May 11, 1949	Rev. Ceslaus M. Jasionowski	Jan. 30, 1960
Rev. Msgr. John E. Rura	Oct. 20, 1949	Rev. Edward J. Shelley	Mar. 12, 1960
Rev. Joseph F. Mahoney	Oct. 20, 1949	Rev. Laszlo Szarvady	Mar. 28, 1960
Rev. Msgr. Peter J. Hart	Nov. 20, 1949	Rev. Msgr. Francis M. J.	
Rev. James P. O'Sullivan	Dec. 15, 1949	Thornton	Apr. 20, 1960
Most Rev. William A. Griffin	Jan. 1, 1950	Rev. Albert A. Tomaszewski	May 3, 1960
Rev. John A. Scheja	Jan. 26, 1950	Rev. John F. Thompson	Nov. 3, 1960
Rev. Thomas M. Flaherty	July 9, 1950	Rev. Alexander F. Maciejewski	Nov. 20, 1961
Rev. John P. Burke	Aug. 4, 1950	Rev. Joseph J. Donnelly	Dec. 9, 1961

Rev. William H. Murray	Mar. 7, 1962	Rev. Francis V. McCusker	Jan. 4, 1970
Rev. William F. Quinn	May 20, 1962	Rev. Ladislaus J. Petrick	Jan. 18, 1970
Rev. Msgr. Francis J. Yunger	June 17, 1962	Rev. Msgr. John J. Foley	May 22, 1970
Rev. Stephen J. Bulvidas	Aug. 31, 1962	Rev. John P. Adamowski	July 11, 1970
Rev. George E. Duff	Oct. 25, 1962	Rev. Msgr. John E. Kelly	Sept. 28, 1970
Rev. Joseph S. Keefe	Nov. 19, 1962	Rev. Msgr. William J. Lannary	Oct. 12, 1970
Rev. Thomas M. Midura	Nov. 19, 1962	Rev. John L. Callahan	Nov. 8, 1970
Rev. William A. Barron	July 23, 1963	Rev. Msgr. Joseph V. Kozak	Apr. 7, 1971
Rev. Msgr. John A. Kucker	Sept. 25, 1963	Rev. Msgr. Pasquale Mugnano	Apr. 12, 1971
Rev. Bernard Carlin	Apr. 7, 1964	Rev. M. A. Konopka	May 5, 1971
Rev. Joseph Doran	Apr. 15, 1964	Rev. Pasquale Parente	Aug. 9, 1971
Rev. Msgr. John F. Baldwin	May 14, 1964	Rev. Lewis A. Hayes	Sept. 22, 1971
Rev. Julius A. Kish	June 15, 1964	Rev. Thomas E. Carney	Oct. 20, 1971
Rev. Msgr. John Goch	July 30, 1964	Rev. Edward A. Corrigan	Oct. 30, 1971
Rev. John F. Welsh	Oct. 9, 1964	Rev. John P. Wessel	Dec. 26, 1971
Rev. Msgr. Zenon Lesniowski	Jan. 9, 1965	Rev. Daniel J. Sullivan	Dec. 30, 1971
Rev. Msgr. William P. Leahy	July 26, 1965	Rev. John A. Dzema	Jan. 17, 1972
Rev. Francis X. Donovan	Sept. 7, 1965	Rev. Wilfrid B. Emmons	Feb. 2, 1972
Rev. Edward C. Mannion	Nov. 14, 1965	Rev. John J. Mackin	June 14, 1972
Rev. J. Arthur Hayes	Jan. 14, 1966	Rev. Msgr. Joseph A. Mulligan	Aug. 21, 1972
Rev. Louis F. Cogan	Jan. 22, 1966	Rev. William H. McKenna	Oct. 18, 1972
Rev. Stephen G. Fech	Feb. 25, 1966	Rev. Msgr. John J. O'Hara	Nov. 12, 1972
Rev. Vincent S. Lenyi	Apr. 4, 1966	Rev. Raymond R. Griffin	Jan. 7, 1973
Rev. Msgr. Charles G. McCorristin	Apr. 12, 1966	Rev. Msgr. Joseph A. Sullivan	Mar. 28, 1973
Rev. Francis X. McGuinness	June 4, 1966	Rev. Joseph W. McLaughlin	June 12, 1973
Rev. Michael F. O'Keefe	July 7, 1966	Rev. Msgr. Francis J. Sullivan	July 11, 1973
Rev. Joseph Halaburda	Nov. 18, 1966	Rev. Chester C. Genecki	Nov. 12, 1973
Rev. Paul A. Cartier	Feb. 12, 1967	Rev. Msgr. Joseph T. Casey	Jan. 31, 1974
Rev. Thomas T. Barry	Feb. 24, 1967	Rev. Stephen A. Buszka	May 7, 1974
Rev. Msgr. Joseph P. Sergel	Feb. 27, 1967	Rev. Walter A. Radziwon	Aug. 1, 1974
Rev. James J. Duffy	Apr. 3, 1967	Rev. Msgr. Martin A. Madura	Aug. 19, 1974
Rev. Paul A. Grieco	June 1, 1967	Rev. Joseph J. Connelly	Aug. 26, 1974
Rev. Msgr. Francis A. Kasprowicz	June 25, 1967	Rev. Thomas B. Dennen	Aug. 29, 1974
Rev. Ignatius Bembenek	July 21, 1967	Rev. Alexander A. Burant	Oct. 20, 1974
Rev. Msgr. William J. Wrinn	Aug. 30, 1967	Rev. Richard McEwan	Aug. 9, 1975
Rev. Joseph S. Keenan	Sept. 29, 1967	Rev. Msgr. Peter J. Teston	Apr. 22, 1976
Rev. Paul J. Kane	Oct. 2, 1967	Rev. Stephen A. Rybacki	Sept. 25, 1976
Rev. James F. McGrath	Dec. 4, 1967	Rev. J. Paul Butler	Jan. 12, 1977
Rev. Charles P. Poltorak	Mar. 31, 1968	Rev. Charles I. LaCavera	Apr. 19, 1977
Rev. Thomas F. Nolan	Mar. 1, 1969	Rev. Msgr. Maximilian F. Wujek	Apr. 30, 1977
Rev. Mitchell J. Cetkowski	May 1, 1969	Rev. John J. Nowak	Sept. 19, 1977
Rev. Edward P. Blaska	July 6, 1969	Rev. Msgr. Thomas C. Ryan	Oct. 17, 1977
Rev. Msgr. Martin J. Lipinski	Aug. 24, 1969	Rev. Michael J. Bacso	Jan. 2, 1978
		Rev. Francis L. Nolan	Jan. 23, 1978

Rev. Anthony J. Huber	Feb. 28, 1978	Rev. William E. Barna	Mar. 19, 1986
Rev. Cornelius J. Kane	Mar. 23, 1978	Rev. John J. Meehan	June 28, 1986
Rev. Melvin J. Stanczewski	Aug. 14, 1978	Rev. Gerald J. Griffin	Aug. 30, 1986
Rev. Msgr. Walter F. Urbanik	Sept. 25, 1978	Rev. Francis P. Gunner	Nov. 24, 1986
Rev. Russell E. Loughman	Sept. 27, 1978	Rev. Stanislaus A. Milos	Jan. 9, 1987
Rev. John J. Reilly	Nov. 24, 1978	Rev. Msgr. Lawrence W.	
Rev. Joseph G. Olsovsky	Jan. 30, 1979	Donovan	Jan. 21, 1987
Rev. John W. McMullen	May 19, 1979	Rev. Paul T. Gluth	Jan. 26, 1987
Rev. Julian C. Rucki	Sept. 3, 1979	Rev. Msgr. John J. McGovern	May 2, 1987
Rev. Thomas J. O'Dea	Nov. 14, 1979	Rev. Msgr. Edward J. O'Keefe	Oct. 14, 1987
Rev. Ladislaus J. Madura	Feb. 13, 1980	Rev. Brian O'Reilly	Dec. 15, 1987
Rev. Msgr. Emmett A.		Rev. Joseph F. Sheehan	Feb. 28, 1988
Monahan	Mar. 23, 1980	Rev. Msgr. Michael J. Kseniak	Oct. 11, 1988
Rev. Henry A. Murphy	May 15, 1980	Rev. Joseph A. B. Wade	Nov. 20, 1988
Rev. Thomas I. Flynn	May 25, 1980	Rev. Michael M. Garry	Dec. 11, 1988
Rev. Walter T. Doyle	June 21, 1980	Rev. Peter P. Johnson	July 8, 1989
Rev. Arthur J. St. Laurent	Aug. 5, 1980	Rev. Msgr. James E. Harding	Oct. 1, 1989
Rev. James A. Russell	Nov. 13, 1980	Rev. Hugh F. McGovern	June 11, 1990
Rev. Nicholas C. Murphy	Dec. 15, 1980	Rev. Msgr. John E. Grimes	July 6, 1990
Rev. James A. Mackenzie	Aug. 3, 1981	Rev. Joseph T. Wade	Aug. 8, 1990
Rev. John J. Eagan	Dec. 7, 1981	Rev. Eugene Lenner	Oct. 18, 1990
Rev. John H. Horan	Aug. 8, 1982	Rev. Robert E. Leahey	Oct. 20, 1990
Rev. James A. Reilly	Sept. 25, 1982	Rev. Francis J. Piccolello	Oct. 23, 1990
Rev. Ladislaus J. Rakvicka	Oct. 20, 1982	Rev. Msgr. Salvatore R.	
Rev. Francis J. C. Janos	Nov. 29, 1982	DiLorenzo	Nov. 17, 1990
Rev. Mario A. Fralliciardi	Jan. 18, 1983	Rev. Msgr. Michael P.	
Rev. Msgr. Maurice P. Griffin	Apr. 2, 1983	McCorristin	Dec. 5, 1990
Rev. Msgr. William A.		Rev. Joseph G. Fox	Dec. 22, 1990
Margerum	June 6, 1983	Rev. Msgr. John T. Muthig	Jan. 6, 1991
Rev. Raymond T. Hurley	July 12, 1983	Rev. John J. Connelly	Oct. 29, 1991
Rev. Alexander Zadewicz	July 13, 1983	Rev. Msgr. Francis L.	
Rev. Michael F. Bakaisa	Sept. 4, 1983	Zgliczynski	Oct. 30, 1991
Rev. Gabriel Ivascu	Oct. 8, 1983	Rev. Msgr. Michael J. Lease	Nov. 6, 1991
Rev. Bernard A. Coen	Mar. 29, 1984	Rev. Peter J. Mooney	Nov. 21, 1991
Rev. Msgr. James T. Connell	Apr. 3, 1984	Rev. Joseph A. Doino	Dec. 30, 1991
Rev. John A. Spisak	June 20, 1984	Rev. Joseph R. Hughes	Jan. 7, 1992
Rev. Msgr. Charles A. McGee	Aug. 27, 1984	Rev. Gerald T. Celentana	Aug. 20, 1992
Rev. Eugene R. Scheg	Nov. 13, 1984	Rev. Edward W. Hughes	Aug. 23, 1992
Rev. Donald J. Reilly	Nov. 23, 1984	Rev. William J. Kokoszka	Sept. 2, 1992
Rev. Francis P. J. Coan	Feb. 10, 1985	Rev. Emanuel G. Gauci	Nov. 23, 1992
Rev. James F. Child	Apr. 16, 1985	Rev. John J. Churak	Mar. 22, 1993
Rev. William J. Bohnsack	Aug. 3, 1985	Rev. James B. Coyle	Apr. 2, 1993
Rev. Francis J. Lyons	Sept. 25, 1985	Most Rev. George W. Ahr	May 5, 1993
Rev. Francis J. Dwyer	Mar. 14, 1986	Rev. Donald E. Hickey	June 28, 1993

APPENDIX C

LIST OF PRIESTS OF THE DIOCESE OF TRENTON

	BORN	ORDAINED
Rev. Msgr. Emilio A. Cardelia (R*-6/81)	Jan. 14, 1906	Feb. 8, 1931
Rev. C. R. O'Shaughnessey (I**-8/23/60) (R-6/73)	Nov. 5, 1907	Feb. 7, 1932
Rev. Msgr. James S. Foley (R-11/77)	Aug. 3, 1908	May 21, 1932
Rev. Eugene V. Davis (R-10/81)	Dec. 27, 1910	Apr. 6, 1935
Rev. Joseph B. Miller (R-8/31/87)	Aug. 13, 1911	May 21, 1936
Rev. Msgr. Edward C. Henry (R-5/77)	Apr. 15, 1912	Mar. 13, 1937
Rev. Msgr. Edmund W. Kreger (R-5/81)	Apr. 6, 1911	Mar. 13, 1937
Rev. Edward P. Atzert (R-6/82)	June 3, 1912	May 1, 1937
Rev. Msgr. Bernard C. DeCoste (R-7/81)	May 29, 1909	May 1, 1937
Rev. Msgr. John M. Wilus (R-10/81)	Feb. 8, 1911	May 1, 1937
Rev. Stephen B. Getlik (R-11/84)	Feb. 10, 1911	June 22, 1937
Rev. Msgr. John J. Endebrock (R-12/82)	Dec. 15, 1912	Apr. 2, 1938
Rev. Thomas P. Ridge (R-1/81)	Jan. 22, 1911	Apr. 16, 1938

	BORN	ORDAINED
Rev. Msgr. Robert T. Bulman (R-4/92)	Nov. 17, 1913	July 27, 1940
Rev. Stephen G. Horvath (R-1/81)	Sept. 9, 1913	July 27, 1940
Rev. Msgr. Paul F. Bradley (R-7/7/89)	May 13, 1914	June 7, 1941
Rev. Charles A. Bulla (R-1/79)	Oct. 16, 1915	June 7, 1941
Rev. Ramon P. Farre (I-7/23/71) (R-9/81)	Aug. 7, 1916	Aug. 10, 1941
Rev. John P. Grabowski (R-6/76)	June 25, 1917	May 30, 1942
Rev. James F. Murphy (R-10/5/81)	Oct. 4, 1911	May 30, 1942
Rev. Anthony J. Pluta (R-5/11/79)	May 29, 1912	May 30, 1942
Rev. Joseph L. Remias (R-12/79)	June 8, 1915	May 30, 1942
Rev. Joseph S. Rucinski (R-10/15/86)	Dec. 6, 1915	May 30, 1942
Rev. Msgr. Thaddeus J. Wojciehowski (R-12/91)	May 30, 1916	May 30, 1942
Rev. Sigismund E. Zalewski (R-5/1/71)	Oct. 6, 1916	May 30, 1942
Rev. William J. Campbell (R-10/84)	July 1, 1914	June 19, 1943
Rev. Msgr. Theodore A. Opdenaker (R-7/1/88)	Sept. 2, 1917	June 19, 1943
Rev. George M. Albano (R-7/27/90)	May 25, 1915	June 3, 1944
Rev. Msgr. George E. Everitt, V.G.	Oct. 11, 1919	June 3, 1944
Rev. Francis J. Porazzo (R-4/12/88)	Apr. 12, 1918	June 3, 1944
Rev. Gerard S. Sloyan	Dec. 13, 1919	June 3, 1944
Rev. James A. Thompson (R-7/1/89)	Jan. 8, 1919	June 3, 1944
Rev. John P. Byrnes (R-83)	Sept. 7, 1916	Mar. 17, 1945
Rev. Frederick J. Clancy (R-12/85)	Dec. 11, 1915	Mar. 17, 1945
Rev. Earl A. Gannon (R-1/86)	Jan. 10, 1916	Mar. 17, 1945
Rev. Vincent A. Lloyd (R-5/86)	Jan. 27, 1914	Mar. 17, 1945

	BORN	ORDAINED
Rev. Msgr. Amedeo L. Morello	Dec. 20, 1920	Mar. 17, 1945
Rev. John C. Petri	Jan. 18, 1919	Mar. 17, 1945
(R-2/3/89)		
Rev. Anthony L. Capitani	Mar. 5, 1920	May 25, 1946
Rev. Robert P. Murray	July 13, 1918	May 25, 1946
(R-11/70)		
Rev. James E. Coley	Apr. 17, 1921	May 31, 1947
(R-8/31/90)		
Rev. Msgr. Joseph A. O'Connor	June 2, 1917	May 31, 1947
(R-6/92)		
Rev. Msgr. Henry J. Bogdan	Aug. 24, 1923	Mar. 13, 1948
Rev. Msgr. Thomas A. Coffey	Sept. 16, 1920	Mar. 13, 1948
(R-9/26/90)		
Rev. Msgr. Thomas J. Frain	Feb. 12, 1921	Mar. 13, 1948
Rev. Msgr. Leonard R. Toomey	Jan. 21, 1922	Mar. 13, 1948
(R-3/92)		
Rev. Laszlo F. Rauch	Sept. 12, 1926	Mar. 13, 1949
(I-3/23/82)		
Rev. Joseph A. Bischoff	Apr. 23, 1915	Apr. 2, 1949
(R-8/81)		
Rev. John B. Cook	May 3, 1922	Apr. 2, 1949
(R-6/92)		
Rev. John E. Sullivan	Aug. 26, 1916	Apr. 2, 1949
(R-12/13/75)		
Rev. Michael F. Venutolo	Oct. 17, 1918	Apr. 2, 1949
(R-4/30/87)		
Rev. James N. Cammisa	Feb. 7, 1914	May 26, 1949
(R-5/27/77)		
Rev. David G. Delzell	Aug. 4, 1924	June 3, 1950
Rev. Msgr. William E. Maguire	May 28, 1924	June 3, 1950
Rev. Msgr. Frederick A. Valentino	Jan. 19, 1925	June 3, 1950
Rev. Msgr. William F. Fitzgerald, P.A.	Jan. 21, 1926	June 28, 1950
Rev. Martin M. Komosinski	Sept. 21, 1926	May 19, 1951
Rev. Philip T. Matera	July 10, 1925	May 19, 1951
(R-10/1/88)		
Rev. William C. Anderson	Dec. 4, 1926	June 7, 1952
Rev. John J. Hendricks	July 28, 1927	June 7, 1952
(Working with S.S.J.)		
Rev. Msgr. Carl A. Wagner	Oct. 3, 1918	June 7, 1952
(R-3/11/87)		
Rev. Edward J. Dougherty	Nov. 19, 1925	May 30, 1953
Rev. William C. Eelman	Feb. 19, 1923	May 30, 1953
(R-3/1/93)		
Rev. Msgr. Joseph C. Shenrock	Oct. 4, 1926	May 30, 1953

	BORN	ORDAINED
Rev. Msgr. Alfred D. Smith	July 27, 1924	May 30, 1953
Rev. Arthur F. Conlon	Sept. 28, 1922	June 12, 1954
Rev. Adam T. Kearns	Sept. 17, 1928	June 12, 1954
Rev. James J. McConnell	July 23, 1926	June 12, 1954
Rev. Charles R. Valentine	Nov. 18, 1927	June 12, 1954
Rev. Harry E. Cenefeldt (I-1/13/71)	Nov. 14, 1927	Sept. 1, 1954
Rev. William J. Bausch	Mar. 3, 1928	June 4, 1955
Rev. Sebastian Carmel (I-12/14/88)	Nov. 10, 1927	June 4, 1955
Rev. Samuel C. Constance	July 31, 1923	June 4, 1955
Rev. Thomas J. O'Connor	Jan. 12, 1930	June 4, 1955
Rev. Joseph J. Miele	Aug. 15, 1925	May 26, 1956
Rev. Edward R. Strano	Sept. 3, 1929	May 26, 1956
Rev. William J. Dailey	July 31, 1931	May 25, 1957
Rev. George E. Deutsch	May 31, 1929	May 25, 1957
Rev. Robert T. Evers, S.S.	June 15, 1931	May 31, 1958
Rev. Justin J. Herbst	June 11, 1931	May 31, 1958
Rev. James J. McGovern	Feb. 29, 1932	May 31, 1958
Rev. Msgr. Armand A. Pedata	Aug. 30, 1932	May 31, 1958
Rev. Joseph J. Procaccini	May 14, 1932	May 31, 1958
Rev. Msgr. George A. Ardos	June 27, 1931	May 23, 1959
Rev. Msgr. James P. McManimon	May 31, 1933	May 23, 1959
Rev. William J. Carton	Aug. 20, 1933	Sept. 19, 1959
Rev. Manuel Fernández (I-8/24/78)	Apr. 23, 1935	Dec. 19, 1959
Rev. Matthew Adackapara (I-10/6/86)	Aug. 1, 1931	May 17, 1960
Rev. Evasio F. DeMarcellis	Dec. 3, 1934	June 11, 1960
Rev. James H. Forker	June 9, 1932	June 11, 1960
Rev. John J. Gibbons	Mar. 22, 1935	June 11, 1960
Rev. Msgr. Leo A. Kelty	Sept. 22, 1934	June 11, 1960
Rev. Louis W. Kralovich	Apr. 9, 1934	June 11, 1960
Rev. William J. Queenan, S.S.	Apr. 9, 1935	June 11, 1960
Rev. Henry F. Schabowski (I-3/23/82)	Mar. 26, 1934	June 11, 1960
Rev. Ernest J. Siska	Oct. 23, 1934	June 11, 1960
Rev. Lawrence K. Kunnel (I-4/4/90)	Jan. 25, 1933	Dec. 11, 1960
Rev. Hugh F. Ronan	Apr. 9, 1934	May 27, 1961
Rev. John V. Bowden	Nov. 21, 1936	May 26, 1962
Rev. Richard P. Brietske	Oct. 14, 1936	May 26, 1962
Rev. Patrick G. Fitzpatrick	Sept. 20, 1935	May 26, 1962

	BORN	ORDAINED
Rev. William P. Gardner	May 30, 1936	May 26, 1962
Rev. Msgr. Casimir H. Ladzinski	Mar. 4, 1937	May 26, 1962
Rev. Joseph A. Radomski	Feb. 10, 1935	May 26, 1962
Rev. Antony P. Poovakulam	Dec. 25, 1934	May 17, 1963
(I-12/14/88)		
Rev. James J. Sauchelli	Feb. 14, 1935	May 24, 1963
(I-12/20/79)		
Rev. William T. Schneider	June 29, 1938	Dec. 17, 1963
Rev. Rocco A. Cuomo	May 17, 1938	May 23, 1964
Rev. John G. DeSandre	Jan. 10, 1929	May 23, 1964
(I-3/22/90)		
Rev. James H. Dubell	Nov. 25, 1939	May 22, 1965
Rev. M. Joseph Mokrzycki	May 26, 1940	May 22, 1965
Rev. Eugene M. Rebeck	Feb. 12, 1938	May 22, 1965
Rev. James J. Roche	June 1, 1939	May 22, 1965
Rev. H. Brendan Williams	Dec. 3, 1940	June 20, 1965
Rev. Joseph M. LaForge	Feb. 18, 1937	Mar. 26, 1966
(I-5/28/75)		
Rev. Ronald J. Bacovin	May 28, 1940	May 28, 1966
Rev. Brian J. McCormick	Nov. 18, 1940	May 28, 1966
Rev. Francis E. Santitoro	Feb. 3, 1937	May 28, 1966
Rev. Charles B. Weiser	May 1, 1939	May 28, 1966
Rev. Henry A. Liguori (U.S.N.)	Sept. 30, 1940	June 8, 1966
(I-9/11/80)		
Rev. Thomas Brennan	June 1, 1931	June 11, 1966
Rev. Frank J. Iazzetta	Jan. 5, 1942	May 20, 1967
Rev. Terence O. McAlinden	Oct. 4, 1940	May 20, 1967
Rev. Anthony M. Carotenuto	Oct. 25, 1942	May 25, 1968
Rev. Msgr. John K. Dermond	Jan. 17, 1942	May 25, 1968
Rev. Michael S. Vona	Jan. 3, 1932	May 25, 1968
Rev. William J. Nolan	Aug. 15, 1939	May 17, 1969
(I-5/28/75)		
Rev. Patrick J. Castles	Apr. 14, 1943	May 31, 1969
Rev. Ronald J. Cioffi	Feb. 1, 1941	May 31, 1969
Rev. Peter J. Flood (U.S.A.F.)	Feb. 6, 1943	May 31, 1969
Rev. Casimir Milewski	Aug. 10, 1942	May 31, 1969
Rev. Walter E. Nolan	Apr. 14, 1933	May 31, 1969
Rev. Robert R. Schulze	June 21, 1943	May 31, 1969
Rev. John F. Campoli	Feb. 29, 1944	Apr. 4, 1970
Rev. Peter J. Loffredo	Dec. 31, 1944	May 23, 1970
Rev. Joseph W. Hughes	May 10, 1944	May 30, 1970
Rev. John J. Zec	Sept. 13, 1944	May 30, 1970
Rev. Gerard J. McCarron	Aug. 26, 1939	June 6, 1970

	BORN	ORDAINED
Rev. P. Francis Magee	July 1, 1941	June 13, 1970
Rev. Matthew T. Thelly	Dec. 17, 1940	Jan. 3, 1971
(I-2/15/87)		
Rev. Frederick W. Jackiewicz	Nov. 5, 1944	May 29, 1971
Rev. Eugene T. Keenan (U.S.N.)	Feb. 28, 1942	May 29, 1971
Rev. Msgr. Thomas A. Leubking	Aug. 25, 1939	May 29, 1971
Rev. Robert J. Schecker	May 28, 1945	June 26, 1971
Rev. James F. Clark	Apr. 28, 1946	May 20, 1972
Rev. Vincent J. Inghilterra (U.S. Army)	Nov. 11, 1942	May 20, 1972
Rev. William F. McKeone	Feb. 17, 1947	May 20, 1972
Rev. Robert J. Parenti	Sept. 30, 1939	May 20, 1972
Rev. John J. Scully	May 30, 1944	May 20, 1972
Rev. Gregory D. Vaughan	June 21, 1946	May 20, 1972
Rev. Feliz F. Venza	Feb. 6, 1946	May 20, 1972
Rev. James J. Brady	Apr. 7, 1947	June 10, 1972
Rev. Michael O'Connor	Sept. 14, 1946	June 17, 1972
Rev. Edward J. Griswold	Nov. 13, 1946	Apr. 7, 1973
Rev. Richard J. Gallagher	Oct. 13, 1944	May 13, 1973
(I-12/23/83)		
Rev. James A. O'Brien	Apr. 1, 1947	May 19, 1973
Rev. Ralph W. Stansley	Oct. 22, 1946	May 19, 1973
Rev. Ronald R. Becker	Mar. 9, 1945	May 26, 1973
Rev. Michael J. Burns	Aug. 28, 1947	May 26, 1973
Rev. Vincent J. Donadio	Oct. 10, 1939	May 26, 1973
Rev. Robert F. Kaeding	May 31, 1944	May 26, 1973
Rev. Paul A. Scaglione	Feb. 3, 1947	May 26, 1973
Rev. Michael J. Walsh	Mar. 31, 1949	June 9, 1973
Rev. Daniel G. Cahill	Sept. 27, 1948	June 17, 1973
Rev. Joseph F. McHugh	Jan. 12, 1946	Dec. 15, 1973
Rev. William M. Dunlap	Feb. 8, 1947	May 18, 1974
Rev. Joseph J. Farrell	June 11, 1947	May 18, 1974
Rev. Joseph L. Ferrante	Aug. 10, 1947	May 18, 1974
Rev. Bernard J. Keigher	Apr. 21, 1948	May 18, 1974
Rev. Jerome McG. Nolan	Nov. 23, 1945	May 18, 1974
Rev. John F. Wake	Jan. 1, 1947	May 18, 1974
Rev. John T. Kielb	Apr. 10, 1948	May 17, 1975
Rev. Anthony F. Krisak	Dec. 9, 1949	May 17, 1975
Rev. Leonard P. Lang	June 16, 1946	May 17, 1975
Rev. Eugene J. Roberts	June 17, 1949	May 17, 1975
Rev. Daniel Sullivan	Jan. 14, 1949	May 17, 1975
Rev. Thomas J. Triggs	Sept. 17, 1947	May 17, 1975
Rev. John P. Flynn	Sept. 16, 1950	June 8, 1975
Rev. James G. Innocenzi	July 13, 1949	Apr. 24, 1976
Rev. Patrick W. Battiato	Mar. 17, 1950	May 15, 1976

	BORN	ORDAINED
Rev. David A. Hillier	Aug. 29, 1950	May 22, 1976
Rev. Philip A. Lowery	Feb. 22, 1949	May 22, 1976
Rev. Thomas R. Rittenhouse	Nov. 12, 1949	May 22, 1976
(R-5/89)		
Rev. Msgr. Joseph R. Punderson	Aug. 6, 1948	Dec. 4, 1976
Rev. John P. Czahur	Sept. 8, 1951	May 21, 1977
Rev. Anthony Stringile	Sept. 13, 1948	May 21, 1977
Rev. Dennis A. Apoldite	May 6, 1951	May 20, 1978
Rev. Andrew Cervenak	Aug. 13, 1928	May 20, 1978
Rev. James A. Conover	Apr. 4, 1949	May 20, 1978
Rev. G. William Evans	Dec. 6, 1943	May 20, 1978
Rev. Francis M. McGrath	July 10, 1950	May 20, 1978
Rev. John W. Russo	Oct. 26, 1952	May 20, 1978
Rev. Francis Zalewski	Apr. 4, 1937	May 20, 1978
Rev. Robert A. Pearson	Apr. 16, 1927	Oct. 1978
Rev. Sergio C. Bicomong	May 13, 1954	Mar. 18, 1979
(I-12/14/88)		
Rev. Edward J. Arnister	July 16, 1953	May 19, 1979
Rev. Joseph A. Halpin	Aug. 13, 1932	May 19, 1979
Rev. Stanley P. Lukaszewski	Oct. 2, 1950	May 19, 1979
Rev. Phillip C. Pfleger	Feb. 3, 1953	May 19, 1979
Rev. Richard L. Tofani	Sept. 7, 1951	May 19, 1979
Rev. Douglas U. Hermansen	Mar. 28, 1952	Dec. 1, 1979
Rev. Joseph A. Tedesco	May 9, 1944	Dec. 1, 1979
Rev. Leonard F. Troiano	Dec. 15, 1945	Dec. 1, 1979
Rev. Kenard J. Tuzeneu	July 22, 1953	Dec. 1, 1979
Rev. Thomas J. Mullelly	Aug. 27, 1952	May 31, 1980
Rev. Joseph C. Glass	Aug. 13, 1953	Sept. 27, 1980
Rev. R. Vincent Gartland	July 6, 1939	May 23, 1981
Rev. Edward M. Jawidzik	Apr. 25, 1954	May 23, 1981
Rev. Stanislaus T. Polczyk	Jan. 6, 1949	May 22, 1982
Rev. Ralph E. Barile	Oct. 8, 1942	Oct. 30, 1982
Rev. Thomas N. Gervasio	Aug. 21, 1956	Oct. 30, 1982
Rev. Michael J. Lynch	Sept. 26, 1954	Oct. 30, 1982
Rev. Richard R. Milewski	Nov. 26, 1946	May 14, 1983
Rev. Timothy J. Capewell	Nov. 11, 1946	Nov. 12, 1983
Rev. John M. Dobrosky	Jan. 4, 1957	Nov. 12, 1983
Rev. Paul S. Rimassa	Dec. 19, 1947	Nov. 12, 1983
Rev. Vincent E. Keane	July 20, 1932	Nov. 23, 1983
Rev. Jacek Labinski	June 27, 1957	May 19, 1984
Rev. Albert Ricciardelli	Dec. 13, 1951	Nov. 10, 1984
Rev. Sam A. Sirianni	Feb. 17, 1954	Nov. 10, 1984
Rev. John S. Christian	Mar. 27, 1940	Nov. 17, 1984
Rev. Leon J. Inverso	July 20, 1942	Dec. 14, 1985

	BORN	ORDAINED
Rev. Richard R. Sweeney	Feb. 3, 1934	May 17, 1986
Rev. Richard D. LaVerghetta	Jan. 18, 1959	May 24, 1986
Rev. John J. Quinn	Jan. 30, 1925	Nov. 15, 1986
Rev. Michael T. Babalya	Oct. 18, 1919	Dec. 13, 1986
Rev. Daniel B. Pienciak	Aug. 25, 1952	May 25, 1987
Rev. David A. Adams	Apr. 11, 1958	May 14, 1988
Rev. Stanley W. Krzyston	Feb. 13, 1953	May 14, 1988
Rev. Charles F. Moore	June 13, 1918	May 14, 1988
Rev. Edward J. Fahey	July 20, 1961	May 20, 1989
Rev. Robert N. Moschini	June 25, 1954	May 20, 1989
Rev. Daniel J. Ryan	Dec. 14, 1951	May 20, 1989
Rev. Daniel F. Swift	Sept. 20, 1961	May 20, 1989
Rev. Kenneth S. Szepesy	Aug. 31, 1956	May 20, 1989
Rev. Robert M. Tynski	Sept. 12, 1962	May 20, 1989
Rev. Daniel F. Gowen	Dec. 16, 1959	Dec. 2, 1989
Rev. G. Scott Shaffer	Dec. 27, 1957	Dec. 2, 1989
Rev. Joseph N. Rosie	Feb. 10, 1963	June 16, 1990
Rev. John Bambrick	Aug. 15, 1964	May 18, 1991
Rev. Kenneth Ekdahl	Oct. 18, 1947	May 18, 1991
Rev. Gerald McBride	Mar. 12, 1932	May 18, 1991
Rev. Michael Sullivan	Mar. 12, 1962	May 18, 1991
Rev. John J. Dwyer	July 6, 1956	May 16, 1992
Rev. Michael Lang	Oct. 31, 1957	May 16, 1992
Rev. Michael G. Lankford	July 1, 1958	May 16, 1992
Rev. Jeffrey Lee	Mar. 29, 1964	May 16, 1992
Rev. James P. Quinn Jr.	Apr. 15, 1930	May 16, 1992
Rev. Brian T. Butch	Aug. 1, 1961	May 15, 1993
Rev. Thomas P. Chester	Aug. 27, 1966	May 15, 1993
Rev. Donald J. O'Brien	May 11, 1926	May 15, 1993
Rev. Eugene Vavrick	Feb. 22, 1957	May 15, 1993

*R = retired.
**I = incardinated.

INDEX